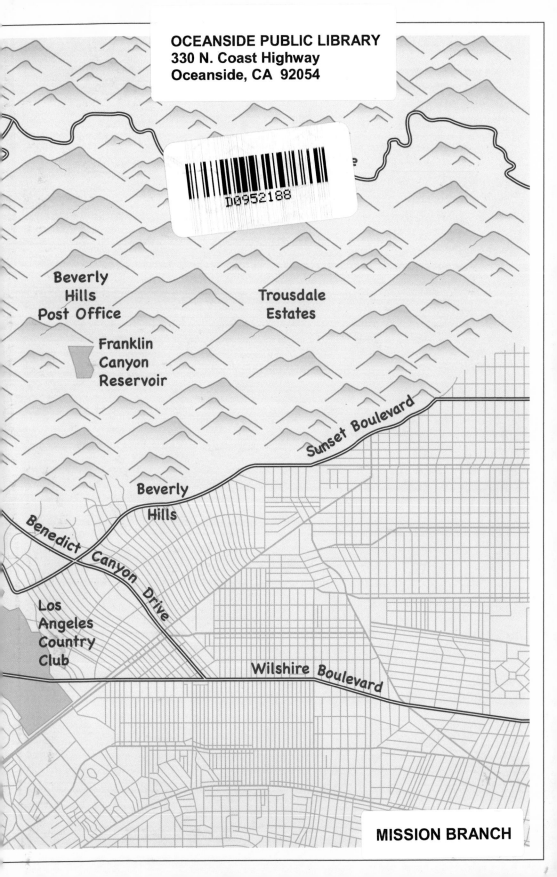

Beverly
Hills
Post Office

Trousdale
Estates

Franklin
Canyon
Reservoir

Sunset Boulevard

Beverly
Hills

Benedict Canyon Drive

Los
Angeles
Country
Club

Wilshire Boulevard

UNREAL
ESTATE

{ THE GREENACRES GATES }

UNREAL
ESTATE

MONEY, AMBITION,
AND THE
LUST FOR LAND
IN
LOS ANGELES

MICHAEL GROSS

Broadway Books
New York

Copyright © 2011 by Idee Fixe Ltd.

Grateful acknowledgment is made to Sheldon Harnick for permission to reprint lyrics from "If I Were a
Rich Man" by Sheldon Harnick and Jerry Bock.

Library of Congress Cataloging-in-Publication Data is available upon request.

ISBN: 978-0-7679-3265-3
eISBN: 978-0-7679-3266-0

Printed in the United States of America

Illustrations and endpaper map by Fred Haynes
Jacket design by Jennifer O'Connor
Jacket photography by Ian Cumming/Axiom Photographic Agency/Getty Images

1 3 5 7 9 10 8 6 4 2

First Edition

For Barbara

And to Patience and Fortitude

I'd build a big tall house with rooms by the dozen,

Right in the middle of the town.

A fine tin roof with real wooden floors below.

There would be one long staircase just going up,

And one even longer coming down,

And one more leading nowhere, just for show.

—SHELDON HARNICK, *"If I Were a Rich Man,"* Fiddler on the Roof

Tip the world over on its side and everything loose will land in Los Angeles.

—FRANK LLOYD WRIGHT (1867–1959)

CONTENTS

Burton Green

Max Whittier

Edwin and Harold Janss

Minnewa and Alphonzo Bell

Charles Canfield and Jake Danziger

Harold Lloyd, Charles Chaplin, and Douglas Fairbanks
at the Beverly Hills Hotel

Neil Steere McCarthy

Diane Stockmar, Dolly Green, and Burtie Green at Stockmar's wedding

Harold Greenlin (left) with Habib Carouba and their
lawyer George Choppelas

Steven Macallum Powers (left), Bernie Cornfeld and friend

Stewart and Lynda Resnick with Barbara Davis (right)

CAST OF CHARACTERS

This book is about sixteen great estates in the best neighborhoods of Los Angeles—the contiguous communities of Beverly Hills, Bel Air, Holmby Hills, and Beverly Park. Of those, seven emerged as the book's main "characters." Five are in Beverly Hills: Grayhall (1100 Carolyn Way), Greenacres (1740 Green Acres Place), Greystone (905 Loma Vista Drive), The Knoll (1130 Schuyler Road), and 9481 Sunset Boulevard, named Sunset House by its latest owner. In Holmby Hills, there is Owlwood (141 South Carolwood Drive), so named by owner number eight, and in Bel Air, Casa Encantada (10644 Bellagio Road), the name used by owner number two. The street addresses of some of these estates have changed over the years for reasons ranging from subdivision to privacy concerns. To aid identification, they are generally referred to by their current addresses.

These trophy homes are not historic relics. All but Greystone are occupied today, and several continue to grow. The owners of Sunset House just swallowed a third neighboring lot. Owlwood now incorporates two more of the great estates on the famous 10000 block of Sunset Boulevard (10060 and 10100 Sunset, both demolished in 2002).

Those last two "ghost" houses—gone but not forgotten—are also featured players in this story, as are seven secondary estates, some still standing, some not, that are intimately connected to the history of this linked bracelet of gilded neighborhoods. But those sixteen estates are really only windows onto the fabulous, sometimes glorious, but as often toxic and corrupt lives of the real subjects of the book—the owners and occupants of those homes over the last century, along with the founders of the four communities and a handful of major figures from the history of greater Los Angeles. Their great fortunes fueled their lust for land, power, prominence, and opulence—and have made these incredibly unreal estates very real, indeed.

PIONEERS AND FOUNDERS

Brian Adler: Developer of Beverly Park North.

Margaret and **Stanley Anderson:** Mother-and-son proprietors of the Hollywood Hotel and founder-proprietors of the Beverly Hills Hotel.

Alphonzo Edward Bell: Oilman, founder of Bel Air, owner of the Santa Monica Mountain Park Ranch, and second owner of La Quinta, which he renamed Capo di Monte (since demolished).

Elizabeth, Minnewa, and **Alphonzo Bell Jr.:** Children of Alphonzo Bell.

Edson Benedict: A pioneer settler of Benedict Canyon.

Pierce Benedict: Son of Edson and the first president of Beverly Hills.

Leonard I. Bursten: First, failed developer of Beverly Park; former prosecutor; convicted tax evader.

Charles Adelbert Canfield: Edward Doheny's partner in the oil business. Leader of the cofounders of Beverly Hills.

Harry Chandler and **Harrison Gray Otis:** Fathers of the *Los Angeles Times*; land owners and investors. Chandler was a cofounder of the city of Hollywood.

Wilbur David Cook Jr.: Landscape architect of Beverly Hills.

Daisy Canfield and **Jacob Morris "Jake" Danziger:** Daughter of Charles Canfield and her husband, a lawyer and cofounder of the Beverly Hills Speedway. First owners of Bel Air. Builders of La Quinta at 801 Bel-Air Road (since demolished).

I. Irving Davidson: Washington fixer. Co-owner of land that became Beverly Park.

Edward L. Doheny: Pioneer Los Angeles oilman, builder of Greystone estate.

Allen R. Glick: Teamsters associate, casino owner and mob front, failed second developer of Beverly Park.

Elliot Gottfurcht: Developer of Beverly Park South.

Burton Green: Oilman, partner of Max Whittier, cofounder of Beverly Hills.

Dorothy "Dolly," Liliore, and **Burton "Burtie" Green:** Daughters of Burton Green.

Hyman Green: Teamsters associate, co-owner of land that became Beverly Park.

Henry Hammel and **Andrew Denker:** Later owners of Rancho Rodeo de las Aguas, then known as the Hammel-Denker Ranch.

Henry Edward Huntington: Son of railroad pioneer Collis Huntington, early Los Angeles trolley car mogul, founding partner in Rodeo Land and Water.

Harold and **Edwin Janss:** Cofounders of Holmby Hills, Westwood, and Westwood Village; owners of Conejo Ranch (later Thousand Oaks, California); benefactors of UCLA.

Arthur Letts: Cofounder of Holmby Hills.

Gladys Letts: Daughter of Arthur and Florence Letts and wife of Harold Janss.

Llewelyn Arthur Nares: First estate owner in Beverly Hills.

Florence Letts Quinn: Estranged wife and heiress of Arthur Letts; later married Charles Quinn.

Arthur Pillsbury: First city engineer of Beverly Hills.

Moses Sherman: With a brother-in-law, Huntington's partner in the Pasadena and Altadena Railway. Cofounder of Hollywood, founder of Sherman (later West Hollywood).

Maria Rita Valdez: The first settler and owner of Rancho Rodeo de las Aguas, which later became Beverly Hills.

Max Whittier: Oilman, partner of Burton Green, cofounder of Beverly Hills.

Benjamin Davis "Don Benito" Wilson: An early owner of Rancho San Jose de Buenos Ayres.

John Wolfskill: Forty-niner and later owner of Rancho San Jose de Buenos Ayres.

FEATURED HOUSES, OWNERS, AND OCCUPANTS

Beverly Hills

Shadow Hill/Grayhall (1100 Carolyn Way)

Harry Dana Lombard: Boston banker, Carole Lombard's godfather.

Douglas Fairbanks: First actor-resident of Beverly Hills, owner of Pickfair.

Caroline "Carrie" Canfield and **Silsby Spalding:** A daughter of Charles Canfield and her husband, the first mayor of Beverly Hills.

Amos Johnstone: Scion of a local real estate family.

George Hamilton: Actor.

Bernard Cornfeld: Retired mutual fund founder, entrepreneur.

Steven Macallum Powers: Penny-stock manipulator, luxury home redeveloper, playboy, best friend of Hugh Hefner.

Philippe Boutboul: Tunisian-born French electronics retailer, special advisor to the president of Burkina Faso, mansion redeveloper.

Mark, Suzan, and **Darcy LaPier Hughes:** Herbalife founder, nutritional supplement guru, alleged pyramid scammer, and his third and fourth wives, both beauty contest winners.

Moussa and **Mahnaz "Lilli" Mehdizadeh:** Persian-born businessman and his wife, a member of the Elghanayan real estate dynasty of Tehran and New York.

9755 Sunset Boulevard (since demolished)

Max Whittier: See Pioneers and Founders.

Samuel Berch: Dairy and ice cream mogul, founder of Arden Farms.

Leo Hartfield: Son-in-law of Samuel Berch.

Dino Fabbri: Milanese publisher.

Mohammed and **Dena al-Fassi:** Brother- and sister-in-law of Saudi Prince Turki bin Abdul Aziz al-Saud.

Greenacres (1740 Green Acres Place)

Harold Lloyd: Silent film comedian.

Nasrollah Afshani, Naim Perry, and **Abdullah Moghavem:** Persian-born investors (never occupied the house).

Bernard Solomon and **Dona Powell:** Budget record mogul and his jewelry- and costume-collector wife.

Ted and **Susie Field:** Marshall Field heir, race car team owner, and entertainment executive and his wife.

Ron Burkle: Supermarket entrepreneur turned billionaire investor.

Greystone (501 Doheny Road)

Edward L. "Ned" Doheny Jr.: Son of the oilman.

Lucy Doheny Battson: Ned Doheny's wife; later, his widow and builder of The Knoll.

Leigh Battson: Lucy Doheny's second husband.

Henry Crown: Chicago industrialist, partner of Conrad Hilton, alleged Mafia associate (never moved in).

The Knoll (1130 Schuyler Road)

Lucy Doheny and **Leigh Battson:** See Greystone.

Dino De Laurentiis: Film producer.

Kenny Rogers: Singer; owner of first lot sold in Beverly Park.

Marvin and **Barbara Davis:** Oilman and owner of Twentieth Century Fox and his socialite wife.

Eric Smidt: Harbor Freight Tools hardware mogul.

9481 Sunset Boulevard (Sunset House)

Francisca Bernard (Mrs. Dionicio) Botiller: Builder, wife of heir to a Spanish land grant fortune.

Frank and **Cecilia Botiller** and **Ida Botiller Lindley:** Children of Francisca and Dionicio Botiller.

Jack Royal Young Lindley: Brother of Loretta Young, informally adopted son of Ida Botiller Lindley.

Dorothy Wellborn "Dolly" Green: See Pioneers and Founders.

Neil Steere McCarthy: Lawyer for Howard Hughes, L. B. Mayer, and others; polo player; cofounder of the Beverly Hills Speedway. Lover of Dolly Green.

Mary Beich McCarthy: Candy heiress, second wife of Neil, painter.

Stewart and **Lynda Resnick:** Former owners of the Franklin Mint; owners of FIJI Water, Teleflora, fruit and nut farms, and other enterprises.

Bel Air

750 Bel-Air Road (the "Beverly Hillbillies mansion")
Lynn Atkinson: Public works builder.
Arnold S. Kirkeby: Hotelier.
A. Jerrold Perenchio: Agent, event promoter, entertainment mogul.

10644 Bellagio Road (later Casa Encantada and Bellagio House)
Hilda Olsen Boldt Weber: Former nurse, widow of glass bottle mogul Charles Boldt, later married to Joseph Otto Weber. Builder and first owner.
Conrad N. Hilton: Hotelier, great-grandfather of Paris Hilton.
Nicky and **Barron Hilton:** Sons of Conrad. The former briefly married actress Elizabeth Taylor. The latter is the grandfather of Paris Hilton.
David Murdock: Conglomerateur and head of Dole Food Company.
Gary Winnick: Former Drexel Burnham Lambert investment banker, founder of the defunct telecommunications firm Global Crossing.

10539 Bellagio Road
Sol Wurtzel: Movie mogul. Builder and first owner.
Woody Feuert: Business partner of costume designer Adrian.
Anthony Norvell: Astrologer, psychic, metaphysician.
Howard Hughes, Elvis Presley, Prince Rainier of Monaco: Sublessors.
Reginald Owen: British character actor.
Dolly Green: See Pioneers and Founders.
Diane Hunt Stockmar: Alleged illegitimate daughter of Dolly Green and Neil McCarthy.
Bill and **Maria Bell:** Executive producer of *The Bold and the Beautiful* and *The Young and the Restless* and his wife, an arts philanthropist.

364 St. Cloud Road

Louis W. Zimmerman: Financier.

Casey Robinson and **Tamara Toumanova:** Writer and producer at Twentieth Century Fox and his wife, a ballerina.

Tony Curtis and **Christine Kaufmann:** See 141 South Carolwood.

Sonny and **Cher Bono:** See 141 South Carolwood.

Larry Flynt: Founder, Flynt Publications, and publisher, *Hustler.*

Holmby Hills

375 North Carolwood Drive (since demolished)

Harold Janss: Builder and first owner (see Pioneers and Founders).

Gregory and **Veronique Peck:** Actor and his wife.

10060 Sunset Boulevard (since demolished)

Edwin Janss: Builder and first owner.

Charles Reese "Jack" Warde: Insurance executive.

William Osco: Pornographic movie producer; husband of Jackie Kong, director.

Ghazi Aita: See 141 South Carolwood.

Roland Arnall: See 141 South Carolwood.

10100 Sunset Boulevard (since demolished)

Hubert Prior "Rudy" Vallée: First owner, never occupied the house.

Jayne Mansfield and **Mickey Hargitay:** Actress and her bodybuilder husband.

Harold Greenlin: Former carny and vaudeville, burlesque, and pornographic theater owner.

Engelbert Humperdinck: Singer.

Ghazi Aita: See 141 South Carolwood.

Roland Arnall: See 141 South Carolwood.

10236 Charing Cross Road (now the Playboy mansion)

Arthur Letts Jr.: Son of Arthur Letts, builder and first owner.

Hugh M. Hefner: Founder of *Playboy* magazine.

594 South Mapleton Drive (since demolished)

Edna Letts and **Malcolm McNaghten:** Daughter of Arthur Letts and her husband. Builders and first owners.

Harry "Bing" Crosby: Singer and actor.

Patrick Frawley Jr.: Owner of Technicolor, Paper Mate, and Schick; right-wing activist.

Aaron and **Candy Spelling:** Producer and his wife; they tore down the house and replaced it.

141 South Carolwood (now incorporates 10060 and 10100 Sunset):

Florence M. Letts and **Charles Quinn:** Builders and first owners (also see Pioneers and Founders).

Joseph W. Drown: Partner of Conrad Hilton, hotelier, first husband of Elizabeth "Bettye" Avery, later Libby Keck, creator and longtime owner of the Bel-Air and Ocean House hotels (the latter the former William Randolph Hearst–Marion Davies beach house in Santa Monica).

Joe Schenck: Movie pioneer, alleged lover and mentor of Marilyn Monroe, pardoned convicted perjurer.

William Myron Keck: Founder and president of Superior Oil; father of Howard Keck, the second husband of Elizabeth Avery Drown.

Tony Curtis: Actor, husband of actresses Janet Leigh and Christine Kaufmann and model Leslie "Penny" Allen.

Sonny and **Cher Bono:** Entertainers.

Cher and **Gregg Allman:** Entertainers.

Ralph and **Chase Mishkin:** Carpet company owner, theater producer.

Ghazi and **Salma Aita:** Syrian-born middleman, hotel owner, and investor and his wife.

Roland and **Dawn Arnall:** Savings and loan owner and subprime mortgage pioneer and his second wife.

OTHER NOTABLE CHARACTERS

Alfred and **Betsy Bloomingdale:** Department store heir, credit card mogul, and Reagan kitchen cabinet member and his socialite wife.

Roland Coate Sr.: Architect of The Knoll.

Vince Conti: Pimp, actor.

Hernando Courtright: Manager and owner of the Beverly Hills and Beverly Wilshire hotels. Close friend of Dolly Green.

James Dolena: Architect of 10644 Bellagio Road.

Robert Farquhar: Architect of 141 South Carolwood and Daisy Danziger's Crestmount.

Heidi Fleiss: Waitress, prostitute, madame, girlfriend of Bernie Cornfeld.

Miles Gray: Haberdashery heir and husband of Minnewa Bell and Burtie Green.

William Randolph Hearst and **Marion Davies:** Proprietor of the *Los Angeles Examiner* and *Evening Herald* and his mistress. Owned 1011 Beverly Drive and 415 Pacific Coast Highway (later the Ocean House hotel and now site of the Annenberg Community Beach House).

Sumner Hunt and **Silas Burns:** Architects of Grayhall.

Charles Hopper: Head of sales in Bel Air during the Depression and World War II.

Howard Hughes: Texas oil heir, movie producer, aircraft manufacturer, airline owner, noted bachelor and eccentric.

Gordon Kaufmann: Architect of Greystone, 10060 and 10100 Sunset, 375 North Carolwood, 594 South Mapleton.

Atwater Kent: Radio pioneer, inventor, engineer, party host, and third and last owner-occupant of 801 Bel-Air Road.

Sidney Korshak: Lawyer; middleman between the Chicago Mafia and unions, Los Angeles investors, and Hollywood studios and producers.

Francis Xavier Lourdou: Architect of 9481 Sunset Boulevard.

Walter McCarty: Cofounder of the Beverly Hills Speedway, founder of the Beverly Wilshire Hotel.

Colleen Moore: First actress to own a home in Bel Air.

Antonio Moreno: Silent film actor, second husband of Daisy Canfield Danziger.

Vicki Morgan: Lover of Bernie Cornfeld and Alfred Bloomingdale, later murdered.

Wallace Neff: Early architectural draftsman in Beverly Hills. Architect of Pickfair renovations, Enchanted Hill, and 10539 Bellagio Road.

Hugh Plunkett: Personal secretary and presumed murderer of Ned Doheny.

Terence Harold Robsjohn-Gibbings: Interior designer for 10644 Bellagio Road.

Enrique "Heini" Schondube: Mexican industrial heir. Third husband of Dolly Green.

Sumner Spaulding: Architect of Greenacres.

Fred Thomson and **Frances Marion:** Cowboy star and his wife, a screenwriter. Builders of Enchanted Hill.

Paul Trousdale: Developer of the Doheny Ranch as Trousdale Estates and other subdivisions.

A NOTE ON GEOGRAPHY

While New York City is defined to a great extent by a contained, vertical geography, and in most of Manhattan at least, an easy-to-comprehend numerical grid, Los Angeles is typically characterized by the word *sprawl*; it is horizontal and both historically and geographically uncontained. But despite the fact that non-Angelenos find the place a geographical bafflement, it has its own logic.

East is downtown, where Westsiders—the wealthy residents of Beverly Hills (its own city, surrounded on all sides by L.A.), Beverly Park, Holmby Hills, and Bel Air—rarely go. Some, without shame, even proudly claim to have never been there. Downtown is where Los Angeles was founded. It's the home of the city's government, of the *Los Angeles Times,* and of cultural institutions (the Walt Disney Concert Hall, the Dorothy Chandler Pavilion, the Geffen Contemporary at MOCA) that are the equivalent of New York's Lincoln Center. Though it is only 11.5 miles from the eastern edge of Beverly Hills, twenty to forty-five minutes away (depending on the time of day and traffic), downtown L.A. strikes many as another country, so far away from the people most likely to appreciate its pleasures—and in many cases, also the people who paid for them—that getting there can seem a dreaded excursion.

Also to the east and southeast are the poorest neighborhoods of Los Angeles, like South Central, which burned in the infamous rioting in the 1990s, and the homes of the Westside's maids and gardeners, many of them Central American, who sometimes travel hours each way by bus to turn grand neighborhoods like Bel Air into Spanish-speaking villages during daylight hours. Their march into and out of the district's wealthy canyons each day is a visual signature of life on the west side of town.

Northeast of downtown Los Angeles are its old-money bedroom communities of Pasadena and tiny, exclusive San Marino; their architecture greatly influenced that of Beverly Hills. Scattered around downtown like brilliant stones on a broken necklace are other former enclaves of wealth, including parts of Hollywood, Windsor Square, Hancock Park, and Los Feliz, as well as hip Silver Lake, home of architectural gems by the modernist master Richard Neutra.

West of the neighborhoods that are the focus of this book, Los Angeles dead-ends at the Pacific Ocean, which is vaster by far than its East Coast counterpart and a tropical aqua rather than the North Atlantic's slate gray. Some of the oceanfront neighborhoods are posh, like Malibu; others funky, like Venice; and some are a mash-up of both, like Santa Monica; but all are desirable for their proximity to the beach, sunsets that blaze redder because of the smog, and their distance from downtown.

As the communities that concern us here were forming, planners envisioned a road called Beverly Boulevard running east to west through the Los Angeles basin, parallel to Mulholland Drive. Beverly Boulevard was merged with Sunset Boulevard in 1933. The aptly named Sunset wends its way across twenty-four miles of this twenty-nine-mile-wide metropolis, a curlicue, not an arrow, running east to west, as well as the dividing line between the hills that define the north side of Los Angeles and the flats that mark the south. Its most famous blocks, comprising the Sunset Strip, are in West Hollywood (also its own city since 1984), between Beverly Hills and Hollywood, which was annexed by Los Angeles in 1910. Rising above Sunset, in both Eastside and Westside neighborhoods, are the steep, fire-prone canyons that reach their apex along Mulholland Drive before tumbling into the San Fernando Valley to the north.

Mulholland, a scenic highway at the crest of the Santa Monica Mountains named for the engineer who brought water to L.A., was already under construction when planners suggested a series of canyon roads running north and south through Benedict, Coldwater, Franklin, Sepulveda, and Higgins Canyons—roughly parallel slashes through the mountains, connecting the basin with the San Fernando Valley on the other side. At the time, the Cahuenga Pass, site of today's Hollywood Freeway, was the only route of consequence connecting the valley to downtown Los Angeles. In 1929, it was said to carry a million cars a month, making the need for alternative routes acute.

The canyons now named Coldwater (originally Cañada de las Aguas Frias, or Canyon of the Cold Waters) and Benedict (originally Cañada de las Encinas, or Canyon of the Live Oaks—later renamed for its first resident, Edson Benedict) got twisty, turny eponymous roads; Franklin Canyon a foreshortened Beverly Drive that never made it to the valley; and Sepulveda Canyon got both a boulevard and the San Diego Freeway, also known as Interstate 405.

South of Sunset, the city flattens and gradually morphs from the mansions of Beverly Hills to a mix of industry and residences in places like Culver City (home of the famous MGM Studios, now the Sony Pictures film and television complex) and finally to the asphalt sprawl of the airport, Los Angeles International, better known as LAX. Landing there on a clear day, one can easily spot the primary features of the Los Angeles Basin: ocean to the west, mountains to the north, downtown to the east, and just north of the ebony towers of Century City (on the former Twentieth Century Fox studio lot), the subjects of this book, the urban oases of Beverly Hills, Holmby Hills, Bel Air, and Beverly Park—all nestled in the foothills, as the early advertising brochures put it, between the city and the sea.

Introduction

On Summit Ridge, Above Beverly Park
November 2009

The greatest frustration in researching this book was the difficulty I had seeing the estates I was writing about, all of which are hidden behind gates, fences, and foliage and visible, if at all, only in glimpses. Most homeowners are understandably disinclined to open those gates even under the best of circumstances. I took a commercial tour of the star homes at one point; was given a second, far more accurate tour by a real estate broker; and repeatedly drove through the communities I'd decided to write about. I was even invited into a few of the breathtaking houses described in the pages that follow.

Beverly Park was the hardest nut to crack because, unlike Beverly Hills, Bel Air, and Holmby Hills, it is what's called a guard-gated neighborhood. You can't even drive through it without being invited in by a resident. So one day, I tried to drive around it, looking for a place where I could see this community that was conceived as a modern update of its neighbors, an update consisting of those fences and gates that keep the curious like me at a safe distance. Like its older siblings, Beverly Park, built beginning in 1985, has a hidden history. Unlike them, it is also almost entirely hidden itself.

Seeking a vantage point, I drove up what was once called Higgins Canyon on Beverly Drive, but that road ended abruptly. I doubled back and tried Franklin Canyon. Turning west on Mulholland Drive, I found the north gate of Beverly Park, but was turned away by a guard. A block further west, I turned south on Summit Ridge Drive and eventually came to an intersection with a sign directing cars to the other two guarded gates of Beverly Park. There were also signs that read PRIVATE PROPERTY and NO TRESPASSING and a squad car from the Bel-Air Patrol, a private security service.

Certain I would only be spurned again and identify myself as a nuisance in the process, I pulled off the road between the two gates and parked on a ridge where, just beyond a low fence, the roofs of the mansions of Beverly Park were all visible in a canyon bowl just below. Finally, I was able to get a glimpse of this protected enclave and see its sprawling homes for myself. I was, frankly, astonished; from above, the large houses all crowded together looked like a suburb, albeit one pumped up on steroids.

Beverly Park is the youngest, most expensive, and arguably most exclusive subdivision on the west side of Los Angeles. That region is so famous it has multiple nicknames, most of them coined by realtors seeking to smear cachet over as many communities—some nice, some not so—as possible. The broad residential zone between the crest of the Santa Monica Mountains and Santa Monica Boulevard, West Hollywood, and the Pacific Ocean includes Malibu and Santa Monica, Westwood, Brentwood, Pacific Palisades, Beverly Crest, Bel Air, Holmby Hills, Beverly Hills, and Beverly Hills Post Office, an L.A. neighborhood that has a snob-appeal Beverly Hills mailing address even though it's not actually in that city. Beverly Park is a neighborhood within Beverly Hills Post Office.

Together, they are collectively the Westside. Its smaller, brighter nucleus, the homogeneous and contiguous estate district made up of the last four of those communities, has been dubbed the Platinum Triangle, though from above, it looks more like a broccoli flower. But another nickname, initially coined to capture greater L.A.'s reputation for spaced-out flightiness, alleged eccentricities, otherworldliness, frivolity, and lack of any ties to what most people consider reality, especially in the realms of ambition and conspicuous consumption, more precisely describes these, its richest and most prestigious districts.

Welcome to La-La Land.

There are certain alluring neighborhoods around the world that are considered the best of the best nests, not just for locals but also for the world's most discerning homing pigeons. These are places that symbolize and consecrate success when their names are uttered in answer to the question, Where do you live? London's Knightsbridge and Belgravia, Monte Carlo, the 7th arrondissement of Paris, the Gold Coast of Manhattan, Connecticut's Greenwich, Florida's Palm Beach, Hong Kong's Victoria Peak, Pacific Heights in San Francisco, and Atherton and Woodside in the Silicon Valley all have their fans and their charms. But the Triangle is in a class by itself, offering the unique experience of country living within a world-class city and boasting easy access (geographically speaking), high quality of life, spectacular beauty, extravagant architecture, a year-round temperate climate, and a world-class concentration of glamour, fame, and fortune. The best homes in those communities are what economists call positional goods, their value determined in large part by their scarcity and how much others desire them.

Let's be clear: La-La Land is not Hollywood. The Hollywood community is part of it, but La-La Land is more than, as the *Beverly Hillbillies* theme song put it, swimmin' pools and movie stars. La-La Land is a figurative geography as much as a real one; it's a place of pregnant possibility and polar opposites, good and evil, American dreams and nightmares, sudden rises and vertiginous falls. So it appeals equally to dreamers and schemers, all of them gambling to survive on an L.A. mountaintop. That group certainly includes directors, producers, actors, and even some writers. But movie and TV people were latecomers to the Platinum Triangle. Initially unwelcome, they have helped make its international reputation as a place with truly great estates, but ironically, few celebrities can afford to live in the largest of them anymore. And Hollywood stories are hardly the most interesting ones in town. The Triangle is the world capital of unbridled fantasy and ambition—sometimes base, but always compelling, whether centered on power, sex, fame, fortune, or all of the above.

Location, location, location, the realtors say. Beverly Hills, Holmby Hills, and Bel Air, the neighborhoods that latecomer Beverly Park apes and aspires to join, were all conceived at the start of the twentieth century to be the most exclusive, prestigious, luxurious, envy-inducing communities on earth. Great homes on large, flat pieces of land with sweeping views in these three hillside neighborhoods soon became the West Coast equivalent of what the author Tom Wolfe memorably characterized, in a bit of literary understatement, as the "good" apartment buildings of New York's Upper East Side. What makes them so good is, largely, that you and I can't live in them and probably never will. Not only that, we will probably never even visit unless we work for a caterer, landscaper, or private security firm, or shell out for a pricey benefit ticket. They are home to the fewest of the few, the self-selected stars of democratic society, those who seek to act on the world's great stages of the theater of ambition.

Sitting adjacent to each other, these four communities (one, Beverly

Hills, a separate, independent city, the others parts of L.A.), comprise a distinct psycho-geographic unit, irrespective of political boundaries. La-La Land is as small as it is special, occupying a mere fifteen square miles, but its size belies its magnetic position in the world's imagination. It is the focal point of a kind of social, financial, and professional desire that exists no-where else. For here, ambition in all its forms runs as hot and uncontrolled as lust. The very visible reward for success is to live in the billionaire's belt around Sunset Boulevard.

The three original communities of the Triangle were all formed by real estate developers between 1906 and 1923. At about 5.7 square miles, the city of Beverly Hills is much larger than its estate district, which begins just south of Sunset and rises up to Mulholland Drive, bordered to the west by Bel Air, to the east by Hollywood, and above it, by the Franklin Canyon Reservoir, long the source of the Westside's drinking water. Bel Air, the largest Triangle neighborhood, at about 6.4 square miles, is loosely bordered by the Getty Museum and Sepulveda Boulevard on the west, Mulholland along the north, Sunset Boulevard to the south, and Beverly Glen to the east. Holmby Hills, shaped like a fist with its index finger pointing south down one side of the Los Angeles Country Club, nestles between Beverly Hills and Bel Air. At four hundred acres, it is comparatively tiny, yet its huge homes on large lots straddling Sunset lead some to call it the most prestigious of the four communities. Their young sibling, Beverly Park, is formally part of Beverly Hills Post Office, which is in Los Angeles but shares the cherished 90210 zip code with Beverly Hills and so, in most minds, is part of the smaller city. About the same size as Beverly Hills, B.H.P.O. sits in a notch mostly north of Beverly Hills between the upper Hollywood Hills and the upper reaches of Bel Air.

Together, they are—and always have been—mecca for the self-invented. Though there is a landed gentry in California, much like the colonial Society-with-a-capital-S of the East Coast, it no longer has the social power or financial leverage to capture the popular imagination—that resides instead with the Triangle's founding fathers, who were descendants of fur trappers, Forty-niners, railroad builders, ranchers, and oilmen of the late nineteenth century, and the descendants, both familial and professional, of the Jewish movie moguls of the early twentieth century. They all made this a community of staggering wealth and set the standards of how it should be spent. Their contemporary equivalents are tech billionaires, rock musicians, financial manipulators, and pyramid scheme operators.

Born out of the alchemical reaction of overlapping booms in oil, railroads, and land in the early twentieth century, the Triangle was conceived for the Los Angeles elite, but it wasn't until the relative arrivistes of Hollywood started buying land and building great estates in the 1920s that its fortunes were assured and vast farms and ranches turned into luxury residences. The Depression and World War II stopped that movement in its tracks, and for years afterwards, the great homes of the area were relegated to white elephant status. But in the 1970s, oil-rich Middle Easterners revived the market, and the odd price correction notwithstanding, the area's luster as an enclave of supreme achievement has been unassailable ever since. It's now occupied by parallel but separate and often opposing societies—quiet, ultraconservative local wealth; some lingering Hollywood glamour and its consort, decadence; and the latest iterations of fast money earned everywhere from cyberspace to infotainment to the lower depths of the financial industries.

They may look askance at each other but they mix and mingle (even in bedrooms); in many ways the apogeal product of their union was Ronald Reagan, the movie star turned politician who emerged as a force in the Republican Party, backed by ultraconservative wealth, and became a Bel Air resident himself in 1989. Though Richard Nixon, another Southern Californian, also moved to La-La Land, and Jack Kennedy and Bill Clinton loved to party there, it was Reagan who was the apotheosis of its will to power. The kitchen cabinet who propelled Reagan to the White House were all Platinum Triangle residents; a few owned trophy houses there. Today, you hear more about its liberal cabal, but for a moment, Reagan's pals ruled the world.

The Triangle population is constantly refreshed by an endless stream of fortune-seeking and -spending East Coasters and foreigners who have made Los Angeles the world's last frontier. For all of them, a home in the Triangle is the ultimate fantasy of arrival. It is rarely acknowledged that, perversely, they hope and believe money can buy the appearance of permanence in a place defined by transience. In most cases, this "arrival" is followed by almost inevitable departure. Unlike the landed gentry elsewhere, rare is the family that holds on to a great estate across generations. Indeed, Triangle mansions are so huge and cost so much to maintain that owners typically downsize, dispose of, or lose them long before inheritance comes into play. The real estate lineage of the homes in this book demonstrates the patterns of Triangle ownership. Some examples:

- On Sunset Boulevard, a mansion built in 1928 by a Spanish land-grant family passes to the personal lawyer of Howard Hughes and Louis B. Mayer and then to a guy who started out running a janitorial service and his wife, who ran a little ad agency. They are now the billionaire owners of Teleflora, FIJI Water, POM, thirty thousand acres of citrus groves, seventy thousand acres of pistachio and almond orchards, and the Neptune Pacific shipping line—and have bought three properties adjacent to theirs to create their own Sunset empire.

- A Bel Air mansion built between 1935 and 1938 for a nurse widowed by a rich older husband was then owned by Conrad Hilton, the hotel chain founder (and grandfather of Paris Hilton). It then passed to the owner of Dole Food, who made a staggering $58 million profit when he sold it in 2000 to a former junk bond trader who'd walked away from a public telecom company's collapse with hundreds of millions of dollars.

- Greenacres, the mansion completed in 1929 by silent film star Harold Lloyd in Benedict Canyon in Beverly Hills, has since been owned by three Iranian businessmen; a record company mogul and his socially ambitious wife; Ted Field, the much-married Marshall Field heir who raced cars in the 1970s and ran Interscope Films and Interscope Records in the late 1980s; and most recently, the controversial supermarket billionaire, alleged model-hound, and former Friend of Bill (Clinton), Ron Burkle.

- In 1949, the Doheny family sold their ranch to a subdivider and their adjacent mansion to a mob-connected businessman who never lived there—it is now empty and owned by Beverly Hills—and moved to a slightly smaller mansion that they sold to the movie producer Dino De Laurentiis, who sold it to the country singer Kenny Rogers, who sold it to the Colorado wildcatter turned studio mogul Marvin Davis, whose widow sold it in 2005 to a guy who sells hardware—*lots* of hardware. He tore it down to cement and studs and has been rebuilding it ever since.

- The veritable Rose Bowl parade that has passed through today's

Owlwood, a huge Sunset Boulevard estate built in 1932, includes a founder of Holmby Hills and his wife's mother, the developer of the Bel-Air Hotel, a movie mogul and convicted tax cheat who seduced Marilyn Monroe there, the crooner Rudy Vallée, the actor Tony Curtis and two of his five wives, pop stars Sonny & Cher and rocker Gregg Allman, Jayne Mansfield, Engelbert Humperdinck, an oilman, a carpet manufacturer, a staid insurance man, a Syrian middleman for military contractors with a taste for hookers, a guy who owned both dirty movie theaters and part of the Jimi Hendrix estate, and a twenty-five-year-old known as the Boy King of Porn. The last two each did time in federal prison. Its current owner is the second wife and widow of one of the pioneers of subprime mortgages.

More than a neighborhood, the Triangle is the seat of a certain set of as-pirations, not all of them the same, but generally harmonious. It is a mirror that both reflects and confirms self-image. But it is also a pleasure pit, and as another of its nicknames, Lotusland, implies, can and has turned status and image into a kind of opium, inspiring addictions just as dangerous and all-consuming.

Just like New York, Paris, London, and Rome, the Triangle has a stratified hierarchy. It is a Darwinian place where the pecking order is so brutal that to stumble is often to die or, even if you live, to quickly disappear, if you're smart, or else linger on as your life shrinks, first in the estimation of others, then, unless you have superhuman strength of character, inevitably in your own.

Why inevitably? Because La-La Land is a make-or-break kind of place. Only certain sorts want to be there and have the nerve, the skills, the resolve, and the peculiar set of delusions to make their evanescent dream come true. How brutal is it? Even movie stars have mostly left the area, leading some to contend that they don't matter anymore since they've effectively been priced out of the molten center of the Triangle's volcanic real estate market. All that matters here is money—or the ability to conjure its appearance out of nothingness.

Appearances may not be everything in the Triangle, but they count for a lot in a place defined by rootlessness and the illusion that wealth and ac-complishment bring security; a city that is philosophically, emotionally, and even physically a fantasy; a place that would turn brown, wither, and die were it not for piped-in water, roll-out insta-lawns, and gardeners who come in every day from somewhere else to sustain its grand illusions. Though it wasn't invented for them, that's why Hollywood types found the Westside a perfect place to settle. Nothing is indigenous in Los Angeles, a quality perfectly captured in the faux-historical pastiche that has come to be seen as the architectural style of the Triangle. Everything and everyone here comes from somewhere else. Impermanence defines the place. The book you are reading is an attempt to give back to this magical kingdom some of the history it has, perhaps willfully, forgotten.

PART ONE

McMansions

1911–2011

{ OVERLOOKING BEVERLY PARK }

Beverly Park

I met Roger, an athletic-looking guy in a college T-shirt and jeans, standing on that ridge where I was looking down on Beverly Park. He was leaning on a Cadillac beside a buxom blonde. They were practicing real estate voyeurism, too.

Roger pointed out Sylvester Stallone's mansion, explaining to his friend that he used to golf with Sly, who'd once told him an amazing story about Beverly Park. I had an inkling what he was talking about. "You know the story?" he asked me—then proceeded to tell us both.

One day, Sly hears some noise, looks out his window, and sees three Cadillac Escalades pumping rap music pulling up to the house next door, which is on the market. "In and out go the Escalades," Roger says. Sly calls the listing realtor, a star herself, Valerie Fitzgerald, a blonde dynamo broker queen (in a town full of them). Who's the buyer? Sly asks her.

It was 2001, and a representative for the rap music mogul and ex-convict Marion Hugh "Suge" Knight Jr. had just made an offer of $15 million for 31 Beverly Park Terrace. He was trying to be quiet about it even though discretion wasn't considered one of Suge Knight's virtues.

When Marion "Suge" Knight, just out of prison, came along wanting in, Beverly Park already sheltered dozens of the richest and most famous residents of Los Angeles. They had come there to escape the celebrity petting zoos the older, neighboring, but ungated communities that inspired Beverly Park had become, constantly besieged by paparazzi and buzzed by star-home-tour vans with their blaring loudspeakers and their all-too-common occupants. These are the very same gawkers and lookiloos who line the pockets of L.A.'s wealthiest by buying their product—whether it's their movies, their music, their gadgets, or their mortgages. So they feel entitled to loiter outside mansions, to press their noses against windows, to try and snap photos of the fortunate few zooming through high, locked gates behind the tinted glass of Land Rovers, Maseratis, and Bentleys. Though it is a product of the same forces (the lust for wealth, power and social status) that drove the development of the older, surrounding enclaves (and indeed the entire Los Angeles region), Beverly Park, with its high gates and guarded gatehouses, draws a much clearer line between the public and the privileged.

Suge Knight was arguably one of the latter, not much different from other Beverly Park denizens of the time like Roseanne Barr, Denzel Washington, Rod Stewart, Eddie Murphy, Martin Lawrence, Haim Saban (of the Mighty Morphin Power Ranger Sabans), Samuel L. Jackson—and Sly Stallone. Like Knight, some of them hailed from what are still called minority populations: African Americans, Italians, and Jews. Some even had police records. But when Stallone heard who was aiming to be his next-door neighbor, he wasn't feeling very inclusive.

He had his reasons. Knight, a former football player, is a major figure in modern entertainment, the kingpin of West Coast hip hop, cohead of Death Row Records, home of acts like N.W.A. (aka Niggaz with Attitude), Snoop Dogg, and Tupac Shakur. But he is also reputedly a former drug dealer who's racked up an impressive criminal record, having been arrested for assaulting a girlfriend and shooting a man in an attempted robbery, and having pled guilty to felony assault with a deadly weapon after breaking someone's jaw with a gun. People say he uses the threat of violence as a business tool, openly carrying weapons. He is also suspected of involvement in the murder of Tupac's East Coast rival Biggie Smalls, aka Notorious B.I.G. Knight had just been released from nine months in prison for a parole violation—and probably had his own good reasons for wanting to live in a guarded and gated high-security community—when he made his offer on 31 Beverly Park Terrace.

What happened next isn't entirely clear, even to the seller, Dorothy Schoelen. The fashion designer bought bare land for $2 million in the mideighties and built what she calls her "dream house" on it, a Mediterranean villa overlooking Beverly Hills with a koi pond in front, an infinity pool in back, another pool indoors under a glass atrium, a sunken tennis court, a patinated standing-seam copper roof, five bedrooms, one of them round, a huge living room over a round breakfast room, a billiard room, playrooms, work rooms, and a library. "Then I discovered the neighborhood was way over my head; it cost way more than I'd planned," she says, so after four years, she reluctantly put the house up for sale, and Suge came a-calling.

"My neighbors had a fit," Schoelen recalls. "They were nervous I might sell it to someone who wasn't right. I didn't know who he was. I don't listen to rap music. To me, it was, if he loved my house, what's the difference?" She doesn't know what Stallone thought or did, either. "But the real estate lady thought it was not a good idea. [She] said, 'I don't think the neighbors would like it.' And the next thing I know, Stallone made an offer. All cash." She doesn't think he topped Knight's bid.[1] Regardless, she sold the place to him.

Roger told a good story, which may even be true. It goes like this:

"So next thing, Suge and his posse somehow show up at Sly's door," Roger says.

"You don't like black people?" one of them asks Stallone.

"No, asshole, I don't like *you*," Stallone says. At least according to Roger. Then he and his blonde slip into his Caddy and head off down Summit Ridge Drive.

Beverly Park is a young community that attracts mostly youngish rich people who want spanking-new houses for their spanking-new money, people like the actress Jami Gertz; the country stars Reba McEntire, Faith Hill, and Tim McGraw; and the athletes Barry Bonds and Magic Johnson, some of whom might have even listened to a Death Row record in their day. Yet a few months later, Stallone sold his extra house for $14,500,545 (a $1,499,455 loss) to the then seventy-nine-year-old Sumner Redstone, CEO of the Viacom infotainment conglomerate. With Redstone in residence, it was a pretty good bet there would be no sleepless nights chez Stallone due to raucous rap parties—or worse.

To many, Beverly Park is a shimmering symbol of La-La Land—its love of the new, of self-invention, and of hiding in plain sight. No house there predates 1986; most are known, if at all, for gargantuan tastelessness rather than architectural distinction, and although its residents are generally rich as Croesus, few are rooted in either family or place. It's "a billionaires' Levittown," the *New York Times* once sneered, where "huge feels just right." But

Beverly Park also offers a window onto the hidden history of a city that is profoundly antihistorical. It is a microcosm of all the forces that made L.A., its roots sunk, however improbably, in rootlessness, civic sleaze, organized crime, and unbounded social ambition. It's a place where self-invention under the sun is nothing new. Its short history is an echo of the only slighter longer history of the Triangle.

Pre–Beverly Park

On colonial-era maps, the site of today's Beverly Park is not shown as private property; it is marked only as public land. In the nineteenth century, it was known as Higgins Canyon, named after one of the homesteading families who settled there. But soon enough, unlike the Benedicts of Benedict Canyon, who remained significant figures in Beverly Hills, they and their names effectively disappeared.

One Beverly Hills realtor says the rough canyon they abandoned was "bottom feeder land," good for little or nothing. But in fact, the Lankershim Estate, a family-owned corporation that bought sixty thousand acres in the southern half of the San Fernando Valley for $115,000 after the Civil War, owned property at the top of Higgins Canyon. And William Augustus Reeder, a onetime Kansas congressman who founded another early real estate dynasty in L.A., and whose descendants are still in the local social register called the Southwest Blue Book (blue for their blood as well as its cover), owned land there, too.

After two thousand acres in Higgins and Benedict Canyons burned in fires in the fall of 1924, Reeder's son Leland told the *Los Angeles Times* that neighboring landholders included the pioneer moviemaker Thomas Ince, then the head of United Artists, the film producer Joseph Schenck, and a New York stockbroker, Edward Francis "E. F." Hutton. Reeder had been buying canyon land above Beverly Hills since 1911. "I didn't even know that we had property there," admits Marylee Reeder, Leland's granddaughter-in-law, who still lives in Beverly Hills. "But everyone had *huge* parcels in those days."

In 1925, a subdivision called Beverlyridge opened in the hills between Reeder's land and some of the earliest Beverly Hills estates to the south; development of the foothills was beginning. Where two decades earlier there had only been homesteaders, now houses sheltering two thousand families dotted the hills between Beverly Hills and Laurel Canyon, which had just been absorbed into the ever-expanding city of Los Angeles.

That year, a paved road through Higgins Canyon was proposed but never came to be, and for a time the city even barred travel on the existing narrow dirt road, less than a mile long. Real estate tourists could still take other routes for shallow glimpses into the surrounding hills, where the variety of residences on display presented "a striking spectacle," the *Los Angeles Times* wrote. But even as Edson Benedict's son Pierce sold off the last piece of his family's ranch for subdivision in 1932, Higgins Canyon remained undeveloped raw land—visited mostly by rattlesnakes, hikers, firemen battling brush fires, joyriding local teenagers, and, in a famous case in 1933, an eighteen-year-old girl who shot herself after failing to find work as an actress. It would remain undeveloped for half a century.

After that starlet's suicide, Higgins disappeared from the local public record until 1956, when the president of the Beverly Hills Thrift and Loan, Morton Gimple Rodin, also a developer, won approval from the Los Angeles City Council to build twenty-two single-family houses there. A few years later, Rodin would be accused of bribing a Los Angeles zoning official with a personal financial stake in canyon land to gain approval of building projects. A few years after that, that official would be publicly defended by an L.A. city councilman who had his own interest in canyon land—and ended up losing his job and his reputation as a result. But that's getting ahead of the story of the land that became Beverly Park.

In their film *Chinatown,* a fictionalization of the diversion of Owens Valley water to Los Angeles, director Roman Polanski and screenwriter Robert Towne exposed the corrupt base of the edifice of power in Los Angeles. That theft of water by the rich for the rich is only one of many scandals hidden in plain sight in L.A. history. The creation of Beverly Park involved another complex conspiracy. It began in 1957 when James Riddle "Jimmy" Hoffa became the president of the International Brotherhood of Teamsters, the giant Chicago-based labor union that had been tied to "Scarface" Al Capone's mob syndicate since its truckers carted liquor during Prohibition. Organized crime became Hoffa's business partner, with the fund holding union members' pensions treated as a piggy bank. Through the Teamsters Central States Southeast and Southwest Areas Pension Funds, gangsters bought into and earned fortunes from seemingly legitimate businesses in Los Angeles and its backyard playground, the nearby gambling town of Las Vegas. If you scratched the surface of L.A. or Vegas, you'd see Chicago, Hoffa, the descendants of Capone, the mob, and its pimps and murderers.

Suge Knight was nothing new.

In 1961, Frank McCulloch, a crusading editor at the *Los Angeles Times,* pointed out a window of his office to the Santa Monica Mountains in the distance and asked two of his reporters to find out who owned the valuable, undeveloped land there. The next May, the paper began publishing a months-long series of exposés that revealed the extent of the Teamsters' influence in L.A., just as the United States Department of Justice, then led by Robert F. Kennedy, was impaneling a federal grand jury to investigate the union, the pension fund, and Hoffa. Though the Teamsters boss was only one of sixteen trustees, he exercised control over the fund's multimillion-dollar investments. Over fifteen months, the series told how the Teamsters had funneled the pension money under their care into, among other things, Southern California real estate. The paper didn't yet cover it, but one such investment was being made at that very moment in its own backyard—in the same Santa Monica Mountains that had inspired its investigation. The first inkling anyone had of the Teamster-financed plan—and the first suggested development for what would eventually become Beverly Park—was an application in June 1963 to build a private golf course and six thirteen-story apartment buildings at the north end of Beverly Drive, the only road into Higgins Canyon.

The Beverly Hills Country Club was its name, an inside joke tribute to a just-closed nightclub and illegal casino in Newport, Kentucky, that billed itself as the "show place of the Middle West" and featured acts like Dean Martin and Frank Sinatra. Its first incarnation had burned to the ground in 1936 after the owner, a bootlegger's driver, refused to sell it to one Morris B. "Moe" Dalitz, Al Capone's Cleveland equivalent. The club was rebuilt and reopened, and it wasn't long before that same owner agreed to let Dalitz and Co. buy it. They ran it until 1961, when it was shut down by protests of local clergy.

But in the meantime, Dalitz had found greener pastures (green as in money) in Las Vegas. Organized crime families from the Midwest had had interests there since the 1930s, and after World War II, the various mobs—Cleveland, Kansas City, New York, and especially Chicago—began setting up western outposts in Los Angeles; their operations in the neighboring cities intertwined. Tony "the Hat" Cornero, who opened the first casino in Vegas, later ran gambling boats in international waters off the Santa Monica coast, frequented by wealthy Angelenos. Benjamin "Bugsy" Siegel, a former bootlegger tied to a New York crime family, came to L.A. in 1937, and allied with local crime boss Mickey Cohen to set up a national wire service reporting race results to illegal gaming establishments. Siegel later owned several casinos and finally opened the glamorous Flamingo hotel in Vegas, where a Capone-era mob lawyer, Sidney Korshak, became Siegel's lawyer, too. Korshak had been sent to Los Angeles in 1945 to become, as his biographer Gus Russo puts it, the primary liaison between the Underworld and the upper world, representing the Chicago Mafia's interests as it infiltrated West Coast—that is, Los Angeles and Las Vegas—labor unions, hotels, legal gambling, and real estate development. One such operation was the second Beverly Hills Country Club, which was conceived two years after its Midwest namesake died.

By 1950, Dalitz's Desert Inn group, a casino partnership between the Chicago and Cleveland crime families, had become a favored recipient of Teamster pension fund financing. Bobby Kennedy had been watching all this for years; at the time of Hoffa's election in '58, Kennedy was chief counsel to the United States Senate's Permanent Subcommittee on Investigations, then known as the McClellan committee after its chairman, Arkansas senator John L. McClellan. McClellan also ran the Select Committee on Improper Activities in Labor and Management, which called Korshak in for questioning the same day Hoffa took over the Teamsters; Korshak walked away unblemished. The next year, when he bought a modern mansion on Chalon Road in Bel Air that was later sometimes guarded by armed men, the mob's influence already reached into the highest places in Los Angeles politics, society, and business.

The parallel investigations by Kennedy and the *Los Angeles Times* slowed the Teamsters-mob endeavor, but didn't stop it. Indeed, even as the *Times* was revealing that $6.7 million in Teamsters pension money had financed Trousdale Estates, an expensive subdivision of the vast Beverly Hills ranch that had once belonged to the oilman Edward Doheny, a front man for one of Trousdale's developers was heading a group buying up nearby Higgins Canyon for the mob.

In his heyday, I. Irving Davidson, now eighty-nine and ailing, was one of Washington's best operators, a guy who made things happen, sometimes for not very nice people. Davidson was close to Hoffa, to New Orleans mob boss Carlos Marcello, and to the American-backed governments, some run by dictators, in Nicaragua, the Dominican Republic, Haiti, Cuba, Israel, Guatemala, Ecuador, and Indonesia. An expediter in the official World War II ammunition program, Davidson later flourished as a government-registered middleman for arms deals, moving guns and jets around the world. But his forte was being a fixer.

Before Davidson got involved in Higgins Canyon, Korshak approached two L.A. developers, Archie Preissman and David May of the May's department store family, about investing in the land. After a few lunches, they turned him down. Then, the Washington lobbyist entered the negotiations. Another member of the Higgins Canyon group was a fellow associate of Hoffa's and recipient of Teamster largesse, Hyman Green, later identified by the *Times* as a "promoter in and out of trouble with Federal authorities but never convicted." As developers in St. Petersburg, Florida, Green and a brother had just been charged with defrauding the Federal Housing Administration.

Davidson and Green teamed up with two gamblers who were neighbors in Trousdale Estates. They'd co-owned a large plot in Bel Air before they bought 155 acres of Higgins Canyon land on April 19, 1962. Though the name Melba Rice was on the deed, she was fronting for her husband, Emanuel J. "Manny" Rice, a wealthy L.A. "businessman," who, in a previous incarnation, had been a Scarface-era Chicago bookie. Rice's partner was Dr. Victor G. Lands, a Los Angeles surgeon. "Manny was the money, Victor was the brains," says Mona Lands, the girl he'd just married, who was twenty years his junior. He expected her to "stay pregnant and barefoot," and didn't tell her anything about his business. But she couldn't help noticing things.

"He was very well respected," she says, "but he loved gambling. He loved the excitement of that world. He was fascinated with the dark side." And she isn't surprised that he got tangled up with gangsters. "It was his nature," she says. "He gambled that way. He was always borrowing to buy something and then borrowing against that."

In 1964, Leonard L. Bursten, a stocky, hard-driving assistant U.S. attorney turned Florida real estate speculator, organized Beverly Ridge Estates Corp. to subdivide Higgins Canyon, financed by a loan of just under $4 million from the Teamsters pension fund. Davidson and Green were behind him, even though a previous Bursten-Teamsters land deal had collapsed; Bursten and Green were suing each other and Bursten was later convicted of tax evasion and disbarred. By then, Hoffa had been convicted, too, in a multimillion-dollar scheme to defraud that pension fund. His troubles had been mounting for several years. In 1962, he was tried for accepting illegal payments from a trucking firm. In 1963, he was charged with bribing jurors in that trial, which ended with a hung jury. A few months later, he and seven associates were charged with conspiracy and mail and wire fraud for obtaining $20 million in loans from the pension fund and siphoning off $1 million for themselves. The next year, Hoffa was convicted and sentenced to five years in prison. His influence waned after he went to jail in 1967, appointing an acolyte acting boss in his absence, but he hung on to his job atop the union until 1971. Hoffa finally agreed to step down upon being pardoned by President Richard Nixon, who'd briefly lived in a Trousdale Estates home sold to him at a "celebrity" discount after he returned to California in 1961 on losing his first run for the presidency.

But none of that stopped the planning for the Beverly Hills Country Club in Higgins Canyon. Neither did angry neighbors, who made their feelings known at the first hearing on the proposed development in October 1964. By then, the plans had changed. The apartment buildings had been abandoned, replaced by expensive single-family homes surrounding the golf course, and the developers had reinforced their ranks, adding four lawyers as directors of the company, superstar golf course designer Robert Trent Jones, and Dean Martin, a patient of Dr. Lands who'd performed at the first Beverly Hills Country Club, as the development's celebrity face. Robert E. Petersen, publisher of *Hot Rod, Motor Trend,* and *Teen* magazines, was named the club's president. Lands was named a director of the golf club, along with Martin and his Rat Pack pal, Frank Sinatra.

Martin, then at the peak of his career with his own TV show, headlined the press conference announcing the 70-par golf course with an unprecedented twenty-two holes—there would be four duplicate par-3 holes to speed play on the course. "The best way for a golf-crazy Italian street-singer to become President of a country club is to start one of his own," Martin wrote to potential members. "The first nine is now being played by a foursome of bulldozers in a beautiful, exclusive mountain rimmed area just five minutes from the heart of Beverly Hills and almost in my own back yard."

The cost of the course was projected at a mind-boggling $15 million ($95.5 million in 2010 dollars) due to the need to raise the valley floor four hundred feet with 10 million cubic yards of soil, about a third of the total excavated for the Panama Canal. The planners promised a moving sidewalk between a Spanish clubhouse and the first hole. It was all going to be paid for by six hundred equity members ("white, Negro, Catholic, Jew, Italian . . . people from every walk of life," Martin promised) who would pay $25,000 apiece for the privilege, presumably to repay the Teamsters fund which, by June 1967, had made two more loans of an additional $4,772,500.

The proposed course—which Martin said would open in 1969—became a national news story. But the two *Los Angeles Times* investigative reporters, Gene Blake and Jack Tobin, who'd made the Teamsters their beat, didn't write about it; in fact, the last story to carry their shared byline had run in January 1963. Their investigation was squelched by members of the Chandler family, who owned the newspaper and had a spider's web of business interests spread all over the region.

It continued to be a good story, though. Shortly after Dean Martin announced the country club, Victor Lands was arrested, one of six men indicted in a conspiracy to cheat card players at the Friars Club in Beverly Hills, a private watering hole for show business and wealthy types. Peepholes had been drilled in the ceiling of its card room, and a spy would watch games and signal confederates playing below. Among the victims were Zeppo Marx of the Marx Brothers, the comedian Phil Silvers, who played television's Sergeant Bilko, and Harry Karl, a wealthy shoe manufacturer who was married at the time to actress Debbie Reynolds and had sold his last home in Bel Air to a friend—the ubiquitous Sidney Korshak.

Lands and his codefendants all pled innocent. Lands's role in the scam remains unclear. He'd chaired the Friars' house committee when it approved the installation of the cheating devices, which were disguised as burglar alarms, and had often played cards at the club, but had sometimes lost money himself. While his five codefendants were eventually found guilty of committing forty-nine felonies, Lands cut a deal, pled guilty to a single count of filing a false tax return (for the same year in which the Higgins Canyon property was assembled), and was fined $5,000 and sentenced to a mere ten days. It later emerged that he'd secretly taped one of his codefendants on behalf of the government. "He was trying to save his life," says Mona Lands. "Most of those guys deserved to be gotten."

Before Lands went to jail, he'd argued with Manny Rice, who wanted to sell the Higgins Canyon property. "Victor wanted to develop it," says Mona Lands. "So Manny sued him right after he went to jail. It was nasty. He got him while the guy was down" and Lands "gave up the property."

Though none of the developers knew it, the death of the Beverly Hills Country Club was preordained. A year before its opening was announced, the developers had decided that they needed a new four-lane road to their club, not only for access, but also because they needed that 10 million cubic yards of soil to fill the valley, which would be theirs for free if they could induce the L.A. City Council to lop off the top of the ridge to build the road for them. Leading the charge to approve the road was the canyon's city councilman, James B. Potter Jr., who warned that if the road wasn't built, those six hundred golfers and their friends would clog the narrow hillside streets. It would cost $154,000 to acquire the right of way, but Beverly Ridge Estates had offered to pay more than $2 million toward the cost of planning and preparing the road if it was approved. It was an offer the city found nearly irresistible, but again, angry neighbors disagreed.

"The road got us involved," recalls Betty Decter, who still lives at the top of Beverly Drive just below the ridge where it was to be built. Decter and her husband, Gerald, who were partners in a mannequin-manufacturing business and dedicated conservationists, became obsessed with stopping the road. They allied with the Beverly Hills city government, which feared a new road to the valley would be an open invitation for invasion, "ruining our fine neighborhood," as one official put it, and organized a neighborhood association. Its membership grew when the grading operation caused a flood that saw hundreds of homeowners evacuated.

The neighbors appeared en masse at the first public hearing on the road. "Out of two hundred families here, one hundred fifty went," says Decter.

"We didn't even know where city hall was before that." Aside from representing the canyon district and sitting on the city council's Public Works Committee, Potter was the son of a state senator. "He was very arrogant," Decter says. " 'Why are you trying to tell me my job?' We didn't know you're not supposed to ask questions. That made us want to look into it." A week later, the developers tried to simultaneously outflank and co-opt them. The *Los Angeles Times* ran an article claiming that 3.5 million cubic yards of dirt had already been moved for the 7,000-yard course, and that former White House press secretary Pierre Salinger, actors Tony Curtis, James Garner, and Kirk Douglas, and director Mervyn LeRoy had signed on as founding members. And Jerry Decter got a letter from the Beverly Hills Country Club, asking if he'd like to play in a new PGA tournament, the Dean Martin Golf Party, to be held at the club once it opened in fall 1969.

Despite the opposition, Potter's committee soon endorsed the road and a few months later, the council followed suit. Instead of giving up, the Decters redoubled their effort. Meantime, three hills were leveled, the valley between was filled in, the grading was nearly completed, and seeding for the fairways was set to begin. Only then did the Decters uncover the Teamsters-mob connection.

"Willie the Icepick?" Jerry said to Betty one day. "*What* are we doing?"

"We were terrified," says Betty. "Jerry would start his car in the morning expecting it to blow up. But we were loudmouths. We told everyone what we'd found." They hoped that would give them some protection.

By summer 1968, the cost of the project had soared nearly 50 percent to $23 million—making the BHCC the world's most expensive golf course—and both Dean Martin and Robert Petersen had quit the project. Clearly, there was trouble in paradise, yet Potter and the city persisted, even as the Teamsters financing was revealed and more legal challenges were filed by both Beverly Hills and neighbors. One found his water lines suddenly cut. Another had a 200-foot ridge on his property bulldozed into the valley. "They didn't care, they did what they wanted," says Robert Dewhirst, who still lives in Beverly Hills. When Dewhirst called in a deputy sheriff, Beverly Ridge workers menaced him with a bulldozer. Dewhirst offered to sell the land, but was spurned, so he filed for an injunction; finally, "the Teamsters" bought the tiny strip of land. "I've always wondered if it was legal," Dewhirst adds, "because the guy who signed the papers was in jail at the time."

In 1969, the Decters and Co. (a group that had expanded to include seventeen separate canyon homeowners' associations) began to get traction. They suggested that Councilman Potter had conflicts of interest: His sister and a member of his staff had both worked for the developers. Potter was then running for Congress; he would shortly lose the Republican primary. Then, the state attorney general opened an investigation into those charges of conflict as well as malfeasance and bribery of public officials by Beverly Ridge, and it emerged that months earlier, at the end of 1968, the Central States Pension Fund had sued Bursten and colleagues for foreclosure on their loans, alleging they'd received no interest or principal repayments, and that in response, Beverly Ridge had declared bankruptcy. Adding to the confusion, Teamsters' lawyers claimed that Bursten had filed that action for bankruptcy protection on his own, without authorization by his board of directors (i.e., the real landowners, Davidson and Green). Nonetheless, Los Angeles kept pushing for its road, even as more city officials came under scrutiny.

That summer, the road was shelved when more of the truth emerged. It turned out that Bursten's offer years before to pay for the road had come with secret strings attached: He'd asked that the city's Board of Public Works not only buy and give Beverly Ridge sixteen acres of land owned by its Department of Water and Power, but grade the tract as well. Potter and a friend of his, who worked as a lobbyist for Bursten, kept pushing the plan even though it was a bonanza for Bursten, who was legally obligated to pay for an access road. For two years, Water and Power officials were kept in the dark about the proposed giveaway. They only found out when Betty Decter started asking pointed questions at a city council hearing.

In fall 1969, Councilman Potter's bank records were subpoenaed; a superior court judge blocked a similar move to examine Beverly Ridge records. A few days later, that judge was arrested for assault with intent to commit murder after stabbing his wife. Subsequently found not guilty by reason of insanity, he was sent to a state hospital for observation and electric shock therapy. Released the next year, he was briefly committed again in 1973, and finally returned to practicing law in 1980, all the while blaming the stabbing on a topical drug he'd been taking for skin cancer.

Beverly Ridge stayed in the headlines and Potter's troubles mounted. A grand jury was convened, a joint federal-state task force was formed to look into the development in Higgins Canyon, and the trickle of information turned into a torrent. It finally emerged that Bursten was only a front man, as were Petersen, Dean Martin, and another early Beverly Ridge officer, realtor Sammy Hess, best known for dating Frank Sinatra's teen-aged daughter, Tina.

Most of the canyon land still belonged to Irving Davidson and Hyman Green. And mob ties and corruption were everywhere. The Teamsters fund's financial advisor, the son of a Capone-era mobster, owned stock in Beverly Ridge and would later die in a mob-style execution. The PR man for Beverly Ridge had served nine months for obstruction of justice for juror intimidation at Jimmy Hoffa's trial. Beverly Ridge had loaned thousands of dollars to Potter, his sister, a local congressman, and a county tax assessor, and had regularly entertained L.A. mayor Sam Yorty and his staff. The finances of the company were, as one report put it, "a bewildering mass of promissory notes and trust deeds." Adding an almost-comic dimension, the well-wired Washington columnist Jack Anderson speculated that the Teamsters were actually behind this scandalous publicity, hoping it would let them squeeze out Bursten et al. and replace them with "insiders" the union could more easily control.

Two months later that suggestion seemed to be confirmed when the Teamsters fund sued Beverly Ridge for fraud, alleging that it had been shocked . . . *shocked* . . . to discover that its money had been used to bribe politicians. And ultimately, the pension fund did end up the only winner in the affair. Bursten, Davidson, and Green all pleaded guilty to fraud and in 1972, the Teamsters bought their land in a public foreclosure sale. But there were still twists to come in the tale of the land that would finally become Beverly Park.

Potter was kicked out of office in 1971. Found guilty of perjury, the county commissioner went to jail for six months. Sentenced to fifteen years in prison, Bursten first underwent ninety days of psychiatric observation. But then, his sentence was abruptly altered to fifteen years probation, with the judge citing "very serious" (nonpsychiatric) medical issues as the cause of his reversal. A telephone call to the U.S. attorney pleading for leniency, made by Murray Chotiner, Jimmy Hoffa's lawyer and a longtime political aide to then president Nixon, went unmentioned. Despite his alleged life-threatening heart condition, Bursten lived another fourteen years.

Davidson did even better; sentenced to only a year's probation after cooperating with the prosecution, he continued his career in "public relations" until serious illness intervened. "Someone once said he had a knack for making coincidences happen," says his daughter Lynne, now a senior advisor at the U.S. Department of State. "He always knew who to call. He certainly knew very colorful people. But he would adamantly deny that he ever crossed the line."

In 1974, the Teamsters sold Beverly Ridge to Allen R. Glick for $7 million, all of which it provided in a loan to their buyer at half the prevailing bank rate of interest, with no repayment scheduled for a decade, and the final payment due in twenty-five years. The reason for this cushy arrangement? Glick was a Teamsters insider, installed because he would be more malleable than Bursten had been. A Vietnam veteran, lawyer, and residential housing developer in San Diego, the thirty-one-year-old Glick was tied in with another wise guy, a relative of a Capone-era gunman who'd introduced him to pension fund officials, who financed his purchase of the Stardust and Fremont hotel-casinos in Vegas. Seemingly overnight, Glick was a star who fancied himself the next Howard Hughes—the only person who owned more casinos there.

Glick was a "straight-arrow naïf," in the words of Mafia expert Nicholas Pileggi, who told his story in the book *Casino* (Glick is called Philip Green in the Martin Scorsese movie). He'd become the property of the crime boss of Milwaukee, a trustee of the Teamsters' pension fund, installed in Vegas to ensure that the mob's skim—the illegal diversion of cash bet in the casinos, a steady source of income for La Cosa Nostra since the 1940s—flowed unimpeded. "The money was handed over to special couriers who made regular trips," Pileggi wrote, "between Vegas and Chicago, where it was distributed to Milwaukee, Cleveland, Kansas City . . ." It was a perfect illustration of how pension fund loans were used for criminal purposes.

A mere few months later the pension fund handed Glick its poison plum—Beverly Ridge. Unfortunately for Glick, his fortunes promptly took a turn for the worse. A Vegas casino he owned filed for bankruptcy, and he was sued by its creditors. Soon he was under investigation by the Los Angeles–based Organized Crime Task Force. Simultaneously, the Nevada Gaming Commission was investigating the man who actually ran the Stardust for the mob, Frank "Lefty" Rosenthal (aka "Ace" Rothstein, played by Robert De Niro in the Scorsese movie). Next, the Labor Department piled on, asking whether the Teamster loans to Glick violated a brand-new pension reform law implemented to curb abuses like those that had already plagued Beverly Ridge. Then, Nevada charged Glick with failing to report loans to his casinos.

Finally, Glick's name surfaced in the investigation of the gangland-style execution of Tamara Rand, a fifty-four-year-old San Diego businesswoman whose safe deposit box was stuffed with $400,000 in crisp new currency. A former consultant to one of Glick's companies, she'd sued him a year before her death after he allegedly refused to give her 5 percent of his gambling shares in return for more than a million dollars she'd loaned him. Rand had just won the right to subpoena corporate documents regarding the pension fund loan and had been killed just after she had an argument with Glick. Pileggi reported that Rand's murder was ordered by Glick's Milwaukee mob boss in order to protect the skim.

Though he was simultaneously fighting Clark County's district attorney, the Justice Department, the Securities and Exchange Commission (SEC), and the IRS, which was seeking back taxes and civil fraud penalties, Glick would hang on in Vegas—and in Beverly Ridge, now renamed Beverly Summit—for a few more years. However, the problems took their toll, and in 1978, a professional manager hired by the government to manage Teamsters assets foreclosed on Beverly Summit, and soon Glick was nudged out of Vegas, too. Ironically, that manager had once worked for the family that created neighboring Holmby Hills almost six decades earlier.

Granted immunity by several grand juries in return for testimony against his Milwaukee mob boss and a dozen other organized crime figures charged with skimming millions from his casinos, "Glick was a devastating witness," Pileggi writes, "precise and incapable of being ruffled." The guilty pleas and verdicts that resulted effectively ended the mob's rule of Las Vegas. Allen Glick then made himself scarce, maintaining to this day he'd been an innocent ensnared.

Beverly Park

In February 1979, the Teamsters finally lost the Higgins Canyon land; the government-appointed asset manager sold off the 355 troubled acres for $7.9 million to a group of about twenty wealthy investors. The only one publicly identified at the time was Henry Salvatori, a multimillionaire oilman from Bel Air and member of the so-called kitchen cabinet of California conservatives who were then within months of placing Ronald Reagan in the White House—though both his family and the developers now say he wasn't involved. The investors did include hair salon mogul Vidal Sassoon, a stereo component manufacturer named Bob Craig, local supermarket owner Bernie Gelson, a local car dealer, and Gerald Breslauer, a Hollywood money manager, as well as a number of his clients, including director Steven Spielberg, then flush with cash from *Jaws* and *Close Encounters of the Third Kind*. (Breslauer also managed Barbra Streisand, *Rocky* producer Irwin Winkler, Jane Fonda, and Michael Caine, among others.) The investor group had been put together by a realtor, Brian Adler, who also recruited a semiretired canyon developer to take charge of the tract.

Elliot Gottfurcht, thirty-nine, promised to meet with government and local homeowners and win their approval of a plan to build a private gated community. Adler says their plan B was to sell the original six parcels separately as ranches. Both men, who later had a falling-out, claim authorship of the idea of the community of Beverly Park. Gottfurcht says he wanted to build something comparable to Bel Air and Holmby Hills. "I had a vision of a high-end enclave," *better* than those neighborhoods, says Adler. "The quality of life on the Westside had changed. I'd grown up in Beverly Hills. I was sensitive to what the upscale audience wanted." In a word, gates. "I was marketing the lifestyle of large flat lots in beautiful settings with controls over house size and setbacks so there would be consistency and maximum appreciation over the years without being too restrictive." Except, of course, when it came to who could get inside those gates.

Adler says he named it Beverly Park Estates after a children's park on the site of today's Beverly Center, where he'd ridden ponies as a child. Despite his vision and his nostalgia, neighborhood protests continued, and Joel Wachs, the city councilman who'd replaced James Potter, hoped aloud that Los Angeles would buy the land for an actual park, but "nobody had the money," says Wachs, now head of the Warhol Foundation. Though it would still take years to build a house there, the so-called Teamsters Tract was finally on its way to becoming a new neighborhood.

Gottfurcht announced an initial plan to build 189 homes, but says he expected to negotiate down to what he really wanted, 80 homes on larger lots. With memories of the floods and illegal grading of 1967 still fresh, "fights, wars, whatever," as Gottfurcht puts it, began again. Neighboring homeowners said they would accept only 46 homes. The city approved 115. In 1982, Gottfurcht was finally given permission to finish preparing the land (which required adding another 1.5 million cubic yards of earth to bring the unapproved grading up to code) and sell 76 building lots. In exchange, he agreed to donate about $400,000 to environmental and government groups and sixteen acres above Mulholland Drive to create a park. "Everyone knew that if they didn't permit this, one day, who knows, something worse might come," says Wachs.

In 1985, with roads, infrastructure, and utility lines in place, Beverly Park went on the market, heralded by a lavish $100 hardcover coffee-table book that sold its not-yet-built homes by showing photographs of the great estates of the Platinum Triangle's heyday, and an over-the-top Rodeo Drive showroom filled with computerized special effects displays that allowed potential customers to take a simulated, joystick-driven aerial tour of the development with photos of those great old houses superimposed on the empty Beverly Park lots.

"It's a fantasy land," Gottfurcht told journalists as part of the $2 million marketing effort. What was inarguable was that for the first time since the Depression and the end of the first golden era of the great L.A. estates, Beverly Park offered the opportunity for the megawealthy to build West Coast dream homes on large, level properties with floor plans and views as expansive as their owners' self-images.

Initially, only sixteen relatively small sites of one or two acres (costing $1 million to $3.5 million each) went on the market in the southern end of the tract, "to introduce the public to the idea," Adler says. Later, plots to the north twice that size would be offered for $5 million. "You have to walk before you run."

But the first lots sold at a snail's pace. Though the south gate of Beverly Park is only 4.5 miles from the corner of Sunset Boulevard and Doheny Drive—about a ten-minute drive—that seemed too far to the pampered denizens of the Triangle. Even after the developers opened a slate-roofed stone gatehouse, its look inspired by the Henry Ford estate in Dearborn, Michigan, Adler "felt resistance to being the first in," so he decided to build a house for himself, and simultaneously moved an architect, a landscaper, and a team of contractors into the gatehouse "to offer a turnkey package," he says. "We would orchestrate their dream houses."

A savings and loan bank that had helped finance the deal bought six lots and began building spec houses. Adler recruited a partner, Marshall Ezralow, the low-key head of a family that had been managing and developing real estate for four generations, and together, they bought four more lots and started planning houses, too. Finally, the country singer Kenny Rogers, who'd developed a sideline in real estate, bought a lot, as did the record company owner Jerry Moss. Though neither of them ultimately built, other boldfaced names and big bank account holders did, including the merchant banker Tony Forstmann, movie producer Jon Peters (who trucked in 150 mature trees for his property), Paul Marciano of Guess, Inc., the fashion line, Sly Stallone's ex-wife Sasha, basketball's Earvin "Magic" Johnson, and the actress Pia Zadora and her husband, Israeli businessman Meshulam Riklis, who lived there while rebuilding the nearby estate Pickfair, once the home of Douglas Fairbanks and Mary Pickford.

Even though unprecedented new fortunes were beginning to accumulate in the early Reagan era, it was still slow going at Beverly Park, and within a year the first investors were looking for the exit, as was Gottfurcht, who began fielding offers for the northern section of the tract, already prepared for homes, as a single entity. UCLA was briefly interested in building 250 condominiums for faculty on 135 acres, but was beaten back by renewed neighborhood protests. After Gottfurcht began marketing a plan to turn the remaining land into four huge megaranches, some with polo fields, Sly Stallone offered $6 million for one, and producer Peter Guber considered building a horse ranch on another, but neither deal materialized. Finally, in 1988, just after a stock market plunge spooked the real estate market, Gottfurcht and the investors sold their remaining interest for $22.5 million to a group led by Adler and Ezralow. Gottfurcht says Ezralow brought in Canada's Belzberg financial dynasty as quiet investors. Though he retained several lots, since sold, Gottfurcht switched gears and went into the software business. He had no interest in living in Beverly Park. "I'm not that kind of person," he says.

Meantime, between 1986 and 1988, homeowners had finally begun moving into South Beverly Park, today the low-key half of the development. Though it shelters a few big names like Richard Zanuck (the film-producer son of the legendary movie mogul Darryl Zanuck), who bought from Kenny Rogers; Magic Johnson, who stayed and built; and actor Samuel L. Jackson, its residents are mostly the lesser-known likes of real estate investors Daniel Blatteis and Paul Daneshrad; David Sydorick, a trader then with junk bond specialists Drexel Burnham Lambert and a classic race car collector; Dr. Mohammad Gharavi, chief of cardiovascular surgery at Providence Tarzana Medical Center; and former Midwest concert promoter Irv Zuckerman.

And with memories of the '87 crash already fading, half of North Beverly Park's sixty-four lots were reserved by the time the house-building team moved into a new north gatehouse in 1990. Rod Stewart, Adler says, was one of the first buyers. "Brian," the singer told him, "I've got people crawling over my walls" in Holmby Hills—even after he'd topped them with barbed wire. "They stole his pool furniture, too," Adler says.

Adler instituted rigid restrictions on what could be built, demanding homes be 6,000 square feet or larger; he expected most would range from 11,000 to 15,000 square feet and be worth about $8 million (in fact, as the economy grew in the 1990s, so did the houses; Eddie Murphy's house, completed in 2000, is 45,000 square feet). Adler promised buyers two new gatehouses, a four-acre children's park (which would become a running joke as it is rarely used by residents with vast acreage of their own), and all the security cameras and armed guards they would ever need (a later buyer likened the private force to Israel's fearsome spy agency, Mossad). The smallest lot initially cost $2.8 million, but by 1990, when the north gatehouse formally opened with a cocktail party and model home tours, lots started at $3.4 million.

So it's no wonder that the development has attracted people of great wealth, great fame, and often, an equally great desire for privacy. A brother of Saudi Arabia's King Abdullah owns three lots near Mulholland Drive (literally around the bend from Jack Nicholson) totaling 55,000 square feet; Bambang Trihatmodjo, the late Indonesian dictator Suharto's second son, is said to have bought two or three (after Suharto family business associates reportedly invested in Adler and Ezralow's purchase of the tract); former Disney boss Michael Eisner bought and sold three properties; mobile home park operator Lee Kort sold his 27,000-square-foot mansion for $36.7 million to public-works builder Ronald Tutor in 2008. Other owners in the north have included Indonesian billionaire Peter Sondakh; the comedian Paul Reiser; California Pizza Kitchen founder Larry Fink; Michael Jackson lawyer John Branca; the St. Petersburg, Russia–based corporate raider Alexander Sabadash; the leveraged buyout specialist Alec Gores; former Marvel Entertainment chairman Avi Arad; tech tycoon and Tesla Motors CEO Ze'ev Drori; baseball's Barry Bonds; Tampa Bay Buccaneers owner Ed Glazer; the former head of Noble Group, a Hong Kong–based commodities trading giant, Michel Harouche; financier and fashion executive Fabian Oberfeld; former studio heads Richard Frank and Mike Medavoy; casino executive Paul Alanis; Beverly Hills plastic surgeon and nose-job specialist Paul Nassif and his wife Adrienne Maloof, whose family owns the Sacramento Kings (and who is a "real housewife" of Beverly Hills); hand tool and hardware mogul Eric Smidt; and *Perfect 10* magazine publisher and Hugh Hefner–wannabe Norman Zadeh.

With all that money and ego in play, it was probably inevitable that conflict would ensue. And the Suge Knight–Stallone kerfuffle was just the first. In 2002, the North Beverly Park homeowners' association sued Robert Bisno, a real estate developer who owned both a home and a vacant lot, after neighbors Steven and Christine Udvar-Hazy (he is the Hungarian-born chairman of the largest for-lease fleet of airplanes in the world) objected to the exterior paint job and gates of the Bisno home, as well as a topiary dinosaur and what the Udvar-Hazys deemed a suggestive sculpture on the Bisno lawn. Brian Adler's sister, a member of the architectural review committee, said it was all "too Vegas" for their quiet community, and Bisno lost the case. Nonetheless, he joined his neighbors in the biggest battle of Beverly Park, which became public in 2008 after a civil war broke out between the separate south and north homeowners' associations over access to the north's Mulholland Drive gate, which had been closed the year before to guests, gardeners, nannies, maids, and contractors working in the south.

In 2006, the northerners had demanded $121,000 a year from their southern neighbors, representing 20 percent of the cost of road and gate maintenance and private security in North Beverly Park, claiming that not only had traffic become a burden but that cars authorized by southerners sometimes drove too fast and sometimes didn't need to be there at all, but were merely using Beverly Park roads as a commuting shortcut. The southerners, upset because some large vehicles could only reach the enclave from the north, refused to mediate and after the north refused them further access, sued for an injunction to open the gates. Adler testified for the south (where he had lived, though he had since sold and moved)—and early in 2009, the southerners prevailed, though their subsequent request for damages and legal fees kept the gates closed well into that year. When the south side relented on that, the north "still stalled," attempting to impose Draconian new rules on gate access, says Steven M. Goldberg, lawyer for the southerners. "We made a motion to hold them for contempt," and after a minitrial on that motion, "the judge was enraged, they caved in," and the border opened again, though the north has appealed both the judgment and the award of legal fees.

Through all of this, life went on behind the guarded gates of Beverly Park. But rich as its residents are, the economic crisis of 2008–2009 had an impact on the enclave. As Gate-gate was playing out, the Real Estalker, a Los Angeles blog, ran a post headlined "The Big Beverly Park Sell Off," reporting that "an unusual and surprising number" of Beverly Park houses had suddenly come on the market. They included the homes of country music stars Faith Hill and Tim McGraw (4 acres, 10,5000 square feet, six bedrooms for $14.8 million); TV mogul Michael Jay Solomon and his wife, Luciana Paluzzi, who played the "Bond girl" Domino in the movie *Thunderball* (house and guesthouse, tennis court, pool and spa, 13,638 square feet, six bedrooms, $19.9 million); Norman Zadeh (6.79 acres, a contemporary with guesthouse, 20,000+ square feet total, eleven bedrooms, art and dance studios, paddleball court, pool, $24.5 million); Robert and Jeanette Bisno (5+ acres, 16,800 square feet, five bedrooms, brick wine cellar, rose garden, pool, sunken tennis court, $25.9 million); Lisa Vanderpump, another member of the cast of *The*

Real Housewives of Beverly Hills, and her husband, restaurateur Ken Todd (seven bedrooms, ten bathrooms, $29 million); Rockstar Energy Drink founder Russ Weiner (5+ acres, 8,448 square feet, six bedrooms, $28 million); and a $31.5 million mansard-roofed spec house, marked down from $49 million, with ten bedrooms, a ballroom, a glass-floored circular library overlooking a 2,500-bottle brick wine cellar, a home theater, spa, gym, hot tub, indoor and outdoor pools, and a permit to build a tennis court.

The pseudonymous blogger, a young man who calls himself Your Mama, added that other properties had been taken off the market—officially, at least—including ones owned by a former bodybuilder and nutritional supplement salesman ($34 million), an Indonesian businessman (ten bedrooms, $29 million), the movie executive Mike Medavoy (five bedrooms, $23.5 million), and George Santo Pietro, a restaurateur and playboy (a spec house later leased to Prince for a rumored $100,000 a month). The Udvar-Hazys' Villa Firenze was also "quietly being shopped around [at] a price so high no one will even whisper it in Your Mama's big ear." By early 2011, some of those houses had sold—but at giant markdowns. The Medavoys got only $12.5 million from an entity called Ragada Corp., and that spec house, too, went to a buyer identified by Real Estalker as "some sort of real estate investor/flipper . . . who may or may not be a front for some other shadowy figure." In real estate circles the buyer was said to be a wealthy Russian. In an update early in 2011, Real Estalker catalogued more fire-sale prices in the gated enclave. McGraw and Hill's house was sold to a pair of Beverly Hills attorneys for $9.5 million; Paluzzi and Solomon's went to Alex von Furstenberg, son of the designing Diane and her late first husband, Egon, for a 45 percent markdown price of $12,999,999; the health-supplement guru sold his house for $21 million to a young private-equity billionaire, Tom Gores, the brother of Beverly Park resident Alec Gores; Santo Pietro's spec house, first listed at $50 million, sold to the owners of a handbag line for $23.5 million; and Zadeh, Your Mama wrote, "unloaded his white elephant" for $16.5 million, reportedly to wealthy Saudis who, less than three months after closing, flipped it back onto the market for $25 million. "Such are the real estate ways of the famous and freakishly rich," Your Mama concluded.

Though it would stave off neither foreclosure on his own home nor personal bankruptcy, Robert Bisno, too, had sold an empty lot he owned across the street from his former house to "Marky" Mark Wahlberg, the rapper–Calvin Klein underwear model turned actor-producer. A famously troubled youth, Wahlberg had once stolen cars, hurled drugs and racial epithets at a group of black schoolchildren, robbed a pharmacy while under the influence of PCP, knocked a middle-aged Vietnamese man unconscious, and permanently blinded another in one eye before he was arrested and tried as an adult for attempted murder (he copped a plea to assault and was sentenced to two years in jail—he served forty-five days); and then, at twenty-one, he fractured the jaw of a neighbor in an unprovoked attack. But by the time he bought in Beverly Park, Wahlberg had turned his life around and redeemed himself; today he is one of Hollywood's most renowned producers and, surprisingly perhaps, one of its most-respected figures.

Which all brings back to mind Suge Knight, who failed to redeem himself either before or since he was blackballed from Beverly Park; instead he has gone bankrupt and continued to skirmish with the law. Who knows what his life would be now had the residents of that crime- if not criminal-free neighborhood given him a chance. After all, as the short but colorful history of Beverly Park and the longer but equally colorful history of the Triangle proves, reinvention is what makes La-La Land go 'round.

PART TWO

Ranchos

1539–1906

{ SPANISH RANCHOS OF LOS ANGELES }

Alta California

They thought it was paradise on earth. The name *California* likely derives from a series of sixteenth-century Spanish novels on chivalry; populated only by Amazonian women, California was the fictional island that inspired Hernán Cortés, the real-life conqueror of Mexico, to send ships north along its Pacific coast in 1539. The explorers didn't find an island, but they discovered the Baja Peninsula.

Three years later, the Portuguese sea captain Juan Rodríguez Cabrillo, an explorer commissioned by the king of Spain, led three ships up the coast from New Spain again, and anchored in today's San Diego Bay. The first white men in California stayed three days, sailed on to discover Santa Catalina Island, San Pedro, Santa Monica Bay, and Ventura, and then steered northwest to take advantage of wind, almost reaching today's San Francisco before finally returning to Santa Catalina, where Rodríguez Cabrillo broke his shin, which became gangrenous and killed him.

Rodríguez Cabrillo was the first, but hardly the last, mostly unremembered figure in the history of what would become known as the Southland, the area around today's Los Angeles, encompassing Los Angeles, Orange, San Bernardino, Riverside, and Ventura counties. Including most of today's California and Nevada, it was a large portion of what would soon be known as "New" or "Alta" (Upper) California, to both attach and differentiate it from Baja, or Lower, California.

Sebastíano Vizcaíno followed Rodríguez Cabrillo, sailing out of the port of Acapulco in 1602 to map the California coastline. His flagship, the *San*

Diego, gave its name to that bay before he too traveled further north. One hundred sixty-seven years later, Spain again sent expeditions north, but this time by both land and sea to prevent British and Russian competitors from making claims on Alta California. Led by Father Junípero Serra, a Franciscan friar, and a Spanish officer, Don Gaspar de Portolá, they established forts, towns, and church missions, which doubled as farms and workshop outposts providing troops with food, horses, leather, and ironwork. Father Serra is credited with taming the California desert but also blamed for setting in motion the genocide of the native Indian population, whom he deemed "lazy savages." Driven from their homes, forced to convert to Christianity and abandon their culture, and thus effectively enslaved, they quickly died off, victims of both colonial brutality and European diseases. By the early nineteenth century, the indigenous population had shrunk to about twenty-five thousand, and a century later, it had virtually disappeared.

The Spanish built a series of missions along the coast from San Diego to San Francisco (San Diego that first year, followed by San Gabriel in 1771, San Juan Capistrano in 1776, San Buenaventura in 1782, San Fernando in 1797, San Luis Rey in 1798, La Purísima Concepción in 1787, and Santa Ynez in 1804), and laid the foundations of future roads and cities as well as the society that would come to rule over them. It was run by *hacendados,* the descendants of Portolà's soldiers, some of whom would be granted the right by the Spanish crown to use vast tracts of land called *ranchos.*

But first, Portolà and his troops passed through today's Beverly Hills in the summer of 1769, finally making camp near a river in what would become Los Angeles. That August, a Father Juan Crespi described their campsite in his diary as a beautiful plain blooming with wild roses. Legend has it that Crespi also named the future city that day, calling it Nuestra Señora la Reina de Los Angeles del Río de Porciúncula, or the town of Our Lady the Queen of the Angels on the Porciúncula River, itself named after the Italian town where Saint Francis of Assissi was born.

More expeditions to Alta California followed. In 1776, Juan Bautista de Anza led the first of two, and five years later, forty-four settlers who'd come with him became the first occupants of the pueblo, or town, of Los Angeles. Felipe de Neve, the fourth Spanish governor of the Californias, created it and two more secular towns, San Jose and Villa de Branciforte. He also commissioned "two low-caste Spaniards, one mestizo, two Negroes, eight mulattos, [and] nine Indians" to build an adobe wall around the town to keep out animals and the Indians they'd displaced. By century's end, Los Angeles was growing more grain than all but one of the other missions and more settlers arrived, including families whose names are still remembered, if only on street signs: Figueroa, Pico, and Sepulveda.

Luis Quintero, a tailor, and Eugenio Valdez, a soldier, had come to California in the same expedition that founded Los Angeles in 1781. Valdez married Quintero's daughter and, at the Mission San Gabriel, their child Maria Rita married Vicente Ferrer Villa, who'd arrived at age six in a separate group. When Valdez retired from the Spanish army, the family used his pension to help finance their move to a vast tract of flat land between Los Angeles and the sea—today's Beverly Hills. Though the crown retained title, veterans of its army were permitted to settle and graze cattle on these ranchos. Passing through this same land in 1769 with Portolà, Father Crespi had noted the water that flowed down from the nearby mountains and gave the property a name, Rodeo de las Aguas, for the "round-up of the waters" that rushed down the canyons and created lakes and swamps in the low plains beneath.

After her husband died, leaving her with eleven children, Maria Rita realized that she needed some proof that she and a relative named Luciano, who'd been the pueblo's schoolmaster, had a right to her land and went to see the *alcalde,* or mayor, of Los Angeles, requesting and winning formal occupation of the tract. In 1821, Mexico gained independence from Spain and a few years later, individuals won the ability to petition for outright grants of land they had previously only occupied. Maria Rita and Luciano had to borrow cattle to meet a 150-head requirement for the grant, but they did and were given 4,500 acres around their houses, which sat near the present corner of Sunset Boulevard and Alpine Drive. Soon, though, Luciano got feisty, moving his house close to Maria Rita's, behaving intolerably, she said, and running off her cattle, and in 1834, the city council ordered him to leave. Maria Rita paid him $17.50 for his share of the land; he threw in a peach tree and some farm equipment.

By then, Alta and Baja California had been split in two and a newly independent Mexico had taken control of both territories. In 1834, Mexico secularized the missions, breaking up their lands into hundreds more ranchos; eight million acres passed to about eight hundred grantees. The first American to travel to California overland, Jedediah Smith, a trapper, had arrived not long before, opening a new trail that became America's gateway to the

Southland. Some of the newly arrived *gringos*—or foreigners—understood that Mexican land grants could be inherited and married daughters of land-owners. Others simply made lots of money and bought land on their own. Rancho San Jose de Buenos Ayres, which would become Bel Air, Holmby Hills, and Westwood, was next door to Maria Rita; it was initially granted to a Mexican but was soon "conveyed" to two Los Angeles *gringos*.

In 1848, after the Mexican-American War, America won control of Alta California and Maria Rita briefly fled her ranch in fear. While she was gone, all her papers were stolen, including her land grant. It would be years before she could again definitively prove the rancho was hers.

The California gold rush began that year and was not only transforming life in San Francisco, but raising expectations to the south as well. Two years later, California gained statehood, and the Land Grant Act of 1851 required that all Spanish and Mexican land titles be officially confirmed. Many ranchos and their owners in the Hispanic gentry were driven into bankruptcy by the resulting legal bills and taxes, and gringos often took over their land. Among those who'd followed Jedediah Smith to California was a fur trapper, Benjamin Davis Wilson of Tennessee. En route, Wilson allegedly survived both bear and Indian attacks; the latter left a Mojave arrowhead in his flesh. He'd intended to go to China but never made it. Instead, he began buying Los Angeles ranchos. In 1852, Wilson, by then known as Don Benito, having married into a Spanish family, bought half of the 4,438-acre Rancho San Jose de Buenos Ayres for $662.75 (six years of land-price inflation later, he'd buy the other half for $16,000).

For a time, Maria Rita held on next door, but life was hard. In 1852, Indians surrounded her house; some of her children ran to a nearby settlement for help, and the attackers were chased off, but again the next April, Indians swept through the area, stealing some of Wilson's cattle. Finally fed up, Maria Rita sold her rancho to Wilson and Henry Hancock, a gringo lawyer and land surveyor. Sources vary on the price, but it was likely between $1,300 and $4,000. Hancock also had his eye on Rancho La Brea to the east; he'd represented its owners, who held a Mexican land grant, in attempting to prove their claim to it. It's said that the pair planned to combine all three ranches and grow wheat in the vast fields. But within a year, Hancock conveyed his interest in Rancho Rodeo de las Aguas to William Workman, an Englishman from Taos, New Mexico, possibly as repayment of a loan.

(Hancock eventually took over Rancho La Brea, where his son later created the still-wealthy neighborhood of Hancock Park.)

The late 1850s were good years in the Los Angeles basin. Its population was growing, augmented by trappers like Wilson, Basque sheep herders, German Jews, French peasants, and Yankees. Wilson enclosed three sides of his 4,438-acre ranch with a four-board fence to keep his ever-more-valuable cattle from roaming; the Santa Monica Mountains served that purpose to the north. But growth slowed during the Civil War, and a drought in 1864 wiped out many fortunes. By then, Wilson had planted two thousand acres of wheat and built a new house near Maria Rita's abandoned adobe, but after one good season, two bad ones followed and he was ready to give up; neighboring ranchers took advantage of the situation and began stealing his rancho's fence boards. During those hard, dry years, cattle died in neighboring fields and were herded to their deaths off the cliffs at Palos Verdes by ranchers who could no longer feed them. But in 1862, Abraham Lincoln signed legislation to bring railroad and telegraph lines from the Missouri River to the Pacific, ensuring California's prosperity—at least for those who could wait.

Then came another promise: oil. In 1865, prompted by some early discoveries elsewhere in California, Wilson helped form Pioneer Oil to buy rights and drill wells on Rancho Rodeo de las Aguas and beyond. But when only a few wells came in, the fever broke. All around the region, ranchos were being split up and sold off. Wilson sold small parcels, but it was almost two decades before he was free of his other rancho, Buenos Ayres, finally selling it for $40,000 in 1884 to John Wolfskill, who'd come to California from Missouri years earlier, seeking gold.

Throughout those years, only sheep farmers prospered—by 1875, there were more than half a million sheep in the county, yielding two million pounds of wool—but dreams of real estate riches kept bubbling to the surface even if oil did not. In 1868, a German apothecary and wool dealer, Dr. Edward A. Preuss, who'd married into a prominent Louisville family, bought the rest of Rodeo de las Aguas from Wilson and Workman for $10,775, and began planting barley. But Preuss, too, grew frustrated and sold off land piecemeal before taking on a partner and creating the De Las Aguas Land Association, which filed plans to create a town, Santa Maria, in what is now the Beverly Hills business district. Their idea—like many a land developer's since—was to subdivide and sell lots, but after a few more dry years, their dream of Santa Maria, too, turned to dust, and they sold the land parcel by parcel to Henry Hammel and Andrew Denker, the brother-in-law proprietors of the United States and Cosmoplitan Hotels in downtown Los Angeles, where "every bed was a spring bed." They used the land to grow lima beans and other food for their guests (and presumably for profit as well). Like his subdivision, Preuss has been mostly forgotten; Preuss Road, which honored the doctor, is today the chic shopping street Robertson Boulevard.

Los Angeles

The railroad changed everything. After May 1869, when a golden spike linking the Central Pacific to the Union Pacific was driven at Promontory Point in Utah, it became possible to travel from New York to Alameda, the terminus of the transcontinental railroad just outside San Francisco. In addition, the Southern Pacific Railroad had been formed to lay rails through California's interior, and in 1876, the first train from San Francisco reached Los Angeles. It was only a few years more before Pullman cars with service equal to that of the best hotels and restaurants linked the coasts. And a decade later, when the Atchison, Topeka and Santa Fe finished its rail line to the West Coast and began competing with the Southern Pacific, starting fare wars that brought ticket prices from Kansas City as low as $1, Los Angeles experienced a spasm of growth, turning from a poor, isolated pueblo into a new city.

The Southland's Spanish and Indian roots lent it a romantic, exotic allure, and as word filtered back east about its weather and fertility (in 1884, California oranges were exhibited at a World's Fair in New Orleans), it became America's last frontier, promising health, wealth, adventure, and a fresh start to anyone who needed it. Midwesterners in particular flooded in, California-dreaming of a Garden of Eden in the desert, bringing with them their Protestant work ethic and small-town values. Real estate auctions, complete with free lunches, became popular tourist attractions. Lots that sold for $500 one day went for a profit the next, and with the first electric streetcar in the United States running in downtown L.A., it was hard to say where it would all end. In 1887, John Wolfskill sold Rancho San Jose de Buenos Ayres for

$438,700 to the Los Angeles and Santa Monica Land and Water Company, which planned a town there called Sunset. In the next few years, sixty similar "paper" towns, envisioned to cover almost eighty thousand acres of the Southland, were laid out. Even then, the developers' dreams went far beyond what could be done, and most would never be built. But few saw they were living in a real estate bubble. When it burst in 1888, only 2,351 people occupied 79,350 lots.

The future Beverly Hills, Holmby Hills, and Bel Air remained bucolic, underpopulated farmland. The Los Angeles and Santa Monica Land and Water Company soon went bankrupt, and Wolfskill got his ranch back.[2] Hammel and Denker, who'd given up their hotel, decreed that a town called Morocco would rise on Rodeo de las Aguas in 1888. It never happened, either, and by 1892 both men had died, leaving the ranch in the hands of Denker's brother and Hammel's widow.

Despite the overreaching of developers, civilization and opportunity were still reaching out to L.A.'s pioneers. Jonathan "Don Juan" Temple, an L.A. storekeeper from Massachusetts, had married into a Spanish rancho family and then expanded its holdings, buying into Buenos Ayres with Workman. In 1868, his brother, Frances P. F. Temple, formed one of the first banks in L.A. with William Workman and Isaias Wolf Hellman, the German-Jewish owner of a dry goods store who'd previously run an informal bank for miners, safeguarding their gold for them. Temple had been Preuss's partner in his attempt to subdivide Rodeo de las Aguas. In 1886, after making several successful investments in streetcar lines downtown, Hellman was one of the founders of the Los Angeles Ostrich Farm Railway, which brought tourists to see those then exotic birds on a farm near the Los Angeles River.

A year later, the Los Angeles County Railroad was formed by a local developer to run a steam line from downtown L.A. through the proposed towns of Morocco and Sunset to Santa Monica and bought the Ostrich Farm line from Hellman. It is evidence of the optimism of the moment that although Sunset (today's Westwood Village) and Morocco didn't exist, Morocco Junction, a train stop, did. On the day the line opened, farm hands stopped work to gawk. And the president of the New York Central Railroad was said to have passed through and predicted that one day, the region would have the biggest population in the United States.

• • •

Others would eventually get the credit, but if anyone was the prime mover behind the Platinum Triangle, it was Henry Edward Huntington. A native of Oneonta, New York, Edward, as he was known, was brought into the railroad business by his uncle Collis, one of the San Franciscans who owned the Southern Pacific Railroad. Edward came to San Francisco in 1891 and inherited a third of his uncle's estate upon his death in 1900, a fortune he greatly increased after selling control of Southern Pacific to E. H. Harriman, a competing railroad tycoon, in 1902.

Tall and distinguished, but shy behind a bushy walrus moustache, Huntington quickly became known in San Francisco as a relentless consolidator of electric street rail lines, and a man who didn't hesitate to devour weak competitors. The year he sold out to Harriman, he moved his operation to L.A. Though one crushed rival soon told him, "You will grab up all the money in Southern California and die and no one will ever know that you have ever lived—just like your uncle—only a hated name," that name lives on, particularly at the Huntington Library, gardens, and museum in San Marino. Land was Huntington's secret but abiding passion. "He really made his money in real estate," says Deborah Johnston, comptroller of the library. "He was an opportunist." But not a speculator. Knowing where rail lines were going was the ultimate inside information for a real estate investor.

During the next decade, railroads throughout the region would merge with such frequency that each new conglomeration was numbered in order to keep them all straight. In 1896, Moses Sherman, Huntington's partner in a short railway called the Pasadena and Altadena, and Sherman's brother-in-law bought the latest successor to the Los Angeles County Railroad, and began replacing its steam road with a two-track electric line from the western edge of L.A. to Morocco Junction, where it connected to the Santa Monica line in 1897. Along the way, a town sprang up around the railroad's car barns, power house, and shops just east of Rodeo de las Aguas, and was named after Sherman (today it is West Hollywood).

The future of Los Angeles was finally sealed in 1898, when the Spanish-American War brought the Philippines under American rule and, the same year, Hawaii was annexed. Whether they'd foreseen the inevitability of a Pacific-coast equivalent to New York or were merely in the right place at the right time, men like Huntington and General Harrison Gray Otis and Harry Chandler, the fathers of the modern *Los Angeles Times,* set the stage for the economic boom that followed. "The marvelous changes that have come to Los Angeles," Chandler's *Times* would soon write, "owe more to Mr. Huntington and his associates than to any other one factor."

More changes. Sherman's other rail lines kept merging in a confusing welter of deals designed to assure their financial viability. But that same year, his Pasadena & Los Angeles (Unit 10) defaulted and was sold to Huntington and Hellman. Three years later they made it the first building block of Pacific Electric, which would become a regional rail colossus within a decade. That's when Huntington moved south to L.A. and began building a headquarters that would become the center of an ever-increasing universe of deals.[3] To an outsider, it would appear that Huntington and Hellman would be competing with Sherman, but they'd actually made a deal to stay off each other's turf. It would not be the last time their interests converged.

Railroads needed oil, and by the turn of the twentieth century, the two rapidly growing industries were increasingly intertwined. The most important oilman in Los Angeles in 1900 was Edward L. Doheny, namesake of Doheny Drive in today's Beverly Hills. He and his partner-in-petroleum, Charles Adelbert Canfield, had met over a poker table a quarter century earlier in New Mexico, when both were young men on the make, prospecting in the Black Mountain mines. Doheny, a slight but tough Irishman from Wisconsin, and Canfield, an indecisive English-Scottish insomniac from Minnesota eight years Doheny's senior, parted company for a while. But when he heard that Canfield had made a fortune—he had discovered one of the largest chambers of silver ore in the legendary Comstock mine in what is now Nevada—and gone to California to invest in real estate and racehorses, Doheny followed. By the time he got there, though, Canfield had lost everything in the real estate collapse and gone back to prospecting. Canfield's wife, Chloe, was reduced to selling their furniture to feed their two daughters and son.

Their luck changed late in 1892 when Doheny spotted a wagon outside his downtown L.A. hotel, loaded down with a gloppy brown substance the driver called *brea*. Under questioning, the man pointed Doheny toward its source. Like Don Benito Wilson before him, Doheny hoped that the tarry stuff, which most still thought a useless nuisance, signaled the presence of oil, and with $400 that Canfield borrowed, leased the oozing parcel of land. Within months, they'd drilled the first successful oil well in L.A., and with the money it produced plus backing from banker Isaias Hellman, among others, began leasing every promising property they could find. An unprecedented oil rush followed. It had taken thirty-five years, but Wilson's dream of a west coast oil boom had finally come true. As railroads switched from coal to oil power and the internal combustion engine set loose the automobile, oil became one of the Southland's leading industries.

In the years that followed, Canfield and Doheny expanded their empires, together and separately, leasing land and drilling wells all over the region. Doheny also invested in the railroads that emerged as their best customers, gaining access to leases on rail-owned lands in Kern County in California's Central Valley, which turned out to be home to one of the state's largest oil fields. With a new partner, Joe Chanslor, Canfield, too, found more oil and began to remake his fortune. They then merged their interests in the Petroleum Development Company and expanded their search to Mexico, where one of their railroad colleagues felt sure they would find more oil—which they did, in vast amounts.

By 1900, there were sixty-five producing oil wells in Kern County, and lots of new oil operators there as well. In fall 1901, many of them came together in Associated Oil, formed to finance a pipeline, but perhaps more important, to try and control local oil prices, which had plunged from a dollar to twelve cents a barrel due to oversupply and competition. Associated included firms owned by Canfield and Chanslor, and among their partners and officers were several who would soon join them in a land venture called Beverly Hills.

Two officers of Associated were Burton E. Green and Max Whittier. Green's father, the deacon of a Baptist church, had brought his family to Los Angeles from Middletown, Wisconsin, in 1886, when Burton was nineteen years old. In the years since, Burton had tried his hand at several businesses, including washing and polishing fruit, dealing in physician's supplies, and buying and selling land in Redlands, California, before returning to Los Angeles to seek his fortune in oil. Whittier had come from the wilderness of Maine to do the same "with fifty bucks and his shoes," says one of the Whittier family's accountants. "But he was a big man and a smart man and he did various jobs, even picked lemons to make a living and advanced a bit and got into the oil business."

Whittier formed the Hardly Able Oil Co. in 1893 at age twenty-six, and after it lived up to its name and failed, he met Green, who had financial and administrative skills he lacked; together they struck oil, as Doheny had, near the Kern River in 1900. Oil-rich land climbed in price from $2.50 to $1,500 an acre. "I felt money so easily made would likely go as quickly," Whittier said. "My better judgment was to hang onto the land."

In 1904, William F. Herrin, general attorney for Southern Pacific, also joined the board, "additional confirmation of the now established fact that the railroad influence is strong in the affairs of the Associated," wrote the *Los Angeles Times*. Southern Pacific had a contract to buy Associated's oil and had recently purchased "large amounts" of its stock. Associated's wells would pump wealth for them all for years to come.

The ties between oil, rail, land, and capital were tightening. Many of these men also ran financial institutions. One day in 1902, a column of advertisements on a single page of the *Times* named Canfield as a director of the Citizens National Bank, Green at Southwestern National, a Huntington associate named Kerckhoff at First National, and Huntington, a director and shareholder in First National. In 1904, Associated Oil's partners spun off a new company, Amalgamated Oil, of which Burton Green was named president. The firms and their leaders then moved even closer together—into a new office in Huntington's Pacific Electric Building.

But bad feelings simmered between Huntington and E. H. Harriman, who'd bought Southern Pacific from him and his uncle's widow. Harriman wanted in to the electric streetcar business. In May 1903, Harriman and Huntington worked out an elaborate compromise that made them partners in Pacific Electric.

Huntington had bigger things on his mind: the synergy between rail lines and real estate. In 1903, Sherman and Harry Chandler of the *Times* incorporated the new town of Hollywood, where they owned about forty-seven thousand acres, and the Hollywood Hotel opened to attract tourists they hoped would like what they saw there and buy land. A month later, Huntington formed the Pacific Electric Land Company to buy and sell properties along *his* railroad lines.

The future value of that land still wasn't certain. Without a reliable source of water, Los Angeles would die of thirst. By the turn of the twentieth century, it was clear that the relative trickle of the Los Angeles River would never sate the thirst of the city some visionaries had already foreseen. Water was the key that would unlock the region's potential. So in 1905, the city's voters were offered and approved a $25 million bond issue to build a water aqueduct from the faraway Owens Valley, between the Sierra Nevada mountains and the desert. Just before that, a syndicate financed by Huntington, Harriman, Sherman (who sat on the city water board), Chandler, Otis, and others had acquired most of the land—approximately 108,000 acres—that the water would pass through in the San Fernando Valley. With investment already in place, that promise of vital infrastructure was the final piece of the puzzle, unlocking the development potential of the whole area, and making possible the Platinum Triangle.

Things happened fast after that. By 1912, the city of Los Angeles was buying up Franklin Canyon, in the hills above Beverly Hills, to use as a reservoir for the water that would begin arriving the next year via a vast system of pipes and aqueducts from the Owens River. Meanwhile, next door, the Hammel and Denker familes had just lost $20,000 in another futile search for oil on Rancho Rodeo de las Aguas when a rumor arose, late in 1905, that they were about to sell out. When the deal closed in April 1906, the land went for $400 an acre, or over $1.2 million. It turned out the buyers, named as "Charles Canfield, the oil man, and associates," had secretly held an option on the land for more than a year, and had drilled thirty wells there, but found oil only in one spot on the boundary of Rodeo and Buenos Ayres (later the site of Beverly Hills High School). That fall, when those buyers formed the Rodeo Land and Water Company to subdivide Rodeo de las Aguas, newspaper reports—though now more accurately describing them as "the Canfield-Huntington-Kerckhoff syndicate"—missed a key detail: Huntington's frenemy E. H. Harriman had a hand in the deal, too.

Rodeo's shareholders included six principals in Amalgamated Oil, among them Canfield, Green, Chanslor, and Porter; several heirs to the Hammel estate; Huntington's longtime associate Kerckhoff; two of Huntington's lawyers (who held a single share apiece); and Huntington himself. Huntington personally owned only 1,349 shares out of 14,000 total, whereas Hammel's widow Mary and her daughter Mathilde McLaughlin held a combined 2,749 shares; but assuming Huntington, his lawyers, Kerckhoff, and his other associates voted together, they controlled the company. Yet the shareholder list also contained two surprises—Moses Sherman with 650 shares and William Herrin of Harriman's Southern Pacific, who held 800. Huntington and Harriman both apparently saw wisdom in the old adage about keeping your friends close and your enemies closer.[4]

Finally, that fall, the group's plans were revealed. Even though Huntington didn't control the rail line through Rodeo de las Aguas, he would still profit from it. Not only would a town called Beverly Hills blossom on the land, with no expense spared in the process, Harriman's Los Angeles–Pacific had agreed to run a new branch line directly through its heart, leaving what was still called Morocco Junction and running north along a new street called Rodeo Drive for a mile to a new stop in front of an as-yet-unbuilt hotel, then turning west along Sunset Boulevard to make, as the *Los Angeles Times* put it, "a bee-line for the sea." On October 21, 1906, an advertisement in the paper announced the formal opening of the subdevelopment. And at the bottom of the page in a small box headed OWNERS, their pecking order was made clear: The first name on the list, on a line all alone, was Henry E. Huntington. Other players, notably Charles Canfield, Max Whittier, and Burton Green, took over from that point, but a century later, Edward Huntington's beneficiary, the Huntington Library, would still have its stake in the Beverly Hills Land Company, the modern successor to Rodeo Land and Water.

PART THREE

Lots for Sale

1906–1932

{ BOTILLER MANSION UNDER CONSTRUCTION }

Beverly Hills

The founding fathers of Beverly Hills were no aristocrats, angels, or heroes. But neither were they the villains they were sometimes made out to be. Like most business visionaries, they fell somewhere in between. Smart and driven, they were also lucky. Guided by self-interest, the desire for profit and position, and, later, for the status that comes with creating something more than wealth, they did well for themselves first and always, but in the process did good for the Southland and its residents, too. It was perhaps inevitable that someone would create Beverly Hills or someplace like it and inspire the creation of Bel Air, Holmby Hills, and even Beverly Park. But the shareholders in Rodeo Land and Water were in the right place at the right time with the right skills and dreams. That eventually made them successful. It didn't always make them happy.

Charles Canfield's last years were an ordeal of grief. In 1902, his wife, Chloe, was murdered at their Los Angeles home while he and Edward Doheny were drilling for oil in Mexico. The killer was the family's former coachman, a twenty-eight-year-old drug addict who shot her on their front porch in front of her youngest daughter after she refused to lend him money. She fought back until the coachman's third shot killed her. On hearing the news, Canfield fainted, and awoke in a permanent state of despair, his already deep-set eyes permanently clouded, his interest in business gone. Family lore has it that his decision to develop Beverly Hills instead of seeking to exploit its potential as an oil field was a way of paying homage to his beloved.

Whether that is true or not, after Edward Huntington set the wheels in motion, it was Canfield, backed up by Max Whittier, driving the train. "Canfield was the man that insisted that everything be done in the best possible manner regardless of expense," the first city engineer, Arthur Pillsbury, recalled at a 1946 group discussion of the history of Beverly Hills. "It had to be perfect. . . . Canfield's instructions were merely this: Make the best subdivision that man can make, regardless of cost." The vision of perfect no-expense-spared luxury was present from inception.

Years later, when he was the last living founding father of the city, Burton Green would be given much of the credit for creating Beverly Hills. But the record doesn't support that. "Burton Green was secretary of the [Rodeo Land and Water] company and had no particular control over the subdivision until after Mr. Canfield's death, at which time street work, tree-planting, building of the hotel, etc. had taken place," said Bert James Firminger, a former Beverly Hills city clerk. Indeed, even the oft-repeated tale that the city was named by Green, after President William Howard Taft visited Beverly Farms, Massachusetts, appears apocryphal. Taft had a summer White House in Beverly, Massachusetts, but not until 1909, long after Beverly Hills was named. Years later, Lee Whittier, one of Max's sons, would tell a family employee that the name was borrowed from "something in Florida." Though there is also a town called Beverly Hills in western Florida, and the Green family had visited Palm Beach in eastern Florida, the real origin of the name chosen by Canfield, Green, and Whittier will probably never be known. But Green's ego is clear in another tale told by one of his three daughters, who said that at one point, he proposed naming the new city Burton Hills.

Egos notwithstanding, together, the Rodeo partners quickly accomplished more than any Southland developers before them. They immediately hired Wilbur David Cook Jr., a New York landscape architect who'd worked for Frederick Law Olmsted, the creator of Central Park, to draft a master plan. Cook is generally credited with the grand vision of a three-layer-cake community. Beverly Hills' foundations sit in the southern part of the city, where 50-by-150-foot lots priced from $700 to $1,500 were laid out for the small dwellings of workers who would serve both the middle-class residents of the "flats" (the flat land between Santa Monica and Sunset Boulevards) and the wealthy, who lived north of Sunset in large estates in the foothills. Their lots were large and deep, starting at 80 by 175 feet and growing to five acres, with the least expensive selling for $900 (a 10 percent discount was offered for purchasers who paid cash, and the same price cut was offered to anyone who started construction within six months). Rodeo initially kept the land below Wilshire Boulevard and on the city's two flanks off the market.

"Below Santa Monica [where the Pacific Electric tracks were located], it was called Beverly," Pillsbury recalled, and above was Beverly Hills. "One was restricted and one wasn't. The theory was that below the tracks the scum lived, and the hoi polloi. Above . . . was the swell part of town." Ironically, some of the "scum" who bought property south of Santa Monica would end up quite wealthy as that neighborhood evolved into the city's business center.

Original Beverly Hills deeds codified another distinction, forbidding nonwhites except as servants. "No part of said property shall at any time be sold, conveyed, leased or rented to or inherited by or otherwise acquired by or become the property of any person whose blood is not entirely that of the Caucasian race," a restrictive covenant read. Nor could nonwhites live on or use Beverly Hills property unless they were "kept thereon by a Caucasian occupant strictly in the capacity of servants or employees actually engaged in the domestic service of such Caucasian occupant." Movie people, who'd begun to colonize nearby Hollywood, were also personas non grata. "We were not supposed to sell to anybody in the motion picture business," said Pillsbury. "We tried to keep them out."

Cook also set aside ten acres for a hotel and land for four parks, a three-acre civic center, a small industrial-commercial zone in the southeast part of the city, and a community nursery where, the founders would later claim, "tens of thousands of young trees and shrubs are being nurtured and nourished until the time when they shall have a part in adding to that greater beauty about them. The wild cherry is there, and the whole family of palms, and the camphor, the sweet-smelling eucalyptus, the pepper . . ."

Cook's street plan, first revealed in November 1906, had been suggested by the realtor Percy Clark, who insisted on a series of gently curving streets shaped like a voluptuous woman's body in a long, clingy dress shown from the neck—today's Elden Way emerging from the bodice-curve of North Crescent Drive—to a hem at Santa Monica Boulevard. Later, some would say the design was based on the actress Clara Bow's body, but that's dubious as she was, at the time, just a year old. As was the California film business, which was born when the Selig Studio of Chicago began filming in Laguna Beach in 1905 to avoid inclement weather. It would be five more years before D. W. Griffith would first shoot in the Hollywood Hills, and six years past that before the big studio era began when Jesse Lasky's movie company, led by Lasky, Sam Goldfish (later Goldwyn), and Cecil B. DeMille merged with Paramount and Adolph Zukor's Famous Players.

Every care was taken to make the new suburb sound as prestigious and well served as possible, even though groceries, liquor, newspapers, and laundry services were still obtainable only by rail on special order. A British-born horticulturist, the first to successfully transplant large trees in Southern California, was hired to work his magic along each of the city streets, and he insisted, over Burton Green's objections, on using one type per street to give a distinctive look, demanding, too, that homeowners not move curbside trees when laying their driveways. Telephone, electric, and water lines were installed. Cement conduits and drains for storm runoff were laid, although sewers, street lights, and gas lines were not yet installed. A brochure, "Between the City and the Sea," was printed, full of renderings of what was to come and flowery sales come-ons.

"It is manifest in the refined design and substantial workmanship of the concrete bridges carrying the drives across the streams," it began. "It is shown in the engineering skill and care which have led the avenues so easily and advantageously over the larger roll of the land. It is told by the thoughtfully executed plans for the drainage. There is proof of forethought in the provision made for abundance of water—water pure and fresh from its natural sources among the mountains, held in readiness in protective reservoirs, millions of gallons of it, and other millions available as needed."

Never mind, for now, that Rodeo was fibbing about all that water.

"It is not in one way but in every way that the earnestness and sincerity and good judgment of the makers and builders of Beverly Hills are shown," this 1907 brochure continued. " 'Tis as though the beauties and possibilities of the scheme had opened more and more before them as they worked and they had been constrained to better and yet greater endeavor." They even claimed a subway would soon be built from downtown L.A., making the journey to Beverly Hills "a fifteen minute spin."

That never happened either.

A few lots were sold; an east-west road that ran from downtown to the town of Sunset was graded, though it remained unpaved for years; and about a dozen company houses were erected to stimulate sales. The first private home in the flats, commissioned by a Henry Clay Clarke, would rise by Thanksgiving 1907, as would the first commercial building, a two-story frame and stucco structure at today's intersection of Burton and Beverly. It held a general store run by a Pegleg Brewster. Then, Llewelyn Arthur Nares, a British-born irrigation and hydraulic engineer turned real estate developer (who'd recently set a record by driving a car from Los Angeles to San Francisco in just over a day), hired Myron Hunt, a Pasadena architect who consulted with Cook, to build the first home in the hills—a twenty-room mansion on a street named Naresborough in his honor. Nares was given the land by Rodeo partner W. G. Kerckhoff in exchange for advice on drainage and engineering problems.

By year's end, there were sidewalks on Crescent Drive and palm trees, sidewalks, and a couple of homes on Cañon, including one whose owner kept a Jersey cow that supplied the handful of residents with milk, and another whose owner grew Concord grapes. Beverly Drive had sidewalks, palm trees, and one home, occupied by a banker; Rodeo had black acacias, sidewalks, and one resident, a corpulent Mrs. Pattee, whose "labored puffings to catch the Pacific Electric cars" were later recalled by Henry Clarke's son Phillip. Pillsbury bought a corner lot on Rodeo for $800 and built a seven-room house for another $2,000. There were still few cars; realtor Percy Clark used a horse-drawn surrey to show houses. His clerk, whose desk was conveniently situated in the Pacific Electric station, also sold rail tickets.

Then it all ground to a halt. An attempt by Easterners to corner the copper market set off a bank run, the Panic of 1907 that paralyzed financial markets, leading to a severe national recession and the eventual creation of the Federal Reserve System. In Beverly Hills, despite the expenditure of about $1 million of the Rodeo syndicate's money, the only tangible proofs of the community's ability to survive were that lovely name, six houses, some bungalows for laborers, and those five roads "of splendid solidity and durability . . . absolutely noiseless and dustless," laid through the bean fields planted in the Hammel and Denker era that still occupied most of the empty lots.

After Standard Oil offered $3,000 an acre for 250 acres of Rodeo land and was refused, the oilmen behind Rodeo started drilling again that spring, made a promising strike on the east side of their property, and immediately announced their intention to dig more wells. But their subdivision had been approved on condition of no more drilling, so Amalgamated Oil had to buy back lots on the fringes of the property from Rodeo. By fall, five rigs dotted the outskirts of the subdivision, including one that capped a gusher between Sherman and the new Beverly train stop. Three derricks also sprouted on the Santa Monica Land and Water company's Wolfskill ranch property. But soon the oil ran out and the rigs were producing mostly water. Fortunately, Amalgamated's wells in Kern County were still paying big dividends, and in 1910, the indefatigable Whittier made a discovery that immediately ensured Beverly Hills' future and would eventually make his and Green's families richer than their wildest dreams.

After hearing that oil was seeping from the ground in western Kern County about sixty-five miles west of Bakersfield, Whittier investigated. He and Green found the owner of the land, who was in New York, but she asked a staggering $1 million for her thirty thousand acres—more than they could pay on their own. So they recruited a local fruit farmer and two real estate speculators, and together formed Belridge Oil to buy the land. Simultaneously, Associated Oil, the larger enterprise of Whittier, Green, and other independent oilmen, took over another twenty-five thousand acres twenty-five miles to the north in Lost Hills. The canny oilmen were betting that the area held vast reserves.

Production from the fields dubbed North and South Belridge waxed and waned over the next two decades, but in October 1930, a surprise gusher proved that their bet had been right. The two real estate speculators sold their shares to the predecessors of today's Mobil and Texaco, but the three remaining partners retained 65 percent of Belridge stock. By 1933, their field was considered the best in California and in the years that followed, Associated and Belridge steadily drilled new wells, and farmed the land as well. "They had a lot of income off that property," says someone who worked for Green. "There was *a lot* of oil up there."

In June 1911, the Los Angeles Country Club moved to 320 acres on the Wolfskill Ranch and became the first private golf course in the area. Its purchase of that acreage in 1904 was the first time since the 1880s that Wolfskill had agreed to sell off any of his land—and no doubt inspired Rodeo's development. There was as yet no road to the course, so when golfers reached the Wilshire–Santa Monica trolley stop, they raised a flag to summon a wagon to take them over the fields. Simultaneously, Rodeo announced plans to erect a magnificent tourist hotel nearby with three hundred rooms and a dozen bungalows to attract potential buyers. "Mr. Canfield figured that was the only way to get a sucker to buy something," said Arthur Pillsbury.

A month later, Margaret Anderson and her son Stanley, proprietors of the Hollywood Hotel, where Max Whittier liked to eat lunch, were lured to

Beverly Hills. Whittier offered them a $323,000 mortgage to build and own a hotel in Beverly Hills; Rodeo threw in the land for free. Anderson's father, a Presbyterian minister, had moved to California in 1874. In 1903, his daughter, a widow with two children, had taken over the just-completed Hollywood Hotel, which sat on land owned by Harrison Gray Otis and others (now the site of the Kodak Theater). By the time she left, she'd enlarged it repeatedly into a 250-room magnet for travelers, a country resort with all the modern conveniences. Rodeo Land and Water hoped she could do the same thing in Beverly Hills—and Anderson didn't disappoint them. She managed to open the Beverly Hills Hotel, a $500,000 Mission-style fantasia designed by Elmer Grey to command a rise overlooking Sunset Boulevard, with considerable fanfare less than a year later.

On April 30, 1912, Anderson's lease on the Hollywood Hotel expired. She'd been warring with its owner for several years over who would pay for improvements, and that morning, she got her revenge when she locked its doors just after breakfast and moved herself, her son, and most of their guests, servants, cooks, and managers to Beverly Hills in time for lunch at her new establishment. She never looked back, and soon, her new hotel was attracting winter vacationers along with the curious, many of whom stayed, bought lots, and built homes in Beverly Hills, returning to the hotel for dinners in what was then the only restaurant in town. It was also for a time the local church, movie theater, and community center. A small train carted guests from the Pacific Electric station up Rodeo Drive to the hotel along a track 1.378 miles long that had been laid down five years earlier. "We had a hell of a time keeping kids from putting grease on the tracks," said Arthur Pillsbury. "The poor thing couldn't climb the hill."

While the hotel was still under construction, several of the Rodeo Land and Water partners began building houses nearby. They'd realized they had to counter the growing impression that their suburb was just another ghost town. Some of their early buyers were growing restive, disturbed by coyotes crying in the desolate hills and howling winds that drove dust and tumbleweeds through the many empty lots.

Burton Green was the first to build, in 1911. Six years earlier, Green had married into the nascent Los Angeles aristocracy when he wed Lilian Wellborn, a daughter of Olin Wellborn, who'd been a captain in the Confederate Army in the Civil War, a Texas congressman, and a powerful federal judge in Los Angeles. They'd since had two daughters, Dorothy Wellborn, or Dolly, in 1906, and then Liliore; a third, whom they'd name Burton (because Green had hoped for a boy so he would have a namesake), was on the way. Lilian was pleased her husband had gone into real estate, which she felt had more cachet than the oil business.

Lilian's sister was married to Roland Bishop, a wholesale grocer and food manufacturer; he bought land across the street and built a house he called Rosewall, a red brick twenty-room mansion surrounded by porticos supported by Corinthian columns, sitting in a lush four-acre triangular hilltop garden surrounded by a four-foot wall lined with hundreds of rosebushes. After living there only four years, the Bishops sold the place to Irving Hellman, a nephew of the railroad-owning banker, who lived there until 1946. (Rosewall was later torn down and replaced by seven contemporary houses, several of which have since been torn down themselves.)

Green's house, a timbered Tudor-style mansion with grand mahogany-paneled entertaining rooms and five bedrooms, each with a private bathroom and dressing room, sat on eleven landscaped acres occupying a full block behind the hotel that also contained a tennis court, a lake, and several pavilions. Huge terraces looked out over the grounds, where Green transplanted full-grown oak and palm trees; his views stretched to the beach at Santa Monica. He would live in that house for more than half a century. As it rose, the *Times* declared it "one of the costliest, as well as one of the handsomest" dwellings in Los Angeles, a suitable nest for one of the founding fathers of Beverly Hills and one of the richest oilmen in the Southland.

At the same time, Charles Canfield told his daughter Caroline "Carrie" Canfield, "move to Beverly Hills and I will build you a house." Her husband, Silsby Spalding, was a stockbroker and they'd been living outside San Francisco, but he'd just been transferred to Los Angeles. So they bought a lot close to Burton Green's on North Crescent Drive, and the next year took up residence in a Southern colonial.

The founding families weren't entirely alone. That summer, a six-room hunting lodge was nearing completion on 11.5 acres on a knoll above them with views of Beverly and the ocean; it was designed by architect Horatio Cogswell for Lee Allen Phillips, an insurance executive and deep-sea fisherman. And Virginia and Harry Robinson moved into a huge home on fifteen acres at the highest point of Elden Way. The Robinsons, he the heir to a department store empire, she the daughter of a wealthy architect and Texas sheep rancher, had married in 1903 and gone on a three-year honeymoon that took them to New York, Europe, and Kashmir. Mrs. Robinson's uncle was a partner in Henry Huntington's Pacific Electric. She is said to have never known how many rooms were in her home.

The day after the Beverly Hills Hotel opened, Rodeo Land and Water began advertising again, relentlessly touting the city's charms and offering lots with eighty feet of street frontage around the hotel for $1,700, with a 10 percent discount for immediate construction. In the months that followed, the ads kept running, and the pace of building increased. "The number of people who passed through [the hotel's] portals into their own homes here cannot be counted, but they were legion," said B. J. Firminger, who married the pioneer resident Henry Clarke's daughter in 1913. Tourists would often rub shoulders with homeowners who came there to attend church and concerts, barbecues and Saturday night movies. The hotel also boasted a school for the children of guests, stables for their horses, and a riding school. Aside from hunting, fishing, drinking, and card-playing, it was the only game in town.

As more people built houses in Beverly Hills, a small commercial center grew up along with it ("Charge it to Burton Green," his daughters would say in the soda shop), and the need for larger schools became acute. When Los Angeles County refused to help, a mass meeting was held to promote the idea of incorporating Beverly Hills. "We had roughly two hundred people," recalled Pillsbury, but they needed five hundred to be certified by California as a small city. Pierce Benedict, who saw the virtue of independence from Los Angeles, donated some acreage Rodeo didn't own, adding to the body count, and others gave more land in Higgins and Franklin Canyons, but there still weren't enough people. So Henry Huntington solved the problem by running a rail spur into Beverly Hills along Santa Monica Boulevard, and bringing with it "a bunch of cars that these *cholos* lived in, the Mexican track workers," Pillsbury said. "We moved them over to Louis Ranch [where Rodeo Land and Water still grew beans]," said landscaper Raymond Page, "and Beverly Hills had enough people to qualify [as] a city." They all signed a petition, which was approved in early 1914 by the Los Angeles government; an election was held and a city requested. Pillsbury made a mad dash by train and car to Sacramento to file the paperwork, arriving late the night the certification would have expired. Beverly Hills was officially incorporated that January 28.

Beverly Hills

The start of World War I in 1914 didn't affect faraway Beverly Hills—at first. But German attacks on ships in the Atlantic soon hit home, and inevitably, America was drawn into the war in 1917. The city's growth stopped again and was "more or less dormant" until the war ended, Pierce Benedict, its first leader, wrote in his *History of Beverly Hills*. But just as dormancy prepares plants for future development, so the mid-decade pause set the stage for what would come. In 1914, Canfield's partner, Doheny, struck oil in Sherman, just south of the modern intersection of Robertson and Santa Monica Boulevards, and not long afterwards began quietly buying land just east of Beverly Hills. He would eventually cobble together ten parcels, five of them in his brother-in-law's name, to form a ranch of more than four hundred acres.

At the same time, Rodeo partner Max Whittier bought 4.5 acres where the first local schoolhouse once stood and started construction on a pink thirty-eight-room Italian Renaissance mansion, which his wife filled with furniture purchased at the 1915 World's Fair in San Francisco. The basement contained one unexpected whimsical touch, a bar hidden behind a painting—which came in handy once Prohibition became law in 1920. The house was graceful and as restrained as Whittier himself; unlike several of his Rodeo partners, Whittier rarely put himself forward. Instead he practiced philanthropy, donating time and money to a host of good causes, and dedicated himself to his home life, raising three sons and a daughter and regularly bringing relatives to California from Maine for family vacations. In the next decade, his name never appeared in the *Los Angeles Times* until 1923, when his wife hosted a benefit on their huge lawn. A mere two months later, she died in their home while Max and their daughter Helen were on a steamboat heading to Asia. "They were Christian Scientists and didn't believe in doctors or hospitals, so she died," says their granddaughter Laura-Lee Whittier Woods.

Whittier rushed home for the funeral. Then, the scene repeated itself two years and four months later when Whittier returned from another trip to Asia with daughter Helen and checked himself into a sanatorium—a facility operated according to the rules of his religion—for what he thought was a common cold. Seized by a coughing fit, he fell into unconsciousness and died at age fifity-eight. Though he was an honorary pallbearer at the funeral, Burton Green neither eulogized his longtime partner nor served on the committee that erected a statue in his honor four years later.

Briefly, the house stayed in the family. "The boys lived there after his death," says granddaughter Whittier Woods. "I was a child there. Helen remained a Christian Scientist, but my father became interested in founding hospitals." Today, his L. K. Whittier Foundation, with assets of just under $90 million, supports colleges and hospitals, and stem cell and nanobiology research that Max Whittier might not have approved of. In 1928, the mansion was sold to Samuel Berch, owner of a large dairy and ice cream maker. The Berches, too, opened the house for good causes, typically Jewish ones. They had only one brush with notoriety, when one of their four daughters ran off to Tijuana at seventeen and married a nightclub performer ten years her senior. The marriage was promptly annulled, and two years later, she married a nice Jewish boy in their garden. When Berch died in 1951, his widow sold the house to another of their daughters, whose husband owned discount department stores, and they lived there over two more decades.

The war years weren't entirely uneventful. They were marked by the first of many crime sprees in the hills of Beverly. In February 1915, the wife and son of the president of the New York Central Railroad checked into a bungalow at the Beverly Hills Hotel. Six hours later it was ransacked while they ate dinner and they were robbed of $75,000 in jewels. Almost exactly a year later, burglars entered the safety razor inventor King Gillette's new twenty-room Mission-style mansion on three acres near the hotel, a mere three weeks after he'd moved in, and got away with a number of important diamond pieces, though they left behind far more valuable art. Two more similar robberies followed that year. Finally, in 1917, Beverly Hills hired its first police chief, and in 1918, a jewel thief was captured and confessed to carrying out a half dozen local burglaries. The casual racism of the newspaper report on the arrest is now startling: "a pair of eyes gleaming in the window . . . a row of white teeth . . . a black apparition. . . . Under the bed they found the burglar, a Negro."

These crimes notwithstanding, the word was out: Beverly Hills was where the money was going. At the corner of Burton and Beverly, a brick commercial building replaced the old wooden one, and Percy Clark moved Rodeo's realty office there. "He had a span of white horses with a surrey that he got suckers with," recalled Arthur Pillsbury.

Shadow Hill (1100 Carolyn Way)

Stanley Anderson of the Beverly Hills Hotel roped in suckers, too, collecting commissions when he did. A few months after Douglas Fairbanks, then Hollywood's newest and most vibrant star, played in a celebrity tennis tournament at the hotel in January 1918, Anderson—and the rest of the world—learned the actor and his wife were separating. The hotelier promptly found him a sublet, a Benedict Canyon mansion called Shadow Hill, on the very same acreage Pierce Benedict had donated to get Beverly Hills certified.

"The morning after [Fairbanks] moved in," said Anderson in 1946, "he called down to the hotel and I'm telling you the truth, he was crying. He said, 'I've never felt so awful. I have to leave Beverly Hills.' " Fairbanks told Anderson he'd gotten calls from several Beverly Hills residents who didn't want "any picture people" in their town. Anderson "happened to know one of the parties, and I talked him out of it." Fairbanks stayed, "and all the rest followed him."

Quite simply, the rest—that is, the movie people who'd been flocking west for ten years—needed a place to go, and thus was the position of Beverly Hills secured. Drugs, homosexuality, and mysterious deaths were shaking the new movie community in Hollywood. In the high-profile category, a year earlier, an actress named Virginia Rappe had been found dead at a party hosted by film funnyman Roscoe "Fatty" Arbuckle; he was charged with murder, but later found innocent. Top stars were encouraged to move out. Beverly Hills, just to the west, was sold as a sanctuary of respectability, away from the Peeping Toms of the press. Charlie Chaplin bought a lot next to the Fairbanks house, Gloria Swanson bought King Gillette's house, and other wealthy movie figures began buying land. Though Charles Canfield died in August 1913, he'd laid the ground for this upturn. He also ensured that Canfields would still hold sway in Beverly Hills after his death. They, too, played a role in the arrival of the picture people.

Shadow Hill had been built in 1915 by Harry Dana Lombard, a Bostonian who'd come west as a banker in the 1880s, made a fortune subdividing Pacific Palisades and the town of Hawthorne, just southeast of today's Los Angeles International Airport, and eventually loaned his last name to one Jane Peters, the daughter of family friends, who became a movie star as Carole Lombard. Harry had bought fifteen acres with ocean views from Rodeo in 1913, just after returning from the first automobile trip around the world. In 1916, after his landscaping had grown in, he and his wife, Henrietta, moved into their new house of rough stone designed by Sumner Hunt and Silas Burns, combining elements of Tyrolean, Provençal, and Italian Mediterranean architecture.

Sublet to Fairbanks in 1918, Shadow Hill proved a perfect trysting place for him and his new lover, the actress Mary Pickford, also married. The pair had bonded when they joined Charles Chaplin on a national war bonds tour after America entered World War I. In 1919, the three stars formed United Artists with director D. W. Griffith to wrest control of their films from movie studios. Some of the meetings that led to their declaration of independence were held at Shadow Hill.

While Fairbanks was in residence, Carrie Spalding, whose husband had gone off to fight in the war, traded the home she and Silsby had built on North Crescent Drive to the Lombards in exchange for the occupied Shadow Hill. It's unknown what inspired the trade, but Fairbanks, Carrie Spalding, and Henrietta Lombard were all on hand one afternoon in October 1918 when the actor opened its grounds for another war bond benefit featuring movie stars like Dorothy Gish, vaudeville and circus acts, gymnasts, rodeo and aerial-stunt performances, a band, a clown, and professional wrestlers and boxers, raising more than $100,000 for the war effort.

It would be several more months before Fairbanks and his wife were divorced. Just after their split was finalized, Stanley Anderson took Fairbanks to see the insurance executive Lee Phillips's hunting lodge on fourteen rustic acres near Shadow Hill. Hollywood historian Charles Lockwood says the director Raoul Walsh and his wife, a silent film star, had looked at it first but were put off by coyotes howling in the distance. A few days later, Fairbanks came by and bought the place for $35,000, even though it lacked electricity and running water. Fairbanks wanted more house than that, though.

He gutted the existing structure, added a new wing, two floors, a private screening room, a bowling alley, a billiard room, five guest bedrooms, a 55-by-100-foot swimming pool surrounded by a cedar hedge, stables, and a garage with a caretaker's quarters at a cost of $175,000. It's said that Fairbanks built an underground tunnel between Shadow Hill and his new home so he could supervise the renovation (and perhaps sneak Mary Pickford in and out unnoticed). Today, a thirty-foot-long tunnel leaves the former Shadow Hill's lower level before ending abruptly. Fairbanks wasn't always loath to attract attention; when the finishing touches were proceeding too slowly for his taste, he had his landscape architect bring in studio lights so work could continue around the clock.

In early March, Pickford finally got her own divorce and married Fairbanks a few days later. Their bridal supper and honeymoon took place in the new house, which a reporter dubbed Pickfair, a name that stuck throughout the couple's reign as the king and queen of filmdom and of Beverly Hills. They entertained all kinds of visitors there, from European royals to Albert Einstein and Babe Ruth. They expanded their home in the early 1930s with the famed architect Wallace Neff. After divorcing Fairbanks in 1936, Pickford lived on there, finally dying an alcoholic recluse in 1979. The house changed hands several times thereafter—among the owners were Jerry Buss, owner of the Los Angeles Lakers; the Israeli industrialist Meshulam Riklis and his sex symbol wife, the actress-singer Pia Zadora; and Corry Hong, a Korean in the software business—as successive remodelings effectively destroyed any traces of its glorious past. As of spring 2011, it had been languishing on the market for several years with a price tag of $60 million.

Beverly Hills adapted quickly to the presence of movie people. "They had these wild parties when they'd start throwing the underwear and the shoes out on the lawn," Pillsbury recalled. "The older natives would start complaining and Charlie [Blair, the city's first police chief, appointed in 1917] would come in." He'd have a couple drinks with the revelers and ask them to quiet down and never arrest anyone who complied. At first Blair took a similar approach to natives who still enjoyed hunting coyote and rabbits in the hills. But finally, gunplay was banned. "This town has kind of built up and you just can't keep on doing this," Blair told Pillsbury one night, putting an end to a hunting expedition.

A civil war of sorts would soon rock Beverly Hills—fought over that most vital of fluids in the Southland, water. Rodeo Land and Water had formed a utilities company in 1914 to separate its land sales operation from the one that provided water, gas, and electricity. Despite its early promises, Rodeo's officials knew they didn't have enough drinking water. "They had cheated the city," said Pillsbury, and by 1922, faced a serious problem. With eight hundred homes occupied and three new families a day moving into town, the existing water supply was insufficient.

Back in 1914, Los Angeles had won the right to lay a water pipe through the Beverly Hills foothills. But just after the new city was incorporated, its leader, called the president then and still under Rodeo's thumb, learned that L.A.'s pipeline easement contained a crucial gap; the city had not acquired the right to lay its pipe across one road in Coldwater Canyon, and Rodeo saw a chance to horse-trade—it would let L.A. through in exchange for access to the city's clean, cold Owens Valley aqueduct water. But then L.A. went to court and won the right to lay its pipe without Rodeo's permission, sending Rodeo back to square one.

When the issue arose again eight years later, the company rejected a proposal that it buy the next-door Hollywood Union Water Company from Moses Sherman and his partners. Urged on by local realtors who feared building would stop until the water problem was solved, Rodeo campaigned to have L.A. annex Beverly Hills, which would solve the water problem, but thwart the will of the new city's citizenry. Pierce Benedict spoke for many when he scorned "the groping tentacles of Los Angeles."

All hell broke loose. The editor of the *Beverly Hills News,* who opposed annexation, was sent a cigar box with three firecrackers inside that exploded when he opened it. On the lid were a skull and crossbones, the letters *KKK,* and a warning: "Lay off the annexation stuff or our next move will be TNT."

A referendum was set and the city's residents chose sides. A group of movie stars, including Fairbanks and Pickford, Tom Mix, Rudolph Valentino, Harold Lloyd (who'd just bought a house on ten acres in Benedict Canyon for his mother), and Will Rogers (who'd recently installed a polo field behind his mansion near the hotel), joined the anti-annexationists, worried a change would threaten both the city's low taxes and their special status as big fish in a small pond. Signs were posted all over town by the pro-annexation-ists, led by Rodeo's latest broker, Frank Meline, a department store window dresser who'd reinvented himself as a luxury realtor, warning that when clean water supplies ran low, the city would be left with nothing but sulfurous water with "laxative qualities."

After Charles Canfield's death, Burton Green had become the largest shareholder in Rodeo, and he took the lead in fighting for annexation. Stanley Anderson was against it and sought the support of Canfield's son-in-law Silsby Spalding, who'd served as a city trustee since 1919, and then quit his job as a stockbroker to become its second president and then its first mayor. Though he controlled a large block of Canfield's Rodeo stock, Spalding had at first stayed on the sidelines. But when he was booed by Rodeo employees at a mass meeting for refusing to take their side, and after Anderson showed him a letter proving that Burton Green had known about the water shortfall all along, Spalding got off the fence and became a leader of the anti-annex-ation forces.

On election day, residents found little bottles of sulfurous water labeled "This is the water you drink!" on their doorsteps, but even that extreme elec-tioneering failed to turn the tide. By a 507–337 vote, the citizenry declined to submerge into Los Angeles. The celebration that followed went on for hours. "I don't think there was a sober person in town that night," said the landscape architect Raymond Page. A brass band marched through town, fire bells sounded alarms, and hoses were connected to fire hydrants; when pro-annexationists emerged from their homes, they were doused. At year's end, Beverly Hills bought Rodeo's water company and authorized a bond issue to install a proper sewage system, buy a modern pumping station and incinera-tor, and build a city hall. Four years later, a new water softening plant opened. And a new era of civic engagement had begun: With help from the city, a group of private citizens led by Stanley Anderson and Irving Hellman even turned the discontinued train line down Rodeo Drive into a bridle path.

At a dinner at the hotel to raise funds for all that, Will Rogers, soon to be named the honorary mayor (Spalding really ran the city), referred to another fresh development while recalling his early efforts to build a church so his children could attend Sunday school. "I guess I made a mistake from the looks of things here tonight," Rogers cracked. "I should have tried to build a synagogue." Not only was Beverly Hills growing, it was growing more open.

Silsby Spalding was the "King of Beverly Hills," said one resident, "running the town . . . a lot of it with his own money, paying for everything that we couldn't afford." Moving into Shadow Hill after Fairbanks left, he and his wife added thirty-seven acres to the estate and called back the original architects to expand the house. Hunt and Burns created a 71-by-56-foot addition with a black-and-white entry hall, a music room, a drawing room, a swimming pool, a bridge between new upper and lower gardens, and a pergola.

"It was a great Dracula-like place to a little girl," says Mary Warthin, a grandniece. The Spaldings had live-in servants and used fingerbowls three meals a day. "Nobody does that!" she raves. "It was very impressive."

Though both Spaldings were "quiet and full of good works," they loved to entertain, says Warthin. "Silsby was an interesting man. He was a drunk in the best social sense. He couldn't help himself. He liked to party a lot. One night he came home with a fleet of taxis and paid them to stay while he entertained [all the passengers]." An accomplished musician, Spalding had installed a gigantic organ in his new music room, with pipes that rose to the ceiling.

In 1924, the Spaldings bought a 1,400-acre ranch he called Rancho Tecolote north of Santa Barbara and soon, Carrie and their daughter Deborah, then a child, moved there full time. After resigning as mayor in 1929, Spalding joined them.

"He was always in the ranching business after that," says Deborah, raising purebred cattle and wolfhounds, growing walnuts and citrus, and riding horses with silver-embellished saddles and tack. But "he always dabbled in stocks, too," and commuted to Los Angeles, where he kept an office. Despite the Depression, he obviously did well, as he kept Shadow Hill, although all but the few rooms he stayed in were shut down. "Nobody was in it," says Deborah. It sat empty until after World War II, when Spalding had one more brief moment of fame when a Japanese submarine fired the only known rounds to hit U.S. soil during the war, aiming for a nearby oil refinery. One round went astray and exploded on Tecolote.

Four years later, Spalding decided to subdivide sixty acres of Shadow Hill and sell sixteen large estate lots, commissioning a hand-illustrated and numbered limited-edition booklet full of impressionistic drawings of the property studded with as-yet-unbuilt homes. Then, he fell ill; Spalding abandoned the project, and he and Carrie moved back in. Mary Warthin visited and called it "a big, shadow-filled lonely house."

He died at Shadow Hill in 1949, says daughter Deborah, whose mother then "moved to an apartment and put the house on the market." The next year, the acreage was sold to a developer backed by what the *Times* called "a representative group of Beverly Hills and Los Angeles citizens" and was broken up into 122 lots. In 1951, the exclusive agent for what was being touted as the New Beverly Hills Park Estates, Leland Reeder, son of the pioneer local real estate man, put Shadow Hill and three surrounding acres on the market for $150,000. Its place in the history of Beverly Hills went unremarked, but not its proximity to Pickfair.

It was eventually purchased by Amos Johnstone, a former New Yorker whose family money came from real estate. Johnstone lived a quiet life there, and would later become president of the surrounding subdivision's property owners' association. Carrie Canfield Spalding died in 1970 at age eighty, living a life of great wealth until the end.

Today, there are scores of homes crowding her once solitary mansion.

Greenacres (1740 Green Acres Place)

Half a mile west of Shadow Hill, the movie star invasion of Beverly Hills was entering its second, extravagant phase. Harold Lloyd, a comic actor in silents since 1912, had become film's first romantic comedy leading man, portraying an eager boy-next-door type who got out of scrapes and then got the girl. By the 1920s, Lloyd was earning a fortune, $6,000 a day, far more than his rivals Charlie Chaplin and Buster Keaton. He also owned his own films, giving him a producer's cut as well.

Lloyd had an eye (behind his trademark round horn-rimmed spectacles) for real estate. So after marrying (and forcibly retiring) his leading lady, Mildred Davis, in 1923, he bought a $125,000 house, including its furnishings and an art collection, in Windsor Square, another early mansion development on the Spanish Rancho La Brea. Immediately, Lloyd's sights turned west to Beverly Hills and Benedict Canyon. His first eleven acres included the original P. E. Benedict home site, which had stayed in the family for sixty years. Lloyd paid $100,000 and installed his mother, a failed actress who'd divorced her ne'er-do-well husband before moving west from their native Nebraska, in a hunting lodge on the property. Later, he bought an adjoining four acres from the widow of Thomas Ince, one of the L.A. film pioneers.[5] The deals were negotiated by Lloyd's uncle and business manager, a former supervisor of the U.S. Forestry Service, who helped him choose the "remark-ably beautiful" property, said the *Chicago Tribune*.

Lloyd began landscaping that property soon after buying it, but it was two more years before he drafted plans for a $2 million estate that would dwarf those of his neighbors, Fairbanks and Pickford, Chaplin, Valentino, and the mogul Carl Laemmle, who'd bought the Ince estate. Lloyd first planned a three-story Renaissance chateau surrounded by a nine-hole golf course, a canoeing stream stocked with trout and bass, a 100-foot waterfall, a 40-by-85-foot 250,000-gallon swimming pool with underwater lighting and its own reservoir to feed it, an open-air theater, a miniature children's estate with its own aviary and monkey house, a dancing pavilion, tennis courts, outdoor bowling and handball, stables and bridle path, a small farm for the estate's kitchen, two acres of greenhouses to supply plants for the seven sepa-rate gardens (which would be tended by sixteen gardeners), a kennel where Lloyd would keep Great Danes, and a dozen fountains. But after the plans were revealed in newspapers, he redid them. "It was too grand," says his granddaughter, Sue Lloyd. "He wanted a home."

Two years later, Lloyd's architect, Sumner Spaulding (no relation to Silsby Spaulding), finished plans for the residence. Sue Lloyd calls it "the house that glasses built." It was still a huge production. Fronted by a 120-square-foot automobile courtyard and loggia, the forty-four-room, twenty-six-bathroom home featured public rooms inspired by a Florentine villa, grouped around a cortile and entered through a hall with a sixteen-foot beamed ceiling, a gold-leaf coffered-ceilinged living room complete with an Aeolian pipe organ, a hydraulic movie screen and a hidden winding stairway to a projection room tucked behind a carved wooden panel, and a wrought-iron and hand-carved oak staircase leading up to the family quarters.

The Lloyds began entertaining there in summer 1929, inviting guests to a wedding shower for an actress friend before the house was finished or the custom-made furniture and custom-woven rugs installed. "One enters through ivy-entwined gates to find oneself in a golfer's heaven," a columnist rhapsodized, "the trimmest of greens and fairways giving way to a bridge built over a tiny, lily-filled lake . . . glimpses of the bluest of water through the trees of a formal garden . . . a scene of breathtaking beauty, the swimming pool, around which lawns, the blue bathhouse and a summerhouse open to the breezes invite one to forget the heat of the city."[6] A later housewarming went on all weekend and ended with revelers wandering the hallways and sleeping in the garden. Seven years (and five of his seven sound films later), Lloyd finally gave the house a name: Greenacres.

Mostly, the house reflected Harold's taste. Mildred only fought with him over his desire to install a bowling alley beneath the entrance foyer. When he bought bowling equipment anyway, Marion Davies, a drinking buddy of Mildred's, suggested she instead install a rogues' gallery of photographs there of everyone they knew, all signed to Harold. Years later, that "friendship corridor" revealed how frozen in time both Lloyd and his estate would soon become: The last picture on the wall was of the young Deanna Durbin, who made her first film in 1936.

Sound didn't kill Lloyd's extraordinary 487-film career; the Depression did. In 1937, he sold his studio west of Beverly Hills to the Mormon Church, which erected its Los Angeles temple there. By 1940, Lloyd was semiretired when he asked Los Angeles County to cut its assessment of Greenacres by more than 50 percent, complaining that it cost him $48,000 a year in up-keep and taxes even as its value had plummeted. Unable to rent it, he lived on there, even after a 1943 explosion and fire destroyed his film vault and the original negatives of many of his silent classics. Following a brief detour into radio during World War II, Lloyd's movie career ended in 1947 after a comeback film directed by Preston Sturges was shelved by Howard Hughes, the oil-and-aviation magnate who'd bought RKO, the last privately owned movie studio. By then, Lloyd had been forced to cut his live-in household staff of thirty-two and some of his sixteen gardeners, allowing parts of the rambling estate to go unmaintained.

Lloyd never admitted he'd retired. Instead, he'd say he was having a good time playing handball, fiddling with microscopes, dabbling in painting, nude and 3-D nude, and celebrity photography, traveling, and managing his real estate. "He bought property as an investment," says Sue Lloyd, and he rarely sold it. His inventory eventually included his bachelor house, his first marital home, a home for his father, three places in Beverly Hills, an avocado ranch in Templeton, California, a beach house next door to Hearst and Da-vies on the Pacific Coast Highway in Santa Monica, and a desert home in Palm Springs.

He also assumed an active role in the Shriners, serving as the Imperial Potentate of the Ancient Arabic Order of the Nobles of the Mystic Shrine in 1949, and helping build and run nineteen Shriners hospitals and burn treat-ment centers for children. That interest was inspired by the serious injuries and burns that almost ended his career in 1919 when a prop bomb explosion cost him the thumb and index finger of his right hand, and left him scarred and partially blind (which led him to adopt his signature glasses). Lloyd was also active in the Republican Party, serving as a convention delegate for Dwight D. Eisenhower and Richard Nixon, and was deeply involved in the Beverly Hills Chamber of Commerce, interests reflecting the down-to-earth character that set him apart from the contemporaries with whom he is most closely associated. "Chaplin was mean and Keaton was a drunk," says Lloyd's granddaughter. "Harold wanted to do things—especially for children. He loved kids."

The Lloyds raised granddaughter Sue after her mother and father's marriage ran into trouble. Her father, descended from old California oil and wine families, grew up a playboy, and after marrying into the Lloyds of Hollywood at Greenacres, in the presence of both Hedda Hopper and Louella Parsons, "forgot he was married," Sue says. Her mother spent a lonely pregnancy at Greenacres, divorced her husband when Sue was seventeen months old, and then, suffering from mental illness, gave legal custody to her parents, who raised, educated, and cared for the girl.

Sue's arrival was a tonic for the Lloyds. Harold's own children, born while he was still making movies, had felt stifled and lonely in the big house, which they considered a mausoleum. "Harold felt guilty because he'd missed out on raising their kids; he was always working. He said, 'I'm going to raise you differently,' " says Sue. Mildred, who'd taken to drinking in her forced retirement, kicked the habit, joined the local PTA, and "came out of her shell."

Sue learned to share Lloyd's love of his house. "He treasured it," she says. "It represented something he needed"—the stable home and family he'd lacked as a child. "He could never say no to relatives; there were people around all the time. And everything was used. Maybe the poker nook wasn't, but it was where he had slide shows. People were so taken with the grandeur, they didn't get it. It was lived in. He knew the name of every tree." Yet he didn't care for the place itself as much as what he filled it with. "Fabrics were in disrepair," says Lloyd, furniture grew threadbare, "but he had all the latest gimmicks. There were ruined rooms with the best hi-fi equipment" and thirty thousand vinyl records, all carefully categorized by his secretary. Lloyd's late-life fascination with stereo led him to install a state-of-the-art system with forty-nine speakers so loud they shook the gold leaf off the living room ceiling.

At age seventy-three in 1966, Lloyd still jogged around the estate and swam daily, and still had a fortune. "I am loaded," he told a reporter, pausing before adding, "with avocations." He smiled. "How's my timing?" He was worth millions. Mildred died in 1969, and Harold followed in 1971, at age seventy-seven. A thousand people attended his funeral. In his will, he directed that Greenacres become a museum of his life and belongings, including his films, paintings, and collection of vintage cars. With typical self-concern, neighbors in Benedict Canyon rose up in protest of anticipated traffic before it was even clear whether Lloyd's estate would manage to create and endow the tax-exempt foundation needed to maintain the place.

Greystone (905 Loma Vista Drive)

By the late 1920s, movie stars seemed to be setting the pace in building up Beverly Hills, but they weren't alone, and neither were they the city's richest or most influential residents. Another investor in local land started building around the same time Harold Lloyd did. His home would not only outshine Lloyd's but remains to this day the largest in Beverly Hills, and was once the second most splendid in California, after William Randolph Hearst's San Simeon. He was also the first in a century-long parade of controversial, politically connected businessmen who ended their lives in the Triangle, living in epic splendor but stained by scandal, their legacies darkened by the lingering impression that their fortunes were founded in corruption.

Like his friend and business partner Charles Canfield, Edward L. Doheny started out a prospector—"a real western cowboy," said his grandson Tim Doheny. "He had some wild times. He was a prospector with a pack mule when Geronimo was knocking them off down there in Arizona." Slight and pale but tough and smart, Doheny always came back from defeat. His first wife suffered from mental problems and their marriage was troubled from the start. During a period of calm in 1893, she gave birth to his only son, Edward Junior, nicknamed Ned. But as Doheny found success in the oil business, his wife felt increasingly alone and abandoned, and finally left him at century's end, fleeing to San Francisco with their son. The couple never saw each other again.

Doheny moved to downtown Los Angeles after the breakup and within

months had improbably fallen in love with the voice of a telephone operator who connected his calls; in summer 1900, he married her in a ceremony
held in his black walnut–paneled private railroad car. Margaret Leslie Davis,
Doheny's biographer, wrote that Estelle Doheny's understanding and refined
demeanor complemented his impatient, blunt personality and thrilled him,
completing his decade-long reversal of fortune. Aghast at his rapid remarriage, his first wife killed herself (the newspapers called it an accident) by
drinking battery acid. Ned, then seven, returned to Los Angeles, where Estelle took over his care.

Canfield lost interest in the oil business when his wife was murdered,
but Doheny remained committed to it, even pawning Estelle's jewelry to
refinance his Mexican ventures when some of his original investors pulled
out. His long absences again strained his marriage, but now he could make
up for that somewhat with a luxurious life for Estelle and Ned. For the then
stunning sum of $120,000, he bought a 10,500-square-foot mansion on
Chester Place, an exclusive enclave of fourteen homes in the West Adams
district of L.A., another property originally owned by Henry Hancock.
The French Renaissance/Gothic Revival mansion had twenty-two rooms,
including reception, music, and dining parlors, a library and a great room,
an ornate central tower reached only by ladders, and a freestanding Japanese
tearoom. Estelle threw herself into refurbishing it, extending its second and
third floors, adding windows and a Pompeian room connected to the tearoom, and landscaping lavish outdoor parlors where the family entertained.

Over the next fifty-eight years, Doheny and, later, his widow would take
over adjacent properties until they owned the entire subdivision and occupied an estate of almost twenty-five thousand square feet. Doheny could
afford whatever he wanted. He sat atop an international energy empire and
was one of the richest men in the world. He invested some of his wealth in
what grew to become the Doheny Ranch, his 429-acre holding on the border
of Beverly Hills, complete with a country home. In 1916, he even agreed to
pay for half the cost of paving the last mile of the future Sunset Boulevard in
"the rising little residential city," said the *Los Angeles Times*. He raised cattle
there and grew oranges, lemons, and avocados.

Unfortunately, Doheny also made a very bad investment around the same
time. He'd met a future member of President Warren Harding's cabinet, interior secretary Albert B. Fall, playing poker in the 1870s. Late in 1921, at his
father's bidding, Ned Doheny, who'd been living in New York and working

for his father's Mexican Petroleum Company, withdrew $100,000 from an investment account and, with his personal secretary Hugh Plunkett in tow, took it to Washington in a black satchel and loaned it to Fall interest-free so the cabinet member could pay back taxes and expand a cattle ranch he owned. Another oilman, Harry Sinclair, also loaned Fall money. Fall then leased several government-owned reserve oil fields in Wyoming to Sinclair and naval oil reserves in California to Doheny without competitive bidding. The oilmen happened to be financial backers of President Harding, who'd put those fields under Fall's control. Inevitably, those leases and loans became the subject of a U.S. Senate investigation.

In 1924, in what came to be known as the Teapot Dome Scandal, Doheny and Sinclair were indicted on federal charges of bribery and conspiracy, Fall was named a codefendant, and Ned, then thirty, was indicted for bribery and faced fifteen years in prison. A civil action sought to annul the oil leases. The charges against Ned were soon dropped but nonetheless, for the next decade, the Dohenys were entangled in court while the press portrayed them as rich crooks. Though the family's reputation would never recover, Doheny père was more fortunate financially. The next year, in the largest deal of its kind, he sold all his oil holdings outside California to the Rockefeller family's Standard Oil of Indiana. Whether out of prescience or a stroke of luck set in motion by his expensively mounting legal troubles, Doheny saved his fortune from the coming collapse of the stock market.

Amidst his troubles, Doheny was also thinking of Ned. In 1926, he and Estelle drafted a grant deed for about a dozen acres of their land, a parcel that unlike their ranch was actually in Beverly Hills, planning to sell it for a nominal $10 to their son and his wife Lucy. Doheny set about building a sixty-seven-room, 45,054-square-foot mansion for Ned, Lucy, and their five children on the land early in 1927;[7] it was a testament to his wealth, his devotion to his son, and his need to find distraction from the scandals swirling about them as well an apology of sorts for involving Ned in them. Doheny may have also hoped it would give his son and their young family shelter from those storms. The family even bought lots to the north and west from a subdivision called Beverly Crest to ensure the estate's privacy.

Lucy Doheny chose architect Gordon B. Kaufmann and landscape architect Paul G. Thiene because they'd just completed another estate near the ranch that she admired. When one of his assistant landscapers asked Thiene what Doheny wanted, he said, "Why, give them everything." Construction continued even as the U.S. Supreme Court invalidated the oil field leases Fall had granted to Doheny. Appropriately, one of the problems faced by the landscapers was oil seeping from the ground.

The house was finished in fall 1928 and cost $3 million to $4 million. The elder Doheny was so happy with it, he gave architect Kaufmann an expensive Cord car in thanks. They named the place Greystone after an estate in Yonkers, New York, owned by Samuel J. Tilden, its governor and a failed presidential candidate. Doheny's Greystone boasted panoramic views stretching from downtown L.A. to Santa Monica Bay. The name fit the English Gothic/Tudor-style Boise sandstone castle with a gray slate roof, vast formal gardens complete with fountains and a cascade, buttressed stone retaining walls, an elaborate porte cochère and arrival court, English lead details, Vermont slate terraces and fountains and a reflection pool—all so imposing it would be compared to a principality, a castle, and a fortress. Years later, it would provide an appropriate film set for Wayne Manor, the home of Bruce Wayne in Tim Burton's movie *Batman,* as well as Harry Osborn, aka the Green Goblin in the Spider-Man movies, and Jack Nicholson's devil, Daryl van Horne, in *The Witches of Eastwick*. The makers of *There Will Be Blood,* loosely based on Doheny, filmed in the Brunswick bowling alley in its basement (which boasted the requisite Prohibition-be-damned bar).

On the ground floor, entered through huge grillwork-covered glass doors, was a full suite of public rooms—a checkerboard Carrara marble–floored reception area with a carved staircase modeled on one in the home of England's Earl of Essex, an oak-paneled library with a barrel ceiling, family and paneled formal dining rooms, a card room complete with floor-to-ceiling murals and a central fountain, and a great room fit for a king with a beamed, two-story ceiling, huge leaded windows, oak paneling, and a massive carved fireplace.

Marble stairs led to the second-floor family quarters with his and hers master suites and sewing, linen, and gift-wrapping rooms. Original letters from George Washington and a framed copy of the Declaration of Independence hung in the hallway. A barber's chair was installed in Ned Doheny's black marble bathroom where a barber would visit "and give everybody a haircut," grandson Tim Doheny recalled. A sitting room where the family often ate had a small balcony from which the Doheny children would launch paper gliders. There were also a billiard room, a screening room, a playhouse for the children, tennis courts, a two-bedroom gatehouse, kennels, stables, a greenhouse, a ten-car garage complete with a mechanical lift, and a servant's wing that slept fifteen. The mansion boasted its own telephone system and two switchboards. The adjacent Doheny Ranch housed a private fire station, a security force, and a water system, which Greystone shared.

There was a playhouse on the highest point of the property for the Doheny children, and it, too, was grand. Transplanted from Chester Place, it was a completely livable house "except that all furnishing and all appliances, including a baby grand piano, were approximately two-thirds scale," said George Malie, younger member of the father-son team that supervised the property for decades.

But really, the whole place was a playhouse for the younger Dohenys. Greystone set a new standard in owner friendliness; it had secret passages between its inner and outer walls to allow electricians and plumbers access to the guts of the house without bother to the occupants. "There were places in the cellar where you could get into the walls. I used to get into the walls real good," Tim Doheny remembered. "You could also get . . . into two trap doors in what they called the maid's quarters . . . which they didn't know. They wouldn't have felt as secure if they had known this little brat could climb through a trap door in their closet at night, which I never did, by the way." Tim never got stuck, but "I dreaded it," he added. "I really did. Nobody would hear you and you would be a skeleton by the time you were found."

The Doheny children would ride in the kitchen dumbwaiters, roller skate across the vast marble floors on the main floor and through the hundred-foot halls in the basement, pick figs from their trees and throw them at passing cars, climb the flagpoles, ride horses (four were kept in plastered stables), fish in ponds stocked with bass, play ball on the vast lawns, and when they got older, rope calves on the ranch. They also rode anything they could find with wheels down the hill to the garage, spent "a lot of time down at the garage keeping those guys from working," and played in the dog kennels, the dairy where four cows produced milk, and in the spring caves that provided fresh water for the ranch and the estate; they had been dug out with picks and shovels by some of Doheny's old prospector friends. "We used to spend a lot of time in those caves," said Tim. "There was all limestone flooring. . . . Beautiful springs, just beautiful water. There were seven on the property. We had little headquarters here and there, which consisted of dirty magazines, a candle, you know. You go out there and smoke and things like that."

Always, though, there was the fear that Lucy Doheny would catch them.

She would ring bells to summon whoever was misbehaving. Each child was assigned a number of rings. "When I heard four bells, ding ding ding ding, it would scare the living shit out of me," Tim recalled, "because I knew exactly what was going to happen; my mother was home, somebody had told her that I had done something, and I'd get my ass home, usually got a spanking. The temptations were there. I took advantage of all of them."

Greystone's temptations weren't only for the children; one wing held a movie theater with another hidden bar behind paneling that rolled up into the ceiling at the push of a button. A sign there read, "We don't serve Mom but we have Pop on ice." More liquor was stored in the basement, near the laundry room, and behind the vault. The booze vault also held vats "for a little home brew," Tim Doheny recalled. E. L. Doheny's solid silver saddle was kept on the landing of the circular stair that led from the billiard room to the theater.

The Dohenys filled the place with grand antique and modern furnishings—chosen to deliver a powerful message of seasoned wealth and taste, though both the fortune and its family seat were new. They likely sought these signifiers not only to convey their hard-won status, but also as a bulwark against the political and legal turmoil that was battering them and blackening Doheny's reputation. If their money, made manifest in Greystone, appeared to be so old it was immovable, it might serve as a totem warding off the forces trying to bring Doheny down.

They also filled Greystone with staff—a veritable army that kept the outside world at bay. The grounds crew numbered between eighteen and twenty-two and the house staff of maids, waitresses, and laundresses was fifteen strong. The kitchen alone required two cooks and maids, mostly to feed all those employees, many of whom lived on the estate. The outside staff had to maintain more than lawns: The waterfalls, lakes, and fountains were all connected to the ranch's private water system and reservoirs and required two pumps to operate. Then there were the drivers—four of them—and the mechanics—five of them—who worked in the garages, including two specially designed to fit the family's pair of sixteen-cylinder Cadillacs, two of only twenty ever manufactured. There were eleven other cars and two trucks and a full machine shop capable of making any part needed for any of them. The Dohenys and their wealth were something new for Beverly Hills. They set a new standard of astonishing excess and outrageous indulgence that put them on a different plane from their fellow Angelenos. They seemed to be saying they were the rarest of the rich, like the Rockefellers and Morgans, untouchable, almost sacred in their castle on its Beverly hill.

They may have been asking for trouble.

There was another price paid for Greystone: a scandalous tragedy on a scale that would become all too familiar in the Triangle. This one revolved around that friend and employee of Ned's, Hugh Plunkett, who'd helped oversee the building of Greystone and whose marriage had collapsed under the strain of his long absences while doing so. At the same time that Ned and his family left their townhouse on New York's East 84th Street and took up residence at 501 Doheny Road, entertaining through the holidays, Ned's father was selling off his properties, eventually raking in about $100 million ($1.25 billion adjusted for inflation) for his oil fields and firms. But that was small comfort; though the Teapot Dome indictment against Ned had been dropped, they were dreading Doheny Senior's criminal trial, in which both Ned and Hugh—who'd delivered Doheny's "loan" to Albert Fall, that $100,000 in a black bag—were likely to be called to testify.

Did Hugh worry he'd be made a scapegoat? Perhaps. Still, no one could have predicted what happened next. Near midnight on Saturday, February 16, 1929, gunshots ended Ned and Hugh's Teapot Dome ordeal and Ned and Lucy's quiet life at Greystone, and opened up a mystery that will likely never be solved.

The official version: An upset Plunkett had arrived at Greystone several hours earlier, and rousted Ned from his private quarters on the second floor. They went together to a first-floor guest room where Ned, in a robe and slippers, made drinks and sat down for a talk that caused Plunkett to grow so agitated that Ned called the family's doctor, who'd treated Hugh when, certain he would end up in jail, he'd had a nervous collapse the previous Christmas Eve. It was later suggested that they were arguing over Ned's proposal that Hugh commit himself to a mental hospital for a rest, a plan that offered the added potential benefit of keeping him out of the witness box at Doheny's bribery trial.

When the doctor arrived at Greystone, he was met by Lucy, who'd heard a loud noise and had come down from the second floor. As they approached the guest room, Plunkett slammed its door in their face and within an instant, two shots exploded. Lucy and the doctor entered to find both men on the ground and bleeding, Plunkett dead, Ned dying next to an overturned chair. Soon, family members, among them Ned's father, converged on the mansion.

What happened next has led to eight decades of debate. The police were summoned—but only after a significant delay—and an investigation, though launched immediately, ended abruptly a mere three days later with the conclusion that Plunkett, in a sudden fit of insanity, had killed Ned and then shot himself. The truth, whatever it was, was not that clear-cut. The only witnesses were Doheny family and staff and their doctor. The detective in charge of the case discovered that Ned's body had been moved and found many oddities—among them, no fingerprints on the gun and contradictory evidence concerning Plunkett's mental state. Ned was buried at Forest Lawn Memorial Park instead of a Catholic cemetery, even though his stepmother was a devout Catholic—leading some to believe Ned may have committed the mortal sin of suicide.

While admitting uncertainty, Doheny's biographer Davis seems to blame the years of legal tension for the deaths of Ned and Hugh. Davis even allows that Doheny Senior could have been to blame. Though Doheny would be acquitted in his trial for committing bribery, Fall was convicted of taking a bribe from him. So Davis gives the last word on the affair to a Doheny critic who surmised that he brought about his own son's death through his zealous pursuit of wealth and power. If so, he paid dearly and continued to; like his partner after Chloe Canfield's death, he was a broken man and died five years later at his home in Chester Place. His $75 million estate was no comfort in the end. Despite his disgrace, or perhaps because of all the notoriety, more than three thousand people attended his funeral. His widow and her sister burned his personal papers.

Some of Ned's descendants entertain another explanation for the events of that night at Greystone: that the gossip at the time, which had Ned and Hugh as lovers, might have been true. "All of us have sort of wondered," says Will Doheny, a grandson of Ned and Lucy (and one of fourteen cousins in his generation). "It could have easily been [true] . . . Ned was not a good guy, apparently. He drank pretty heavily." Two of Ned's brothers-in-law were pallbearers for Plunkett, who was buried not far from Ned at Forest Lawn.

Despite inheriting Ned's $15 million fortune, more than ample to allow her to move, Lucy continued to live at Greystone, and was remarried in the house three years after her husband's mysterious death. Lucy "was very hard," says Will. "She was nicknamed Sweetheart. It was a misnomer." She

and her second husband, a divorced investment banker named Leigh Battson who had helped sell off E. L. Doheny's oil properties, would remain at
Greystone for decades, raising their five children and many grandchildren
there. Battson added a gun room and sauna to Greystone after World War II
and painted over some of the woodwork in the public rooms. Their parties
would mix figures from Los Angeles, San Francisco, and New York society
and British aristocrats with movie folk like Bob Hope, Edgar Bergen, George
Murphy, Adolph Menjou, Bing Crosby, and Jules Stein. And their grandchildren still talk about their Easter and Christmas parties.

In 1949, Lucy decided to sell the Doheny ranch (where the actress Loretta Young had been living for several years in the family's old white ranch
house) because "it was a real burden to try and manage and maintain," Tim
said.[8] The developer Paul Trousdale bought the ranch in 1955 for more than
$6 million after his condition that it be annexed by Beverly Hills was met
(Trousdale paid just over $400,000 in fees to get the chic Beverly Hills ad-
dress). Tim Doheny felt Trousdale "decimated" the hills where he'd played
as a child, and "pushed all the ridges into the canyon" while grading his
subdevelopment.

It's unclear whether the Dohenys knew that Trousdale's backers were the
Teamsters. They were likely happy with Trousdale Estates, the development
that resulted. Considered the epitome of midcentury modern chic, Trousdale
housed both Frank Sinatra and Dean Martin, and has staged a comeback in
recent years, once again becoming a fashionable neighborhood. The Battsons
kept Greystone, its grounds, and a nearby ten-acre knoll off Schuyler Road,
where they planned to build a smaller, yet still grand new home. Finally,
twenty-six years after her husband's death, it was finished, and Ned Doheny's
widow left the scene of the crime.

9481 Sunset Boulevard

Shortly after Greystone began rising in the hills, an extravagant French chateau was built about three blocks away by Francis Xavier Lourdou, a French-
born architect who'd relocated to Los Angeles and found clients in its new
upper class. Though they weren't as rich as the Dohenys, the family that
built it was older and redolent of the patrician past of the Southland—and

they were equally if not even more dysfunctional. The style of the house was appropriate, for its owners could trace their passage to Sunset Boulevard back to France, though the source of the money that paid for their architectural extravagance was New Spain. As with the Dohenys, they would soon find that their inheritance did not include peace and happiness. Fortunately, thanks to Los Angeles' rabid appetite for the new, their old money didn't attract attention to their family drama, even though it played out mere steps from busy Sunset Boulevard.

The first Botiller in North America came to Mexico from France in the late 1700s, escaping the French Revolution in his own sailing ship, presumably without much money since one generation later, Juan Antonio Botiller, a Baja, California, blacksmith, died in poverty along the Anza trail. He'd joined the march north from Mexico as a soldier of God seeking to find an overland route to northern California and help build Franciscan missions there. Botiller's wife survived the march and brought their children first to the mission at San Diego and later to those at San Gabriel and Santa Barbara.

The Botillers received lots of land in thanks for their family's services to Spain and Mexico, including today's Pebble Beach and Cypress Point and part of Rancho de Los Alamos y Agua Caliente at the southern end of California's Central Valley. A large family, the Botillers appear to have raised cattle and grown wealthy from the hide and tallow trade, selling skins and fat for cooking, candles, and soap, so Jose Vicente Botiller was raised in privilege in Santa Barbara; besides his own significant ranch lands, he built one of the earliest mansions in downtown L.A. on 8th Street and Main and owned one of the first carriages in town. On his death, his wife, Juana Maria Reyes, from an old Spanish family, inherited land that he owned in downtown and southern Los Angeles.

The family's land would be divided among ten members of the next generation and its fortune, tied up in lawsuits, became "an inextricable mess," according to the L.A. *Times* in 1909, shortly after the share controlled by one of those ten branches was estimated to be worth $234,000 (or more than $5 million today). But one son, Dionicio, who'd grown up with private tutors, managed to rise above the familial strife. He became a real estate investor and operator and in 1863, at age twenty-one, was elected as a Democrat to the Los Angeles City Council, where he served two terms and later, eight years as county assessor. In 1877, Dionicio married Francisca Bernard, daughter of a Swiss businessman who'd sailed around Cape Horn to California seeking gold and ended up owning a brickyard, a vineyard, and a hotel in downtown L.A. Francisca was also the granddaughter on her mother's side of one of the founders of colonial Los Angeles, whose family owned Rancho La Ballona, today's Marina Del Rey, Playa del Rey, and parts of Culver City. Francisca's mother built a Los Angeles landmark, a Gothic–Moorish–Art Nouveau chateau that still stands south of MacArthur Park near downtown. A taste for architecture ran in the family.

Dionicio and Francisca had six children, of whom only three survived them: Ida, Frank, and Cecilia. In 1907, Ida married Angus Reginald Lindley, the youngest lawyer ever admitted to the California bar. They were childless and lived with Ida's parents and siblings. Dionicio Botiller died in October 1915, and soon after that, Ida and Angus took in a neighbor boy who lived around the corner, John Royal Young, known as Jack. He was the future film and television star Loretta Young's brother.

Loretta and Jack's parents had broken up, and her mother had returned to her hometown of L.A., where a brother-in-law worked in the film business, to open a boarding house. Angus may have been Gladys Young's lawyer. When Gladys announced she was moving away, the Lindleys offered to adopt Jack, who'd begun spending more time at the Botiller house than he did with his own family. He called Ida and Angus Mama and Papa Bear. His mother refused the adoption but let him stay with the Botillers whenever he wanted, which turned out to be most of the time. (His sister Loretta was similarly taken in by the silent film star Mae Murray, who also tried but failed to adopt her.)

"From that point on, Jackie really belonged to both families," Loretta later wrote. "The Lindleys never formally adopted him, but they did change his name to Jack Young Lindley, first because he needed it for a passport, and then just because it seemed appropriate. They educated him beautifully, took him to Europe many times, and allowed him to be with us whenever he wanted." Jack Lindley eventually became a lawyer and one of his sons, David, would gain notice as a guitarist in the Southern California singer-songwriter Jackson Browne's band.

After Dionicio's death in 1915, his son Frank ran his estate. A ledger he kept of the property he'd inherited lists seven downtown Los Angeles tracts—including a nine-block stretch on the north side of the current Flower and Fashion districts—that are today worth many millions of dollars, and five properties in greater Los Angeles County, including several in the

San Fernando Valley; pieces of the colonial Rancho Conejo, which straddled western Los Angeles and eastern Ventura counties; and thirty-five acres in the former Rancho Tajauta, which is now Willowbrook, in South Central Los Angeles. So there was plenty of money to go around. In 1921, Francisca and her three children took an eight-month trip around the world.

Angus Lindley died at age forty-two in 1924. Three years later, Francisca decided to bring her remaining family together under one expansive roof and commissioned a 16,621-square-foot mansion with nine bedrooms for herself, her children, and Jack Young Lindley, at what would eventually become 9481 Sunset Boulevard, on the north side of the street between the two outlets of the U-shaped Mountain Drive. Her architect, Lourdou, had gotten his start with the Paris firm that designed the Eiffel Tower.

It is a testament to how much things had changed in Beverly Hills that the building of this remarkable H-shaped mansion passed unnoticed in the mainstream press. It was Lourdou's last commission; he died just shy of a year after filing the plans. They showed a 100-by-100-foot house with a full basement, two and three stories tall. It held twenty-two rooms and seven tiled bathrooms and was to be built of structural steel and stucco-covered brick with tasteful gray cast-stone doorways, windows, and balustrades. Guests would arrive through seventeen-foot-tall black iron gates, up a curving driveway to a wrought-iron and marble canopy over an entrance approached by marble steps and flanked by stately cast-stone columns. All of it, right down to the fleur-de-lis-trimmed wrought-iron doors and balconies, was designed to evoke the Petit Trianon at Versailles.

Compared to the Spanish colonial, American colonial, Hansel and Gretel, and Plantation-style houses that were its architectural neighbors, it was in a class apart, distinguished by the academic discipline of its classical façades, with their perfectly proper and meticulously crafted and detailed stone parts. Although the Botiller mansion was more elaborate and less austere than the Petit Trianon, it exhibited the same classical restraint, and nodded to the ideal of nobility in architecture, with serene horizontal lines and harmonious proportions set permanently in its stone construction.

Around it, pond-dotted gardens held fountains supported by baby cherubs; within were mahogany and oak paneling and trim, ornamental ceilings, even in the staff quarters, a gold-leafed music room, a foyer surrounded by ten Corinthian columns with a curving wooden staircase, five white marble fireplaces, four more of cast stone, an elevator, a water-softening system, steam heat, a rooftop sun room, a ballroom, and either a theater or a swimming pool in the basement (sources differ on what was finally installed). There was also a separate two-story garage. Excavation began that fall. Lourdou died the following April and was replaced by his son George Gustav, who oversaw the completion of the job and filled the place with museum-quality French furniture. Francisca Botiller got to see it finished but didn't have much time to enjoy it; she died in the house in spring 1929, two weeks after moving in.

Though no record of the total cost of the house exists, many subcontracts were filed with the city and give an idea of what Francisca spent. Excavation cost $3,895 (the equivalent of almost $49,000 today); carved stone, $10,080 ($126,000 today); steel, $2,200; lumber, $3,580; the elevator, $3,200; sashes, doorways, and glass, $6,196; terracotta, $1,060; plumbing and heating, $8,800; electric wiring, $2,470; sheet metal, $2,312; marble, tile, and terrazzo, $2,821; flooring, $3,475; carpentry and stairs, $6,200; cement floors, $732; masonry, $15,000, and plaster work, $11,675. Lourdou's fee went unmentioned.

None of the Botiller descendants alive today lived in the house. Frank was a pathological ladies' man and left behind a troubled legacy for the family. "I only met my father once, when I was about four," says his illegitimate son Robert Melsted, now seventy-nine, who was born Frank Drew Botiller Jr., but later took his mother's maiden name. He vaguely recalls visiting the house on Sunset and noticing that it had an elevator. "There was a lot of fighting," he says.

Janet Clifford is Frank Botiller's illegitimate daughter. Her mother had met Frank's best friend, Henry Blumenberg Jr., a womanizing borax-mining magnate, while modeling in a fur shop, and married him. Then she had an affair with Frank and gave birth to her son and a daughter before Blumenberg died when Clifford was two years old. "I never knew [Frank] was my father until I was nineteen years old," Clifford says. "My mother married another fellow. Then Frank lived with us for about ten years. After he moved out and died, my mother told me that he was my real father. It did not bother me one way or another because I never liked him. He always looked like a bum from Tijuana. He only dressed up for family meetings" of the D. Botiller Company that controlled their inheritance; Frank rarely bathed, and was "always making passes and grabbing at me."

"They were very eccentric people," adds Bobbie Hofler, Frank Jr.'s daughter. She never knew of her aunt Janet's existence until they met while she was doing genealogy research. Hofler thinks Frank Sr. "was more a playboy type. He kept 8-by-10s of women signed, 'Thanks for a good time.' " She says her father visited Frank Sr. until her mother forbade further contact. At one point, their mother showed up at the house on Sunset and "Ida threw knives down the stairs at her," Clifford says. Frank lived with his sisters for a while, but the siblings became estranged and he moved out. Estrangement ran in the Lindley family, too.

Ida Botiller Lindley died in 1947 at age sixty-eight. Frank and Cecilia inherited and sold the house two years later, shortly after giving their parents' home downtown to the Archbishop of Los Angeles for use as archdiocesan offices (it has since been demolished). As far as their descendants know, whatever was left of the family's land and fortune was similarly bequeathed to the Catholic Church. "But there's still some money in trust," says Hofler.

Relatives give differing accounts of the last of the Botillers. One says Frank owned land in Thousand Oaks and died there of a heart attack in 1952. Another says he lived in a big house in Pasadena. His death certificate puts him in West Hollywood. "The will said I got 6 percent or $60 a month, whichever was larger," says Robert Melsted. "I got a call. 'Will you contest the will?' I said no. Maybe I should have. I knew Frank was a shyster and he had shyster lawyers. But I wasn't going to go back through all that. I still get $60 a month."

Cecilia moved first to a bungalow at the Beverly Hills Hotel and then to either Hancock Park or Pacific Palisades, where Frank Jr. and Janet Clifford tried to visit, seeking to connect with their aunt, but she refused to see them. The only memory Clifford took away "was a limousine with a chauffeur in the driveway." John Lindley, son of the almost-adopted Jack Young, made it inside and recalls his aunt as "a nice little old lady" with a house "just jammed with antique furniture, European, kind of gaudy." She died in 1990.

"My dad was pretty silent about everything," says John Lindley. "No circumstance is ideal that I know of." Great houses aren't always homes for happy families.

Pre–Bel Air

In 1901, Charles and Chloe Canfield's younger daughter Daisy, sixteen, was pretty and willowy, with full, sensuous lips and dark, smoky eyes. That summer, she left Los Angeles by train—with a chaperone, of course—en route to Boston, where she planned to study at the Conservatory of Music. She never arrived. Instead, she went to Salt Lake City, where she secretly married Jacob Morris Danziger, nineteen, the son of a tailor. The Canfield and Danziger families had lived six blocks away from each other in Los Angeles, and Jake had been "a sort of clerk, a yeoman type in Charles Canfield's office," says great-granddaughter Mary Warthin. His romance with Daisy was unknown to their parents, who learned of the elopement a few weeks later when the couple sent telegrams revealing the news.

"TWO CLEVER YOUNGSTERS," headlined the *Los Angeles Times,* which reported that "Jakey" had left Los Angeles one day after Daisy, en route to Philadelphia, where he planned to go to college and become a lawyer. Five days later, Jake's father Morris revealed that his son had written him from Philadelphia to say that they were settled there and happy. Eight months and two days after that, Daisy gave birth to a daughter they named Daisy, too.

Despite the circumstances of their marriage, both families embraced the couple. Danziger's father swore he'd support them even if Jake decided not to work. When he graduated from the University of Southern California law school and won admittance to the bar in 1903, Charles Canfield brought him into the oil business, and by 1908, Jake was a well-known lawyer and oilman when he filed a suit seeking commissions on an oil deal he'd arranged. By that time, he'd made enough money to invest in Canfield and Doheny's Mexican oil plays, and eventually he quit his job as the lawyer for the Santa Fe Railroad's oil department to work full time with his father-in-law.

Canfield kept his family close. Not only did Jake work for him, they also vacationed together at his mansion on the shore at Del Mar between San Diego and Los Angeles. Upon Canfield's death in 1913, Danziger was named executor of his estate, which was valued at $9 million, likely an understatement. "Danziger took Canfield's place on all the boards of directors," said Beverly Hills engineer Arthur Pillsbury. He became a rich man and an even richer woman's husband; Canfield's four daughters each immediately inherited $1 million (or almost $25 million today).[9] So when John Wolfskill, who still owned Rancho San Jose de Buenos Ayres, died that December, they could easily afford to buy the portion of his rancho that seemed least appropriate for subdivision, running from the north end of the flats near the Los Angeles Country Club up into the hills, including a large flat knoll perfect for a mansion. Years later, Danziger would boast that he'd resisted his father-in-law's demand that he buy Beverly Hills land because Rodeo wanted too much for its lots. Instead, he'd say he paid next to nothing for the Wolfskill land—variously reported as 600 acres for $28,800, 1,700 acres for $34,000, or 2,000 acres for $96,000. Late in 1918, Danziger would buy another 468 acres of the foothills from Wolfskill's heirs.

In January, Jake announced plans for La Quinta, his and Daisy's thirty-five-room, twelve-bathroom house, "the largest and most expensively equipped" home in Southern California, said the *Los Angeles Times*. Sitting seven hundred feet above the flats, the 250-foot-long fireproof Italian-style villa was going to be covered in soft gray stucco, its interior walls paneled in floor-to-ceiling mahogany and oak. The plans included both heat and then-new air conditioning, fireplaces in every room, a swimming pool and pavilion, extensive gardens, and elaborate hillside staircases. Danziger ran gas and telephone lines in from the Beverly Hills Hotel. Eventually, he would add a golf course, tennis courts, stables, a trout hatchery, and a casino with cards and roulette tables. All told, Jake and Daisy were said to have spent $1 million on the place (about $21.3 million today).

Behind the perfect façade, though, the Danziger marriage was troubled—and so was Daisy. Though the once handsome Jake had turned fat, balding, flat-faced, and thuggish-looking, with a strong resemblance to the Chicago gangster Al Capone, he was a successful womanizer and cheated on Daisy whenever he could—even at his father-in-law's house in Del Mar. Friends and Canfield domestic workers told her of his infidelities; they separated in 1907 and again in 1908 and by 1915, after giving birth to three children, she'd grown plain-looking and, by all accounts, quite cranky.

Daisy found comfort in her gardens, which were run by a full-time botanist and were so elaborate it was said to take days to see them all. She was also an avid philanthropist, serving as finance chairman for a local tuberculosis group and working with the Red Cross, for which she devised a market selling various crafts, trinkets, and other donated items that was so successful the concept was rolled out nationally. But a 1918 photo of her in her Red Cross uniform shows a face marked with ineffable sadness. That year, she and Danziger separated for the last time, though they still shared their mansion. It was big enough to accommodate their estrangement, at least for a time.

The separation hardly slowed Jake down. In 1919, he helped Cliff Durant, a race car driver and son of the founder of General Motors, organize a group that bought two hundred acres just south of today's Wilshire Boulevard from Rodeo Land and Water for $1,000 an acre to build a speedway—a car racing track—designed to put the name of Beverly Hills in headlines around the world. To get financing, Jake called a meeting that included, among others, the movie moguls Cecil B. DeMille and Jesse Lasky, and Jake's brother-in-law Sil Spalding. "When one of these groups shot, the rest shot, see?" Pillsbury recalled. "He said, 'Now listen gentlemen, we are going to raise $200,000 while we sit at this table.'" Turning to his brother-in-law, Jake then declared, "You're going to take forty."

The mile-and-a-quarter speedway with a raked track made of two million feet of boards more than served its purpose, attracting more potential home buyers to town—as many as fifty-five thousand to each race—and earning the partners a return of nearly 20 percent a year. It closed in 1924, "when [the land] became so valuable that we couldn't hold it any longer," said Pillsbury. It was dismantled, and the seven million feet of lumber used for the roadbed, fences, and stands was sold for $25,000 to the junk man who carted it all away. The speedway syndicate sold the land to several of its members; Pillsbury helped subdivide it and not only made huge, easy commissions, but bought himself a corner of Wilshire and Santa Monica Boulevards for $27,500, which three years later he sold for $145,000. Another buyer, Walter McCarty, built the Beverly Wilshire Hotel on the site after Margaret and Stanley Anderson's hotel exclusive with Rodeo expired in 1924.

Stanley Anderson, too, made a small fortune investing in land. He bought the corner of Beverly Drive and Santa Monica Boulevard for $1,850 (just over $23,000 today) and in 1946 boasted of turning down an offer of $1 million for it. Between 1919 and 1927, the value of land in downtown Beverly Hills climbed from $1,000 (or $12,345 today) to $435,000 (or $5.37 million) an acre.

Danziger likely made money on the deal, too, but he got nothing from Daisy after she filed for divorce, pointedly serving her husband on Christmas Eve, 1921, charging him with cruelty and citing "at least" two instances of infidelity, one at Del Mar, and the other in New York, where their daughter was in school. The complaint alleged that Jake had "squandered large sums on luxuries for his female companions . . . spent many evenings away from home and associated himself with women of dissolute character." Daisy moved into an apartment she'd leased from her Episcopal priest near Hancock Park, far from her husband, and asked the court's permission to resume her maiden name. Her complaint stated her belief that they shared no property. "Mr. Danziger has his property and I have mine," she told a reporter.

Two days later, Jake concurred, calling the divorce "the inevitable adjustment of incompatible ideals." He admitted that her ideals were high "and I have not been able to measure up." Though he claimed her complaint left "a wrong impression of my qualities," he said he would not contest the divorce and added the dubious claim that he and Daisy remained friends. A decree was granted with blinding speed and a mere two weeks after she sued, Daisy was granted her divorce and custody of their two younger children. Under California law, it would all become final in a year.

Danziger remained a vice president of the Canfield-Doheny oil companies after the divorce. But he moved east, leaving their mansion to Daisy, and by 1923 he was remarried to an Edith Wake; they lived in an apartment on New York's fashionable corner of Fifth Avenue and 57th Street. (One newspaper report said he married a Mrs. Estrella Bishop that same year, but the veracity and fate of that marriage is unknown.) Jake and Edith returned to Los Angeles in 1924 and he got back to business, joining the committee formed to complete Beverly (later Sunset) Boulevard from Beverly Hills to Santa Monica and putting together a group of investors, including his former brother-in-law "Black Charley" Canfield, to build a concert and convention hall. Olympic Auditorium opened the next year with a boxing match followed by a season of opera. Once again, Danziger hired Arthur Pillsbury as his builder.

Pillsbury, still working almost exclusively for Burton Green at Rodeo, was glad to moonlight for Jake; by then, he'd come to consider Green quite unpleasant. "They were all scared of Green," Stanley Anderson said. One day, during the construction of the speedway, the water lines running to the site were mysteriously shut down; Pillsbury rushed to Green's house to demand they be turned back on. Green denied he'd had anything to do with it. "The only time I ever called Green a liar," said Pillsbury.

He felt differently about Danziger. Like his late father-in-law, Jake ordered that no expense be spared on his jobs. So Pillsbury liked him "in spite of the fact that he is of Jewish descent," he said in 1946. "He is one of the few of his race I have ever liked." Jake was also generous, paying Pillsbury "three times any amount I had ever hoped to get," he said. "He treated me white."

Barney Oldfield, a race car driver, felt differently and in 1926 filed a lawsuit against Jake and his new wife over a piece of property; the case went on for seven years before Oldfield won. The tangled litigation even included an action pitting Danziger against his second wife—one of many lawsuits the apparently litigious couple would engage in over the next decade. Danziger's legal troubles were both civil and criminal. In 1929, he was arrested and jailed in Tijuana, Mexico, when he broke into a property after he lost control of it and was ordered to repay half its construction costs to investors.

When he accompanied "Black Charley" Canfield's ex-wife to court in 1932 (she was seeking back alimony), the two men got into a scuffle and young Canfield pulled a gun on him. A sheriff confiscated the gun, revoked Canfield's carry permit, and forced the pair to shake hands.

Then, in the 1940s, Jake was found guilty of twelve counts of mail fraud, conspiracy, and violations of the Securities and Exchange Act for defrauding investors out of $50,000, and at age sixty-six, after three years of appeals, was sent to federal prison for fifteen months. When he died in 1954, he still had enough money to own a waterfront home in La Jolla, California. In one last curious twist, the son of a Jewish tailor was buried in a Catholic cemetery.

Jake outlived Daisy, but arguably, she out-*lived* him. By spring 1922, she was back in her estate alone, entertaining grandly, perhaps celebrating her new-found freedom, but also having a last hurrah there. That June, she closed on a sale of La Quinta, at that point reported to be 1,700 acres, for $2 million, to developers who were said to be planning a high-class residential subdivision, complete with a hotel and a polo club. Then, one day short of a year after filing for divorce, it was revealed she was acquiring a new husband.

Antonio Moreno was a member of Hollywood's reigning triumvirate of "Latin lovers," ruling the box office with their smoldering good looks, notwithstanding the fact that all three were homosexuals. The others were Rudolph Valentino and Ramon Novarro (who were reportedly lovers; among Novarro's prized possessions was an inscribed sterling silver replica of Valentino's prodigious sex organ). At the time, their sexuality was a closely guarded secret.

Moreno came from Madrid where, at age fourteen, he'd met two men who were taking a grand tour of Europe together: Benjamin Curtis, a nephew of New York's then mayor Seth Low, and Cuban-born Enrique de Cruzat Zanetti, a Harvard-educated lawyer, who would later marry and divorce and then spend the rest of his life traveling, looking at art, and practicing Sufism.

"My huge admiration for them, lavishly expressed, and my breathless interest in all they told me about America evidently caught their fancy," Moreno would later say in a ghostwritten and endearingly revealing movie magazine autobiography. "They made a chum of me. . . . I dared to tell them things I didn't even dare to tell my mother, for fear of hurting or shocking her. They were men. They would understand. I liked men better than I liked women. . . . I even went so far as to make brave enough to invite them to my house where, with great ceremony, I presented them to my mother. I somehow felt that this was a Great Occasion. I felt it even more when, after our dinner, Mr. Curtis began to talk very earnestly to my mother about a subject that was of intense interest to me—myself. He said a great many things about me that I did not understand and am not sure that my mother quite did, either. Flattering things. I hadn't had many flattering things said of me before. I wasn't used to it."

The pair immediately put the teenager in a private school and then invited him to New York, where he found more sponsors and eventually a job working backstage at a theater; inevitably, the handsome youngster landed onstage and within a few years, was making silent films in Hollywood, usually playing a romantic hero. He was dubbed an "It" boy by no less an authority than the woman who coined the term to describe sex appeal, author

Elinor Glyn, and went on "studio dates" with costars like Gloria Swanson and Pola Negri.

At first, Daisy and Moreno refused to confirm reports they were engaged, even as their nondenials made it plain what was happening. A "visibly moved" Moreno claimed he'd been a family friend for years, adding, "If I could say that I was engaged to Mrs. Danziger, I would be the happiest man in the world. . . . Like a Spanish cavalier I would throw myself at her feet so she could walk upon me. . . . She is more to me than anything in the world." Six weeks after that splendid performance, they were quietly married in her Hancock Park apartment. She was already building a palatial new twenty-two-room home she'd call Crestmount above the Silver Lake reservoir between Hollywood and downtown L.A.

Moreno's "friends in the film colony were on the verge of proclaiming him a permanent bachelor," noted the *Times* in a glancing reference to his sexual preference. Rumors—never published, of course—soon spread through Hollywood that the marriage had been arranged by his studio. Her family doubts a story that circulated at the time that she'd met him when she invested in films. But they are less dismissive of the sham-marriage scenario, which was later revealed in several authoritative books. In *Heroes, Lovers and Others: The Story of Latinos in Hollywood,* Clara Rodriguez writes that Moreno "initially resisted the pressure from his studio (and possibly from his agent as well) to marry for the sake of his public image, but eventually he gave in, and Daisy Canfield Danziger was selected to play the part."

Moreno's version of the event is somewhat more romantic: "Perhaps it is not given to every man to meet his Ideality. It was given to me. A woman, gracious and poised, lovely and cultured, intelligent and charming—my wife. . . . We have built a home in California and we are, I dare to prophesy, going to 'live happily ever after.' "

Or, at least, for a few years.

By the time Jake Danziger returned to Los Angeles, Daisy and Tony were ensconced in Crestmount, establishing themselves as a magnetic force bringing Hollywood and L.A. society together at regular Sunday afternoon parties in what was called "the most beautiful house in Hollywood," a "hilltop palace . . . designed for entertaining upon a large scale" with "tapestried furniture, golden hued velvet hangings . . . oriental rugs . . . and the loft ceilings . . . of dark wood that is polished and inlaid." Describing "the picture stars and social lights" who came there—Charlie Chaplin, Sam Goldwyn (who had anglicized his name), Buster Keaton, B. P. Schulberg, and Norma Shearer among them—as "mocha and java," the columnist Grace Kingsley joked that "they have the same bootleggers and that in itself is a real bond."

Again, though, the marriage didn't last. "He would appear and disappear," says Mary Warthin. "He would go to the bullfights when he wasn't working." Which happened more often as the 1920s ended, sound movies came to dominate Hollywood, and Moreno's fortunes declined. "I'd love to see Hollywood toss the spoken word out the window," he groused. In January 1929, he and Daisy deeded Crestmount to the Chloe P. Canfield Memorial Home, the "hospitality center" for intelligent Caucasian girls aged six to twelve, which Charles Canfield had endowed in his will in memory of his murdered wife. The Morenos moved into an apartment while building a new home in Laughlin Park, a small gated enclave near Griffith Park, northeast of Hollywood, where many silent stars had lived in the early days of the movies. Three years later, though, they separated, and both moved out, citing "temperamental differences." Daisy, devastated, wrote a friend to say that Tony had left her and predicted she wouldn't live out the year. She also predicted a reconciliation.

Less than a week later, after a party celebrating her daughter Elizabeth's wedding anniversary at the Beverly Wilshire Hotel, Daisy and Elizabeth had a fight and Daisy stormed off with her escort, a twenty-one-year-old nephew of Moreno's sponsor Enrique Zanetti, who was visiting L.A. Daisy's right arm had been injured—a fact that led some to speculate she'd had a physical altercation with her estranged husband—so she let the young man drive her Cadillac, suggesting he take scenic Mulholland Drive so he could see its splendid view of Los Angeles. On a foggy, twisty part of the road, he tried to turn on the car's brights, but extinguished the lights instead and within seconds, drove through a wooden guard rail. The car plunged 150 feet into a box canyon, flipping over. Daisy's escort, despite five broken vertebrae, managed to climb out of the ravine and get help, but it was too late. Thrown fifty feet from the car, Daisy Canfield Moreno was dead at age forty-seven.

Moreno reeled when given the news, and never remarried, though he eventually managed to find regular work again as a character actor and remained in Beverly Hills. Daisy's son-in-law told a complicated, less than honest version of the deadly evening's events at an inquest. His story, which eliminated many details told within the family, was sufficient to halt the investigation and have the death ruled an accident. The cause of Daisy's injured arm and the fact of her fight with her daughter were never revealed. A day later, Daisy was cremated at a funeral attended by a hundred friends, Moreno, and his stepdaughters. He and the children eventually inherited about $1.3 million (or $20 million today). A year after Daisy died, her brother, Black Charley, tried but failed to challenge her will. In 1964, when Moreno was ailing, his then companion, Mary Westbrook, sought to take over his estate, but was stopped by the children. Though he'd lost large sums in an unsuccessful subdivision of his own, called Moreno Highlands, he still left them $1.1 million when he died at age eighty in 1967.

In 1950, the Chloe Canfield home in Silver Lake closed and was sold to an order of Franciscan nuns who kept Canfield's dream alive by caring for orphaned, homeless, and court-placed girls. Damaged in a 1987 earthquake, it has since been rented out for film shoots and to pop musicians for use as a home and studio. Though he likely didn't know the tragic history of the family that built it, a member of the band Papa Roach, which recorded there, noted perceptively (if profanely) that the estate "was completely fucking haunted."

Bel Air

When Daisy Canfield kicked Jake Danziger to the curb and a year later left their vast estate just west of Beverly Hills forever, she neither knew nor likely cared that she'd set in motion the creation of the second great estate community in Los Angeles, billed by its creator as "The Aristocrat of Suburban Development . . . meeting the ideal conception of what the exclusive suburban home should afford."

Like Charles Canfield, Max Whittier, and Burton Green of Beverly Hills, La Quinta's buyer had made his fortune in oil.

Alphonzo Edward Bell was born in Los Angeles, but like most of the men who built the city, his roots lay in the Midwest. His mother and father had moved to California at the urging of her brother, an adventrepreneur who'd spent twenty-five years in Panama and Nicaragua running a river boat, a trading post, and a hotel before coming to Los Angeles in the 1870s to invest in real estate. Alphonzo was born just after his parents arrived in 1875. Initially, his father ran his brother-in-law's farms and cattle ranches, but soon owned his own 350 acres south of Los Angeles, today the towns of Bell and Huntington Park.

"A typical Scotch Presbyterian of his era . . . serious, pious, honest, and very strict," according to Alphonzo's biographer John O. Pohlmann, Bell's father wanted the youngest of his nine children to become a minister and brought Alphonzo up sober and self-reliant. His youthful exuberance found its outlet on the family's tennis court, one of the very first in California;

Americans had organized their first national tournaments only a few years earlier.

Alphonzo's father was one of the founders of Occidental College, and his son enrolled in the Presbyterian school at the precocious age of thirteen; he studied there until he graduated at nineteen, serving in the student senate, working on a campus magazine, playing tennis, football, and baseball, and becoming a star pole vaulter. He spoke at graduation, extolling the virtues of education and religion, and condemning the evils of alcohol. Then he entered a theological seminary to study for the ministry. But after two years, he withdrew, convinced he was too shy and private to be a minister, but also, his biographer thinks, because he wanted to pursue both real estate and tennis. By 1900, he was winning championships, and a few years after that, he was ranked one of the top ten players in America. He won two medals at the 1904 Olympics.

His closest friendships were formed on the court. Men he played with became his lifelong business associates. In 1902, he married Minnewa Shoe-maker, a like-minded, religious Kansas City girl he'd met at a Los Angeles tennis tournament. "She was a cute gal, very pretty and spunky," says her grandson Rex Ross III, who called her Mamo. The family cherished the story of how she'd captured Alphonzo's heart by taking the wheels off his wagon when he planned to go to a picnic with another girl.

While in school, Bell had inherited 110 acres of farmland from his uncle, who called him "Phonzie." He subdivided, investing the profits in more land. In 1908, he and Minnewa moved to one of his properties in Santa Fe Springs near his father's land, where he built a large house with a clay tennis court on two hundred acres. Still industrious, he grew orange and lemon trees, alfalfa, oats, hay, and barley—earning enough money to hire two household servants and a multitude of farmhands, drive a Hudson, and become the moving spirit behind the Hacienda, a local golf club. While planning it, he visited the Westside to see how the Los Angeles Country Club watered its lawns.

Drilling for water to irrigate his crops, Bell discovered *brea,* the same goop that led Edward Doheny and Charles Canfield to their fortune. A few years later, oil companies started drilling in Santa Fe Springs, and Bell tried to entice them onto his land. In 1917, Union Oil bought a lease, and two years after that, sank its first well. It was just in time; Bell had defaulted on his mortgage even as he began building a beach house, revealing a profligate fault in his pious façade. He continued to believe that Union would strike oil, even as the drilling went deeper and deeper without results.

Finally, late one night in 1921, an explosion of mud and gas heralded a gusher on Bell's land, cloaking him in oil and unfettered joy. By 1923, the Santa Fe Springs field would be producing a sixth of America's oil (Burton Green's Amalgamated also had wells there), and despite a steep drop in the price of oil due to the field's astonishing productivity and another, even larger strike the same year outside Long Beach, Bell's leases earned him about $25,000 a month ($320,000 in 2010 money). His biographer estimates that over the years, he netted the current equivalent of $250 million. News of his good fortune spread so widely he was forced to hire bodyguards to protect his three children after receiving kidnapping threats.

Those threats weren't the only troubling repercussion of the oil strike. In spring 1922, the Bells were driven from Santa Fe Springs when Union's second well caught fire and threatened their home. They moved into the Beverly Hills Hotel, bought ten acres next to the Doheny Ranch for $50,000 (about $633,000 in 2010), and announced plans to build a $100,000 estate there. But just less than three months later, and for reasons unknown, Bell's plans changed—radically. Frank Meline, who had taken over Beverly Hills lot sales for Rodeo Land and Water, brokered a deal for Bell to buy Jake and Daisy Danziger's sprawling La Quinta estate—the $2 million purchase price (which would be more than $25 million today) set a local record.

Sixteen months later, the Bell family moved into Jake and Daisy's former home on twelve acres Alphonzo Bell had decided to keep for himself. Bell filled the house with furnishings and a dozen servants, its stable with forty horses, and its garage with cars; he would eventually own two Rolls Royces, a Phaeton, and a Packard, all serviced by a full-time mechanic. It was a sophisticated place where Minnewa Bell loved to host formal dinners for guests in evening clothes. Yet "the country was still wild," wrote Alphonzo Jr., their youngest, then seven, describing how mountain lions would wander across the much diminished though still spacious grounds on which Bell spent, according to his son, $1 million. He converted Danziger's gambling cabin into a proper children's playhouse; turned a bare hillside into a one-acre copy of Babylon's terraced Hanging Gardens (at $75,000—almost $950,000 today—"the world's costliest private vegetable garden," said the *Times*); re-landscaped the estate's already luxurious gardens; added a tennis court with a surface made of redwood blocks (replaced with concrete after they swelled in the rain), a swimming pool, and a rock house that sometimes contained a bear; and surrounded it all with a wall a mile and a quarter long and between four and twenty feet high made of six thousand tons of gray sandstone and yellow flagstone quarried from his mountain land. Bell wasted no time; the next year, he built a forty-eight-office mission-style headquarters for his real estate interests (later the nucleus of the Hotel Bel-Air).

A new Alphonzo E. Bell Corporation was formed and Meline announced the opening of sales in a new subdivision, "a community of gentleman's estates" named Bel Air. Brochures promised that "the last word in improvements will prevail throughout," including buried water, gas, electric, and phone lines—a first in Los Angeles; its own reservoir, connected to the Los Angeles aqueduct; "a complete system" of "dustless" bridle paths and engineer-designed roads with views planned by a landscape architect; and "artistic bridges" designed by an architect known for churches. Bel Air would be a sanctuary. Though clearly inspired by the success of Beverly Hills, Bell positioned it differently. Bel Air would be "highly restricted" and "protected from undesirable developments by natural and imposed restrictions," its literature promised. It all reflected Bell's contradictory personality. "He wanted to get into society and [buying that house] was a way to do it," says Douglas Waldron, a cousin. "He used to love to show off. He loved that life—parties with fancy people—but he was also very religious. I don't know how he reconciled it. He was lively but he just had certain beliefs. We used to have to hide the wine."

The first batch of 128 fully improved Bel Air lots between Sunset Boulevard and Bell's own estate ranged from three-quarters of an acre to more than ten acres and cost $7,500 to $30,000 ($91,500 to $366,000 in 2010 dollars). Deeds required a minimum expenditure of $15,000 on houses (unlike Rodeo Land and Water, the Bell Corporation didn't build spec houses) and a formal architectural review. There was also a vetting process for purchasers. "References are required," an offering explained, "and credentials are carefully investigated." Bell quietly directed that no sales be made on Sundays, and neither movie people nor Jews were allowed to buy. Nonwhites were also barred, as in next-door Beverly Hills.

The first movie person who tried to buy was turned away, even though he'd gone to college with Bell. Fred Thomson, a cowboy star, and his wife,

Frances Marion, Mary Pickford's favorite screenwriter, tried to purchase a tract. Marion's biographer, Cari Beauchamp, quotes Bell's reply: "I'm terribly sorry you became an actor, Fred. I've made it a law—not one acre of my land is to be sold to actors or Jews." They bought twenty-four acres in Beverly Hills instead. Years later, Bell's son and namesake Alphonzo Jr., who'd gone into local politics and so had reason to sugarcoat his father's legacy, would claim that the second sale in Bel Air was to a Jew, but that can't be substantiated.

Bell wasn't done buying land himself. A few weeks after the Bel Air announcement, he made another, even more epic deal through Meline, paying $5.4 million to buy the Santa Monica Mountain Park Ranch. Formed by Moses Sherman and his partner, though later sold to others, it was a vast twenty-two thousand acres of farm and cattle land, covering thirty-five square miles from the Los Angeles Country Club to the ocean and extending two to four miles into the southern slopes of the Santa Monica Mountains. With that purchase Bell (and several partners) owned all that was left of two colonial ranchos, San Vicente y Santa Monica and Boca de Santa Monica, following the initial development of Brentwood (first settled in the 1890s), Pacific Palisades (where homes began springing up in the 1920s), and several other communities.

The tract, some of which was destined for further subdivision and development, some for investment, included seven thousand feet of ocean-front property just north of Pacific Palisades, and Topanga, Rustic, Emerscal, Kenter, Santa Ynez, Sepulveda, and Mandeville Canyons, as well as ridges soon to be serviced by the new Mulholland Highway with vast views of the San Fernando Valley. Some 2,500 acres of it were annexed to Bel Air, where Bell had decided to build another country club, financing it by personally underwriting a $500,000 mortgage. He soon began selling, too; one 200-acre tract went to the actor-humorist Will Rogers, who turned it into a ranch and polo field. Eventually Bell and a small group of partners would sell off 6,000 acres for a total of $9.3 million ($113.4 million today). They intended to subdivide the rest into large estates, even though they could have shoehorned a hundred thousand small homes onto the land. They expected their estate district would one day stretch all the way from Beverly Hills to the Pacific.

With those big deals done, the Bells took off for Europe early in 1924, staying more than three months and coming home inspired to name the streets of Bel Air after places they'd seen in Spain, Tuscany, and France. The former La Quinta was thus renamed Capo di Monte, and that mile and a half of oceanfront that Bell and Meline were developing was named Castellamare, after a Neapolitan port. Bell also started building the Bel-Air Bay Club, a private beach club, on thirty-one acres there, with membership limited to Bel Air homeowners.[10] He just kept spending. After opening Bel Air's bridle trails in spring 1925, he built a horse ring, grandstand, and stables, complete with accommodations for grooms ready to "bring mounts to your door," and began staging an annual horse show.

In 1928, Bell added to his land holdings again, buying eight thousand acres in Colorado, which he named the Bar-Bell Ranch; he raised saddle horses, cattle, and silver fox and ran a trout hatchery there, hunted deer, fished, and taught his children and grandchildren to love the outdoor life as he did. He loved it so much he bought another property south of Mount Whitney in the High Sierra, where he built a campsite among the boulders with beds made of pine needles laid down in log frames; the family would spend several weeks there every summer. And then, in 1935, he bought another ranch of 2,300 acres nearer to Bel Air in the Coachella Valley. The extremes represented by his residences were expensive symbols of his at once pious and extravagant character. His son would later claim to have been so embarrassed by their wealth that he hid on the floor of the Rolls when he was taken out shopping as a boy.

Bell's character may also explain why Bel Air sales started off slowly and then ground to a halt during the Depression. Many potential purchasers were reluctant to buy because of Bell's quirks: He wouldn't allow drinking in the one restaurant on his land or in either of the Bel Air clubs, and when members took to carrying flasks, he banned them, too. Bell could afford his quirks; he continued to make money from real estate investments, and oil royalties kept pumping out of the ground in Santa Fe Springs. The liquor prohibition didn't end until his death.

As Bel Air's promotional brochures implied ("Bel Air is different," said an early one. "Like the painting of an artist, it is the dream of one man—Alphonzo E. Bell"), Bell proved to be more visionary despot than businessman. "Perhaps you, too, may some day turn your back upon the clangor of steel on steel to establish your place of work in the hills where flows the air which God made to be breathed by Man in his image," was no typical real estate come-on.

Which is not to say that Bel Air was a flop. Bell produced lavish brochures and later a newsletter, the *Bel-Air Progress,* full of gentle sales exhortations, some signed by the proprietor himself; articles extolling Bel Air's landscaping and climate; hand-drawn renderings of new homes; and news of their owners, who were relatively anonymous compared to the show-offs who were flocking to Beverly Hills, but numerous nonetheless. Among them were a builder of dams, a dentist, a botanist, an architect, two hoteliers, a banker, a real estate investor, an insurance salesman, a retailer, a Pasadena piano store owner, the city attorney of Phoenix, a politician, and executives from the copper, clay, oil, electricity, aviation, citrus, and textile businesses. Not one of their names would ring a bell today. But they could afford houses that cost far more than Bell's minimums; by 1927, several six-figure residences were rising in Bel Air.

A few picture people did sneak into Bel Air in its early days, Bell's prohibition notwithstanding. One was a movie director, J. Leo Meehan, who'd previously edited a Pasadena newspaper. He was followed by the film star Colleen Moore and her husband, John McCormick, a theater executive turned producer, who convinced a Chicago businessman to direct-sell them the unfinished twenty-six-room Spanish house he was building on 1.68 acres for a reported $250,000, thereby evading Bell's screening. Bell could not have been happy when Moore's presence, her tiled swimming pool, her tennis court, and her screening room began getting regular mentions in newspapers.

Moore remained in Bel Air after splitting with McCormick a year after buying the house on St. Pierre Road. And in 1934, she sublet it to Marlene Dietrich. Moore would ultimately sell it to another actor, Robert Stack, for a mere $100,000 in 1945. Despite his profession, Stack was more to Bell's tastes. His late father, J. Langford Stack, had been a millionaire polo player, but he'd caused a scandal when he was divorced by his socially prominent wife in 1921. She testified that he drank to excess, mistreated her, and, said the *Times,* "paraded half-clad before friends and relatives in their home." The divorce wasn't for keeps and they remarried in 1928, shortly after Langford Stack was diagnosed with a fatal illness. By 1945, when Robert Stack moved in, both the times and Bel Air had changed considerably. The stock market crash of 1929 and the grinding years of the Depression and war that followed caused many changes in the world, some of them for the better. Though Alphonzo Bell might not have agreed, the loosening of Bel Air's restrictions, stated and otherwise, not only ensured its survival as an enclave of wealth, but set the stage for unimagined glory.

Bel Air

As the Roaring Twenties neared their end, Alphonzo Bell was just getting started. But, like Icarus, his success led him to tempt fate and either ignore or underestimate the other equally rich and powerful people in the lush garden communities of the Triangle, where beautiful surroundings often hid ugly competing agendas and lured the ambitious to fly ever-closer to California's beckoning sun.

Late in 1927, with Beverly (today's Sunset) Boulevard nearly complete from Los Angeles to the ocean, Bell announced that he would borrow $3 million to begin development of his remaining twelve thousand acres adjacent to the first developed parcels of Bel Air. Shortly after that, the Los Angeles Planning Commission received his request to rezone about five hundred acres of his property deep in today's Topanga State Park so Bell could quarry rich limestone, shale, and clay deposits there and make concrete to use for roads and infrastructure throughout the area. Immediately, all hell broke loose. Bell, knowingly or not, was challenging the established order of power in L.A.

The two dominant newspaper publishers in the region were Harry Chandler, who owned the *Times,* and William Randolph Hearst, proprietor of the *Los Angeles Examiner* and *Evening Herald.* Chandler, whose reach extended throughout the Southland, had friends and investments in what was known as the Cement Trust, a group of local concrete producers who didn't appreciate a new competitor, particularly one whose limestone was said to be of higher quality than theirs. Hearst also had reason to want to frustrate Bell.

In his autobiography, *The Bel-Air Kid,* Alphonzo Jr. wrote that his father had refused to sell a Bel Air lot to Hearst, who not only owned a film studio, but lived adulterously, if openly, with its star attraction, his mistress, Marion Davies.[11] Hearst's publisher at the *Herald* also owned property near the proposed quarry. Though normally fierce antagonists, the major newspapers in Los Angeles joined forces to fight Bell's proposed cement plant and railed against him on a regular basis. Only a local Beverly Hills newspaper and the small *Los Angeles Illustrated Daily News,* where the editor was allegedly encouraged by a bribe from Bell, took his side.

Even after Bell revised his plans to include a pipeline to send crushed, quarried rock to ships at sea for processing into concrete elsewhere, hundreds signed petitions against his plans, their doubts and anger stoked by the press and mass mailings claiming that the cement operation would be the first of many industrial encroachments on residential districts in Los Angeles, and would foul the air with dust and assault the senses with noise. In response, Bell argued the quarry would be three miles from the nearest neighbor, built on land that was otherwise uninhabitable, would create eight hundred jobs, and would bring down the local price of cement by more than half. Small wonder the *Beverly Hills Citizen* concluded that the Cement Trust was behind all the anti-Bell publicity.

The fight played out into fall 1929, a period that saw both the Dow Jones Industrial Average and personal debt in America, Bell's included, soar to unprecedented—and ultimately unsustainable—levels. "He was overextended," says a grandson, Ralph Tingle. Though stocks continued to rise through September, property sales in Bel Air were weak, with some blaming the concrete fight, others a vague sense of economic uncertainty. On the surface, life at the Bells' went on as always. Their eldest daughter, Elizabeth, returned from her first (and only) year at Finch, a finishing school in New York, and the family spent August at the Bar-Bell Ranch in Colorado. Bell's younger daughter, Minnewa, named for her mother, entered Mills College in Oakland that fall.

On October 29, the stock market crashed and stock prices kept falling for a month. Though it's hard to imagine how things could've gotten worse, at 5:30 p.m. on Thanksgiving, November 28, young Minnewa, home from college for the holiday, struck two women with her Packard roadster as they left a streetcar near the corner of Bedford Drive and Santa Monica Boulevard. She killed the first instantly and sent the second to the hospital, where she, too, died. Hysterical, Minnewa had driven her car into the curb, where the Beverly Hills police found her behind the wheel. They kept her name from the public until the next day, and insisted it was an accident and that alcohol wasn't involved—a coroner's inquest held a few days later arrived at the same conclusion. The talk—never confirmed—was that her father had paid a six-figure bribe to hush things up.

A week after the accident, the Los Angeles Planning Commission approved Bell's concrete plant by a 3–2 vote and sent the matter to the city council for final approval. It was a Pyrrhic victory, though. The Hearst press, determined to keep pressure on Bell, attacked anew with cartoons that implied he was a gangster, and also took aim at the planning commission, saying its chairman had been spotted at the Bel-Air Bay Club wearing women's clothes. Hearst went after the Beverly Hills police, too, forcing a grand jury investigation into Minnewa's crash, and then ran advertisements seeking witnesses who would say she was drunk—a charge sure to reflect badly on her abstemious father. But though two witnesses supposedly came forward, none actually appeared before the grand jury, which again exonerated the girl. "Nothing is sacred to Mr. Hearst," the pro-Bell *Beverly Hills Citizen* editorialized, "not even a man's fireside." Even Chandler's *Times* agreed with the Bell forces this one time, calling the attacks on Minnewa "vicious yellow journalism" and "reprehensible tactics," though warning darkly that approval of the cement plant "would be a severe blow to our good name abroad as well as a serious inroad upon our security at home."

Early in 1930, the city council gave Bell another ray of hope, approving the quarry; a few days later the mayor of Los Angeles ratified the decision. But Bell's battle still wasn't over. Immediately, opponents began a petition drive in an attempt to force a public referendum on the plan. They needed 25,801 signatures, but when petitions were submitted with 44,000 names, only 25,300 could be certified. A lawsuit was filed but before it was decided, Bell blinked, announcing a tentative sale of all his remaining land west of Bel Air, including the planned quarry, reportedly to Eastern financiers who planned yet more gentlemen's estates, for a price variously reported at $8 million to $10 million.

Bell's shaky finances got a further boost in the early 1930s when he sued two oil companies, claiming they'd allowed Santa Fe Springs oil to drain away or be siphoned off, and won nearly $1.4 million in settlements. But just a few weeks after his eldest, Elizabeth, married in January 1931, the deal to sell his thousands of acres fell through, and "under cover of darkness," as Chandler's *Times* put it, Bell laid a pipe through his oceanfront property to a buoy 150 feet offshore, apparently preparing to start quarrying rock. A judge quickly authorized the referendum against the quarry and after the city council reversed itself and took away Bell's permit to build it, he dropped the plan forever.

Bell had lost six years of his life and his good name to the cement-plant fight. His son Alphonzo Jr. considered it his biggest mistake. Senior "had prejudices," says grandson Rex Ross III, referring to his stubbornness, rather than his anti-Semitism or hatred of liquor, "and if he hadn't he would have made a deal with Chandler and he would have stayed in big business. Junior always said it was too bad he didn't go along."

"The real estate business in general and my father's in particular was in a shambles," Alphonzo Jr. wrote of the Great Depression. The oil flow from Santa Fe Springs was "winding down—new investment ideas were needed. My father was forced to be more open to such ideas than he was in the past." Though he continued to live like the relatively rich man he still was, he nonetheless had to make changes.

In September 1931, Bell Sr. effectively retired, handing sales in Bel Air and its beach club to Charles B. Hopper, a longtime real estate man and Beverly Hills resident. Bell would devote the next decade of his life to quiet philanthropy, particularly at his alma mater, Occidental College, where he became president of the board of trustees. His wife gave her time to the Beverly Hills Women's Club and a garden club in Bel Air. Bell's retirement was a turning point for Bel Air. Hopper, a pro, set some stringent conditions before agreeing to take on the job.

"[Bell] learned instantly that my terms would require some regretful concessions on his part," Hopper wrote in a memoir. Confronted with Bell's rules about the Sabbath, Jews, and movie people, "I told him very frankly that these were absurd conditions and proceeded to hand him back my contract. 'You can at least keep the movie people out, can't you?' he pleaded. 'No,' I insisted. . . . As I had clearly foreseen, movie actors and executives moved in by the score." Of course, the truth is, some were already there— with enough money, most rules can be bent, if not broken.

But Hopper had his own standards. He agreed with Bell that architectural harmony was necessary for the preservation of Bel Air's special character. "You want a distinctive house," he told prospective buyers in a sales brochure notable for its soft sell. "Don't forget that there is a far finer distinction in aristocratic humility than there is in insistent calling attention to yourself. The latter impresses some but those whose opinions in such matters is worth having, are attracted rather by an evident regard for neighborhood harmony."

Hopper set out into the woods with an axe in hand to notch trees where new roads would be run, new home sites prepared. "Thus, we lined out Stone Canyon Road," he wrote. "The bulldozers followed, making way for the eventual steamrollers." Over the next few years, he made way for more roads into lateral canyons, opening up more of Bel Air for what Hopper called the "few well-to-do people who might have been inclined to indulge in expensive items which would possibly never again be offered at such reasonable prices" due to the Depression, which inspired precious little indulgence elsewhere. Hopper considered Beverly Hills his biggest problem, as it had a two-decade lead on Bel Air and "there simply weren't enough people of great means to populate both areas." Hopper saw that in order to compete, Bel Air had to remain different—even if those differences were no longer the ones Alphonzo Bell had decreed.

Though the remaining full-acre lots surrounding the golf course sold quickly, sales slowed again once they were gone. But Hopper regularly opened new tracts with even larger lots and relentlessly promoted them, and slowly, buyers appeared, either "movies," as he called film people like Sol Wurtzel, a Fox executive who bought, or "individual prospects of definite means," as he called the lower-profile buyers.

By 1933, the economy notwithstanding, sales and construction had picked up. In fact, one of the signature mansions of Bel Air was about to be built. Lynn Smith Atkinson, an engineer and public works contractor, had started a construction company as a young man and was immediately successful enough that he took in his uncle Guy as a partner. Guy Atkinson would soon spin off a company of his own. "Lynn was more the promoter, Guy was more the contractor," says John F. Whitsett, Guy's grandson. Together and separately they were credited with building some of California's first highways, the Pardee Dam that provided water for Oakland, Alameda, and Berkeley, and Arizona's Coolidge Dam. Guy went on to build the Grand Coulee Dam and Southern California's Metropolitan Water District aqueduct, the largest public works project in the area during the Depression.

Guy tackled the last of those projects alone because, at age thirty-eight, Lynn retired, allegedly blaming ill health, and channeled his energy and contracting skill into a private dream. "Lynn was a risk taker and liked challenges," says Whitsett; "big projects, big houses, big cars, big yachts. Lynn had, and spent, substantial wealth." After buying six and a half acres on Bel Air Road for $45,000 (about $726,000 today), he was reported to be spending $225,000 (about $3.6 million) on a new 21,000-square-foot French neoclassical mansion designed by Sumner Spaulding, architect of Greenacres. "He was a real kook," says Arnold "Buzz" Kirkeby, son of a later owner. While planning the house, "he sat on a hillside for a year tracing the wind and the sun."

In the end, the house at 750 Bel Air Road would cost much more than predicted, given its marble entry hall with a twenty-eight-foot ceiling, sprawling public rooms with eighteen-foot ceilings, a ballroom with an orchestra stage, a dining room decorated with frescoes and two Baccarat chandeliers, a paneled library with hidden bookshelves, billiard and garden rooms, six lavish bedroom suites (including identical wings for Atkinson's two daughters), silver and fur vaults, a pipe organ, and four acres of gardens, complete with swimming pool, tennis court, manmade 150-foot waterfall, and a landing pad for helicopter-like autogyros.

Atkinson's engineering skills were evident in the way the house sat on its hill, displaying its two top stories in front, and a third only in the rear, where the lower-level ballroom, with its own terrace, looked out over the gardens. Below that, accessed by an elevator that ran from the second floor to seventy-five feet below the house, were two cream-walled, echo-filled tunnels, one leading to the swimming pool, the other to the landing pad. "They were super," says the granddaughter of a later owner, "creepy and cool." But it was the gold-plated doorknobs and hinges that became the talk of the town—and the defining feature of the house. It was often claimed that Atkinson spent between $1.6 and $2 million, but he would later give sworn testimony that he spent only $576,000 on the property.

Regardless, Atkinson's home was the most expensive to go up in Bel Air during the Depression. And, perhaps, the oddest, as the Atkinson family never moved in. A legend sprang up that Atkinson built the house without his wife's knowledge, brought her there for the first time for a party unaware it was her own housewarming, and only then learned she hated extravagance.

The realtor and estate historian Jeff Hyland has debunked that story, writing that Berenice Atkinson collaborated on the house with her husband. After it was completed, Hyland continued, Atkinson learned that under an odd local law, his real estate taxes would triple if the family moved in, so suffering from "financial woes," the Atkinsons remained in their home in Hancock Park.

In fact, a family member says, money, health, and family issues combined to keep the Atkinsons from moving in. A later owner of the house says Berenice Atkinson "was too ill to move in. . . . It's sort of a sad story." Buzz Kirkeby thinks Berenice refused to move unless the house was fully staffed and furnished, which Atkinson could no longer afford, because he'd depleted his fortune building it.

Ultimately, the Atkinsons used the Bel Air estate only for parties and entrée to the Bel-Air Country Club. As late as May 1941, "titian-haired" daughter Doris could be found hosting a "badminton-tennis-swimming shindig" there. "Father Lynn watched the younger set as they served them up on the sunlit court, scampered down the woodland paths beside the enchanting waterfall that cascades down for hundreds of feet, or played eye-black games of 'keep-away' in the tiled pool," a social columnist reported. "Exhausted sportsmen imbibed frosted beer and soft drinks in the dusk, then gathered about the great horse-shoe table with its bright red cloth to enjoy a supper of mammoth proportions. Just as the moon came up, stringed minstrels appeared to entertain with Viennese waltzes." If Atkinson was indeed going broke, he was going in style.

After her car crash, Minnewa Bell transferred to Sarah Lawrence College in New York, but lasted only a year before returning to Bel Air, where she spent another year at UCLA and then abruptly married Miles Gray at Capo di Monte. An MIT graduate, Gray was the son of a wealthy shirt and tie manufacturer (whose ex-wife, a millionaire's daughter, went on to marry the developer of Grauman's famous Chinese and Egyptian theaters). Alphonzo Jr. considered his sister's new husband a hobnobber, but his family was wealthy and social and knew scandal and tragedy; one of Miles Gray's uncles killed himself after falling prey to what his parents deemed "evil influences." He'd last been seen checking into a hotel with a divorcée ten years his senior.

Initially, Minnewa seemed to be settling down; she joined the Junior League, held swimming, tennis, and barbecue parties with her sister and brother-in-law in Bel Air, and was part of the west side's smart social set, earning gossip-column mentions alongside friends like Ned Doheny's widow Lucy Battson and Burton Green's third daughter Burton, who'd taken the name Burtie. Whatever the cause of her 1929 car crash, drinking was definitely a part of her life with Gray—Alphonzo Jr. called him "not much more than a good looking drunk"—and on Christmas Day 1932, they were in another Beverly Hills accident that nearly severed her ear when he ran into another car. No one alive knows whether Minnewa was drinking when she killed those two women, but relatives acknowledge that later in life, she was, as one puts it, "a raging alcoholic."

"My mom felt terrible [about the deadly 1929 crash]," says Rex. "It put a big dent in her life, and people drink because of things they can't deal with."

She and Miles kept up appearances for slightly more than two years before calling it quits. At the divorce trial that followed, she testified that he belittled her card playing and once threw her out of their car near the Bar-Bell Ranch, driving away and leaving her alone in the Colorado wilderness for an hour. "I got to thinking I was the most impossible person in the world just because he was always telling me I was," she complained. After their separation, she moved home with her parents; he kept their rental in Beverly Hills.

Gray wouldn't be alone long. Four months after the divorce was finalized, he was stepping out with Burtie Green. She called him Snowshoes and he called her Pieface. Theirs was a tight-knit social set, and sophisticated enough that despite the divorce, Minnewa's sister Elizabeth, known as Bobbie, and husband Ralph Tingle, the owner of a Hudson dealership, regularly partied with Gray and Green—and worse, as far as her father was concerned. "They partied . . . and he wanted them to read the Bible every day," says grandson Rex Ross. Tingle "drank excessively," wrote brother-in-law Alphonzo Jr., the only Bell child who did not find rebellion in the bottle.

Their life was an endless round of days at the races, jaunts to Catalina Island and Palm Springs, where Burtie's parents had a house, private dinners, and nightclub nights at Trocadero, Mocambo, and Cocoanut Grove. Just as movie stars had infiltrated Bel Air, so did they mix with local young society. At a 1936 luncheon, Miles and Burtie joined Cesar Romero, Fay Wray, the Cole Porters, various Dohenys, and a Vanderbilt relation. Miles and Burtie formalized things with a "very large, brilliant ring," as a column put it, followed by a quiet July wedding attended only by the principals, a minister, and his wife. Minnewa Bell went unmentioned in the newspaper reports of the wedding party at the Greens' and the honeymoon cruise to Hawaii.

Painful though Minnewa's marital misadventure must have been to the Bells, there was worse to come. Sometime after midnight on a Tuesday morning in February 1936, sister Bobbie, then twenty-six, and her husband Ralph, twenty-seven, died when he drove home drunk from what the *Times* called "a gay party at a fashionable Beverly Hills hotel." Their speeding car, one of the powerful Terraplanes that Tingle sold at his dealership, smashed into a Pacific Electric train at the corner of Santa Monica Boulevard and Holloway Drive and was thrown fifty feet by the impact. The Tingles died immediately. A passenger, a young Australian they were driving home, was hospitalized with multiple fractures.

The newspapers noted that the train crew was exonerated. Left unsaid was who was driving and what caused the crash. Alphonzo Sr. identified the bodies, took in the Tingles' two children, Ralph Jr., three, and Diane, four, and taught young Ralph to ride and fish. Ralph's cousin Douglas Waldron, a few years younger, says they all had the run of Capo di Monte. "It was a big, dramatic place," says Waldron, "with lots of land, lots of stairs, and fun places to play and hide." They especially loved creeping around in the service corridors tucked behind the walls.

Two months after her sister's death, Minnewa Bell was spotted "losing sleep" at the Trocadero club, in the company of Miles Gray's new sister-in-law Liliore Green. It would be two years before she found another husband, "named Burnside," her brother later wrote. He was an Englishman, an advisor to the producer David O. Selznick, and "an actor, an agent and a liar. He had a running mouth full of false, name-dropping, self-aggrandizing tales that began with lines like 'I told Mr. Zanuck...'" That marriage lasted ten months and ended after Minnewa complained in divorce court that he stayed out until all hours, drove dangerously when he was angry at her, was rude to waiters in restaurants, would not speak to her for a week at a time, and said being married had hurt his career. Two years after that, she married a doctor, Rex Ross Jr.

Minnewa and the Green sisters, with Gray attached, were often thrown together, swimming in a very small pond as the daughters of Bel Air and Beverly Hills. Compared to the Bell girls, though, the Greens seemed low-key. There were no tragic car crashes giving brief glimpses behind the mansion walls on Lexington Avenue. But the Green sisters' lives were simply more slow-motion affairs. Burtie's marriage to Minnewa's second ex was just the beginning.

Bel Air

As part of a general downsizing, Alphonzo Bell sold Capo di Monte early in 1941 to Louis Lurie, a San Francisco developer (he built the city's first movie theater and then nearly three hundred office buildings) who dabbled in backing Broadway plays and Hollywood films. Lurie almost immediately sold the estate to Atwater Kent, a retired inventor and engineer who'd invented an early ignition system for cars and later became the largest manufacturer of radios in America, for a mere $65,000 ($942,000 today), "the greatest bargain of the past 20 years," according to Hedda Hopper. Though a teetotaler and a vegetarian, Kent was also a starstruck movie fan, and his frequent parties for hundreds of guests both during and after the war were said to have "skimmed the cream of the Southland's social, motion picture and diplomatic sets." He famously announced, "People are my pleasure." All of them mourned in 1949, when the gregarious and generous host died of cancer at age seventy-five. His doctor said he'd suffered from "a malignant condition . . . for some time." His parties hid his pain.

Alphonzo Bell, too, was nearing the end of his life. After selling Capo di Monte, the Bell family moved into a small suite of rooms at the Bel-Air Club for a year while planning and building what Rex Ross III calls "a miniature version of Capo di Monte," a new fourteen-room home in the seventh tract to open in Bel Air. "By contemporary standards, it was quite grand," he says. Minnewa and Rex Jr. lived about a hundred yards away and paths ran down the hill to Alphonzo Jr.'s home, later sold to Burt Lancaster. Bell had already sold most of the Bar-Bell Ranch and used the proceeds to buy his farm in Coachella Valley; it brought in good money from fruit, vegetables, and cattle. He also kept his home in Palm Springs.

Bell's last independent business decision was to sell 18.5 acres just beneath Capo di Monte to a hotel developer in 1944. That fall, Bell suffered a severe stroke after which he was never the same. He moved to Santa Fe Springs, where he built a small house on his very first piece of land, leaving wife Minnewa behind in Bel Air. "They didn't get along so well in later years," says Rex Ross III. After a second stroke returned him to the hospital for almost a year, much of it spent in a coma, Bell moved in with his daughter Minnewa and her husband. The next year, Alphonzo Jr., just out of the military, stepped in and took over what remained of his business. "Dad never told me to take charge," he wrote, "his mind was off in the sky somewhere. He was in a very sad shape."

The Alphonzo E. Bell Corporation was in debt and Alphonzo Jr. had to sell assets to pay it off. He also believed that one of his father's old associates was cheating the family, and further worried that anything that was left would be lost to taxes when his father died. Desperate, he sold all the remaining undeveloped land in western Bel Air, 3,200 acres, to developers, who took quick advantage of the lifting of wartime restrictions. By summer 1947, forty-six new homes were under construction.

Shortly before Bell died that year, his son had convinced him to rip up his will and create a trust to protect his remaining $6 million in assets. Alphonzo Jr. then moved the family interests entirely into its oil business, taking a risky but successful plunge on an oil lease that "made Bell Petroleum a sizeable little oil company," he wrote. To further bolster the family coffers, in 1951 he sold the remaining 11,600 acres of the ill-fated Santa Monica Mountains tract to William Zeckendorf, a New York real estate operator, for $3.3 million. Their remaining land would stay in the family for years and Junior would shortly become a force in the local Republican Party, eventually winning a seat in Congress.

In 1950, Minnewa sued to divorce Rex Ross, once again charging extreme mental cruelty. She said that despite his income he'd refused to contribute to the support of their seven-year-old son. Four months later, she dropped her suit, but Ross promptly sued her on the same grounds, asking for custody of the boy and their community property, including oil leases. He charged that she'd left him for an old family friend, Elliot Roosevelt, son of the late President Franklin Delano Roosevelt, who had already been married three times to Minnewa's four. Though they had in fact been seeing each other for months, Roosevelt called Ross's charge "perfectly ridiculous" and "disgraceful." After Ross was stopped from physically removing their son from the parochial school where he was enrolled in Miami, Minnewa, who'd filed a new divorce action there, flew in and told reporters she had no plans to marry Roosevelt. Two months later, a Miami newspaper said they were going to marry as soon as the Ross divorce was finalized, and finally, in March 1951, the couple admitted that they'd bought land together in the Florida Keys and planned to marry as soon as possible. Details of the Rosses' custody agreement filled newspapers nationwide, though the judge sealed the records of their marital battle, saying only that "a little slapping" had been the cause of the breakup. One clause in the agreement stated that both were fit parents, once again papering over Minnewa's drinking.

Roosevelt applied for a license to wed just hours after the Ross divorce was finalized. Roosevelt's brother and sister-in-law were among the few guests at the ceremony, held in Minnewa's rented Miami house. Their marriage lasted fourteen years, longer than the Bell trust, which was split into three in a welter of litigation, pitting the Bell and Tingle children against each other.

Nine years after he bought Bell's mountain acreage, Zeckendorf, facing bankruptcy, would sell the land for $8 million to a group of East Coast investors led by the Lazard Frères investment bank. And in 1972, Congressman Alphonzo Bell Jr. would play a decisive role when the state of California bought most of the land to turn it into a park, forever protecting it from development. The elder Minnewa Bell, who'd abandoned Bel Air for a penthouse at the Beverly Hilton Hotel, died in 1979, shortly after celebrating her one-hundredth birthday at the Bel-Air Hotel. She'd come into her own after her husband's death, even developing a taste for the Silver Fizzes served at the Bel-Air Country Club's bar. "She said she'd never had so much fun," Ralph Tingle recalls.

Her daughter had divorced Elliot Roosevelt in 1960 in Colorado, where they'd lived for several years on what remained of the Bar-Bell Ranch. Like all of Minnewa's husbands, Roosevelt drank, and "he carried on," says Ralph Tingle. "He thought of himself as a big shot. They had terrible fights." Rex Ross adds that Roosevelt "turned bad. He tried to take control of her assets."

Four years later, Minnewa made news for the last time when she was arrested and charged with falsely reporting a bomb on an airplane after a desk agent told her it was too late to board. After pleading guilty, she was fined

$250. Minnewa Bell would never settle down, instead going on to marry "a series of escorts [because] in her era you didn't live with, you married," says her son, who counts eight husbands altogether. "Alcohol was always a factor. She was in and out of dry-outs" and died in obscurity in 1983 in Pima, Arizona. Her brother divorced, remarried, lost his $15 million share of the proceeds from the 1981 sale of the family oil company in bad investments, and died at age ninety in 2004 "almost penniless," says his nephew Ralph Tingle.

And what of the Danziger-Bell mansion, Capo di Monte? After Atwater Kent's death, its contents were auctioned off by his family. Five thousand sightseers pushed into the previews but Kent's seventy-piece art collection, valued as high as $2 million, sold for only $20,000, and the house with all its furnishings went for a mere $113,000 after bidding on the building alone stalled at $93,000 and was suspended. Though the eventual buyer, an auctioneer, told a newspaper he would subdivide the land and keep the mansion for himself, it was soon sold again privately, then put back on the market complete with preapproved plans for subdivision, but attracted no takers. Finally, in 1950, after another failed offering, it was demolished. All that remains today are Bell's perimeter wall and a garage, long since converted to a residence. All the Bell family's later Bel Air homes are gone, too, burned down in a great fire that swept through Bel Air in 1961. Capo di Monte "was a huge place, dramatic, bright and sunny, green, verdant, opulent," says cousin Douglas Waldron. "You couldn't see any other houses." Now, they are all you can see.

That was not how Alphonzo Bell had once dreamed it would be. Neither was it likely that he foresaw the tragic effects his once seemingly limitless oil money would have on his family. Instead of living lives of piety and moderation, his daughters chose excess. And instead of winning immortality as the founder and namesake of Bel Air, Bell would be remembered, if at all, as just another specimen of the special strain of hubris that seemed to thrive in these "verdant, opulent" canyons between the city and the sea.

Holmby Hills

Like the Bells, the Greens, and the Dohenys, the Janss family often appeared in gossip columns, even in the depths of the Depression. Not only were they rich and social, they'd just founded and colonized the third, smallest, and to many, most desirable community in the Platinum Triangle, Holmby Hills. Unlike the Bells, Greens, and Dohenys, however, they'd left their family's biggest scandal—a case of mail-order fraud—in the past before becoming icons of luxury real estate.

But the story of Holmby Hills begins with Arthur Letts. The enclave is named for Holmby Lodge in Northamptonshire, England, where Letts was born in 1862; it had been his upper-middle-class family's home for centuries. After several years' apprenticeship to a dry goods store owner, Arthur and a younger brother decided to seek their fortune in the new world, informing their parents only after they'd boarded a steamboat in Liverpool en route to Canada, where Arthur would get a job in a Toronto department store and then serve in the military.

Decamping to Seattle after his discharge, Letts worked in another store until it burned down, inspiring him to pitch a tent nearby and open one of his own. By the mid-1890s, with $500 to his name, Letts moved to Los Angeles, borrowing money to buy the premises and stock of a bankrupt retailer on the fringes of the downtown business district. Over the next decade, his Broadway Department Store (named for the street it was on) grew as he took over neighboring buildings and finally built a store of his own from scratch. With the fortune he made, Letts also built two mansions in Hollywood. The first was called Holmb. The second, a grand mock Tudor estate, was called Holmby House; its forty acres of formal gardens were filled with rare trees and flowers, a tribute to his avocation, horticulture.

Civic minded and a club man, Letts followed the injunction of old money: His family name appeared in the newspapers only when his daughters, Gladys and Edna, married. Letts had many investments, and though he rarely spoke about them, one would make him famous. Over the six years since John Wolfskill's death, many suitors had approached his family, seeking to buy and subdivide what remained of Rancho San Jose de Buenos Ayres. But the Wolfskill heirs were "difficult to approach and hard to please," wrote Letts's biographer. "Besides, they wanted all cash." In 1919, in a lightning raid, Letts secured a deal for the land with a $500,000 certified check and a promise to pay three times that amount on transfer of title. His purchase of what had been, until then, the most sought-after 3,296 acres in west Los Angeles earned him unaccustomed headlines. Much of the land was flat, making it extremely attractive for building—and Letts had realized that one day soon a vast suburb would cover his new acreage. But his assurance that development would begin immediately was premature.

There is little doubt that Letts's purchase gave courage to Alphonzo Bell, whose deal to buy what became Bel Air followed two years later. But Bell was quicker off the mark. In 1920, Letts transferred the Wolfskill acreage to the Janss Investment Company, co-owned by one of his sons-in-law, Harold Janss. "It was a present to Harold on the birth of Betty, his first child," says an in-law. "They may have couched it as a sale." The Janss company had been in the subdivision business in and around L.A. for two decades and had experience that Letts lacked. They owned both land and water distribution systems and had already developed several even larger tracts, among them the 47,000-acre Lankershim property in the San Fernando Valley, which it split up into smaller farms. What made their success surprising was that both the company's founder and one of his sons were medical doctors who'd had a change of calling.

Peter Janss had come to America from Denmark at age twelve in 1870 and helped pay for his own education by selling fruit trees to his neighbors. He was a doctor in Chicago before moving to Los Angeles in 1893. In 1898, he began investing in real estate subdivisions. He was apparently already well connected in town by then; his sixteen-year-old son Edwin joined the Los Angeles Country Club that same year. Edwin followed his father into medical school in Chicago. After further studies in Vienna, Edwin returned to Chicago in 1906. He wouldn't stay long.

That summer, Edwin Janss got a call from his father asking him to abandon Chicago for Los Angeles to take over his fledgling real estate company. The likely reason was that Peter and his brother Herman, another doctor, were peripherally involved in a mail-fraud scandal—Herman has bought into a company selling phony impotence remedies at extortionist prices—and Peter wanted to take off on a world cruise. "I wonder if Peter was getting out of Dodge," says Larry Janss, a great-great-grandson. Herman Janss came west, too, becoming a specialist in farmland; the company expanded and a move to Edward Huntington's Pacific Electric building followed. Edwin's success in guiding the company through the economic troubles that resulted from the Panic of 1907 convinced him to give up medicine for business. It wasn't long before younger brother Harold quit college and joined the family business, too. In 1911, the company had revenues of $1.5 million, the equivalent of $34 million today. To celebrate their success, the Janss family gave a barbecue for 250 fellow real estate professionals on a historic ranch near the latest valley subdivision they were managing, Van Nuys.

"Beef fresh from steers but a few hours removed from peaceful existence on the fat pasture of the Sheep Rancho and done to a turn over wood coals was passed in heaping pans, constantly replenished, down long tables laden with frijoles, enchiladas, and everything else hot and Spanish and dear to the palates of a generation now departing," rhapsodized the *Times*. "Mingling with every exclamation of wonderment and satisfaction at the marvelous transformation of the old valley into a modern home center was a genuine sigh that the times when such feasts were common affairs had departed."

One secret of the Jansses' success before Holmby Hills was buying huge tracts of land and selling lots of lots at low prices to working-class people, sometimes on installment plans requiring payments of as little as $5 a month. Their first development soon boasted a population of sixty-five thousand. They also bought the Conejo Ranch, ten thousand acres in Ventura County, for $22 an acre. Long a family getaway, the Jansses finally turned it into the middle-class suburb of Thousand Oaks in the 1950s; it was their last development.

Another key to the family's rise was forging powerful local alliances through both business and marriage. All three Janss children married well. Harold married Arthur Letts's daughter Gladys, whom he'd known since he was six years old. Harold's sister Henrietta married into a California pioneer family, the Bralys, and her daughter Doris would later marry into another old clan, the Hollisters. Edwin's wife, Florence Cluff, was from a San Francisco family that was well-enough established that its members were "disdainful of her Southern California marriage," says her granddaughter Dagny Corcoran. "Florence was this tiny thing, just a pistol," says Larry Janss, who called her Gong-Gong. "She was kind of a bitch. The Cluffs were the bluest of blood. It was annoying that she'd fallen in love with this ruffian. She forgave him every day."

Presumably, the other Cluffs were assuaged as the Jansses formed business associations with the wealthy likes of General Otis, founder of the *Los Angeles Times,* and his protégé Harry Chandler, the Harrimans of Southern Pacific, and the Letts family after Harold married into it. "Nothing was overlooked," says a brief biography written for the Janss family in 1978. Though that biography goes on to say that Letts sold all the Wolfskill property south of Wilshire Boulevard to the Janss interests in 1922 and the remainder of the property "soon after," deeds indicate that Letts kept a stake in the land, while letting the Janss family oversee its development.

The Jansses drew up plans for the Wolfskill land, beginning with a development called Westwood, where in 1922 they began selling lots on streets bearing English names in homage to Letts. Then, they shifted their attention to the more valuable land north of Wilshire Boulevard, and in an action that combined generosity, Machiavellian cunning, and a keen sense of self-interest, conspired to give 385 acres to the University of California for the establishment of a new campus. "There was no reason to move there," says Dagny Corcoran, "so his concept was that the university would create jobs and be the basis for a community."

There are several versions of the story of how they won the school, but they differ only in detail. "It was probably Harold because Ed wouldn't have been this clever and conniving," says Larry Janss. "He had a friend, Tanner, who owned a livery company. He'd got wind that the regents were looking for property for a second university and they were coming to look at one in Pasadena and one in Palos Verdes, both superb. So Mr. Janss concocted a plan and called Tanner, who'd be providing limousines, and plotted to rent them for the day. Tanner provided uniforms, Janss provided drivers."

En route to Pasadena, the driver interrupted the regents, and told them how wise they were to choose Pasadena, where the weather was great nine months a year. What about the other months, the regents asked. Summers are really hot, said the driver. "Then on to Palos Verdes," says Janss, where the driver explained that winters there were cold, blustery, and foggy. "The turd was floated in the punch bowl," says Janss. En route to the train back to San Francisco, the driver suggested the regents might want to stop at the Letts ranch. The only difference there, he said, "the sun shines at just the right angle so the weather is perfect twelve months a year," Larry Janss continues. "The driver asked if they wanted him to find out who owned it now and the hook was set." Thus UCLA came to the Rancho San Jose de Buenos Ayres.

The Jansses offered the land for $1 million, effectively giving the university a gift of $3.5 million. Alphonzo Bell, realizing this would only be good for Bel Air, too, added more land valued at $250,000. These moves assured the success of the community the Janss family would soon build around UCLA, Westwood Village. A day after the announcement, "thousands of people" visited the site, the Janss brothers' assistant Evelyn Schmidt recalled. In the next four days, $1 million in home sites were sold.[12]

The UCLA campus would open just before the stock market crashed in the fall of 1929. The Westwood Village commercial center, Westwood Hills (now known as Little Holmby) for the upper middle class, and the even more affluent Holmby Hills had all begun taking shape in the meantime, with home sites priced as low as $800 near Pico Boulevard to the south, and as high as $150,000 in the 400-acre estate section, where lot sales began in spring 1925. Like the founders of Beverly Hills, the Jansses wanted to create a community with room for both rich and the relatively poor who would work for them, and gave consideration to the amenities each economic group would expect, deeding parcels of land to Los Angeles to create Holmby Park and De Neve Square, a pocket park just north of Sunset Boulevard, but also installing bridle trails and selling a parcel in Holmby Hills to the Los Angeles Equestrian Club, which opened a polo field and stables there before a single home had been completed.

Holmby Hills was the jewel of the development, a "residential masterpiece," according to the Janss company, which also boasted that it had a microclimate cooler than Beverly Hills, and that its home sites set among gentle knolls would be easier to build on and more accessible than lots in the ravines of Bel Air. The Holmby Hills sites offered elevated views "without steep grades," as the company put it, making the comparison clear without direct insult to the neighboring estate communities. By May 15, Janss claimed that half of the initial offering of sixty-seven lots, none smaller than three-quarters of an acre, some as large as nine acres, had been sold at prices ranging from $17,000 to $30,000 an acre. By July, fifty-five lots were spoken for, streets and utilities—buried underground, of course—were going in, and three homes were under construction. Two of those were inside deals; among the first buyers were Edwin and Harold Janss.

10060 Sunset Boulevard

Life took a strange turn in the Arthur Letts household in April 1923. Letts, then sixty-one, had a nervous breakdown that was blamed on overwork after a trip to San Francisco. His "devoted" wife was reported to be at his bedside and his prognosis was said to be good, but none of that was true. Five weeks later, Letts abruptly filed for divorce, claiming his wife had deserted him a year earlier. News reports said they'd already made a property settlement. Five days later, Letts died of double pneumonia.

A mere four months after that, Florence Letts, the "devoted" widow who would shortly inherit half her husband's $17 million estate, was reported to have remarried in Paris. But when Florence returned to Los Angeles a few days later, she adamantly denied the report, said she'd left the country after her husband's death only to rest and "get away from the old surroundings for a time," recited her itinerary, and concluded, "And that's all there is to be said." And that pronouncement put an end to the affair. When Florence Letts did remarry, the event passed virtually unnoticed. A year after the phantom Paris marriage, she reappeared in the social pages as Mrs. Charles H. Quinn, the wife of a railroad engineer nine years her junior.

Meantime, the Letts children (who each inherited a sixth of the estate less 10 percent earmarked for charity—the equivalent of $25 million each today) took control of their father's empire, including his interest in the Westwood–Holmby Hills development. The family had previously lived in proximity to one another on Winslow Square, near today's Silver Lake district. In short order, Letts's son, his son-in-law, Harold and Edwin Janss, and Florence Letts Quinn would all be Holmby Hills homeowners.

Edwin and Harold built the first houses in what would become Holmby

Hills beginning in 1923, both hiring Gordon Kaufmann as their architect, spending $100,000 and occupying their new homes before any public sales of lots took place. The estate historian Jeff Hyland has written that the brothers sought to "set the standard of the level of elegance, style and expense that prospective estate-lot buyers were expected to equal in their residences." Harold, who'd moved fourteen times in fourteen years, built a twenty-room pastiche of Tudor and Mediterranean styles, with a brick chimney, slate roof, bronze gutters, English gardens, and a log playhouse complete with utilities, tennis, and a pond in front. It was set on a hillside property north of Sunset (then still Beverly) Boulevard at 375 North Carolwood; terraced gardens led to a stable in a ravine below the house.

Simultaneously, Edwin built a twenty-room Spanish Revival hacienda on four and a half acres at 10060 Sunset at the intersection of Carolwood, a half mile from his brother and backing onto the Los Angeles Country Club. Both homes were low-slung and featured recessed second-floor balconies, likely outside the bedrooms, says the architectural historian, Sam Watters. Edwin's had five bedroom suites, a pool and pavilion, lath houses for orchids, European tiles, a lily pond, several cottages, and a hydraulic lift and gas pump in its garage. Around the houses were bare, dry hills. In early photographs, says Larry Janss, the mansions look like "blisters on raw land."

The brothers were "very close, very close," said their assistant Evelyn Schmidt. "They worked together on everything." They shared a love of golf and lived close to each other both in Holmby Hills and on their ranch in Ventura County, but their looks and personalities were distinct. Edwin was tall. Harold was shorter, balding, and more charming and "loved cigars, whiskey, and golf," says Edwin's granddaughter Pat Gregson. "Edwin did more work than Harold. Harold didn't work that much."

"Ed was the businessman," says Lett Mullen, Harold's grandson. "Harold was the front man, the proselytizer." He preferred the Royal Hawaiian resort on Waikiki Beach to working. He liked it so much, in fact, he later redecorated his house in homage. Harold was gregarious and social. In 1944, he even filled in for a *Los Angeles Times* gossip columnist who'd gone on vacation. Edwin, in contrast, was a traditional family man. "A gentle giant," says grandson Larry, "very tweedy, pipe-smoking, with two or three of us in his lap at a time."

Though both brothers had long held a place in local society, Harold's family had been far more public about it. Through the 1930s, his three daughters, Betty, Virginia or "Ginna," and Gladys, were often in the public eye, particularly Ginna, described as a "delectable" aspiring nightclub singer, and a "Teutonic beauty" who was briefly linked in the columns to a Nazi diplomat in Los Angeles; after World War II, she fled California for Greenwich Village, where she pursued her singing career. "She was Auntie Mame," says Lett Mullen, her nephew. Betty was the serious one. Gladys, the baby, was shy.

In spring 1933, Harold would head to Reno to dissolve his marriage of twenty-two years to Arthur Letts's daughter Gladys on the grounds of cruelty. "They were just unhappy," says grandson Lett Mullen. "She'd built a house in Beverly Hills at Foothill and Elevado. When she was angry she'd stay there." One night Harold walked in and found Gladys with an opera singer.

But that all came later, once Holmby Hills was established. Initially, following the lead of Arthur Letts Sr., the Janss brothers' houses went up without Beverly Hills–style fanfare and without Bel Air–style restrictions. There was no liquor ban in Holmby Hills. Family legend has it that Edwin Janss's sons Ed and Bill sold lemonade spiked with Prohibition-era rum from a stand on Sunset Boulevard. Their niece Pat Gregson and her brother Eddie "would steal Danish beer" from the refrigerator at 10060 Sunset, sneak to the nearby sixth tee at the Los Angeles Country Club, and sell bottles to golfers for a dollar each. After Edwin got wind of it, the venture folded, but it wasn't liquor he disapproved of. "All Janss males loved their cocktails," says Larry Janss.

Even more than in Bel Air, however, discretion seemed important to the Holmby Hills developers, whose press releases rarely named lot buyers. Jewish people weren't barred. Milton Baruch, a local steel executive and Jewish community leader who had enough money and influence to get a tennis court installed on his property overnight so he could host a match between the champions Bill Tilden and Harvey Snodgrass, was one of the first to build a house. Neither, clearly, were show-biz types persona non grata. The proof of that: In 1932, the era's Elvis bought a house there.

10100 Sunset Boulevard

Hubert Prior "Rudy" Vallée's radio variety show, the *Fleischmann's Yeast Hour*, had gone on the air two days after the stock market crash, transforming him from $60-a-week itinerant musician to a $20,000-a-week star. The smooth, sophisticated, white-tie-and-tails crooner, saxophone player, and band leader from Maine was a sensation. Flappers mobbed the tall, blue-eyed, wavy-haired star at public appearances, where he would sing through a megaphone, and he allegedly took full advantage of his fame. "People call me the guy with the cock in his voice," he would boast late in life. "I've been with over 145 women and girls." Behind the scenes, he was known as a pugnacious bully with a taste for combat and a penchant for attracting litigation for everything from breach of promise to recovery of wages by fired employees, but the former Yale philosophy student quickly became a movie star, epitomizing the urbane, swank style that said "upper class" in his era.

Vallée had come to Hollywood to make his first film in 1929; he lived in a small apartment and flew home to New York with a $55,000 fortune. His film career sputtered in the early 1930s but he starred in George White's *Scandals* on Broadway, and apparently still visited the West Coast, since in 1931 at age thirty, he married his second wife (his first, a coffee heiress, had just won an annulment after a mere three weeks of marriage), a smoky-eyed brunette starlet named Fay Webb whose father was the police chief of Santa Monica. It was the beginning of a rough patch of road.

A week after the wedding, Vallée's mother died and the couple went east. Within months, Fay was back in L.A. Rudy lured her back to their apartment on Central Park West in New York, but then she went home again. And again. "Life is just one railroad train after another," she said. "I know every fence post between here and New York, no fooling."

Problem was, Rudy had no time to come west, and one of his fans in New York had threatened her. Or so it was said the first time she came home. By her third trip, the message was different. "I hate New York," Fay told reporters. "And all the glitter and glamour of the Great White Way can't keep me from being lonesome." She still called her parents' house home.

A month later, early in 1932, Rudy said he had no time to visit California and Fay's family expressed their unhappiness—in the newspapers. A day after that, Vallée flew in from New York with the humorist and honorary mayor of Beverly Hills, Will Rogers. Vallée was seen vainly trying to find Fay at the airport. The next day he was photographed, posing dutifully for the newspapers with Fay and Chief Clarence Webb. While in town, he defended himself against yet another lawsuit, the twenty-third separate claim that he'd stolen authorship of his most popular song, "I Am Just a Vagabond Lover." Then, instead of returning to New York as planned, he bought a house. Briefly, it seemed he would be a vagabond no more.

Number 10100 Sunset sat just east of what would soon be Florence Letts Quinn's house, on the Los Angeles Country Club. It was what had become the standard Holmby Hills mansion, a sprawling fifteen-room southern Mediterranean surrounded by a landscaped garden. The one-and-a-half-acre lot had been deeded to a builder named Rolland Van Ness and the Sun Lumber Company in December 1928. The house that he built—whether on spec or for a customer who backed out has gone unrecorded—was called Tres Palms. The Vallées said they planned to move in the following July. And shortly after the purchase was announced, Rudy took part in a newspaper roundup of recent property purchasers who were asked why they bought in the depths of the Depression. His answer seems calculated to please his bride:

"We both like to live in California," Vallée said, "as we feel it is the ideal happy medium in climate and temperament in people. We went house hunting with no definite idea of what we wanted and this is the house we looked at first, and although we looked at many others between the time we decided to purchase it and the time of actual purchase, we found none quite as attractive in every way, shape and manner. . . . California is our idea of a perfect place to live."

Despite the Depression, the relatively small size of Holmby Hills, and the fact that it was restricted only in terms of buying power and taste made it a slow but steady success. The most notable deed restrictions there were ones that forbade subdividing lots for fifty years, required minimum setbacks from the street, and banned any commercial structures, thus assuring the neighborhood's character.

Certainly, neither the presence of film stars nor Jews hurt Holmby Hills. A year after it opened for business, the first three batches of lots were gone, the last thirty lots were on the market, and a new branch of Beverly Boulevard, which had previously ended at Santa Monica Boulevard, running through Holmby Hills and Westwood, was nearing completion (it would soon be renamed and disappear into Sunset Boulevard), as was a gatehouse for Holmby Hills; the Jansses were so pleased with the results, they touted the proximity of Little Holmby (then Westwood Hills) to Holmby Hills as a selling point for its smaller lots. And by 1935, film stars like Claudette Colbert and Constance Bennett would be building houses, too.

Oddly, the first real boasting about Holmby homes was done by the heretofore reticent Letts family. An architect's rendering of a mansion Arthur Letts Jr. was planning to build, also adjacent to the Los Angeles Country Club, appeared in the *Times* in 1926, and six years later, when Florence and Charles Quinn decided to build their house between Edwin Janss's and the Vallées', it was touted as "the year's largest residence, costing $150,000" in a newspaper headline.

Arthur Letts's daughter Edna and husband, Malcolm McNaghten, also hired architect Gordon Kaufmann to build them an eclectic house nearby combining elements of Southern colonial and French provincial architecture and a huge landscaped garden with terraces, elaborate walkways, and a Chinese gazebo. The Depression notwithstanding, the Letts family was openly enjoying its wealth. Shortly after the McNaghtens moved in, their home was the scene of a massive debutante party for their daughter Jane, "the first debutante in Los Angeles this season to make a formal bow to Dame Society," according to the *Times*. Thanks to real estate, the Depression was less than depressing for the Janss and Letts clan.

Arthur Letts Jr. had inherited serious wealth—and got even richer after he sold the Broadway Department Store to a group of executives led by his brother-in-law for a reported $10 million. Letts, who'd lived until then in a Cotswolds-style farmhouse in Hancock Park, retired to run his father's estate and its many investments, and was determined to build the greatest home in Holmby Hills, one that reflected his lofty stature in Los Angeles.

Situated on a knoll at 10236 Charing Cross Road, three lots north of the McNaghten house, with views of not just the country club, but Beverly Hills and downtown Los Angeles, Letts's new property already had a magnificent location. He gilded that lily with a 14,000-square-foot Tudor-Jacobean manor house with a rough stone façade; impressive towers, windows, and double chimneys; a jaw-dropping driveway and automobile entrance; and mixed Old English, Georgian, and French interiors, reflecting the eclectic taste of the times. The grounds, planted with some of the best specimens from his father's home, were equally spectacular. Years later, the mansion's third owner would make it infamous. Hugh Hefner paid the second owner (an industrialist who developed instruments for oil, space, and medicine),

$1.05 million for the estate in 1971, setting a record. Ever since, it's been known as the Playboy mansion.

Next door to Arthur Jr. in what had become by 1932 a virtual Janss-Letts family compound wrapping around the entire north end of the Los Angeles Country Club, Edwin and Harold Janss built a home for their mother, Emma, Peter Janss's widow. It was originally a rambling twenty-room, five-bedroom Monterey-style house with a rear courtyard on one and a half acres at 10224 Charing Cross Road. Ed and Harold's sister, Henrietta Braly, the widow of a businessman, moved in to care for the elderly Mrs. Janss, and promptly became an up-and-comer in local society, renowned for her garden and her parties, which attracted the likes of Harry Robinson, Charles Hopper, and the actors Tony Moreno, Irene Dunne, Walter Pidgeon, and Ralph Bellamy. When Etta Braly died suddenly in 1935, her daughter moved in and took over the care of Emma Janss, adding a new wing with bedrooms for her children and a governess. After Emma Janss died in the house at eighty-seven in 1944, the family sold it.

141 South Carolwood Drive

It was Letts Sr.'s runaway bride Florence who built what would eventually become the greatest estate in Holmby Hills at 141 South Carolwood, right next door to her son-in-law Edwin. Had it actually existed, the mansion at 10086 Sunset occupied by Gloria Swanson's character Norma Desmond in *Sunset Boulevard* would have sat between them.[13] "The ten-thousand block" of Sunset was made world famous in that 1949 script by Billy Wilder, Charles Brackett, and D. M. Marshman Jr. But the homes there were not really the "great big white elephants . . . grandiose . . . gloomy, forsaken," described in the script. At least, not yet.

Florence and Charles Quinn (she'd dropped the Letts name), who'd been living in a downtown L.A. hotel between frequent jaunts to Europe and the East Coast, bought their four acres within walking distance of her three children's homes in 1932, and hired architect Robert Farquhar, who'd designed Daisy and Tony Moreno's Crestmount, to build them a $150,000 12,000-square-foot Italian Renaissance mansion. That was the equivalent of $2,344,000 in 2010, indicating the Quinns got a bargain; for their money, they got a lot of house, too, a sprawling L-shaped red-tile-roofed mansion with a separate guesthouse surrounded by endless flat lawns, gardens, and fountains. Florence bought an entire elaborately carved, pine-paneled 1740 Georgian drawing room from the Fortescu family's Castle Hill in Devonshire, England, which had been removed in a nineteenth-century renovation and stored in an outbuilding until the 1930s. She installed it in her new house, which she filled with Chippendale and Hepplewhite furniture, including pieces from the reigns of Charles II, Queen Anne, and George I, some covered with seventeenth-century needlework; jade, amethyst, and lapis lazuli objects and jars and bowls from the Ming dynasty; and paintings by Joshua Reynolds, Thomas Lawrence, Henry Raeburn, and Boucher.

On her death at age seventy-seven in March 1944, much of her fortune went to her children, but Florence also donated the Georgian Room and 124 of her best pieces of art to the Huntington Library's art gallery; a secondary collection of decorative arts, including more rare jades and French and English gold and silver tableware and utensils, went to the University of Southern California. The remaining furnishings and twenty other carved paneled rooms were sold with the house in November 1945.

The buyer was Joseph W. Drown, who had simultaneously bought 18.5 acres in Bel Air from Alphonzo Bell. Drown would shortly become a force in shaping the second era of the Triangle's history. In the process, much of its backstory would simply disappear, but if Arthur Letts Sr.'s biographer is right, that would not have bothered the father of Holmby Hills.

"Isn't the present the greater romance?" he wrote. "Isn't today more wonderful, with its hurrying thousands eagerly building homes and erecting cities where haciendas once stood, than yesterday, with its half-nomadic civilization moving at ox-cart pace over the barren hills, with here and there a casa of sun-baked bricks, or an occasional hut of mud. . . . [Arthur Letts] knew that the soil which the pioneers held so cheaply, and from which they drew so little, divided into city lots, with their gardens and their fruit trees, would produce more for the sustenance of the people than ever was done in the happiest of the days of old—even if it did mean that the great Rancho San Jose de Bueynos Aires would become but a memory, an incident blended in the vital history of this great epoch of city building!" He might have been speaking for all the La-La Land founders.

Visionary, opportunistic, and profoundly dysfunctional, the families that pioneered the Platinum Triangle bought its barren hills for a relative song, primed the canvas of the communities they created, and sketched the outlines of what they would become. What they would not become, curiously enough, were monuments to the memory of their creators. Like the Spanish land-grant families before them, they were swept aside, if not entirely forgotten, in a place that favored those, like Arthur Letts, who lived in the moment, neither dwelling on the past nor worrying much about the future.

The first families of the Platinum Triangle sometimes seemed determined to self-destruct on a scale proportionate to what they'd achieved. Minnewa and Elizabeth Bell started young and surely broke their father's heart along with the bodies of themselves and others. Their counterparts in Beverly Hills and Holmby Hills mostly squandered their opportunities—unless, like the Whittiers and Carrie Canfield Spalding, they moved out of the towns their fathers had started, or like Edward Huntington, the Platinum Triangle's prime mover, never even moved in, preferring to count his rail and real estate profits at his estate in San Marino. Though they would eventually find ways to make a lasting mark on Los Angeles, the Green sisters would fritter away fortunes on multiple marriages and social lives that were, ultimately, much ado about nothing. And the Jansses, though latecomers to the development game, would not escape unscathed.

Instead of establishing themselves, digging roots, and making permanence (of their families, of their legacy) a priority, as their East Coast counterparts and a handful of Angelenos like the Chandlers did, the founding families seemed content to reflect the nature of their place, accepting and even embodying the notion that nothing could take root in the desert soil of L.A. They were like the rarefied, pampered hothouse flowers their forebears planted in their irrigated desert—birds of paradise come to mind—that blossomed brilliantly with proper care, but proved too fragile to survive on their own for very long.

And that may be their most important legacy. There is one remarkably consistent pattern in the history of the Triangle and it starts right here with the Canfields, the Greens, the Bells, and the Jansses. In each of their stories, the lavish scale of their wealth and the excesses of their indulgence presage misery in equal measure, whether in the form of depression, divorce, alcoholism, loneliness, suicide, or multiple pathologies, all mixed together. As their mansions and communities matured and changed hands, the same patterns would repeat again and again, suggesting that the antihistorical attitudes so prevalent that they have come to define Los Angeles stem from an absolute refusal of those who are drawn there to heed such cautionary tales. Lost in the illusion that grand mansions will protect them from unhappiness and mortality as easily as from the weather, they find it unfathomable that the pesky attributes of the human condition affect rich as well as poor.

Denial, to twist the well-worn phrase, may well be the most powerful river in Los Angeles. Like everything else, it's just a question of how much of it you can afford.

PART FOUR

Great Estates

1932–1959

{ HILDA BOLDT WEBER RESIDENCE, BEL AIR }

Holmby Hills

10100 Sunset

The early adopters had taken their places in Beverly Hills, Bel Air, and Holmby Hills. The style of the three communities had been set. Though their future prosperity was less assured than it had been before the stock market crashed, the prognosis wasn't bleak, and efforts were soon under way to ensure that development didn't falter. In Bel Air, for instance, Charles Hopper recruited the then up-and-coming builder, Paul Trousdale, offering his clients 75 percent off any lot on which construction began within four months. Despite the anemic economy, Hopper managed to sell $9 million in Bel Air lots during the 1930s. He was successfully swimming against the tide. And he wasn't alone. Easterners were still heading west, some lucky enough to have fortunes that had survived the crash. And they weren't going to let a mere economic downturn—or even a major meltdown—stop them from building the homes of their dreams in the one place in America where too much was still not nearly enough.

Rudy Vallée's performance as a happily married man closed thirteen months after his wedding to Fay Webb, the Santa Monica police chief's daughter; they never did move into their new Holmby Hills estate. In late August 1932, when rumors of a split surfaced, Vallée was on tour with his band, the Connecticut Yankees, and Fay was with her parents in his apartment in the Art Deco landmark 55 Central Park West in New York. The crooner's attor-

ney said the couple was suffering a "wide divergence of temperament" and a
Reno, Nevada, divorce was imminent.

At midnight a few nights after the attorney spoke, they reportedly signed
a separation agreement, witnessed by Chief and Mrs. Webb, and the three
Webbs left New York the next day on the Twentieth Century Limited. Fay
Vallée was bound for Reno. Rudy's lawyer, Hyman Bushel, whose clients
included Babe Ruth and Dorothy Lamour, claimed to be playing referee.
He said the couple had agreed to a settlement of their finances and real estate holdings, but refused to be specific, except to add that he believed they
would avoid "the unnecessary unpleasantness frequently attendant upon a
situation of that kind," and pass along their wish that they "be relieved from
the constant pressure for information concerning the unfortunate turn that
their marital affairs have taken" and "spared if possible the necessity for any
further publicity as to matters which are and which they would like to be of
private concern to themselves."

Two days later, the Vallées were back in the headlines, though, this time
due to a midnight reconciliation just hours after Fay reached Nevada. "We
love each other more than ever now," she said, calling herself "a little fool to
even think of a divorce." Back in Santa Monica, she said they planned to see
each other again in a month, when she would visit New York, and that Rudy
was planning a California vacation in January 1933. They had yet to furnish
their new home—she and Rudy were joint owners—but their gardener and
his wife were house-sitting. In fact, the reconciled couple met up again three
weeks later in Cleveland, where Rudy's band was playing. They were photographed making cow eyes at each other. Fay then joined Rudy's band on
tour. And that December, Chief Webb announced that the happy couple was
coming west again, not for that planned vacation but rather so Rudy could
make his second movie. There were still no plans to occupy 10100 Sunset.

That second film got bogged down, too, and this time, Rudy went on
the road alone with the Connecticut Yankees, giving interviews, wistfully
musing about giving up singing and finding some time for himself. In April
1933, Chief Webb traveled east to resolve yet a new "little difficulty" with
the battling Vallées. Friends of Fay let the public know she'd never torn up
their signed separation settlement. Chief Webb's rescue mission failed. Two
days later, the couple announced another split, and this time it would be
permanent.

"I'm going to remain in California the rest of my life, I think," said Fay.

Her troubles were just beginning, though. At the train station as she and her father were leaving New York, she was served with a $100,000 lawsuit by a woman who claimed Fay had tried to seduce and had "improper relations" with her husband, an "acrobatic" dancer who'd been a school chum of Fay's in Santa Monica. Arriving in Chicago, she dismissed the charge as "quite amusing, really," and used the occasion to emphasize that a reconciliation with Rudy was "absolutely impossible." To confuse matters further, the dancer denied he was married.

Unfortunately for Fay, Rudy had secretly recorded her phone calls with the dancer. Unfortunately for Rudy, he was still married when, late that summer, an accident in a rainstorm started talk that he was having a dalliance of his own. He was en route to a show in Virginia Beach when he crashed his car in Delaware. Several musicians were along for the ride, but the only one hurt was Alice Faye, a teenage torch singer, who was in the front seat. Alice was sixteen when she'd joined the cast of *Scandals* in 1930. Rudy, the star of that show, was quick to notice her; an entrepreneur as well as a performer, he'd just opened his own talent agency and thus had a professional reason for his interest, but she was also a beauty. So he might have had unprofessional ones, too.

Alice Faye and Vallée had reunited when he hired her to sing with the Connecticut Yankees the winter after his first breakup with his wife. Despite his reputation as a stern boss, they got along fine and he became her Svengali, remaking her as a satin-clad vamp, to the delight of his audiences. He liked her so much he paid her salary out of his pocket when Fleischmann's Yeast, his sponsor, refused to pick up the tab. So it was only natural for newspapers to hint at a romance when they learned she'd been in his car, though it's never been proven that they had an affair.

When the initial choice for one of the female leads in Vallée's third film, a screen version of *Scandals,* dropped out of the picture, Alice was sent for and found herself playing two parts, a wanted one in the movie and an unwanted supporting role as the other woman in the Vallée divorce. Stories connecting Rudy and Alice were soon appearing regularly in newspapers. After overhearing their chatter as they left a nightclub together, one gossip columnist noted, "It really seemed quite domestic."

Though the divorce was already a mess of lawsuits and countersuits, early in 1934, it grew even uglier. Fay Webb's lawyers threatened to sue Rudy and demanded proof of his charge of her fling with the dancer, claiming Rudy and Alice Faye had "conducted themselves improperly during 1932 and 1933 at 12 different places, from Asbury Park to Tampa and Atlanta." En route back to New York after finishing the suddenly all-too-appropriately-titled *Scandals,* Rudy responded, "The whole thing's a stick-up."

Newspapers all over the country covered every chess move as Fay added a fourth "other woman" to her list of his dalliances and itemized her demands, including five servants, a secretary, regular massages, and home maintenance, though her only home was the still-unfurnished 10100 Sunset. Poor Alice Faye denied any involvement other than letting Rudy cry on her shoulder. "He had to have someone to talk to about his troubles, and I was that someone," she said.

Rudy teased the press with hints of tawdry revelations to come. He admitted his brother had begun recording his wife's phone calls after she spent two hours behind closed doors in her dancer friend's dressing room less than a month after their marriage, and promised that when those recordings emerged, "somebody will jump out a window and it won't be me." A dark cloud passing over his face, he added, "Some of the stuff I had to listen to was very painful."

Fay was holed up in the very same suite at the posh Biltmore in Santa Barbara where they'd honeymooned two years before. That didn't do her much good; a few days later, she was confined to a hospital in an "unstrung nervous condition," according to her doctor.

The wrangling continued, with Fay's team insisting Rudy had cheated her by hiding a million-dollar income; a judge would later peg his annual income at the equivalent of almost $2 million today. Throughout 1934, Fay remained under medical observation. Her acrobatic dancer friend and his wife—they *were* married—joined the Vallées in Splitsville. The dancer immediately remarried.

The final chapter of the sordid celebrity drama opened in spring 1935 when Fay, after losing an appeal to set aside an earlier, unfavorable separation agreement, finally filed for divorce on the only grounds allowable in New York, cruelty. A few days later, despite Rudy's formal denial that he'd been cruel to her, it was granted. Fay signed a quitclaim deed on 10100 Sunset in favor of Rudy's lawyer, Hyman Bushel. She was free, though not long for this world.

In November 1936, after undergoing abdominal surgery Fay developed peritonitis and fell into a coma. She died two days later, at age twenty-nine.

Upon hearing the news in a nightclub, Rudy started sobbing, laid down his baton, and went home. But he didn't attend the funeral, instead sending Clarence Webb a telegram professing undying love for his daughter. "It was the same with Fay," Webb responded. "She would say, 'I still love Rudy.' " A thousand mourners spilled into the streets from the funeral parlor. Rudy sent a pillow of gardenias and orchids fringed with heather that sat at the head of Fay's coffin. As she stood beside the open casket where Fay lay in a pink lace evening gown, Winifred Webb, Fay's spinster aunt, dropped dead.

Fay never got the chance to live in her dream house at 10100 Sunset. Five months after her death, Hyman Bushel sold the never-occupied mansion for $60,000 to a grocery store executive from Chicago who would add more rooms, a swimming pool, and tennis court to the estate. Eleven days later, Vallée was convicted of assault and battery on a newspaper photographer who'd snapped a photograph of him leaving a local theater with a showgirl. Vallée's third marriage, in 1943, to actress Jane Greer, lasted eight months. His last, in 1949, proved charmed, and ended only with his death in 1986. He had his last hit in 1943, but continued to make movies and appear on television and on Broadway. In the 1980s, he sometimes opened shows for the disco group the Village People.

14

Bel Air

10644 Bellagio Road

It's possible to disagree over which is the best house in Bel Air, but most would agree that the one that rose on a flat hill above the Bel-Air Country Club in 1934 is a strong favorite. And most would agree that the woman who built it, Hilda Olsen Boldt Weber, was a most unlikely candidate to have done so.

The money that built the house came from Charles Boldt, who grew up in Louisville, Kentucky, the son of a carpenter. After attending business school, he got a job as a bookkeeper at a bottling company, but left to pursue a dream to have a business of his own, and founded the Muncie Glass Company in Muncie, Indiana, a bottle-making factory. By 1900, when he turned thirty-two, Boldt had moved to Cincinnati and expanded the re-named Charles Boldt Glass Company. In 1911, the firm owned an eight-acre plant with eight hundred workers making not only bottles, but also labels, caps, cases, and more, and was one of the largest industrial concerns in the Ohio Valley. By the end of the decade Boldt had nine bottle-making factories all around the country. A 32-degree Mason and a Republican with "a well-balanced character," Boldt was a model middle-American entrepreneur, a stolid fellow who plastered down his wavy hair and had conservative taste in clothing and about $10 million in the bank.

Life changed for Boldt in 1919, when his first wife died and Prohibition decimated his business, which had mostly made liquor bottles. The Cincinnati plant closed and Boldt retired, selling a share of his business. Then he suffered a heart attack and ended up in a New York hospital where things started looking up—he fell in love with a nurse who took care of him. A year later, he married the Chicago-born Hilda Olsen, a kind, frumpy-looking woman with dark hair, a high forehead, close-set eyes, and a bow-lipped mouth a bit too small for her prominent nose. She was seventeen years younger than her new husband.

Seeking a healthier place to live and determined to join the new society of California, Boldt took Hilda to Beverly Hills in 1922, where they stayed at the Beverly Hills Hotel while shopping for a house. Boldt soon bought twelve acres across the street from Harold Lloyd's Greenacres for $20,000 and hired the architect Elmer Grey, who'd designed the hotel with his partner Myron Hunt, as well as Edward Huntington's mansion in San Marino, to create and build a half-timbered two-story Elizabethan-style love nest, complete with swimming pool, outbuildings, and garden.

The Boldts' 6,000-square-foot house was 138 feet long, with twenty rooms, four full bathrooms, four powder rooms, a two-story entrance hall with exposed roof trusses, public rooms with oak wainscoting, a mahogany dining room, and a library with floor-to-ceiling oak bookcases. Surrounded by terraces with sweeping views, it also had its own incinerator, sewage plant, and vacuum cleaning system and was estimated to have cost $100,000.

But a year later, Boldt returned to New York after Owens, the company that made the machines he'd used in his bottle factories, merged with Boldt Glass; he was named chairman of the executive committee and began engineering a series of mergers with competitors that reinvented the company. He sold the Beverly Hills house and bought the Hudson River estate of a paper manufacturer. But Boldt hadn't abandoned California. In May 1928, he bought a sixteen-acre estate with a twenty-two-room house, guest cottages, and all the expected amenities on the so-called Riviera of Santa Barbara, overlooking its mission, and that fall bought a 171-foot yacht, too, renaming her *Hilda*. The Boldts boarded in Havana that Christmas and a crew of eighteen took them through the Panama Canal to Santa Barbara. According to the Hollywood historian Charles Lockwood, Hilda had lofty social ambitions that had not been met among the movie folk in Benedict Canyon, and she believed they could be better realized in Santa Barbara, where Midwestern millionaires like her husband spent their summers.

The Boldts added servants' quarters, an Art Deco swimming pool, and nearby, a building they called the Teahouse, with a bandstand and, hidden behind a faux wall, a bar backed by a mirror rimmed with Tiffany glass. A closet next to it held a dumbwaiter later owners assumed was installed to dispose of liquor in a hurry, since the Boldts owned the house during Prohibition, when raids on private parties, even ones held in a building called the Teahouse, were not unthinkable. Beneath the dumbwaiter was a 150-foot tunnel leading to a hidden walk-in wine cellar.

The next year, business again brought Boldt back east where he worked "long and arduously," *Time* magazine reported, to arrange a merger of his business, by then called Owens-Illinois, and Continental Can, its equivalent in the manufacture of tin cans. He succeeded on October 9, 1929, but early the next morning, died of a second heart attack in his New York hotel room. Two weeks before the stock market crashed, Hilda Boldt returned to Santa Barbara with her husband's body, grieving but extremely rich. Thanks to her late husband's last deals, she would stay that way—for the moment.

One of Hilda's first moves was to put her yacht on the market, attracting no less a personage than Howard Hughes, a twenty-two-year-old Texas oil-drilling-equipment heir—he'd inherited $17 million (the 2010 equivalent of $215 million) from his father, Howard Sr. Hughes made a splash upon arriving in Hollywood by becoming a movie producer and romancing countless actresses. He was then courting Billie Dove, one of the more important women in his life, and upon hearing she loved the ocean, took her out on the *Hilda* three weekends in a row, allegedly test-sailing the yacht to see if he wanted to buy it. When he tried to borrow it for a fourth weekend, Boldt rebelled, demanding $450,000—the equivalent of nearly $6 million today. A Hughes aide talked her down to $375,000 and a subsidiary of the Hughes Tool Company bought the *Hilda*.

Then Hilda acquired a new husband—a suave, well-groomed German, Joseph Otto Weber, who'd been her chauffeur and butler; they married in 1933. According to Lockwood, the arbiters of Santa Barbara society were aghast (or a little envious, or perhaps both), and Hilda found that her social position, tenuous to start, had eroded. That's when she decided to move back to Los Angeles, or more precisely, to Bel Air, where Charles Hopper had recently taken over sales from Alphonzo Bell, and was aggressively marketing empty lots. In March 1934, Hilda dropped a mind-boggling $100,000 on two of the best, totaling nine and a half acres on a rise nestled between

Bellagio and Stone Canyon roads, surrounded on three sides by the Bel-Air Country Club.

Most houses that offer more than rudimentary shelter are in some sense acts of ego. Trophy houses say, "Look at me." Trophy houses in trophy neighborhoods demand the world do that. Hilda Olsen Boldt Weber's new house, four years in the making, screamed her need from its hilltop. She rented on nearby Stradella Road during its construction. In 1935, she hired Benjamin Morton Purdy, a landscape architect, to prepare the property and then took off for a months-long trip to Europe. The next year, she brought in Russian-born architect James E. Dolena, who specialized in classical and moderne residences, both quite distinct from the prevailing California-Mediterranean style, to create a house he would describe as "modern Georgian with Grecian influences." She also had her new husband sign a quitclaim deed, acknowledging that the estate was hers alone.

Hilda dreamed big. In 1936, she offered her Santa Barbara place to President Franklin D. Roosevelt for use as a summer White House. Finally, Roosevelt responded that although he gave it "mighty serious thought," as "most of us here in Washington wanted to go to Santa Barbara . . . the world situation won't permit me to leave." Simultaneously, Hilda sued Santa Barbara County for the return of $7,170 in taxes, claiming that under a new California tax law, the local payments represented double taxation. She lost, but her effort showed she could be as careful as she was profligate with her inherited fortune.

Her profligacy was clear in fall 1938 when she was handed the keys at the close of construction of the most magnificent estate erected in Los Angeles since the start of the Depression. Boldt's hilltop held a very formal forty-room, 35,000-square-foot mansion; a gatehouse; a two-story, five-room guesthouse with hand-rubbed wood paneling, men's and ladies' wings, and marble floors throughout; a swimming pool; tennis and badminton courts with their own spectator galleries; a greenhouse; a doghouse reached by a rosebush-lined lane; and a two-story garage that held eight cars and servants' quarters. Hilda even put in a tunnel direct to the Bel-Air Country Club fairways. "The main house is almost the size of two football fields," its next owner would later say, "but the allocation of space . . . becomes an object of symmetry and beauty."

The rich yet spare interiors were a collaboration of a Santa Barbara design studio and Terence Harold Robsjohn-Gibbings, a New York–based British decorator. The designer of the iconic modern-day Klismos chair, Gibbings, *Departures* magazine has said, was "a darling of the international beau monde; an Englishman who championed the cause of American design independence; a rarefied snob whose furniture scored with the middle-class masses; a rabid foe of retro styles who led his own Greek Revival." His style was at once classical and Art Deco, a studied yet streamlined nod to an elegant past. The furnishings he made for Hilda were the ultimate expression of his moderne reinvention of classical elements from sphinxes to Ionic columns, all custom-made from English sycamore, black walnut, acacia, and other rare woods.

The copper-roofed house featured a classical Italian fountain in the motor court that faced the elegant Chippendale-motif portico with its four stately two-story columns and a delicate wrought-iron balcony over the imposing front door. In the rear, floor-to-ceiling glass doors and windows overlooked statues set among rare plants, multiple patios, a terraced lawn, and stairs leading to the pale-blue-tiled pool, the pool house, and tennis court beyond. The H-shaped ground floor opened onto an oval reception room with Indian bronze figures of Devi and Siva; there was also a long gallery, a living room decorated with panels by Jean Baptiste, a dining room paneled in green-black walnut inlaid with ivory wood with concealed pin lights in the ceiling to light floral centerpieces, a smaller living room with a round bar and an eighteenth-century Viennese clock, a library, and a card room. In the powder room, a huge Blackamoor statue offered visitors cigarettes and perfume. There were only four bedroom suites upstairs (reachable by elevator, of course), two for the Webers—her bathroom was green marble with gold trim and had a massage room as well as a maid's room, Otto's featured Italian marble and a steam bath—and two for guests, connected by a sitting room with its own kitchen and massage, ironing, and breakfast rooms.

Hilda's bedroom was movie-star ready with yellow silk-upholstered walls as soft as pillows and a quilted satin headboard shaped like a mermaid's tail. Every room had a fireplace. A hundred cabinetmakers spent a year on the walls alone; they used sixty-six different kinds of wood.

The estate had five kitchens, one with five sinks and a warming oven that held a hundred plates; a separate "spice" kitchen with a special ventilator for smelly food; a cold room with coils in the marble walls for desserts and salads; a kitchen by the pool—and the house could easily seat and feed two hundred. "In a home of this size it would be thoughtless to have only one [kitchen], making the servants walk endless steps," said Hilda, the former nurse.

Off the pantry was a silver-polishing room next door to the silver vault, which was lined in billiard cloth and boasted labeled drawers that rolled on ball bearings. Out of sight were a laundry that could handle the needs of twenty-five families, enough electrical power for a thirteen-story building, a workshop, and wine and fur vaults. There were also twelve servants' bedrooms. Each was private and floored in marble. One new employee spent his first night awake, worrying he'd accidentally been placed in a guest room. "Most big homes have extra wings and scores of useless rooms, but no conveniences for owners and no thoughtfulness for servants," said Hilda.

Everything in the interior was designed and made for the house, explaining both the time it took to build (there were four thousand separate designs for interior details) and the $3 million that architect Dolena later said it all cost (the equivalent of $44.8 million today), of which only a tenth was spent on the earthquake-proof reinforced concrete, brick-faced, stone-finished house itself. Hilda would soon be spending another $1,800 a month (about $27,000 today) on household staff, gardeners, maids, a cook, a butler, and a house man.

The Webers had a housewarming dinner-dance just after Christmas 1938. The seated dinner for 250 cost $50,000 (the equivalent of $640,000 today), with $5,000 of that spent on Christmas and table decorations alone. The guest list was light on the sort of social moths who fluttered around the Dohenys, Greens, or Jansses. The Beverly Wilshire developer Walter McCarty, Dolena, and Robsjohn-Gibbings were the biggest names around the table.

Regardless, Hilda loved giving parties, and lots of Los Angeles big shots passed through and were impressed. Louis B. Mayer, the head of MGM, said, "If I had not gone inside myself I would not have believed such a residence existed in the world." But L.A. society didn't embrace Hilda and Otto, who hit their social apogee eleven months after the housewarming, when Doll Hart, whose daughter had married first one of William Randolph Hearst's sons and then William S. Paley, the founder of CBS, gave a cocktail party in Hilda's honor. Chatterbox, the social gossip column in the *Times*, noted that her "life story reads like a fairy tale." Oddly, the writer didn't bother telling it.

In 1940, the Webers opened their doors to *Architectural Digest*, which devoted eighteen pages to the house. They also hosted a charity event and the elder Minnewa Bell, Arthur Letts Jr.'s wife, and a sprinkling of Westside society came. But a big photo spread of that affair showed guests whose faces were dour at best, even somewhat disapproving. The ladies "came away impressed," said the *Times,* but Hilda and Otto only rarely made the social columns thereafter and then only in passing. The Webers were apparently not as appealing as their house. Indeed, when people did talk about them, their comments were usually critical. Realtor Jeff Hyland recounts that Bel Air sneered at how Hilda sometimes answered her own door, let the staff call her by name in front of guests, overspent on the parties those guests nonetheless attended, got swindled in an oil deal, and enjoyed betting on horses and cards just a little too much. The Webers were living proof that it took more than real estate, no matter how special, to fuel a smooth, successful social takeoff.

Meanwhile, that house and those habits were draining Hilda's bank account, so in 1942, she started divesting assets. The Santa Barbara property was sold to a buyer who donated it to the Marymount School, which has occupied the premises ever since. Then, in 1949, Hilda and her house were the subjects of a rare long profile in *Coronet* magazine. "The House Where Dreams Come True" described the place in intimate detail. "Guests never want to leave and neither do the servants," her butler was quoted saying. It wasn't apparent, or even mentioned, but Hilda's dream had turned sour; her house was already for sale for $1.5 million when that article ran.

Over the next two years, as the price dropped by half, Cedric Gibbons, a movie art director, and his wife, the actress Dolores del Rio, Louis B. Mayer, and William Randolph Hearst were said to have considered buying it, but none would commit. Another possible buyer, the Texas hotelier Conrad Hilton, initially resisted in 1950 even though the price had by then been reduced to $400,000. But his oldest friend and associate, Bill Irwin, pushed him hard, telling him how the future shah of Iran had sought to buy it before Weber was willing to part with it, even getting caught sneaking onto the grounds one day to show it to a friend.

"Look, Bill," Hilton replied, "the Prince of Iran is used to palaces. I started out in an adobe room in back of a store." But Irwin was having none of it, telling Hilton that not only was the house a bargain, it was a necessity for a man in his position—he'd reached the pinnacle of the hotel business a year earlier when he bought New York's Waldorf-Astoria. "It all sounds too pretentious," Hilton grumbled, but then he wavered. "If it ever gets down to $250,000, I'll take a look at it." Some deals were just too good to refuse. And sure enough, a few months later, the price had dropped again, and Hilton spent a morning there alone. "I had to know if the house and I would suit each other," he recalled in his autobiography. "It was a case of love at first sight." But he could still bargain. When a desperate Hilda agreed to drop the price to $225,000, Hilton bought the house and all its contents save for her linens and the breakfast room silver and china. "I couldn't resist it," he later said. It was "one of the fabulous houses of the world."

Understandably distraught at the loss of her foothold, however tenuous, in Westside society, Hilda and Otto gave one last party, a "house-cooling" bash "with fifty Southland society guests invited" and then returned to Santa Barbara—this time to a common, rented bungalow. According to Hyland, who heard the story from Hilda's broker, she then gambled away what little money she had left.

Accounts of her last days differ. Her broker said that while spending a week with her sister in a modest house in Pacific Palisades, Hilda tapped Conrad Hilton for a loan of $10,000, but lost it all that same day at Santa Anita Race Track. Otto Weber, meantime, had driven down from Santa Barbara to meet his wife in L.A. In one version of the story, Hilda's sister told Otto that the day before, Hilda had said she was going to Hollywood for a premiere and then spending the night with friends. But when Otto called them and learned she'd never turned up, he went to the police and reported her missing. Another account claims she'd withdrawn a large sum of money from a Santa Monica bank and vanished.

A missing-person search had already begun when Hilda called her sister, professed amazement at all the fuss, and said she'd merely changed her plans. Wanting "to be by myself for the night," she'd slept at the Beverly Wilshire Hotel. The whole affair was considered sufficiently odd that the *Times* ran it on page three, misdescribing Hilda—though surely she'd have been glad—as a "wealthy society figure." Back home in Santa Barbara ten days later, while Otto was out for an afternoon walk, Hilda wrote him a ten-page note, swallowed a bottle of sleeping pills, and climbed into her bathtub. When Otto returned, he broke down the locked bathroom door and found his sixty-five-year-old wife in the tub, her head submerged. Firemen and the local sheriff arrived but it was too late; Hilda was dead. Otto told the sheriff she'd been in ill health for three years, ever since hurting her back in a train accident.

Friends told the *Los Angeles Examiner* that she'd also been brooding over the "stupid mistakes" that led to the loss of her fortune, first among them building the Bel Air house. Detectives said the suicide note went further, complaining that the sale of the house was still in escrow, that Hilton had taken advantage of her, that regardless, "most of the money realized from the sale will go toward paying back taxes," and that she regretted ignoring friends who'd urged her not to build it, but rather to put her inheritance into a trust that would have assured her a long, comfortable life. The note also named several Santa Barbara society figures who Hilda felt had snubbed her since her return there in modest circumstances.

Finally, Hilda begged Otto to forgive her for "leaving when life no longer holds any interest for me. . . . Don't think me a coward. It takes courage to go through with this. I love you."

After her cremation and interment in Charles Boldt's mausoleum, it emerged that Hilda Weber still had some assets—albeit in furniture and objects she'd left in storage. In June 1952, a Beverly Hills auctioneer offered the contents of her Santa Barbara house and some items from the Bel Air house, too, including those bed linens, in a four-session sale featuring eighteenth-century French and English furniture, Meissen and Sèvres pieces, Chinese jades and ivories, rugs and carpets. "Any description would be inadequate," the auctioneer boasted, "and could not possibly do justice to these furnishings." The press apparently took him at his word. The auction went unreported and its results are unknown.

According to Hyland, Otto Weber remarried, moved to Chicago, and became a bartender, so perhaps his story had a happy ending. And even though she lost it far too quickly, Hilda's home at 10644 Bellagio Road, which Hilton named Casa Encantada, or House of Enchantment, still stands as her magnificent monument.

Holmby Hills

594 South Mapleton

Edna and Malcolm McNaghten were the first of the six Letts-Janss households to sell their home in the informal family compound in Holmby Hills, though they moved only four doors down the street. Malcolm McNaghten was in ill health and contemplating retirement from the Broadway Department Store. The buyer of their house at 594 South Mapleton was the crooner and actor Harry "Bing" Crosby.

Like Rudy Vallée, Crosby was a soft-singing product of the radio and record-player age, and like Vallée he had a public image that was substantially at odds with reality. Der Bingle, as he was called, sold himself as Mr. Smooth, a nonchalant Irish Catholic homebody, beloved as a typical dad who happened to have a great voice. However, his private life was filled with "casual cruelties and uncontrollable demonic impulses," as the critic Charles Marowitz once put it. *People* magazine has described life in the Crosby family's Holmby Hills mansion as "a Hollywood Gothic horror story."

The Crosbys moved to Holmby Hills in January 1943, a mere week after their previous home on four acres in the Toluca Lake neighborhood of North Hollywood burned down. Defective wiring sparked a fire as Crosby's wife, Wilma, who'd been a professional dancer known as Dixie Lee before marrying Bing, was taking down their Christmas tree. An alcoholic, Dixie was used to being left alone by her husband; also a drinker, he regularly cheated on his wife and sometimes beat his children. They were rarely seen together.

Bing had spent the afternoon playing golf with Fred Astaire at the Bel-Air Country Club and was just sitting down to dinner at one of the famous Brown Derby restaurants when he got a call and learned that his twenty-room home had burned to the ground with several thousand gawkers watching. His wife had pulled their four children, aged three to nine, from bed and sent them to a neighbor's house before huddling under a blanket to watch the colonial mansion go up in flames taking with it all of Bing's copies of his records, his beloved pipes, and golf and horse-racing trophies. Crosby coolly finished dinner before driving home to comfort his family and view the charred remains.

In 1945, a reporter from the *New York Times* described the Crosbys' new home as "a small place as mansions go: two-storied, stone and L-shaped on one of the seventy Holmby Hills, an expensive tract which stands with its back to Beverly Hills and its nose in the air over Westwood." But the new home didn't change the sad secret facts of Bing's life. Dixie Lee had drunk herself into deep trouble at age forty, and the multitude of distractions that came from Bing's success hadn't helped their marriage. The Crosbys briefly separated in 1950. The couple known as Hollywood's ideal mother and father reconciled and kept their family's happy image intact, but they couldn't do the same for her health; she fell into a coma after abdominal surgery in 1952 and died of what her doctor called a "generalized cancer condition." Bing's mother moved in to care for the boys.

Having diversified and invested wisely in everything from oil to sports teams and real estate, Bing was said to be a multimillionaire, but the following year, he briefly put his home (as well as another in Pebble Beach and his sixty-five racehorses) on the market, saying he'd done it in order to pay $1 million in inheritance taxes due on Dixie's estate. Contradictory as ever, Crosby also claimed he'd stopped drinking right around the time he was in a car crash that resulted in cracked vertebrae and a million-dollar lawsuit that alleged he'd been driving drunk (the State Highway Patrol said he wasn't and the case was ultimately settled out of court for $100,000). And he publicly flirted with the idea of retirement even as he also hinted he might do a TV show and signed up to appear in a slate of back-to-back films: *White Christmas*, *The Country Girl* (which led to several dates with costar Grace Kelly and an Oscar nomination), and *High Society*. The result was a career renaissance; Crosby was as canny as he was contrary.

In 1957, he secretly married Kathy Grant, a starlet three decades his junior who immediately produced his fifth son. The youngest of his four boys by Dixie—all of whom had deeply troubled relationships with their father—immediately moved out. The eldest, Gary, who was older than his father's new bride, hired his father's longtime housekeeper after Kathy fired her. But family troubles aside, Bing's career was still crooning and he sang his way into the mid-1960s, appearing in more films and numerous TV specials, seemingly invincible, even in the era of the Beatles and the Rolling Stones.

The Crosbys had two more children and remained in Holmby Hills until 1963, when they sold the house and moved to a new one on a golf course south of San Francisco. Bing's film and recording careers ended shortly thereafter, though he would resurface now and again, even joining the glam rocker David Bowie for an acclaimed duet of "Little Drummer Boy" shortly before his death in Spain in 1977, just after he finished eighteen holes of golf. By then, the critic Gary Giddins wrote, "he had become a Norman Rockwell poster, an irrelevant holdover from another world." Yet one who, despite his personal troubles, remains a beloved icon.

Crosby's Holmby Hills house would have two more owners before it, too, came to be considered an irrelevant holdover. The next was Patrick Frawley Jr., a blue-eyed, ruddy-faced businessman who was trading up from a home in Bel Air. Frawley, who got rich manufacturing Paper Mate ballpoint pens and Schick razor blades, was an American original, even though he was the Nicaragua-born child of an Irish Catholic father and French-Spanish mother. Sent to live with relatives in San Francisco so he could get an American education, Frawley dropped out of school and returned to Managua to work with his father, who ran insurance, import-export, and banking businesses. At eighteen, he made a $300,000 deal, his first, between U.S. Rubber and the Panamanian government. When World War II began, he went to Canada, enlisted in the Royal Canadian Air Force, and married.

After the war, he and his wife settled in San Francisco, where he took control of a company that made parts for pens after its owners defaulted on a loan. He gambled $100,000 on its latest innovation, leak-proof pens loaded with fast-drying ink, called the innovative product the Paper Mate, and became a millionaire. In 1953, Frawley launched a $2 million ad campaign for the pens starring celebrities like George Burns, Gracie Allen, and Zsa Zsa Gabor. Six years after his breakthrough, which revolutionized the writing implement business, he sold the company to Gillette for $15.5 million.

After becoming an American citizen and president of Eversharp, which owned Gillette's competitor Schick, the razor manufacturer, and introducing another successful product, the first stainless steel razor blades, Frawley evolved into a corporate tycoon; in 1961 he took over Technicolor, the Los Angeles film processing company, and shortly thereafter gained personal control of Eversharp by buying up its shares and stocking its board with confederates. Schick's blades were made in Cuba until Fidel Castro took over the island nation and expropriated Schick's factories that year, turning Frawley into an arch anticommunist and a vocal and financial supporter of conservative politicians and causes, beginning with then vice president Richard Nixon. Frawley and Alfred Bloomingdale of the department store family then put on the largest anticommunist youth rally in history, where the entertainers George Murphy (a song-and-dance man and Frawley protégé), John Wayne, Pat Boone, Ronald Reagan, Dale Evans, and Roy Rogers appeared before a hundred thousand schoolchildren. Frawley subsequently became a nationally known figure of controversy when he tried to cancel a million-dollar advertising deal with ABC after it ran a program he felt was anti-Nixon.

Frawley was renowned for his business prowess if not always for his politics or ethics.

In 1964, Frawley and his large family (seven daughters and two sons) were settling into Bing Crosby's old Holmby Hills house when he personally bought and mailed copies of the book that launched Barry Goldwater's right-wing campaign for president, *A Choice, Not an Echo* by Phyllis Schlafly, to forty thousand Roman Catholic priests, accompanied by a letter on Eversharp-Schick letterhead criticizing the press, attacking liberal foreign policy, and assailing the Democratic Party's approach to civil rights legislation. Shortly after that, he was tangentially involved in what investigators termed a criminal libel conspiracy, a politically motivated attack campaign— sometimes described as more savage than anything that happened in the McCarthy era—that successfully targeted a moderate Republican senator, Thomas Kuchel, ending his public career.

Frawley financeed his activism personally, and he used about $1 million a year in corporate funds to, in his words, "fight communism full time" and elect a conservative president. Frawley, along with other like-minded tycoons, organized American Businessmen for Barry Goldwater and TV for Goldwater-Miller, hiring the actor-turned-pitchman Ronald Reagan as their spokesman, giving him the platform from which he ran for governor of California two years later. Frawley then promoted a Reagan presidential run in 1968.

The winner that year proved to be Richard Nixon, but Frawley and his political friends had seen the future. The group of California conservatives who brought Reagan to power included Frawley; Bloomingdale; Henry Salvatori; Taft Schreiber, an MCA executive; Holmes Tuttle, a car dealer and realtor; Tom Jones, the chairman of the defense contractor Northrup; Henry Singleton, a former OSS (Office of Strategic Services) man and engineer who cofounded Teledyne, the conglomerate that made everything from unmanned aircraft to Waterpik shower heads;[14] Earle Jorgensen, who turned a scrap steel distributorship into a giant industrial concern; drugstore owner Justin Dart; corporate lawyer William French Smith; and A. C. "Cy" Rubel, the president and chairman of Union Oil. Many of them lived in the Platinum Triangle—giving lie to the conventional wisdom that the estate district west of Los Angeles was the beating heart of flaming liberalism.

Though his political activities were controversial, they didn't hurt him professionally for many years. Only when it was revealed that George Murphy, the former actor and Technicolor executive, had remained on the company's payroll and carried its credit cards after his election to the U.S. Senate from California did Frawley pay a price for his beliefs; he was forced out of his job in 1970. He sold Schick that year, retaining ownership only of a Seattle hospital he'd bought after its enzyme therapy cured his alcoholism. He spent the next two decades expanding it into a chain of treatment centers, and lived long enough to see Ronald Reagan become president in 1980 and serve two terms in the White House.

Bel Air

10644 Bellagio Road

Far more controversial, although by necessity far less well known, was another local group with shared interests—though their ties were not political but financial. Their wealth was a by-product of organized crime—specifically, of that series of decisions made before and after World War II by the heirs to Al Capone to open shop in Los Angeles to launder their ill-gotten gains and, more importantly, legitimize themselves. They were the predecessors of the quasi-legitimate businessmen who would put together the land that became Beverly Park. Though they failed in that attempt, over the course of the second half of the twentieth century, they would plant their hooks deep in the Southland.

In summer 1945, simultaneous with the end of the war, two significant mob-tainted figures moved from Chicago to Los Angeles. As reported by Gus Russo in his encyclopedic book *Supermob,* Mafia lawyer Sidney Korshak rented his first home in Los Angeles, in Coldwater Canyon, that summer, and shortly afterwards, bought a house in nearby Encino. A son of Jewish immigrants from Kiev, Korshak was the nephew of a Chicago saloon owner and real estate investor who had also dabbled in an arson-for-hire ring. Another uncle was involved in local Chicago politics, as was one of Korshak's older brothers, Marshall. His other older brother was a junkie and minor criminal. Their father was a successful contractor. Sidney became a lawyer in 1930 and allied himself with Jake Arvey, a lawyer and political kingmaker who ran a notoriously corrupt ward politics operation—nothing out of the ordinary for Chicago. The ties between Arvey and organized crime were many. The Capone mob provided protection for Arvey's operations and, in turn, Arvey and his firm represented some of the mob's businesses, including a wire service that provided horse-race results to illegal gambling rooms around the country.

Korshak was a partner with, as well as a lawyer for, hoodlums from the beginning of his career and became an important advisor for the mob as it moved into real estate deals like Beverly Park, as well as legitimate labor unions and hotel and entertainment businesses. Korshak also grew close to Jules Stein, the ophthalmologist turned Capone-connected nightclub owner and agent who founded MCA, and Lew Wasserman, Stein's chief lieutenant. Stein had preceded Korshak to California, buying Misty Mountain, the Beverly Hills estate of the silent film director Fred Niblo, in 1940.[15]

According to Russo's detailed dissection of his career, Korshak also represented Benjamin "Bugsy" Siegel, a New York mobster tied to the East Coast bosses Meyer Lansky, "Lucky" Luciano, and Frank Costello. Siegel had actually been the pacesetter, moving to Beverly Hills in the mid-1930s to set up gambling operations and run the mob's wire service there. Raffish and handsome, he was taken up by a Countess Dorothy di Frasso and entered Hollywood society, though after years of legal difficulties, Siegel would set his sights on Las Vegas, where he hoped to build a legitimate gambling business. Korshak would be involved in that business long after Siegel was murdered by gunmen who fired shots through the living room window of his latest girlfriend, Virginia Hill's, home in the Beverly Hills flats in 1947, shortly after he managed to open the still-unfinished Flamingo hotel-casino. Though he'd effectively invented the modern Las Vegas Strip, Siegel had spent and lost too much of the mob's money at the Flamingo, exceeding his $1.5 million budget by $4.5 million. Simultaneous with his murder, three of Lansky's henchmen took over the place. Officially, Siegel's murder remains unsolved.

Korshak also rubbed up against the movie business, fixing a "leak" when a mobster indicted on extortion charges involving MGM studios and a corrupt theatrical stage employees' union was threatening to point fingers at Chicago. That earned him a reward—a job as the mob's liaison and master fixer in Los Angeles. As Russo wrote, "The movie extortion case left the Chicago underworld shaken and more resolute than ever to transfer its cash westward, into real estate and other legitimate businesses. . . . California seemed to mandate that its citizens recreate themselves . . . with its lax law enforcement and legal double standard for the wealthy . . . [it] had the perfect climate, literally and figuratively, to expand their enterprise. . . . Los Angeles, in particular, was known as a city receptive to both hoodlums and Jews." This was the beginning, but hardly the end, of the mob in L.A.

The second Chicagoan, a friend of Korshak's, Arnold S. Kirkeby (who would later buy Lynn Atkinson's "house with the golden doorknobs") was neither Jewish nor a hoodlum. He wasn't even Italian; he was Norwegian. But long before Beverly Park, he had people wondering about mob connections to La-La Land. Born in 1900 in Chicago, Kirkeby started his career as a teen-age messenger with an investment house on La Salle Street, Chicago's Wall Street, and owned his own bond-dealing business by age twenty. Two years later, Kirkeby had sixteen employees and an annual trading volume of $16 million. Five years after that, he owned a 75-foot schooner, raced his own planes, set daredevil air travel records, and had started the Chicago-Tampa Development Company during a Florida land boom to build a suburb out-side Tampa, Florida. There, he first spied Carlotta Cuesta, the daughter of the cofounder of the Cuesta Ray cigar company. Carlotta had just been crowned Queen of the Gasparilla at an annual festival celebrating a local pi-rate. Kirkeby courted the Cuban-American beauty and married her in 1928. This proved to be good for him professionally as well as personally; soon, he'd be doing important business in Cuba, leading to suspicions that have lasted for decades that he was also doing business with the mob.

After a 1933 military coup in Cuba, its leader, Fulgencio Batista, made a group of American criminals his secret partners in running gambling on the island. Many believe Kirkeby was involved in that from the beginning, in league with the mob. What is demonstrably true is that after the securities business went south in the Depression and his bond firm went bankrupt, Arnold Kirkeby pivoted, went into the hotel business, and a decade later, ended up owning Cuba's Hotel Nacional for a dozen years.

In 1937, a few months after his wife's wealthy father died, backed by a Chicago paving contractor and bucking the headwinds of the Depression, Kirkeby leased Chicago's iconic Drake and Blackstone hotels from Metro-politan Life Insurance. Kirkeby then bought the four-hundred-room Town House hotel in Los Angeles, originally built by Edward Doheny for $2.5

million—Kirkeby paid $1 million for it. In 1939, he leased the Gotham Hotel in New York, as with all the others, from Metropolitan Life. Then he bought the Biltmore in Tampa out of receivership for $275,000—it came with an island in the Gulf of Mexico as a sort of gift with purchase. And in 1941, he paid $1.25 million to buy outright Chicago's Blackstone. In total, Kirkeby controlled 2,314 hotel rooms by then. Either he was still a daredevil, had very deep pockets—or both.

As the war wound down, Kirkeby slowed down, but didn't stop trading properties. In 1943, he was reported to have bought the Stevens Hotel in Chicago, the world's largest, from the U.S. Army for $5.25 million in cash. But he quickly sold his 15 percent share to the partners who'd financed him, then turned around and sued them for a $100,000 transaction fee and was countersued for alleged "fraud, duress and compulsion" in seeking that payment. He would ultimately win $40,000. But long before that settlement, Conrad Hilton swooped in and bought the Stevens at a $2.25 million premium early in 1945.

Tall, vital, and oozing charisma and energy, Conrad Nicholson Hilton's first brush with business had come before World War I when he was seventeen and dropped out of military school to work in his father's general store in San Antonio, New Mexico. When Connie, as he was known, was twenty, his father, who'd been the town's top businessman, suffered a financial reverse and the young man, who'd resumed his education, dropped out of school again to rejoin the family firm, shilling passengers on incoming trains and offering to carry their bags in an attempt to fill rooms in a five-room boarding house his father opened in their family home. After brief stints in the local legislature, running a small bank, and serving in the army in World War I, Connie moved to a Texas cow town where he tried to buy a bank, failed, and bought a flophouse instead with $5,000 of his own and another $45,000 he'd borrowed. Connie and L. M. Drown, a friend of a friend he brought in as his operating partner, renovated it into a more respectable enterprise and ran it successfully enough that he was able to expand, buying more hotels in Fort Worth and Dallas. He would always maximize the use of space, hire and empower the best employees he could find, and mix his own funds with those of lenders and investors, setting a unique managerial style he would never abandon. In 1920, he broke ground for the first hotel he'd build himself, the Dallas Hilton, the cornerstone of the Hilton hotel chain. Hilton married the same year and quickly produced his first son, Conrad Jr., better known as Nicky.

For a time, Hilton opened a hotel a year. He also had two more sons, William Barron (now best known as Paris Hilton's grandfather) and Eric Michael. Then he suffered business and personal losses, including a 1931 default that saw him lose most of his hotels to a lender and a 1934 divorce, but by 1937 he'd won back five of his eight hotels and was soon expanding again. By the time he bought the Stevens Hotel, he'd moved to Los Angeles, built a Spanish stucco-and-tile house on Bellagio Road adjoining the Bel-Air Country Club, and married Zsa Zsa Gabor, twenty-two, an aspiring actress who'd been Miss Hungary of 1938. By then he also owned the Sir Francis Drake in San Francisco, the Plaza and Roosevelt hotels in New York, and Hiltons in Abilene, Longview, Lubbock, and Plainview, Texas; Long Beach, California; Albuquerque, New Mexico; Dayton, Ohio; and Chihuahua, Mexico. That year, in a Christmas buying spree, he acquired the Ambassador in Los Angeles for $6.2 million and the Palmer House in Chicago for just over $19 million.

In spring 1946, the Hilton Hotel Corporation was formed, combining all his separate hotel corporations. Though he had a number of powerful partners, Connie was the corporation's biggest shareholder; it went public on the New York Stock Exchange a year later.

At the same time Hilton was buying the Stevens in Chicago, Arnold Kirkeby's lease on Chicago's Drake ran out and he snapped up control of the second most famous hotel in Beverly Hills, the Beverly Wilshire. Kirkeby decided to move nearby, and in summer 1945 acquired Lynn Atkinson's house in Bel Air for a mere $250,000. It's unclear, even to his family, how he came to own it.

A local gossip column once claimed that Atkinson gave the house to Kirkeby in repayment of a gambling debt. Carla Kirkeby, Arnold's younger child, says her parents told her that Atkinson had run out of money to finish the house, borrowed it from Kirkeby, and, unable to pay it back, lost the house, his collateral. Her father "didn't want to take the house," she says. "He said he'd never make another loan like that." Kirkeby's son Arnold, known as Buzz, believes that the kooky Atkinson took the loan for an ill-fated wartime engineering brainstorm—floating islands he proposed to sell to the U.S.

Navy. But the war ended, the navy was no longer interested—if it ever had been—and Atkinson "handed over the keys to the house."

Understandably, he did so with a heavy heart—his daughter Doris once told Carla Kirkeby that her father moved into an apartment on Wilshire Boulevard with a view of the house and sat staring at it for hours on end through binoculars. In summer 1961, having moved again, he leapt from his twelfth-floor apartment in the Le Corbusier–inspired Park La Brea complex east of Beverly Hills. A note found near his body blamed the infamous Los Angeles smog that had exacerbated his pulmonary emphysema. "I have lived here for almost fifty years in perfect physical condition except for smog-affected lungs that make life too miserable, but if my passing shall accent a need for a change, it will have served a good purpose," wrote the sixty-six-year-old. Atkinson's wife, unmentioned in the news report of his death, had apparently predeceased him.

Kirkeby's L.A. shopping spree recommenced in 1945, when he bought the Sunset Towers apartment building at a liquidation auction for $620,000 in cash. The next year, he acquired New York's Warwick Hotel; Hampshire House, a luxurious apartment-hotel; and a controlling interest in the landmark Sherry-Netherland as well as the Saranac Inn in upstate New York. Meanwhile, back in Bel Air, he and Carlotta were living it up, throwing parties attended by the likes of Clark Gable and Hedda Hopper, who compared their new house to Versailles. In summer 1948, they hosted a ball attended by Conrad Hilton, who came with Ginna Janss; Hilton's ex-wife Zsa Zsa (they'd broken up after their house burned down in 1944), who came with George Sanders; Gable; Angela Lansbury; Esther Williams; retailer Bernard Gimbel; and Mike Romanoff, the beloved restaurateur who falsely claimed to be a Russian prince. "Never in all our meandering have we witnessed such a buffet," a *Times* columnist wrote, "and never such magnificent jewels and clothes."

Kirkeby's ties to top-tier L.A. may have been solid, but soon, an event at his Hotel Nacional in Cuba proved his ties to the mob as well. The so-called Havana Conference, complete with a concert by Frank Sinatra, who arrived with two of Al Capone's cousins, was organized by Meyer Lansky at the Nacional so that Lucky Luciano, who'd been deported from the U.S. after a prison term, could attend. It's remembered as a historic conclave of American Mafia leaders, including Frank Costello, Joe Adonis, Albert Anastasia, Vito Genovese, Tommy Lucchese, and Joe Bonnano. Among the topics discussed: Luciano's appointment as *capo di tutti capi,* or boss of all bosses of the mob; the Mafia's future in the narcotics trade; and what to do about Bugsy Siegel. Though the death sentence the bosses imposed on Bugsy was delayed by Lansky's pleading, it would be carried out a few months later.

In the 1950s, two journalists, Art White and Robert Goe, began researching the Chicago–Los Angeles criminal nexus both on their own and for the Los Angeles Police Department; author Gus Russo discovered White's heavily footnoted reports in storage at the Chicago Crime Commission while researching his book on Sidney Korshak. Their research was, Russo discovered, funded by elements of California's Democratic Party, working on behalf of Los Angeles mayor Sam Yorty, who'd grown concerned that the mob was infiltrating that city's politics as it had long done in Chicago. Among their investigative targets were Meyer Lansky, Arnold Kirkeby, and Conrad Hilton.

Kirkeby's alleged links to the mob, though impossible to prove beyond a doubt and dismissed as "baloney . . . hooey," by Buzz Kirkeby, have nonetheless attained the status of received wisdom—and evidence of the cosmopolitan sophistication of their Triangle community. "Most well-to-do Angelenos knew where the Kirkeby money had come from, and they didn't care," Jeff Hyland wrote in his coffee-table book *The Estates of Beverly Hills.* "The Kirkebys were considered to be on the top rung of Los Angeles society." And Kirkeby climbed higher still when he sold the Nacional, as well as the Beverly Wilshire and New York's Gotham, for over $10 million and used the proceeds to buy Westwood Village from Harold Janss for the bargain price of $6.5 million a few months later.

Holmby Hills

10060 Sunset Boulevard

The good life had mostly continued in the Janss compound in the intervening years. Harold Janss's daughters were still fixtures in the gossip columns,
their trips to the mountains, to Europe, and to Hawaii (their father's favorite
bolt-hole) lovingly chronicled. But there was turbulence, too. Edwin Janss's
daughter Patricia, only twenty-five, was killed in a car crash in Yosemite
National Park just after Christmas 1938. Her mother blamed Patricia's husband, George Gregson, who'd been driving when the car plunged down a
150-foot embankment, but she allowed him to move into 10060 Sunset
with their two children anyway.

The next year, Harold's daughter Gladys married a utilities executive, but
she quickly got divorced, married a broker in 1950, and got divorced again
in 1953, charging her husband with repeatedly staying out all night, giving her an ulcer. Edwin's son Bill married a San Francisco socialite in 1940.
That same year Ginna Janss sang at the Santa Barbara Biltmore (where Tony
Moreno was in the audience) and the Beverly Hills Hotel—and later took
off for her two-year stint in Greenwich Village, where she sang in a nightclub. Betty Janss married briefly in 1943. Ginna Janss did the same in 1962.
But the most sensational match of all was made by Edwin's grandson Eddie
Gregson. In 1958, at age nineteen, he eloped with May Britt, a stunning
twenty-two-year-old Swedish actress he'd met a month earlier. They lasted
nineteen months in a 10060 Sunset guesthouse before splitting up. (Britt

immediately married the African American actor-singer Sammy Davis Jr. on the rebound, almost wrecking his career in a country—and a city—that still looked askance at interracial marriage.)

Meantime, the Janss Investment Company had broken in half in the midfifties, when Harold decided to leave the company. He took Westwood Village and his brother kept the ranch in the Coachella Valley. Harold then sold his Westwood holdings, which included twenty buildings, fifty stores, an office building, a garage, and fourteen parking lots, to Arnold Kirkeby. "My grandfather thought $7 million was wonderful," says Lett Mullen. "He had no idea. No question, the Edwin side [of the family] got the better deal."

Both Janss brothers retired. Edwin died in 1959 just after May Britt and his grandson were divorced; he was seventy-seven. Harold spent the rest of his life having fun ("He loved to give parties," his assistant Evelyn Schmidt recalled) and died at home in 1972 at the age of eighty-two. Edwin's sons Edwin Jr. and William turned the family ranch in the San Fernando Valley into the suburb of Thousand Oaks, bought and expanded Sun Valley, the Idaho ski resort, and developed Snowmass near Aspen, Colorado. In 1961, Florence Janss, Edwin's widow, moved to Wilshire Terrace, the first co-op apartment building in Beverly Hills, and the last stop before the nursing home for many of the Triangle's most social citizens.

But Florence didn't stay in her apartment for long; her boys had the architect Cliff May build her a house in Thousand Oaks, where she lived until 1981. When she died, to avoid "a huge tax event," all the properties still owned by Janss Investment were valued and split up among the family's fourth generation. Edwin Jr. ("an eccentric genius," according to his niece Pat Gregson) raised lemons, avocado, and cattle, became a racehorse breeder, a noted art collector, and an underwater photographer before committing suicide in 1989 after he was diagnosed with terminal cancer. Janss Corp., which was run by one of Edwin Sr.'s grandsons, was the last firm to bear the family name; it was liquidated in 1995, ninety-nine years and nine months after Peter Janss first went into the real estate business, killed by the burden of millions of dollars in debt incurred in that decade's real estate slump. Most of the remaining Janss properties—a shopping mall and apartment and commercial complexes—were turned over to creditors. "It was a wonderful old company," said William Janss Sr., "but it was time to move on."

For all their accomplishments and advantages and despite their relative low profile, like so many of the Triangle's founding families, the Jansses didn't fare wonderfully. Edwin Jr. wasn't the only suicide: Ginna Janss, Eddie Gregson, and Harold's granddaughter Barbara all killed themselves and Betty and Gladys both tried, says Dr. Michael Lain, Barbara's widower. "They're a genetic bundle of suicides." Many suffered severe depression—and the latest generation feels the repercussions. "We are a very dysfunctional family," one of Edwin's grandchildren admits. "There are nine of us and we don't talk to each other."

Arnold Kirkeby's seemingly charmed existence took a mysterious turn a decade into his years in Bel Air. In 1958, he suddenly put up for auction twenty-nine Impressionist and post-Impressionist paintings he'd collected, by a magnificent roster of name-brand artists: Picasso, Cézanne, van Gogh, Monet, Modigliani, Matisse, Renoir, Degas, Utrillo, Bonnard, Pissarro, Manet, Morisot, Vlaminck, Signac, and Rouault. He'd never collected before, but a neighbor, C. Michael Paul, a financial hustler who sometimes dealt in art, talked Kirkeby into a buying trip to Europe where "he bought about forty paintings in one swell foop," says his son Buzz. Less than a year later, they went for a bit more than $1.5 million at the Parke-Bernet auction house before a crowd of two thousand. Five thousand more who'd asked for tickets were excluded. Collectors came from around the world and for their trouble saw sale records set for many artists. Yet the sale came in well below the advance estimate; art's big-game hunters sat on their bidding paddles. It was said that Kirkeby collected the right names but not the right pictures. He'd paid $185,000 the year before for a Picasso he sold for $152,000. Three years earlier, it had sold for $45,000.

Why, someone asked, was Kirkeby selling pictures he'd bought but a year before? "For personal reasons," he muttered. But in truth, he'd sold them in a fit of pique on learning that California was going to charge a "use tax" if he brought them home—an echo of Lynn Atkinson. "He said, 'Screw them, sell 'em,' " says Buzz. He kept only a few. "They were Monopoly pieces for him," says granddaughter Nancy. "He did not care about art at all."

Then, late in 1961, the Kirkebys were victims of a robbery: $225,400 in jewelry, including a $150,000 diamond necklace, was stolen from their house while they were at a dinner party; two maids and a butler slept on the grounds, unawares. Both the master bedrooms were ransacked before the burglars found a "secret wall" that hid the jewels.

Just three months after that, Arnold Kirkeby was killed at age sixty along with ninety-four others when an American Airlines flight from New York to Los Angeles crashed on a gorgeous day after a perfect takeoff, falling nose first into Jamaica Bay and exploding. It was called the worst crash in the history of commercial aviation. The explosion was so devastating that the medical examiner said it would be inhumane to permit relatives to see the remains of the dead. Kirkeby's body was never recovered. Obituaries revealed that by then, he'd sold off most of his hotels to concentrate on interim finance, lending money short-term to businesses. Despite the brevity of his interest, the *New York Times* described him as "an ardent collector of modern art."

After American Airlines was found negligent, Carlotta Kirkeby sued on behalf of herself and her daughter, then sixteen, and four years later won more than a million dollars in a jury trial, a record in a negligence case. Because the award was for compensation, the Kirkebys did not have to pay any taxes on it. Arnold, worried about Carlotta's ability to maintain their estate, had directed in his will that she should sell it. But now that money wasn't an issue, she kept it. She also kept silent on the Mafia insinuations that continued throughout her life.

Shortly after his death, one of Kirkeby's last deals came back to haunt his widow. A producer friend had asked his permission to film exteriors for a TV situation-comedy pilot; Kirkeby read the script, thought it was ridiculous, but agreed, assuming the show "would go nowhere," his son says. But when it debuted in fall 1962, *The Beverly Hillbillies* was an instant hit. The show, about a "poor mountaineer" from the Ozark swamps named Jed Clampett who discovered oil on his land and "moved to Beverly—Hills that is," ran for nine years. No matter that the house the Beverly Hillbillies supposedly lived in was actually in Bel Air.

Eventually, Carlotta Kirkeby was forced to put her foot down and stop the exterior shooting after the house began attracting so many fans—some of whom rang the doorbell asking for Jed, Jethro, Granny, and the other Clampetts—that police had to guard it on weekends, the family had to shoo picnickers from their lawn, and Carlotta would sometimes drive down the hill to beg the hawkers on Sunset Boulevard selling maps to stars' homes to black out the Beverly Hillbillies references. "She did not find it amusing at all," says granddaughter Nancy. "It got to the point she didn't answer the door." A reproduction mansion was finally built on a studio set.

The fame that came from *Hillbillies* was probably no help when Carlotta took up the cause first championed by Lynn Atkinson and tried to have the latest tax assessment on her house—most recently valued at $1.06 million—reduced in 1965. Though the *Los Angeles Times* covered the hearing and used it as an opportunity to repeat the story of the house, it did not report on the tax appeals board's ruling.

Whatever their decision, Carlotta kept her name, her fortune, and her mansion until her death and in the interim became a regular at society parties and watering holes like Palm Beach and Rancho Santa Fe. Betsy (Mrs. Alfred) Bloomingdale would walk into the White House in 1975 and remark, "This looks just like Carlotta Kirkeby's house in Bel Air." Hers was a life—and death—Hilda Boldt Weber would have envied. When she died of cancer in 1985, Carlotta was reported to be "in her late 60s or early 70s," and was described only as "a philanthropist" and cofounder, with Burton Green's daughter Liliore, of CHIPS (Colleague Helpers in Philanthropic Service), aka the Colleagues, an elite group of socially prominent and charitable women in Los Angeles. Carlotta's children put the house on the market less than three months after her death, asking $27 million, a world record price for a private home. "I wish we'd held on to it," says Buzz Kirkeby, "but you can't imagine what it cost."

To drum up interest, they loaned it out for a series of heavily publicized benefits, including a dinner dance hosted by Elizabeth Taylor for AIDS research. It also served as a set for the Sylvester Stallone film *Over the Top* before it finally sold in fall 1986 for $13.5 million, half the asking price—still allegedly the second-highest price ever paid until then for a Los Angeles home.

The buyer, A. Jerrold Perenchio, was a Hollywood agent who evolved into a sports promoter (he'd organized a heavyweight title bout pitting Joe Frazier against Muhammad Ali in 1971, and a famous "Battle of the Sexes" tennis match between Bobby Riggs and Billie Jean King), then became a television production executive, partnering with Norman Lear and Bud Yorkin and buying and selling entertainment companies, culminating in his purchase of Univision, the largest Spanish-language television network in the United States. That deal made him a billionaire. Long before any of that, though, he'd married into the Green family. As an ambitious UCLA student who'd made a small fortune producing fraternity parties, he'd met and soon married Robbin Gardner Green, a great-niece of Burton's.[16]

In 1986, about to marry his third wife, Jerry Perenchio spent two years gutting and redoing the house, replaced the copper roof with slate, hired the legendary Henri Samuel of Jansen to redecorate, and solved the problem of *Beverly Hillbillies* fans besieging his estate with several simple, if expensive, expendients. He bought two adjoining lots (including one with a Wallace Neff house on it) for a total of $6.65 million more, installed a wall in front, a tall hedge around the entire property, and moved the front entrance from 750 Bel Air Road around the corner to Nimes Road, blocking the famous view through the gates known to TV fans everywhere. Perenchio later bought several more adjacent lots, adding to an impressive real estate collection that is said to also include at least a dozen lots and a private golf course in the gated Malibu Colony on the Pacific Ocean, and an apartment in midtown Manhattan.

Luckily, Perenchio gives lots of money to Republicans; one of his next-door neighbors in Bel Air is Nancy Reagan, who has been there since the end of her husband's presidency. Originally 666 St. Cloud, the address of her home was changed to 668, allegedly because Nancy feared the biblical association of that number with Satan in Revelation 13:18. The Reagan retirement house was found by Kitchen Cabinet spouses Betsy Bloomingdale and Marion Jorgensen and purchased just before Perenchio bought his place by a large group of Reagan friends and associates (it is now in the name of a family trust). Reagan's 6,500-square-foot house, with three bedrooms, a library, dining room, barbecue room, pantry room, two servants' rooms, a heated swimming pool, and a three-car garage, is "modest by local standards," said *Time* magazine. A mere acre large, the property is truly overshadowed by Perenchio's beast of an estate behind it. Ironically, Reagan's home is regularly pointed out by guides on tours of stars' homes, while on one recent excursion, the guide ignored Perenchio's hidden estate but claimed that a totally unrelated, though column-fronted house in Beverly Hills was the "real" Beverly Hillbillies mansion.

Holmby Hills

141 South Carolwood Drive

The Triangle has never lacked for visionaries, schemers, and dreamers willing to gamble big on bringing new heights of exclusivity and luxury to the neighborhood. One such man was Joseph W. Drown, who bought Florence Letts Quinn's home at 141 South Carolwood in Holmby Hills just after picking up the Bel Air stables and offices from Alphonzo Bell. At the very beginning of his career in hotels, Hilton had hired Drown's father, known only as L. M. Drown, to run his very first hotel, giving him a share in the business in exchange, even sleeping beside him in chairs in the hotel's office in order to free up more beds for paying customers. Joe, one of L. M. Drown's three sons, "had all his father's acumen plus an eagerness to back his judgment by taking a gamble," Hilton wrote in his autobiography. Though he could never talk L. M. into anything risky, "Young Joe Drown and I did some exciting things together."

The slender, dark-haired, blue-eyed Joe was born in Chicago, raised in Colorado Springs, Albuquerque, and San Diego, and moved to Texas when he was twelve in 1919. At nineteen, he became a summer desk clerk in a Hilton hotel at $75 a month and, he later said, "became ensnared in the hotel business." Within four years, Drown had become a vice president of the Texas chain, but when Hilton's hotels went bust in the Depression and were taken over by a rival from Galveston, Drown went with them and two years later became president of a third hotel chain with properties stretching from Virginia to New Mexico. Developing an expertise in hotel finance, he next worked for a Dallas investment bank that specialized in hotels, but also spent time in South America, says his son-in-law William Franklin Hopkins, "and made a bunch of money in oil."

In 1939, shortly after Connie let go of the lease on his very first Hilton in Dallas, he and Drown, who'd partnered on a number of hotels, both moved to Los Angeles seeking greener pastures. Hilton had bought his first California hotel two years earlier and had just opened a Hilton in Long Beach. Drown had acquired the rights to one of the vast tracts of land in Mandeville Canyon that Alphonzo Bell had sold off after he bought the Santa Monica Mountain Park Ranch. He also bought the lease for one of the largest hotels in Hollywood and, with his old boss Hilton, took a lease on another Los Angeles hotel called the Clark. Over the four years they ran it together, they made a million dollars profit. By 1941, Drown was hobnobbing with stars and the likes of Greg Bautzer, the Hollywood attorney and ladies' man whose contacts reached into the highest echelons of Hollywood as well as the murky underworld.

When war broke out at the end of that year, Drown won a contract to provide food to West Coast aircraft factories for the U.S. government, but remained in the hotel business, too. In 1943, he partnered with Hilton and others in buying the landmark Plaza Hotel in New York. He also bought the lease to the Hayward Hotel in Los Angeles and the first important hotel built on the Las Vegas Strip, El Rancho Vegas. That same year, Drown married an actress-without-credits named Elizabeth "Bettye" Avery. They'd met at the racetrack. She was nineteen, Miss Oklahoma of 1939, and a starlet wannabe. "He told me he saw a beauty in a lavender blouse, approached her, and one thing led to another," says their daughter Francisca, known as Frandy. "He had to buy her out of her movie contract." She gave up a lead role opposite Gary Cooper as Lou Gehrig in *Pride of the Yankees*.

Elizabeth had a house of her own and initially didn't move in with Drown. He lived in Sunset Towers, the apartment building Arnold Kirkeby would soon buy where Bugsy Siegel hung out at the bar, Howard Hughes kept mistresses, John Wayne kept a cow on his balcony, and rich kids like Connie Hilton's son Nicky and stars like Mae West, Greta Garbo, Errol Flynn, Jean Harlow, and Frank Sinatra came and went. When Elizabeth got pregnant, she moved in.

But a few months after she gave birth to their daughter and they were photographed for a Mother's Day newspaper photo feature, Elizabeth was in court getting divorced. She charged that her husband "hated marriage . . . didn't like having a wife, didn't want a wife, didn't need a wife." He wanted it over, too, and pronto, and offered her $28,000 a year until 1948, $18,000 annually until 1955, and after that, $8,000 a year for ten more years if she'd go and take their daughter with her. "I heard [that when] she was pregnant, [she] picked up a newspaper and read about Joe dating Ava Gardner, and I think that was the last straw," says Frandy. "He said one time in jest, but it was true, that he just hated seeing a woman in the hall more than once. Once, he and mom were at a cocktail party with a lot of women. She asked him what he was doing and he said, 'Standing here wagging my tail.' He had a black sense of humor. He loved women. There were always women around."

Unlucky in marriage, Drown did better in Bel Air, where he transformed Alphonzo Bell's Bel Air real estate sales and Bell Oil offices, a tearoom called the Sycamore, and the Bel Air community stables into the secluded Hotel Bel-Air. Like its much-larger counterpart in Beverly Hills, what became a sixty-two-room hotel set among lush gardens full of ficus and palm trees and reached via a bridge over a lake traversed by swans, was in the news even before the first guests arrived.

To avoid an injunction against the hotel opening, Drown, through two front men, his architects Burton Schutt and Denton Scott, had to promise that a third of the rooms would be reserved for members of the armed services or people deeply involved in war industries at a discount. There were also pre-opening battles with the Bel-Air Association, which fought both the construction of a proper hotel building (the tearoom became the lobby) and changes to the existing structures, such as installing bathrooms, closets, and patios. Luckily for Drown, accommodating them ensured the discreet charm and extraordinary individuality of the establishment; it's been called, quite rightly, the world's first boutique hotel. After opening that August, Drown made nice with the neighbors by letting those without their own swimming pools use the hotel's.

But Drown's troubles weren't over. In short order, he would be accused of profiting from a plot to defraud investors in the El Rancho in Vegas and of co-owning the Beverly Club, a restaurant with a secret casino, with mobster Johnny Roselli. According to the website of the Cornell University School of Hotel Administration, which gives out a prize named for Drown every year, he also had an unreported interest in the Desert Inn in Las Vegas "in the early days of development of that resort city." If so, that was another instance of his keeping bad company; when the inn's founder ran out of money before completing the hotel-casino, he was bailed out by mobster "Moe" Dalitz's Mayfield Road Gang from Cleveland, which quietly took majority control, leaving the founder in place as front man. Another regular and alleged secret shareholder was the many-tentacled Sidney Korshak. A decade later, the heirs of Chicago's Capone mob would buy into the Desert Inn, too.

In 1947, Drown paid $750,000 for the massive Santa Monica estate of Marion Davies, a fifty-room Georgian mansion on the beach with two swimming pools and several outbuildings, and converted it into a hotel. He spent $800,000—keeping three two-hundred-year-old parlors from an Irish castle and turning the estate's fabled Gold Room, paneled in 14-karat gold leaf, into a bar, and a library with paneling from the Earl of Essex's manor into a screening room. He opened his sumptuous new resort hotel and private beach club, Ocean House, in 1948, and then ostensibly retired.

Selling his interests in the Bel Air and Vegas hotels to "a syndicate of Chicago investors," he kept an option to manage the first for thirty years and buy it back in thirty months at his discretion. Among the investors who took on the Vegas hotel, renting it for ten years with an option to buy for $3 million, was Beldon Katleman, a central figure in the Friar's Club card-cheating scandal that ensnared Victor Lands of Beverly Park.[17] Also in Vegas, Drown joined a raffish group in a failed attempt to buy Bugsy Siegel's Flamingo Hotel in 1949; his partners included a notorious gambler, a lawyer who represented various mobsters, and another former partner of Hilton's.

In the meantime, Drown had bought and sold the Florence Letts Quinn house at 141 South Carolwood, his passage so brief it has been mostly forgotten. He bought the place furnished two months after his divorce, paying an unknown sum, then swept in and out of Holmby Hills in less than eighteen months, selling the place to a movie executive, and moving to a home on Stone Canyon Road next door to the Hotel Bel-Air, where he lived the rest of his life.

"I had a playhouse there," says his daughter Frandy. "I grew up in the hotel, climbing the roof, playing with the swans, hiding in the canyon, swimming in the pool." Later, when she married, Frandy and husband William Franklin Hopkins lived across the street in another house Drown owned. Even in his dotage, Drown was still a player. "He was great-looking," says

Hopkins, who recalls his father-in-law as a ladies' man, "out on the Strip with all the gals." But at the end of his life, Drown evolved into "a real loner," Hopkins says. "He'd walk down to the hotel, get drunk every night, and go home."

Drown continued to shuffle hotels like cards, sometimes in partnership with Hilton, for years. The duo also opened a firm to lease airplanes, run by Drown and Hilton's son Barron. On his own, Drown became a developer, buying and selling industrial sites and suburbs, some of them on the vast acreage in Mandeville Canyon that had once belonged to Alphonzo Bell. Drown did take back ownership of the Hotel Bel-Air and ran it for decades, but he sold the Ocean House to the state of California for $1.1 million in 1960, though he continued operating it, too, until 1965.

David Price, today a Los Angeles entrepreneur who owns and operates small airports, was hired by Drown in 1961 and ran several companies for him over the next two decades, learning business and meeting the likes of Barron Hilton and Howard Hughes in the office Drown kept in his house next door to the hotel. "He was always honorable," says Price, "a man of his word" who "had a lot of girlfriends, all good-looking and young," "did like to drink," and still had an interest in a Las Vegas casino, where Price was once sent to try and "work something out with the people operating it," he says, chuckling. "They all had Italian last names."

Just before his death in April 1982, Drown agreed to sell the Hotel Bel-Air for $22 million to Caroline Hunt, daughter of Texas billionaire H. L. Hunt. The sale finally closed after his death at seventy-five following open-heart surgery and a boardroom-and-court battle with the family of the Wall Street arbitrageur and takeover artist Ivan Boesky, who owned the Beverly Hills Hotel at the time and offered $2 million more than Hunt. Hunt won because Drown had insisted the hotel be sold to a family whose interest in it would be "as devoted and fervid" as his own. The proceeds of the hotel sale went to a charitable foundation Drown had set up years before with an initial donation of $60 million.

19

Bel Air

Casa Encantada (10644 Bellagio Road)

Marital mishaps were hardly unknown in Conrad Hilton's family. His first wife, the mother of his children, responded to his workaholism and frequent absences by having an affair, inspiring him to divorce her. She died in 1940 when she fell asleep at the El Paso Hilton while smoking a cigarette. Family chronicler Jerry Oppenheimer reported that she was "apparently inebriated." After meeting Zsa Zsa Gabor at Ciro's, a nightclub on the Sunset Strip, early in 1942—she was with ladies' man lawyer Greg Bautzer—Connie offered her $20,000 if she'd run away to Florida with him, an offer she refused, though she did allow that she might marry him. Four months later, she did.

The newlyweds moved into separate bedrooms in his first house on Bellagio Road in Bel Air, quickly started fighting over money, and soon grew hopelessly estranged. Zsa Zsa ended up in a psychiatric ward, possibly at Connie's instigation, but got her revenge, she later claimed, when she started having sex with her tall, handsome, brown-haired stepson Nicky. Later, she'd say that Conrad raped her, inadvertently siring a daughter. Connie denied paternity and late in 1944, they separated after their Bel Air house burned down and was rebuilt. At their divorce trial, Zsa Zsa testified that he'd moved back in a few months earlier, but when she asked him to fire his butler, who'd been fresh to her, he refused. "When the house was rebuilt, he returned with the butler," she said. "I did not go back." She left with a mere

$300,000, most of it paid out slowly over ten years, and stock in a couple of hotels.

Hilton was still in that Bel Air house late in 1949 when his twenty-three-year-old namesake Nicky started dating the seventeen-year-old child star grown up, Elizabeth Taylor, who'd just finished *A Place in the Sun* with Montgomery Clift. Nicky was Taylor's third beau in eighteen months. By February 1950 they were engaged. Hedda Hopper declared the couple a studio put-up job; the engagement was encouraged if not arranged to hype ticket sales of Taylor's latest film, *Father of the Bride*. Connie, who'd become nationally known a few months earlier when he bought the lease on New York's Waldorf-Astoria Hotel for $3 million, was so excited by the news that he gave gossip columnists a wedding date before Taylor could tell her best friends. Connie naively asked the reporters to keep it a secret; he was not yet as sophisticated as his newest hotel.

Taylor began taking lessons in Catholicism because Connie wanted a church wedding. As they made their way across America on a trousseau-buying trip with Taylor's doting mother in tow, the Hiltons grew even more famous. Connie gave Elizabeth shares in the Waldorf as a prewedding present. It was a publicity coup. But unfortunately, the *coup de foudre* at the center of it all proved to be a passing fancy.

Taylor and Hilton married before seven hundred guests in an MGM-engineered ceremony in May 1950; a troop of policemen held the huge crowd of gawkers at bay. A reception followed at the Bel-Air Country Club. It was said that Nicky planned to go to work for Joe Drown at the Hotel Bel-Air after a European honeymoon. But when they got back to New York late that summer, all was not well. The arguments had begun en route to Europe on the *Queen Mary*. Nicky had infuriated Elizabeth with his drinking and gambling. Nicky was said to have physically attacked her, tossing chips in her face, maybe even punching her to the ground. Young Hilton wasn't used to playing second fiddle to a film star. Back in Los Angeles, they borrowed Barron Hilton's home; Nicky's brother and his wife were expecting their third child and had moved to a new place in Brentwood. Nicky was supposedly renovating his apartment.

In December, a month after Nicky's father bought Hilda Boldt Weber's estate, Taylor's studio announced that she'd moved out on Nicky and was in seclusion at her parents' home. "Elizabeth and Nicky are both spoiled and should have been spanked years ago," Hedda Hopper declared. A studio spokesman insisted they hadn't separated, but right after Nicky returned from a business trip with Connie, Taylor announced plans to file for divorce, which she did a mere ten days later, "seven months, seven days and 17 hours after the ceremony," as Hopper put it.

Elizabeth charged Nicky with cruel and inhuman treatment and extreme mental cruelty. Early in 1951, she won her case after testifying that he'd stayed up until all hours, ignored her, cursed at her, and refused to attend film industry functions. Taylor waived alimony, but was allowed to keep her wedding presents. She also won permission to return to her maiden name and was soon rumored to be dating the director of her next film. The Hiltons have been world famous ever since.

Nicky briefly moved in with his father at Casa Encantada, but life wasn't enchanted for him; he spent the next few years attracting publicity, most of it bad, as he ran through an endless parade of willing starlets, strippers, beauty queens, and just plain females—most anonymous, but some as well known as Natalie Wood and Joan Collins, and, according to papers filed in their divorce suit, the actor John Wayne's wife Esperanza. Nicky also abused liquor and sleeping pills and got into fights in Sunset Strip nightclubs; in one, Joe Drown allegedly left him with broken bones. In 1954, Nicky ended up in jail after punching and kicking policemen summoned to his latest apartment by neighbors fed up with his drunken screaming and fighting. "I can buy and sell the lot of you," the twenty-seven-year-old fumed at cops who dragged him off to jail, where he gave his occupation as "loafer" and offered a sergeant $1,000 "if you'll cool off this beef and let me go." He ended up in rehab at the Mayo Clinic. The cure didn't take.

In his book *House of Hilton,* Jerry Oppenheimer paints Connie and Nicky as Oedipal competitors, with Connie always on top. One night at dinner at Casa Encantada, Connie, Nicky, and Mamie Van Doren, the young man's latest date, ate off solid gold plates served by countless retainers while Connie—whose hotel empire was by then expanding internationally—smoked Cuban cigars, belched and farted audibly, and ignored the buxom starlet to berate Nicky, demanding that he return to live in Casa Encantada's pool house.

In 1958, Nicky married Trish McClintock, the teenage daughter of a Tulsa, Oklahoma, oilman shortly after a drunken tussle that left brother Barron with a fractured leg. Settling down in Beverly Hills, Nicky produced two sons, tried to toe the line, and at age thirty-nine in 1965 accepted his father's offer (or more properly, reward) of Barron's seat on Hilton International's board and later, a mostly ceremonial job atop its executive committee. He and Trish moved to an 11,000-square-foot house on two acres on Delfern Drive in Holmby Hills, taking a place among the mansion owners of the Triangle. Barron, two years Nicky's junior and by then the father of eight (including Paris Hilton's father and Jeff Hyland's partner, Rick Hilton), got a new job too, but one with considerably more responsibility: his father's former post as president of the domestic Hilton Hotels. Connie remained chairman of the board, but gave up active management.

Briefly, it seemed that the playboy Nicky might find a life and fade from the public eye. But soon enough, he returned to his crash course with fate. A lifelong contest with Barron for their father's attention came to a head late in 1966 when Barron engineered a deal to sell the international hotel division to TWA in exchange for shares in the airline. Nicky was not only out of a job, he felt betrayed by both father and brother and responded to Barron's play by descending again into a haze of pills and drink. He and Trish had separated once before; now, she filed for divorce a second time. During a brief reconciliation, Nicky attempted suicide and, his wife told Oppenheimer, "went off the deep end."

Summoning Connie, Trish tried to engage him in saving his son. Instead of paying attention, the eighty-year-old fished for compliments on a new wig he'd bought to hide his balding pate, insisting it was his real hair. "Conrad was brilliant in business, but he had a hard time with everyday life and relationships," says a family member. "He was very Germanic. That was his upbringing. He couldn't relate. He wasn't cold but that made him look cold."

Furious at his brother (whose deal with TWA turned out to be the worst of his career—the hotels flourished; the airline did not) and depressed over his inability to satisfy his father, Nicky went into a sharp decline. In a desperate attempt to break his downward cycle and convince him to get help, Trish sold the Holmby Hills mansion and left yet again. Nicky moved into a split-level in Coldwater Canyon above Beverly Hills, where he died four and a half months later early in 1969, at age forty-two. A thousand people—Zsa Zsa Gabor and Dean Martin among them—attended his memorial service.

The official cause of death was heart attack, but Trish suspected that was concocted by Connie to cover up an overdose. Another relative insists that the real cause of Nick's death was the sale of the international division: "It killed him. He couldn't get over it." Barron would always deny that he had anything to do with it. "But I think he did," the relative says. Barron Hilton's granddaughters Paris and Nicky are hardly the first Hiltons to become notorious in La-La Land. They are merely upholding a family tradition.

20

Holmby Hills

141 South Carolwood Drive

Enter Marilyn Monroe. Joe Drown sold 141 Carolwood to Joe Schenck, who knew the mob as well as anyone in Los Angeles. Schenck and his younger brother Nick were Russian émigrés in America. As boys, they'd sold newspapers on the street, then worked in and earned enough money to buy their own pharmacies in New York. At age twenty, though, Joe wandered into a Bowery vaudeville theater and befriended a local entertainer, Irving Berlin: show business! He and Nick sold the drugstores and became theater owners, first vaudeville, then movie. They joined forces with Marcus Loew, expanding into talent management, real estate, nickelodeon, and finally, movie production during World War I. The extroverted Joe had a knack for production; Nick specialized in "inside" matters like administration and film distribution. When Loew acquired a studio in 1919, Nick joined him and Joe set out on his own.

The Schencks were gamblers and Joe bet on talent—he had a lucky hand. As an independent producer for Paramount and First National, he discovered or worked with Buster Keaton, Fatty Arbuckle, John Barrymore, Mary Pickford and Douglas Fairbanks, Corinne Griffith, and Constance and Norma Talmadge, the last of whom he married in 1916. They moved to Los Angeles the next year, and secretly separated in 1927. (They finally divorced in 1934, blaming Schenck's devotion to business, and remained friends. Talmadge married George Jessel; Schenck was briefly involved with Merle Oberon but never remarried.)

While younger brother Nick stayed with Loew and became president of the parent company that owned MGM, Joe Schenck was the first president of Chaplin, Pickford, and Fairbanks's United Artists, then formed Twentieth Century with Darryl F. Zanuck (financed by Nick and Louis B. Mayer) and subsequently merged it with Fox studios. He was a father of today's Hollywood film industry.

In 1921, Joe lost a fortune when Fatty Arbuckle was accused of raping and killing that dancer at a wild party; though Arbuckle was never convicted, his remaining Schenck-produced films were banned, and even after the ban was lifted, nobody wanted to see them. But the brothers had already made a fortune—$20 million by some accounts—with another million coming in annually.

The mob was around, of course. At Twentieth Century Fox, Johnny Roselli was Schenck's bookie and Joe was in charge when the mob-run union for backstage workers started demanding payoffs from the studios. Everyone paid protection money, $550,000 in all, but only Schenck was indicted—the designated Hollywood scapegoat. In court, his extravagance, bad manners with help, and bad luck at cards all came out. He paid big bills for his girlfriends and entertained lavishly. He'd loaned his mansion to a gambler who used it as a casino. Convicted of tax fraud and facing a $250,000 tax bill, three years in jail, and a $20,000 fine as well as a perjury indictment, Schenck cut a deal. The mob-connected union bosses got years in jail—but after Sidney Korshack intervened, the scandal didn't reach Chicago. Schenck pleaded guilty to one count of perjury and was sentenced to a year and a day in federal prison.

Schenck had resigned as chairman of Twentieth Century Fox when he was convicted, but since the whole industry knew he'd taken the rap, he returned to the studio as head of production following his parole in 1942 after four months in prison; he stayed at Fox for a decade as a producer. After he completed three years' probation, he was given a presidential pardon by Harry Truman, restoring his citizenship rights; that was kept secret for more than a year.

It was four years into his return engagement at Fox that Schenck bought 141 South Carolwood from Joe Drown. He furnished it in a manner described as spare—perhaps because he considered the stars, starlets, and Hollywood players he filled the place with sufficient decoration.

Schenck would not be the last man to live like a pasha at 141 South Carolwood. But he set a high standard. Though no one alive can say for certain, it seems reasonably clear that he began an affair with a neophyte starlet named Marilyn Monroe there. According to legend, she spotted him leaving the studio in his limousine, flashed him a flirty smile, got his card and a dinner invitation in return, and quickly became a regular Carolwood visitor. What went on between the aging Hollywood lion—by now he was sixty-eight—and the young blond actress, who'd either just been or was about to be dropped as a contract player at Fox after playing bit parts in only three films, has been a subject of speculation and argument ever since. When asked on the record if she'd been intimate with Schenck, Monroe denied it, but others say that privately, she admitted otherwise.

Monroe's countless biographers have chimed in on her time chez Schenck, "a weathered bear of a man, aging but active, a *bon viveur* who rightly saw himself as one of Hollywood's grand old men," according to Anthony Summers. "Joe was not a handsome man," wrote Fred Lawrence Guiles. "What impressed her most was his sturdy physique; he had the slightly hunched look of a beefy wrestler. With a perpetual squint and an upside-down smile—from biting down on so many cigars—he had begun to resemble an aging Chinese warlord." According to Guiles, Schenck was by then semiretired, devoting most of his time to friends, whiskey, and cigars.

A collector of women and a generous host, Schenck invited Monroe to Carolwood for Sunday brunches, large dinners, screenings, and late night, high-stakes card games "attended by top studio executives, producers and directors," wrote Barbara Leaming. In exchange for access to "Uncle Joe's" friends, Leaming continued, "the women were expected to make themselves available" and "he was happy to pass her around." But eventually "Schenck took a special liking to her." She became, in Darryl Zanuck's phrase, "Schenck's girl," which, wrote Guiles, was the kiss of death at Fox: "As a consequence, Zanuck despised her." Delivered to Carolwood in Schenck's limousine, Marilyn became a regular presence behind his chair at card games and later, after her contract with Fox ended, "even briefly moved into the guest cottage in order to be nearby when he wanted her at night."

Summers went into detail, explaining that such proximity was necessary because at age seventy in those pre-Viagra days, Schenck's desire rose unexpectedly and often only briefly. According to biographer Jane Ellen Wayne, Schenck could achieve an erection only if his doctor gave him an injection, so at first Monroe would merely undress and let him fondle her. Later, though, Wayne says, "it was an exchange of champagne dinners and fellatio," quoting Monroe's comment to an unidentified friend: "Sometimes it took hours. I was relieved when he fell asleep."

Sex aside, Schenck was more personal mentor than professional rabbi for Monroe—he did nothing for her in her first sojourn at Fox—but there's no doubt that he played a small but vital role in turning Monroe's stalled career around after that. Having taken her into Carolwood late in the summer of 1947 when her contract ran out and Fox decided to drop her, the next year Schenck announced it was time she started making movies again and prevailed upon Harry Cohn, a fellow veteran from the silent film days, to sign her up at Columbia Pictures, which would also let her go. Finally, in 1949, she won attention with a walk-on role in a picture called *Love Happy* at her third studio, United Artists. She followed that with small, high-impact parts in *The Asphalt Jungle* and *All About Eve,* which won her a second chance at Fox. She remained close to Schenck throughout, moving in and out of his guesthouse.

In 1951, Leaming wrote, Schenck proposed to her and promised her his fortune after he learned she was sleeping with a married director, Elia Kazan. Though she turned him down, he then engineered an encounter at a luncheon with Fox president Spyros Skouras—Darryl Zanuck's in-house rival—to ensure that her contract, which was about to expire, would be renewed. Though Wayne writes that she then moved into a hotel and left her post as Schenck's mistress to play the same role for Skouras in 1953, the year of her breakout performances in *Niagara* and *Gentlemen Prefer Blondes,* she would still be photographed at Schenck's home.

Their bond was a strong one. Years later, she would tell the writer W. J. Weatherby about listening to Schenck's stories: "He was full of wisdom like some great explorer," she said. "I also liked to look at his face. It was as much the face of a town as of a man. The whole history of Hollywood was in it." Norman Mailer took this up when he wrote his meditation on Monroe.

"The likelihood is that Schenck and Monroe had, or at least also had, some sort of genuine friendship; if there was sex, it was not necessarily the first of the qualities he found in her. We are not going to know," Mailer wrote.

At age seventy-one, Joseph Schenck left Fox to manage its movie theater chains and the investments he'd made over many years in real estate, racetracks, and a Mexican casino. He also served as a bank director until he retired in 1957 after a stroke from which he never recovered. He'd sold Carolwood a year earlier, moved to the Beverly Hilton Hotel's penthouse, previously occupied by Greg Bautzer, and put all his furniture up for auction. Later, after a heart attack, he bought a house in the flats where he died in 1961 at eighty-three, surrounded only by his household staff. Sam Goldwyn, Mervyn LeRoy, David O. Selznick, Harold Lloyd, Irving Berlin, and Buster Keaton were all at his funeral. He left most of his $3.5 million estate to his brother. The gossip columnist Louella Parsons was one of several recipients of $10,000 bequests. There is no mention of Marilyn Monroe in press reports on his will.

Schenck had sold his estate at 141 South Carolwood several years earlier to William Myron Keck, the founder and president of Superior Oil, in February 1956. In a curious twist of fate, a half dozen years before that, Keck's second son Howard had married the ex-wife of Joseph Drown, who'd sold Carolwood to Schenck. Keck added some notable decorating touches to the house. Apart from installing an indoor swimming pool and a bowling green on the expansive lawns, he adapted Schenck's paneled screening room so it doubled as a bomb shelter, and also installed gold sink fixtures in the shape of oil derricks in a marble-walled guest bathroom.

The son of an oil field worker and an autodidact, William Keck, known as W. M. to friends and Killer Keck to foes, quit his first job selling sandwiches on the Baltimore and Ohio railroad at age twenty and moved from his native Pennsylvania to Southern California after catching a glimpse of his first gusher. He worked as a roustabout, tool dresser, driller, and wildcatter in the oil fields, learning "the business literally from the ground up," according to his official biography, and in 1921, formed Superior Oil as an independent drilling contractor, sometimes taking oil leases in lieu of payment. Within two years, Keck and Superior were drilling wells of their own and striking oil in, among other places, the Santa Fe Springs field that made Alphonzo Bell rich. By 1924, Keck was one of the nation's leading independent oilmen with sixty-six producing wells scattered across the Southland.

Keck resigned as chairman of Superior in 1962, handing the reins to his son Howard, a race car and thoroughbred owner. W. M. Keck died two years later at his Holmby Hills estate after a brief illness. When his will was filed a few days later, it emerged that his fortune, valued at $180 million, was the largest ever recorded in California, beating that of William Randolph Hearst by a factor of three. Nearly $80 million was placed in trust for a foundation he'd started dedicated to encouraging science and technological research, which also received title to the Carolwood house. Additional trusts benefited four colleges and universities and one church. His children, correctly assumed to be independently wealthy, got nothing. Howard Keck was clearly doing all right. He bought the film director Howard Hawks's ranch deep in the canyons of Bel Air, 105 acres on Moraga Drive.

Despite their good fortune, Keck's heirs were famously unhappy. "They all hated each other," says a relation by marriage. William Keck Jr. and his younger brother Howard had shared control of the family's Superior stock in their father's will, but were frequently at odds; in echoes of the Hilton family, their father had set up a rivalry between them. Howard wouldn't fly in the same corporate jet as his brother, so even when they were on matching itineraries, each had his own Gulfstream. In 1981, William Jr. was forced to leave the board under a mandatory retirement rule; he died within a year.

In 1983, Superior became a takeover target after another of Keck's children, Willametta Keck Day, upset by Howard's ways, began an effort to convince fellow shareholders to stage a takeover. Her animosity, too, was said to source back to childhood; family legend had it that Howard had killed young Willametta's pet ostrich by forcing an orange down its neck. After a year of family infighting—Willametta, who'd set the feud in motion, then called its plot twists unbelievable—Mobil bought Superior for $5.7 billion, about a quarter of which went to the feuding Kecks.

And still, the fussing wasn't finished; the constant battles earned the Kecks repeated comparisons to the Ewing family of the television soap opera *Dallas*. After years of litigation, the Kecks made their last public splash at the end of the 1980s, when Howard and his wife Libby, Joe Drown's ex, split up. While they were getting divorced, Libby charged her butler with stealing a painting from her latest French chateau-style home on Bellagio Road in Bel Air and replacing it with a high-quality photograph, and then, after he was exonerated, sued him for $31 million for theft, slander, invasion of privacy, and infliction of emotional distress. In an article on the imbroglio, the *Los Angeles Times* said it combined "betrayal, theft, family jealousies, illegitimacy and, behind it all, pure greed" and reported that the family strife had already cost $12 million in legal fees.

The butler's trial brought many unsavory and embarrassing details (including Libby Keck's monthly expenditures of $5,000 for groceries, $3,300 for dinners, $1,200 for lunches, $10,000 for dinner parties, and $25,000 for clothes and accessories and an allegation that Howard Jr. was not his father's biological son) out of the shadows. It is perhaps no surprise that following their divorce and a forced auction of their belongings in 1991, the litigious Kecks retreated behind the screen of their wealth and confidentiality agreements.

Howard Keck died in 1996 and an obituary said that a family spokesman wouldn't even name survivors. The most prominent Keck in the Triangle today is Willametta's son, money manager Robert Day, who is also the head of the Keck Foundation. Day is barely known outside his social circle and likely prefers it that way.

Beverly Hills

9481 Sunset Boulevard

Now, as their founders dreamed, Beverly Hills and the rest of the Triangle had become elite playgrounds for California's wealthiest players. And no one played harder than the Green girls, Dolly, Burtie, and Liliore. The princesses of the royal court of Beverly Hills, by the mid-1920s, they'd become the most celebrated sister act in La-La Land.

The eldest, Dolly, who was petite and freckled and wore her dark hair in a stiff helmet that focused attention on her huge eyes and upturned nose, had started making social noise as a Marlborough schoolgirl in 1920. After graduating, she went east to the Bennett School in Millbrook, New York, and by 1925, was including younger sisters Liliore and Burtie in her revels. Dolly was welcome everywhere from Pasadena to Palm Beach, Florida.

The girls followed a well-trod path for the wealthy. As Liliore and Burtie tested the waters as young hostesses in their own right, Dolly joined the Spinsters, a group of socially prominent unmarried young women, and began dabbling in amateur theatrics and fashion. Soon, all three sisters would embark on a disastrous serious of multiple marriages. Between 1928 and 1938, Dolly and Liliore would both marry twice, and Burtie would marry Minnewa Bell's ex-husband Miles Gray.

One of the girls also had a notable extramarital adventure. During her short-lived second marriage, Dolly started an affair that would continue for years, despite the fact that her lover was also a devoted husband and family man. Neil McCarthy, a lawyer for Cecil B. DeMille, Louis B. Mayer, A. P. Giannini and his new Bank of America, and Howard Hughes, hung on the same social rung as the Greens, and Dolly's and Neil's paths started crossing in the late 1930s in places like the Santa Anita racetrack, the Diamond Horseshoe Ball at the Mocambo nightclub, dinners at McCarthy's client Mayer's home, and even at Neil and Marguerite McCarthy's mansion where Dolly was a guest at dinner parties.

Dolly soon divorced her second husband; she was no shrinking violet, and not even the start of World War II could dim her light. In 1942, Neil McCarthy set up a blood bank, staffed by the Hospital and Recreation Corps of the Red Cross, better known as the Gray Ladies for the gray dresses and veils they wore as uniforms. Among the most devoted volunteers at the unfashionable location on South Western Avenue was none other than Dolly, now calling herself Mrs. Green Walker (using her second husband's name), who regularly worked in the administration office. Good works and bad marriages would henceforth be constants in the Green sisters' lives.

The end of the forties spelled the end of many marriages in the Greens' charmed circle. Liliore married a third time, but thirty-five days later, her husband, only forty-five, died while taking a steam bath. Burtie divorced Miles Gray and followed him up with a yearlong marriage to a New York doctor. Somewhere along the way, McCarthy moved out of his family home in Hancock Park. How and when Dolly and Neil became more than friends is unrecorded: McCarthy's relatives aren't sure, and Dolly's aren't talking. Hedda Hopper revealed Dolly's ongoing indiscretion for the first and only time in a 1949 gossip column. Hopper called her "Neil McCarthy's friend" in an item about a dinner party she'd had at her latest home, on Mountain Drive in Beverly Hills, for the American ambassador to Britain attended by McCarthy's client Mayer, Jack Warner, and Douglas Fairbanks. Never again would they be so closely associated—unsurprising considering how much power each wielded separately—though clever columnists would take to listing their names together, sometimes discreetly separated by others but still in the same paragraph, for the next several years.

Dolly's and Neil's intimates knew what was going on. "She wanted to marry him," says Patricia Brown, executive director of Burtie's Burton G. Bettingen Foundation, "but he wouldn't"—most likely because he couldn't bring himself to divorce Margeurite. Then, in 1949, Dolly bought another mansion—Frank and Ida Botiller's pile at 9481 Sunset. "She's bought the

French chateau," wrote Hopper. "The place cost a million, but Dolly picked it up for $50,000."

She didn't keep it long. Fourteen days later, in a transaction no one wrote anything about, Neil McCarthy, who'd handled the purchase for her, owned it. Dolly told McCarthy's grandson Michael Gless that she got a bad case of buyer's remorse on discovering she could hear traffic on Sunset in the master bedroom, and McCarthy bought it from her. His daughter Rosemary Bullis adds that Dolly made no money: "She sold it to my father for $50,000." Neil's new house was just a block from Dolly's.

Neil Steere McCarthy was a grandchild of Irish immigrants who'd come to America in the 1850s. A son of a Phoenix blacksmith, Neil was an equestrian from the age of four and a football player in high school. He graduated at sixteen and went to the University of Michigan. In 1908, at the age of twenty, Neil worked his way to London on a freighter and served there as an assistant coach for the U.S. Olympic track team at the fourth modern Olympic Games. Back in America, McCarthy completed a law degree, moved to L.A., where he got a job in a law office, and then came back east to marry a woman he'd met in college, Marguerite Mead Gilbert, a descendant of a Mayflower family from Binghamton, New York. Her mother objected to a union so far beneath her. Her father, a judge, took her to breakfast and put $50 in her purse but wouldn't walk her down the aisle.

They produced four children in seven years. Before the first came, Neil made partner at his law firm. A disciplined teetotaler, he would wake at 4 a.m. He would later be remembered for eating dinner each night promptly at 6 p.m. at the Los Angeles Country Club. At the time, though, Neil and Marguerite sometimes subsisted on a can of beans, which they'd split for dinner.

Family legend has it that Neil got involved in the film industry by accident when he picked up the phone one day, answered a caller's legal question, and was hired as general counsel for the Jesse L. Lasky Feature Play Company, the partnership of the moving picture pioneers Lasky, Cecil B. DeMille, and Samuel Goldwyn. In 1916, it merged with Adolph Zukor's Famous Players and several other film and distribution companies and became Paramount Pictures.

McCarthy's movie star clients eventually included Rudolph Valentino, Spencer Tracy, Katharine Hepburn, Edward G. Robinson, Ethel Barrymore, Fred Astaire, Gene Kelly, and Cary Grant. He was a founder of the Brown

Derby restaurant, helped form the Screen Actors Guild, and played a role in bringing the Olympics to Los Angeles in 1932. Within a decade of his arrival in L.A., McCarthy was known throughout the film industry—and eventually came to represent Louis B. Mayer and MGM as well. But he wasn't just a mouthpiece; McCarthy was an equal. He, Lasky, and DeMille all served together on the board of the Commercial National Bank of Los Angeles; he was on the board of the Hollywood-California Hotel with silent film director Fred Niblo and several of William Randolph Hearst's executives, and also had an equity stake in the movies. DeMille once famously said they had a bond that "only death could break." In fact, it survived them both; late in his career, McCarthy made a deal that gave him a cut of the royalties from two of DeMille's last pictures, the 1949 production of *Samson and Delilah* and *The Greatest Show on Earth* from 1952; seventy-five years later, his seventeen grandchildren still share the fruits of that arrangement.

McCarthy was another exception to the rule that kept movies and society apart in the early days of Los Angeles. In truth, the two mixed freely everywhere but Bel Air, especially in the bedroom and in sporty pastimes, which is where the then still happily married McCarthy began crossing social boundaries. He and Lasky were among Jake Danziger and Silsby Spalding's partners in building the Beverly Hills Speedway. McCarthy also had a lifelong involvement with racehorses and would counsel his client Mayer when he, too, decided to enter racing, helping Mayer build a $5 million equine portfolio that made him the winningest racehorse owner in America by 1945.

McCarthy built a home on two lots on South Muirfield Road in fashionable Hancock Park in 1924. With more than seven thousand square feet and ten bedrooms, it was big enough for his family of six. Neil wanted a Spanish house but Marguerite insisted on an East Coast colonial with six columns out front; she consented to green shutters decorated with shamrock cutouts to honor McCarthy's heritage.[18] Marguerite designed the understated interiors of the mansion, which also boasted two full kitchens and a huge yard with a long, unheated swimming pool that McCarthy would empty of water in winter and use to practice polo, setting up a wooden horse in the deep end, hitting the ball against the shallow end, and watching it roll back.

Their parties were renowned and guests included stars as well as clients. The McCarthys were close enough to Joan Crawford that they would let her be secretly married in their home in 1942. Early in her career, Crawford had appeared at Muirfield Road when McCarthy wasn't home. Realizing her husband's secretary had confused his appointments, Marguerite invited Crawford to sit by the pool; she donned a white satin swimsuit and settled in. "I didn't know what to do, so I sat with her all day," Marguerite would tell her granddaughter. Finally, a chauffeur came to pick Crawford up. Or so it seemed. "I don't have a chauffeur," Crawford whispered. "That's my father."

"That's all right," Marguerite answered. "I don't have a chauffeur, either."

Marguerite McCarthy was a down-to-earth woman, an accomplished cook and hostess, and in the 1940s would publish *The Cook Is in the Parlor,* a guide to doing both at once; her family believes she invented the recipe for Chex party mix. But the McCarthys were also part of the Hollywood high life. In 1935, Judy Garland auditioned for MGM in McCarthy's parlor. About a decade later, he insisted that his neighbor the jazz singer Nat "King" Cole attend a party, waving off Cole's fears that a black performer wouldn't fit in with their swell white friends. At least part of their lavish lifestyle was paid for by Neil's most famous client, one he would keep for less than two decades but who would nonetheless ensure that he was remembered long after both of them were dead.

Howard Hughes arrived in L.A. in 1925 with his inherited fortune and a first wife, Ella; one of his first moves was to hire McCarthy as his lawyer as he tried to break into the movie business. Initially Hughes and Ella lived at the Ambassador Hotel, but two years later, after his first attempts at film production proved profitable, Hughes leased and later bought a house a few blocks from McCarthy on South Muirfield Road, backing up onto the Wilshire Country Club, where Hughes played golf.

McCarthy established offices for Hughes at Hollywood and Vine and found an accountant, Noah Dietrich, who'd previously worked for Edward Doheny in New York, Harry Chandler in the San Fernando Valley, and the Jansses in Westwood; he would become Hughes's closest aide and within a year would warn McCarthy that Hughes's young marriage was being threatened by proximity to Hollywood actresses. In 1927, McCarthy sent a letter to Hughes urging, "Try to be a good boy." But by fall 1928, Ella had moved home to Houston and started divorce proceedings.

In 1927, McCarthy sent Hughes a bill that gave a snapshot of the sort of work he was doing. In fall 1926, Hughes had hired Lewis Milestone, a Russian director who'd just declared bankruptcy to escape a contract with Warner Brothers, to direct *Two Arabian Nights,* a film that would win him an Academy Award—and make big profits. For arranging that, McCarthy billed Hughes $12,500 (the equivalent of $155,000 today). The bill also covered negotiations for actors like Fay Wray and Rod La Rocque (McCarthy charged $500 for each), the hiring of Noah Dietrich ($250), and the creation of the Caddo Company, a local subsidiary of Hughes's Texas drill bit company (another $250). Right from the beginning, Hughes questioned his legal fees. McCarthy pushed back and usually won. But he also believed in his new client—a faith Hughes initially justified. In 1930, Hughes released *Hell's Angels,* a film with Jean Harlow he'd codirected over three years. It was about his favorite avocation, flying—he would shortly become an aircraft manufacturer, too—and even though he was a first-time director, it proved to be a hit; suddenly he was more than just the new rich kid in town, though the cynical scenarist Ben Hecht would still dismiss him as "the sucker with money."

McCarthy handled more than movie deals for Hughes. Early in 1931, he suggested that Hughes and his latest girlfriend, Billie Dove, move to Nevada so the actress could get a quickie divorce from her jealous husband, a director. Introduced by Marion Davies, the actress and the heir had had an on-and-off affair interrupted by his dalliance with Carole Lombard and hers with George Raft. They spent two weeks living incognito in a Nevada shack before McCarthy decided the ploy wouldn't qualify her as a resident of Nevada after all. Hughes stuck with his lawyer nonetheless and back in Hollywood, McCarthy got Dove her divorce, with Hughes paying the $20,000 tab; one Hughes biographer, Charles Higham, has alleged that Hughes also bought off Dove's husband, negotiating him down from the half million he wanted for leaving quietly to $325,000 in cash. According to Higham, McCarthy packed the money in a suitcase and made the payoff personally. Despite the price he paid, Hughes proved unable to commit and never closed the deal with Dove.

As his public profile (and private catting around) increased, Hughes became a target for con men and extortionists like the girl who threatened to kill herself on his doorstep if he didn't see her. He gave her McCarthy's address. McCarthy had become a trusted advisor in all aspects of Hughes's famously complicated life; so it was galling to McCarthy, in 1932, when Hughes decided to stop making movies and demanded a 50 percent reduction in McCarthy's retainer. At first, he agreed to a 25 percent cut, but when Hughes kept pressing to pay less, he reversed course, demanding his full retainer. "I do not know intimately your financial condition," he concluded in a long letter bursting with hurt feelings. "I presume that there is enough money coming in to pay me. . . . As I said to you before, Howard, and as I think you know, I would work for you for nothing if you did not have the money to pay me, but there is no justification at present for my agreeing to take less." His argument apparently won the day, for Hughes's file on the matter ended with that exchange. McCarthy's children cherished stories of how he stood up to Hughes, who called them "the brats who answer the phone."

Once, Hughes called at 3 a.m., demanding McCarthy come to his house immediately. "I'll see you at 9 a.m.," McCarthy responded, "and I'll return your retainer." Next morning, says great-granddaughter Bridget Gless, "Howard Hughes was in Neil's office, hat in hand."

McCarthy's next big job for Hughes came right after he traded the *Hilda*—the yacht he'd bought from Hilda Boldt Weber—for a new one, the *Rover*, the fifth biggest in the world. Another Hughes biographer tells the story of how Hughes picked up a Pasadena society girl named Nancy Belle Bayly and took her on board, then promised her a twenty-first birthday she'd never forget. Their night began with drinks at Trader Vic's and continued with dinner and dancing at the Cocoanut Grove, a nightclub in the Ambassador Hotel favored by movie people, where they were joined by Pat DiCicco, a talent agent who doubled as a gangster, bootlegger, and pimp and was known as Charles "Lucky" Luciano's man in Hollywood. Leaving DiCicco, the couple was driving back to the *Rover* when Hughes's car struck and killed someone. As rubberneckers watched, Hughes put the girl on a trolley car and sent her to his house with orders to wait for him. Police arrived and Hughes refused to speak until his lawyer came, so he was checked for sobriety and injuries and taken to jail, where he was booked on a charge of negligent homicide based on eyewitness accounts. He identified himself as a manufacturer and gave his address as Houston. After McCarthy arrived, Hughes finally submitted to an interview and was sprung the next morning.

Hughes had refused to give the police Bayly's name, but DiCicco told reporters who she was, and along with Hughes, she appeared at an inquest a few days later, corroborating his testimony that he'd been driving responsibly and the crash was unavoidable. After an interview with McCarthy, an eyewitness changed his account of what had happened, retracting his claim that the victim was in a safety zone and Hughes was driving erratically, saying instead that the victim stepped right in front of Hughes's car. A six-man jury exonerated Hughes in eighteen minutes.

While continuing to work for Hughes—even becoming his hatchet man in corporate intrigues in Texas—McCarthy's own social star continued to rise, particularly after one of his daughters married into one of California's oldest families, the Amestoys, who'd owned the rancho that became Encino. His stature was reflected in his latest crop of clients, who included the likes of Helen Vanderbilt, aka Mrs. Cornelius Vanderbilt Jr., and Betsey Cushing Roosevelt, aka Mrs. James Roosevelt, wife of the eldest son of the president; both were seeking divorces. The start of the war did nothing to dim the McCarthys' social life, and parties continued at the Muirfield Road house, where showers heralded the births of grandchildren and two Great Danes, Posey and Tagus (the McCarthys also bred dogs), kept vigil by the fireplace.

Howard Hughes kept up his demands on his lawyer. By 1940, having set several world air-speed records flying his own experimental planes, Hughes had returned to moviemaking, and McCarthy was forced to handle matters when his most important client interfered so much on the set of his come-back film, *The Outlaw,* that the director Howard Hawks left and Hughes replaced him. Though the conventional wisdom is that Hawks quit, Mc-Carthy denied it to Dietrich in Houston. "Hawks was displaced because he was not doing this picture as instructed," he wrote. "It was he who refused to follow economical moves which I suggested at the very inception."

The McCarthys and Hughes were no longer neighbors; in a dispute over whether he should pay California resident taxes, Hughes had sold his house on Muirfield Road (where he'd lately shacked up with Katharine Hepburn) and moved into a rental adjoining the Bel-Air Country Club. But Hughes still had great faith in McCarthy, as he made plain when he put him in charge of a project then known as the Flying Boat, later better known as the Spruce Goose. In summer 1942, after German U-boats had sunk a huge number of American supply boats, the shipbuilder Henry Kaiser caused a sensation when he proposed to build a fleet of huge flying transport planes to safely move troops and supplies to Europe. But Kaiser had no aeronautical engineers, so when he heard that Hughes did, he approached the younger man to design planes he would produce. Captivated by Kaiser's energy and reputation, Hughes agreed to partner up, and they announced their intention to build five hundred flying ships. Hughes put McCarthy in charge.

The effort to build the plane hit any number of snags, not least Hughes's desire to finish *The Outlaw*. Hughes was also distracted by another plane, the D-2 fighter-bomber, which he'd begun developing before Pearl Harbor. The U.S. Air Force had decided against investing in it—the D-2 had failed in its first flight tests and was scrapped. But after a secret intercession by Elliot Roosevelt, the president's second son and Minnewa Bell's future husband, the air force agreed that if Hughes redesigned it for photoreconnaissance, it would buy a hundred of them.

In 1944, the U.S. government decided to cancel the Flying Boat. Hughes and McCarthy mobilized to save it, even though the project had been plagued with delays and, as his biographers Donald L. Bartlett and James B. Steele put it, "Hughes had not demonstrated the slightest ability to build it." One air force major general had done all he could to keep the Hughes contract alive, and Hughes had jokingly wished aloud that the officer had a twin brother he could hire to run his aircraft division; the officer replied that he'd like the job for himself.

As he fought to save the Flying Boat, Hughes heard from that major general, who really did want a job—with a three-year contract and a $50,000 advance payment. Hughes dispatched McCarthy on a personal mission to Washington to tell the officer, as nicely possible, that there was no job to be had. Over dinner, McCarthy delivered the news; the major general asked for a loan and financial guarantees amounting to $200,000, instead. Afterwards, McCarthy and Hughes agreed that was impossible, and that Hughes should deliver the bad news himself.

But when McCarthy got back to Los Angeles, the officer called him. Hughes hadn't made the call and when McCarthy explained that there would be no loan, the major general exploded. Hughes blamed McCarthy and badgered him relentlessly through the summer, trying to get him to make peace with the officer and ensure that Hughes's deal for the photo-reconnaissance plane would survive. But McCarthy, concerned for his health, decided enough was enough and stepped back. He quit both the Hughes Tool Company board and his job as Hughes's lawyer. Hughes would later say they parted on "very bitter terms."

McCarthy's resignation had a profound effect on Hughes. He had a nervous breakdown, the first of many he would suffer before his death; he spent the ensuing months establishing a pattern he'd continue for the rest of his life, shuttling between hotels in Las Vegas, Reno, and Palm Springs, where he registered under assumed names and disappeared. Many of the strange, obsessive traits that would come to define him appeared right after he lost his lawyer. Hughes sent an assistant to comb through McCarthy's files. Then, seven months after McCarthy quit, Hughes sent him a check for $6,250 with a request that he continue to work for Hughes Tool. McCarthy returned the money.

It was right around the time of his break with Hughes that McCarthy—perhaps feeling the loss of his mother, who'd died at eighty-three in 1942, or perhaps suffering from empty-nest syndrome after all his daughters had gotten married and his son had gone to war, or maybe because of the yawning vacuum left where his most important client had been—let Dolly Green Walker alter his life, possibly sexually, but certainly domestically. In 1945, Neil moved out of South Muirfield Road, away from his wife, and into a house in Bel Air.

McCarthy asked for a divorce but Marguerite wouldn't agree. "She was devastated, heart-broken, but very smart," says their granddaughter, actress Sharon Gless. "Women of that generation tolerated, they didn't divorce. She said, 'I'd be much better off as the present Mrs. McCarthy.' "

"Who told you that?" he asked.

"The finest attorney I know—you," she answered.

For years to come, the family would reunite for Christmas and Neil and Marguerite would appear together when it really mattered—like the Los Angeles Country Club's fiftieth anniversary party. They even continued to call each other Mammy and Pappy. But Marguerite soon moved herself back to the East Coast, where she started writing the cookbooks that made her famous in her own right.

Neil ended up at 9481 Sunset a few years later, though the house wasn't as incredible then as it became. The Botiller siblings had let it get so run down that bees had taken up residence and built hives in the ceilings and behind the imported boiserie. "You could hear them!" recalls McCarthy's daughter Rosemary Bullis. "The honey dripped out of the paneling and onto the floor." Sharon Gless remembers that one honeycomb remained in the ceiling of the library years later; McCarthy would spread its honey on toasted Irish bread every morning. To solve the problem of the traffic noise from Sunset, McCarthy moved a Louis XV bed and an equally valuable desk into the rear ballroom on the ground floor, stuffed its closet with some of his clothes, and made it his bedroom, rarely using the upstairs. On hearing where McCarthy was sleeping, Dolly Green said, "Why didn't I think of that?"

Gless says McCarthy never used the formal living room with its gold and brocade décor, either. But daughter Rosemary loved the aristocratic furniture that the Botillers had sold with the house. "It was breathtaking," she says, "all original French pieces and Savonnerie rugs." Great-granddaughter Bridget loved the massive foyer with the sedan chair McCarthy used as a phone booth best. No one knows what happened to the basement swimming pool allegedly installed by architect Lourdou. By the 1960s, the basement was full of McCarthy's Howard Hughes files and the fruits of a late-in-life obsession with auctions. "He bought [china] plates in bulk," says Sharon Gless. "He was crazy about auctions."

He was also crazy about Christmas trees. Even those who didn't know Neil knew his house on Sunset because of them. There were three altogether, a living one in the front yard, another on top of the roof outside the ballroom—"you could see that one for miles," says Sharon Gless. "And then, the largest tree you've ever seen in the foyer, so big it had to be decorated with fishing poles."

McCarthy's attention was now mostly given to his horses and the track but he kept a hand in the law. He continued representing Cecil B. DeMille and many performers. He represented Chrysler, the carmaker, says Bridget Gless, and Hernando Courtright, the hotelier who at different times ran both the Beverly Hills Hotel and the Beverly Wilshire, and in between, helped develop Century City. The Neil McCarthy salad, a variation of the Cobb with chopped beets, is still on the menu in both hotels. McCarthy favored the famous Polo Lounge at the Beverly Hills, eating lunch there almost every day. His booth was the second on the right as you entered.

Neil also did a lot of family law work, representing Lana Turner in a 1952 divorce and Ava Gardner when she shed Frank Sinatra in 1953. An old friend of Jack Kelly's, whom he'd met through their shared love of athletics, McCarthy put up Prince Rainier of Monaco at 9481 Sunset the night he arrived in L.A. in 1955 to secretly court Kelly's actress daughter Grace. The next year, Neil reviewed a prenuptial agreement for the couple at the prince's request, says Bridget Gless.

Dolly Green and Neil McCarthy didn't stay an item long. But she wasn't his first lover, nor would she be his last. "He'd had a couple of affairs," says Bridget Gless. "He was a bit of a rogue." They were still rubbing shoulders in 1951, though, sharing the pinnacle of Los Angeles society, attending dinners with the likes of Louis B. Mayer, Clare Boothe Luce, the Jules Steins, and the screenwriter Charlie Brackett, who'd recently coauthored the script for *Sunset Boulevard*, set in a fictional mansion just a few blocks west of McCarthy's chateau.

In 1954, the McCarthy family put on an extraordinary public show of support for Marguerite, who'd returned to California and taken up residence in Carmel. CLOSE-KNIT MCCARTHY CLAN TO OBSERVE DAY, read the Mother's Day headline on the society page of the *Los Angeles Times*. "Mrs. Neil S. McCarthy will spend the day in Carmel answering long-distance calls and opening packages from her children and grandchildren," its society editor wrote. "Mr. McCarthy is recuperating from an illness and will spend the day quietly here at his home [in Beverly Hills]." Accompanying the article was a photograph of Marguerite with sixteen of her twenty-one children and grandchildren. Around the time of that article, Neil asked Marguerite to take him back. She refused.

22

Bel Air

Dolly Green was finally out of Neil McCarthy's life; in 1955, she would marry again, this time tying the knot with Enrique "Heini" Schondube, a Mexican playboy with German ancestry and plenty of money. Having entered international society in the 1930s as a founder of Acapulco's exclusive yacht club, Heini made a fast first impression in L.A. with virtuoso party hopping and the purchase of Charlie Chaplin's fifty-five-foot yacht *Panacea*. There's no proof of this, but it's said that he went everywhere with a mariachi band trailing behind him—and that the musicians doubled as his bodyguards. It's not inconceivable that he needed them. His father's heavy machinery business had been blacklisted by the Mexican government during World War I for suspected ties to Germany—he'd been shot to death a decade later by antigovernment rebels. Then, during and just after World War II, son Heini was accused of having Nazi ties.

Schondube's entry into Beverly Hills was likely arranged by his friend Hernando Courtright, who'd led the group that had bought the Beverly Hills Hotel a few years earlier. Margaret Anderson had sold it in 1928, two years before her death. The buyer, a restaurant operator, promised a million-dollar upgrade financed by mortgage bonds, but in 1933, lost the hotel to his bondholders. The hotel's future wasn't secured until 1937, when Bank of America foreclosed and sent in Courtright, a bank vice president, to whip it into shape to sell it. Instead, in 1944, Courtright organized a group to buy and upgrade the place, investing in a new wing and more of its famous bungalows. When Schondube, a recent widower, came to town, he and Courtright, who'd just lost his wife in a divorce, became running buddies. When Heini headed back to Acapulco on the *Panacea,* Dolly Green followed. The following spring, Heini followed her to her new thirty-room country mansion, a spread called Far Afield on the beach in Montecito. They married in spring 1956. That was a happy year for the Green sisters. Burtie, too, had married yet again, to an old flame Bill Bettingen of Pasadena, the son of a wealthy Canadian lumberman and grain broker. For a time, all three Green girls settled into the lives of wealthy, middle-aged society women.

Their mother, Lilian Wellborn Green, died in 1957 after at least a decade in seclusion. "She wasn't allowed out and about," says a relative. Family intimates differ as to why. One says she suffered from mental illness. Another believes she suffered a stroke late in life, never completely recovered, and also developed mild dementia. A third says she'd had a nervous breakdown and been institutionalized. No one still living knows for sure. "The kids were kept in the dark," says a fourth.

Rodeo Land and Water, the company that created Beverly Hills, had disbanded by then, and its only remaining holdings were some tiny pieces of Beverly Hills and the "right of reversion" to Southern Pacific's right-of-way through town, which passed to the families. A generation later, they incorporated the Beverly Hills Land Company, which still exists today.[19]

In 1958, Burton turned ninety, and Dolly, Liliore, Burtie, and Burtie's children all gathered on Lexington Road to share cake and champagne. Then Dolly and her husband returned to Montecito, where they'd been living full-time. Two years later, most of the family gathered for Burton's ninety-second birthday; each occasion was a fresh opportunity for the newspapers to retell the old apocryphal story of Green as the man who'd founded and named Beverly Hills.

It was two more years before Dolly Green returned to Los Angeles, and when she did it was to Bel Air, not Beverly Hills. In 1962, she and Heini moved into the Bellagio Road mansion Wallace Neff had built thirty-two years earlier for the movie executive Sol Wurtzel in a bowl-shaped 1.3-acre property. Wurtzel had slipped by Alphonzo Bell's edicts against Jews and movie people by buying an empty lot from a couple who'd decided against building when the stock market crashed.

Neff's semicircular Florentine-style four-bedroom mansion was underwhelming from the front, but magnificent behind, where the public rooms—an oval entry foyer led to a step-down living room, a formal dining room, a garden room, and a solarium—all overlooked loggias, terraces, and two regal staircases that cascaded down the rear of the house to a wide green lawn that led to the Bel-Air Country Club. A paneled library adjoined the master bedroom suite. Though the lot was small, the views gave the impression of a much larger property; a few years later, Neff added a swimming pool to the west of the house. Dolly bought the house from Reginald Owen, a British character actor, and his wife, the daughter of a tsarist princess. The man who'd sold it to them was one of the oddest characters ever to pass through the Bel Air gates.

Late in life, Anthony Norvell would be known by his last name only and would achieve minor celebrity as a psychic and astrologer-to-the-stars, a speaker at the fiftieth anniversary of Rudolph Valentino's death, an author, and a regular lecturer at New York's Carnegie Hall where, he often falsely claimed, a bronze plaque honored him as "the twentieth-century philosopher." En route to that special niche, he'd hit some speed bumps.

The son of a Greek immigrant, Norvell first gained fame as Mahlon Norvell in the midst of the Depression, when he made "psychic" predictions to the press about movie stars that sometimes came true. In the 1940s, he tried his hand at stage acting, but gained more renown when he was arrested for violating a Los Angeles city ordinance against fortune-telling, went to trial claiming he was an ordained minister of the Inter-National Constitutional Church (whatever that was), and was found guilty and sentenced to five months in prison or a $75 fine. He appealed; the verdict was upheld.

Norvell did speak at Carnegie Hall, performing there twelve times in its main auditorium and recital hall between 1946 and 1974, but anybody could rent it back then. He also spoke around the country on topics like "enriched consciousness" and "the power of your subconscious mind." And he was apparently successful since, in 1953, he bought Dolly Green's future house at 10539 Bellagio Road for a reported $125,000, as well as a twenty-two-unit apartment building in Brentwood for which he paid $250,000 and another with twenty-eight apartments in Beverly Hills for $275,000—his total investment the equivalent of $5.2 million today.

The next year, Norvell was in court again when he was sued by a woman he'd conned into loaning him $10,000 to open an art gallery on Sunset Boulevard. She won a bit less than half that, but Norvell hardly blinked and within weeks was back to lecturing, calling himself the pastor of the Cathedral of Mind Science and Divine Healing (whatever *that* was).

In years to come, Norvell would claim to have advised Mary Pickford, Conrad Hilton, J. Paul Getty, Aristotle Onassis, and the young Howard Hughes, whom he swore in an unsigned affidavit that resides among the Howard Hughes Papers he'd first met in 1932 and continued to see three or four times a year until 1972. Norvell also claimed to have had George Sanders, Marilyn Monroe, Tyrone Powers, and Nicky Hilton as house guests in Bel Air, and to have sublet the mansion to Hughes, Elvis Presley, and Monaco's Prince Rainier.

Dolly Green bought the estate in 1962 and it was hers for the rest of her life. She decorated the mansion in scarlet, gold, and ivory brocade and painted her furniture, much of it Belle Epoque designs by François Linke, "by herself, with a paintbrush," says Hutton Wilkinson, a Los Angeles interior decorator and designer who met her a few years later. "She liked Zsa Zsa décor, very very fancy, ormolu French. There were fake plastic roses everywhere. The house was kind of a mess."

Dolly was "tight with everything but what went around her neck," Wilkinson continues. Every Christmas, she would buy herself whatever piece of jewelry was on the cover of the Van Cleef & Arpels catalog. "She was also a compulsive window shopper," Wilkinson confides. "She would pass a department store and then call and say, 'I'll take everything in the last window.' "

Burton Green died at his home on Lexington Road in 1965 at age ninety-six. His will added money to trusts already established for Burtie's two children, left small sums to eight employees, and split the remainder of his $10 million estate among his three daughters. Dolly divorced Enrique Schondube the next year, though she continued to use his name, writing to him on his seventy-fourth birthday in 1973, "My name is still Schondube!" But to most of those who knew her during and after her marriage to Heini, she was, and would always be, simply Dolly Green.

Dolly never remarried, but she continued to lead an active social life, sometimes escorted by another wealthy Mexican in L.A., a gay man-about-town named Alfredo De La Vega, who co-owned the La Fontaine apartment building in West Hollywood. De La Vega, whose friendships ran the gamut from the young Jack and Pat Kennedy and Nancy Reagan to James Dean and Greta Garbo, would be shot to death in 1987, at age seventy-five, by an intruder in his apartment.[20]

In fall 1979, the Green sisters got considerably richer when they and the other remaining shareholder auctioned off Belridge Oil and its 376 million barrels of proven oil reserves to Shell for $3.65 billion—the then richest corporate deal in history. The selling families were tight-lipped about their windfall, but one of the Green sisters—they each made about $230 million; all would soon appear in the *Forbes* 400—did speak out, though she refused to be identified. "When you have all you want, some more doesn't mean that much," she said.

That didn't stop Burtie and Dolly from spending some of their new-found fortune very quickly and in a very public way. Early in 1980, at her latest husband's urging, Burtie bought John Wayne's six-bedroom waterfront house in Newport Beach for $5 million. A few months later, Dolly made a splash at a thoroughbred auction, paying $2.2 million for five horses, one of which, a progeny of the 1964 Kentucky Derby winner Northern Dancer, cost $1.4 million. Though Dolly had been a regular at L.A. racetracks since her Neil McCarthy days, she'd hidden her past so well that the *Los Angeles Times* said she'd never been seen at a Southland racetrack and "no turf people had heard of her." Asked where she lived, all she would say was California. When she amended that to Los Angeles, she added, "But please don't print that." the *New York Times,* too, would call her "a complete stranger to the racing world." She didn't stay that way for long; in the next five years, Dolly would spend another $10 million on thoroughbreds.

Dolly and her sisters, though, had grown apart. "They didn't socialize with each other," says a family retainer. "I won't say they all approved of what the others did." Dolly had her horses. Burtie and Bill Bettingen had an antiques business—Burtie was thought to have the best taste of the sisters. Liliore simply disappeared from public view.

Burtie's husband Bill died in 1983 and his widow went into a steep decline, locked behind the walls of Wayne's Newport Beach house and another at the highest point in Beverly Hills, on Lago Vista, overlooking Franklin Canyon reservoir with a view from the ocean to downtown. Burtie told friends it stood on the very spot where Burton Green had laid out the first streets of his city. Legends persist, of course, and those of the Greens were no exception.

They all stayed close to home in their last years. Liliore also lived in seclusion at her massive place on Doheny Road with five bedrooms, six fireplaces, a gatehouse, swimming pool, and its own pine forest, and died there in 1985.

Though she was posthumously described as a recluse, several people close to the family say she suffered from Alzheimer's disease, a problem her wealth could not cure. Yet she managed to make an impact after her death, splitting all but $10 million of her $250 million fortune among five schools and two hospitals. Pomona College, Stanford and Marymount universities, Loyola, CalTech, the Hospital of the Good Samaritan in Los Angeles, and the Menninger Clinic in Kansas had few if any ties to their benefactress or her family, and spokesmen for several said they were baffled by the gifts of $40 million each with no strings attached.[21]

The remaining $10 million went to Burtie's two children and to a handful of friends and employees. She also gave a ranch in Ventura County, where she'd raised about fifty jumping and show horses, to their trainer. Liliore's Beverly Hills home, where she'd lived for almost a half-century, was sold to Merv Griffin, the entertainer, owner of television's *Wheel of Fortune* franchise, and real estate investor, for $5 million cash. Liliore's belongings, including a valuable cellar of fine wines, were auctioned off in 1986.

Sadly, the story of Burtie's old age is the kind that's all too common among the aging wealthy, who often tend to surround themselves with vulture-like lawyers, accountants, and other retainers, whom they sometimes find preferable to self-interested family and friends. Burtie's children were long gone, though relatives and friends disagree on why. "She made the children think California was evil; they were both shipped off," says one family intimate. "She was so dogmatic, spoiled, rich, demanding, alcoholic, overweight, on pills, and hard to be around she drove them across the country," says a member of her last husband's family. Regardless, she was left at the mercy of her paid staff.

Patricia Brown, who went to work for Burtie after her last husband's death, derides the Green family's retainers, all but one now dead, as "horrible people with big reputations" who tried to "separate [Burtie] from her children and stepchildren. They tried to separate the sisters. They played on old hurts." Why? "Jealousy. Power. . . . There's no question they were robbing Burtie blind. They discounted her because she was an alcoholic, but she was charming and brilliant and kind. They came in and fed her liquor." Burtie was also taking psychoactive drugs, Brown says. "They wouldn't tell her how much money she had. She got suspicious and she stopped drinking and started asking questions, and the staff went crazy." Even at the end of her life, a relative agrees, Burtie would not stand for being manipulated.

Just before her death, Burtie tried to seize control of her finances. "She kept asking for a CPA, but the staff refused to hire one," says Brown, who discovered that checks Burtie had authorized to various charities hadn't been written. "She loved signing philanthropic checks," says Brown, who followed up and was told the checks weren't prepared because there were insufficient funds in Burtie's account to cover them. "But Burtie had instructed her bank manager to transfer $20 million," Brown says. Burtie decided to replace her lawyers, but she never followed through. Dolly had also "tried to leave, but they presented her with a huge bill and she decided she couldn't. . . . I was tired," says Brown. "I said, 'We're never going to know the truth.' These people wouldn't tell her where her money was. She died shortly thereafter. It was suicide. But some might say she was murdered." Shortly after Burtie's death, Brown adds ominously, her own apartment was burglarized.

Brown ended up in charge of the Burton G. Bettingen Corporation, a foundation she has run to this day, and she believes that its mission says a lot about her patron and the things she really cared about. Despite her wealth, Burtie "felt she was the most unlucky person in the world," says Brown. "Her self-confidence and self-image were damaged. She was crippled and deformed with arthritis. She felt she was Quasimodo. People said she was a hypochondriac; she made lists of her mental and physical ills." The other sisters "had a wonderful life, up to a point," says Brown. "Burtie's life was hell all along."

Brown is reluctant to share her thoughts on what caused Burtie's suffering, but the story of their relationship hints at childhood trauma. Brown and Burtie met just after Brown, who came from a Southwest Blue Book family, had broken up with a fiancé and heard through mutual friends that Burtie was looking for a philanthropic assistant. "She wanted someone to help her be a good steward of her money," says Brown. "I thought that was doable." A series of conversations ensued. "She'd breakfast, I'd lunch," says Brown. "She'd have cocktails, I'd have milk and cookies." Burtie asked questions like, "Have you ever had a crisis of faith?" Brown noticed about two dozen Bibles in her bedroom. "I hired you because I was going to kill myself," Burtie told her, saying she'd always trusted the wrong people and had never been aware of her alternatives.

"What about other people who are blinded by hurt and nightmares and making wrong choices?" Burtie asked. "How can I help those people?"

She decided to focus on runaways, particularly girls. "She felt they ran away because of unwanted sexual attention and secrecy," Brown says. "Then she said she wanted to use her whole estate to help them, to provide psychological, medical, and addiction services, education and vocational help, life support if they couldn't live at home, and to work against child prostitution. For someone so isolated from life, Burtie had an incredible vision to devote her last year to trying to plan to use her wealth to let others lead full, joyous lives and see their own potential, power, and ability to be productive and happy."

Brown says that the Green family retainers didn't just interfere with Burtie; they also tried to have Dolly declared incompetent when she decided to take charge of her estate and give her money to charity. They rewrote Dolly's will to include themselves, Brown says, fired her butler after accusing him of stealing, and scared her personal maid, Maria Rivera, so thoroughly that she called Brown to warn that "bad things" were going on. Brown arranged to meet Rivera but she didn't show up. Later, one of the family retainers told her the maid had died en route to her family home in Mexico.

Through all this, Dolly lingered. One friend called Brown to say "they'd taken away her medicine and she wouldn't die." It was all a mess. Dolly and Liliore had always hated Burtie's children, Brown says. Now, all that was left of the Greens were Dolly, those kids, and the staff, each with their own idea about how the $750 million Green fortune should be divided. (The one member of the family's support team who is still alive asks not to be identified. He denies there was any friction and, asked about Patricia Brown, says only that "the name is sort of familiar.") The infighting and money-grabbing was about to get even uglier.

23

Beverly Hills, Bel Air, and Holmby Hills

Dolly, the eldest of the Green sisters, died last, of a heart attack ten days after a stroke in September 1990. She was also blind and had breast cancer and had been suffering cognitive problems for five years. She requested that her age—eighty-four—be omitted from her obituaries. It was also misstated on her death certificate, which shaved off three years.

The disposition of her estate got no notice in the press, unlike Liliore's, which had generated national headlines. Dolly's Bellagio Road house was sold the next year to Bill Bell, executive producer of the soap operas *The Bold and the Beautiful* and *The Young and the Restless*. He paid $4.78 million—considerably less than the $6.9 million asking price.[22] Dolly's brief obituary in the *Los Angeles Times* flew in the face of the facts of her life. It claimed that she'd startled her parents by refusing a coming-out party and that she preferred studying languages or the law "to a life of parties and dinners and teas." Rather than detailing her life of parties and multiple husbands, it stressed her late-in-life role as a racehorse owner and her philanthropy.

Like her sisters, Dolly died with a fortune—well over $200 million. Most of it went in small tranches worth between $2 million and $10 million to thirty-two different organizations working for children, who got the largest chunk of her fortune, and then in order of decreasing sums to animals, hospitals, the environment, the church, the blind, veterans, and finally, Goodwill and the Salvation Army, which each got 1.1 percent of her fortune. Unlike her sisters, however, Dolly also died with a secret—a supposed illegitimate daughter.

Diane Melanie Hunt Stockmar had been encouraged to call Dolly her aunt, but Stockmar believes Dolly was really her mother and that she was cut out of Dolly's will by the same family operatives Patricia Brown describes. Stockmar is convinced that she's the product of Dolly's affair with Neil McCarthy. She has no conclusive proof of this claim, but she tells a compelling story spiced with intimate details few outside the two families know; there is considerable evidence of a long and close relationship between her and Dolly and she has several photographs that reveal the two shared a startling resemblance.

As far as she knows, Stockmar was born in June 1947. Though the world was breathing a sigh of relief and the rich were spending again that spring after years of war and the Depression, Dolly Green was uncharacteristically absent from the social columns in the six months before Stockmar's birth, appearing in the *Los Angeles Times* only twice, once with McCarthy after both attended a gala dinner at L. B. Mayer's.

Over the years, Stockmar claims, she became Dolly's protégé and secular confessor, hearing stories the Green heiress rarely told anyone. Dolly was not only "born with a silver spoon in her mouth," Stockmar writes in an unpublished manuscript, "she was blatantly proud of that fact."

All three Green sisters were terribly spoiled, Stockmar says, but Dolly was the worst, and her attention span suffered from the way her father indulged her, buying her pets and extravagant toys that would be forgotten in a matter of days. Because Dolly hated school, Green hired tutors for her. Since one of her girlfriends had a chauffeur, Green got her one of those, too. When Stockmar turned eighteen and snuck a boyfriend into her bedroom at Dolly's house, she learned that Dolly had done something similar, having her first affair with that chauffeur in the backseat of her Cadillac, where Burton caught her. The chauffeur was fired. Dolly continued to be indulged.

Stockmar says Dolly told her she divorced her first husband because "he beat her [to] within an inch of her life." She heard about the trip to Europe that followed, and also Dolly's boasts that she snuck out of their hotel and slept with many men there until the night her father caught her "reeking of booze and sex" and shipped her back to California. According to Stockmar, Neil McCarthy broke up Dolly's second marriage. "They were like sparks doused in kerosene," she says. "They were mad for each other. Crazy, unbridled, hot." Dolly wanted to marry Neil and decided to become "purposefully pregnant" five years later, to "force the issue of his divorce."

Stockmar can only guess the details of her birth, but she claims that a well-connected lawyer was able to get copies of her sealed adoption papers, filling in some of the story. She believes she was born without paperwork in the house on Mountain Drive, delivered by a nurse and Dolly's longtime maid, Maria Rivera, and that she lived with Dolly as her daughter in a bedroom decorated for her with a circus-tent motif for eighteen months before it became clear to her mother that McCarthy was not going to marry her, and her usefulness ended. She says McCarthy suggested Dolly place her in an orphanage called Merryvale after he saw the child hiding behind a Chinese lacquer screen outside the room in Dolly's house where they sometimes made love. When Dolly told her father McCarthy's plan, he sympathized, expressing the hope that the little girl would soon forget the first year and a half of her life, just as he had no memories of his infancy. The Greens even retained psychologists to assure them that would be the case. "He loved me," says Stockmar, who claims she often visited Burton Green on Lexington Road.

Then, late in 1948, Dolly's father got a call from the district attorney of Los Angeles, who'd heard what was going on from the lawyer the Greens retained to place the child at Merryvale. The DA said he had a better solution to the Greens' problem; he knew a middle-aged couple who had one adopted daughter and wanted another. Ralph Van Nice Hunt was an executive of Douglas Aircraft and lived at 360 Rockingham Drive in Brentwood (later the home of O. J. Simpson) with his wife Marie and daughter Penny. The next day, the Hunts met Dolly and shortly thereafter, a deal was struck. But, Stockmar claims, the process was complicated and took six months to complete, so it was only after her second birthday that she was "packed up to go play with Penny Hunt."

What caused the delay? Stockmar's theory is that Dolly's cover story—that she'd taken in a one-year-old foster child to induce McCarthy into marriage and given the girl up when he refused to divorce—needed to be documented, so a birth certificate had to be produced that named a mother other than Dolly and would satisfy the officials who had to approve a transfer of custody, first to Merryvale and then to the Hunts. And so Stockmar, whom Dolly called Beau, assumed the identity of the child of a twenty-nine-year-old actress-singer named Heather M. McDonald and a John Dahlinger.[23] "The baby died," Stockmar thinks. "Burton Green arranged to buy the dead child's papers." While the Hunts' adoption was in the works, Dolly was apparently "restless and impatient" to be "relieved of the responsibility for the child," according to a letter the Greens' lawyer sent to Neil McCarthy.

Finally getting custody and making Beau their own, the Hunts renamed her Diane Melanie Hunt. She didn't see Dolly Green again for five years. But Dolly wasn't ready to admit defeat in her campaign to win Neil McCarthy. Six months after divesting Beau/Diane, she bought 9481 Sunset and sold it to him, making him her neighbor. And it turned out Dolly and Diane weren't done with each other, either. Stockmar believes Dolly and her adoptive mother made a deal that Dolly could reappear as Diane's godmother once the child forgot her.

At first, it appeared that wouldn't happen; Stockmar says she suffered bouts of screaming and crying, demanding her mother back, and that even beatings didn't stop them. Finally, after four years of anguish, Maria Rivera, Dolly's maid, suggested a solution; she urged Dolly to move the Hunts into what Dolly considered a small house—most would have called it a mansion—that Burton Green owned on Strathmore Drive in Holmby Hills as a change of scene, to remove a painful reminder of what Diane still considered her abduction. Simultaneously, she and her new sister Penny were enrolled in the nearby prestigious and private Westlake School for Girls. These moves, Stockmar says, were "what the doctor ordered," and soon, Marie Hunt announced that she was taking seven-year-old Diane to lunch to meet her godmother.

"Call me Aunt Dolly," she said over lunch at Perino's, a chic Beverly Hills restaurant. Little Diane sat poker-faced, sure she should give not a hint of her mixed delight and distress at this sudden turn, and her reticence won back the woman she believed to be her real mother. "They were convinced I didn't know," she says. "I wanted Dolly in my life. If these were the terms—okay." Afterwards, they all returned to Mountain Drive in Dolly's red Cadillac. Ultimately, Dolly would leave McCarthy behind, at least as a neighbor, and buy the former Sol Wurtzel house on Bellagio Road that she'd first seen when Howard Hughes rented it.

Lavishly decorated in Dolly's favorite colors and filled with rare first editions, what social wits call Louis Louis antiques, and furniture covered with sheets to protect them from Dolly's beloved boxers, who had the run of the place, that house became the scene of regular meetings and, later, sleepovers, with fifteen-year-old Diane occupying a back bedroom done up in white moiré piped in gold and spending hours in the paneled library listening to Dolly's stories of how Elvis Presley had used the room to house his pet chimps. It soon became clear to Diane that Dolly "did not lead the most motherly of lives," she'd later write. "She was mostly out carousing with men until all hours of the night," recounting her adventures to her "goddaughter" afterwards while sipping her favorite drink, Korbel, a cheap ersatz champagne produced in California. Dolly drank it on the rocks. She typically wore a silk dressing gown, her nails painted bright red, her hair perfectly coifed in the dressing room off her bedroom, where a full beauty salon was set up so her hairdresser from Elizabeth Arden could come to her.

Third husband Schondube was already in the picture, but it was a while before Dolly introduced Diane to the "dreamy, divine Spaniard" she'd married. "She could be your daughter, not your niece," was his first comment on meeting her, Stockmar says. She believes that introduction—and perhaps that remark—spelled the end to the second act of Dolly and Diane's relationship; the couple soon decamped for Santa Barbara, where they would spend most of their time. Diane says that was okay with her as her teenage years were generally happy, diverting ones, spent with the children of Holmby Hills whose parents were rich and famous and invited her to their mansions and movie shoots.

But when the Hunts took Diane to Paris for her sixteenth birthday, the sights she saw there—especially the great paintings and antiques—inspired her to write a series of postcards to Dolly, pleading for a reunion. On her return, she got a call inviting her to Santa Barbara, where she arrived to find Dolly and Heini fighting. Later that day, Dolly confessed that her "dreamy" Spaniard was a philanderer, but that since she'd converted to Roman Catholicism for him, she could not get divorced. (It was a perfect religion for her, thinks a relative, "full of red and white and gold and ceremony.") For the next two years, Diane says, she became Dolly's confidante and the catalyst that helped her overcome her reluctance to divorce. One night, Heini got drunk and attacked her and "Dolly threw him out," Stockmar says. "The 'divine Spaniard' became the 'filthy Mexican.' She told me she was going back to Green because Dolly Schondube couldn't get restaurant reservations."

Once, during that stay in Santa Barbara, Stockmar says, Dolly briefly opened up to her, quizzing her about what she knew and when she knew it. "You were my mother, weren't you?" Diane asked.

"I knew you couldn't have forgotten," Dolly said.

"I believe she felt remorse," Stockmar says. "We'd never really talked, I was going off to college. We had a sit-down, talking like adults, and then we or she pretended it hadn't happened. It didn't need to be revisited."

Stockmar left California at age nineteen to marry in Colorado the same year Dolly divorced Schondube and moved back to Bel Air. Though Dolly came with Burtie to Diane's wedding (where they were all photographed together), and they spoke often on the phone, they didn't see each other for years. Dolly had sent the Hunts $100 a month after the adoption, Stockmar says, and after she went to Colorado, she got a yearly Christmas check of $1,000, except in 1980 when Dolly celebrated her new Belridge-funded wealth by sending $3,000 instead.

Unbeknownst to Stockmar, she'd also been left money in Dolly's wills since at least 1962, when she got $25,000. In that same will, Elinor Logan, an assistant in the Green family's office, was left $5,000. Early in 1965, Dolly drew up a new will. Neil McCarthy, previously unmentioned, got a day bed that had once belonged to Madame de Pompadour, Diane's bequest rose to $50,000, and Dolly's office assistant Logan's jumped to $10,000. Eight months later, Dolly executed a codicil, dropping Heini Schondube's bequest from $400,000 to $100,000, and upping Diane's to $100,000 and Logan's to $20,000. In a new will in 1968, Logan's bequest rose to $50,000 while Diane's stayed the same and Neil McCarthy's bequest vanished.

Over the next seventeen years, Dolly would change her will often, reflecting who was in and out of her life, and adding new bequests for staff members. Diane stayed in the will until at least 1985. That year, Stockmar attended a school reunion in L.A. and called Dolly, who said she had the flu, sounded disoriented, and wouldn't see her. Stockmar claims that the maid, Maria Rivera, told her that once off the phone, Dolly seemed confused as to whom she'd been talking to. Though she sometimes telephoned and left messages in the months that followed, they only connected once; after that, Stockmar says, Dolly never returned her calls.

More than a year later, the Stockmars flew to Los Angeles for a visit, got Maria on the phone, and in a furtive, whispered conversation, arranged a visit the following Sunday when the household staff would be at church. On arrival, Maria took them to Dolly's room, where they discovered the Beverly Hills heiress in a wheelchair, blind, "talking to imaginary friends." She seemed to mistake them for the Hunts, asking if they'd come to take her baby away. "You can't have her," Dolly supposedly said. "I've changed my mind."

Says Stockmar, "I will never forget that moment; it has haunted me all this time."

On the way out, Diane noticed that the framed photos of her that had once been displayed in the house were gone. "Maria said Mrs. Logan [who'd become Dolly's assistant] didn't want to be forced to look at me any longer," she says, "and since Dolly was blind, she would never know they were gone." Later, she says, she learned from Maria that someone on the staff had told Logan she'd been there. Maria also warned that Logan had taken charge of Dolly's life, forbidding anyone to see her. Though she felt uncomfortable with the situation, Diane returned to Colorado, keeping tabs on Dolly through Maria.

Nine months after her visit to Bellagio Road, Diane wrote to Logan about Dolly's condition. "I said I was alarmed." She got a remarkably detailed response. Logan spoke of her devotion to "our dear Dolly" and her family. "Dolly has been failing for several years prior to 1986 which you mentioned," she wrote. "Her memory was gradually going and she had no remembrance of her many good friends. She really had to rely on me to fill her in. She was quite an actress, as you know, so she managed to carry things off in a crowd. I believe that her eyesight was going, her brain was going also. . . . By March, 1987, we had to hospitalize her because she was refusing to eat, etc. We pulled her through and from then on have had her home with nurses around the clock. The doctors have not specifically diagnosed her condition as Alzheimers, however, the symptoms seem similar. It is a dementia of some kind. . . . Dolly hallucinates and seems to be living in her own little dream world."

What Logan didn't tell Stockmar was that in August 1986, when Logan felt she was already failing, her brain going, Dolly had changed her estate plans one last time. In a new codicil to her will, many of her bequests changed radically. Elinor Logan and Maria Rivera were willed $3 million each, accountant Hugh Mullen and a maid named Yolanda each got $2 million, two chauffeurs who doubled as bodyguards got $1 million each, and, in what appeared to be a last-minute change of heart, one recipient of Dolly's largesse was eliminated: A $300,000 bequest to Diane Hunt Stockmar, though included in the typewritten document, was crossed out by hand. Dolly's shaky initials confirm her decision to disinherit her daughter/goddaughter/niece. It was that will, in which Logan and Mullen were named Dolly's new executors, that was filed in Los Angeles County two days after her death.

Maria Rivera didn't live to see that sad day or get her million dollars. Stockmar says they last spoke by phone in 1989, and her description of their conversation, though different in some details, echoes the recollections of Burtie's assistant Patty Brown. "She sounded really worried about things that were going on around the house," says Stockmar, "and she was afraid." Stockmar suggested she quit, pack up, and move home to Puerto Rico. "I then received a letter from Elinor saying how tragic it was to relate the news of Maria's death."

Stockmar's next contact with Logan was similarly bleak. "Our Dolly has died," she recalls Logan calling Colorado to say, before adding that Stockmar shouldn't bother coming to the memorial service the next day, "as she did not mention you in her will."

The day after Christmas 1990, Stockmar's lawyer wrote to his counterpart at the Green estate to say that she had "substantial reason to believe that she is the natural daughter of Dolly Green," suspected she'd been cut out of the will and hoped to open a conversation to rectify matters. "We were trying for a settlement," Stockmar says. "We didn't want to go through litigation." Less than a month later, unsatisfied, she formally challenged Dolly's last will and codicil.

In one of their responses, and contrary to Logan's earlier account, she and Mullen insisted that Dolly was competent to make a will, suffered no mental disorder or delusions or hallucinations in 1986 when she wrote it, was in "reasonably good health," and "sharp as a tack." They claimed that her last bequest changes were "prompted, perhaps" by the deaths of Burtie and Liliore and that she was particularly motivated to make gifts to "the office staff," that is, themselves. They alleged she asked Mullen to put together a gift list that totaled "someplace in the range of $10 million," and that in a meeting with one of her lawyers after the new documents were drawn up, she upped her gifts to a maid and secretary and deleted Stockmar because "she had already done enough for Diane and . . . they had not been in close contact with each other for some time."

The response then recounted the sad end of Dolly's life in great detail, her January 1987 visit to a glaucoma specialist that left her suicidal, her last visit to the family office that February, the hiring of round-the-clock nurses shortly afterwards, a March call to her lawyers from one of the chauffeurs saying Dolly wanted to revise her will again, and the way "Respondent Logan was asked to help guide Dolly's hand to the line on which she should sign (since she could not see well enough to find the line)." One last curious feature of the executors' response to Stockmar was their answer when asked whether Dolly believed Diane to be her daughter. They objected to the question, they replied, "because its use of the term 'daughter' is vague and ambiguous." But they answered anyway, asserting that Dolly did not, at any time, believe that.

A few weeks later, Stockmar accepted an offer to settle her dispute for $175,000 plus any taxes that might become due on that amount. "My sister had just died," she says. She and her husband "had financial challenges with our business. I don't think we were logical or stable. Had we been, we wouldn't have settled." She claims her lawyer in Los Angeles delivered a message from the Green gang implying that she might be killed if she pressed her case, referring to the then recent 1990 murder of the wife of a U-Haul heir in nearby Telluride, Colorado. Contacted for comment, that lawyer first claimed in an e-mail not to remember the case at all, and after being shown evidence of his deep involvement, refused to even entertain questions about it, writing in an e-mail, "I remember the case now (vaguely). But I have no memory of the details." Most of the lawyers who represented the family and the estate are either dead, similarly profess not to remember, or refuse to discuss it.

"I think we're lucky to be alive," Stockmar says. "These were *not* nice people. People with that much money could arrange a hit. I dropped the will contest. But I did not sign a gag order. They wanted me to." To this day, she's convinced that Elinor Logan and other staffers conspired to not only cut her out of Dolly's will, but also to increase their own bequests from their impaired, dying employer.

Stockmar's story has flaws in it; she's told various versions over the years that have sometimes contradicted each other and gone against documented facts. "I'm not infallible," she says. Nor has she been without her own legal troubles. Twelve years after Dolly's death, a dispute with a partner in a Vail, Colorado, art gallery led to Stockmar's arrest on nine felony counts, charged with theft and fraudulent use of credit cards. Five years later, the charges were dismissed after Stockmar paid the partner $20,000. "The evidence got so bad, we couldn't prove the case," the local district attorney told the press. Diane says she made the payment at the DA's request "to put an end to it. I'm not embarrassed by it." Her accuser, though still angry, wouldn't comment on the record.

• • •

The final distribution of Dolly Green's estate took place in 1993. Her physical property was valued at almost $17 million and much of it was sold off at a pair of auctions, advertised with lavish catalogs. The estate paid $71.5 million in taxes to the United States and almost $24 million to California. Another maid and a chauffeur-guard were both given the houses they lived in, which Dolly had owned, and the family staff and a handful of others received their cash gifts. Under law, Logan and Mullen received a bit over $150,000 in payment for their services to the estate above and beyond Dolly's generous bequests. They asked the court for another $100,000 "for their extraordinary services rendered." The estate's lawyers were paid more than $280,000.

Dolly left some money to Burtie's kids. The rest went to those thirty-two charitable organizations in a symphony of philanthropy. Among the beneficiaries were the Wildlife Waystation, a refuge for abandoned and neglected animals on a mountainside in the Angeles National Forest (it got $2.6 million, which took it out of the red for the first time in years), and the Ark Trust (which gave out an annual Dolly Green award for pro-animal artistic achievement before it merged with the Humane Society).

One of Dolly Green's bequests stands out. The Dolly Green Research Foundation, which she'd set up years earlier, got only 1.7 percent of her fortune, but (aside from a chair for a professor of ophthalmology that she endowed at UCLA at the request of Jules Stein) is the only entity to which she attached her name. Though her life had been one long party, it was her horses she wished most to be remembered for. The foundation provides funding for research into health issues facing thoroughbreds. Neil McCarthy had died by then, but if there's a heaven, no doubt his Irish eyes were smiling.

Beverly Hills

9481 Sunset Boulevard

Neil McCarthy's life shrank after the end of his affair with Dolly Green. Once when granddaughter Sharon Gless was house-sitting, she asked him if he wasn't lonely in his big house. "No!" he replied. "Who's better company than I am?"

He still had his routines, like daily lunch at his table in the Polo Lounge and dinners at the Los Angeles Country Club. In 1959, the year he turned seventy, he gave an interview to the *Los Angeles Times* sports page saying it was his horses that kept him going. "Breeding them, racing them, buying and selling them get me out in the open, keep me active, provide relaxation and give me something to do that I love doing," he said. "What better prescription for good health can you get?" He kept thirty mares and three stallions at his 400-acre ranch northwest of Los Angeles, and stabled ten racehorses at Hollywood Park. He kept horses too old for breeding or racing, too, and ended up with 250 of them.

Mortality nibbled away at him. He had the first of a long series of strokes that would plague him for the rest of his life. He was a pallbearer at Cecil B. DeMille's funeral in 1959, and then again for DeMille's widow a year later. There were also family troubles; the first hint of them came in 1964, when his son, Neil Dillon McCarthy, also a lawyer and briefly his father's partner, sued him for nonpayment of $7,500 in legal fees for representing him in a tax dispute. Father and son settled the suit eight months later.

Marguerite McCarthy, Neil's long-estranged wife, died at her home in Carmel in 1966. Despite his departure, McCarthy had remained devoted to her. "She hated planes," recalls great-granddaughter Bridget Gless, "so he insisted she be driven back to Los Angeles in a hearse because she wouldn't have wanted to fly." McCarthy also wouldn't allow an obituary to run until after she'd been buried.

Finally free to love openly again, McCarthy found his second wife at the Los Angeles Turf Club a year later. Mary Beich Myers was the heiress to a candy fortune and a well-regarded painter who some considered the American Mary Cassatt (even thought Cassatt was American, she lived most of her life in France). A down-to-earth, pretty blonde divorcée with two sons, "she made him very happy," says Sharon Gless. The couple married in the living room of 9481 Sunset in June 1969 with a horse trainer and grandson Michael Gless as witnesses. The happy occasion set off another family squabble.

Beich "was not well received" by two of Neil's three daughters and his son, says Michael Gless, who convinced his mother not to get involved when her siblings sued to appoint a conservator to oversee Neil's $9 million in assets, claiming that his mental capacity was impaired; he'd had six strokes by then. McCarthy was livid when he learned what the kids were doing. "I've worked for every dime I have and I'll be damned if anyone will take it away from me," he vowed to Sharon.

The children brought a doctor into court who testified that losing $250,000 a year on horses was proof their father was not of sound mind. "He kept every horse," says Michael Gless. "He couldn't kill them. His feeling was it was *only* $250,000." The judge ruled in McCarthy's favor and as Neil walked from the courtroom, he asked his grandson to redraft his will, disinheriting the three children who'd sued him. He also demanded they return some gold and silver polo and racing trophies he'd given them as keepsakes. He gave them to his new wife, who mixed her paints in them.

McCarthy's final upraised middle finger to his estranged children may have been "Leprechaun in Versailles," a four-page spread of color photographs of the newlyweds and their mansion in the *Los Angeles Times* magazine the next fall, including shots of Mary descending the grand staircase into the foyer, and the upstairs loggia where she kept her easel. The story ostensibly promoted a one-woman show in Paris of Mary's paintings, but with its catalog of his possessions ("a set of Louis XVI fauteuils . . . Limoges tea service and silver, shell-shaped bun-warmers . . . mahogany commode with a Sèvres medallion . . . boule-embossed Blondin piano and the dining table [set with] 24-carat gold Czechoslovakian cups, English china and magnificent Napoleon Capo de Monte plates"—some bought from the Botillers, some at auction), it was also clearly Neil's way of saying, "I'm still standing."

That said, he didn't stand for long. He had two more strokes after the one that so worried his children, and the second one killed him in June 1972. Shortly before that, his granddaughter Sharon had come to him with some big news. She'd been offered a contract by Universal Studios and brought it to Neil, asking him to look it over and wondering aloud about the offered $180-a-week salary. "I made $200 as a secretary," she told him.

McCarthy burst out laughing. "This is *my* contract!" he said. "I drew up the first contract-player contract and this is it. Sign it. You're not in a position of power."

"Then he died," Gless says sadly. "He never saw me perform." But Gless has been a successful actress ever since and was also, apparently, the last contract player ever to sign the contract her grandfather drafted.

Neil McCarthy did see Dolly Green again, though. During his last hospitalization, she visited him every day, with Mary's blessing, bringing him flowers from her garden.

Upon his death, Mary Beich McCarthy got 9481 Sunset and lived there alone for five more years. But she didn't get something else she wanted: a space next to Neil and his first wife on their mausoleum wall at Holy Cross Cemetery in Culver City. She'd reserved it, but daughter Marjorie Gless wanted to be interred there. "I went to the business office at the cemetery and was told the spaces were all gone," says her son Michael. "Mary had reserved it, but she hadn't paid for it." He wrote a $15,000 check on the spot, thus ensuring his mother would be buried there.

McCarthy's most colorful client, Howard Hughes, intruded on Mary Beich McCarthy's widowhood just once. After McCarthy quit as his lawyer, Hughes's behavior became ever odder, even as he continued pursuing his interests in aviation and film, gaining control of the RKO studio in 1943, crashing another plane in 1946, and trying to sell RKO the next year to a syndicate that included several men with mob ties, a deal that fell apart after those ties were revealed in the *Wall Street Journal*. Sidney Korshak, who negotiated for the buyers, believed that Hughes kayoed the deal so he could keep their deposit. In the years that followed, Hughes won and lost control of TWA, the airline, but rarely went to his own office, working instead from houses and hotel suites, including Marion Davies's Ocean House in Santa Monica; Howard Hawks's Bel Air house; several homes in Bel Air, including the one later bought by Dolly Green; a leased house in Palm Springs; a suite at the Bel-Air Hotel; and two bungalows at the Beverly Hills Hotel. After the 1950s, he was almost never seen in public.

In 1966, Hughes moved into the penthouse of the Desert Inn hotel in Las Vegas, buying it, allegedly, when the owners asked him to vacate for a high roller. He then invested heavily in casinos and eventually came to control 28 percent of all gaming revenue in Clark County and 35 percent of all the hotel rooms on the famous Vegas Strip. Some say the mob's control of Las Vegas ended with Hughes's arrival, but author Gus Russo thinks it remained, albeit in the shadows, and that Sidney Korshak settled his score with Hughes over RKO there, causing the Texan to lose millions to the mob's ongoing casino-skimming operations.

In 1972, Hughes sold Hughes Tool to the public and consolidated his other holdings in the new Summa Corporation. By then, he'd moved to the Bahamas, and later Managua, Nicaragua, and was more famous as a crazy recluse than for any of his considerable prior accomplishments. Hughes died in 1976, either in the Fairmont Princess hotel in Acapulco or aboard an air ambulance returning him to Houston so he could die in the United States. His $2.5 billion estate was held up for seven years due to questions over the legitimacy of a purported handwritten will. That December, Summa officers contacted Mary Beich McCarthy and asked if any of her husband's files were still in their house. Various drawers and filing cabinets were opened, and the searchers found an unsigned Hughes will among the papers in the basement; dated 1938, it left his fortune to the Howard Hughes Medical Institute for medical research. Asked if McCarthy also had a safe, his wife said he did. A locksmith was brought in to open it, and there, the Summa officials found a signed and dated codicil that did not refer to a prior will and had no new will attached to it. "It was therefore invalid," says Michael Gless, a lawyer, who learned from the Summa men that if the unsigned will that gave everything to charity was declared valid, there would be no taxes due on the estate, but if Hughes was judged to have died intestate, the estate would have to be split among a large group of cousins and one or all of the states of California, Nevada, and Texas, which all claimed Hughes as a resident. In the end, that's what happened.

That multitude of Hughes cousins likely ended up happy. Neil McCarthy's children not so. The only child in Neil's will, Marjorie (Michael and Sharon's mother), got a quarter of Neil's estate; Michael also got a quarter and Mary Beich McCarthy got the other half as well as the Sunset Boulevard house, which she eventually sold for about $750,000. Mary then moved to Arizona and in the process, "my [great]-grandfather's things" all disappeared, says Bridget Gless. Sharon Gless concurs: "Mary walked away with my debutante gown, my mother's wedding dress, all of that sort of stuff was in there." Michael tried to buy some antiques and gold plates McCarthy had won at Hollywood Park, but Mary sold them. None of them know what happened to McCarthy's antiques. "My mother said, 'Let it go,' " Sharon says—and they did. Mary Beich McCarthy died in 2002.

25

Beverly Hills

Greystone 905 Loma Vista Drive

The founding generation of Beverly Hills, Bel Air, and Holmby Hills died with Dolly Green. The greatest estates had all passed into the hands of other great fortunes by then. Starting in the 1950s, people referred to them as white elephants and asked if it was possible to save them from "the great ivory hunters who shoot gunite from astride a bulldozer" and replace great mansions with "stucco cartons," as the *Los Angeles Times* would put it in 1965. The last to fall from the hands of the family that built it was the largest, Greystone. Lucy Doheny Battson sold it in 1955.

Lucy and Leigh Battson didn't abandon Greystone because it was out of date, though it was, but rather because "the kids grew up and they all had their own houses," says grandson Will Doheny. "The place was just too much for them." It is indicative of what they considered normal that they then hired the eminent architect Roland Coate Sr. to design and build his last commission: a thirty-five-room 27,000-square-foot house on ten acres adjacent to Greystone. Called The Knoll, it was the largest estate to rise in Los Angeles since World War II.

Less than a minute from Sunset Boulevard, The Knoll nonetheless seemed a private fantasy once visitors passed its eagle-topped columns and gilded iron gates. The circular motor court with an elaborate fountain at the center led to the grand foyer with its white marble floor, mirrored columns, and sweeping staircase up to the six bedroom suites (there were thirteen baths in all). The Battsons also had an oak-paneled office suite, a pine-paneled library, a large den, a banquet-ready formal dining room (served by two industrial-strength kitchens), an indoor swimming pool, a vault, a separate dining room for staff, and several staff apartments. Two guesthouses, one with an adjacent tennis court, a thirteen-car garage, and a forty-eight-foot outdoor pool, pool house, and gazebos, flanked the main residence, which also boasted a granite bar and to the rear, floor-to-ceiling Palladian windows looking out over gardens to the city beyond.

As she packed to move, Lucy Doheny Battson stripped Greystone of much of its décor, taking fixtures, statuary and decorative items, several fireplace mantels and hearths, even the library paneling and Ned's barber chair. "She decided to divide up the liquor" stored in Greystone's basement wine cellar, Tim Doheny recalled in a 1984 interview on file with the Beverly Hills Historical Society: "I was only twenty years old and didn't get any. She had to stick to her beliefs." Tim, for one, wasn't sad to see the place pass into other hands. "It's very pretentious and people just don't think in those lines today," he said. "It's something you could get away with then, but [aside from] rock stars and some others, few people are that pretentious today. . . . I was always embarrassed by it, always. Some members of my family weren't but I was. I spent most of my youth trying to live it down."

The next owner of Greystone, Henry Crown, a building supplies millionaire from Chicago, apparently didn't know what to do with it, and in fact never even moved in. So when it wasn't rented out as a film set (*Forever Amber, The Disorderly Orderly,* and *The Loved One* were shot there), Greystone sat empty, slowly becoming a ruin. Rain poured through broken windows, damaging plaster; paint was peeling; carpets were damaged and infested with moths; the grounds were overgrown; and rodents alone enjoyed what had once been the finest residence in Beverly Hills. The movie studios that rented it agreed to pay Crown's Park-Grey Corporation to keep it in shape, but "those funds were not used for that purpose," according to a later, carefully worded city-generated report.

"I leave the doors unlocked, otherwise kids would smash the windows out," a caretaker told the *Beverly Hills Times,* pointing to a chandelier that had been vandalized. "They get in and just wreck everything." They'd even stolen the pins from the bowling alley and the key to the projection room. "I'm fighting kids all the time." Just a few days earlier, he'd chased off a dozen who'd left behind beer cans and whiskey bottles.

Eventually, Crown sold a single acre at the highest point of the property to a friend for about $60,000, and then approached the city to propose that if it would not buy the rest from him, he would subdivide it. Two years later, after getting no response, Crown filed subdivision plans to erect twenty-five houses on the property, forcing the issue. Crown rejected the city's first offer of $1 million payable over twenty years, but late in 1964, agreed to sell Greystone for $1.1 million. Voters balked; the city renegotiated and finally managed to win voter approval by promising to finance and build a much-needed water reservoir on the property. A citizen's committee considered forty proposals before leasing the house to the American Film Institute (AFI), which paid the city only $1 a year, but rehabilitated the mansion using 1929 photographs from *Architectural Digest* as their guide. In 1971, Greystone's grounds were opened to the public as Greystone Park. In 1982, AFI vacated, but since then, the estate has been well maintained and used as a film location and site of fund-raisers, weddings, corporate events, concerts, and even a day camp.

The movie-ready image of a ruined Greystone is a compelling one, but that empty, echoing house on a hill was the exception, not the rule. The way of life it epitomized was endangered, but the decadence Greystone symbolized wasn't gone, it was simply evolving. The Doheny mansion is best seen as a ritual sacrifice, the house that had to die (at least as a residence) so that others might live.

By the start of the 1950s, Beverly Hills, Bel Air, and Holmby Hills were already quite changed from the communities originally envisioned by their founders. Beverly Hills had those swimming pools and movie stars, there were Jews in Bel Air, and actors sometimes even played golf at the Los Angeles Country Club, right in the backyards of the Janss and Letts family homes of Holmby Hills. But the essence of the idea that had brought them and others to the Triangle, the idea of an Eden blooming in a bean field, an enclave where the wealthy and accomplished could be with their own kind, had survived, and would also survive the inevitable downsizing and redefinition of what constituted the very best of the good life that followed World War II.

On the East Coast, those old determinants of social position, blue blood and inherited money, were being challenged by red-blooded immigrants with their fresh ideas and newly minted cash. The Triangle had been created by fresh faces with new money, but they, too, would be supplanted in years to come. Just as water came from the Sierra Nevada to irrigate the land, newcomers would keep coming to California, some to seek their fortunes, some to spend them. All would find the Triangle to be fertile ground for its main preoccupation of self-invention. Some would seek to carve out new lives in an extinct past, others to sustain the illusion that its fading glories were their present. But they would all prove to be transient, coming and going, rarely leaving a trace behind. The estates would change, redecorated to reflect the changing lifestyles of its residents. But an essential truth remained: Here, big dreams live, sustained by big money; here, too, inevitably, they die.

PART FIVE

White Elephants

1958–1979

{ MICKEY HARGITAY AND JAYNE MANSFIELD IN THE PINK PALACE }

26

Holmby Hills

10100 Sunset Boulevard

The first era of the grand Los Angeles mansion was over. They didn't build 'em that way again for half a century after World War II. Nor, for the next two decades, would Triangle real estate be owned by the same sort of people. There were still stars enough to keep the public fascinated and maps of star homes selling briskly on street corners off Sunset Boulevard. But though it wasn't yet entirely clear, the Hollywood types who bought significant mansions in the sixties were the last of a breed; they saw themselves as exemplars of a sort of mythic glamour that was already on the wane. In retrospect, they were both caricatures and dinosaurs, the last rulers of a kingdom that would shortly face its own extinction. In their place late in that decade and into the seventies would come a motley, decadent crew who saw the Triangle as a playground, a fountain of fun for those rich enough to drink from it, a no-holds-barred, rule-free zone where you could have it if you could dream it. For them, the great estates were like gambling chips in Vegas, won and lost in games of ambition, ego, power, desire, and divorce. Even in apparent decline, the Triangle remained a crucible of excess, where native and foreign, rich and famous, accomplished and notorious were all mixed up—and more often than you might expect, crossed paths on the manicured lawns and in the grand foyers of great mansions.

Just as, in Norma Desmond's words, the pictures got smaller, so did the new houses off Sunset Boulevard. "Even uninhibited Hollywood has begun to pursue soberer tastes," Peter Bart wrote in the *Los Angeles Times* in 1966. "Though the movie stars still live in the grand manner, most have taken refuge in smaller, more modern homes requiring fewer servants and lower upkeep. Many have fled over-publicized Beverly Hills." One Beverly Hills realtor groused, "The stars move out and the dentists and psychiatrists move in." But Bart also noted exceptions to the new rule, the few who "still hanker for the old glory days." In the early sixties, just before the counterculture of sex, drugs, and rock 'n' roll overwhelmed American society, it took a special kind of personality, simultaneously nostalgic and aspiring, to live up to, as well as live in, the great estates of west L.A. Though the houses were bargains in a sense, often being sold for a song, they were mind-bogglingly expensive to maintain.

Vera Jayne Palmer, the future Jayne Mansfield, was one of those special personalities. A buxom, wasp-waisted platinum blonde who gave her measurements as 40-18-35, she'd grown up idolizing movie stars and in 1954 came to California to become one. Her last idol was Marilyn Monroe, who'd stayed next door to Jayne's eventual home at Joe Schenck's 141 South Carolwood. Mansfield would be touted as the movies' "next Monroe" before the first one had even left the stage.

Jayne was seventeen when she married Paul Mansfield, the high school sweetheart who'd gotten her pregnant in her senior year. Six months later, they had a baby they named Jayne. Back from a stint fighting in Korea, Paul accompanied his wife to Hollywood, where she sold candy in a movie theater while she screen-tested at studios. When she failed to get a contract she hired a press agent and started shedding clothes, pioneering the attention-getting faux-gotchas of coy underwear and nipple slips that the publicity-hungry still resort to today. To keep things focused on her even when she was clothed, the preternaturally PR-conscious Jayne, at age twenty-one, adopted pink as her signature color. Rudy Vallée's sedate Holmby Hills home would soon be remade as Mansfield's Pink Palace.

First, though, Jayne had to get rid of Paul Mansfield, and when Warner Bros. offered her a contract, she did, initiating divorce proceedings the same day she signed her starlet deal. Though Warner dropped her before her first film was released, Jayne became a star when she inadvertently won a legitimate stage role her legend says she didn't really want; allegedly trying to sabotage her own reading, she caricatured the dumb blonde movie star lead of a planned Broadway musical spoof. She not only impressed the director, but invented the calculated character she would portray on and off camera for the rest of her career—a bodacious yet innocent blonde bimbo. Jayne would appear in 452 performances of *Will Success Spoil Rock Hunter?* at New York's Broadhurst Theater. The savvy starlet also managed to secure a semipermanent place in the media; she was a pioneer—and something of a philosopher—of celebrity self-invention. "Celebrities don't do; they are," Mansfield said, setting the stage for the likes of Paris "That's Hot" Hilton. In November 1955, Jayne appeared on the cover of *Life* magazine, famous mostly for being famous. Four months later, top photographers voted her the "Most Dangerous Woman in America." Though she would enjoy many intoxicants over the years, publicity would always remain her drug of choice.

Twentieth Century Fox was feeling the abrupt absence of Monroe, who'd left Hollywood for New York, where she was trying to reposition herself as a serious actress. Its executives pounced and in spring 1956 started grooming Mansfield with small dumb-blonde roles, and then her first dramatic part in a movie based on a John Steinbeck novel.

Her private life took off that May, too, when she went to see Mae West's nightclub revue at the Latin Quarter in New York and got a load of body-builder Mickey Hargitay, a former Mr. Universe from Budapest via Indianapolis who was one of several muscled chorus boys in the aging diva's stage show. In an apocryphal tale, when the waiter asked Jayne what she wanted for dinner, she pointed at Hargitay and said she'd take "the beefsteak on the end." After the show, she sent him a message, inviting him to her table. Both were married (Jayne's formal divorce had been delayed by a paperwork problem), but that didn't matter. Jayne had met her match.

When West, then in her seventies, got wind of what had happened, she laced into Hargitay, dismissing Mansfield as a "phony Hollywood blonde" who was using West to get attention. Mansfield's response was column-ready: "I wonder, when was the last time anybody took *her* picture in a bikini?"

The press loves a catfight, and Jayne and Mickey played this one for all it was worth. Mickey told his wife that Jayne had promised him leading-man roles in movies, and asked for a divorce. Mae West decided she wanted to keep him and ordered him to drop Jayne and join her at her next engagement in faraway Syracuse; he did. When West found out that he was still calling Jayne nightly, though, she ordered him to go straight to their next date in Washington without stopping in New York to see her. This time, he disobeyed.

West demanded he renounce Jayne and say he was only in it for public-ity, and a press conference was called, but Mickey defied her, announcing instead that he was "very much in love" and that he and Jayne were discuss-ing marriage. Another of Mae's musclemen responded by punching him out. Hargitay had the former wrestler, described as West's boyfriend, arrested for assault. After that, Mickey and Mansfield were inseparable, moving back to California when Jayne finished her play, though maintaining the illusion of separate residences while they disposed of their respective spouses. "It was like seeing two big beautiful animals at play," a reporter wrote of the Jayne-and-Mickey show. Her advisors were dubious, but she knew what she wanted.

The Girl Can't Help It, with Jayne in her first starring role backed by early rock performers like Little Richard, Gene Vincent, Fats Domino, and the Platters as well as the jazz chanteuse Julie London, was released that De-cember and her dreams of movie stardom suddenly came true. Testing her new status, she demanded Mickey play her boyfriend in her next movie, a film version of *Will Success Spoil Rock Hunter?* The role was a walk-on, but to Jayne, putting her lover in it proved she was now a star.

Jayne's rookie year at Fox was, sadly, the high point of her film career. In 1957, her photo appeared in newspapers more than two thousand times. Though female reporters were skeptical, her breasts were catnip to the gen-tlemen of the press. At one point, New York's *Daily News* is alleged to have banned her as overexposed; years later a columnist at the same paper would issue a similar ban on Paris Hilton. Both efforts proved futile.

A few days after her divorce from Paul Mansfield was finalized, Jayne married her muscleman on January 13, 1958 (the zipper of her dress broke during the reception), and the very next day, finalized the purchase of 10100 Sunset Boulevard from the wholesale grocer Harry Kanter and his wife, who'd bought it from Rudy Vallée. Jayne paid the entire $76,500 purchase price out of an $81,340 inheritance she'd received from a grandfather and put the house in both their names, but told the press it was Mickey's wed-ding present to her. Really, it was an investment in her career.

The fact that the Kanters had let the place get run down worked to her advantage. Not only was she able to buy a movie-queen-ready house "with rooms and rooms and rooms," as she put it, for far less than it would have cost otherwise, but Hargitay, once a carpenter and plumber, was eager to become general contractor and turn the place into her dream.

Their move from a small house high in Benedict Canyon (decorated with a hundred magazine covers featuring Mansfield) to the mansion offered countless new publicity opportunities, and the couple took advantage of every one. That fall, they even posed at a card table set up in their bare living room, facing the massive fireplace where Mickey was storing barbells—the only décor. But Jayne's marriage was weighing down her career, although her incandescent image, buoyed by her bountiful, rambunctious breasts, made that less than obvious for the moment. Her studio would have preferred her unmarried and under its control. Instead, she initially gloried in being Hargitay's wife, and then in the years that followed, disdained him as slow and cheated on him so promiscuously, even her fans started having doubts about her.

The trouble began soon after the couple married, when Hargitay's first wife—who apparently believed the tale that Mickey had paid for the Vallée house—sued for additional child support and Jayne and Mickey responded by pleading poverty; they said that though they'd spent $100,000 to upgrade their new mansion, they couldn't afford furniture and were cooking on a hot plate and sleeping on foam pads on the floor in the servants' quarters. A police lieutenant from Laguna Beach promptly took up a collection to buy Jayne and Mickey a bed. Once the first Mrs. Hargitay was out of the way, they furnished the mansion by writing to hundreds of household purveyors requesting samples and promising free publicity to everyone from furniture companies to a garbage-disposal maker. The disposal ended up in the garage, along with a lifetime supply of Firestone tires.

In the coming months, while Jayne traveled the country promoting herself, Mickey painted the eight-bedroom, thirteen-bathroom house and the walls around it pink, the paint mixed with quartz dust so it would glitter in the sunlight, and installed wrought-iron gates decorated with the three-foot-high initials J and M entwined in a heart; inside, there were pink shag carpets and pink furniture, a white marble fountain that sometimes spouted champagne, a pink marble kitchen, a mirrored bedroom matching Jayne's pink mirrored headboard with a heart-shaped red canopy above the bed and pink fluorescent lights below, a piano painted with cupids, and more cupids, marble ones, on pedestals and adorning the walls. Mickey installed a heart-shaped bathtub, a heart-shaped swimming pool surrounded by pink terrazzo tile, with two heart-shaped islands in the middle and "I love you Jaynie" in huge mosaic tiles on the bottom, heart-shaped gardens, and, in the living room, a heart-shaped pink Norwegian marble fireplace mantel. Only the carved wood ceilings and doors remained the same as they had been in the Vallée era. The parade of reporters Jayne invited over to see the work in progress often met Mickey pushing a wheelbarrow or plastering a wall. Guests were asked to remove their shoes before stepping into the ankle-deep living room carpets—also "promoted."

When he wasn't working on the house, Hargitay worked as Jayne's second banana in a nightclub act she developed. He was her willing slave. Though the house had a call system for multiple servants—upstairs and downstairs maids, a butler, a cook, a houseboy, a gardener, and a chauffeur—a maid, a housekeeper, and Mickey were all Jayne needed. "My marriage is everything," she told her best friend May Mann, who reported the conversation in a posthumous biography. That was true—for the moment.

In mid-1958, Jayne told Twentieth she was pregnant and having the child—another example of the personal determination that worked against her career. Mickey Jr. was born late that year (Mickey Sr. gave Jayne a pink Cadillac to celebrate) and a second son, Zoltan, followed in summer 1960. The back-to-back pregnancies wreaked havoc on Jayne's status as a sex symbol, and she was reduced to appearing in low-budget films in England and Italy, cutting ribbons at drugstore and supermarket openings, and appearing at bowling alleys for sums ranging from $1,000 to $2,500; she was usually paid in cash or goods and for the rest of her life argued with the Internal Revenue Service. But to her fans and herself, she stayed a star, even walking an ocelot with a pink bow on a leash and taking pink champagne baths for photographers. Thanks to her devotion to image maintenance, she and Mickey remained $25,000-a-week headliners in Las Vegas even as her brief movie career fizzled.

It appears Jayne finally got the studio's point about Mickey, though, as she began a protracted effort to dump him in 1962. First, she filed for divorce. Mickey got the news from reporters; they reconciled two days later, and soon were off to make a movie in Rome, where she again dumped Mickey and took her married Italian producer as her lover, the first in a series of Svengalis. Then she took Mickey back and he recreated a few feet of Rome's Appian Way in their driveway to remind her of their brief reconciliation. Then they separated again and she tossed him out. He bought a house in Trousdale Estates and signed away his share of the Pink Palace.

As the number of her lovers mounted, she who'd lived by public attention began to slowly die by it; the overpublicized Jayne may have been the first star squelched by the perception that she was all image, no substance. Making matters worse, Mickey's presence had hurt her career, and now his absence—where's the beef? you might say—appeared to do the same. More important, Jayne realized she still depended on him, even if other needs were being fulfilled elsewhere. "If he would only be my manager," she whined to May Mann. They were back together in Holmby Hills by Christmas. But as soon as Mickey reverted to unpaid houseboy, Jayne fell out of love again.

Early in 1963, Jayne took a step that briefly spurred ticket sales but hurt her in the long run—appearing topless in the movie *Promises! Promises!* Stills from the film appeared in *Playboy* magazine. While she was filming, she and Mickey edged toward divorce again, a process that accelerated when Jayne took a new lover, a Brazilian singer who then joined her on a trip to Juarez, where she got a quickie divorce from Mickey. That year, "she was on a merry-go-round," wrote Raymond Strait, another friend turned posthumous biographer. "She dated every available bachelor." But none of them satisfied.

Whether she really loved Mickey or just needed his skills around the house, by the time the topless film was released he was back and she was pregnant again. In January 1964 she gave birth to a second daughter, Marie, who as Mariska Hargitay would go on to star in television's *Law & Order: Special Victims Unit*. She has consistently refused to discuss her mother in interviews. Perhaps that's because she was rumored to be the daughter of one of Jayne's lovers, perhaps because she never got to know her, perhaps because of how Jayne lived in the three brief years they shared. Shortly after Mariska's birth, "Jayne was near collapse," Strait wrote, "popping pills and chasing them with bourbon."

By that time, Mansfield could find work only in small-town theaters, often recreating parts originated by Marilyn Monroe. In spring 1964, she broke up with Mickey again after falling in love with Matt Cimber, her director on a dinner theater production of *Bus Stop*. She cast him as her latest Svengali and married him that fall, even though there were questions about the legality of her Mexican divorce. As wedding presents, she and Matt bought a townhouse in New York and a red Ferrari; though it's unclear who paid for them, they acted as if she were still a star even as her career neared its nadir. She decided against renting out the Pink Palace; rather, she'd keep it for vacations in L.A.

Meantime, Mickey had taken baby Mariska away from Jayne, demanding $25,000 and a share of their eleven pieces of real estate aside from the Pink Palace before he'd bring her back. That earned him $70,000 but also a fistfight with Cimber on a Manhattan street corner over visits with his children. Jayne bore another son with Matt but couldn't stay married, filing divorce papers yet again in summer 1966.

Mickey soon returned, but again not for long. A twenty-year-old South American college kid Jayne hired as a bodyguard was her next lover. Then came Mansfield's last boyfriend, Sam Brody, the lawyer who represented her in the never-concluded divorce from Cimber. He supposedly fell in love with her but spent his time manipulating her when he wasn't beating her up. "He has a terrible picture he'll blackmail me with," Jayne told her friend May Mann. Her downward spiral accelerated, fueled by Brody's abuse and a continuing dependence on alcohol, amphetamines, and lately, a new drug, LSD.

When Jayne and Sam were in residence, the police were regular visitors to the Pink Palace, checking on reports of domestic violence. That fall her second son, Zoltan, was mauled by a lion at a publicity photo shoot and she was fired from her latest job, a nightclub act tour of England and Ireland. The next year, Brody's wife named Jayne as his "41st other woman" in a divorce suit. Jayne countersued and also sued Matt Cimber for harassment, and separately for assault and battery; he countersued alleging she owed him management fees. Astonishingly, things then took a turn for the worse: In summer 1967, her sixteen-year-old daughter Jayne turned up at a local police station, covered with bruises, and asked the cops to protect her, alleging that Brody had beaten her with a belt at her mother's instigation.

A hearing on the beating of the younger Jayne, who was sent to stay with a relative of her father, Paul Mansfield, was scheduled but postponed after Brody lost control of his Maserati on Sunset Boulevard, a few blocks from the Pink Palace, breaking an elbow, a leg, a thumb, and two teeth; it was to be held when Mansfield and Brody returned from a nightclub date in Louisiana. She played her show but the hearing never happened. In the middle of the night on June 29, 1967, en route to an early morning television show in New Orleans, Mansfield, Brody, and their driver were killed instantly when they rear-ended a truck spraying mosquito repellent thirty miles outside New Orleans. Mickey Jr., Mariska, and Zoltan, asleep on the floor of the backseat, survived with minor injuries. The gruesome tragedy—an untrue story that Jayne was decapitated, first purveyed by local police, persists—was spun by newspapers as fated; her death sold more newspapers and magazines than she ever did movie tickets. Having determinedly turned herself into a risqué cliché, she died in the center ring of a tawdry circus of her own making.

Mansfield's messy life left a messy estate that continued to generate headlines for years. Her mother, Hargitay, and Cimber all sought control of her body and her property. A New Orleans court decided Jayne's Mexican divorce was invalid and gave Mickey the right to dispose of her remains. But a California court ruled that Cimber was her husband for inheritance purposes (she'd left no will), and he promptly installed guards around the Pink Palace to keep Mickey and his children out. Apparently, Cimber then relented a bit, as Hargitay's children and their nurses were allowed to stay for several months. Little Jayne remained with those relatives of her father's and tried to become an actress, posed for *Playboy*, and then dropped from the public eye. Cimber raised his son, Antonio, and continued his career as a director of exploitation films, documentaries, and most notably, *Butterfly*, in 1982, starring Pia Zadora and financed by her then-husband Meshulam Ricklis, who went on to buy and effectively raze Pickfair. *Butterfly* won multiple nominations for Goden Raspberry, or Razzie, Awards as one of that year's worst movies.

The Pink Palace went on the market while the children were still in residence; the prurient and curious waltzed through, posing as buyers. The price dropped but still it sat unsold for a year as pipes burst and rats moved in. Potential buyers noted a certificate from the Church of Satan naming Jayne a member. It was said Sam Brody had been cursed in their last months after he and Jayne went to visit the notorious Anton LaVey, head of the devil-worshipping group, and Brody insulted him when LaVey named Jayne a high priestess of his cult. Zoltan's mauling, Jayne's accident, and a series of further misfortunes followed: car crashes and the deaths of many who'd been in her circle. None of that helped sell the house but finally, it and its contents, 264 items of Jayne's furniture and clothing, were disposed of for $180,000 in August 1968. There was still $70,000 due on the mortgage.

Mickey Hargitay remarried, raised his children, and continued to work as a contractor, landscaper, and actor; he last appeared on his daughter Mariska's TV show in 2003 and died three years later at age eighty. Mae West had already had the last laugh. She outlived Mansfield by more than thirteen years, dying at eighty-seven in 1980. In her obituary, Jayne Mansfield was dismissed as a "Mae West imitator."

Beverly Hills

Grayhall (1100 Carolyn Way)

Mansfield was hardly the only movie star in the neighborhood. Bill Hamilton, brother of the perennially tanned actor George, fell in love the first time he laid eyes on Shadow Hill, the former home of Silsby and Caroline Canfield Spalding, even though the subdivided estate was much smaller than it had been in its glory days. It was being sold by Amos Johnstone, who'd lived there for a decade. Bill decided George had to buy it.

Bill was the first child of Anne "Teeny" Stevens, a Southern belle who would eventually marry four times. For convenience's sake, Bill had taken the name of his mother's second husband, his first stepfather, George William Hamilton, a bandleader better known as Spike. Teeny's second son, whose father and namesake was Spike, was the reason Bill was house-hunting. A devilishly handsome, dark-haired young man, young George had recently returned to Los Angeles for his second grab at the brass ring of movie stardom and his brother Bill had followed, determined to mold him, Queer-Eye-for-the-Straight-Guy style, into a star and then ride his coattails. Their mother was hard on Bill's heels.

Teeny, who claimed descent from one of the first families of Virginia, "had scratched more men off her list than a major league baseball talent scout," George later wrote in a memoir, and his older brother Bill "had some sexual identity issues"—to wit, he was flamboyantly gay. George's father had been left behind in 1947 after Teeny caught him in a Cleveland hotel bed with the singer in his band. Seeking a new, preferably rich, husband, she tossed a coin to decide whether to head to Hollywood or Palm Beach, and the West Coast won. It was the home of Buddy Rogers, an old beau who'd married Mary Pickford and lived in Pickfair (just up the street from Shadow Hill). She was determined to see Buddy again, and even if he was no longer the man of her dreams, she was sure there would be another in the vicinity.

On that first trip, the Hamiltons moved into a series of rentals, first east of and then in Beverly Hills, and plotted their conquest of Hollywood. Teeny dated movie people like Ronald Reagan and Howard Hughes, Bill dressed her, and George attended school, but in 1949 their "Hollywood idyll ended," George wrote, when his mother ran out of money and returned to the South to regroup. A stint in New York followed where Teeny sometimes fed her boys out of doggie bags from the legendary nightclub El Morocco, and George learned to mix martinis and look like he'd been born in a dinner jacket. By 1957, after attending dozens of schools and working at a series of odd jobs, George had decided on a career as a Hollywood star—not an actor, a star—and returned to Beverly Hills with two friends and $90 in his pocket. He found an agent and won his first movie role and some television bit-part work that led to an offer of a seven-year contract from MGM.

Early in his career, Hamilton decided that he had to project "the illusion of grandeur," so despite making only $500 a week, he rented a Rolls Royce and dressed his gardener as a chauffeur; then "Hollywood began buzzing about George Hamilton," he wrote. He later bought a 1939 Rolls built for King George VI of England and rented it out when money was short. By 1962, a magazine would report that he owned 75 Italian suits, 50 English sports jackets, 120 silk shirts, 150 pairs of pants, and 75 pairs of custom-made shoes. His next film, *Where the Boys Are,* about spring break in Fort Lauderdale, Florida, got the rest of the country buzzing, too, which is when his brother Bill showed up and convinced George to buy a mansion to hold all those clothes. He got Shadow Hill for only $135,000.

"It was a different world then; Hollywood had changed," Hamilton says. "It was a town amazingly at a loss for glamour and it had happened overnight. It had suffered a death blow but no one had pronounced it dead yet. What our life there had been in 1947 to 1949 was far more glamorous and I was in search of that glamour." He cast himself as a well-mannered rich boy dabbling in pictures, nudged along, he admits, by his brother and mother, both in their way stage mothers, who saw George poised to play out their dreams.

Hamilton was engaged to marry actress Susan Kohner, who'd played opposite him in his second movie, and whose father was an agent representing European stars like Greta Garbo, Marlene Dietrich, and the director Billy Wilder. She was "sexy and sizzling," he wrote, "and she loved me." Then his brother showed up and everything went awry.

Hamilton blames the house for breaking up his engagement, believing it made Kohner's father wary of him, perhaps correctly. Susan was a serious actress. The house proved that Hamilton was unserious and incompatible with her; he wanted to be a celebrity. "He fell into that idea easily," admits Kohner, "but he had a sense of humor about it, which was his saving grace."

Her father didn't get the joke.

The negotiation for Shadow Hill was "not difficult," says Hamilton. "Nobody wanted it. These were white elephants." He put down 10 percent and his agents at William Morris arranged a loan for the balance. Credit was easy in those days. "I was worried but Bill said, 'They'll have to find you work to get even.' He was very cunning."

He renamed the house Grayhall after its entry. "The first thing I saw was the gray hall," he says. "I entered the realm of movie stars before the first world war." George moved into a three-room master suite—effectively his bachelor apartment—and his mother and brother immediately set up house in a separate wing (though a swinging bookcase connected her bedroom to George's suite) and hired an ancient butler. Kohner never moved in; they broke up shortly after George took up residence—"a great relief to Teeny and Bill, who were living it up at Grayhall," Hamilton wrote—and for the next ten years, George reigned as a leading Hollywood bachelor.

Bill immediately redecorated, removing a Rathskeller-style kitchen with a table suspended on chains from the ceiling and the roller-skating rink that the previous owner, a tinkerer, had installed in the ballroom for his kids. Then he started filling the place with furniture bought on a shoestring. "He had a sleight of hand with décor," says Hamilton. His mother had similar skills with people. "She filled it with movie stars," like her old friend the silent film star Mae Murray and Gloria Swanson, who were more than happy to enjoy the Hamilton family's largesse—financed by George's borrowing against his movie star future—and help raise the family's social profile by attracting other greats of old Hollywood.

The *Los Angeles Times* would later describe the house as "somewhat seedy," but nonetheless "a throw-back to the Jean Harlow era." Hamilton agrees. "I was living in a 1920s movie in the 1960s," he says. Teeny, just divorced from husband number three, even arranged a walk across the street so George could meet Mary Pickford (while Teeny visited her old flame Rogers). Pickford swilled Scotch and milk through dinner. "Who would have guessed that Pollyanna was a lush?" Hamilton wrote of that brief encounter.

Later, Pickford wrote him about his house, admitting that she'd "lived there in sin" with Douglas Fairbanks, and found it dark and oppressive. Hamilton savored the vestiges of Fairbanks's tunnels to Pickfair and also an innovation of Silsby Spalding's: "He put an alarm system in the wine cellar that ran to city hall because he'd get drunk and one time he locked himself in there for days." There were still bottles from 1918 in that cellar when Hamilton moved in.

Two events in 1965 changed Hamilton's life, one for the better, the other for better and worse. "I got a call from a woman named Canfield," he says, "who had original furniture from the house and wanted to return it." There were Aubusson carpets, a Gobelin tapestry, and a pair of Sèvres vases that the Duc de Richlieu had long before given to the Princess Lamballe, Marie Antoinette's confidante at Versailles. The Spaldings had bought them at auction in 1916 for $700. The Canfield heiress agreed to let George pay off the $28,000 asking price over time. "That started the task of making the house into a museum," says Hamilton. "After that, whenever I went to a movie set, my brother said, 'Bring back chairs, not postcards.' Bill had an uncle who'd married a French countess and he'd gone to Paris and seen real stuff, so he knew and taught me an appreciation for the real thing. Bill and mother had a theory that if you filled your eyes with beauty, it would come to you." Bill later bought him Jerome Bonaparte's bedroom suite. George paid, of course. He was making just over $100,000 a year, but it barely covered expenses. "It costs him everything he makes to support that house," his friend James Mitchum, the actor Robert Mitchum's son, told *Life* magazine. "It's like a giant slot machine that does not pay off."

Hamilton had always been handsome, courtly, and well dressed despite his mother's roller-coaster finances. Among his dates in his youth were the heiresses Caterine Milinaire, Topsy Taylor, and Charlotte Ford, who went on to marry Stavros Niarchos; like all his girlfriends, the last stayed friends with George and introduced him to Lynda Bird Johnson, twenty-one, shortly after her father Lyndon became president. Lynda invited him to a state dinner at the White House. He was intrigued, believing that inside the bookish college girl was "a babe trying to get out."

His visits to the LBJ ranch that spring and their very public nights out (including a trip to Acapulco, appearances at the Sugar Bowl and the Academy Awards, a night dancing the frug at the famous Beverly Hills disco the Daisy, a Broadway opening, and a twenty-second birthday party for Lynda at Grayhall attended by Tony Curtis, Samantha Eggar, Greer Garson, Natalie Wood, Elke Sommer, Bobby Darin, Jill St. John, and Eddie Fisher, who sang) helped her emerge from the shadow of her more vivacious younger sister, Lucy, who'd already gotten engaged.

It was also a publicity coup for George, who found his price and his fame rising. By 1966, he was raking in half a million dollars a year. But dating the president's daughter in the midst of an increasingly unpopular war in Vietnam also brought him undesired attention. Some were sure he was using the First Daughter for publicity. Others brought up his draft status; he'd been declared ineligible for the armed services since 1961, as he was allegedly the sole support of his mother. Antiwar activists (and likely, some who were merely jealous) turned against him and he was ordered to take a physical exam; ultimately he avoided the draft because by then he was twenty-seven, too old to serve.

Finally, though, it wasn't war, but sex that killed the romance. A friend of his mother's who was in trouble with the IRS threatened to "out" his brother as a homosexual. That would not have been good for Lyndon Johnson. Hamilton avoids the subject of who broke up with whom, but a year later, Lynda agreed to marry the far more suitable marine Charles Robb, who was later elected governor of Virginia.

Hamilton's acting career and finances went south in 1968, when the illusion of glamorous Hollywood became unsustainable, replaced by the gritty new rebellious films of directors like Martin Scorsese, Francis Ford Coppola, and Robert Altman. But George also met his first wife, Alana Collins, a statuesque blonde fashion model from Houston, that year in Acapulco; she was with another man and ignored George. "He thought I was snotty," she says. "I was just shy. I didn't fawn. I didn't know how to behave around a movie star."

A year later, they bumped into each other again at an L.A. disco, the Candy Store, and George asked her on a date that began at Grayhall. "I pulled up and I thought, 'My God.' I'd never seen a house like that except from a distance," Alana says. "He showed me the ballroom. I thought, 'Who the hell needs a ballroom?' It was kind of over the top and fascinating."

They went out on a second date, then flew to New York together. Alana was going back to work, George to Europe, and he invited her along, but she turned him down. She didn't know him well enough, she said. The next day, her modeling agent, Eileen Ford, told her she had a job in London; she called George, they arranged to meet in St. Tropez, "and we fell in love," she says. For the next year, they had a bicoastal relationship, but by 1970, she'd moved into Grayhall.

He'd been "trying to find a way to move away, get away," Alana says. He'd slowly realized that his life there was financially unsustainable. He'd been reduced to renting Grayhall out for parties when he could, making brief appearances with his mother as part of the bargain, says a sometime girlfriend. "Anne would walk around claiming descent from 'Lady' Hamilton," one amused party guest reports.

"I was desperate to get out from under that lifestyle," George admits. "My mother and Bill hired minions to work for me from a mental institution. A driver, a butler, a cook, five or six of them all the time, half of them impaired somehow." There were advantages to living in a house that size. "You don't have to keep them clean," Hamilton says. "You just move to another room." But there were also drawbacks. "You'd leave your wallet in one room and not find it for three days," he continues. "People have no idea." Mostly, though, George just couldn't afford it anymore. It wasn't only the house; his family was running roughshod over his finances. "Mother and Bill had bookkeepers and accountants and secretaries working for me but doing their bidding. I'd go away, come back, there would be more furniture—and I'd have to go to work again to pay for it. They said, 'You don't realize what it's worth.' In the background, always, I didn't have my own life. I always wanted to escape. I didn't want to deal with the madness."

George thought he'd be fine living with Alana under the same roof as Bill and Teeny—the house was that big. They weren't so good with it, as it turned out. Bill and George fought, and the fights escalated as it became increasingly clear that George was going to sell Grayhall. It was unofficially on the market, he says, but finally it was openly offered at $475,000, then price-chopped to $369,000 and simultaneously available for rent for $4,000 a month furnished. But Bill would tell potential buyers that it wasn't for sale, was under reconstruction, had a cracked foundation. "All not true," says George. Then a realtor brought a buyer who made a serious offer, and George's decision to accept it led to a memorable shouting match with his brother on the grand staircase. "My mother and brother had invested their lives and they wanted to keep it and stay," George says. "They lived through me."

The buyer wanted to keep some of the furniture. Bill insisted it was his. Finally, George gave him a choice: He and Teeny could keep the house or the antiques. Bill chose the latter. Their sale at auction paid for two houses in Palm Beach and their living expenses for the next half a dozen years. George finally got $300,000 for Grayhall and, simultaneously, $500,000 from an investment banker for another estate he'd bought as an investment—stabilizing his finances and paying for a move to a Palm Springs house he bought from Gloria Swanson. But he wasn't finished with big L.A. estates yet. He was just taking a break.

28

Holmby Hills

141 South Carolwood Drive

Hamilton's friend the actor Tony Curtis was following a similar trajectory—both in his career and in real estate—though he eventually gained acclaim as an actor, not just a pretty-boy movie star. Curtis was born Bernie Schwartz in the Bronx, the child of a Hungarian immigrant tailor who was frequently evicted from the shops where he and his family slept, and a schizophrenic mother who beat him and his two brothers. During the Depression, he and his brothers were briefly placed in an institution when their parents were unable to care for them (one brother, Julius, would be hit by a truck and killed in 1938). Bernie grew up skinny and the target of bullies, which eventually turned him into a showboat who would disarm those who might beat him before they got around to it; his good looks, slight stature, family troubles, and religion all made him a target on the streets. They also turned him into a loner who spent whole days in movie theaters watching Leslie Howard, Cary Grant, Errol Flynn, Humphrey Bogart, and James Cagney. At fourteen, he wrote a six-page letter to the Hollywood gossip columnist Hedda Hopper asking how to become a movie star.

Three years later, in 1943, he dropped out of high school and joined the navy, spending two years in the Pacific and occupied Japan before returning stateside at Christmas 1945. He took advantage of the GI Bill to enroll in drama school, began playing small parts in live theater, and in 1948 went west as a twenty-three-year-old $75-a-week contract player with Universal

Studios, choosing the stage name Tony Curtis. At first, he found it hard to live down his roots, thanks to a thick Bronx accent he couldn't shake. But as much as they'd hurt him in the Bronx, his looks helped him in Hollywood, where he became a favorite of movie magazines and the young female fans known as bobby-soxers. Curtis soon won starring roles, and although he lived in an apartment three blocks from the trolley to the studio, bought a Rolls Royce with $1,000 borrowed from his agent.

"If that car was a big junk, I still would have bought it," he told a reporter. "It was a symbol. I wanted it because it was something that I could wear as a badge to say, 'Look how goddamned successful *I* am.' I wanted to get back at a lot of people in Hollywood who gave me a hard time when I started," he said—from the studio acting coach who singled him out for ridicule to the so-called friends who mocked his accent at parties, mimicking an unfortunate line reading from his first big role as the title character in *The Prince Who Was a Thief*: "Yondah lies da castle of my faddah."

Curtis acquired another symbol when he started romancing Janet Leigh, a blonde ingénue whose acting career had begun a year before his. Although Leigh had already been wed twice—her first marriage at age fourteen had been annulled; her second ended in a divorce after two years—she was a rising star and a major catch. Leigh and Curtis married in 1951 and were soon known as Hollywood's perfect couple.

At first, they lived modestly in an apartment on Wilshire Boulevard, and Curtis sounded more level-headed about real estate than he was about cars in a 1953 interview. "A lot of people around here buy beautiful houses for which they can't pay," he told Hedda Hopper. "I couldn't do that. I don't want to have to make a picture just to get money for a mortgage." Nonetheless, by 1955, they'd moved to a house on Coldwater Canyon Drive in Beverly Hills.

Hopper wrote that they started their careers "about on an equal basis," but by then Leigh's had outpaced her husband's as she won meaty roles while he played lightweight parts, even if they were leads—rather like George Hamilton. In the mid-1950s, Curtis had a personal crisis, decided that although he was well paid, he was no more than a pretty vegetable, and entered psychoanalysis to work things out. Four years and $30,000 in shrink bills later, he pulled out of his tailspin, renegotiated his contract so he could make better films for other studios, and "tried to learn something about acting."

By the end of the decade, he'd accomplished all that—and been voted the most popular actor in the world—thanks to weighty roles in films like *Trapeze* and *Sweet Smell of Success* (both with Burt Lancaster); *Mister Cory,* directed by Blake Edwards; *Kings Go Forth,* with Frank Sinatra and Natalie Wood; Stanley Kramer's *The Defiant Ones,* for which he earned an Oscar nomination for best actor along with his costar Sidney Poitier; and two back-to-back comedy classics, Billy Wilder's *Some Like It Hot,* in which he costarred with Jack Lemmon and Marilyn Monroe, playing a Prohibition-era saxophonist who masquerades as a woman to escape from Chicago mobsters, and *Operation Petticoat* with Cary Grant.

Canny in business, Curtis also negotiated gross percentages of the revenues of many of his best films, so by 1959, he was earning $1 million a year, making investments in land and art and living in a $200,000 eighteen-room mansion on Summit Drive with a pool, bathhouse, and badminton court. He counted the rooms to be sure of their number, never forgetting the one-and-a-half-room apartment in which he'd been born. "All of a sudden I wake up one day and I'm the master of an estate," he told a reporter that year. "Man, it's kookie."

Kookie, perhaps, but now that he didn't need to worry about a mortgage, it wasn't enough. Especially around new friends like Sinatra, Dean Martin, Jerry Lewis, and Sammy Davis Jr. (who later bought the Summit Drive house). That group of stars had inherited the Rat Pack label from the original glittery group that met at the Holmby Hills home of Humphrey Bogart and his wife Lauren Bacall, including Cary Grant, Katharine Hepburn and Spencer Tracy, David Niven, Judy Garland, and others. They all set a less than domestic example with their world-class carousing. "To be included in this circle," Curtis said, "was a wonderful feeling for me." But it also drove him to gamble, indulge in extreme egotism and excessive spending, and suffer bouts of paranoia, hypochondria, and paralyzing self-doubt. And then came infidelity.

Late in 1961, Curtis was on location in Argentina making *Taras Bulba,* a film based on Gogol's novel about Cossacks in the Ukraine, when he fell for his love interest, a seventeen-year-old Austrian-born actress named Christine Kaufmann, who'd been making movies in Europe since she was seven. Back in Beverly Hills the next spring, he left Janet Leigh; the couple divorced that July. Two months later, after getting a second divorce in Juarez, since California divorces still barred split couples from remarrying within a year, Leigh did just that at the Sands Hotel in Las Vegas. Four months after that, Curtis, then thirty-seven, married Kaufmann, who'd just turned eighteen, at the Riviera in Vegas with Kirk and Ann Douglas as their best man and matron of honor. Still riding high professionally, Curtis bought a series of ever-more-elaborate houses for them to live in, one in each of the Triangle neighborhoods: the first on Loma Linda Drive off Coldwater Canyon for $175,000 in 1963; the next, in 1965, a twenty-two-room white stucco Mediterranean home with a red Spanish tile roof at 364 St. Cloud Road in Bel Air, which he jokingly called Villa Schwartz; and finally, Florence Letts Quinn's mansion at 141 South Carolwood in Holmby Hills in October 1966.

Houses were a way of keeping score. "We were all kind of chasing each other," he said of his friends, who bought estates as if they were raising the stakes in poker.

When he bought Carolwood, Curtis and Kaufmann were living at the St. Cloud Road house, which Kaufmann says she found. "I'd met Ruth Gordon the actress and her husband Garson Kanin at an early dinner party. They liked me because I was pretty but not stupid. I toured the house with Garson. He said, 'This house suits you. Tony will have to grow into it.'"

Like so many in the area, that house came with a fascinating backstory. It had been built in 1929 by Garrett van Pelt, a Pasadena architect, for Louis W. Zimmerman, who'd been a broker in Chicago, where he was one of the least known but most successful financiers of his time. Between 1925 and 1929, he made a fortune estimated at between $10 million and $75 million—a range equivalent to $125 million to $937 million in 2010 currency.

Though he lived in Chicago, Zimmerman was a Wall Street speculator. After starting his career in import-export, he'd segued into the markets, moving in and out of commodities like wheat and later stocks like RCA and Montgomery Ward, cashing out early in 1929. That year, he paid $500,000 to build his house in Bel Air "to give his only son a better playground," according to a 1930 book.

His house passed through the hands of several others at a significant discount from its cost before it was bought for $65,000 by Casey Robinson, a writer and producer at Twentieth Century Fox, and his wife, Tamara Toumanova, who'd come to America at age thirteen, hailed as "the baby ballerina." In 1955, she found a "little black book" in her husband's laundry. It "contained the names and addresses of some ladies; they were not mutual friends of ours," she testified at her subsequent divorce trial. "I asked him who they were, but he had no explanation. A few days later, he packed his bags and moved out." Toumanova got the house in the divorce.

The day Kaufmann and Curtis moved in, a press agent sent them a photo of Sonny and Cher, then riding high on the pop music charts, with a note formed ransom-style from cut-out magazine letters, reading, "May your life always be sunny and you have a lot of cheer." Kaufmann would soon have cause to remember that clumsy pun of a welcome.

Kaufmann and Curtis quickly had children and when she was pregnant with their second, "we needed a bigger house," she says. "Tony needed the space. I realized, alas too late, that children bothered him because he wanted to be the child. But he's fun. And we had a lot in common. I love to move. I love to decorate."

In summer 1966, while still living in Bel Air, Curtis gave a prescient interview to the *Los Angeles Times* on the set of a film called *Don't Make Waves*. "When you have a mansion, a beautiful young wife and a Rolls in the garage, you can get to thinking you're awfully cute," he said. "And in no time, you find yourself in a TV series that's cancelled."

Forty-four years later, six months before his death in 2010 at age eighty-five, married to his sixth wife, who was half his age, and living in Vegas, Curtis looked back on his next mansion—141 South Carolwood—as if it were a dream. "Who'd have thought I'd end up in that house," he said. "I began in the back of Schwartz's Tailors in New York, cleaning and drying. We went from one house to another. Houses became spiritual places for me. Just to say 'Carolwood' is mind-boggling." After he bought it in 1966, his other houses faded from memory. "I hardly remember it," he said of 364 St. Cloud Road. "Aren't I a terrible fellow?"

Curtis learned from his lawyer that the Carolwood house—which he did remember, as he'd dated Marilyn Monroe when she was bunking in Joe Schenck's guesthouse—was on the market. William Myron Keck's estate financed the arrangement, which Curtis recalls was worth $300,000, but thanks to a tax dodge, all he had to pay was $15,000—representing prepaid interest on the loan—and the same amount each year. At the end of five years, he could either buy the house outright or sell and take a profit. "I couldn't turn it down," Curtis said in 2010.

When he first walked through it, the house was empty except for a pool table in the basement, but it was still full of paneling, gesso, and marble.

There was also Joe Schenck's gracious screening room, complete with a bar with a door that disappeared into its paneling; a bomb shelter; a garden room Curtis later filled with ferns; an indoor pool with a retracting roof, waterfall, and dressing rooms; and a string of guesthouses, including Monroe's. "There was a balcony overlooking the entry hall," Curtis recalled. "I was told Mrs. Keck fell off there and died." Interior decorator Ron Wilson heard a wildly different version of a similar story: "Supposedly, his wife shot the old man on the stairs for having an affair with his male secretary," says Wilson, who began his career working for the Kecks' decorator. Wilson's version is possible, Curtis's is not: Keck's first wife died in 1936, long before he moved into the house, and his second wife survived him.

True or not, the story didn't cool Curtis's ardor. "I didn't want to know about ghosts," he said. "I didn't want to interrupt buying that house. I was a gangster out of New York. I knew I had to grab it. . . . I didn't know I was an aristocrat, but I thought I was, that in my heart, I was the Count, and these houses became cloaks and when I pulled them on they became me, not the other way around. Aristocracy is in your soul. You don't acquire it; it's there and the atmosphere you live in is part of it."

Curtis said he did nothing to the house. Christine Kaufmann begs to differ. "Obviously, I was a lot younger than he was, but I was also more mature and educated," she says. "I was a star at nine, I grew up in film and theater, I spoke five languages, I'd lived in Italy. I wanted to create my own space, even at nineteen." Kaufmann loved Carolwood because it reminded her of Tuscany; she says she decorated it herself with signed eighteenth-century furniture and the art Curtis had begun collecting. Kaufmann recalls that they had a Picasso and a Balthus. Curtis also made art of his own, converting an outbuilding into a studio where he painted and made Joseph Cornell–style boxes.

Briefly, their life there was joyous. "We had lots of dinners," she says, with guests like Gregory Peck, Burt Lancaster, Sharon Tate and Roman Polanski, Raquel Welch, and Jack Lemmon. But Kaufmann found stars to be "disagreeable people," she says. "I liked writers like Henry Miller," another dinner guest. "There was a certain glamour before the drugs took over. People came in long dresses and it wasn't ridiculous then. Beautiful women and interesting men. The romantic part of the house was that I loved Tony's friends, both male and female. So for a very brief while, it was a good house."

Even though to her it had no history. "As a European, I've lived in buildings six hundred years old, so everything in America was papier maché."

The fashion photographer Melvin Sokolsky, who first shot pictures of Kaufmann on the set of *Taras Bulba,* was close to the couple. He and his wife stayed at Carolwood with Kaufmann when Curtis was away, often enough, in fact, that they gave Curtis a new pool table detailed with rosewood in thanks. The house "was in much better taste than most in Hollywood, classier than any I'd seen," Sokolsky says, recalling the matched oak paneling and a door hidden in the entry foyer, with a powder room behind. "It was big for a couple but not for a Hollywood couple. Most people in that business have a coterie that gives them an identity."

Soon, though, Christine's life wore thin. "Being invited and inviting was what kept the marriage going," she says. "The house was beautiful but in a funny way, it made certain things transparent." One night, Tuesday Weld, the actress, took Kaufmann aside and said, "You're twenty-two. Are you going to be the hostess with the mostest for the rest of your life? You're not forty. Get the fuck out of here."

Says Kaufmann, "She couldn't understand how, at my age, I'd be happy with a child, married to a man I didn't love. Our house was beautiful but it was an empty shell. Every woman with a revolutionary spirit wanted to leave her husband then. I was just one. I once wanted to leave but I couldn't drive, I couldn't even open the gate, I couldn't escape if I wanted to. It felt like a strange prison. I had a view into the future. I started to despise him."

To Kaufmann, Curtis's fantasy that he was lord of the manor was mere narcissism. "Narcissists expect their environment to become them," she says. "He'd have been happier in Hungary in short pants, watering his garden. Instead he was a movie star but not somebody who really enjoyed it. That house was so splendid. It need[ed] people with a certain spirit and a couple who could communicate, but that spirit wasn't there anymore."

One night when Curis was in Las Vegas performing, Kaufmann went dancing with one of Dean Martin's sons, Dean Jr., and her husband heard about it and called her.

"Leave my house," she says he ordered, "and you may not take anything."

"I said, 'Stick it all up your ass,' " she recalls, "and I took my dresses and the children." Kaufmann left Carolwood Drive on the Saturday after Thanksgiving. Curtis suffered after she left, walking the empty halls of his house sure he'd find an intruder, keeping loaded guns in his bedroom just in case, staring at the fish in his twenty-six-gallon aquarium, playing with a miniature auto-racing set in his basement, and sometimes going to discos with celebrity pals like the pop musicians Sonny and Cher.

Kaufmann insists she walked away from all that without regrets, but more than forty years later, just before Curtis's death, she still betrayed a lingering bitterness. "He has only prostitutes with him in his world," she said. "That's all there is."

29

Holmby Hills

10060 Sunset Boulevard

Next-door neighbor Douglas Warde, son of an insurance executive who'd
bought the Edwin Janss estate at 10100 Sunset in 1962, remembers Tony
Curtis as very nice, never getting upset when local kids hopped his fence
to explore the bridle path that ran beneath his art studio. Warde doesn't
remember the man who bought Jayne Mansfield's home in 1968, and no
existing account of the house's history includes him, though it is often falsely
claimed that Cass Elliot of the Mamas and Papas and the Beatle Ringo Starr
lived there—presumably separately. But Harold Greenlin, that 1968 buyer,
was a harbinger of things to come in Holmby Hills—and the rest of La-La
Land, too.

Greenlin appeared on the national show business radar in 1949 as the
operator of the Alameda Theater, a 385-seat burlesque house in Sacramento,
California. He bought an ad in *Billboard* magazine that fall, offering to
sell a ten-year lease on the theater for $28,000, pitching its "low overhead,
low rent, no stage hand[s], no musicians, no local heat." Candy sales covered
the cost of the shows, he noted, adding that he would finance half the purchase price for the lease. His ad said he had other interests that required his
full attention, and promised the Alameda would be "a gold mine for a live
operator."

The emphasis on candy was telling. Greenlin, a native of San Francisco,
had grown up in the world of burlesque and carnival girly shows, starting

his career in the Depression as a candy butcher doing what was known as the candy pitch. Candy butchers sold candy and programs inside strip shows, keeping the crowd happy and spending with the "pitch," in which the butcher announced that every box of candy had a prize in it, but one contained something of great value—a watch or a wallet, for instance—that one lucky patron would get for just a few cents. In truth, all of the prizes were worthless.

"It was a way of selling what didn't exist," says Roger Forbes, who worked with Greenlin in the early 1970s, and ended up a multimillionaire and a principal in a national chain of strip clubs. "That was the era he came from."

By the 1940s, Greenlin had pitched enough candy to start buying theaters of his own. He'd also developed a humpback that he blamed on a fall, and married a stripper who called herself Shalimar and had learned the fan dance from the famous Sally Rand. With her he fathered a daughter, though he left her and her mother behind by the time Sharon Greenlin was six years old. Shalimar would continue stripping, and Sharon wound up in a foster home. In the next several years, Greenlin's name would pop up often in show business trade magazines as the operator of the Liberty, another theater with strippers in Stockton, California; as a publicity agent for Jennie Lee, who styled herself the "Basoom Girl"; and as the operator of a chain of what were known as triple-feature grind houses, movie theaters in the South and Southwest that operated thirteen hours a day, showing soft-core pornography and other exploitation films.

By 1959, Greenlin's wife had tired of the carnival life, reclaimed their daughter from the foster home she'd grown up in, and tracked Harold down in New Orleans, where he was living with another stripper, a tall, glamorous dancer named Rita, and her son by another man, and running a French Quarter club called Vavoom. Rita called herself his wife and used his name, though it's unclear if he'd ever gotten divorced. "I didn't like her," says his daughter Sharon. "She let her stupid poodles poop on the floor. I was close to her son, though; we both felt abandoned." Uncomfortable with his two "wives" in one city, Harold moved Sharon and her mother to Dallas, and put his first wife through nursing school. She was an LVN—a licensed vocational nurse—for the next thirty years and didn't see Harold again for almost half of them.

In 1964, Greenlin was operating the Gayety, a "nudie" theater in Toledo, Ohio, when he was sued by local prosecutors seeking to shut it down as a public nuisance. After three judges reviewed fifty-one minutes of a two-hour film he'd shown in the theater, they ordered it destroyed. Perhaps sensing that Ohio wasn't ready for his wares, by the late 1960s, Greenlin had moved his base of operations back to the West Coast, where he owned and operated theaters specializing in soft-core pornographic films in Seattle, San Francisco, and Los Angeles. Among his employees was a doorman named Jim Mitchell, then a film student who would go on, with his brother Artie, to make "nudie" shorts for Greenlin before segueing into hard-core pornography and eventually producing one of the pioneering classics of the genre, *Behind the Green Door,* starring an Ivory Snow model named Marilyn Chambers.

According to a biography of the Mitchell brothers, Greenlin was "pure show-biz, a fabled character in the world of burlesque. . . . Everybody loved [him] because he was colorful and funny as hell, but he was a treacherous man to do business with. The word was, if [he] gave you a cashier's check, it was not necessarily money in the bank."

Harold and Rita did pay the Mansfield estate $180,000 for 10100 Sunset Boulevard and its contents in August 1968. According to the official "chain of title" documents, he didn't own it long, though. Two years later, the Greenlins were sued by an L. M. Kenworthy, who appeared to have obtained the deed to the house in a marshal's sale in 1970 for a mere $5,011.60. The following June, the deed was assigned by Kenworthy to a Jack McDonald, who passed it on to an R. J. Huisman in summer 1972. Huisman held it for four years before the deed passed to a Frank and Barbara Doherty, who sold it thirty-six days later to an A. G. Dorsey. That tangled web of transactions hid the fact that Greenlin continued to own it, says Gary Culver, then one of Greenlin's Seattle attorneys, but later disbarred and sent to prison after he was convicted of eighteen charges of conspiracy, theft, forgery, and perjury in a complex land fraud. Culver's story of his involvement with Greenlin and the purchase of the Mansfield house seems to be another example of a complex real estate deal with a whiff of fraud around it.

Rita Greenlin, Culver says, "had a great desire to move up in the L.A. scene," and Harold bought the Mansfield house as a means to that end, "almost all in cash," which Culver says Greenlin had accumulated by skimming box office receipts at his theaters. Greenlin initially hoped "to make a friggin' fortune auctioning off Jayne Mansfield's underwear," Culver says, "but Rita decided to be prim and proper, so there was no auction." She gave Mansfield's brassieres to Goodwill instead.

Culver says Greenlin, "a tough guy," had "wandered into my office one day when I was green behind the ears." At the time, Culver was working for William L. Dwyer, a well-known Seattle trial lawyer. "We were among the first lawyers to make inroads in pornography," Culver says. "We'd represented Lenny Bruce. We had no idea what we were turning loose."

Just after he bought the Mansfield house, Greenlin caught the attention of a Seattle prosecutor engaged in what was then called a smut crackdown. Raymond "Tiny" Becker, the manager of the Rivoli, one of Greenlin's theaters, was arrested in spring 1969, charged with maintaining a public nuisance and exhibiting obscene material. The next year, the manager of another of Greenlin's Seattle theaters, the Embassy, was also arrested after vice squad officers watched part of a documentary film it was exhibiting, *Pornography in Denmark,* made by director Alex de Renzy about the world's first porn trade show in Copenhagen, following the legalization of adult porn there in 1969. "The picture explicitly depicts lesbianism, fellatio, cunnilingus, and every detail of conventional sexual intercourse," said *Time* magazine, making it the first hard-core porn film ever legally shown in America.

When the copy of the film that Greenlin's theater had shown disappeared, he was threatened with contempt of court, ten days in jail, and a $300 fine if he didn't explain where the print was and why it had not been produced. Compounding Greenlin's legal problems, the film's distributor sued him, contending that it had been shown in Seattle without permission—they wanted it back, too. Greenlin was on the edge of the sexual revolution in America, and an experienced lawyer was a good thing to have.

Later that year, Greenlin also stuck his oar into the waters of the cultural revolution. The Seattle-born rock music sensation Jimi Hendrix had just died at twenty-seven, suffocating on his own vomit after mixing sleeping pills and wine. Greenlin, Culver, Tiny Becker, and several others approached Hendrix's father Al and a Hendrix family friend and civil rights activist, Freddie Mae Gautier, offering to set up a Jimi Hendrix Memorial Foundation to donate land to the city for an outdoor concert venue, a Hendrix museum, and a summer camp for underprivileged children. Al Hendrix, unsure whether he would get any money from his son's estate, gave his permission in exchange for the title of vice president of the foundation, $1,000, promises of "a white woman every month," Culver claims, and a further $100 a week. Those payments ended after only a month. "Not one among us gave a shit about Hendrix," Culver admits. "We had no idea how big a deal he was. It was just a money-making proposition."

According to *Jimi Hendrix: Electric Gypsy*, a biography of the guitarist, Greenlin and his associates rented offices, leased twenty telephone lines, sought sponsors to buy advertising in a Hendrix photo book, sold official Hendrix merchandise and foundation memberships, and staged a few concerts. But, the authors Harry Shapiro and Caesar Glebbeek charge, most of the money was used to bail out another of Gary Culver's clients in a land deal gone bad. Soon, employees went to the police with that information and more, charging that the Hendrix Foundation was breaking laws related to its tax-exempt status, and it emerged that Tiny Becker had a police record. The foundation's charitable status was revoked and within a year, the offices were emptied. One of the principals later killed himself after he was indicted for armed robbery, and in 1973, Becker's wife, a Mormon, killed him with a .38 revolver during a domestic squabble.

Culver believed that officially the Mansfield house was sold by the Los Angeles marshal to satisfy an unpaid debt of Greenlin's, but that he remained in residence during what was called a redemption period, during which he could repay the debt and reclaim the house. In fact, Kenworthy, the first owner listed in that complex chain of title after Greenlin, worked for him in a lab where he processed short porn films known as loops, many of them filmed in the Mansfield house, says Habib Carouba, now a retired theater owner, but at the time another Greenlin employee.

Greenlin taught Carouba the theater business, but they didn't always see eye to eye outside the office. "He'd have a whole bunch of women up there, going in the pool," Carouba recalls. "It was a mess to me. To him, it was fun. I think he tried [to have sex with the dancers who came around], but . . . he liked to get abused." His power and his cash were likely a large part of his appeal as he was short and fat, had a hump, a bulbous nose, a protruding lower lip, small eyes beneath big, dark bushy brows, and an Eddie Munster hairdo, and often wore a girdle under flashy, mismatched clothing. "He liked to eat popcorn and play the organ," says Adele DeCampli-Cirkelis, who danced in his theaters for years as Viva La Fever. "He was just into having fun." She recalls a stripper named Honeychile whom he'd sit and watch, bouncing up and down on his bed, and another named Ruby Tuesday who complained when he gave her hundred-dollar bills because they were too hard to cash.

Cash was likely Greenlin's Achilles' heel; it attracted the wrong kind of attention. "He was always in some kind of trouble with the IRS," Culver says. But in the past, he'd known a federal judge in Las Vegas who could make his tax problems vanish. Unfortunately, that judge was no longer on call when he saw trouble on the horizon that he feared would not easily go away, so "he wanted the house out of his name," Culver says. Greenlin tried to sell 10100 Sunset in 1971, putting it on the market for $285,000 even though he didn't formally hold title to it. Jack McDonald, who was listed on official documents as the purchaser of the deed from Kenworthy that year, "never existed," Culver continues. "That was me. I held the title in trust, though it was never in writing." The transfers were "meaningless," Culver admits. "They were done to muddy the water and avoid a huge IRS tax lien, $300,000 or $400,000." The next owner was R. J. Huisman, which was Culver's wife's maiden name.

Somehow, it's unsurprising that Culver's ex-wife Rose Huisman Culver, briefly the owner of record of the house, tells a somewhat different story. She says the Culvers had loaned Greenlin money "and he went belly up and couldn't pay, so we took possession of the house. We never moved in, though. We stayed in Seattle because we had four kids, and I didn't want to raise children in Hollywood with all the drugs and goings-on." They did visit, though, says their son Frank, who remembers the house as "pretty cool," with its rolling lawn, big gate, tiled pool, heart-shaped bed, and a stash of liquor-filled chocolates that he found one day; they made him sick.

Greenlin was still trying to become a somebody in Los Angeles, and in June 1971, made what may have been his boldest move yet—buying a weekly newspaper, the *Los Angeles Citizen News,* out of bankruptcy (in part with money borrowed from Culver) and announcing a quixotic plan to use it to compete with the city's two major dailies, the Chandler family's *Times* and Hearst's *Herald-Examiner.*

"I realized . . . that Harold was more intent on seeing his name on a masthead than on making money," says Culver. "He ran it like a carnival," and they had a falling out over Greenlin's failure to repay the $50,000 loan Culver had made to him. Greenlin's onetime colleague Roger Forbes thinks Greenlin "pictured himself as a Hearst," and ruined his life chasing that dream. "He grabbed money anyplace he could to pump it into that paper. That's probably what put him in prison."

Rose Culver says the Greenlins next moved to Las Vegas; Rita definitely did, and remained there the rest of her life. Harold "would be here and there," shuttling between two homes in Vegas, one in Hawaii, and an apartment in Seattle, says Habib Carouba, who'd by then risen from protégé to partner. Often, his travels made no sense. Once, Greenlin bought a Lincoln Continental for their company, drove it from Los Angeles to Las Vegas, parked it at the airport, flew back to L.A., and promptly forgot about it. "We'd paid $10,000 cash and he forgot it!" Carouba marvels. "He was a very complicated man."

In 1976, Harold was arrested in Las Vegas after a two-year investigation and charged with fifteen counts of tax evasion between 1970 and 1973. The investigation was conducted by an organized crime strike force. No evidence Greenlin was involved with the mob was ever made public, though policemen who interviewed his ex-wife warned her that his daughter should "keep her mouth shut because if she doesn't, there are people out there who'll make sure she never talks again," Sharon Greenlin remembers.

Certainly, Greenlin had dealings with organized crime. He told Roger Forbes he was once held out a window upside down by the Mafia distributors of another early porn film, *Deep Throat,* who'd come to collect their revenues. They knew Greenlin had a habit of "transferring films around the country, playing them in theaters he wasn't supposed to," Forbes says. "He'd spend $500 to beat someone out of $100." And at some point, Greenlin sold "theaters across the country to some strange people," continues Forbes, who insists Greenlin wasn't mobbed up, but allows that he dealt with "people who were. *Everybody* knew people."

It seems likely Greenlin saw his arrest coming. In July 1976, Barbara and Frank Doherty, who Culver and Carouba agree was a Greenlin lawyer, allegedly sold 10100 Sunset Boulevard to A. G. Dorsey, better known as the English pop singer Engelbert Humperdinck. James Verdon, who'd worked for Greenlin for twenty years, says Humperdinck had been looking for a place in Las Vegas and heard about Greenlin's house from a broker they shared there, who put the deal together. At least some of the proceeds went to repay Culver's loan for the *Citizen News.*

Three months later, in a federal court in Seattle, Greenlin copped a plea to one tax-related count, but later tried to withdraw from the deal after prosecutors sought the maximum three-year term. In 1977, he was denied bail and led out of a Seattle courtroom in handcuffs. According to Carouba, he spent about a year in the Lompoc Federal Correctional Complex, north of Santa Barbara.

In 1981, Greenlin was arrested again. He and three others, two of them lawyers who were free on bail in a separate fraud case, were charged with writing $200,000 in bad checks on a nonexistent bank. Greenlin and an accomplice were arrested while the two lawyers fled, only to be arrested while trying to flee the Bahamas on a stolen yacht, and Harold went back to what Culver calls "the iron bar hotel"—this time, the Federal Correctional Institution on Terminal Island, California. He emerged, by all accounts, a broken man who never recovered his nerve or his fortune.

"Everything was taken from him," says Sharon Greenlin. "We went to nothing. He'd kept everything in his hip pocket. He never wrote anything down. He thought he could get away with anything. Most of his life, he did, so that's how he operated. But whatever he'd had went away."

After his release, Greenlin bounced between Seattle, Las Vegas, and San Francisco, where he partnered again with his long-ago protégé Carouba at the Market Street Cinema, until they had problems with police raids. "He took off with some money, went to L.A. for a couple of months, and left people in jail," Carouba says. "I got them out, put things back in shape. He wanted to come back and I said, 'You're a dime short.' He started working for me. It wasn't really work. I took him in, like my dad or my brother. I paid his rent. He liked big cars. I got him an old car. He'd get so many tickets, they'd take the car. I'd get him another. I think I got him seven or eight." Greenlin died of cirrhosis of the liver in 1992 at age seventy-seven. Carouba paid for his funeral. Rita Greenlin died two years later in Las Vegas.

"There's nothing you can say about my father that would surprise me," says Sharon Greenlin. "But you have to understand that in a family that walks on the shady side of the street, a lot of things aren't told and you don't want to know, because then you can't tell and you can't get in trouble."

Greenlin was a casualty. And sui generis. But he wasn't entirely an aberration. Some of the hustlers who were moving into the neighborhood were just more accomplished players than he was.

30

Beverly Hills

Grayhall (1100 Carolyn Way)

Playboy magazine founder Hugh Hefner bought what had once been Arthur Letts Jr.'s estate in Holmby Hills for the record-setting price of $1.05 million in February 1971. A month later, George Hamilton sold Grayhall to Bernie Cornfeld, an Istanbul-born, Brooklyn-bred financier. It probably wasn't a coincidence.

Apart from being competitive friends, Hefner and Cornfeld were both empire builders, though they built very different empires. Hefner's *Playboy* is today a shadow of its former self, but is still a formidable brand known around the world, and its eighty-five-year-old founder remains a world-class celebrity and renowned, if Viagra-assisted, rake; he also remains in residence in Holmby Hills. Cornfeld, on the other hand, is long dead, and his biggest brand, Investor Overseas Services (or IOS), a force in mutual funds, is forgotten, known if at all only to students of business history or, more specifically, the history of business frauds. Its collapse coincided with Cornfeld's arrival in Beverly Hills. Like so many before and after him, he'd come there to reinvent himself.

Reinvention was Cornfeld's specialty. He'd done it himself, and he'd done it for the many who believed in him, believed he would make them wealthy beyond measure, believed in the promise contained in the line he used as he raised billions of dollars in the mid-1960s, "Do you sincerely want to be rich?" Cornfeld was briefly the King of Finance. Grayhall was supposed to be the stage for his next act. Instead it became the scene of his downfall.

It may have been inevitable that Bernie Cornfeld ended up in Beverly Hills. His father, Leon, had been an actor and a film producer, a Romanian-born Louis B. Mayer with offices in Vienna and Istanbul, where Bernie was born Benno Cornfield in 1927 to Leon and his second wife, Sophie, a Russian. Two half-brothers from Leon's first marriage ended up in the movie business. After an accident ended his acting career, Leon and Sophie moved to America, where Leon briefly taught German literature in Rhode Island until the Cornfields separated. Sophie then took Bernie to Palestine for a year before returning to live in Brooklyn, where she worked double shifts as a nurse while Bernie, her only child, attended public school, sleeping at night in the same room as his mother until he was fifteen years old. As a boy, he said, he collected spare change on behalf of the Abraham Lincoln Brigade, which fought against the fascists led by Francisco Franco in the Spanish Civil War; this early commitment to progressivism would later return as a sales pitch: he called IOS "people's capitalism," designed to "convert the proletariat to the leisure class painlessly."

Plump, shaped like a fireplug, and standing only five feet five inches, Cornfeld—when he changed his name is unknown—grew up the center of his mother's attention. He earned pocket money working for a fruit stand, selling lollipops, and running a guess-your-weight-and-age concession at Coney Island. Years later, a carnival scale would grace Grayhall as a reminder.

Cornfeld spent at least one season in the 1940s at the Camp of the Three Arrows, a communal summer colony for Jewish socialists, sleeping in a barn, playing sports, and enjoying art classes, lectures on politics and social welfare, group discussions called schmoozes, concerts, plays, and dances. Though he'd described his mother as a tsarist, at those gatherings in Putnam Valley, New York, he got a further education in socialism. After two years as an assistant purser in the Merchant Marine, Cornfeld entered Brooklyn College in 1948, when the campus was a cauldron of left-wing political activity; he led a group of student socialists who worked to draft the leftist Norman Thomas to run for president against Harry Truman, Thomas Dewey, and the progressive candidate Henry Wallace.

Cornfeld dove into the factional disputes that pitted various left-wing groups against each other, displaying more ego than ideological resolve. Simultaneously, he dealt with a stammer that had plagued him for years (and would continue to do so for the rest of his life when he was tired), consulting a psychotherapist who lured him into a study group that analyzed human behavior and motivations, and emphasized the way some people compensated for feelings of inferiority by striving for superiority. Its focus on "the engineering of emotional relationships," as Cornfeld's biographers described it, became "the real interest of his life." That psychologist would later describe him as a manipulator. By the time he graduated with a degree in psychology in 1950, Cornfeld had earned a reputation for ambitious manipulation in several areas. He tended to chase extremely desirable and apparently inaccessible women. And he saw himself as an organizer of others, though he'd yet to decide what he was organizing them for. While figuring it out, he took to the sea as a purser again.

Back in New York in 1953, Bernie began to pursue an advanced degree in social work, but left school for good after a friend from Three Arrows and Brooklyn College introduced him to the founder of Investors Planning Corp. (IPC), an early mutual fund sales organization that offered what seemed a socialist dream: a way for common people to get a piece of the capitalist pie while not tying up their investment money. The company would buy gold shares back for cash on demand. Cornfeld accepted a job as a salesman, then had second thoughts and went to Philadelphia, where he spent nine months as a social worker. But the idea of mutual funds kept tugging at him and by the end of 1954, he'd returned to New York and IPC. He pulled a group of friends together to rent a ten-room apartment with a triple-height cathedral-ceilinged living room in the famous Hotel des Artistes there, installed both his mother and an orgone box—the psychologist Wilhelm Reich's device that was alleged to improve both health and sexual energy—and threw himself into the task of making money from the IPC organization, which required not just selling shares of funds but recruiting other salesmen. Soon, Cornfeld wanted to move up faster than IPC allowed. So late in 1955, he quit and for no apparent reason went to Paris, where he met a girl and decided to stay.

At the time, the Dreyfus Funds, run by a charismatic stockbroker named Jack Dreyfus, was the preeminent name in mutual funds. Cornfeld had met Dreyfus while he worked for IPC and wrote to him from Paris, offering to create a sales organization in Europe for him, targeting U.S. servicemen stationed in Europe as the customer base. When Dreyfus agreed, Bernie created Investors Overseas Services (IOS) with $300 in working capital, and ran an ad in the Paris edition of the *Herald Tribune* seeking "people with a sense of humor" to come and work for him. Cornfeld realized that the postwar exile community in Paris might provide him with an army of salesmen looking to make a quick buck by selling fund shares to GIs on contractual installment plans for as little as $25 a month. His latent evangelism had found its message and its flock.

By 1959 IOS had become a major feeder of money into the Dreyfus funds. Aside from recruiting through his ads, which ran regularly in the *Tribune,* Cornfeld also recruited old friends and acquaintances. Eventually, several members of his old Boy Scout troop, veterans of Three Arrows, and friends from the Maritime Service's purser school joined the IOS sales force, and the psychologist who'd helped him overcome his stutter became a speaker at IOS conferences. Bernie's charisma, his soft sell, and his knowledge of psychology were his most potent recruiting tools. The idea of making easy money didn't hurt, either. But Cornfeld's operation did attract unwanted attention from French authorities. So in 1958, he'd loaded his corporate records into his 1947 Chrysler convertible and moved IOS to an apartment in Geneva, Switzerland, which was, as his biographers put it, "the center of the international flight-capital business." A year later, he registered IOS in Panama, out of reach of most securities regulators. Then, using tools ranging from soft-spoken charm to a volatile temper, he taught his growing ranks of salesmen how to win the confidence of customers, and convinced them to invest heavily in IOS themselves, laying the basis for what some would come to consider—too late—a pyramid scheme. Cornfeld, to the day of his death, believed what he was doing was legitimate.

The truth is that Cornfeld and his right-hand man, a Harvard cum laude lawyer named Ed Cowett, were expert at maneuvering in the cracks between the laws of different countries and avoiding taxes, regulation, and financial oversight. Two books were written about the complex web of companies and investment vehicles Cornfeld created over the next decade. Suffice it to say, not only innocents, but many savvy investors, financial operators, and well-respected social and civic types (from James Roosevelt, eldest son of Franklin Delano Roosevelt, and C. Henry Buhl III, a General Motors heir, to Count Carl Johan Bernadotte of Sweden's royal family, the Paris-based Rothschild family, and even the pope, who gave Bernie an audience in 1969) were lured into getting involved in one way or another. They also believed in the goods Cornfeld was selling as, starting in 1960, IOS launched funds of its own, investing their assets around the world, eventually becoming a vital cog in the world's financial system. As his sales force expanded, so did his customer base, from GIs to expatriates of all nations—including some who were breaking the laws of their countries, but couldn't resist the lure of the wealth they saw being generated by Wall Street. Eventually, IOS would even expand into the third world, where it actively sought out "rich and frightened people," Bernie's biographers wrote, "who had reason to fear . . . their fellow countrymen. Such people wanted to get their money out. . . . This was the basic source of the money that made IOS rich."

Sales doubled annually and in 1962, Cornfeld inaugurated his most famous product, the Fund of Funds, composed of shares of other mutual funds. It was "the phenomenon of phenomena," a London *Times* correspondent raved. And that was before Cornfeld had the radical idea of investing the assets of the Fund of Funds mostly in other IOS funds, generating double the management fees. Reinvesting its profits and diversifying into insurance, banking, real estate, energy, and investment services, IOS built its revenues to $300 million in 1964, $100 million in the first quarter of 1965 alone. Then, IOS began using the money in its funds for its own investments, for short trading, as loan capital, and to develop other IOS businesses, spurring even greater growth. But it also regularly bent and broke local laws of securities and finance in the countries where it operated, most notably by raking in flight capital, money illegally removed from troubled or heavily taxed countries by the wealthy seeking to protect their assets, or hidden by Americans living overseas and seeking to avoid paying taxes. "It was all about money-laundering businessmen handing over cash to IOS to hide it from tax-men, ex-wives, present wives, future wives, business partners or police," Canada's *Financial Post* would later report. When Cornfeld bought his first airplane, staffers joked it was the first in the fleet of Capital Flight Airlines.

Finally, IOS became too big to ignore. Brazil, India, Pakistan, and Greece looked askance at its operations. In 1967, IOS made a deal with the U.S. Securities and Exchange Commission to drop charges in exchange for its agreement to shut subsidiaries there and stop selling shares to Americans anywhere in the world. That same year, Bernie threw a handful of pens into the face of a Geneva bureaucrat and called him a son-of-a-bitch, and the Swiss forced Cornfeld to move much of his head-office operation back across the nearby border into France. The *Times* of London reported that the French government, coveting "the considerable local spending power" of the IOS staff and the chance to "mobilize the vast hoarded savings of the cautious French . . .

may even have made the first approaches" to IOS. More likely, an IOS source planted that story to tweak the Swiss. The new IOS headquarters in Ferney-Voltaire was soon dubbed Bernie-Voltaire.

IOS had been very good for Cornfeld. And Bernie was very good for the financial journalists who covered him, delighting them with lavish entertainment at his castle and Gucci wallets as Christmas presents. In turn, they burnished his image. *Time* magazine caught up with him in spring 1965 and, in a story pegged to the $2 million IOS takeover of Cornfeld's first employer, IPC, catalogued the fruits of his labors, which included a Lancia Flaminia convertible; a forty-two-foot Corsair sailboat; a lakeside villa called Bella Vista where IOS was headquartered; a Gstaad ski lodge; Chateau de Pelly, a thirteenth-century fifteen-room stone castle, complete with moat and drawbridge, built by a Crusader in Haute Savoie, France; and the fifty-room Villa Elma on Lake Geneva, once part of the Château de Penthes, former residence of the Empress Josephine, which Bernie bought from the estate of a Cartier heir. It housed ten horses, two Great Danes named Pounim and Scheina (Mug—as in face—and Beautiful in Yiddish), a pair of ocelots, a basset hound, and a Chinese houseman. *Time* also noted "his penthouse office with red silk Empire furnishings and swarms of attractive, multilingual secretaries . . . [and] his worldwide force of 2,000 salesmen," who were rewarded not just with commissions, but also with lavish parties at Bernie's baronial residences. Among the swarm of attractive assistants was a University of Geneva student, Diane Halfin, who would soon marry a German prince and become Diane von Furstenberg, the fashion designer.

By the end of the decade, Cornfeld had more, much more. There was an apartment in Paris, three in New York, a townhouse in London's Belgravia, and a second chateau in Switzerland; a Rolls, a custom-built Lincoln, a Cadillac, and the Corvette Stingray he'd bought to replace his aging Chrysler; and a full wardrobe in each residence; the one in Geneva contained seventy suits, a hundred shirts, and thirty pairs of shoes. "I deliberately went out and created an image I thought most people wanted to emulate," he said.

Bernie had opened a New York–style Jewish delicatessen on the ground floor of the IOS building in Geneva; corned beef and pastrami were flown in from New York and a local baker provided passable, if imperfect, rye bread. There were also girls, whole stables of girls, wherever he went. Cornfeld, though he still lived with his eighty-two-year-old mother, who occupied a self-contained apartment in his Geneva villa (and had a Rolls of her own), usually traveled with three or four girls at a time, and he could constantly restock his shelves from the acting and modeling school he owned in Paris or the model agency he bankrolled in New York.

Cornfeld first flirted with the business of beautiful women in 1965, when a New York bachelor-stockbroker who was close to Jerry and Eileen Ford, heads of the eponymous model agency, and Dorian Leigh, a postwar super-model who then ran a Paris agency associated with Ford, recruited Bernie to bail out Leigh's business, which was on the verge of insolvency. "I went to Geneva and met with Bernie," Jerry Ford said in a 1994 interview. "He was at the top of the world. He had two cheetahs. He'd just apparently insulted a Rothschild by keeping him waiting for 45 minutes while he was upstairs with a girl. He was a fascinating little guy. He stuttered, couldn't complete a sentence, but he was a terrific salesman. A character. He thought he was running the world."

Cornfeld was a fan of the Fords, as well. "They had absolutely stunning women, and every time I was in town, they would organize a party and let the girls know these were people they should be marrying, or if not marry-ing, then fucking," he said in a 1994 interview. But when he looked over the financials of the Leigh and Ford operations, he decided they were rinky-dink and would interest him only "if they were combined with agencies all over the world and turned into a large public company."

Despite the penny-ante nature of modeling, Cornfeld bought TMI, a New York agency, a few years later, and installed Dovima, another retired model like Leigh, to run it. "I don't think I got involved with one girl from my agencies," Cornfeld said. "I had a lot of distraction and who needed an agency to get girls, really?" He was cultivating his female crop for his im-age, not sex; though legend had him frolicking in regular orgies, he actually tended to be a serial monogamist with stable girlfriends like Dewi Sukarno, the ex-wife of Indonesia's president for life, and the actresses Victoria (then Vicki) Principal and Pamela Tiffin, rather than a stable of them. The retinue of girls was an essential element of his calculated projection of success, just like the houses, cars, and planes. He even gave Principal a Rolls Royce for her nineteenth birthday in 1969. Though he professed to believe in "sexual anarchy," he also claimed he wanted to get married "someday," but didn't have the time. "If you get married, you have to be prepared to spend a lot of time with your wife," he said. One longtime girlfriend believed his first romance had been so disastrous he'd vowed to never become emotionally involved with another woman.

By 1967, Bernie's personal style had changed, too. Longtime employee Bert Cantor, who wrote a memoir of his years as a vice president at IOS, recalled his first sight of the "new Bernie" disembarking from a dark blue Lincoln Continental limousine in front of a New York restaurant: "A slim young man wearing Edwardian clothes with a lace jabot and lace showing at the cuffs got out. . . . The old Bernie was a short, plump, generally rumpled man wearing conservative, off-the-rack business suits, white button-down shirts, and Ivy League neckties. He usually looked as though he had slept in his clothes—often he had." The new Bernie wore a beard and was likely to appear at a disco in a red-trimmed white Nehru suit and love beads, carrying a small red fox in a custom-made basket or hopping out of a helicopter in jodhpurs and a flowing pink Pierre Cardin scarf. Asked how he'd gone from portly to pint-sized, Bernie replied that he'd not lost his taste for big, unhealthy meals, but had learned a weight-loss trick, perhaps from his model friends: "Throw it all up," he told Cantor. "You never gain an ounce."

Cornfeld bought a share of the Guy Laroche fashion house in Paris and then invited Oleg Cassini, an Italian nobleman turned American dress designer, to visit Villa Elma, and offered to help him expand his business. Cassini, also a world-class rake, was impressed despite himself. "There were so many girls," he raved in his autobiography. "He kept both houses stocked with them in the same way that certain trout streams are stocked by the state. They were there to be caught; Bernie kept two or three off limits, but the rest were fair game. . . . Some of the girls were pretty, others merely proximate; but quality seemed not to be a concern of Bernie's in this and many other areas. He was interested, primarily, in consumption. He was an insatiable consumer."

Cassini spent a year working out a deal with Cornfeld for a new fashion business based in Italy with boutiques all over the world and sometimes joined his caravan as it careened around the world. "He was a very generous host," Cassini wrote. "A weekend with Bernie could begin in Switzerland and end anywhere in the world. He had several jets on call at the airport at Geneva. Bernie liked to travel and to buy. There was a secretary with him at all times, carrying a briefcase with $50,000 in cash for shopping." The secretary, Bernie told Cassini, also shared his bed.

Cassini claimed to have introduced Principal to Cornfeld, and they also shared a link through another of Bernie's girls, Peggy Nestor, who would drift in and out of Cornfeld's life. Nestor is said to have borne the first of Bernie's three daughters (two of them out of wedlock), though another of his girlfriends suspects the child wasn't really his. One of Peggy Nestor's sisters, Marianne, would secretly marry Cassini in 1971, according to *Vanity Fair* writer Maureen Orth, who noted that the couple gave Bernie's London address as their own on their wedding license.

By the late sixties, the money to pay for Cornfeld's fun was mostly coming from Germany, where he'd started out selling Dreyfus funds to U.S. servicemen; however, he ended up selling so many IOS fund shares to German nationals that by 1969, 60 percent of its business, about $100 million a month, half of it in cash, was being generated there, according to Cantor.

The IOS system had been designed to turn its salesmen into zealots and it reached its apotheosis in Germany. As they rose in the IOS hierarchy based on the revenue from their share sales, thousands of salesmen (known as investment counselors) earned not only their own commissions but a piece of the commissions of those beneath them in the structure, and finally, the right to buy shares in the parent company; this was considered the pot of gold at the end of the IOS rainbow, and it made many of its sales managers millionaires, on paper at least.

Not that there wasn't still real cash to burn, and Cornfeld did, entering the investment banking business in the late sixties by both underwriting offerings and making large investments via its funds in everything from the hot conglomerate stocks of what became known as the Go-Go era on Wall Street to real estate, oil exploration, and hotels. One IOS manager invested in the stock of a conglomerate controlled by Cornfeld's pal Delbert Coleman that operated Las Vegas casinos. The deal for Coleman to buy control of the conglomerate, set up by Sidney Korshak, resulted in investigations by the Nevada Gaming Control Board, the American Stock Exchange, and the SEC, which eventually charged Coleman, Korshak, and others with stock manipulation. The conglomerate's shares promptly dropped from a high of over $100 to $12.50 a share.

On the surface, IOS seemed like a giant cash machine. "We were larger than American Express," Cornfeld claimed in 1964. It had more than a million customers in more than a hundred countries, twenty thousand employees and salespeople, a hundred different business units including five banks, four insurance companies, and eighteen mutual funds, and on some days could boast that it accounted for 5 percent of all trades on the New York Stock Exchange. With almost $2.5 billion under its control after a decade of steady growth, the assurance of the true believers may have been understandable, but it was also a grand illusion.

When Gramco, a rival offshore fund, went public, allowing insiders to sell their shares, the pressure was on for IOS to follow suit so that company insiders could cash in and turn their paper fortunes (Cornfeld was reputedly worth $100 million by then) into real ones. An initial public offering, or IPO, of 11 million shares at $10 per was scheduled for fall 1969. The big cash-out would relieve the pressure and add millions to the IOS coffers. Bernie predicted IOS would soon sell for $50 a share, would hit $4.5 billion in fund sales in 1970, and have $15 billion under management by 1975. But the 1969 market was a bubble that had grown just big enough to burst. The Dow Jones Industrial Average had peaked late in 1968 at about 1,000, fallen sharply, then recovered. Then, right around the time IOS went public, stock values began declining steadily and continued to drop into spring 1970. There was no sudden crash but by the time the bear market hit bottom, 33 percent beneath its peak, $300 billion in equity had vanished. Though its share price initially spiked to $19, IOS wasn't spared. Indeed, it was hurt proportionally hard since the go-go conglomerates whose stocks its funds had favored were overleveraged and sustained the most damage.

Some IOS executives—Cornfeld among them—sold what shares they could and walked away with huge sums; 490 insiders pocketed $55 million (Bernie's take was $8.2 million). However, others, including IOS itself, kept buying shares after the stock price weakened; in order to prop itself up, the company spent $20 million of its $52 million IPO windfall buying in its own stock. Despite those efforts, by April 1970, IOS shares were selling for under the IPO price and its downward slide was accelerating. IOS, Cornfeld's biographers concluded, was "supporting itself into a state of collapse." With an ever-greater share of its revenues going to the sales force in commissions and overrides, there were ever-fewer profits to prop up the edifice.

Not that you'd have known it, looking at the IOS excess. Bernie gave away five thousand bottles of his own Chateau Pelly de Cornfeld Champagne at a 1970 New Year's Eve party in Geneva. Then, in February, he flew to New York to address a conference of 2,300 businessmen and money managers sponsored by *Institutional Investor,* a magazine distributed to the investment trade. In what would later seem an act of extraordinary hubris, he spoke from the podium and at a subsequent press conference of the problems depressing the value of American securities—the Vietnam war, urban and racial violence, and pollution—but mostly blamed his antagonists at the SEC, saying its "destructive, ill-conceived, and headline-seeking attack" on the financial community had undermined faith in American markets and convinced IOS to stop investing in American stocks and shift its attention to markets in other countries. Bernie predicted that the inevitable result would be severe damage to the American economy.

The attendees applauded him like a rock star. And even more than before, he was acting like one, not just courting but feeding the press. Two days after the *Institutional Investor* conference, for instance, he announced his $500,000 purchase of another Swiss castle, this time the eighty-room eighteenth-century former home-in-exile of Charles I, the last Hapsburg emperor. Cornfeld no doubt savored the irony that he bought it from the same U.S. government he'd just excoriated. A few weeks later, twisting the knife, he deemed the SEC obsession with IOS "psychiatric." It was around that time that Bernie's mother secretly opened a bank account into which she deposited thirty Swiss francs a month. "Some day," she said presciently, "my son is going to have nothing and he is going to need this."

Ed Cowett had taken over the chief executive role so Bernie could roam free and dream big. Bernie dreamed of an IOS credit card and an art-buying fund, continued developing the Cassini fashion line, was talking about going into the food and prefabricated playground businesses, and began producing movies; just after the *Institutional Investor* conference, he hopped onto his white Falcon jet with a clutch of TMI models and a magazine writer in tow and flew to Acapulco to meet with Hugh Hefner, who arrived on his black DC-9, the Big Bunny, with a clutch of Playboy bunnies, to discuss a joint venture. One of many IOS real estate schemes, this one was a $15 million 512-unit Playboy condominium on the resort's famous bay. The presence of a journalist on Bernie's jet indicated that he had a personal agenda, too: to put himself on a par with Hefner, arguably the world's most-envied man.

Taking up residence in a Las Brisas villa called Nirvana, Bernie and his harem waited for Hefner; the girls then partied through a weekend while the two alpha males circled each other, sniffing and one-upping at every opportunity. Then, they flew to Chicago together on the Big Bunny, where

Bernie sniped to the writer Julie Baumgold when Hefner was out of ear-shot, boasting that a new plane he'd just ordered would "be infinitely better worked out" than Hef's. "Everything about the Playboy mansion is essentially scruffy," he said. "One of the girls brought me up to her room and my God! He has them in dorms. Eight to a room and bunk beds."

After that, Cornfeld headed back to Geneva. What made Bernie run home? Cracks had appeared in the IOS foundation and he realized they threatened his empire. IOS Ltd.'s much-vaunted stock had begun to drop shortly after it peaked at $19. In early April, shares were trading at $12.50. Then within days they plunged to $7.75. And IOS Management Ltd., a separate company that administered IOS mutual fund investments, had dropped, too, from a high of $66 to $25. Rumors were flying: Cornfeld had cancer; he'd committed suicide; he was being forced out by Cowett, who decided he'd become a liability; redemptions were rising ("baloney," Cornfeld told a reporter); IOS was dumping American stocks, driving down the market ("Don't blame it on me—blame it on the SEC"); German banks, furious that IOS had drained local depositers' saving accounts, were staging a bear raid on its stock, selling borrowed shares in the hope of buying them back later at a depressed price; and worst of all, IOS was running out of cash. "We are not in trouble and the rumors aren't true," Cornfeld insisted. But the L.A. *Times* added a telling coda to his denials: "It was evident . . . as Cornfeld spoke from the bar of his mansion in the wee hours, that a party was in progress."

Late in April, IOS was reorganized to address the crisis, even as IOS Management Ltd. lost another 10 percent of its value. Friendly journalists were recruited to tout the company's virtues: "The world needs Cornfeld," proclaimed London's *Observer*. Still, by month's end, the IOS share price had sunk to $4.50, and the *Wall Street Journal* was wondering aloud whether IOS, not the SEC, wasn't "a factor in the recent U.S. stock market decline." And it wasn't only America—markets were plunging all over the world. Two days after that, with the stock dropping even further, IOS laid off hundreds of employees.

It turned out that secretly, a week after Cornfeld's *Institutional Investor* speech, the company's controller had finished crunching its numbers and discovered that annual profits were far, far below expectations; the company was going to lose money in 1970. By April, the news had spread to a group of top executives, and worse, they learned that all the profits of the IPO were gone, spent propping up the stock price, IOS banks, and other entities and loaned to company insiders, including a guarantee of almost $5 million to buy Bernie that plane that would outdo Hefner's.

In the early days of May, the IOS board met for seven straight days, desperately seeking a solution to the crisis, a savior, a miracle. Cornfeld tried to hang on; he raged, he cajoled, but the board voted him out, offering to rescind its action only if he would resign as chairman. A resignation letter was written. Cornfeld signed it, but then he tore it up. A new chairman declared his resignation effective anyway and so, in weeks to come, he struggled in vain to take back control of his creation. But he was out and IOS was in play, and a cast of contestants ranging from eminent bankers to the sleaziest financiers circled the wounded animal, attracted by the scent of money, for despite all the problems and all the redemptions—effectively a run on IOS by its depositors—there was still at least $1 billion left inside. The ultimate victor was Robert Vesco, an engineer (he designed the first aluminum grille for an Oldsmobile) turned financial engineer, whose International Controls Corp. offered IOS financing in exchange for control of the company. He thought it was worth $2.8 billion.

Cornfeld sued, spewed venom at his former colleagues, and barricaded himself in his Geneva villa—all in vain. The Fund of Funds, the operation that had made IOS famous, suspended redemptions on most of its remaining assets. In September, the board chose Vesco.

The strain on Bernie showed. Victoria Principal turned up in a London courtroom in early December, suing Cornfeld for assault and seeking an injunction ordering him to stay away from her when he returned to London a few days hence. She testified that some months earlier, during the showdown with the board, he'd slapped her, and that the violence had escalated when she'd announced she was leaving him. "In a violent temper, he punched me into a chair and slapped my face," she said in an affidavit read in court. When she started screaming, he put his hands around her throat, stopping only when the telephone rang, and she escaped while he was distracted. The injunction was issued, but a few days later, her lawyers announced that the pair "had come to some private arrangements," and they reportedly reconciled, albeit only briefly. A London newspaper reported that Principal had "a nervous breakdown of sorts" immediately after that but she had one lasting gift from Cornfeld, the acting course he'd paid for at the Royal Academy of Dramatic Arts. She went on to star in the television show *Dallas*.

In January 1971, Cornfeld finally gave up, leaving the IOS board and selling Vesco his shares in the company for $5.6 million. But Vesco's take-over wasn't good for IOS. In June 1972, a block of preferred IOS shares was sold for one cent a share. That year, Vesco fled the United States after he was accused of looting $250 million from its accounts. IOS went bankrupt in 1973. Vesco remained a fugitive until he died in Cuba in 2007. His biographer reported that eventually, 95 percent of IOS investors recouped 95 percent of their money, albeit "in post-inflation dollars, without interest."

After making his deal with the devil Vesco, Cornfeld hopped a plane for the Bahamas en route back to Acapulco. He was a man on the move. A few months later he was working out of an office on Park Avenue in New York and staying with Oleg Cassini. Bernie was said to be wheeling and dealing again, taking an option on ten thousand acres near Palm Springs, where he planned to build a Southern Californian version of Rome's Cinecittà called Cinema City. When asked what happened at IOS by a friendly reporter, he blamed his partner Cowett and professed to be undaunted, but reacted with petulance when challenged; in other words, he was still Bernie.

Maybe the SEC heard Cornfeld was coming, because four days before he closed on the purchase of Grayhall in 1971, it permanently barred him from the securities business in America. Cornfeld responded through lawyers, insisting he'd never violated any laws. One of those he blamed for his ouster from IOS agrees. "I really liked Bernie," says Henry Buhl, a director. "I thought he was honest. We were taking business from all the banks. This brash, ugly little Jew who was living in a castle with a harem, flying to Acapulco! It was not done. So everyone was out to get him. But the downfall was internal dishonesty. Cowett was the crook. I would never say it was Bernie." But, Buhl adds, "He was reckless."

Regardless, the SEC bureaucrats needn't have worried. California's charms quickly distracted Cornfeld. "Bernie immediately became a friend to me," says George Hamilton, who met him when he showed up at Grayhall with his real estate broker—and a pack of girls—and agreed to buy the estate. "He was that kind of person. He'd immediately make you feel important, as if he'd known you a long time. It's the social worker thing. It's not calculated. He was nice, but amoral." A year later, when Alana and George married in Las Vegas (Elvis Presley's manager Col. Tom Parker was best man and Alana's dog was maid of honor), Cornfeld flew to Greece to meet them on their honeymoon "and took us to Israel," Hamilton continues.

Upon their return, the newlyweds visited Grayhall, where Cornfeld had left the downstairs intact, installed his mother in the servants' quarters, and renovated what had been the attic. "He was trying to become Hefner," says Hamilton. "That was his greatest wish. He could get on with life and not feel sorry for himself." Toward that end, he'd copied what he'd disdained at the Chicago Playboy mansion. "Little bedrooms, like dorm rooms, cubbyholes," says Alana, "for all the chicks he had hanging out."

There were twenty-two bedrooms in all. Writer Carolyn See once visited what she described as the Poor Man's Playboy Mansion. "The bottom floor was filled with men playing backgammon," she wrote. "The furnishings were opulent but vulgar. I went upstairs, and just under the roof were maybe a dozen attic rooms, each furnished with a mattress and a bureau. It was mid-afternoon and about 110 degrees. Every room held a sweating young woman in a shorty nightgown, one of them with a baby, none of them talking, just waiting for the night to cool off or for one of the men to finish his game and come upstairs for sex."

Bernie, needless to say, didn't see it that way. "It was kind of a girl's shelter," he explained. "I liked having the girls around. It was a good-sized personal harem." It was clear to Hamilton that Bernie was still willing to share them. "You can keep your bedroom," he told the actor. "That's very nice, but no," the newlywed Hamilton replied. The only other thing he remembers from that last tour of the house was "a huge number of books full of stock certificates."

A year later, a writer for the *Chicago Tribune* would call Grayhall "a kind of limbo" where Bernie, "deposed and languishing," lived "in self-imposed exile." The house was full of massive antiques, old ancestral portraits, tapestries, statues, leather armchairs, some thrones, a chandelier the actor Laurence Harvey sold to Bernie, pinball machines from the Chicago Playboy mansion, a jukebox, a pool table, and a den lined with color photos of Bernie, "Bernie in repose, Bernie with girls . . . " Bernie's bedroom had red velvet walls, a four-poster bed, and a mirrored ceiling.

Bernie, the writer implied, didn't do much but owned a lot, including one new toy: a piece of Bob Guccione's *Playboy* competitor, *Penthouse,* in which he'd invested. Otherwise the catalog of Bernie's possessions included the same old assortment of houses, cars, and basset hounds; the fashion houses of Cassini and Laroche; model agencies; and unspecified "other businesses."

Bernie insisted the latter did not include dirty movies—currently booming due to newly popular videotapes—despite rumors to the contrary, though he did allow that he'd "made some movies lately," none of them terribly successful. He'd also been sued by the U.S. government for allegedly selling gold without a license. "If they think I've got $12.5 million in the U.S. where they can get their hands on it, they must be out of their minds," he railed. "If they really had anything, they would have filed a criminal complaint."

Bernie was planning new, crested electric gates for the house, closed-circuit television throughout, and a better screening room than the one he already had in the basement. But the guests didn't seem unhappy with the place or the food provided by Bernie's cook at an unspecified friend's birthday party (which had been cancelled, but went on anyway). All were watched over by armed security guards, who were needed because the old gates were always open, the front door unlocked, and every light in the house on. As Bernie wandered from room to room, the *Tribune* writer clocked the guests. Women outnumbered men by a factor of four to one, but they were mostly young girls without last names or the ex-wives of more famous men, whereas the men in attendance included Warren Beatty, Hugh O'Brian, and Roman Polanski, some of whom seemed to be there to fish in Bernie's girl pond.

The open doors led to some unwanted guests. Bernie would tell the story of how Vanessa Redgrave invaded the house one day seeking a donation for the Palestine Liberation Organization. As she charged upstairs to a room full of Empire period furniture and a portrait of Napoleon, Bernie clambered out to the balcony and up a tree to hide among its branches.

Bernie's first big business venture in Los Angeles was a nightclub-restaurant-retail complex called the Paradise Ballroom just over the border in West Hollywood. It would crash and burn in under a year, plagued by mismanagement and a scandal in which a club employee was charged with sexual assault on a former Playboy bunny.

Bernie's next blips on the public radar (aside from his frequent appearances in the ongoing IOS coverage) were set off by fresh criminal complaints. In February 1973, he was arrested and hauled into magistrate's court in London, charged with the attempted rape and indecent assault of a nineteen-year-old American girl at his home in Belgravia. Valli Davis claimed that she'd flown to London from America to apply for a job in the stables of Bernie's chateau in the foothills of the Alps. He flew in from Paris to meet her and promptly made advances, which she rejected, she said. "He put his arm around me and tried to kiss me, but I jerked my head away, saying I was working for him on business only," she testified. Bernie replied that what was happening was "part of the business." She kept saying no but slept in his house nonetheless. "As I lay in bed later, he came into my room, naked. It was really frightening. I said everything I could think of to get him out. That I was going to be sick, that I had a venereal disease. Finally, he said, 'Oh boy, I've hit the jackpot.' I grabbed my purse, ran for my coat, and escaped onto the street."

Cornfeld, for his part, had told the police he'd been encouraged to expect sexual congress and believed that was why the girl had come to his home. Then, his lawyer told the court, while Cornfeld was out on bail, he'd gotten a phone call from the girl's mother, intimating that money might make the problem go away, and after that, a letter from a lawyer floating a $25,000 sum as "psychologically palatable" recompense. Then, the price dropped to $15,000. Bernie's lawyers suggested he'd been the victim of a preconceived scam, and the magistrate seemed to agree. Finally, Bernie pleaded guilty to indecent and common assault and was fined £400 for the former offense and £50 for the latter. He was found not guilty of causing any actual harm.

Back in Switzerland, Bernie found himself under arrest again two months later on charges of fraud, dishonest management, abetting speculation, and misappropriation after thirty Swiss citizens, all ex-employees of IOS, brought those charges and separate civil suits against him. Under Swiss law, he was liable to be held for three months while the case was investigated. In fact, he was held for eleven months before he was released on payment of five million Swiss francs ($1.64 million in 1974 dollars) in bail—the highest in Swiss history—some of it provided by George Hamilton and Tony Curtis. The financially liberal Swiss had proven tougher than America's SEC.

During his prison stay, he had an active correspondence with his friend Al Capp, the "Li'l Abner" cartoonist. In one of the letters that was later sold at auction, he condemned the two books that had been written about him, saying they were "libelous at worst and at best have missed the point." He told Capp he'd sued the London journalists who'd written one of them, though he would get no satisfaction. The other, he claimed to Capp, was "full of inaccuracies and trivia." He didn't sue the author, former employee Bert Cantor, he continued, because he was fond of him.

In later letters, he revealed his prison reading list, heavy on humor books and the potboiler novels of his Beverly Hills neighbor, Harold Robbins; reported he was in good health and good spirits; and fulminated about the Watergate scandal and Robert Vesco's illegal campaign contributions to Richard Nixon, which led to the indictment of Nixon's fund-raising chairman, Maurice Stans, and his attorney general, John Mitchell. "It isn't generally recognized but IOS was involved in selling Americas [*sic*] largest export its securities," he wrote to Capp. "We were the biggest in the business. How Mitchell and Stans go on trial and Vesco who destroyed the company and robbed its assets goes on spending the money hes [*sic*] stolen. Its [*sic*] all related."

Cornfeld also commented on Swiss justice and the case against him. "Here one is assumed guilty until proven innocent no matter how absurd the charges," he wrote. "I wish you could have been present in court yesterday. The attorney for some of the plaintiffs in his pleading mentioned my relations with Vicki Principal, Audrey Hepburn Julie Christy [*sic*], Dewi Sukarno but not a scrap of evidence that I had committed a crime that would warrant their holding me. The circus would have been more amusing if I were released after the comic performance. What passes for Justice here has determined that my release was 'premature.'"

Cornfeld left Switzerland right after his release, which did finally come. He would later say his jail time sobered him and made him realize he wanted a wife and family. Nonetheless, his first priority was a party at Tramp, a posh London disco, the start of a monthlong binge of celebration. Paunchy and showing some gray hair, he then returned to Grayhall with his entourage, vowing to clear his name. He'd written a memoir in prison and retained an agent to get it published. It never was. And it turned out Bernie's troubles weren't over, either. With Vesco on the lam and Ed Cowett dead, felled by a heart attack at age forty-four just days after Bernie was sprung from prison, he was the only one left to take the rap, and so was generally blamed for the collapse of IOS and seen as one of the world's great financial villains. Several years later, he'd talk to Vesco on the phone. "They're not going to bump me off," Vesco said of the IOS investors, "they're going to bump you off because you sold the stuff to them."

Yet he could still generate headlines—and, apparently, deals. In November 1974, he took over a failing land development firm based in Nebraska and Arizona, claiming he was going to revive it with $20 million from wealthy Kuwaitis. That deal was never mentioned again after the FBI raided Grayhall in January 1975 and threw Bernie's secretary into prison for using a "blue box," a device that allowed the user to make long-distance telephone calls for free. Cornfeld said the raid "wasn't especially disagreeable," even though two of the devices and four of his address books were confiscated—he claimed not to know whom they belonged to.

"It's a huge house," he said. "There are a lot of people staying here." He added, in faux sorrow, that the agents had arrived just after a *Playboy* centerfold photo shoot concluded. But a few months later, Bernie was indicted, accused of defrauding the local phone company by making 343 calls for free.[24] When he went to London instead of surrendering for trial, the local police threatened to extradite him. For a man used to dealing with sums in the billions, the penny-ante charges would have been laughable had they not been so symbolic of his swift fall from financial grace.

31

Beverly Hills

Grayhall (1100 Carolyn Way)

It's unclear when Vicki Morgan entered Bernie's life. The striking five-foot ten-inch blonde Glamazon is pictured in the *Los Angeles Times* hugging a beaming Bernie in front of a Rolls Royce in a photo illustrating a May 1974 story on him. *Time* magazine said she moved into Grayhall in 1975 when she briefly separated from her powerful married lover, Alfred Bloomingdale, the grandson of the eponymous department store's founder who was a valued member of then governor Ronald Reagan's kitchen cabinet. Bloomingdale and Morgan had met in 1970; he'd paid for her divorce and stayed with her for years, writing checks of up to $18,000 a month to her, even secretly bringing her along on trips abroad with his wife. Though Alfred often promised to get divorced, she knew he never would.

Instead she got fine homes, cash, clothes, and cars, and an education in the manners and mores of the American upper class. She also learned the art of negotiating ever-higher sums for the kinky services she provided—Bloomingdale's extramarital tastes ran to the exotic. She even convinced him to rent a separate apartment solely for the group-sex and S&M scenes to which he was addicted. She seemed reconciled to it all, once even buying him fifteen prostitutes for his birthday. "I paid for them myself," she told him, though the money had come from him.

The relationship lasted, and Alfred's payments to her kept coming for twelve years, though their sexual relationship was an off and on thing, interrupted by the odd separation, a nervous breakdown that saw Vicki institutionalized for five months, and several other men, two of whom she married. One she didn't was Bernie Cornfeld. They'd been introduced, Vicki's biographer Gordon Basichis writes, by another girlfriend of Bernie's who'd known Vicki for years. Once, Vicki had even lunched at Grayhall with Alfred and been given a Bernie-led house tour. Basichis writes that when Betsy Bloomingdale saw her husband kissing Vicki in Beverly Hills, put her foot down, and said he had to stop seeing her, Vicki threatened to sue him if he stopped supporting her. She was relieved when Bernie's then girlfriend, hearing of her plight, invited her to stay with them in Belgravia. Upon arrival, Bernie took her to dinner and out shopping. "Determined to teach Bernie a lesson," for she was sure he wanted to have sex with her, Vicki spent $30,000 of his money, all the while teasing him mercilessly. Finally, she refused to indulge him when he crawled into her bed, instead sending him back to his girlfriend. She'd already called one of her ex-husbands, a much-older gambler, who appeared the next morning to snatch her from Bernie and escort her back to Los Angeles.

The story makes little sense, as she'd soon be photographed lavishing affection on Bernie. According to Basichis, the return engagement with Bernie followed shortly thereafter when she broke up with Alfred, again, and Bernie offered her a room at Grayhall, promising that she could install her own locks on the door and a private telephone. He would later tell *Time* magazine that he gave her a very special bedroom, linked to his by a secret passageway, likely the same one George Hamilton had given his mother. According to Basichis, Vicki would string him along for more than a month before letting him into her bed after Bloomingdale repossessed the Mercedes he'd given her and Bernie replaced it with a yellow Maserati.

A trip to Switzerland and France followed, but all was not perfect. On a houseboat in the south of France, they started to argue; she realized she missed Alfred. She decided to return to Los Angeles; Bernie tried to stop her. She told him she was tired of his ego, his retinue, his circus—as if her life with Alfred had been much better. He made her promise to return to Grayhall and wait for him. She agreed, and he followed, but they lasted only a few days before she left again, taking the Maserati as well as all her belongings. Desperate, she called Alfred, who offered to start paying her again if she dropped the suit. She agreed so long as he never asked her to participate in kinky sex again. While they were dickering, Bernie found her in the Holiday Inn room where she'd been hiding out, and demanded the return of his Maserati. "Tell him you've come back to me," Alfred told her on the phone. "He won't give you any trouble." The affair with Alfred started up again. Shortly afterwards, when Bernie was busted for his blue boxes, Vicki was summoned to a grand jury and lied, saying she'd never seen him use one. But when he refused to pay for the lawyer she'd brought with her, she accepted immunity and ratted him out to the FBI. She and Bernie never spoke again.

A sad footnote to this episode: Vicki's biographer alleged that though she then had another affair (this one with the king of Morocco), drifted into alcoholism and drug abuse, and got married, divorced, and married again, Bloomingdale never stopped wanting her. She demanded a million dollars to break her last engagement and Alfred agreed, though he said he'd have to pay her over time, and she returned even though she knew in her heart that she'd never see the money. Then she left and got married after all. And after that, her life *really* disintegrated. She began a lesbian affair and started snorting heroin, eventually landing in a mental institution for a spell. One of her visitors there was Alfred Bloomingdale, who revealed he was dying.

In mid-1981, Alfred was hospitalized, and nine months later went home to die. Still, he and Vicki kept in touch, and when Betsy discovered that she'd visited their mansion on Delfern Drive in Bel Air, she posted guards, Basichis claimed, demanded Alfred's power of attorney, and cut off Vicki's checks. But Alfred had signed two contracts promising Vicki $10,000 a month for two years and giving her half of his interest in a franchised pizza chain, and with those in hand, she hired the celebrated attorney Marvin Mitchelson, who'd recently set the so-called palimony precedent that said that unmarried couples had financial obligations to each other, and sued Alfred and Betsy Bloomingdale for $10 million. In an accompanying deposition, she revealed everything about their affair, including tabloid-ready allegations of kinky sex.

Alfred died a few weeks later; Betsy, undaunted, refused to settle and the whole mess went public. Thirteen months later, her lawsuit still unresolved, Vicki Morgan was clubbed to death with a baseball bat in her bed by a gay man she'd met in the mental institution who was renting a spare room in her San Fernando Valley condo. He confessed to her murder, and a year later was convicted, found sane, and sentenced to twenty-six years in prison, where he died of AIDS in 1991. Six months after his conviction, a jury awarded Morgan's fifteen-year-old son and heir $200,000 on one of those contracts with Bloomingdale. The rest of Morgan's claims were dismissed by a judge who said she wasn't entitled to payment for sexual services.

Bernie loved it all and told a reporter writing about Morgan's death that he remembered her fondly; he was beyond embarrassment. One must imagine that had he lived, Bloomingdale would not have been beyond a little embarrassment, as Morgan's murder led to revelations that he'd been investigated in the 1960s for links to the mob, paid out thousands in blackmail money to hush up his habit of beating prostitutes, and had lost an appointment as Reagan's ambassador to France because his political cronies all knew of his affair with Morgan. But political loyalty finally trumped discretion in Bloomingdale's case; shortly before he fell ill, he was appointed to Reagan's Foreign Intelligence Advisory Board. Rumors Morgan had videotapes of Reagan-era officials at S&M parties with her and Bloomingdale died down after *Hustler* magazine's gadfly publisher Larry Flynt offered a reward for them and none turned up.

In what can only be regarded as a happy ending, twenty years later, Betsy Bloomingdale remains ensconsed in her Holmby Hills mansion, a sacred figure in American society at age eighty-five.

32

Beverly Hills

Grayhall (1100 Carolyn Way)

After spending eight months on the lam in London and Mexico, Bernie Cornfeld returned to the United States, surrendered to federal authorities on the blue-box charges, and was released on a measly $10,000 bond on three counts of wire fraud. He was allowed to keep his passport. AT&T added a $1 million civil suit to his lengthening list of legal problems. A few months later, he was convicted and sentenced to a $3,000 fine, $2,000 in restitution, and two years in prison, though after his conviction was upheld on appeal, he spent only six weeks in Lompoc, the country club prison near Santa Barbara.

It was around the same time that Bernie submitted to another form of confinement, one perhaps even more unexpected: marriage. Bernie met Lorraine Dillon in 1975 through a mutual friend in Paris, where she was working as a model. Bernie was renting a *piano nobile* near the Place de l'Étoile. Dillon lived nearby "under the eaves" of a less grand building, she says. Invited for a drink, she passed through a twenty-foot-high doorway into an "incredibly grand" apartment lined with "boiserie and everything." She got nervous when Bernie said "C'mere, baby, I wanna show you something," and led her to his bedroom, but was charmed when he opened the door to reveal a goat standing on a small Louis XV sofa, eating its stuffing. "He'd rescued it from the mountains of Morocco," she recalls. "He said he'd been there with

Jane Fonda. He was taking it to his castle. He was sincere. He had a big heart. Then, he took me out to dinner. That was our first date."

The following weekend, Bernie invited her to a friend's house on Ibiza and she took along a girlfriend, another American model, as her chaperone. "It was still hard warding him off," she says. "But I had such a great time, I kind of fell for Bernie. He was so brilliant and witty." More trips followed. Lorraine and Bernie brought his goat to his castle, then went to St. Tropez, where Bernie helped Lorraine sell off a batch of caftans she'd manufactured in hopes of starting a business and leaving modeling behind. "I was very touched he'd be bothered," she says. Back in Paris, he offered to renovate his original IOS office, which he still owned, as an apartment for her. Then he returned to Beverly Hills, where she followed and was only momentarily nonplussed to find a bubbly Canadian girl named Celine in residence along with a pair of teenaged sisters. Quickly Lorraine realized this was all part of Bernie's life. "Then I discovered I was pregnant. I was very worried. This was moving faster than I understood. He wanted to get married and have the child." As soon as the blue-box trial ended they got married under a chupa at Grayhall. Tony Curtis was Bernie's best man. Lorraine was seven months pregnant.

Bernie wouldn't admit it, but his money was running out. "He always had financial problems," says Lorraine. "He was cash poor; there were never huge sums that could be spent." Yet his annual expenses were $2 million a year, and he had to make that somehow. He rented Grayhall out to the producers of the Barbra Streisand version of *A Star Is Born,* and a year after he married Lorraine, he put the house on the market for $2 million and also offered his French castle for $1.5 million. There were always new businesses, too—an electronic game manufacturer in 1976, a projection TV company in 1977—but none ever gained traction. "Cornfeld is obviously groping for . . . some way to fill the void," the *Washington Post* observed, watching the one-time king of mutual funds dandle his newborn baby girl on his lap.

Finally, in fall 1979, Bernie went on trial in Switzerland, appearing in court in a suit and beach shoes without socks. Prosecutors charged that he'd manipulated IOS accounts to show false profits, failed to tell employees who bought IOS stock that insiders were selling their shares, falsely implied that important financial institutions stood behind him, and cynically failed to reveal that the stock market was a bad investment at the time of the offering.

But they also refused to ask the jurors for a guilty verdict, apparently aware that their case was more emotional than factual. Bernie's lawyers portrayed him as a scapegoat for the real villains, Cowett and Vesco, and after a brief trial, he was acquitted.

He wept on hearing the unanimous verdict. Few recall today that he'd already agreed to let his record-setting bail be used to reimburse the civil complainants. "I want to be able to tell my three-year-old daughter that I am not a swindler," he said at the time. He told the court he had only $4.4 million left, most of it in his illiquid real estate.

Bernie had started cheating on Lorraine when she was pregnant, sometimes in the house. "He couldn't maintain it," she says, "so things fell apart." He had a friend who Lorraine decided was his procurer, who would call late at night and ask, "Is she asleep yet?" Once when that happened, Lorraine crept out of bed and went downstairs. "He had brought three girls and a Yorkie to distract them," she says. "It was all set up, in place, all these people were regulars. A constant parade, coming and going. He wasn't like that in Europe. It all had to do with California and that house. . . . As soon as he got there, creepy, unsavory people would be around."

After a few years Lorraine had had enough and demanded the right to cheat, too. "He gave it lip service," she says. "He said, 'No kids that don't belong to me.' But when I actually had an affair, he went ballistic." Two years after they were married, Lorraine moved out for a year, to Laguna Beach, an hour and a half away. Then she returned for three more years, before leaving again, sort of, moving into a house about a mile north of Grayhall with their daughter. In 1985, Bernie bought Max, a flailing model agency in Los Angeles, for $200,000 and put Lorraine, who'd returned to her maiden name, in charge, giving her all the stock. It would be four more years before they were divorced in 1980. Bernie's life had always been wild. After Dillon left, it would take a turn for the wilder. But by then, life all over the Triangle had taken a turn toward the wilder side, too.

Holmby Hills

141 South Carolwood Drive

"We never knew how or why we got invited to a party at Tony Curtis' house. We'd never met him before and we didn't have any mutual friends." So Cher wrote in her memoir, *The First Time*. But as she and her then husband and singing partner Sonny Bono drove up the long driveway on Carolwood Drive in Holmby Hills to celebrate Tony's birthday in 1967, Cher gasped. Curtis's new house was the most magnificent thing she'd ever seen.

"Son," Cher told her husband, "some day we're going to live right here in this house."

"My dahlings, my dahlings, come in," Curtis said in a voice half Bronx, half Cary Grant. He had on a black velvet suit, a white silk shirt, and a long black scarf, well into his Count of Carolwood phase. Sonny and Cher spent the evening wandering through what they would call the Big House, agog.

"We've never seen anything like it," Cher told Tony when he found them again.

"Come tomorrow," he replied. "I want to show you my other house."

Cher, born Cherilyn Sarkisian, was the daughter of a part-Cherokee maid and a hard-drinking, heroin-addicted gambler of Armenian extraction; they divorced when she was five months old. Her mother became a bit-part actress and married many more times. At one point, incapable of taking care of Cher and her sister, she even placed them in an institution.

"My earliest memory is when I was six and my mother said to me, 'How are we going to pay the rent?' " Cher once told *Redbook* magazine. When she was eight, her father went to prison. When she was eleven, her parents remarried. Eventually, they'd marry and divorce three times. In between, her mother married a millionaire builder and Cher spent five months in a big house in Beverly Hills with a pool and servants. But in 1960, Cher's mother married a bank manager in Encino, California. At sixteen, in 1962, Cher got her driver's license. "A very big deal for me," she wrote. "I could get out of Encino." One night in Hollywood in her adoptive father's car, she was run off the road by a white Lincoln Continental convertible. Behind the wheel was Warren Beatty. She ended up in bed with him at his house in Trousdale Estates. Not long after that, she dropped out of eleventh grade and started taking acting classes. That fall, she was in a coffee shop on Hollywood Boulevard when a little guy with a Prince Valiant haircut and puppy-dog eyes came in.

Salvatore Bono came from Detroit to California and shortly after dropping out of high school, decided he wanted to write songs. He took odd jobs in the meantime, ended up a record promotion man, and got a job at a record company owned by the eccentric pop genius Phil Spector, who'd made his wife Ronnie a star with the Ronettes. When Sonny walked into the restaurant—reports vary on whether it was a blind date or sheer happenstance—Cher was a sitting duck. Sonny soon left his wife, and Cher moved into his place when he offered her a bed rent-free in exchange for help around the house. One night, she had a bad dream and asked to join Sonny in his bed. "Yes, but don't bother me," he said.

Cher had a great big contralto voice. Sonny put her on records as a backup singer; she's on many of Spector's greatest hits. The pair were soon in love or something like it, and in 1964, they got married in Mexico and started making their own records, met some high-powered managers, and became Sonny & Cher. Sonny also set her up with a record deal of her own. It was the beginning of the folk-rock moment in pop music, and Cher covered Bob Dylan songs. Then, together, they recorded Sonny's "I Got You Babe," it went to number one, and "in one day our lives totally changed," Cher said.

Invited to perform at a private party for Jackie Kennedy by the hosts, the New Jersey socialites Jane and Charles Engelhard, Cher was "discovered" by Diana Vreeland, the legendary *Vogue* editor, who asked her why she'd not yet been in magazines and invited her to be photographed by Richard Avedon. "We were only supposed to do two pictures but we ended up spending ten days and Vogue ran twenty pictures," Cher recalled. Sonny and Cher bought a $75,000 plastic-décor model home in Encino and moved in without changing a thing. Cher kept making hits and with Sonny recorded "The Beat Goes On," which kept the duo at the top of the charts.

They bought Tony Curtis's spare house on St. Cloud Road right after that party at Carolwood at the end of 1967, agreeing to pay $250,000 for it on the spot. "She just loved that house [on Carolwood]," Curtis said in 2010. "But she saw St. Cloud and wanted it very much so I decided to let her have it."

"We decorated our new house in a very traditional way," Cher wrote. "I guess we were trying to appear established. We were nouveau riche but better nouveau than never." Anyone familiar with their fur-vested hippie look would have been shocked. The house had a huge entry hall with an elaborate crystal and bronze chandelier and travertine marble floors, a ground floor loggia, a columned second-story gallery, a 25-by-45-foot living room with Venetian commodes and baroque carved mirrors, and an 18-by-26-foot dining room with eighteenth-century Spanish portraits looking over a massive dark wood table that sat twenty. The breakfast room was a green and yellow riot of floral prints surrounding a floral chandelier, the bedroom featured an elaborate dark wood four-poster bed draped with yellow silk, and only the library had rock-star touches: a sheepskin rug and two black leather sofas. Their kitchen was featured in *House & Garden* magazine. "Nothing could be less far-out, more Doris-Day-American than the kitchen in the Bonos' refurbished 1930's Hollywood mansion," it said, "all spanking-new gas equipment, ceramic tile, wood cabinets and pretend-tile wallpaper." Said Sonny, "Cher and I adore the house but we don't take it seriously." Sonny let his ex move into their old place in Encino.

Then, Sonny & Cher hit a dry spell. Seemingly overnight, the couple tumbled from the folk-rock elect to the hopelessly uncool. At twenty-two, Cher was passé. "Hippies thought we were square, squares thought we were hippies," Cher would later say. But anyone who'd seen their home would have known that they were some new hybrid. "It is especially surprising to find young people with an appreciation of this way of living," *Architectural Digest* noted, "when many of their contemporaries have little feeling for most things that are representative of the period and the social structure that produced this kind of house."

Attempting to reinvent his wife, Sonny mortgaged the house, spent the proceeds and their savings, and then borrowed more to produce a movie he'd written in which Cher played a hooker. It was a flop and they ran out of money. Making matters worse, they owed hundreds of thousands of dollars in back taxes. Sonny scrambled and kept them in their mansion. But none of his schemes restored their luster and meantime, their expenses had increased when they'd had a daughter, Chastity (a happy event that followed two miscarriages and finally led them to marry properly and officially). So Sonny booked them into nightclubs where they started over by opening for the likes of Pat Boone; their act proved a popular and durable one, a squabbling couple in love.

In 1971, Sonny and Cher guest-hosted for *The Merv Griffin Show* and were such a success that CBS offered to make a pilot of *The Sonny & Cher Comedy Hour*. It debuted that summer and was a surprise hit. Sonny played a dim but eager sad sack, picked on by a deadpan, towering Cher, dressed in drop-dead Bob Mackie gowns showing off her model-perfect body. Sonny also found Cher a new producer, Snuff Garrett, who happened to live near them in the Bel Air house once owned by Colleen Moore. He gave Cher a new sound and she started making hits again with "Gypsies, Tramps and Thieves." Their show was picked up and they returned to CBS in triumph at the end of the year. "Today," *Life* magazine declared, "she is a high-gloss prime time sex symbol, officially one of the world's ten best-dressed women, and her records (alone and with Sonny) are back on the charts—two in this year's top 50. She is seldom seen twice in the same pairs of shoes." By June 1972, Sonny and Cher were not only back on top, they'd also moved from their Tony Curtis starter house into his Big House.

34

Holmby Hills

141 South Carolwood Drive

Christine Kaufmann left Tony Curtis in November 1966, when she was pregnant with her and Tony's second daughter. Presumably he had a fling around that time—almost exactly nine months later, an eighteen-year-old girl gave birth to twins she claimed were Tony's; though he never admitted paternity, he paid her an $8,700 settlement. Before he and Kaufmann divorced, he was engaged to the future third Mrs. Tony Curtis. Leslie "Penny" Allen, twenty-three, was a New York model. Her fiancé was forty-one.

They courted in New York, in Boston where Curtis was making a movie, and then in L.A., where Allen visited several times. In one of two memoirs he later wrote, he recalled asking her to marry him as he showed her the Carolwood estate. She joked that she would if he had an elevator. He did, hidden behind paneling in the foyer. "We got on it and rode up to the second floor and by the time we got there, she said yes," he wrote. A few days after Kaufmann won a California divorce, Tony and Leslie hopped a plane to Vegas, got married at 2 a.m., and left town two hours later; they'd planned a big wedding at the Carolwood house the next day.

There, Leslie Curtis found, to her delight, a three-room women's dressing suite off the master bedroom, still done in pink marble and eighteenth-century French silk, and a sitting room with walls covered in nineteenth-century toile de Jouy. "I was so grateful no one had touched it," she says. The house was "echoing" but "a jewel, absolutely immaculate. You felt transported. I felt very at home there."

Leslie says Tony fought to have a family life, bringing his four children together there whenever he could. "But the house didn't lend itself to a close family life," says Leslie. "It was too grand and too spread out. You could starve to death getting to the kitchen." She laughs aloud at Curtis's claims that their relationship was troubled from the start and that he slept with several of his costars right after they married. "Why would he say that?" she wonders. "Maybe he wanted to think of himself as a great Don Juan?" In fact, they had two more children and stayed together fourteen years.

Leslie has great memories of life on Carolwood. Tony's desire to be part of the A-list rubbed off on her. "There was a society, a wonderful society," she says. "I was entranced by people, in film and not. I was able to meet them because of the marriage." But much as she loved her Holmby Hills moment, Leslie Curtis knew it was unreal. "I was a bird in a cage," she says. "It was a very rarefied life." Sometimes, she'd get so lonely she'd talk to the neighbors, the Wardes, through the hedges. "I thought we should get a smaller, less public house. People would be looking through our gates at 7 a.m." Both she and Tony hated the traffic on nearby Sunset, the star-home-tour buses, and the people climbing their fence "to see Tony Curtis's house." When Tony got an acting job in London, they bought a smaller, modern house in a cul-de-sac in Bel Air and put Carolwood on the market. Leslie Curtis thinks there was no economic necessity to sell, but "Cher had said if you ever sell, you have to let us know," and Tony offered to sell it to her in mid-1972. He was asking $1 million. Sonny and Cher reportedly paid $750,000.

At the end of his life, asked why he sold it, Tony seemed to at once deny and acknowledge that he had to. He could have paid off his loan from the Keck estate and kept it, he said, but "I decided I didn't want to do it. It had too many memories. Things began to fall apart and I began to lose interest in it all. I had to grow. It was not a tragedy. Sonny & Cher came by. It was going to be hard to give it up but it was easy. I made some money on it, too, but that wasn't the reason I sold it. I had to walk away from it. I couldn't continue to afford it. By the end, it was very difficult to maintain it, so I let it go, like a bird, I let it fly out of my hand. But I'd had the best of those houses."

Although both Sonny's and Cher's names appeared on the deed when they bought the house, Leslie Curtis recalls quite clearly that "only Cher was involved in the conversation. Cher was the motivation behind it. She came twice. He didn't. It was her decision." Leslie and Tony both saw something the world didn't know yet. "There was trouble in paradise on St. Cloud Road," she says. "Sonny had a roving eye." And for the first time in her life, Cher was beginning to think and look out for herself.

"She used to say, 'Put your money under your feet. Buy real estate,'" recalls Leslie. Cher certainly had strong feelings about Carolwood. Leslie recalls a meeting where Cher's lawyer made a lowball offer and Tony insisted on more. Cher's voice boomed out of the lawyer's speakerphone: "I want that fucking house."

"People ask why you need anything larger than twenty-two rooms," Cher once said. "You don't *need* any more than a living room, kitchen, bedroom, and bath. But what you *want* is something else again." She'd worked hard for her money and felt entitled to spend it however she wanted.

So Sonny and Cher moved in and the Curtises left for their new house in Bel Air, which, though smaller (only eight thousand square feet), had a family room, an eat-in kitchen, and bedrooms all close to one another. "We were very excited to move into Sarbonne Road," Leslie says. "It was a wonderful time of our lives. We were like any regular family." They even drove around Bel Air looking at other people's mansions. Of course, they took those family drives in a Rolls Royce convertible.

This idyllic picture of family life notwithstanding, Curtis fell prey to cocaine addiction in the late seventies. The couple soon separated, and the Sarbonne Road house went on the market in summer 1981 at $3.5 million. A year later, the price was dropped to $2.95 million. In between, Tony and Leslie were divorced.

Tony's acting career would never regain the heights it hit before his first divorce and remarriage to the teenage Christine Kaufmann. In 1984, he entered the Betty Ford Center to try again to kick the drug problems that began with marijuana and sleeping pills in the 1960s and ended with an eight-year addiction to cocaine. His youngest son would later die of a heroin overdose. Two more divorces, three marriages, and any number of houses followed before Curtis died in 2010 at his last home in Las Vegas, which he shared with his sixth wife. He never again lived in the kind of splendor he'd enjoyed in Holmby Hills—and for a long time, he seemed bitter about it. "I don't need anything fancy," he said while shacked up at the Playboy mansion after he and Leslie divorced. "Everybody used to go on about what a great house [Carolwood] was. Maybe it was to them, but to me, it wasn't a home; just a place to be. I don't need that anymore. I plan to live simply." In truth, the choice was no longer his, and he likely knew it.

35

Holmby Hills

141 South Carolwood Drive

The Carolwood estate was a stage for great drama. Tony Curtis had arrived there as a top-ranked star with a new wife, and left a fading one with one broken marriage and another coming just a few scenes later. The house passed to two stars of equal wattage as they hit the peak of an unlikely yet much-celebrated comeback, and ever so briefly, Sonny and Cher Bono were happy there. Cher even began taking lessons in entertaining from a socially savvy friend. But she barely got a chance to try out her new skills before it all fell apart for them, too.

Sonny and Cher's business partnership lasted longer than their marriage, which began crumbling in fall 1972, backstage at a Las Vegas appearance at the Flamingo where, after a sleepless night, Cher confessed to Sonny that she'd fallen in love with their guitar player and wanted a divorce. Sonny responded with a plea to keep their lucrative partnership intact, but Cher demanded he cancel their last two Vegas shows. According to Bono's autobiography, Cher slept in their room with the guitar player that night while Sonny had sex with the guitar player's wife. The next day, Cher and her lover flew off to San Francisco; she stayed only a night before returning to Holmby Hills, but the breach proved irreparable. "One night we were together and the next night it ended," Sonny later said. "And we were separated from that time on."

The breakup was a long time in coming. For years, Sonny had played the self-written part of El Primo, making all the decisions and handling their money, while Cher went along, even when he refused to let her play music in the house, play tennis (he didn't like the game), go to the movies, or make her own friends. Whenever she'd showed signs of independence, he'd pushed her back in her place. By the time of the epic fight in Vegas, she was so miserable she'd dropped to under a hundred pounds.

Cher told Sonny he'd have to move out and he refused. "CBS told them they could split up but neither of them could move out or their show would be cancelled," says Cher's decorator and former friend Ron Wilson. So for a year, they lived in separate wings of the huge house, maintaining the Sonny & Cher façade in order to maintain their income. "He moved his ugly girlfriend into the far end of the house and had me redo it," says Wilson. "I was really close to Cher. I asked her, 'How can you allow this?' "

"I don't care," she replied. Soon, she found a lover, too.

In fall 1973, David Geffen, a manager of musicians who'd started the record company Asylum, which became the hottest label of the early seventies, branched out with a group of partners, opening a nightclub, the Roxy, on Sunset Boulevard. Geffen attended its opening night show by Graham Nash and Neil Young with Bob Dylan, Robbie Robertson, and their wives. Cher arrived alone just after Young began playing and asked to join Geffen's table. It was love at first sight—for Geffen, at least; however improbably, according to Tom King's Geffen biography, Cher didn't know who he was.

Geffen invited her to dinner the next night at his home, a few blocks from hers. Noting the address—he was renting a mansion from the director Blake Edwards and his wife Julie Andrews—she wondered how he was able to afford it. Regardless, after dinner, she spilled out her heart and told him she and Sonny barely spoke offstage. She was desperate for a divorce but worried about Chastity. Geffen revealed that he'd had sex with men and was afraid of women, but desperate for love and certain he'd find it only with the opposite sex. Finally, supposedly, Cher asked him what he did for a living and learned he was a millionaire music mogul, the chairman of Elektra-Asylum Records, home of best-selling acts like the Eagles. Cher decided she'd never felt more comfortable with a man. The next day, Geffen told his therapist he was in love with her.

In a matter of days, the couple consummated their romance. "We were really crazy about each other," Cher said defensively when confronted with questions about (the later openly gay) Geffen's sexuality. And as sure as she got into his bed, Geffen got into her business, effectively taking over her life and giving her the management and direction Sonny Bono had provided until then. Only he talked to her instead of at her. Geffen's forte was managing women.

Sonny's romance with one of his secretaries had heated up—she would soon attend a skiing event in Sun Valley with Sonny and Chastity, hosted by Janet Leigh and the Janss family—but when Sonny got wind of what was going on, he demanded Cher leave the mansion. She didn't. Geffen found her a new lawyer and a therapist.

Back in Las Vegas that fall, Sonny and Cher had another backstage fight. She told him he'd have to move out of Carolwood and he refused. This time, there was no turning back. She left, instead, renting a five-bedroom beach house Geffen found on Carbon Beach in Malibu for herself and Chastity, taking nothing but her clothes and her Porsche. Geffen also went through Cher's contracts and found they were outrageous. In 1972, she'd signed a five-year agreement creating Cher Enterprises; though it bore her name, Sonny held 95 percent of the stock and his lawyer the rest. Cher had agreed to work where and when Sonny and the lawyer wanted, and let their corporation collect everything she earned. "I started reading what I had signed and I got really pissed off," she said. "My head for business is nil. I just didn't care. All I wanted was to work, sing and be stupid." But those days were over.

Geffen coached Cher for her final confrontation with Sonny in his CBS dressing room; she told him they were through, the show was through, and she wouldn't be performing with him anymore. He chased her down the hallway, King wrote, where she told him any further discussion would have to be with Geffen who, Sonny realized, had taken over for him in the office as well as the bedroom. Now Sonny was seriously pissed off too.

In February 1974, just before the final taping of *The Sonny & Cher Comedy Hour* and one last concert appearance together, Sonny filed suit for a legal separation. Cher struck back with a birthday party for Geffen the next day (at which she sang "I Got You Babe" with Bob Dylan) and, a week later, a suit for divorce for irreconcilable differences. She also filed a civil suit against Sonny and his lawyer. The allegations were startling to a public unaware that Cher had been, effectively, Sonny's puppet.

In her suit, Cher compared her condition to slavery, said Sonny "unlawfully dominated and controlled" her, and asked the court to invalidate their contract for violating the Thirteenth Amendment to the Constitution's ban on involuntary servitude. Sonny countersued for $5 million to force Cher to live up to their deal.

Two months later, the couple's TV show was cancelled after Geffen quietly told CBS they'd be able to replace it with a Cher solo show. Then, Cher announced she wanted to return to Carolwood and ordered the staff to remove Sonny's belongings from the master bedroom. She thought the house was so big, they could cohabit without seeing each other. Sonny protested to their divorce judge that her refusal to abide by her contracts and do their TV show meant he would be unable to "amicably live under the same roof" with her.

In court, Cher said she'd moved out because Sonny had moved his girlfriend in. A month later, Sonny was given sole occupancy of the house and Cher was ordered to steer clear. Sonny agreed to sell it to Cher for half its value, but when she didn't pay him, he remained in residence with his girlfriend. So, late in the evening of July 8, when Sonny was at a recording session, Cher, her lawyer, Geffen, and two security guards moved her back in and threw all of Sonny's things and his girlfriend out of the house. The girlfriend called Sonny and when he called the house to protest, Geffen got on the phone, telling him armed guards had been posted and adding, "Go do whatever the fuck you want to do about it."

What Sonny did was go back to court, demanding Cher's eviction for, among other things, living there "openly and notoriously" with Geffen. "I am fearful that Cher's lifestyle with David Geffen has had and will have an extremely detrimental effect on Chastity," he worried in court documents. But the next day, Cher won the right to the house and Sonny was ordered to stay away.

The last episode of *The Sonny & Cher Comedy Hour* aired in May 1974. Despite, or perhaps because of their troubles, it remained one of the top ten shows on television. Sonny had no such luck flying solo; he made a deal with ABC for his own variety show, which debuted that fall, failed, and was cancelled within three months.

Cher and Geffen were plotting Cher's return to television and records—and talking marriage. Geffen showered gifts on her, including a diamond ring, and delighted in taking her out in public and causing a sensation. They appeared at the Grammy Awards and flew to Aspen on a corporate jet that belonged to Elektra-Asylum's parent company, Warner Communications. Warren Beatty and Jack Nicholson came along. Cher wanted a condo in

Aspen and Geffen promised it to her as a wedding gift. Back home, Geffen began redesigning a house he'd been planning in Malibu to accommodate her and her world-class wardrobe.

Geffen was on top of the world, having recently signed Bob Dylan to Asylum and convinced the legendary music executive Ahmet Ertegun to merge his Atlantic Records with Geffen's labels and form the world's greatest music stable. The magazine writer Julie Baumgold, five years after her coup accompanying Bernie Cornfeld and Hugh Hefner to Acapulco, was able to pull off another one; Geffen gave her total access to him and Cher for a cover story in *Esquire* magazine.

The result was predictably revealing and embarrassing for all concerned: "Cher's tongue is deep inside Geffen's mouth," was one line that stood out. " 'Feel my ass,' she says to Geffen. 'Hard as a rock.' " That exchange followed Geffen's agreement to buy her that Aspen condo. Baumgold also revealed that the last year had been so trying that Geffen was chain-smoking and Cher was getting fat and breaking out.

The story revealed a power couple in love, capturing Geffen driving up to Carolwood, opening the iron gates with a remote control, and driving into what was now *his* home, too. "The house is rich and dark," Baumgold wrote. "Large furniture on ball-and-claw feet looms from the boiserie under elaborate moldings, cartouches and paintings of the draped-shepherds-relaxing-against-columns school. Relying heavily on Chinese export, assorted Louis, and Brunschwig & Fils fabric, the house achieves a clobbering gloom. . . . Geffen has plans; he has already seen an architect about opening the house up, knocking through a wall of paneling and putting in a pyramid skylight." Of Geffen and Cher, Baumgold concluded, "It's a glorious love surrounded by much tumult." Unfortunately, by the time the story appeared months later, the tumult had triumphed.

In February 1975, Sonny amended his year-old suit against Cher, adding a charge that she and Geffen had conspired against him and asking for $14 million in lost revenue, $10 million in punitive damages, and $13 million from Geffen for contractual interference. "There were times when I wanted to kill David Geffen," Sonny said. The day after he filed his amended suit, a *Los Angeles Times* gossip columnist reported that Geffen and Cher had broken up.

Cher had been second-guessing herself about Geffen while having an affair with a bass player, which Geffen heard about and forgave her for, Geffen's biographer claimed. But after a long, Geffen-financed vacation in Europe, Cher decided to break it off anyway. In response, Geffen revved up his Cher management machine to try and prove his worth to her. But now, "there appeared to be no romantic connection," King wrote. "Geffen and Cher were simply lonely friends who were helping each other get through tough times."

Though he tried hard, Geffen finally proved unable to reinvent Cher as a top solo act. Her first post-Sonny LP was a failure, and her new show's performance was less than scintillating. But despite that and her domestic dramas—after she announced she didn't want the condo in Aspen and didn't want to marry him either, Geffen moved out and into the Beverly Hills Hotel—she still won the cover of *Time* magazine, which pointed out that post-Geffen she'd installed a big neon sign reading *Cher* over her Carolwood fireplace and invited four hundred people to a party there. "Nobody in this town lives like *that* anymore," an anonymous invitee sniped. Apparently, Cher did.

Late in June 1975, Sonny and Cher's divorce was made official in a five-minute court appearance, although their financial settlement was left very much up in the air. A month later, the court invalidated Cher's unfair contract with Cher Enterprises, accepting her argument of involuntary servitude, and ordered that she was entitled to all the income she'd earned since leaving Sonny, the Carolwood mansion, a Ferrari, and a $1.75 million life insurance policy. They split their other liquid assets (after Sonny was first forced to return $735,000 to their joint checking account), Cher paid Sonny $450,000 for his share of Carolwood, and Sonny walked away with the house on St. Cloud Road in Bel Air (they'd tried but failed to sell it for $395,000 in 1972), another in Palm Springs, and at least six cars, including a Ferrari newer than Cher's. Cher got physical custody of Chastity, though Sonny was granted equal time with her.

In the meantime, Cher had met Gregg Allman; the two quickly struck up a passionate relationship; Cher, whom Sonny had always shielded from drugs, didn't know Allman was a man with a problem. Make that two problems: cocaine and heroin. "We were a disaster waiting to happen," Cher wrote. Yet three days after her divorce from Sonny was finalized—and despite the fact that the new relationship led to a fight with Geffen, who stopped speaking to her—she asked Gregg to marry her. They took a Learjet to Vegas and were wed in her lawyer's suite at Caesar's Palace. They both later said they instantly regretted it. Cher claimed she cried all the way home—and then went back to work on her new TV show.

Nine days later, Cher filed for divorce. "When I called [Gregg] to tell him," she said later, "he was so high he didn't even understand me." Less than a month after that, when Gregg went into private drug rehabilitation, she withdrew the divorce suit—and put his name on the deed for 141 South Carolwood. He got clean, briefly, but then went on tour with his Allman Brothers Band and inevitably fell off the wagon. Cher would later recall her fury when friends of his snorted coke off her antique coffee table. Gregg would tell Cher he was going out for an hour and return three days later. Her producer joked that they were making a variety show but living a soap opera. Her ratings took a nose dive.

In mid-November, Gregg sued for divorce in his native Georgia. Cher promptly went out with Geffen again. Then, at the end of the year, Cher called Sonny and said she wanted to work with him again and after four weeks of negotiations, they settled their remaining differences, dropped their lawsuits, and announced that they would begin performing on TV and on stage together again. Then, in a plot twist as unexpected as it was worthy of Cher, she discovered she was pregnant by Allman. By New Year's Eve, she and Gregg had reconciled again and he'd dropped his divorce suit.

The breakups and makeups continued until July 10, 1976, when their son, whom Cher named Elijah Blue, was born. Just a few weeks later, Cher sold 141 South Carolwood, which was probably wise, as the new Sonny & Cher show was cancelled just after that. "We only used three rooms," Gregg had observed. "It was like living in a hotel only we weren't getting any rent for the rest." Cher, Chastity, Elijah Blue, Gregg, and Cher's mother all took up residence in a temporary rental, a two-story Spanish-style house in the Beverly Hills flats. Listed at $1.2 million ($1.5 million furnished), the Big House on Carolwood sold for $950,000 to Ralph and Chase Mishkin. He owned Hollytex, a carpet business; she was a theatrical producer. They called it Owlwood, the name by which it is still known, after the owls that inhabited the property.

Gregg and Cher would never come close to Sonny & Cher, though not for lack of trying. In 1977, they even recorded an album together, *Two the Hard Way*. First Sonny & Cher went on the road with an entourage that included Gregg, Chastity, Elijah Blue, and Sonny's latest girlfriend. Then Cher and Gregg went on a tour of their own and played concerts together in

Europe. On the road, though, Cher found that Allman was drinking again; she left the tour and broke off with him for good.

Gregg and Cher were divorced the next year and she got the legal nod to drop both Sonny's and Gregg's last names; henceforth, she would be just Cher. By all accounts, Gregg Allman has had little or no contact since with Elijah Blue, now a musician and visual artist. In 1979, Cher cowrote a song about Allman called "My Song (Too Far Gone)." As she sang it in concert, a film of little Elijah played on screens behind it—shot by Sonny Bono.

After selling Carolwood, Cher bought a 4.5-acre lot in Benedict Canyon, and designed herself a Moorish-style six-bedroom home, which she finally finished in 1982 (after so many changes that her architect quit) at a cost variously estimated between $3 million and $10 million. The next year, she sued the *National Enquirer* for $5 million for claiming it was haunted. She would later say that house, which she lived in for a decade, was the only one she was ever emotionally attached to. But its comforts discomfited her; she preferred to be less content. She also bought a four-bedroom log cabin in Aspen, where she spent weekends with her next rock star flame, Gene Simmons, the cofounder of Kiss, and years later, she bought a second Aspen home, an elaborate adobe villa.

Sonny retained ownership of the house on St. Cloud Road, and in 1978, sold it to the controversial publisher of *Hustler* magazine, Larry Flynt, who moved to Los Angeles after he was convicted on obscenity charges in Cincinnati, became a born-again Christian, and then was shot and paralyzed. Flynt turned the master bedroom suite into an armored vault with a bulletproof electric door and a diesel generator to open and close it in a crisis, added upholstered red velour to the elevator walls and a mirror to its ceiling, and installed a gym-disco and gold-plated bathroom fixtures to match his wheelchair. He kept a lipstick-red heart-shaped bathtub from the Sonny and Cher era.

Sonny retired from show business and opened a restaurant in Palm Springs, where encounters with the local government inspired him to run for mayor. He won. In 1994, he was elected to Congress as an advocate of the Newt Gingrich–era Republican Party's Contract with America. He died in a skiing accident in 1998 and his fourth wife, Mary, succeeded him in a special election—and has been reelected ever since.

In 1985, Cher moved to a rental house in Malibu and put the Benedict Canyon home on the market for $5.9 million, which dropped to $4.7 million and was raised again to $6.5 million before the comedian Eddie Murphy bought it for about $6 million in 1988. By then, Cher had transformed herself into a movie star with compelling appearances in films like *Silkwood* (which won her an Oscar nomination as Best Supporting Actress), *Mask,* and *The Witches of Eastwick.* She won a Best Actress award that year for *Moonstruck.*

Her movie career has continued at a less frantic pace, and Cher, now sixty-five, has an ongoing sideline in developing and selling luxury homes. Her first Malibu house, also Egyptian-style, went on the market in 1996 for $9.9 million. That led the *New York Times* to dub her "the grand champion . . . at parlaying mortar into money," claiming she'd built or renovated sixteen homes in the previous two decades. It was a tossup whether she was better known for those renovations or her physical ones: She was one of the first Hollywood stars to openly admit to having had plastic surgery. "She was sure she was a descendant of an Egyptian," says decorator Wilson, "so she started changing her face and built her Egyptian house. She simply liked to change."

Cher went on to build several more, ever-larger properties, "to prove to the world how successful she was," says Wilson, who later became estranged from her. Her second house in Malibu, an Italian-inspired palazzo with a pool and tennis court that she finished in 1999, was initially listed in 2008 for $45 million. She built another house in Hawaii, since sold. She now divides her time between the Malibu mansion (which is still quietly for sale as a so-called pocket listing) and a one-bedroom duplex bachelorette pad on a high floor at Sierra Towers, a condominium tower on the Beverly Hills-West Hollywood border.[25] Cher bought her pied-a-terre from David Geffen. Her neighbors there include her best friend, the jewelry designer Loree Rodkin, Elton John, who owns two apartments, Diahann Carroll, Matthew Perry, P. J. Harvey, Joan Collins, and renter Jane Fonda. Past residents include Peter Lawford, George Hamilton, Stanley Chais (who funneled Hollywood money to Ponzi schemer Bernard Madoff), Vincent Gallo, Sidney Poitier, and Lindsay Lohan, who famously drove her car into a tree on Sunset Boulevard, just over the Beverly Hills line. "There are hookers and drug dealers in and out at all hours," says one resident, who doesn't seem to mind.

Cher's tenure in Holmby Hills wasn't very long, but it left her with a passion for trophy real estate that's been the longest, most stable love affair of her life.

Beverly Hills

The Knoll 1130 Schuyler Road

It was a star of rare, outsized ambition who still wanted one of the great estates of the Platinum Triangle. It was a star producer who next bought one. He was at that point also rare for not being American-born. But foreigners were about to light a fire under the local real estate market, bringing prices to a boil and making white elephants red hot. "When people need to get money out of a country and need a safe haven," says one local realtor, "Beverly Hills is always on their list."

"Our relocation to Los Angeles was a long and elaborate process," Dino De Laurentiis told his biographers Tullio Kezich and Alessandra Levantesi. That process began in 1939 when De Laurentiis, a diminutive twenty-year-old former actor and prop man, produced his first movie. After a pause during World War II, when De Laurentiis allegedly deserted from the Italian military and hid on the island of Capri until Allied troops invaded Italy, he became one of the most influential producers in Italy, a pioneer of neorealism. De Laurentiis married one of his stars, Silvana Mangano, and teamed up with Carlo Ponti, the husband of Sophia Loren, to produce films by Roberto Rossellini, Vittorio De Sica, and Federico Fellini, whose *La Strada* won an Oscar for Best Foreign Film in 1956 and catapulted them onto the world stage.

Ponti and De Laurentiis then entered Cecil B. DeMille territory, producing epic spectacles with international casts: *Ulysses* with Kirk Douglas and Mangano and *War and Peace* with Henry Fonda and Audrey Hepburn. After the two producers ended their partnership, De Laurentiis won his second Academy Award for Fellini's *Nights of Cabiria*—which later inspired the Broadway musical *Sweet Charity*—and set up his own studio, Dinocittà, on the outskirts of Rome, where he began coproducing films with foreign partners, directors, and stars, like Roger Vadim's sci-fi spoof *Barbarella* with Jane Fonda. His most prestigious film of that era was Franco Zeffirelli's *Romeo and Juliet,* a British coproduction with an Italian director that won two Academy Awards.

In the early seventies, De Laurentiis, Mangano, and their four children, who until then had divided their time between a sixty-room Roman villa once owned by Pope Innocent XIII and a summer house on the French Riviera, moved to New York to escape Italian tax laws. He continued to produce films with old colleagues like Fellini and Ingmar Bergman, but also dabbled in the New Hollywood, producing minor work by new directors like Robert Altman and William Friedkin, and made more traditional mass-market movies that brought in big money: Charles Bronson action films like *The Valachi Papers* and *Death Wish,* Sydney Pollack's *Three Days of the Condor,* and Sidney Lumet's *Serpico.*

Finally, in 1976, at age fifty-six, De Laurentiis went entirely Hollywood, producing a heavily hyped remake of *King Kong.* Though he wanted to cast Cher in the female lead, she was pregnant with Elijah Blue at the time, so he went with an unknown fashion model, Jessica Lange, in the role originally played by Fay Wray. Simultaneously, he bought a house in L.A.; of course it wasn't just any house—it was Leigh and Lucy Doheny Battson's The Knoll. Life imitated his Kong casting conundrum: It wasn't his first choice, either.

"Quite early on," De Laurentiis told his biographer, "we found a splendid villa in Bel Air." It was actually Harold Janss's house on North Carolwood in Holmby Hills, which had been sold to a developer, who'd renovated and put it back on the market. After De Laurentiis put down a deposit against the $1.5 million price, he delayed his move to do some further renovations. Then, when he showed up to close, "we had an unpleasant surprise waiting for us—a surprise by the name of Warren Beatty," he recalled. According to De Laurentiis's account, Beatty had "taken possession of the property to shoot interiors for his film *Shampoo.*" A friend of production designer Richard Sylbert's says the unpleasant surprise was even worse than that. Sylbert had dug up the back lawn that Beatty's costar in the film, Julie Christie, says "looks like it goes on forever," and installed a grotto complete with an outdoor Jacuzzi for a long party scene that included pot smoking and nudity. "The owner was greedy; Dino was out of the country and they figured they could get away with renting it," says Sylbert's friend. But De Laurentiis found out.

"This irritated me beyond measure," he said, "for two very specific reasons. First, I've always refused to allow anybody to shoot a film in my house, and that includes me, too. And second, Mr. Beatty hadn't even bothered to alert me, let alone obtain the necessary permission." Though the sale was in escrow—meaning all the documents had been signed and De Laurentiis's deposit paid—he was able to cancel the contract and get his money back. Gregory and Veronique Peck soon bought the house, and Dino and Silvana went looking again.

It took only a few days to find The Knoll, which had been listed a year before by Lucy Battson and her ailing husband Leigh at $3 million, until that time the highest ask price for a single-family home in Beverly Hills. After it had languished on the market for many months, De Laurentiis, who thought the price was "insane," offered $2 million in cash. "Take it or leave it," he recalled. "It was a classic shot in the dark." The price included the Battsons' $800,000 worth of furnishings.

The Battsons said yes and proceeded to downsize to a 5,000-square-foot two-bedroom apartment in Wilshire Terrace, taking over the former private restaurant for residents on the ground floor of that rare L.A. cooperative apartment building to create a new home with two walled, terraced gardens with European fountains designed by the landscape architect David Jones.[26]

Unfortunately for Dino De Laurentiis, his move to Los Angeles coincided with a sharp drop in his creative output. He released a single film in 1977 and the big-bucks flops *Hurricane* and *Flash Gordon* in 1979. It wasn't until 1981 that he again put his name on hits—*Conan the Barbarian* starring Arnold Schwarzenegger and Milos Forman's *Ragtime*. By the time of their release, he'd sold The Knoll to the singer Kenny Rogers.

Like Sonny and Cher when they bought Carolwood, Rogers was then at the pinnacle of the pop world and was moving from a starter mansion. Raised in a Houston, Texas, housing project, he was a musical chameleon who'd hopped from jazz to folk to acid rock to country and staged innumerable comebacks during a peripatetic career. The onetime New Christy Minstrels and First Edition singer had reinvented himself as a solo act after the latter band broke up in 1974, and he landed in a career trough that saw him selling guitar lessons via TV commercials. At the time, he was flat broke after his third divorce, living in a $300 rental apartment in L.A. that he could no longer afford. He imagined himself ending up working in a car wash on Ventura Boulevard in the San Fernando Valley. He earned an unexpected windfall when First Edition's black-and-white leather stage outfits were stolen from his car; Rogers collected $3,000 insurance and lived off it for months. "It saved my life," he says.

But Rogers, always a musical opportunist, saw a path to pop stardom via country music and pursued it, earning a solo record contract in 1976, when the economy was in shambles but the music business was still capable of alchemy. By 1980, at age forty-one, despite gray hair and a paunch, he was back on top, a superstar earning $18 million a year on the heels of a double platinum album (*The Gambler*), television specials, and multiple hits and country music awards. In 1979, he bought that starter mansion, a 1938 Paul Williams house at 616 Nimes Road in Bel Air that had had only one owner before him, and gut renovated it; the son of a carpenter, he'd studied architectural drawing in high school and decided to be his own general contractor. A Leo, Rogers named the house Lionsgate and installed two carved stone lions before the front gates. "I always have to have a project," he'd later say, explaining his zeal for buying, renovating, and selling that began, much like Cher's, in the Platinum Triangle.

The money kept rolling in. In 1980, the *Washington Post* described him as "a teddy bear holding four aces" in a profile fixated on his ten-passenger Lockheed Jetstar (bought on credit) and seven-seat Hawker-Siddeley jets. There was also a 120-foot yacht, a 360-acre property in Georgia that contained a 120-acre lake, and a three-acre compound in Malibu, purchased and redecorated in a mere seven weeks so Rogers could give it to his latest wife as a Christmas present.

Even though Lionsgate was finished, Rogers decided one bedroom needed redoing and called in Cher's decorator, Ron Wilson. After a walk-through, Rogers decided to overhaul the whole house, adding a summer pavilion, an iron-and-glass outdoor elevator, beds with custom canopies, and more. "He spent a fortune," says Wilson, who claims Rogers demanded he not take on any other clients while in his employ. "He made me promise I'd be there every day. I think he was afraid to be alone."

Job done, Wilson told Rogers that De Laurentiis had put The Knoll up for sale six months earlier and urged his new client to see it. "Just look at it," he said. "You'll never see anything like it." Rogers "walked in the door, stood in the entry, and said, 'This is my house,'" Wilson continues. "Bel Air wasn't big enough, so they moved." Rogers didn't blink at De Laurentiis's $14.5 asking price for the estate and its furnishings. "It was eleven acres in the middle of Beverly Hills—nothing else like that," he later told *Vanity Fair,* justifying setting a new record price for a private home in America. No fool, he hoped to make back most of it by selling Lionsgate; he listed it for $12 million.

To Wilson, Dino's Knoll, essentially unchanged since the Battsons' day, was "a huge, dumb house, very badly built," with "extraordinary details" like a Lalique crystal powder room, but done in "hideous, heavy taste." Rogers embarked on another gut renovation, creating a huge dressing room for his wife out of a batch of maids' rooms, but also ripping out and replacing those Lalique walls, original fireplaces from Greystone, some "gorgeous furniture, Moors worth jillions," says Wilson, who claims he begged Rogers to keep it all. "The S.O.B. wouldn't listen." So Wilson got rid of it, and fast, selling some of the more valuable pieces—a pair of Italian neoclassical commodes, a Louis XV bibliothèque, and a pair of Venetian rococo armchairs—at Sotheby's.

Rogers remembers things quite differently, insisting the house was empty when he saw it. "True or not, it's a story," he says, "and if Ron's got that detail, God bless him. Lalique is so not me. I think I have really good, expensive taste, but it's not fragile, it's more manly." Kenny and Marianne Rogers moved in at the end of the year, just in time to welcome their first child to their new, "all-white fantasy" nursery.

Rogers recalls giving Lionel Richie a tour of the vast interior of the house in a golf cart. "I was responsible for Lionel leaving Tuskegee," he says. "I had two 4,000-square-foot guesthouses." Richie moved into one for two years. Though a realtor would claim Rogers never lived in The Knoll, he begs to differ. "I loved that house," he says. "It was spectacular. No way I wouldn't live in it."

He clearly appreciated the symbolic value of living on one of the largest properties in Los Angeles. "It's representative of success," he says, "and people who come from nothing have to go through that when they can afford to."

Although Dino De Laurentiis continued making movies of quality (David Lynch's *Blue Velvet*) and movies that found commercial success (*Red Dragon* and *Hannibal Rising*), his deal-making career may have peaked the day he sold The Knoll. He pocketed more than seven times what he'd paid for the property five years earlier, likely making up for some of the disappointment he must have felt over the decline in his producing income in the years he lived there. By 1986, when he was splitting his time between a new studio he'd built (and would later lose) in North Carolina, and a five-year-old mansion with a half-mile-long driveway on eight acres in Beverly Hills Post Office (bought from the potboiler novelist Harold Robbins), he was far better known for big-budget flops like 1984's *Dune*.

Personal tragedy also took its toll. In 1981, his son Federico was killed in a plane crash. "My father still to this day can't speak of him," De Laurentiis's daughter Veronica said nearly twenty years after Federico's death. The strain of the loss helped end his marriage to Mangano. In 1988, De Laurentiis and Mangano divorced and his De Laurentiis Entertainment Group went into bankruptcy, chased by the Furies of litigation. He lived for many years in Tower Grove in Beverly Hills with his second wife, Martha Schumacher, also a producer, but was apparently ailing. In 2010, the website for their current venture, the Dino De Laurentiis Company, had not been updated in three years. De Laurentiis died that year at ninety-one.

Beverly Hills

Greenacres (1740 Green Acres Place)

The foreign newcomers to the Triangle weren't limited to movie folk migrating to their mecca. Some saw it, even in this white elephant era, as a great place to invest. Around the same time De Laurentiis moved into The Knoll, several of them became the second owners of Greenacres.

After silent movie star Harold Lloyd's death, it briefly looked as if his last dream for his estate would come true—the Beverly Hills City Council was leaning toward approving the Harold Lloyd Foundation Trust's proposal to turn what the *Los Angeles Times* called the "hilltop barony" into a motion picture museum and film research center, though some members wondered if it could sustain itself on income from the limited tours and two monthly fund-raising events the city would allow. Lloyd's Benedict Canyon neighbors remained opposed, though, so the council left the plan hanging in uncertainty. According to Lloyd's will, the trust had another year to establish the museum and raise an endowment to support it; if it didn't, Greenacres would be offered, in turn, to the city, UCLA, USC, Los Angeles, the state of California, or any charity that could afford the upkeep. If all else failed, it was to be sold for subdivision, with the proceeds earmarked for education.

Briefly, the house did operate as a museum—showing life as it was lived in the kind of house "crazy movie people built in the crazy Twenties," as the script of *Sunset Boulevard* put it. Little had changed since Lloyd died—even the famous Christmas tree remained, supported by a lead pipe and bamboo rods, its needles brown but frozen with fireproofing, dripping with five thousand ornaments from Lloyd's collection. "One year when we were putting them up," his caretaker recalled, Lloyd said, "There's something missing." He pulled out photos of the tree from an earlier year, pointing to ornaments that hadn't been hung. "Sure enough, there was a tray we forgot," the caretaker said. "He had a marvelous memory, that man."

The estate took out a $400,000 mortgage from City National Bank and negotiated a deal for visits with Grayline and other tour bus companies. Granddaughter Sue Lloyd planned a fund-raiser for the museum's endowment. But the city imposed a limit of two hundred visitors a day, and zoning variances were never granted. For two more years, Lloyd fought for her museum. Local bigwigs like Howard Hughes, Jules Stein, and Lew Wasserman took her side, but they only delayed the inevitable; ultimately the money wasn't there to repay the bank, the $47,000 a year in annual taxes, and salaries for the skeleton crew of two gardeners and Lloyd's housekeeper of fifty-five years.

Sue, along with Harold's best friend Richard Symington, the millionaire owner of Muzak and the father of the modern rebirth of body-piercing, hoped to get the city to take over Greenacres, as it had Greystone, but Beverly Hills didn't want a second white elephant. "I tried everything," Lloyd says, still upset thirty-five years after she lost control of the house. In May 1975, after City National learned that four parcels the Lloyd Foundation had planned to sell to repay the loan couldn't be sold under then prevailing zoning rules, the bank foreclosed on the loan—by then, the trust reportedly owed $675,000—and decided to sell Greenacres.

Even as the bank was collecting the $250,000 letters of credit it required in advance from bidders, Sue was still trying to save the house. She'd gotten several stars, led by Debbie Reynolds, to agree to stage annual benefits if the loan could be paid, and in the run-up to the sale, gave a series of interviews that mixed determination with desperation. But nothing could stop the auction.

"It might have been scripted from an old silent movie melodrama," wrote the *Washington Post*. "The scene: Mortgage banker at the door, ready to foreclose. Auctioneer at the block, ready to sell to the highest bidder. Sweet, young granddaughter, trying desperately at the last moment to save Granddad's old homestead from becoming just another subdivision."

Sue Lloyd's hopes of saving her grandfather's museum dream were dashed, but her biggest fear—that the mansion would be torn down—didn't come to pass. On the day of the sale, the day before her twenty-third birthday, a number of qualified bidders appeared, and two bids were made that the auctioneer deemed worthy of consideration by the Lloyd estate's trustees. One was an all-cash offer of $1.1 million from an unidentified group of investors, the other a bid of $1.6 million with $700,000 in cash down, made by a realtor, allegedly on behalf of Nasrollah Afshani, sixty, an Iranian who'd recently moved to Beverly Hills and was seeking real estate investments.

Afshani, who'd made a fortune importing cast iron into Iran from Poland, had left his native country in 1973, six years before its revolution, after planning his move for four years. "He kind of foresaw what was going to happen," says his son Shahram, who believes that while the shah of Iran was still in power, his father felt early stirrings of Islamic fundamentalism and the anti-Semitism that came along with it. In 1969, Afshani had driven from New York to Los Angeles, looking for someplace to resettle his family, and decided on Beverly Hills, where the climate and topography resembled that of the suburbs of Tehran.

Afshani wasn't actually looking for a mansion; he was seeking to invest in shopping malls when his realtor told him about Greenacres. "It was really a no-brainer," says his son. "Sixteen acres in Beverly Hills with a huge beautiful house for only $1.6 million"—$400,000 less than it had cost to build forty-six years earlier. According to a newspaper report on the auction, Afshani was accompanied by a silent, smiling partner dressed all in white, described as an electric parts distributor in Iran. His identity remained a secret for years.

Before, during, and after the auction, Sue Lloyd was "trying to throw monkey wrenches into every piece of the transaction," says Shahram Afshani. She claims that moments before the bidding began, Howard Hughes offered to pay off the loan, but the bank wouldn't call a halt to the proceedings.

Despite her misgivings, a few days later, with Sue Lloyd's consent, the trustees unanimously okayed the sale and stripped the house of its furnishings. Three months later, two thousand lots of Lloyd's belongings, including a 1925 Rolls Royce Silver Ghost, a 1924 Rolls limousine, a 1935 V-12 Packard, a Steinway piano, a Brunswick pool table, and even an archway from the house, were sold at an auction attended by Lloyd, Debbie Reynolds, and Afshani and his wife. The tension in the room was palpable as Lloyd made her unhappiness with Afshani clear. "He thinks we stole the chandeliers," she told a reporter. Reynolds bought the pool table, Lloyd a breakfast set and some chairs. And the auctioneer was left complaining that he could have made more than $122,000 had Harold Lloyd not had a fixation about keeping everything he owned in original condition, even when repairs were needed.

Initially, Afshani and his son-in-law and business partner Naim Perry rented the house out for movie and television shoots, and a party for Paul McCartney's band Wings ("which I went to, funnily enough," says Sue Lloyd). Then, in 1977, they presented a plan to the city to carve sixteen luxury home sites from the estate, preserving the mansion on one five-acre parcel, and adding a new access road. They said they had already spurned several offers for the mansion, and that some members of their extended family might build homes on the property. In a curious footnote, it emerged that four of the five acres on which the mansion sat were in Los Angeles, not Beverly Hills. The latter approved the subdivision, but required that the five-acre site that held the mansion itself remain intact as long as the house remained, and declared that, in the event it was ever subdivided, Beverly Hills would not allow access from within its borders. Though it was tentatively approved in 1977, the subdivision would remain in limbo for another two years.

Holmby Hills

10060 Sunset Boulevard

In the seventies it seemed no one cared where money came from—Iran, Italy, or even the world of pornography—as long as you had enough of it. Jack Warde, the staid insurance-man owner of 10060 Sunset Boulevard, often joked that if someone would just offer him $1 million, he'd sell the old Edwin Janss estate in an instant. When Cher paid $750,000 to Tony Curtis for the house next door, Warde saw a glimmer of hope. With the proceeds of the sale of his insurance brokerage, he'd built a house near Palm Springs in the California desert. And after fifteen years on Sunset, with his youngest boy in college, the house finally began to seem "just too big," says that son, Douglas. So he put it on the market at a price his son believes was fourteen times what he'd paid in 1961, $1.75 million.

Perhaps Warde knew who William Osco was and didn't care. Or perhaps he felt that with Harold Greenlin already in residence two doors down, Osco would just be more of the same, only slicker, younger, and richer. He was the new, pretty face of pornography, a genuine master of the oily oeuvre.

Brown-eyed and handsome in a way, Bill Osco, who wore his straight brown hair fashionably long, was a native of Akron, Ohio, a child of a beautician and a barber; he came to Los Angeles at age eighteen with a rock band called the Poor Boys that "didn't go nowhere," he says. He hoped to be an actor "but no one would look at me." He'd later say he was briefly married, that he lived "in the seedy armpit of Hollywood," ate his meals at the famous hotdog stand Pink's, and was so friendless, he'd spend his days sitting alone on benches, "because he didn't have the nerve to talk to girls," says Jackie Kong, who would briefly be his wife. "I was young and I believed him."

Osco says he attended Los Angeles City College for two years and Cal State for a third before he went to work full time. He claims he found his métier after a chance meeting with Andy Warhol at a party. "I never heard of the guy but we hit it off pretty good," Osco says. "He showed me some of his films and I said, 'Shit, anybody can do that.'" Osco hooked up with a cameraman who lived in the same boarding house. An MIT dropout, Howard Ziehm was in a rock band, too, and Osco offered to manage them. The pair moved into film after Osco revealed his desire to make a motorcycle movie.

"But I was a horndog and wanted to make sex films," says Ziehm, and soon they were shooting hundreds of "beaver loops"—brief silent movies of naked women. Ziehm made the movies and Osco made the deals. Within two years of forming Graffiti Productions, Osco and Ziehm had turned an initial pooled investment of $85 into a small fortune. Osco would claim—dubiously, says Ziehm—they'd made $1 million each. Regardless, they invested their profits buying "art" theaters—a euphemism for porn theaters—first in L.A., and then in Tucson, Phoenix, Portland, and Seattle. "No brain cells needed for that," says Osco, who foresaw that those theaters would become cash machines as porn became chic.

After Alex de Renzy's hard-core breakthrough via the "serious" documentaries *Pornography in Denmark* in 1969 and the next year's *A History of the Blue Movie,* Osco and Ziehm made their first feature. A knockoff of de Renzy's lascivious landmark, *Hollywood Blue* was billed as "the real Hollywood, the forbidden scenes the censors slashed including private erotic films of the stars," but was really just a compilation of clips that sought to recreate Kenneth Anger's naughty banned book, *Hollywood Babylon,* on screen. The scenes, both pornographic and not so, included 1920s stags, Hedy Lamarr's nude dip in *Ecstasy,* Fay Wray's sexy turn in *King Kong,* footage of Ronald Reagan ogling Jayne Mansfield, an introduction by Mickey Rooney, an interview with June Wilkinson, a clip from a film in which a woman writhes on the floor in her underpants (allegedly from a soft-core film by Marilyn Monroe but actually starring a look-alike), and a hard-core clip of a homosexual hookup featuring a man said to be television's Rifleman, Chuck Connors.

Wilkinson later alleged that she and Rooney were tricked into appearing, offered $1,000 to do interviews without being told what they were for. "I was totally aghast," she said. "They did the same thing to Mickey Rooney and he was so disgusted by it that he actually left Hollywood for quite some time." A Loyola University theology professor and crusader for wholesome family life sued to get Osco to remove a clip of a lecture he'd given to the Society of Jesus.

In the frenzy over the new dirty movies, Osco's film became famous. And they followed it almost immediately with the first full-length scripted hard-core porn film ever made. Though directed by Ziehm, *Mona: The Virgin Nymph* was billed as a "film by Bill Osco" and granted serious scrutiny by New York's *Village Voice*. "Bill Osco may well turn out to be the Federico Fellini of the porno film," it wrote, saying his work "shows the same combination of fascination and revulsion that characterizes *La Dolce Vita*." The plot focused on a high school nymphomaniac determined to indulge her desires yet remain a virgin until her wedding. The *Voice* film critic praised "the grubby nature of Osco's vision" and his "unmistakable touch." More important, perhaps, it cost $5,000 and earned them $100,000 when they sold it and *Blue* to a dirty-movie distributor. Osco claims *Mona* grossed about $13 million. "It never stopped playing," he chuckles. Whether that's true or not, it was a landmark. Years later, *Time*'s film critic Richard Corliss would dub it "the *Jazz Singer* of fuck films."

Osco and Ziehm's next movie, about another high school nymphomaniac, inspired another lawsuit, this time from Ravi Shankar, the sitar player, who claimed that a clip of his recent performance at the Monterey Pop Festival was used without permission. It also inspired no less an authority than the *Los Angeles Times* Hollywood gossip columnist Joyce Haber to write, "It's surprisingly funny, amazingly well-photographed, interestingly performed (if that's the right word for the acrobatics therein)," and to declare the new porn genre "eye-opening, mind-shattering." Thus began a love affair in print with Osco, who hoped to use Haber's support as a pivot into working with real stars in a real movie. "We wanted to do something big," Ziehm said.

Haber announced that their next project would be a non-porn but still X-rated parody of Flash Gordon. In fact, they'd already shot porn segments for it, run out of money, gone back to making hour-long hard-core movies to raise funds, and caught the attention of the Los Angeles police, who, in a smut crackdown, issued warrants for their arrest on various charges, including oral copulation and statutory rape, and seized all of Ziehm and Osco's negatives. The legal wrangling went on for many months, says Ziehm, who was desperate to finish the film they called *Flesh Gordon*, sell it, and get out from under his mounting debts. Finally, the beef was settled when Ziehm agreed to let the cops excise and keep the negatives for every hard-core scene in the new film, ensuring that it would be, as Osco had claimed to Joyce Haber, soft-core.

As Osco and Ziehm kept cranking out sex films for money—"a feature every ten days," Ziehm has said—Haber kept an eye on Osco's career, noting that he'd cast himself as an actor in their first non-porn film, about two cocaine dealers. "I figure if I'm an actor maybe I'll get to meet Raquel Welch," the twenty-five-year-old told her early in 1972. That summer, she profiled Osco in a full-page article in the newspaper's Calendar section headlined, "Dishing the Dirt with Boy King of Pornography." Claiming he'd washed his hands of dirty movies, Osco told Haber he admired Aristotle Onassis, Hank Aaron, Elvis Presley, and Adolph Hitler ("He had more power than anyone"), had changed his mind about Raquel Welch ("the most untalented actress on the screen"), and was now obsessed with Barbra Streisand and wanted to date her. Osco revealed an ambition to become "the biggest movie tycoon in Hollywood. Within three years, I will make myself a superstar." He also told Haber he'd tried but failed to buy Jayne Mansfield's house when Harold Greenlin had briefly put it on the market a year earlier. He says he was unaware that the seller was a colleague in porn.

Osco "had a way of getting himself into kind of nice houses," says Ziehm. After failing to buy the Pink Palace, he landed in a gold-plated mansion on Delfern Drive in Bel Air that he rented from a millionaire Korean, where, Osco sometimes claimed, Elizabeth Taylor and Nicky Hilton lived during their ill-fated marriage. Connie Stevens lived just up the block, as did Glen Campbell and the Bloomingdales. Osco lived there for a time with Ziehm's sister, who'd become one of his girlfriends. Another was a beautiful blue-eyed blonde neophyte starlet, Kristine DeBell.

Osco hosted touch football games (his team was called the Delfern Dykes) and regular parties for hundreds there, organized by the actress Sally Kirkland, a friend of DeBell's. The parties attracted the likes of Robert De Niro, Al Pacino, Francis Ford Coppola, Martin Scorsese, Steve Tisch, Roger Corman, John Paul Getty III, Bob Dylan, Mama Cass, Ringo Starr, Mick Jagger, Alice Cooper, and Cher. "I was only too happy when my friend's boyfriend offered me his mansion in Bel Air," says Kirkland, who doubled as the cheerleader for the Delfern Dykes. Like many of their guests, Kirkland was unaware how Osco made the money he spent on them.

"Anyone in Hollywood was invited," says Stefani Kong Uhler, Osco's future sister-in-law and a frequent guest. "There was never any food, just a crush of people. Let-me-meet-everyone-in-Hollywood kind of parties and they were all so high, they didn't notice there was nothing to eat."

Osco and Ziehm's partnership ended badly. "I'm not going into detail," Osco says at first. "I'm not into drugs at all or drunken alcoholics. We had different lifestyles. It just ended." Ziehm, who denies ever being "messed-up on drugs," is more specific. "I caught him pilfering," he says. "I was brain-dead from exhaustion, struggling to finish *Flesh Gordon*, giving out IOUs, and he's driving a Rolls." And giving those parties in his Bel Air mansion.

Ziehm says they finally parted ways after his wife discovered that Osco was showing the then new *Deep Throat* in their Idaho theater, run by members of Osco's family, and stashing the profits in a private bank account instead of with Graffiti Productions. He also thinks Osco was skimming cash from their L.A. theater. "I found proof and tossed it on his desk," Ziehm says. "He could look you right in the face and tell a bald-face lie. I bought him out. He was a pretty damn good businessman but if he could make a buck honest or dishonest, he would choose dishonest."

Osco denies it all. Messed up or not, Ziehm eventually finished *Flesh Gordon*, and Osco helped him find a distributor for the film. Osco even submitted *Flesh* for an Academy Award for Special Effects (no award was given that year and Ziehm suspects it was a snub aimed at *Flesh*).

Osco's next film helped pay for his ever-richer lifestyle. *Alice in Wonderland* was an X-rated, though initially soft-core, musical version of the Lewis Carroll tale, starring DeBell as a repressed librarian who has a sexual awakening when she steps through the looking glass.[27] Released in summer 1976, it made money—Osco claimed, however improbably, that it grossed more than $20 million on a cost of only $300,000—but did not make him happy. Indeed, shortly after its release, he sneered at his adopted hometown: "I hate this city; I'm only here to make money and make movies," he said. "I don't like plastic, and that's what people in this town are—plastic and whores." Nonetheless, Osco ran ads in the show business trade papers promoting a Best Actress award nomination for DeBell, but all she won was her producer's heart, moving into Delfern, which the L.A. *Times* described as a pretentious Greek-statued mansion with a living room filled with gilt cherubs and baroque antiques.

For his next act, DeBell told the *Times,* Osco was planning a parody of *The Wizard of Oz.* That never got made, but Osco did get to live in Oz, or at least 10060 Sunset, which he bought from Warde in spring 1977. His brother and DeBell moved in with him, as he sought to finance *Peewee Pigskin,* a *Bad News Bears* knockoff starring football great turned actor Jim Brown—another unlikely stab at a legitimate movie. It didn't happen, either, and DeBell moved out. She doesn't remember why. "I was in a drug-induced coma then," she says.

Osco barely had time to catch his breath before he found his next girlfriend, Jackie Kong, eighteen, a daughter of the actress Anita Loo, who'd been a lover and stayed a friend of Marlon Brando's; he was close to Jackie, too. Like so many in Hollywood, Osco was fascinated by the reclusive Brando. So when he was introduced to Loo and her daughters by Jim Brown one night at Dan Tana's, an old-school Italian restaurant, Osco became a regular visitor to their home (originally built for Jean Harlow's mother).

That Thanksgiving, Osco gave Jackie a ride home from a party, stopping at 10060 where "he dropped to his knees on the lawn and asked me to marry him," Kong says. "I was from a broken home. I had no frame of reference about marriage. The more I pushed him away, the more he pursued me. Marlon was like my stepfather. He thought Osco was a bad character. He called Osco and said, 'Don't marry her.' Then, of course, he wanted to marry me all the more." So, even though "people tried to bribe her not to marry him," as Jackie's sister Stefani puts it, she said yes. "He was very flash," yet "one of the most unappetizing people in Hollywood," Stefani continues. "But they thought they could have beautiful kids. L.A. is that kind of town."

Osco may have seen something else in Jackie Kong—a replacement for Howard Ziehm. Brando had inspired Kong to be a filmmaker, giving her a 16-mm camera for her seventeenth birthday. Kong would learn that Osco had ambitions, too, the very sort that might lead him to covet Brando's goddaughter. "He wanted the biggest house in Holmby Hills," Jackie says, "the longest limo." He would take those limos back to Pink's for hotdogs to demonstrate—to himself as much as others—how far he'd come.

Kong and Osco got married on Christmas day 1977 in Hawaii, and Jackie got pregnant a few months later. Quickly, she says, she had to grow up, and began to see her husband for what he was. "Had I gotten to know him I would never have married him."

The marriage soon soured. There were always girls around who hoped to become porn stars. Osco's brother lived in a guesthouse and Kong and Osco both say he was not only selling drugs, but growing high-grade marijuana on the grounds. Although Osco repeats that he was always antidrugs, Kong says, "he had a weird fascination. He was tied to the idea of being lawless." One day, agriculture officials showed up to inspect oak trees on the property. Everyone breathed a sigh of relief when they walked right past the pot plants. That may have been the high point—no pun intended—of their tenure there.

Holmby Hills

Owlwood (141 South Carolwood Drive)

While Bill Osco's circus played on, the house next door changed hands again. "My grandmother would not have approved" of the next owner of 141 South Carolwood, says a granddaughter of Edwin Janss. Ghazi Aita "was a very elusive dude," said Greg Hagins, who ran the estate for him and lived there for twenty-one years. Indeed, Aita didn't buy the house from Chase and Ralph Mishkin himself; it was purchased in July 1978 by Magdalenian Investment NV, an investment advisory firm based in the Caribbean tax haven, the Netherlands Antilles.

Though he lived in Holmby Hills for fourteen years, few who encountered him there are sure who Ghazi Aita was or how he made his fortune. His mark on the public record is similarly mysterious: One of the few places his name comes up is on the website of the tiny Republic of San Marino, where he is listed as one of its ambassadors-at-large, appointed in 1998. But a spokesperson for its Foreign Affairs Department says it has "had no official contacts with him in the last few years."

Aita came to Los Angeles in about 1977, frequently staying in Bungalow #2 at the Beverly Hills Hotel. He'd previously lived in London, Paris, and Monte Carlo. Ostensibly, he was a retired banker. Yet he wasn't retiring. A tiny man, about five foot three, he wore glasses, a hairpiece, and lifts in his shoes, had a V-shaped gap between his front teeth, dressed in obviously expensive clothes (he wore custom-made robes sewn from a particular kind of terry cloth), and preferred they be in outré colors like light green or purple; his Rolls Royce was purple too, says Hagins. "He looked more like an entertainer than a businessman," says a business associate. "He wasn't ugly, but he wasn't attractive," says Carol Ann La Vella, his longtime office manager and bookkeeper. "And he had a good personality." He spoke six languages.

Little else was known about him, and he seemed to prefer it that way. But over the next few years, as he gathered a team of lawyers, accountants, and employees around him and began doing deals and investing in real estate, they picked up hints of how he'd become wealthy and caught glimpses of how he was occupying himself in "retirement."

Hagins said Aita worked at Swiss banks in Geneva and Zurich before retiring to California in his midfifties. "He loved the weather," said Hagins. "He loved discos. He loved tennis. He loved California girls." Aita told Hagins he'd made his fortune buying water rights and "drilling for water" in Saudi Arabia. "He did other stuff, arms, under the table," said Hagins. Aita told one associate that he'd made his money during World War II (when he would have been a teenager) by buying sugar on the advice of an uncle who anticipated shortages. He told a real estate broker he hired that he'd once been in the rug business. And he told yet another that an uncle "was the person who brought radio to Syria," that broker says. The general consensus was that he had also married well; his wife, Salma, was from a wealthy and possibly royal Syrian family.

When he arrived in Los Angeles, Aita already had ongoing business relationships with a number of Middle Eastern financiers, some of whom had deep connections with the ruling family of Saudi Arabia, and have since been described as arms dealers. One of the few people with direct knowledge of Aita's first deals in California is his office manager, La Vella, who was working at Northrop, the aircraft manufacturer, when Aita showed up one day with a proposition for her boss. He was putting together a deal to build a compound in Saudi Arabia for American contractors training Saudis to fly and maintain American jets like Northrop's F-5.

About a year later, after Aita's deal was made, La Vella's boss quit to run the venture and Aita hired her to replace his executive assistant, working out of the grand estate he'd just bought from Chase and Ralph Mishkin. Aita had heard about the house from a new L.A. friend, Steven Macallum Powers, another of those scheming, self-invented men of appetite and ambition in the mold of Cornfeld and Hefner.

• • •

Whippet-thin, with dark bushy eyebrows, a full head of hair, and a ready smile, Steve Powers is known today, if at all, as a former hanger-on at the Playboy mansion "with a legendary playboy reputation," according to Hugh Hefner's biographer Steven Wells. But he'd made himself into a player of sorts in L.A. even before Hefner moved west from Chicago. In the late sixties, Powers, the son of a single mother who ran a bar in Westwood, was studying for a master's degree in behavioral psychology at UCLA when he met some lawyers doing so-called shell deals, buying public corporations without assets, liabilities, or ongoing business, and merging private companies into them to avoid the costs normally associated with public stock offerings. Shells also sometimes hid securities frauds. "I didn't want to get a job, so I went with them," Powers says.

In December 1970, even though Powers "had no money, no car, no place to live," he says, he pulled off a shell game of his own, buying the moribund Keck Oil Co. of Los Angeles for $500 raised by selling his sperm. He renamed it Keck First Leisure because *leisure* was then a hot buzzword in the stock market. Before the new company was approved by the Securities and Exchange Commission for relisting on a public exchange, "the stock shot up to seven cents," he wrote in an unpublished memoir. "I then acquired a small bottling company that was also losing money and the stock went up to fifteen cents. I then acquired a small commodities option trading company. . . . The stock shot up to $22 a share, the fastest growing stock in the nation that year. . . . I went from a net worth of minus ten bucks to $30 million in only four months. I was rich beyond my wildest dreams."

But he was also in trouble. In October 1972, shortly after Powers bought the Coldwater Canyon house once occupied by Tony Curtis and Janet Leigh, and a Rolls Royce, his companies were featured in a *Forbes* magazine exposé revealing that they were subjects of "an intense fraud investigation" by the SEC, which soon halted trading in First Leisure's stock. In that *Forbes* story, Powers claimed he'd gotten advice from none other than Bernie Cornfeld. Cornfeld denied he'd ever met Powers. Their paths would cross soon enough.

Just after the *Forbes* piece appeared, Powers resigned, and started throwing parties—indulging in the myriad pleasures of the L.A. scene: "I invited celebrities and attractive women and it escalated as I got to know people." He actually met his alleged mentor Cornfeld when "he had a big party and

I climbed through the bushes and crashed," Powers admits. Cornfeld apparently didn't mind; they would soon grow close.

But before that, Powers made friends with Ghazi Aita, who also had a taste for attractive women and a good party. Forcibly retired from the securities business, Powers began investing in mansions in the years after First Leisure—buying, renovating, renting, and selling them, owning as many as ten at a time, he claims. He would give parties in the houses, full of beautiful young women and celebrities, to entice high rollers to want to buy. A broker Powers worked with brought Aita to one of them, thinking the rich Syrian might become a financial backer for Powers's real estate plays.

"I had ten girls living with me at the time," Powers says. "He was unbelievably impressed." Over a subsequent dinner, Aita ordered Powers to get rid of his other investors. "He became my chief. He was interested in girls. Fun and girls. He had no other reason to be in L.A. He was in and out of town then and after that first party, he called every time he came." After Aita put money into a house Powers had bought at 800 Bel Air Road (later sold to Jerry Perenchio, who tore it down and added the land to his Bel Air aerie), the Syrian told his new partner he wanted a mansion of his own. "I checked around," Powers says, and learned the Mishkins' Owlwood was on the market. "He liked it, of course."

A mere eight days after listing it, the Mishkins sold it to Aita—and built themselves a new house in Bel Air. All they knew of their buyer was that he was a legal resident of Monaco. "It was all cash," says Chase Mishkin. "He had the money. We took it." This change of hands did not please the neighbors.

10060 Sunset Boulevard

Jackie Kong hated Ghazi Aita immediately. "He'd bring all of Pips [a private backgammon club] home at 2 a.m. and play music on a PA system all over the grounds," she says. "The Beach Boys. I hate the Beach Boys. And I was pregnant, so I was really pissed."

But she had other reasons to be pissed. Bill Osco had borrowed money against his already-mortgaged property and put it up for sale because he "really couldn't afford to live in such an expensive home," says Kong. Osco says he was entertaining offers to subdivide when Aita offered to buy the place to keep it from being split up. "I don't think Ghazi spent ten minutes thinking about that property and he never set foot on it. He bought it to protect Carolwood," says an Aita lawyer, Thomas Childers.

Osco agreed and a sale was made (this time to another shingle company, Carolwood Investments) for about $4 million, closing at the end of 1979. After leaving 10060 Sunset, the Oscos moved into a series of rentals and Bill went back to the frustrating game of trying to make movies. Kong, who describes herself as "a go-getter," did the same with a little more success. She wrote a horror script, *The Being*, and managed to get some minor stars—Martin Landau, José Ferrer—to appear in it. Osco forced his way into a part as well; Marianne Rogers played his girlfriend after her husband Kenny invested $250,000 in the project. Robert Downey Sr., Kong's mentor and the director of *Putney Swope*, helped her edit it "to save it," she says. It bombed anyway. Kong blames Osco. "Landau said he was the worst actor ever."

Kong managed to make a second film in 1982, *Night Patrol*, now a cult favorite, by using friends who were willing to defer payment as actors and crew and filming only on weekends. Osco got a producer credit even though he hadn't raised the money or made the deal to get the picture made. "He was there if you did the work," says Kong. "He's an opportunist. I was trying to keep a marriage together because I had a child."

In 1984, just as *Night Patrol* was set to open, Osco moved his business and family to Idaho and declared bankruptcy—"thinking he could do it quietly there," Kong says. "He had a lot of lawsuits going on." He was also in trouble with taxes. The *Los Angeles Times* reported that he owed the IRS $200,000, MGM Labs $75,000, and his lawyers almost $43,000. According to Bill Ziehm, the IRS had been after Osco since just before *their* corporate divorce: "He was forced to make a deal with me to settle with the IRS. He cleared up the first case and then did it again."

Kong moved back to L.A.'s Marina del Rey, leaving Osco and their daughter in Idaho, and initiated a do-it-yourself divorce. All she wanted from Osco, she says, was her daughter. She got a development deal and soon after that was offered a multipicture deal, all without Osco's involvement, and was waiting for a green light to start her next movie. In 1986, feeling sorry for Osco, Kong found them a Malibu house in disrepair, inhabited only by a pack of feral cats, but with one and a half acres of beautiful grounds that they could buy for only $375,000.

But soon, it wasn't just the IRS on his tail; the federal government had started looking into his affairs. "It took me totally by surprise," says Kong, who was busy finishing her third film. "He was away most of the time. His primary residence wasn't Malibu. He was doing something in Idaho and Arizona."

Osco insists the problem was his brother, who was "fucking around with that marijuana shit. If they'd researched, they would have known how anti-drug I was." But he also allows that "eventually, it turned into taxes."

Kong says Osco hadn't paid taxes on the sale of 10060 Sunset and was "hiding money, not using his name on anything; the house is in his mother's name so I have no claim on it, he borrows against the house to the tune of $800,000. Then came the last straw." The FBI came to Malibu, looking for Osco, "coming through the gate," says Kong. They had a search warrant, guns, safe-cracking tools, and infrared scopes. It was a coordinated three-state search of all his property. That's when she learned about his out-of-town businesses, an adult bookstore called Niks and Naks and the Desert Skies Motel, both in suburban Boise, Idaho. Kong fled, first to her mother's house, then to Europe, where she put their daughter into private school. On her return, she found he'd sold her car and pocketed the cash.

In 1987, the couple finally divorced. Kong got a loan to pay off Osco's debts on the Malibu house, found a buyer, and sold it in 1990. "I paid the capital gains tax," she points out. In 1991, a California court ordered Osco to pay Kong $25,000 for jewelry the IRS had seized from her; he also owed her $99,000 in past-due child support payments. In February 1991, he was arrested for solicitation and lewd conduct in North Hollywood. "That was me and a girl," he admits proudly. "We were in a restroom. She was giving me a blowjob." But that was nothing compared to what happened two months later, when Osco, his mother, and his best friend were all charged with a massive tax fraud.

In October of that year, after refusing a plea bargain, a jury found Osco guilty of committing eighteen felonies stemming from money skimming, illegal property transfers, and concealing assets to avoid paying about $50,000 in federal income tax. The charges included tax evasion, filing false returns, bank fraud, bankruptcy fraud, and conspiring to defraud the United States. His mother and friend were convicted along with him, the latter charged with operating Osco's Idaho businesses as a front for him. Osco was sentenced to three years and ten months in prison, his mother to eighteen months. "You know how the Feds are," Osco says of the convictions. "They blow everything up." He insists the businesses weren't his but his friend's; he was just trying to help out, and the jury convicted him only because they heard his brother had been dealing marijuana.

While his codefendants surrendered to serve their terms, Osco disappeared, taking his and Kong's twelve-year-old with him. "I had to take care of my daughter," he claims. "She didn't want to be with her mother." Kong is sure he had the getaway planned. "I offered him some time with her before he went to jail," she says. "When I returned, no one answered the phone so I drove out to Malibu. She was gone and his place was empty."

Several months later, the U.S. Marshals Service informed Kong that they'd tracked Osco down to Costa Rica, which had no extradition agreement with the United States for tax crimes. (Bernie Cornfeld's IOS successor Robert Vesco had gone there for the same reason after the collapse of the company.) Kong went to Costa Rica to look for her daughter, canvassing bilingual schools with her photo. "I didn't realize he didn't put her in school, so I couldn't find her," she says.

Osco finally resurfaced in Ohio, under arrest, in 1995. He'd returned to visit relatives, one of whom turned him in. "I get a call from my daughter in Ohio asking for a plane ticket back to L.A.," Kong says. Osco went to prison, where he remained until March 1999. He insists he did his time in a country club prison where, through "a lot of connections," he was given "special treatment," though there is no evidence of this.

Out of prison, Osco helped produce a late-night cable documentary on the adult film industry. Two years later, he was arrested again near a toilet in a public park in Costa Mesa, California, for solicitation of a lewd act and after pleading guilty, was sentenced to a $270 fine and three years' probation. "That was somebody else with my ID," he insists. "I lost it or it got stolen, one or the other. I got it taken care of. I didn't get no probation." The Costa Mesa police think that's unlikely. "In general," says a spokesman for the department, "the identity of individuals who are arrested is screened and verified," and the same process repeats during the judicial process.

Just as the probation from the Costa Mesa incident was ending, Osco tried to make a comeback, staging a live version of his *Alice in Wonderland* in the San Fernando Valley and then bringing it to Theater Row on New York's West 42nd Street. Osco says it was a hit and played for more than six months to sell-out crowds. The Newark *Star-Ledger* headlined its review

"An All-Time Stinker" and deemed the effort "pathetic . . . coarse, occasionally incoherent . . . stupid and badly written." *The Village Voice* said it was "excruciating . . . inexplicit yet unrelentingly icky." Theater records show it closed after two months due to a breach in the rental agreement. Osco's behavior there was icky, too. "He tried to make us get naked," says an actress who quit the show, adding that he also tried to hide the costume of another actress who wouldn't undress, and made sexual advances.

Though he lives on in Southern California, Bill Osco has never again entered the public eye. "I've been traveling around, just having fun," he says. "I got a couple things I've been approached to do. I'm thinking about it. I'm doing okay. I have no complaints. I never have to work again, put it that way."

Who knows what that means.

Holmby Hills

Owlwood (141 South Carolwood Drive)

10060 Sunset Boulevard

10100 Sunset Boulevard

Steve Powers moved into 10060 Sunset after his buddy Aita bought it from Bill Osco, and remained until he was usurped by Tom Childers and Dan Zerfas, two lawyers who became Ghazi Aita's partners in real estate development. Not to be discouraged, Powers set up an office in the pool house. Real estate development wasn't his, or Aita's, only interest. Indeed, it often seemed to those around Aita that investing was a sideline to his main preoccupation, girls, specifically the ones memorably described as model-actress-whatevers, who were happy to do whatever with rich and generous men between modeling and acting jobs.

Some of the people around Aita believed he only kept Powers around because the Playboy mansion regular knew the right kind of girls. Was he a procurer? "No question about it," says Zerfas. But Greg Hagins said Powers was an amateur at the procuring game—and Aita was about to meet a pro. Vince Conti was known around L.A. as the best friend of the actor Telly Savalas, who cast him as a detective named Rizzo on his hit TV cop show, *Kojak.* Conti calls himself a photographer, but comes close to admitting he's committed the crime he went to jail for, pimping.

When they were introduced by an unnamed friend, Conti had the impression Aita was "was one of the richest guys in the world," he says. And Conti had something Aita wanted. "There were no frickin' girls prettier than the ones hanging around me," Conti says. He claims one of them was a famous film star. "I brought her up there [to Carolwood]," says Conti. "His wife was never there. You want to call it pimping, go ahead. I just introduced them and he was very generous to me."

Conti evades the direct question of whether Aita was paying women for sex. "I don't want to go into it," he says. "They were taken care of." But finally, he can't help himself. "If a girl was loose, she'd do it for money, ferchrissakes."

No one really knows what Aita and the girls Powers and Conti brought him did behind closed doors, but they left a strong impression on all who watched the passing parade and came to understand the rhythm of life at 141 South Carolwood. Or rather, the two different rhythms of life in the house: the one that prevailed when Salma Aita was in town, and the other that started up as soon as she left or when Ghazi flew in alone, as he often did, for a week or a month.

The house wasn't quiet when Salma was in residence. "She came every summer," says La Vella, "and she made Leona Helmsley look like a Sunday School teacher. She was the kind who was put here to shop and make people's lives miserable, and she did good at both." She was known to throw things at her maids and hit her dogs. "She'd have you in tears," says La Vella. "Bipolar, we'd call it today."

Aita rarely socialized when his wife was in town. "When she was there, he'd paint or play the piano," says La Vella. "She found her own amusements. When she gave parties, he'd make himself scarce." When Salma was in residence, there were butlers and chefs, but when she left, they disappeared. "He didn't want them seeing what went on at night," said Hagins.

Though Aita enjoyed visiting neighbors like Hugh Hefner (until they had a falling-out over a girl) and the producer Robert Evans, "his real friends were Middle Eastern," said Hagins. Several Saudi princes were in Aita's orbit. "But they'd bring security with them," said Hagins. "He stopped inviting them because he didn't like that." Aita appeared to share his women with his Arab friends.

Usually, though, Aita's nights were spent with Powers or Conti and a pack of girls, the younger the better. "Vince brought two or three girls a night," said Hagins. "They never came twice unless they were exceptional.

They'd go to [fashionable restaurants like] Morton's or Spago for dinner and Ghazi would pick one and take her back to the house. Vince took the rest."

When Salma was in residence, "he'd have to meet the girls at the Hilton," said Hagins. "I went with him so she'd think we were shopping. When she was there, he was in hell." But Salma Aita was no fool. "One day one of his little bimbos called and told her what was going on," says La Vella. Salma responded, "Didn't he pay you well?"

In the early 1980s, Aita "made a lot of money," said Greg Hagins. "He went from fairly to very wealthy. From asking what things cost, [he progressed] to cost was no question, just find it." Hagins assumed that money came from his dealings with and on behalf of the Saudis. "I saw pictures of them meeting in tents—a bunch of really scary guys," he said.

Dan Zerfas and Tom Childers created a partnership, Somerset Co., to invest in real estate; through Somerset, and also personally, Aita put money into property in Jackson, Wyoming; Santa Fe, New Mexico; Foster City, outside San Francisco; and several other deals, including the historic Pan-Pacific Auditorium in Los Angeles, onetime home to ice shows and Elvis Presley concerts, which they hoped to convert into a hotel.

The secrecy that shrouded Aita extended to Somerset. Though he lived next door for a year and was a partner in Aita's property investments, Tom Childers was never clear whose money the partnership was spending. "I always had a nagging suspicion it wasn't what it seemed," he says.

According to La Vella and Hagins, those local investments were only a small part of a larger enterprise of unknown dimensions centered in the banking havens of the Dutch West Indies and Switzerland. Then, in the mid-eighties, something went wrong in Aita's paradise. He fell out with one of his powerful Arab friends, got tangled up in several lawsuits, and stopped traveling to the Middle East. "All at once, he was afraid to go," says La Vella. "He was afraid for his life." The social calls from Saudi royals stopped at the same time. Aita's Arab partners "would call," said Greg Hagins, "and he'd shake his head like, 'I'm not here.'" There was a recession in the Middle East at the time, but that didn't seem to be the problem. La Vella heard there was "some big deal he'd wheeled and dealed somebody important out of."

Two years later, Aita was enmeshed in more litigation, this time suing a partner in his land investment outside San Francisco. He lost, and the resulting animosity ended his partnership with Zerfas and Childers. By that time, Aita's ego had grown along with his wealth and sense that he could flaunt convention with impunity. He stormed out of a postopera dinner in Santa Fe, furious because he felt he'd been badly seated. He deserved better; not only was he rich, he'd become a diplomat. According to Hagins, Aita bought himself the title of United Nations Ambassador for the Most Serene Republic of San Marino, a tiny (sixty square kilometers) landlocked state within the borders of Italy, in exchange for $6,000 a month. He remained in that post for a year, San Marino's last as a nonmember observer state at the UN, giving up the title when it became a member state. He was then named ambassador-at-large, the post he still held early in 2011.

Roberto Balsimelli, the honorary consul of San Marino in New York, says Aita got and kept his posts "because a person with his power, knowledge, and possibility could help a lot."

"If he paid something, it was some kind of donation in support of the expenses of the consul general," says the consul's son. (The San Marino consulate is the Balsimellis' small home in suburban Elmont, New York.) So did he help with expenses? "Most likely," says Balsimelli Sr. "Why not?"

Why would Aita want the job, though? Greg Hagins suggested diplomatic immunity was a factor. "Ghazi was arrested several times," Hagins wrote in an e-mail. "He was Never Prosecuted (Dip Low Mat)." Many of those who surrounded Aita knew of his weakness for women. And it was common knowledge among his inner circle that his weaknesses went beyond a fondness for young demi-prostitutes. "A couple filed police reports about biting and nasty things," says Daniel Zerfas, who hired a lawyer for Aita to make the charges go away. "I'd enjoyed and admired him but it turned out to be pretty ugly."

On one occasion, Carol Ann La Vella got a call from another of Ghazi's lawyers saying there'd been "a mishap the night before and Ghazi would be arrested and he needed to pay somebody off," she recalls, "and I had to sign this check. They tried to keep it from me, but the lawyer finally told me what he'd done. His teeth were involved and she [the girl] was not particularly happy."

Zerfas and Childers weren't the only associates who broke with Aita. Next to depart was Vince Conti. A new procurer named Heidi Fleiss seemed to be edging onto his turf. Conti had legal troubles of his own. "No way" did Fleiss replace him, Conti insists. "I went to jail. I introduced a guy to a girl. The girl said I pimped her and the fucking jury said I was guilty." Luckily for Conti, Aita was either very loyal or wanted to keep the man who'd long brought him women close and quiet. When he got out of jail after nine months, Aita "took care of me," says Conti, whose food, rent, and clothes were paid for by Aita for several years afterwards. "But I never saw him again and one day he disappeared."

Heidi Fleiss got arrested, too, in June 1993. When some of her Gucci appointment books, seized by police but written in code, were shown on television, Carol Ann La Vella thought she saw a date "I had set up," and realized Aita was a Fleiss customer. After that, "Ghazi went incognito," said Hagins, "changed his license plates," which had read GAITA, "and stopped having girls in the house. He thought he'd be named, so he lay low in New York. He'd only come back for a week or two at a time. He turned into a choirboy."

In the late nineties, Salma Aita fell ill, suffering from Alzheimer's disease, and Aita put Carolwood and 10060 Sunset on the market as a unit in fall 1999, asking $58.9 million for the combined properties on eight and a half acres. The estate took four years to sell. In the meantime, Aita divested his collection of twenty-three Persian, Turkish, Egyptian, and Caucasian carpets and Islamic prayer rugs, built up over twenty-nine years, at Christie's in London, in the fall of 2001, earning over a million dollars. Salma died not long afterwards. Aita remained in residence in Holmby Hills throughout the long slog to a sale. According to one of his real estate brokers, "he stayed up late, played a lot of poker and backgammon, went to Las Vegas."

The actual sale was mysterious; his brokers insist they don't know to whom they sold Aita's house. They dealt only with the unnamed buyer's lawyer. And apparently for this mysterious high roller, two houses weren't enough. The lawyer told them he would need to buy "the house on the corner, too."

That was the old Jayne Mansfield house, which now belonged to singer Engelbert Humperdinck. It had been on and off the market for thirteen years, listed during many of them with Aita's pair of brokers. "He wasn't sure," says one of them. "He loved his house."

Humperdinck was born (and legally remains) Arnold George Dorsey in Madras, India, just before the start of World War II, and moved to England as a boy. At seventeen, he started performing at a local singing contest, and soon went professional as Gerry Dorsey. After a stint in the military, he recorded his first song. It was a flop, yet he continued his career until 1965, when an old friend, who was managing the crooner Tom Jones, suggested he take the stage name Engelbert Humperdinck, after a nineteenth-century German opera composer. Friends called him Enge.

By 1966, he'd grown his signature lush sideburns (later stolen, he claimed, by Elvis Presley) and was recording again, and the next year he topped the British pop charts with the ballad "Release Me," which kept the Beatles' two-sided hit, "Penny Lane" and "Strawberry Fields Forever," from the top of the pops. Seven British hit singles followed, and though they didn't score in America, the handsome and smooth Humperdinck became a television and touring star there, with well-produced stage shows featuring celebrity impressions and his signature crooning. Those shows made him a hit in Las Vegas, especially with women, after Dean Martin, whom he imitated, promoted his first appearance at the Riviera. His signature gimmick was to mop his onstage sweat with a handerkerchief and end the show by giving it to a woman in the audience. A second appearance on the U.S. pop charts in 1976 with "After the Lovin' " won him a coveted Grammy nomination— and convinced him to move to the States and become a tax exile to avoid Great Britain's onerous levies on his earnings.

That July, a Las Vegas real estate broker Humperdinck shared with Harold Greenlin showed him Polaroid photos of 10100 Sunset Boulevard and said it was available for a good price. When Humperdinck learned it had once belonged to Jayne Mansfield, he was shocked; they'd performed together in a club in Bristol, England, years before, and after having dinner together, the blonde starlet had invited him to visit her Pink Palace. He also thought it was an appropriate home for a man who'd been dubbed the King of Romance. ("They say I had an affair with Jayne Mansfield," he'd later tell an interviewer. "I'm not saying it's true or not. I'm away from home a lot and things happen.") He bought it and spent six months renovating, spending a total $1.9 million, he claimed in his autobiography, *What's in a Name?* though that's unlikely as he paid only $233,500 for the house.

"The Pink Palace was beautiful, but very dilapidated and a little on the dark side," Humperdinck wrote. Though the property had "unbelievably beautiful" trees, they "cast too much shade," so the grounds needed work as well. Greenlin had kept the place a shrine to Mansfield, leaving pin-up photos lining the staircase. Humperdinck also "inherited a naked bust of her, but unfortunately," he wrote, "missing her left nipple! When the builders were taking down a wall in the house, they came across a lot of memorabilia and personal stuff that Jayne had stuck to the walls. . . . One of the rooms was called the 'copper room' for its ornate copper ceiling, while the ceiling in Jayne's office was covered in red leather pads. Once, when there was an earthquake, one of the pads came off and underneath it, we discovered a hand-painted ceiling from years before."

Humperdinck is quite candid in some respects. In his book, he admits to excessive drinking and regular infidelity; over the years he'd fend off or settle multiple paternity suits stemming from his on-tour womanizing, and his wife is said to have joked that she could have papered their bedroom with the lawsuits. But he doesn't mention that he bought the Pink Palace from Harold Greenlin.

After he and his family moved into 10100, they had the sense they weren't alone. Only when they did roof repairs did they discover that "a tramp," as he put it, was living in the attic, raiding their refrigerator at night, and sometimes leaving catnip for a cat he'd inherited from the realtor. And then there were the ghosts—"little children dancing around the living room" almost nightly until "they disappeared one day for no reason that we could come up with." His wife missed them terribly and "genuinely pined for their return," Humperdinck writes. "They kept her company." But another kind of spirit also haunted the place, and after twenty-seven years, drove them to sell. In that time, his family counted forty-nine fatal accidents on the twisty stretch of Sunset Boulevard just outside their still-pink home. The last, in which a boy was killed at the end of their driveway just as their same-aged son was learning to drive, finally convinced the crooner's wife it was time to leave.

Humperdinck put a fresh coat of paint on the house, keeping it pink, and listed it for sale for the first time in January 1990, asking $8 million and claiming, in another outrageous lie, he'd bought it from a spinster who lived in one back room. By March, he'd taken it off the market, explaining, "It means too much to me." In 1992, he dangled it again, that time at $7.2 million. In 1997, it went back on the market at $3.95 million, and his brokers advertised the fact that Mansfield's shag carpet, gilt balcony, pink bathroom tile, and other decorating touches had been preserved (though the bottom of the pool had been refinished, obliterating Mickey Hargitay's tiled love note). When it didn't move quickly, Enge went on the home shopping network QVC, giving a guided tour with a camera crew.

By then, his wife had returned to England, where they lived in a grand Victorian mansion originally built for the Duchess of Hamilton in 1856 in Enge's hometown of Leicestershire; that house had its own pub, driving range, wishing well, fountains, and a swimming pool emblazoned with a crest that read in French, "One God, One King." But the master of the house was still a tax exile, living mostly in a home on a Vegas golf course and the deteriorating Pink Palace, with its old-fashioned kitchen and leaking foyer. When he was in L.A., he spent most of his time at the Bel-Air Country Club, where he shared a locker with the actor Joe Pesci. When he wasn't, one of his three sons (the Dorseys also had a daughter) lived there alone with a piano on which George Gershwin allegedly wrote "Rhapsody in Blue."

In 2000, the Pink Palace came back on the market, listed this time at $5 million. For the first time, however, an alternative was offered—the brokers told potential buyers they could also buy Owlwood and 10060 Sunset in separate but simultaneous transactions. The total asking price for the three houses was $63 million. Just after September 11, 2001, Humperdinck cut his price to $4.75 million. He didn't need the money; he was said to be worth as much as $150 million at the time, thanks to multiple reissues of his recordings and constant career maintenance, including an album of dance remixes (the video for one of which was filmed in the Pink Palace) and a comic ballad, "(Fly High) Lesbian Seagull," that he recorded for the Beavis and Butt-head movie.

Drew Mandile, one of the realtors, says the deal to sell the Pink Palace and Owlwood happened fast once it happened, taking only thirty days. But it took somewhat longer to close. Though the sale was already in the works, late in 2002 Humperdinck gave an interview threatening to take his house off the market and rebuild it to make it worth "a vast amount of money." By the time that interview was published, though, an entity called Davis Carolwood Holdings had closed on 141 South Carolwood and 10060 Sunset, and shortly after that, a second entity called Burns Sunset Properties acquired 10100 Sunset. Before he left the house, Humperdinck invited Jayne Mansfield's husband and children over for one last visit. Mickey Hargitay refused, saying, "The house died when Jayne did."

Some of their kids accepted the offer. "We hadn't been back in thirty-some-odd years," says Mickey Jr., "and we were able to take a few little things." He got a wrought-iron railing with decorative hearts and an ornamental copper shield from the fireplace in the pool house, engraved with a note from Mickey to Jayne reading, "My love will flame for you forever." It now sits in his Los Angeles backyard. Humperdinck moved first to Brentwood and three years later to a $3 million mansion at the very top of Bel Air Road, just shy of the Stone Canyon Reservoir.

The buyer of the great new combo estate on Carolwood and Sunset went to great lengths to remain anonymous. Drew Mandile insists he never met the actual buyer, never even knew a name. "You won't see his name anywhere, on anything. He never signed any documents. We sold to a bunch of attorneys." Those lawyers refuse to comment even though the buyer's name did eventually surface.

Despite the years it took to sell his house, Ghazi Aita was so pleased, he tipped his brokers an extra 1 percent in commission. He kept a New York apartment for another four years before selling it for $3.3 million in spring 2006. The buyers had no direct contact with him. By then, he was living on the Riviera in Monte Carlo, in a full-floor penthouse at a top-notch condo called Les Floralies, a block away from the city's famous casino. Early in 2011, Aita still lived in that Monte Carlo apartment, and was greeted as Your Excellency as he remains an ambassador of San Marino. But though he used to phone regularly, he no longer called his former employees in Los Angeles. "It's not like him," said attorney Barry Fink, who reported his former client was ailing and in and out of hospitals. Some worried that in Monte Carlo, that famously sunny place for shady people, he might die and nobody would know.

41

Beverly Hills

Grayhall (1100 Carolyn Way)

Steve Powers fell out with Ghazi Aita, too, around 1985. By that time, though, his focus was back on the man he'd claimed as a mentor, Bernie Cornfeld. A year earlier, Cornfeld had signed an agreement with Powers, in his self-proclaimed protégé's role as redeveloper of great Hollywood mansions. Powers promised to get a loan for Cornfeld in excess of $3 million, pay half the cost of servicing the debt, renovate Grayhall around him, add a tennis court, redecorate, and then sell it. When he did, Cornfeld would get the first $4.15 million after expenses, and Powers would pocket half of any profit beyond that. Powers also got the right to lease the estate to temporary residents when he could for a minimum of $50,000 a month, as well as to rent it out for movie shoots and parties. Powers brokered a mortgage on the house through a bank called Progressive Savings and Loan.

To Powers, gaining control of Grayhall was akin to capturing the Holy Grail, and he paints it that way in the unpublished memoir he's written about his conquest of his dream castle. Much of the book is sheer fantasy, from his claim that the house was also known as Grail Hall, because it incorporates bits of Cornfeld's Chateau de Pelly, which Powers believes was the "original Holy Grail castle," to another that the house is cursed and has "killed off or destroyed most of the womanizers who owned it, beginning with Douglas Fairbanks Jr." But Powers's book does give a clear picture of the power a house can have over people, whether they are men of wealth or the hangers-on who are attracted to them. "Girls would do anything to live in the mansion," Powers wrote of Grayhall.

The Gospel according to Powers has it that there were a handful of "major party mansions" in 1980s Los Angeles. They belonged to what he termed "five million dollar mansion boys": Hefner, Aita, the producer Bob Evans, Kenny Rogers, Leonard Ross, Wilt Chamberlain, Jerry Perenchio, Jerry Buss (the womanizer who was the latest owner of Pickfair and the Los Angeles Lakers), the investor and casino and studio boss Kirk Kerkorian, and Cornfeld. Powers styled himself as the only man in L.A. regularly invited to all of them.

"Every week, dinner at Grayhall on Thursday, Friday at Hef's, Saturday brunch at Evans's, Saturday night movie at Evans's mansion, Sunday night at Hef's," he wrote. "Girls on the Beverly Hills Diet only ate at these regular affairs and a few other assorted events and parties and never had to pay for food. . . . Kenny Rogers always had sophisticated and high-class socialites at his parties. Bob Evans collected the super-models and actresses. Wilt Chamberlain was good for the younger teeny-boppers, and my Arab partners had a bevy of Caucasian blondes and, of course, Hef had everything." Powers was a knight in his own fairy tale, dueling his way into their ranks. Only later would he conclude, "The bigger the mansion, the bigger the ego and the smaller [the] soul."

Powers paints Cornfeld as a Hefner wannabe, a girl-crazy guy drawn to California to engage in a duel of wealth and charisma with the Playboy founder or, at the least, ape his lifestyle. "These two virtual gods were the rulers of the world's most beautiful goddesses," Powers wrote. "In Europe," he adds, "Bernie was bigger than Hefner. To be a run-of-the-mill guy in L.A. wasn't what he wanted."

While Powers looked up to Hefner, he had a love-hate relationship with Cornfeld. He felt Cornfeld "had a charisma that was sort of Christ-like," he writes. "His charms, his power and his magic were everything I longed for. . . . He was the appropriate hero for that period of my life: rich and ruthless." But Powers also saw through him. "Really dysfunctional women liked Bernie; they swarmed around him, sucking on his power or perceived power. I found it all amusing. Here was a squat, balding, overweight man who . . . could safely walk down the streets as the 'Invisible Man' to the entire female population. But when he cast his spell of charisma, money and power they seemed to fall. Every relationship, man or woman, was to him a chess game to be won or lost. The idea of feelings never entered his head or heart."

Bernie was bound for a fall, and if Powers could trip him up, it was his chivalric duty.

By this time, Bernie's happy family had split up and his latest business ventures seemed dicey at best. Around the time his wife Lorraine moved out of Grayhall, Cornfeld had gone into the nutrition business, pulling a shell game himself by taking over a troubled public company and merging it with a private one that pushed health food and vitamins. He swore off red meat, too. "I want to continue to have sex into my 60s, 70s and 80s the way I still have sex in my 50s," he said, explaining his new enthusiasm. *Forbes,* which revealed his new plan, opened its story with a brief scene at a Grayhall party where an emaciated babbling pimp announced, "I supply the greatest women in the world." After a quick tour with stops to see Bernie's bedroom and his collection of ancestor portraits—Bernie called them "Uncle Hymie" and "Cousin Max"—the writer concluded that though "the luxury remains . . . the fire seems burned out."

But a fresh ember had come on the scene. Heidi Fleiss—not yet a procurer—was the nineteen-year-old daughter of a Los Feliz Hills pediatrician whose patient list included Bernie and Lorraine Cornfeld's daughter; Heidi worked as a waitress at Cravings, a restaurant on Sunset Boulevard, and had a yen for older men. So when she was invited to a party at Grayhall around Christmastime 1984, "the two of them fell head over heels for each other instantly," wrote Jennifer Young, the daughter of actor Gig Young and ex-wife Elaine, another Beverly Hills real estate broker, in *Once More with Feeling,* a 1996 book about local party girls and prostitutes. Young had talked Fleiss into going to the party. "I saw Bernie, this little man who looked like Santa Claus," Heidi later said. "I was like, 'Ah, my life, easy street.' Little did I know it was the roughest street I was ever going to travel. I was so young when I fell in love with him."

It wasn't long before Fleiss moved into Grayhall and became Cornfeld's top concubine. He gave her a do-nothing job at Max, the modeling agency he'd bought for his soon-to-be-ex-wife, and a new life unlike anything she had ever experienced—trips to Europe and the Caribbean on private planes, chauffeured cars driven by Bernie's pair of black-leather-clad female chauffeurs. A bisexual, Heidi would sometimes go to bed with Bernie and other women.

An L.A. prostitute named Linda described the scene chez Grayhall in the book *You'll Never Make Love in This Town Again*. "Bernie was known for giving shelter to at least a half-dozen nymphets at a time, innocent young ladies in need of a place to stay," Linda told the authors. "The girls would parade around his house in outfits ranging from 'fanny panties' to sexy, revealing lingerie, to spandex bodysuits. And at times, the firm-breasted, lithe beauties would unabashedly parade around in the nude. . . . He let the girls do pretty much what they wanted. All he expected was to enjoy the view, and if the girl was right, partake of her bounty once in a while." Favorites were given the keys to one of his collection of cars. Heidi's was a classic Mustang ragtop.

Even after she walked in on Bernie having sex with another member of his female flock and claimed to be furious, Fleiss insisted to Young that "she loved him so much, she didn't know what to do." She would later call him the only real boyfriend she'd ever had. But for Bernie love wasn't as simple as it was for a twenty-year-old woman. "We weren't really a couple in that sense—it's not my thing," he would say after her 1993 arrest for pandering, pimping, and narcotics possession, "but we were good friends. We saw a lot of each other."

"She made more out of the relationship than there was," Lorraine Dillon agrees. "It became a convenient way for Heidi to explain all the money she had." But Lorraine's daughter by Cornfeld, Jessica, would later say Heidi was "like an older sister to me." "Heidi was very much in love with him," Jessica adds. "His relationship with her was quite unique. He identified with her very strongly and looked out for her."

Certainly, Heidi and Jessica Cornfeld shared a taste for the life Bernie provided. Years after her father's death, his daughter would "write" a paean to him in Great Britain's *The Mail on Sunday*—published under her name, it was actually written by a journalist who interviewed her, she says, and embellished her tales of her afternoons and weekends at Grayhall. Her own home was empty after school—Dillon was at Max Models—and Grayhall was more fun. But she didn't like to sleep there, wondering what might have happened in her bed the day before.

Today, Jessica stands by most of the *Mail* piece. She considered the mansion "an adult playground" with its "vast ballroom with a 70 foot ceiling, a private cinema, a soda fountain and a Jacuzzi in the basement where there was an enormous painting of a virgin being offered to a well-endowed dragon," she wrote. "He opened his doors to everyone: rich, famous and infamous, from gangsters to mechanics, movie stars to academics. I remember Cher coming to stay with 27 matching pieces of Louis Vuitton luggage. The Jackson family were regular visitors and Tony Curtis often sat at our dining table. . . . Once when *Dynasty* was being filmed at the house, I asked Joan Collins, dressed in a figure-hugging scarlet satin gown, whether she was wearing a wig. Her body heaved in fury. . . . When Madonna was making her video for "Who's That Girl?" at our home, she made the mistake of criticizing the house. Sitting opposite me at lunch, she announced, 'I don't like this house. It gives me bad vibes.' . . . I was nine years old and, until that moment, Madonna had been my idol. I got up, threw down my napkin, stormed around the table and said, 'Well, I can't wait until you're done here either! And I wish you'd fuck off right now.' . . . But although my father had countless celebrity guests and legions of women, he always made sure I knew I was the most important person in his life. When I was born he gave me a diamond pendant to wear near my heart and we had our own special rituals: he would always give me the foam off his cappuccino and make me strawberry milkshakes, while I would always give him the last bite of my ice cream. . . . On nights when I couldn't sleep, he'd take me for a drive in his yellow Excalibur. . . . He spoilt me rotten." Today, Jessica cringes at the Madonna anecdote. She doesn't curse anymore. "I was terribly precocious," she says. "And the house did have bad vibes."

Jessica's childhood took her to three of L.A.'s great estates. A "major childhood hijink was trying to break into Greystone," she says. And she visited a school friend whose parents had bought Greenacres. She loved its Versailles-like child-sized village. "I spent many happy hours there."

Cornfeld gave Jessica a menagerie of pets: a cat, two dogs, a goose, and a monkey called Mazel Tov, and when she turned sixteen and asked him for a party, he gave her hefty quantities of Ben & Jerry's ice cream, candles, matches, cigarettes, rolling papers, hashish, marijuana, Bailey's Irish Cream, Malibu rum, and an injunction to "just have a good time." He also took her to Disneyland with Heidi Fleiss. Briefly, she thought they'd get married, but that was before Heidi's troubles.

For her part, Fleiss would rhapsodize about the twelve-course meals she and Bernie shared "with wines so old they're before George Washington's time," "waking up in Bernie's castle and looking out a window that some king once looked out of," visiting "homes with staircases of 24-karat gold. And soon it became normal," she told Hefner's *Playboy*. "I guess I got into it so young that I got caught up and expected things to be like that forever. . . . In a real sick way I was fascinated by something other than Bernie's helicopters and jets and chateaux. The fascination with the bizarre made the transition [to prostitution] easier."

Heidi and Bernie finally broke up in 1988; she'd found another older man, Ivan Nagy, a minor television director. By then, Bernie seems to have woken a latent entrepreneurial instinct in Heidi. "He was the smartest man I'd ever met," she told *People* magazine. "I mean, he was this genius in so many ways, and the things I learned from him and the lessons . . . He was always trying to make me a better person and make me understand things." She briefly worked in real estate but then moved into prostitution after Nagy set her up with L.A.'s reigning procurer, Elizabeth Adams, known as Madam Alex. At first Heidi worked as a play-for-pay girl but, remembering Bernie's lessons, after Adams taught her the tricks of the trade, she became her assistant and eventually her replacement.

Before Fleiss took over, Adams grossed about $50,000 a month. The first month that Fleiss managed the ring, she said she made $300,000. Then Heidi became the new queen of the high-end Hollywood whore business after Madam Alex went to jail in 1991 (alleging that Heidi had stolen her client list). She was so successful, she moved from a West Hollywood apartment to a $1.6 million Beverly Hills home. It wasn't Grayhall, but her neighbors included Bruce Springsteen and Jay Leno.

Then Heidi got arrested, too, sending clients like Ghazi Aita into mourning, as well as panic that they would be outed as clients. Local police begin investigating her in February 1993. In June, Heidi sent four call girls and a bag of cocaine to meet three clients who turned out to be undercover agents. The vice sting was a coordinated effort of the Los Angeles and Beverly Hills police and the state's alcoholic beverage control agency and attorney general's offices. The arresting officer had won Heidi's confidence by assuring her he and his pals, all posing as Hawaiian businessmen, just wanted straight sex. "I don't want to see a llama coming through the house," he assured her.

Fleiss pleaded not guilty, refused to name her clients (though many would later be identified), and sixteen months later was found guilty of three pandering charges and sentenced to three years in jail and a small fine. Seven months later, she was also found guilty in federal court of eight counts of conspiracy, money laundering, and tax evasion and sentenced to an additional thirty-seven months. She served three years and was released in 1999. When last heard from, she was running a Laundromat called Dirty Laundry in Pahrump, Nevada.

By the time Heidi went to jail, Cornfeld was long gone from Los Angeles, living in London in much diminished circumstances. His final fall from financial grace, and the story of his departure from Grayhall, began when he was still involved with both Fleiss and Steve Powers. Unable to concoct a scheme that would let him relive the glory days of IOS, he was slowly but steadily going broke. But he was also obsessed with keeping up appearances, and that meant keeping *his* Holy Grail, Grayhall, though it became a dead weight dragging him down even faster.

In February 1986, Cornfeld's Grayhall Inc., which owned the estate, borrowed $206,000 from a friend, Howard Mann, a New York City precious metals dealer, secured by the house, to help Cornfeld pay his mortgage debt and forestall a foreclosure from the bank. For the next sixteen months, Bernie and his lawyers maneuvered frantically to keep him in the house. That fall, Grayhall Inc. filed for voluntary bankruptcy and made a deal to repay the mortgage bank.

Cornfeld, Mann, and Powers agreed to pay down the debt together and in exchange, Cornfeld signed a document he would later claim was coerced, promising Powers an additional $100,000 on the sale of the house—it was finally on the market for $9 million—in exchange for his $30,000 contribution to the debt service. But Cornfeld "never lived up to the new agreement with the bank," Mann says. "He never came up with a nickel." Mann was under the impression he hardly had a nickel to spare at that point. "He was really broke," Mann says, "but he always had connections and all of a sudden $15,000 would come in."

In March 1987, the bank began a foreclosure action, and to stop it, Mann paid another $30,000 on the loan. In return, Cornfeld gave Mann the deed for the house and filed a motion to have the bankruptcy case dismissed. A welter of deal making and breaking followed but Cornfeld was unable to stop the bankruptcy. The bank scheduled a foreclosure sale for April 30. Two weeks before the sale, Cornfeld's crony Mann tried to put Grayhall Inc. into involuntary bankruptcy, apparently an attempt to stop the bank from fore-closing. When Cornfeld failed to borrow more money and Powers failed to service the loan, the bank won a court order to proceed with the sale.

One day before it was scheduled, all concerned agreed that if Powers took over payments on the loan and attempted to refinance it, he would get 75 percent of the proceeds of a sale. In return, Cornfeld promised to move out of the mansion and into the pool house by June 15. This time, Powers brought the loan payments current, halting the sale, and moved to dismiss the involuntary bankruptcy case. He believed he'd won Grayhall. Cornfeld felt he'd been coerced, but believed he had a chance to regain the house because the latest deal with Powers had to be approved by the bankruptcy judge. Cornfeld and Powers were now openly at odds.

On May 1, 1987, Powers overstepped, giving himself power of attorney for Grayhall Inc. Then he told the L.A. *Times* he'd bought Grayhall and planned to move in and begin hosting dual-mansion parties with his friend Lakers owner Jerry Buss, across the street in Pickfair, with guests shuttling between their houses through the long-closed Fairbanks-era tunnels. His lawyer told the *Times* Powers had saved the day by appearing with a cashier's check "on the doorstep of the foreclosure hearing" to pay the overdue debt.

Though Powers had saved his house, Cornfeld, still in residence, ob-jected, arguing in bankruptcy court that Powers had no standing to interfere in the bankruptcy action, had improperly tried to reorganize Grayhall Inc., had fraudulently issued new stock in the company, diluting Bernie's owner-ship to 25 percent, and had apparently stolen some Grayhall Inc. stationery. Powers repeated his demand that Cornfeld leave the premises (he'd failed to move into the pool house as agreed) and started a new action to evict him and his harem.

Apparently, in their obsessive attempts to bring each other down, neither paid attention to the bank, which renewed its threat to foreclose. Cornfeld then filed a new lawsuit, asking the courts to cancel all his agreements with Powers, restore his ownership of Grayhall, restore him and his board and officers to their rightful positions, and award him legal fees. Now, Bernie claimed Powers had purposely put him in financial distress in an attempt to "brazenly and improperly usurp" Grayhall.

"I wanted the house," Powers admits now. He'd lost a Playboy Playmate girlfriend to Cornfeld, and seethed over it. "Losing my woman to . . . Cornfeld violated my ego and pride so I mobilized all my money, power, and contacts to stage the greatest fight of my life," he writes in his unpublished memoir. "And so the great war of mentor and heir to the kingdom began."

But Powers suffered a setback that fall, when Bernie won his case and just under $10,000 in legal fees. "Crazy things happened" then, Powers says now. "Bernie was in the house, he asked to stay, he wouldn't move out. He didn't pay the mortgage. My credit was fucked up. I tried to get a judge to kick him out. I had to get legal possession. I had Bernie sign a contract to rent the property to do a movie."

Powers actually rented out Grayhall for a nude photo shoot. On October 23, 1987, when Bernie was away in France, Powers used that shoot as a Trojan horse for a takeover raid on the house. That morning, the photographer, some assistants, and security guards arrived, and after ordering the caretaker, a UCLA senior, to keep all the men in the house away, set to work photographing a naked model. Two hours later, Powers, his lawyer, and about twenty-five men and vehicles, including armed guards and electricians, stormed the estate.

According to Bernie's subsequent application for a restraining order against Powers and more than a hundred others, the invaders had locked the always-open entry gate with a chain, and eight to ten uniformed security guards, plus the president of the security company and "a number of other sizeable men in civilian clothes," were posted around the property.

Cornfeld's lawyer surveyed the scene and called the Beverly Hills police. Lorraine Dillon, who'd been alerted to what was going on, joined the circus at the gate, driving up in a car with a mobile phone, and called the police, too. Powers, meantime, told whoever would listen that what he'd done was legal, waving his contract to shoot the nude photos and cursing out Bernie's lawyers.

Finally, more than two hours after Powers's arrival, the police showed up. Inside, there was chaos and confusion as locksmiths frantically changed Grayhall's locks, and moving men with trucks removed the personal possessions of the occupants, some of whom were in obvious distress, complaining through the gate that men had pointed guns at them, first telling them not to move, then ordering them to leave the premises, leaving their things behind. Hubert Cornfeld, Bernie's nephew, who was staying at Grayhall while convalescing from larynx-removal surgery for cancer, chimed in that the invaders had kicked down his bedroom door. When the caretaker joined the protests, a security guard was ordered to handcuff him and escort him off the property.

By then, some of the things removed from the house—including files, books, and papers from Cornfeld's office—were being loaded onto a truck. A police watch commander ordered Powers to open the gate and leave, but he refused. Finally, after ninety more minutes of argument, the gates were opened and the police convinced the intruders to leave.

Powers wasn't done yet. Late that afternoon, he called Cornfeld's lawyer, alternately pleading and threatening, claiming he was in dire financial straits, had no choice, and would be back to take the house again. The lawyer told him that in the interim, Bernie had posted armed guards of his own on the premises.

Two days later, Bernie and his houseguests struck back, suing for a judgment that the house was his and $10 million in damages and asking for a temporary restraining order against Powers et al. in the meantime to stop any further attempts to take the house. He won that round.

Powers's lawyer, Brian Oxman, insists their actions that day at Grayhall were all justified and aboveboard; most of the dramatics described in Bernie's complaint and the accompanying depositions are "a total fiction," he says. "I saw no armed guards. No weapons. There was no disturbance of the peace." No one kicked in doors, touched anyone's possessions, or ordered anyone in the house around.

Cornfeld's attorney stands by his account. "It was not fiction," David Rudich insists, brusque and affronted. "What Steve Powers and Brian Oxman did was not correct, not proper. Mr. Cornfeld was returned to occupancy of the premises and that's all I want to say."

But it was a Pyrrhic victory. Bernie was out of money, out of time, and out of luck, and his mother's pin-money account wasn't going to save him. "He was so broke the only thing he had that was unencumbered was his mother's 1962 Chevy convertible," says William Brownstein, another lawyer who represented him. "He said he'd give it to me. I got absolutely nothing." Yet Bernie hadn't lost his chutzpah. "He talked about all the different women in his place. He said, 'Come over, check 'em out.' That's how I was to get paid. I guess that's how it was done in the old days, but that wasn't me. Looking back, I wish I'd gone. Who knows where that would have led. He wasn't a crook. The problem was the whole Hollywood deal. You lose sight of reality when you're in with those people."

• • •

In November 1987, the *Los Angeles Times* reported that Grayhall was back on the market, listed by Cornfeld for $6.85 million. But its ownership remained unclear: Powers told the paper Bernie was "an owner, but I'm trying to buy him out. He is living in the house and I'm trying to get him out." It's also unclear how Powers finally got possession of Grayhall, but he claims he did and lived there for a year, though Bernie was also there the whole time.

Powers says that shortly after moving in, he staged "one of the most sumptuous and extravagant Hollywood parties ever held," attracting the Saudi middleman (and sometime partner of Ghazi Aita) Adnan Khashoggi, a Saudi prince, and Albert of Monaco, Kirk Kerkorian, Bob Evans, Tony Curtis, James Caan, Warren Beatty, Elizabeth Taylor, Michelle Pfeiffer, Bill Cosby, Magic Johnson, Wilt Chamberlain, Jim Brown, O. J. Simpson, Kenny Rogers, Berry Gordon, Hugh Hefner, George Hamilton, and even his housemate Bernie Cornfeld. He felt it was his entrée into the Beverly Hills elite.

But Powers admits it didn't turn out the way he had hoped. At some point in the evening, Zsa Zsa Gabor, the former Mrs. Conrad Hilton, shot him a condescending glare that said, he wrote, "You are a fake, a pretender." And well aware that he *was* pretending, he took the message to heart. By the end of that year at Grayhall, Powers was a changed man, determined not to succumb to the curse he believed hung over the house. "I thought of it as a thing that brought me bad luck," he says, "so I thought, I'll be glad to get rid of this problem. The decadence of it all! I was being drawn in more and more and knew I had to break the cycle. I hoped I could become more balanced and more of a real person."

According to Powers's memoir, the answer to his prayers—a buyer for Grayhall—also attended his big party. Among the guests, he writes, was Philippe Boutboul, whom Powers alternately describes as "a minion" and "the money man for the King of Burkina Faso," the former French colony of Upper Volta in central Africa, and the French ambassador to that nation. "He represented the king," Powers insists in an interview. "The money came from the king." Unfortunately, Burkina Faso has no king; Boutboul was actually special advisor to its president.

The child of a *pied noir,* a French-Jewish native of Tunisia and a French mother, Boutboul came from a comfortable family and grew up in Paris, living above a movie theater owned by his grandfather. Philippe became a DJ at fifteen, built his own sound system, and played at balls in French castles.

Around the same time, he made his first trip to Beverly Hills with his father and "made love for the first time there," he says. "So I've always been attracted to California."

Back in France, Boutboul opened an electronics shop and quickly expanded until he owned sixty stores. He manufactured speakers in California. "I went there all the time," he says. At least, he did until he was twenty-four, when he lost his stores and fortune. "I realized quickly and young that when you have money, you're the king, and when you don't, you're nothing," he continues. "I decided to make a fortune again." He headed to Africa, to the Congo, where he started importing and selling plastic bags, and then concrete "and went on to bigger businesses," he says. "I was fortunate to get to know a few heads of state and they asked me to help them." When he returned to Beverly Hills, it was as an advisor to President Blaise Compaoré of Burkina Faso, holding a diplomatic passport. His father had just died and he was at loose ends, looking for something to do.

Boutboul recalls that he first met Steve Powers at a party Boutboul hosted in a house he'd just renovated. "I would do parties with Michael Jackson, Stallone, Lionel Richie, a lot of actors," says Boutboul. Powers invited him to see Grayhall and he arrived during a *Playboy* photo shoot. "A girl naked on the snooker table," Boutboul says. "I wanted to look at the property. Of course I looked at the girl as well." And then he saw the other girls. "Maybe fifteen or seventeen women. Every bedroom, one or two stunning beautiful girls. Bernie was in the middle. It was crazy."

Once they had a live prospect, Cornfeld and Powers stopped fighting and started negotiating. After the sale to Boutboul, Powers, Cornfeld, and their bankers made an out-of-court settlement of their differences. Powers describes a subsequent trip to Europe on the alleged African king's plane. The loan of the plane for two weeks "was part of the price," Powers says. "So me and Bernie and a bunch of crazy guys went to the South of France." In his memoir, he writes that the trip included stops in Geneva (for a visit to the Chateau de Pelly), St. Tropez, Monte Carlo, and Ibiza.

In truth, says Boutboul, he'd chartered a plane (albeit one emblazoned with the words *Burkina Faso* and sometimes used by the president) because Bernie had left his female houseguests behind at Grayhall along with his furniture, and Boutboul needed to get them out so he could begin renovating. "It was a beautiful property in miserable shape. So I went with Bernie to his castle and spent one or two days there. It was a beautiful, stunning castle but not very comfortable. It wasn't heated. It was too cold for me. And that was the end of it. The journey stopped."

Cornfeld's American journey stopped then, too. His daughter Jessica says her father had "a run-in with the IRS" and spent the next eighteen months avoiding the United States before "he sorted it out." Despite all that had happened, Cornfeld and Powers appear to have parted as something resembling friends. "Powers got cash out of Boutboul," says Lorraine Dillon. "Bernie got out with quite a good sum." Which helped him pay for his remaining properties in Europe and his daughter's British boarding school tuition and maintain the illusion of his lifestyle.

That was hardly the end of Bernie Cornfeld's troubles—or his attempts to reinvent himself. Early in 1989, he was subpoenaed in a case that saw IOS liquidators claiming damages from Credit Suisse for facilitating Vesco's grab of the company's cash. He used the opportunity to tout a new mutual fund he'd been trying to start, claiming he had access to $3 billion, but needed $100 million to get it going. "Yes, I am still a multi-millionaire," he told the *Times* of London, claiming he was building condos in Florida and also owned a fifth of a British company developing superchargers for cars. A few months after that, he popped up again at his French chateau, where he said he was planning a village and a golf course while advising unnamed mutual funds. Howard Mann also recalls "a thing in Cyprus," he says. "He sold shares in a bank and misspelled its name on the stock certificates." Asked if Cornfeld's later activities were all scams, Mann chuckles. "He tried. He didn't get away with any."

Bernie then dropped from the media radar until the end of 1992, when he was back in the headlines, claiming to be buying the troubled MGM/UA movie studio. But Credit Lyonnais, the owner, wanted nothing to do with him. Two years after that, he was back with what appeared to be another shell game. In concert with a small American brokerage firm, he was trying to privately sell shares in a Florida drug company. Like the MGM deal, that one soon disappeared. He was working again, says his ex-wife, making $100,000 per deal, but in the end "people pocketed the money."

In September 1994, Bernie collapsed in a restaurant in Eilat, Israel, and was hospitalized in Tel Aviv, paralyzed and in a coma from a stroke. Cornfeld never spoke again. Lorraine and Jessica "traveled back and forth to look after him," his ex-wife says. Sixty of his friends raised more than $100,000 to pay the expenses of his three-month hospital stay. Finally, he was stable enough to be flown home to London, but spent seven more months in critical condition before taking a steep, rapid turn for the worse. Bernie Cornfeld died of complications from his stroke on February 27, 1995. Prison authorities refused to let Heidi Fleiss attend his small funeral. She was devastated, says Jessica Cornfeld.

By the time Bernie Cornfeld died, few in L.A. remembered him or the era he personified. It had been a time when people like Tony Curtis and Ghazi Aita bought houses in the Platinum Triangle in order to inhabit fantasies or, like Curtis's friend Cornfeld and Bill Osco, to bolster shaky realities. It was a time of textbook decadence everywhere in America, but even more so in Beverly Hills, Holmby Hills, and Bel Air, where the residents had the money, the will, and sometimes both to explore the heights of self-indulgence and the depths of hedonism. But they eventually hit bottom and found their fantasies undone by financial distress, drugs, drink, divorce, despair, or physical and spiritual exhaustion. Their casual ties to real life and to others left them casualties. Even their real estate finally proved unreal and unsustainable—and inevitably slipped into the hands of others.

As that assumption-defying political product of the Triangle, the ultra-conservative actor turned Goldwater supporter Ronald Wilson Reagan, left California to take office in Washington in 1980, a great change swept across America—and the Triangle, too. It was morning again, as the Reaganites put it, and that was as true on and around Sunset Boulevard as it was in the rest of the country. Houses have no memories, no nostalgia for who's been and gone. So when their owners hit bottom, they bounce back, passing into new hands, new lives. In the last three decades, many of La-La Land's greatest estates were returned to the sort of people for whom they'd been conceived.

Like their immediate predecessors, those new owners were both good and bad—sometimes simultaneously. But thanks to the prosperity produced in the Age of Reagan (or as some had it, the new age of greed he inspired), their homes no longer seemed to be impractical, costly burdens like the sacred white elephants Asian rulers gave to those who displeased them in order to ruin them. Returned into the hands of a new sort of monarch—ruthless kings of business—these white elephants became domesticated pets, playthings, mere markers of material success. But they were still somehow unreal, for their owners were once again the possessors of impossible fortunes, rich beyond the wildest dreams.

PART SIX

Trophy Houses

1980–2011

{ THE LYNDA AND STEWART RESNICK RESIDENCE, BEVERLY HILLS }

Beverly Hills

Greenacres (1740 Green Acres Place)

In 1980, America was mired in problems both foreign and economic: Iran, an energy crisis set off by rising oil prices, Jimmy Carter flailing in his race for the presidency against Ronald Reagan, and unemployment, down from 1975 highs, set to spike again. Yet in the Platinum Triangle, the prices of mansions, depressed for years, had begun a steep upward spiral that would slow now and then but not stop for thirty years. Neither earthquakes nor mudslides nor recession could stay the desire for status-seeking through living space, fought over with limitless funds.

By 1981, realtor Jeff Hyland would report that there were forty-nine mansions on the market for $3 million or more between Doheny Drive and the Pacific. That was, of course, the moment when Dino De Laurentiis sold the house he'd bought five years before for $2 million and made a $12.5 million profit. The day after buyer Kenny Rogers signed that contract, Hyland asked him if he'd walk away for a $5 million profit—a record-setting $19.5 million. Rogers declined.

"When you're that wealthy, money doesn't matter anymore," Hyland told the *Los Angeles Times*. "And when you have the greatest house in town, there's nowhere else to go." Overnight, the white elephants of the Platinum Triangle became sparkling trophies, advertisements for those who dwelled atop the mountain of American wealth.

It's not that you had to be rich as a Doheny—or even a Kenny Rogers—

to buy a white elephant. But no longer were they bargains. No longer could a Steve Powers hope to land one with lawsuits and bluster. Never again would a porn merchant buy one of the great estates. Performers were priced out of the great estate market, too. Like George Hamilton, Tony Curtis, Cher, Kenny Rogers, and even Bernie Cornfeld, people would still buy dreaming of what their mansions would do for them, psychologically and socially. But now, at the high end, they would also be thinking about what they could do for their mansions. In the process, like Hilda Boldt Weber, they'd be demonstrating what they were made of.

Such was the case with Dona Powell and Bernard C. Solomon. Solomon was a record guy, an accountant turned budget-end classical music mogul. And Dona, the second of his four wives, was a gal with some taste and a yen to be known for it. But they were nobodies in L.A. Until, that is, they bought Harold Lloyd's Greenacres.

In 1979, the Afshani family and Naim Perry, the Iranians who'd apparently bought Greenacres at auction, finally got permission to subdivide it. They began to look for financing, but they had no desire to sell Lloyd's house. They spurned all offers on the mansion itself; they were making money renting it as a film set and felt no need to sell. But Bernie Solomon wouldn't take no for an answer. He offered $3 million. No. "He kept coming back, back, back. We did not want to sell at that price," says Shahram Afshani, a son of Nasrollah, who'd led the group that bought the house. "It was worth significantly more. Mr. Solomon somehow notified Naim Perry that bad things would happen to him and his kids if he did not go through with the sale. He finally found a way."

Naim Perry was a serious property holder in Los Angeles, with two office buildings on Wilshire Boulevard. But bad things had already happened to him that year; he was revealed as a key agent in the sale of lasers to the shah of Iran. Those lasers had just fallen into the hands of Iran's new Islamic revolutionary government, enhancing the unstable nation's nuclear capability. So he might have been wary of any threat against him or his family. But regardless of any fear he may have felt, when subdevelopment finally started in 1981, Naim Perry built a home right next door to Solomon and lived there many years. "I had to pass the house every day," Sue Lloyd says of the Afshani-Solomon interlude at Greenacres. She missed the house so much, it hurt. "I couldn't go in. It broke my heart."

This was one of the domestic dramas the movie star homes tour guides don't tell you.

Bernard Solomon was born in New York in 1925 and grew up working in his Russian-Polish parents' grocery store in New Rochelle. His father was a handsome philanderer, his mother uneducated and cold to Bernie, preferring her elder son, according to Bernie's first wife, Teri. "They taught him to work at seven," says Dona Powell, his second. His job? Counting the money.

Solomon hated his home life so much that despite winning a scholarship to New York University at fifteen, he went to the University of Cincinnati to get away. But at seventeen, he was drafted into World War II, where he served as a medic in Europe until he got hit by a truck and sent home. He ventured to Los Angeles for his older's sister's wedding and stayed, earning an accounting degree at UCLA at nineteen and at twenty, passing the state exam to become the youngest CPA in California history. In 1949, Solomon joined a big accounting firm.

Solomon met first wife Teri when she was a precocious seventeen-year-old UCLA co-ed. "I'm the only wife [of four] who married him without money," she says. "And the only one who didn't consummate before marriage." They started life together in a tiny apartment far south of Beverly Hills.

In 1952, Solomon was assigned to Gene Autry, radio's famous Singing Cowboy, who'd just started a television show, to handle an IRS audit of the singer's 1947 returns. "I was only 25 or 26," he told Autry's biographer, "and they made me grow a moustache so I looked older." Solomon's father had just died and Autry became a stand-in, taking a liking to the young accountant and hiring him away from the firm to do internal accounting and audit the books for his movies. Teri and Bernie moved closer to Beverly Hills.

In the late 1950s, Autry formed Challenge Records. When their team had a worldwide hit in 1958 with "Tequila," an R&B instrumental by the Champs (the only lyric was the word *tequila*, spoken after each bridge) that sold six million records, money came pouring in. Solomon negotiated Autry's purchase of Four Star, music publisher for acts like Johnny Ray, Buck Owens, Merle Travis, and Patsy Cline, and Autry made him a partner; it was his first ownership stake, and he liked the taste of it. A 4 percent share of Challenge followed. Soon, Solomon increased his stake in both firms to 25 percent.

Solomon went to Europe to sell foreign rights and while there, the couple started collecting art—even though Bernie was color-blind. They bought a Renoir for a mere $30,000. "I knew art," Teri says. "Bernie knew money." They looked for investment art, specializing in Impressionism.

Working in the record business, Solomon couldn't help but notice the success of record clubs, mail-order subsidiaries of major labels like Columbia and RCA, that lured in customers, particularly in rural areas underserved by retail stores, with free vinyl records in exchange for a commitment to buy more. "Why can't there be a record club of independent labels?" Solomon wondered.

He'd been doing accounting work on the side for Alfred Bloomingdale at Diners Club and "met with Al and his wife Betsy in Hawaii," he told Autry's biographer, winning a nod to start a Diners record club. Its first record of the month (advertised in the Diners Club magazine, of course) was "Mack the Knife" by Bobby Darin. Teri, who'd worked in the registrar's office at UCLA, quit to run the office.

Three years later, larger clubs started poaching Bernie's labels. "I had no capital," Solomon said. "I had the name, that's all. So I sued them and we settled." With the proceeds, he bought one of the labels he'd distributed, Everest Records. By then, he'd sold his stakes in Challenge and Four Star and moved to a house in lush Mandeville Canyon, once part of Alphonzo Bell's holdings.

Everest Records started as the expensive hobby of Harry Belock, whose Belock Instrument Corporation made computerized weapons systems for the U.S. military. Belock loved classical music and sound recording technology, and aspired to make the best stereo records on the market. Unfortunately, that cost him about $1 million, and though his recordings were highly prized by music lovers, that meant financial trouble. So in a series of deals beginning in 1961, Solomon took over Everest, sold off its equipment, and began re-releasing its master recordings on low-quality budget-priced vinyl discs. He paid off the purchase within two years.

Solomon was on a roll. "He bought small, idealistic record companies as they went broke," says Teri, and soon owned several classical music labels as well as Tradition Records, which recorded Pete Seeger, Odetta, and Lightnin' Hopkins.

He began taking regular trips to Europe, buying or leasing tapes of concerts—some of which he didn't have clear rights to release on record.

"Bernie," says a later partner, Mark Chayet, "was generous to a fault, but he took liberties." In 1963, Pablo Casals, the cellist, sued Everest. Four years later, a Russian concert organization accused Solomon of releasing unauthorized concert recordings. "They were a pirate company," says Herman Krawitz, then the assistant general manager of New York's Metropolitan Opera. "They were in the business of evading copyright and avoiding payment."

Late in 1968, Solomon sold Everest to Pickwick, a publicly traded group of budget record labels, for an undisclosed amount of stock. Those shares soared in value around the time that Teri Solomon, pregnant with Bernie's second daughter, decided her husband was cheating on her. "He was the sweetest nice man you'd ever want to know, but he had bad taste in women," says Stan Schneider, an employee and friend who'd later take over Solomon's accounting practice.

Dona Powell was seventeen years younger than Bernie. She grew up on Beverly Drive in Beverly Hills, the granddaughter and daughter of home builders, or so she said one day in 2010, sitting in the lobby of the Beverly Hilton, where she was living while renovating her small condo in Century City. The Hilton is "like Greenacres," she explains, "but I don't have to pay the twenty-seven servants." Powell wore a Dolce & Gabbana blazer accessorized with an Hermès scarf and a Valentino bag and glasses, and flicked her long dark hair to reveal her low-cut blouse and impressive bosom. Her earliest recollections, she says, are of eating breakfast at the Polo Lounge and running around a building lot in the hills behind the Beverly Hills Hotel while her father staked out their house.

A relative who no longer speaks to Powell says that while all that's true, it isn't the whole truth. The home on Beverly was one of several spec houses built and sold by Dona's father, moonlighting from his day job as an inspector for the Los Angeles Department of Building and Safety. The Powells actually "lived in the valley," the relative says.

Dona (pronounced Donna) says she was a champion debater at North Hollywood High School. "In every category, I was first, and to tell you the truth I barely prepared. I decided to be an actress. I screen-tested, but when I realized the commitment—I wouldn't be walking in and picking up a gold medal—I decided I wasn't interested. I didn't want to spend my life going from character to character." She attended Valley College in Sherman Oaks, and married while there.

"I was a beautiful teenager," she says, showing her décolleté again. "Smart. I needed nothing but a smile. A beautiful little trophy." She and her first husband, Christian Henry "Hank" Lass, a descendant of a Spanish land-grant family, married in Hawaii about 1965 and returned to socialize with the likes of Steve McQueen, Elvis Presley, Paul Newman, and Jay Sebring and Sharon Tate, who would be two of Charles Manson's killing spree victims just a few years later.

Lass "was hot, funny, gorgeous, charming, an international playboy with hundreds of acres in trust," says Dona. "I was a little girl married to a very rich man." They broke up six months after having a daughter. "They were very similar personality types," says the estranged relative. "Pretty egocentric. I don't think it worked out well."

Dona says she was fascinated by Lass's land, in particular a lot he owned in Bel Air. "I wanted the house, not the life," she says. "I wanted my world." But she was stuck in his and says it wore thin. "That life was decadent," she says vaguely. "He said he wanted to settle down, but you can wish and hope and not be able to do it. I never took drugs. I like reality as it is."

So she divorced Lass and entered law school. She would later claim in a press release that she did that at UCLA, but it has no record of her attendance and she now says she was misquoted (by her own publicist) and actually attended the University of West Los Angeles Law School, founded in 1966. It will neither confirm nor deny her attendance there.

Dona didn't last long in law school, regardless; she gravitated to a different power nexus. To get to her divorce lawyer's office, Dona had to pass the office of Far Out Productions, a team of concert promoters and music producers. After she'd waltzed by several times, eliciting howls of approval, Dona says, she accepted an invitation to lunch from one of the partners, Jerry Goldstein ("Kids are always hungry"), and then joined him one night at a Jerry Lee Lewis show at the Whisky à Go Go, where he introduced her to Bernie Solomon, who was thinking of investing in Far Out and was helping to underwrite the filming and recording of the Jimi Hendrix Experience's last show together, a February 1969 concert at London's Royal Albert Hall.

Bernie was separated, living in an apartment on Wilshire Boulevard, and dating his secretary, Dona says. "I was dating people like [A&P supermarket heir] Huntington Hartford. I wasn't dating ordinary people. I like men who are highly intelligent and in play. I won't give you the list."

"She played them against each other," says Teri Solomon. "Bernie was very competitive."

That winter, when Goldstein had a Christmas party and Huntington Hartford took Dona but then disappeared, "I had no one to talk to but Bernie," she says. "Bernie had a brain." The next spring, they went to dinner and he told her he was going to marry her. "He was bold," she says, remembering him returning the next morning with flowers. "I sent him away." He came back that afternoon.

Dona says that at the time, she was engaged to Bernard Gelson, founder of the Gelson's supermarket chain (and briefly, a co-owner of Beverly Park), but even though Solomon "had the personality of a gravedigger" and was "the poorest man I knew, our brains clicked. I fell in love. I went to his house in Palm Springs." He had a van Gogh, a Cassatt, a Monet of Waterloo Bridge. They had hot sex and moved in together. "I always enjoyed older people," she says. "You can learn from the dinosaurs."

But Bernie wasn't sure what he wanted and dithered over what to do, causing wife Teri several months of personal torment. "He wanted to come back," she says. "I'd had enough."

Ultimately, Teri and Bernie and Dona and Hank Lass all divorced the same day; Bernie paid for Dona's divorce and they got a license to wed. "It was a takeover deal," Dona says, adding that she gave up alimony and child support from Lass in exchange for their daughter. The Solomons' art collection and his Pickwick shares were sold, the proceeds split up. Their van Gogh, *Pietà (after Delacroix),* was sold to the Vatican Collection. "He'd bought those paintings at unbelievable prices," says Stan Schneider. "He would have been a multimillionaire if he'd stayed with Teri." Instead, in June 1971, Bernie married Dona at the Bel-Air Hotel. Bernie's oldest daughter, Cori, recalls that she wanted to dance with her father, but the bride forbade it. "I walked out crying," Cori says.

To Cori, Dona was Cinderella's stepmother. "She forbade him to see his kids, so he picked us up at school," she says. Schneider's relationship with Bernie changed, too. "I didn't see him much during that marriage," he says. "He started living large. People hadn't known him. With Dona, he was out there; people knew him." But not his old friends. Dona cut her new husband off from his past. "They had new friends," he says. "His family wasn't around much, either."

Dona describes their love as a grand passion that ignited her new husband. "He was very sexual, possessive, obsessed, passionate," she says. "Like you cannot believe." She doesn't mention Bernie's two children, but says he adopted her child and they had three more in the three years that followed. And he let Dona, who'd collected glass and jewelry as a single woman, start buying serious art to replace what he'd sold. But her kind of art. Old Masters.

Bernie wasn't easy. He had to be the center of attention. Yet he didn't like to stand out. "He had a profile lower than the bellybutton on a worm," says Dona, but "he liked making money. I could spend it on what I wanted. He trusted me. He understood value."

They needed a house. The one Dona loved the most, Neil McCarthy's 9481 Sunset, had just been sold. But Sonny and Cher were breaking up and Sonny was willing to rent out 364 St. Cloud Road. Dona negotiated that deal and their next to buy a house on Bel Air Road near Jerry Perenchio and the Reagans. Then she restored it. "I'm an art collector," she says. "I see architecture as an art form." She also appreciated the art of the deal. "I worked with the lawyers. I called the banks." They bought it for $370,000 and sold it five years later for $2.6 million, she says.

The Solomons also practiced the art of spending. When their middle son was born in 1973, Bernie bought Dona a $200,000 Fabergé cuckoo egg to celebrate; made for Czar Nicholas II, it came complete with a cuckoo that sang and moved its wings and beak. And in 1975, Bernie bought Everest Records back from Pickwick for $1.3 million, much of it financed with loans.

His next takeover was Greenacres. Dona says the purchase was all her doing, beginning the moment she heard it was near foreclosure and rushed to the estate, bluffing her way inside. "As the front door opened," she says, "it became an obsession, my raison d'être. It couldn't be torn down." But it had also become clear it wasn't going to survive as the museum Lloyd had wanted and was going to be sold. Dona vowed to save the house.

At the auction, Powell says they won the house with an all-cash bid, but bidding then began again with borrowing allowed and, Powell claims, a cousin of hers who was advising Afshani whispered that the Iranians wanted the land surrounding Greenacres, not the house itself, and would sell it and the small plot of land it sat on to her and Bernie afterwards, so they let the Iranians win. "We negotiate for the house, agree on a price, they renege and raise the price," she says. "When Arabs say yes, they mean maybe."

Finally, the mysterious man in the white suit at the auction, Abdullah

Moghavem, a silent partner of the Afshanis and Naim Perry, agreed to sell the house to the Solomons. (Like his partners, Moghavem is Persian, not Arab.) But the sellers didn't see eye to eye. Shahram Afshani denies Moghavem was in on the deal while Moghavem's son Afshin insists he was actually behind it, adding only, "Other people tried to create fame for themselves off of that purchase." Afshin Moghavem adds that the Afshani family's claim that threats were made against Naim Perry is "a gross misrepresentation."

Clearly, the transaction was fraught for all concerned. "We took possession when the subdevelopment was approved," says Powell. "I went to the house that day and walked through. The land was all bulldozed. I think they did it for spite."

Two years later, their renovations complete, the Solomons launched a press blitz, inviting reporters to Greenacres to show what they'd done with the place "at considerable, though undisclosed, cost," wrote Ruth Ryon, the real estate reporter for the *Los Angeles Times*. Bernie had replaced Harold Lloyd's rogues' gallery of friends with the jackets of records he'd released. The former taproom with doors based on King Tut's coffin was transformed into a disco.

But they also honored the estate's past, recreating Lloyd's Christmas tree for their own holiday party, during which a guest returned a plaque reading "Control Switchboard: Harold Lloyd Estate," which they restored to a room that also held plaques naming the architect, engineer, and electrical contractor. "We put in all new electric lines," Bernie said, "and we had to get new gas lines up to the eleven fireplaces." The original stove was repaired and the checkerboard rubber tile floor of the kitchen reproduced.

Dona claimed she'd sanded, cleaned, and taken over Lloyd's library, filling it with research books for her expanding art, jewelry, Hollywood fashion, and antique collecting. Woodwork throughout the house was rewaxed and resurfaced to duplicate Lloyd's original color scheme, the original contractor was hired to reproduce pewter and gold-plated door handles and hardware, missing pipes were replaced in the organ in the living room, and the room's flaking gold-leaf coffered ceiling was removed and recreated with new materials that wouldn't be shaken loose by the organ's vibrations. The garden room, painted with leaves, birds, flowers, and angels, was touched up, and the remaining garden was restored by the original landscape architect.

Harold Lloyd's furniture, sold at auction, was replaced with what Dona called "the Solomon Collection" of antiques, tapestries, paintings, art glass, textiles and costumes, and English silver. It even had its own curator. The indoor staff of ten included a live-in policeman and a bodyguard (augmenting a computerized security system), and five gardeners toiled outdoors, where the Solomons hoped to rebuild torn-out fountains and add walls and gates where the property had been truncated. The couple later claimed to have spent $3 million on the restoration, hiring as many as thirty craftsmen at a time.

"Why did we buy the house?" Dona asked a reporter. "It wasn't that I cared for Harold Lloyd. I never saw one of his films. But Greenacres is a copy of the Villa Gamberaia near Florence and I view it as a work of art." (Powell's lack of interest in Lloyd didn't go over well with his granddaughter. "Dona Powell was full of herself and insensitive," says Sue Lloyd, who thought her renovations were "showy" and "all about her.")

In another interview, Dona made clear she was serious about her new career as a collector, reeling off museums to which she'd made loans, claiming she was inspired to collect by her grandfather, beginning while in college, and explaining her philosophy ("go straight to the top") and her sense of mission. "The collector has a special duty to research, catalog, conserve, teach and share," she said, claiming that in the two-plus years since she'd owned it, eight thousand visitors had passed through the downstairs rooms of Greenacres. "We don't really own anything," she concluded. "It is our duty to protect the pieces in our collection for future generations."

In fact, Dona's primary concern appeared to be promoting herself. "She wanted to be the grande dame," says Stan Schneider. "She's an attractive woman but a piece of work. She became well known in town." But not well liked.

She gave those interviews in 1981 as other houses built by Afshani and Perry started rising on the subdivided Greenacres land—and they were all in service of her next real estate ambition, a quixotic attempt to buy or lease Ned Doheny's Greystone, which had just been abandoned by the American Film Institute and was again sitting empty. Though UCLA and Beverly Hills were negotiating to make it a retreat for artists-in-residence at the university, the Solomons offered to lease it for ninety-nine years or buy it for $8 million and restore it (at a cost they figured to be another $7 million) to use as their next home and a private museum for their collections, which they vowed to open to the public—periodically. Greystone's extensive parking lots, an amenity lacking at Greenacres, would allow that. They wanted to move, they said, because Greenacres had too many windows, and the light threatened their paintings and tapestries.

The offer won them a lot of press and a photograph in the *Times* next to a Rodin they owned. But, says the relative who won't speak to Dona anymore, "people in the city didn't like Dona too much and they made sure she didn't get it," despite the $150,000 the city had to pay annually to maintain the place. In a strong rebuff to the Solomons, in spring 1982 the mayor of Beverly Hills said she'd put Greystone on the market before selling it to them. "There have been many people who have expressed an interest in the property for private purposes," the mayor said, "but they have not been given the kind of attention the Solomons have sought." They'd "exerted a great deal of political pressure to have their offer favorably and exclusively considered." But noting that the landmark status of the house qualified buyers for a 25 percent tax credit and depreciation allowances, she added that she preferred a buyer who would "acquire and restore it for the public benefit" versus one seeking "their own personal and financial benefit."

A citizen's committee was formed to make recommendations after a searching study of the house. Though Dona lobbied Tim Doheny to speak on her behalf, he told the committee, "I've always felt the best thing for this house is for the City to control it."

Sometimes, even in the Triangle, money and hustle aren't enough. In fall 1984, Beverly Hills decided to transfer title of the mansion to a newly formed Greystone Foundation in order to end its days as a political football. Yet the city council never formalized that, and new proposals for the estate, including one that would have turned it into an art museum, went nowhere; today, the vast house still stands empty and is still owned by Beverly Hills.

In the wake of their failed attempt to buy Greystone, Dona and Bernard Solomon split up. That wasn't the only reason, but it deepened the malaise in the power couple's marriage. Bernie moved out, first into a hotel, then an apartment near Beverly Hills High School, where his boys could visit easily. "He was a sweet, gentle man and it was horribly ugly," says Mark Chayet, who met Bernie at the time and became his partner in a cassette company as well as a friend. "I was party to quite a bit of disgraceful behavior on his wife's side."

Greenacres "broke up our marriage," Powell says flatly. "He liked to live in a tiny house. He did not want my lifestyle." Later, Powell returns to the subject of their breakup and the role Greenacres played in it, recalling her husband's recoil the first time a newspaper paid attention to her. "It was very hard to be married to a man who wouldn't give me the freedom to be recognized for what I'd done. I'd studied [Greenacres] for four years. I appreciated the art form. It needed to be restored properly. To Bernie, it was nonsense, it was ego."

Chayet and four of Bernie's relatives insist that infidelity caused the breach. "Dona was a horrible runaround," says his fourth wife, Barbara, who adds that Bernie came to believe that the hard way: "He caught her a couple of times." She says that Bernie told her he served Dona with divorce papers at a party at Greenacres, "in front of everyone."

Other relatives whisper behind their hands about family scandals far worse than those they are willing to discuss openly, whatever those may have been. The breakup was devastating and its aftershocks continue to reverberate through the extended Solomon family. "It was a terrible time in his life," says Stan Schneider. "It never went away. It lasted three times longer than their marriage. It was on his mind constantly."

All agree that Dona's ambition became intolerable to Bernie. "She had a quest," says a relative. "She wanted to be very important. She wanted to be wealthy. She wanted the biggest house in Beverly Hills. I don't know if they could actually afford it. She wanted everything. And it became an ego battle. You come from nothing, you get too much, and it goes to your head." At the end, says the relative, "it wasn't pretty."

Bernie and Dona's divorce dragged on until summer 1986. After Bernie moved out, Dona held on to Greenacres for a time, renting it out as a set for the TV show *Dynasty*, the movie *Commando* starring Arnold Schwarzenegger, and corporate parties, and loaning it to causes that sometimes honored her in return. As the couple fought, they started selling assets like her Fabergé cuckoo egg, which was sold at auction for $1.76 million to the publisher Malcolm Forbes. After a fall 1985 minitrial held because Bernie wanted to sell Greenacres and Dona didn't, the estate went on the market at $12 million (soon dropped to $9 million). One of the selling points, according to broker Jeff Hyland, was the fact that it straddled the Beverly Hills–Los Angeles border, sitting in both cities simultaneously. Thanks to the listing, Dona got her photograph in *Life* magazine in spring 1986, posing in a Marion Davies gown from her collection.

That was her last hurrah at the estate. By fall, Greenacres had gone in a court-ordered sale to an heir to Chicago's Marshall Field retailing fortune. Ted Field, the son of Marshall Field IV, paid Dona $3.7 million for her half and traded Bernie a Malibu beach house for his. "Bernie was terrified that if I kept the house, he'd have to pay for my lifestyle," says Powell. "We'd had a $20 million offer years before but we had to sell it within six weeks. We didn't need money. We owed very little." She adds that she offered to pay more for it than Field did, "but the court wouldn't hear it."

In fact, says a broker involved with the transaction, Los Angeles Superior Court—in the person of Judge Joseph Wapner, future star of television's *The People's Court*—had probably heard far too much about Greenacres by that point. Dona had interfered with so many showings of the house—"She'd say, 'I'll outbid you—don't buy it,' or 'The house is haunted,'" says the broker—that Wapner finally decided to be on site whenever it was shown.

With the sale to Field, Dona Powell's public profile was significantly diminished. No longer the chatelaine of Greenacres, she moved first to Grayhall, leased from Bernie Cornfeld for $18,000 a month, then to a house on Mountain Drive once owned by Dean Martin, and reinvented herself as a jewelry designer. In 1989, her collection of royal, historic, and film-related jewels, billed as "world-renowned," departed on a tour of department stores sponsored by her newly formed Dona Corp., which sold replicas of some of the pieces. A press release for the tour touted her Collection-with-a-capital-C, and described her as "a leading philanthropist and fifth-generation Californian" whose art collection included works by Rubens, Van Dyck, Raphael, and Lucas Cranach the Elder. Articles about her at the time were illustrated with a cleavage-baring Helmut Newton portrait she'd commissioned. One story boasted that Dona Corp. was "a multi-national concern involved in virtually every field of media communication, music and entertainment."

The same press release for her line that claimed she'd studied law at UCLA also cited her "extensive background in visionary business projects," her purchase of "literally thousands of master recordings" of old music (Bernie went unmentioned and she said they were golden oldies rather than classical performances), and her role as coproducer of Goldstein and Gold's Jimi Hendrix film before "multiplying her music and film earnings with shrewd stock market projections."

Powell's jewelry design career lasted several years, but her circumstances were reduced and shrinking. By 1994, the *Times* would describe her as "once the wife of a wealthy man and reluctant to spend too much."

• • •

Dona never remarried. Bernie did, immediately after their divorce was finalized in 1986. His third wife, Colette, was his youngest son's first-grade
teacher. They moved to a ranch in San Luis Obispo and to Victoria, Canada,
where she bore him his last child, another daughter. "He'd had enough of the
legal badgering," says his friend Chayet, and moved "to get away." Almost
immediately, though, Colette fell ill with Lou Gehrig's disease, which finally
took her life in the midnineties. Bernie returned to L.A.

Solomon's fourth wife and widow, Barbara, had met Dona Powell when
she was married to Hank Lass and shopped in a boutique where Barbara
worked as a salesgirl. Later, "we double-dated a lot," says Barbara Solomon,
"but I stopped talking to her because of the way she talked to people. 'Do
you know who I am?' That kind of thing."

Barbara and Bernie met when he got back to Los Angeles. One of his
sons by Dona was dating Barbara's daughter, and asked Barbara if they could
give him her phone number. They married in 1998, and after she refused to
give up her condo apartment on Wilshire Boulevard and move into his latest house in Bel Air, he bought the penthouse in her building (his daughter
Cori, who'd gone into real estate, brokered the deal), "and we lived there
until he died," she says.

Even when he owned Greenacres, "Bernie was a pisher compared to Harold Lloyd," says Stan Schneider. Post-Dona, he was even less wealthy. "He
had a little office in Century City for a few years, then he worked out of his
apartment," says Schneider. He was content to sell a couple records at a time
"and he'd ship direct from the pressing plant. He had no overhead. He did
everything himself and he made a living." He still attended art openings,
loved leafing through auction catalogs, and went to the movies every day.

"He'd made millions," says Mark Chayet, "but the business was no longer
throwing off money. He slowed down. He was financially diminished. He
sold off his art just to maintain." In the late nineties, he had quadruple-
bypass heart surgery but didn't change his habits, so his health started to fail.

After collapsing on a trip to England, Bernie Solomon spent his final days
in the hospital and died in 2007. Dona, who'd disappeared from Bernie's life
during his last marriage, soon reappeared, picking up where she'd left off—in
court. "She'd fought everyone," says Teri's daughter Cori. "She was entitled
to fifty percent; he offered her sixty but she wanted eighty. She would've
ended up with a lot more money if she hadn't sued." Cori guesses that Dona

got $4 million in the divorce. Then, a year after Bernie's will was filed for probate, "she sued again."

Bernie expected that, says Chayet, who was named a trustee of the estate. Solomon's will contained a clause mandating that if Dona made a claim against the estate, legal fees would come out of her children's inheritance. Nonetheless, the litigation continues to this day and Solomon's estate remains unsettled. "She's suing for a couple million in back alimony and child support," says Barbara Solomon. The decades-old legal dispute over ownership of the Hendrix movie and recordings continues, too, with Powell still claiming to be an owner. "We'll all die and it will still be in litigation," says Stan Schneider. Says Barbara Solomon, "I could care less. I'm not worried. It's kind of a joke." There's only "a little" money left, she adds.

Dona Powell doesn't believe that. "Bernie was, shall we say, a bit protective," she says vaguely. "He had twenty-eight bank accounts when we got divorced." She adds that she never saw their tax returns, didn't know where he kept her bank accounts, let alone his, and was unaware that she had power of attorney over several Swiss bank accounts he'd opened. She also mutters darkly about the circumstances of his death and about his widow, who had some legal problems of her own when she was younger.

When asked what she is suing for, Powell turns coy. "I can't tell you because I don't understand," she says. "It's not for me. It's to protect my children and grandchildren." Then she abruptly changes the subject to her friendships with presidents Reagan and Ford. "I have pictures with them," she says brightly. "I was close to their families, to royal families, to the Rothschilds."

Though he sold off all his art over the years, Solomon's business interests survived him. "Now, it's basically licensing" the recordings he owned, says Schneider, whom Solomon named his executor. Bernie was "content" in his last years. "The kids by everybody came, siblings and nephews. He was sweet, a hamisch little guy. I never saw him get mad in forty years. He had a lot of fun. I envied him the balls it took to buy a Fabergé egg. He'd go out on the edge to do that. The accumulation of wealth was not his aim. To live and have fun—that was his thing."

It's unlikely he ever spent a moment mourning the loss of Greenacres.

Bel Air

Casa Encantada (10644 Bellagio Road)

About three miles to the west, Conrad Hilton was all business, almost to the day he died. Seven weeks before his ninety-first birthday, Christmas 1978, Hilton had a stroke. Just after New Year's, he was hospitalized with pneumonia and two days later he died. His obituary writers, unaware of his stroke, said he'd been in his office two days before his death. Hilton was survived by his third wife, four children, fourteen grandchildren, and a thriving Hilton Hotels Corporation, which had seen a 69 percent gain in net income the previous year, thanks in large part to two newly expanded properties in Las Vegas—the old Flamingo and the Las Vegas Hilton. His most famous descendant, named for his first international hotel, never met him; Paris Hilton wouldn't be born until February 1981.

Casa Encantada went on the market in fall 1979, priced at a record $15 million. "After Mr. Hilton died," said a secretary for the estate's attorney, "we got so many calls from real estate brokers saying Mr. Hilton had promised each of them the listing that the family decided to give it to none of them. We didn't want any hard feelings. Anyway, we feel the house will sell itself."

The house and, as his son Barron put it, "essentially all of his wealth, principally in the form of Hilton Hotels stock," then worth about $164 million, had been left to the Conrad N. Hilton Foundation, founded to assist Roman Catholic nuns. Barron would fight for years for the right to buy that stock at its 1979 price, finally prevailing in 1988, when its value had risen to almost $700 million. In an out-of-court settlement, Barron got 4 million shares outright and another 6 million in a charitable trust (that reverts to the foundation on his death), and the foundation got the remaining 3.5 million shares; the battle solidified Barron's control of Hilton Hotels. Like his father, Barron committed to giving most of his fortune to the Hilton Foundation. In 2007, he gave it $1.2 billion in proceeds from the sale of Hilton Hotels to a private equity firm, and he is set to bequeath 97 percent of his net worth, then estimated at $2.3 billion, to the charity at his death.

Conrad's widow, the former Mary Frances Kelly, an old friend whom he'd married in 1977 when she was seventy-four, moved to a condo on Wilshire Boulevard. Before she left she rented out Casa Encantada as a set for the television miniseries based on the novel *Scruples,* about a wealthy woman and her ritzy Beverly Hills boutique. Hilton's secretary, who'd lived in a guesthouse for thirty-five years, had retired, and his head butler planned to leave when the house was sold. The indoor staff of thirteen (down from sixteen in the years when Hilton entertained), many of them in residence, remained, as did six gardeners.

Despite its beauty and provenance, Casa Encantada had still not sold itself in summer 1980, when Barron Hilton sought to stir up interest by staging a charity event there benefiting the City of Hope, a medical center that had long been a favorite cause of his father's. At the same time, rumors were floating around the real estate scene that he was raising the asking price to $17 million. For a minimum donation of $1,000, 650 guests were invited to tour the house and grounds and have dinner in a tent set up in its gardens, all supposedly honoring the Hollywood song-and-dance great Gene Kelly.

It's not clear if David Murdock was there; though he'd been a presence on the Los Angeles social scene for some time, Murdock wasn't mentioned in coverage of the events. But three months later, he'd signal his arrival as a social and financial force to be reckoned with in L.A. by buying Hilton's house of enchantment. It was just what the spin doctor ordered when he bought it—a walled estate perfect for guarding the privacy of an already-wealthy man whose stated goal was nothing less than to build the most profitable privately owned company in America.

As a child and teenager in the Midwest during the Depression, David H. Murdock watched his father travel around selling generators to impoverished farmers. Suffering from undiagnosed dyslexia, David dropped out of high school; it's said he worked as a riveter, in a hatchery, hoeing cornfields, cleaning poultry coops, and pumping gas before he was drafted into the army in 1942. He washed out of Army Air Forces cadet training after balking at an officer's order to clean up grease on a floor and spent the war as a gunnery instructor. A fellow soldier set him on his course in life when he convinced Murdock to try reading again; he got hooked on biographies of America's wealthiest businessmen and determined to join their ranks. Ashamed of his lack of formal schooling, he became an autodidact.

Released from the service in 1945, Murdock landed in Detroit, where he bought a greasy spoon restaurant with $900 borrowed from two finance companies and an equal amount in a loan from the seller. He sold the diner eighteen months later, doubling his money, and then became a salesman, says Lillie Murdock, who would shortly become his first wife.

Lillie was simultaneously studying for a master's degree in biology and a beauty parlor operator's license when she met Murdock in a hotel elevator in Lansing, Michigan. "I had always wanted to leave that area and thought about the West Coast," she says. They bought a trailer and ended up in Phoenix, where he turned down a job selling shoes because he wouldn't kneel at anyone's feet, instead picking up a cue at a dinner party from a friend of a friend of Lillie's, a real estate man who "stated that what Phoenix needed were houses," she continues.

Murdock joined forces with a carpenter and became a home builder. He was in charge of financing the operation but he also dug ditches. It wasn't long before he'd graduated to building strip malls and medical offices in the rapidly expanding southwestern city. One of his then partners told *Fortune* years later that he "was a bulldog with ambition who struck some people as obnoxious, but he knew how to take an idea and make it go."

A short, fit, impatient man with bushy eyebrows, a booming, deep voice, a contemplative nature, and native shrewdness, Murdock was driven to make up for his lack of education with business success. "I used to think it was a sense of power and prestige he wanted," a friend would tell the *Wall Street Journal*. "Now I think maybe all of this is the report card he never got. By doing all these things, he's showing the world he can make straight A's."

Early on, Murdock realized that he shouldn't build on speculation and sought to sign up tenants in advance. In 1959, determined to find a bank as an anchor tenant in a new office building he was planning, he convinced a group of local businessmen to help him start one. It inspired the first of his very few failures and left him with a preference for private over public companies. Financial Corp. of Arizona, a publicly traded group of financial businesses, stumbled badly during a slump in Arizona's real estate market in 1964. After selling off its various businesses and paying off loans, Murdock (like his shareholders) emerged poorer but wiser. "I was quite young and everyone was saying I was a genius and I started to believe it," he later mused. He'd also lost his first wife to a divorce. "Like so many men, he wasn't the most perfect husband," Lillie Murdock says, diplomatically, about his extra-marital adventures.

Murdock managed to hold on to about $10 million in real estate, $3 million in cash, and some handy tax losses, all of which he used to reinvent himself as, to use his phrase, a free-form entrepreneur. He also reinvented himself personally. In Texas he'd been introduced to Gabriele Bryant, a German-born beauty with dark hair, wide, even features, and impeccable taste, and made her his second wife shortly before they moved to Los Angeles in 1967. They first took an apartment in Sierra Towers, then moved to Hancock Park, and finally settled into a 10,000-square-foot Georgian colonial that had been built by architect Roland Coate in 1933 for David O. Selznick and his wife, L. B. Mayer's daughter Irene, on the corner of Cove Way and Summit Drive, atop one of the Beverly hills. The Selznicks lived together through the filming of *Gone with the Wind* (Tara's chandelier ended up in the house), and Irene Mayer Selznick kept it after their separation and 1948 divorce. In the years since, Barbara Hutton and Katharine Hepburn were said to have lived there, and after the original two-acre parcel was subdivided, Sammy Davis Jr. owned it before Murdock.

By the early 1970s, the Murdocks had three children (one from Gabriele's first marriage, whom Murdock adopted) and had established themselves in local society. In 1973, Gabriele was photographed for the *Los Angeles Times* at a Versailles-themed party she chaired for the Diadames, a women's charity. To plan for it, she and David went to Versailles for a week; she researched the court of Louis XIV while he, the *Times* piece said, "worked his way through a briefcase of papers." She was the creative force behind the couple. "She had exquisite taste," says interior designer Erika Brunson, a friend and god-mother of their children. "She was definitely the mover and shaker behind the houses. She decorated to the great objection of David at times; he didn't always agree but she persevered. She was instrumental in buying the most exquisite pieces."

Gabriele was rich, but she wasn't happy, says a friend. "David was extremely possessive. He never let her out of his sight." At one dinner, Gabriele showed off a brand-new pear-shaped diamond ring Murdock had bought her. "Yeah," Murdock said from across the table. "She's gonna have to work that one off."

In the seventies, while he was continuing to develop buildings in places like Des Moines and Omaha, Murdock started acquiring construction suppliers, first picking up a brick maker and then cobbling together a conglomerate of tile businesses. "You use your imagination in fitting the pieces together," he'd later tell *Fortune*. "It's like tinkering with an old car and adding parts to make her go."

Murdock continued to buy, split up, and sell companies so cleverly that by 1979, when he gave that first lengthy interview to *Fortune,* it valued his holdings at about $225 million and described him as "a corporate collector"; apart from his huge real estate interests in seventeen states, his holdings included the Chicago, Rock Island and Pacific Railroad; oil, steel, textile, and forest product stocks; and prosaic makers of paint cans and sewer pipes, which, Murdock claimed, he bought for a song because Wall Street found them dull. They all earned, *Fortune* estimated, $20 million a year.

Murdock was (and remains) private, a workaholic who rose daily at 5:30, exercised regularly, and was obsessive about healthy eating. But he wasn't dull. He had feisty opinions. One quote he gave to *Fortune* would haunt him for years, reminding him of the value of a low profile. "It's useless to give more money to the poor," he said, "because they only lose it." He also hired Richard Nixon's former chief of staff, H. R. "Bob" Haldeman, as a vice president of his empire when the latter was fresh out of jail for conspiracy and obstruction of justice in the Watergate scandal. And in the year Ronald Reagan seemed to have every conservative in California on his side as he ran for president, Murdock chose to become a major fund-raiser for a rival, former Texas governor John Connally.

Murdock worked out of an office stocked with fine antiques, conducting meetings using antique canes as batons. Besides his home in Beverly Hills, he owned a 1,200-acre working ranch in Hidden Valley, north of Los Angeles, where he raised purebred cattle and Arabian horses. Found after a three-year search, it was decorated so well by Gabriele, with English furniture, Murdock's favorite Chinese porcelains, folk art, and Brunschwig & Fils fabrics, that *Architectural Digest* would feature it in a 1987 piece. That spread was an early hint of the conflict between the private and the proud (and not just house-proud) Murdock.

Murdock made two more important purchases in 1980, both of which reinforced the idea that, despite that fear of publicity, he wanted to be known as a man of taste as well as wealth. He dropped about $10 million buying Stair & Co., a prestigious London and Manhattan antique retailer (one of the sellers was his neighbor, MCA founder Jules Stein). And then, he bought Casa Encantada, paying $12.4 million for it. Though conservative, he proved he wasn't hidebound when he renamed it Bellagio House and let Gabriele remove all the Robsjohn-Gibbings furnishings that had been built in by Hilda Boldt Weber. Seventy pieces were sold in a two-part auction at Sotheby Parke Bernet that raised about $700,000.

They redid the place in the same style as their ranch, "Georgified," in the words of one person who saw it, describing the new George III décor. Though some decried the loss of Hilda Weber's unique furnishings, it, too, would eventually be featured in *Architectural Digest*. Along with a new sixteen-story tower he was building at the corner of Wilshire and Westwood Boulevards as a corporate headquarters for his David H. Murdock Development Company and Pacific Holding Corp., the purchase signaled an open intention to become a big-money player in L.A. The Murdock Plaza, as the building was known, was the first time he put his own name on any of his building projects.

Its top floor contained the Regency Club, a private dining club and an alternative to downtown L.A.'s highly restrictive Jonathan and California Clubs, which still existed, long after the days of Henry Huntington. Murdock had created similar aeries for the elites of Phoenix and Omaha and Lincoln, Nebraska. Wealth and reputation were the criteria for entrance, not birth, sex, or religion. But he didn't tolerate the casual dress habits of most Angelenos; jackets and ties were strict requirements. "We discriminate, I guess, against the slobs," said the head of Murdock's membership committee. Nonetheless, more than half of L.A.'s leading industrialists, as well as Arnold Schwarzenegger, Kenny Rogers, and O. J. Simpson, were soon counted among its one thousand members.

A private elevator from Murdock's antique-filled office took him to lunch most days; like his club, his dress—tailored suits, starched cuffs, perfectly knotted ties—was a reflection of his buttoned-up persona. "I'm a very traditional individual as far as aesthetics are concerned," he said. Murdock, wrote the *Los Angeles Times,* "had managed to insinuate himself profoundly into the economic, political and social life of the city at a pace only Los Angeles would tolerate. . . . He is less like Horatio Alger than like the characters in the Ayn Rand novels he's read." Asked if he'd ever run for office, his reply was succinct. "Why would I? I have my own world, don't I?"

Shortly after moving into Bellagio House, Murdock made his most public move yet, earning a front-page story in the *Wall Street Journal*—he put together a deal to have Occidental Petroleum buy Iowa Beef, and came away with a 2.8 percent share of Occidental, which made him the company's top shareholder, barely edging out its chairman, Dr. Armand Hammer. The *Journal* painted him as a greenmailer, one of those eighties corporate raiders who bought stakes in companies in the hope management would pay a premium to be rid of them. But he was really chasing deals, and the excitement of reinforcing his self-image. "Anything man's mind can imagine, he can do," he told the *Journal.*

In 1982, Murdock bought Cannon Mills for $414 million. Had they known how he'd dealt with Conrad Hilton's furnishings, the employees of Cannon, long a family-run, paternal business, might have had a warning of what was to come. An immediate cost-cutting drive saw benefits cut and thousands laid off, some with only a half-hour's notice; an ultimatum was given to survivors to work harder or lose their jobs, too. Elderly part-time workers were forcibly retired and others were told they had ninety days to buy company-owned housing they'd previously rented. Three years later, Murdock claimed victory after beating back an attempt by the Amalgamated Clothing and Textile Workers Union to organize Cannon's workers—and promptly sold off most of the company.

Several years after that, pensions at what remained of Cannon were cut because Murdock had invested pension pool assets in a junk-bond-holding insurance company that was seized by regulators. Though Murdock later wrote checks from his own pocket for nearly $1 million to cover some of the shortfall, bitterness lingered among retirees and former employees. Murdock may not have been close to the Reagan administration, but he was a poster child for its unemotional approach to American business.

Murdock's next fight was with Occidental's leader Hammer, allegedly his friend—the pair owned a $1 million Arabian stallion together. In 1984,

Murdock threatened to break a promise to limit his Occidental holdings to 5 percent of the company, signaling that he disapproved of Hammer's leadership. Occidental finally paid him a $60 million premium over and above the $135 million value of his stock to get rid of him; Hammer later described him as a "business barracuda." Murdock promptly bought an apartment on New York's Fifth Avenue for a record $6.5 million.

But the high didn't last. Gabriele was diagnosed with cancer and after a long stint at the Mayo Clinic with Murdock by her side, died at age forty-three. "I went everywhere in the world trying to figure out how to save her life," he said. "But it was impossible. With that, I said, 'What I want to do is find a cure for cancer.' " Gabriele's death spurred an interest in brain, nutrition, and biotechnology research, which became his philanthropic focus. Another heartache followed the same year, when their eldest son from Gabriele's first marriage drowned in an accident at twenty-three.

Though devastated, Murdock didn't falter in business. Within a year, he'd beaten another corporate raider, Irwin Jacobs, and taken over a troubled 104-year-old real estate company called Castle & Cook, which owned almost the entire 90,000-acre Hawaiian island of Lanai, and Dole Food, the pineapple and banana company that had been born there. Dole also owned 60,000 acres on other Hawaiian islands, 6,600 acres in California, and plantations in Thailand and the Philippines, where most of its fruit was grown. Murdock's first announcement on becoming its chairman and CEO was a plan to convert Lanai from farmland to a luxury resort with two hotels and villas for the rich. Though islanders griped about his condescension and self-importance, he shrugged off their criticisms and, as he always did, continued full speed ahead. The resorts would open a few years later, gaining praise and, as expected, the patronage of America's wealthiest; Bill Gates would rent the whole place for his New Year's Day 1994 wedding.

Murdock hired his neighbor Kenny Rogers for $17 million to make commercials for Dole, inspiring tattletales at his advertising agency to tell *Adweek* magazine that he wasn't an ideal client. "Unilateral thinking is a trademark of the impulsive Murdock," it wrote. "Former [agency] staffers tell of embarrassing public rages. At the office, they knew immediately which way the wind was blowing. . . . He began to throw pens or pencils at them during agency presentations." He fired and rehired his agency at least three times before moving to another, earning him a nod as the worst client of 1987.

It's doubtful he cared; that year, *Forbes* pegged his net worth at $800 million and growing. In 1991, *Fortune* upped that to $1.8 billion, and by 1992, another of his development projects, the Sherwood Country Club in Thousand Oaks, north of Malibu, had attracted former president Reagan and President George H. W. Bush as members, ending his exile from the Republican inner circle. That year, too, he remarried, tying the knot with Maria Providencia Ferrer, the daughter of Rosemary Clooney and José Ferrer, who was half his age. His third marriage lasted less than five years, and in 1997, Ferrer and Murdock had what his next wife calls "a very nasty divorce"; she reportedly walked out with $40 million and a San Jose ranch. Two years later, Murdock met another beautiful dark-haired girl. Tracy Yates Hayakawa, a part-Japanese former model thirty-eight years his junior, had first married the Iranian-born Rodeo Drive retailer Bijan Pakzad after appearing in his advertising campaigns. On meeting Murdock, she segued into decorating—she has said he helped her find her "interior design enlightenment."

"When I was married to David, we built a lot of homes together and hotels," she said. "David has a very feminine side and he loved to shop. When you shopped with him you didn't buy one, you bought a dozen. And we had so many homes and projects going on, it didn't matter if we made a mistake; we'd just put it somewhere else." His idea of mail-order, she added, was Christie's and Sotheby's auction catalogs. The couple were together for five years, but married for only one. After the marriage ended, Tracy set up a company for interior design, event planning, property management, and real estate consulting and ran a boutique with her daughter by Bijan. "We had an extraordinary relationship," she says, "but they all deteriorate. You can probably imagine he's very difficult to be with. He's very driven. You know, he's a billionaire, what can I tell you?"

At the end of the nineties, as he approached age seventy-five, Murdock went into a slump. He'd long since sold Murdock Plaza to Ted Field, the Marshall Field heir who lived at Greenacres and who had also bought the Selznick estate from him. Now, *Forbes* reported, losses at Lanai, expenses at Sherwood (where he'd sold only 160 of 630 building lots), and his second divorce had combined to drain his fortune, forcing him to sell stock and borrow millions. "At one point in time every great man in history has said, 'Damn the torpedoes,' " Murdock responded; his opinion of himself was as high as ever. He had no plans to retire, either. "My dad died at 93," he told the magazine, "but he didn't take care of himself." He was still at it in 2000, when he took Castle & Cook private after raising his bid by 13 percent, and in 2002, when he tried to take Dole Food private, too, after an oversupply of produce caused its publicly traded shares to plummet. Again, he succeeded after raising his bid.

If he was in any financial trouble, Murdock's September 2000 sale of Bellagio House to Gary Winnick, a wealthy businessman who lived in Brentwood, probably helped; the complex, record-setting deal included $26 million worth of land and cash adding up to about $94 million. Winnick had made several ever-increasing offers before Murdock succumbed.

"I've got to do this," he finally said to broker Jeff Hyland. "I'd be foolish if I didn't."

Murdock was hardly finished with real estate. He got Henry Salvatori's former property at 457 Bel Air Road from Winnick as part of the deal. Winnick had bought Salvatori's thirty-three-room Georgian colonial Paul Williams house for about $16.5 million a year earlier and torn it down. Instead of building, Murdock sold the lot to Beny Alagem (a former Israeli tank commander who'd founded computer maker Packard Bell Electronics Inc. after buying the name out of bankruptcy).[28] In the same deal with Winnick, Murdock also picked up an adjacent one-acre lot on the corner of Bel Air's Copa de Oro Road. A few months later, he sold the corner for $3 million. A descendant of General Otis, the founder of the *Los Angeles Times,* would eventually take over that property for $7.25 million and build a new house there, which was sold in 2009 for $22 million. "[Murdock's] philosophy is, don't get attached and if you can make money, sell," says a friend. Yet, for obvious reasons, he has regretted selling his great estate on the commanding hill overlooking the Bel-Air Country Club and all of Los Angeles.

Looking for a new place to live, Murdock paid the fashion designer Mossimo Giannulli $10 million for a place about five minutes to the west—the former estate of George Getty II, a 1927 house on Bel Air's Chalon Road with 9,627 square feet of floor space. The house had some dark history. Getty, the eldest son of oil billionaire J. Paul Getty, died there in 1973 after overdosing on liquor, uppers, and downers. News reports said he'd accidentally stabbed himself in the abdomen with a fork during a barbecue at the house, and then locked himself in his room after a family quarrel. His wife later found him unconscious on the bedroom floor and he was taken to hospital, where he was admitted under a false name and address and died fifteen hours later.

A spokesman for Getty Oil quickly blamed the death on a cerebral hemorrhage, but the county coroner ruled the death a probable suicide after it emerged that he'd announced he planned to kill himself. That was a gruesome year for the Gettys; in the interim, George's nephew Paul Getty III was kidnapped in Italy. The kidnappers cut off their captive's ear and sent it to the family with a ransom demand. Murdock's new home had one curious detail: bulletproof windows.

Today, despite continuing issues at Dole, which he took public again in 2009 during a liquidity crunch (in 2010 it was still trading 20 percent below its IPO price), Murdock remains supremely wealthy, number 130 on the 2010 *Forbes* list of the four hundred richest Americans, with a fortune of $2.7 billion. He splits his time between Bel Air and a 2,000-acre estate near Sherwood and is a sought-after if superannuated bachelor in L.A. But despite his wealth, the last few years cannot have been easy for him.

In fall 2004, he lost another son, David II, at age thirty-six, when the young heir (who'd followed in his father's footsteps and begun developing spec houses, albeit Bel Air mansions) turned off the Santa Monica Freeway in his Ferrari and ran into a tree at 2:30 a.m. His father had recently bought him a 7,881-square-foot six-bedroom 1942 estate from another Marshall Field heir for $16 million. Another Paul Williams house, it had once been the home of Everett Crosby, Bing's brother. Young David had proved as unsentimental as his father, tearing it down along with the houses on two adjacent lots on Perugia Way and getting approval to build a 35,000-square-foot Georgian mansion on the 4.5 acres he and his father had assembled. In the wake of David's death the house was never built. Murdock "can't bring himself to do it," says a friend, and listed the land at $22,950,000 instead.

Murdock's trials were not yet over. His sole surviving son, Justin, a college dropout, passed through a phase in his late twenties and early thirties during which he performed at Los Angeles clubs as Eliphas Horn, the black-caped devilish half-beast front man of a Goth band, and made the papers for getting into bar brawls. He seemed to settle down when he went to work in mergers and acquisitions at Castle & Cook and Dole, where he served as vice president of investments, and ran a pharmaceutical company into which he and his father poured millions. But he remained a player on the local celebrity social scene, too, hosting annual Halloween parties at Murdock Plaza with Ted Field, dating singer Avril Lavigne and Donald Trump's daughter Ivanka, and allegedly endangering the existence of the rock band Aerosmith in 2009 when he partied a bit too hard with its substance-troubled singer Steven Tyler.

In fall 2010, the *New York Post*'s Page Six column reported that the young heir, his family's pharmaceutical company, and Castle & Cook were being sued. The plaintiff, a company executive, alleged that Justin had made derogatory remarks about women, called her a whore, described outré sex practices to her, said she needed "a good pounding," and simulated sex acts at meetings. He also allegedly forced her to book sex dates for him; pay, without reimbursement, for hotel rooms for him and "interns or models for alleged" photo shoots for the company; and use her own e-mail address to open a Facebook account for him, under the name Cobra McJingleballs, that included racist images among its photos. He allegedly once told her that her job was to sit "under my desk sucking my cock." Finally, he supposedly warned that if the company failed, he'd send her to "the bottom of the Pacific Ocean in concrete boots."

A friend of Gabriele Murdock's blames David for all these troubles. "It's a very tragic family," she says, "and it's easy to see why. The man was a monster." Even though he announced the closing of the Regency Club in spring 2011 when its lease expired, Murdock, now eighty-seven, is clearly not slowing down. "Retire?" he asked a writer not long ago. "Retire to what? Old age? To nothing? To give everything up? I just plan on continuing. I have no knowledge of why anybody would retire."

44

Beverly Hills

The Knoll (1130 Schuyler Road)

No matter that they came from many places, the world of the owners of the great L.A. estates was still a small one. Justin Murdock's social set included not only his Halloween party cohost Ted Field, who bought Greenacres from the Solomons in 1986, but also a son of the man who next owned The Knoll, Marvin Davis. Both were entertainment moguls: Davis moved to Beverly Hills in 1984 after buying the Twentieth Century Fox studio, and Frederick Woodruff "Ted" Field was a film producer and the cofounder of the wildly successful Interscope Records. But Davis and Field were as different as their homes.

Marvin Davis wasn't born wealthy, but by the time he was a teenager, his father, Jack, was a politically connected millionaire living on New York's Central Park West, and Marvin attended a prestigious private school. Liverpool-born Jack Davis had worked his way into the dress business and founded what became one of the largest dress companies on Seventh Avenue.

Though he remained a garmento, Jack Davis had also started investing in oil wells; in 1939, while on vacation in Miami Beach, he'd met Ray Ryan, a mob-connected hustler, gambler, and resort and casino owner from Evansville, Illinois—according to *Vanity Fair*, they'd saved a drowning swimmer together—and Ryan convinced Davis to put some of his fashion profits into oil wells. When some of those wells came in, Jack Davis founded the Denver-based Davis Oil in partnership with Ryan. They mostly drilled dry holes, but eight years later, Ryan gave Marvin a job where he learned how to run an oil company, and after returning to New York to marry Barbara Levine, a lawyer's daughter, and honeymooning at the Beverly Hills Hotel, they moved to Denver. There Marvin, overweight but six feet four and handsome, with blond hair and blue eyes, slowly took over his father's oil interests. Between 1967 and 1976, Jack Davis set up a series of trusts for Marvin and Barbara's five children and transferred his half interest in Davis Oil to them.

Marvin got off to a slow start in Denver, drilling dozens of dry holes, too, but he'd inherited his father's sales skills, and he came up with a way to insure against losses by convincing others to invest in his wells, sometimes raking in more than they cost to drill, allowing him to profit even from failure. Eventually, he'd codify these as "a fourth for a third" deals, in which three investors covered the entire cost of a well (drilling rights as well as the cost of drilling) and, like him, got a quarter of the profits.

To his credit, Marvin also learned from his early failures, becoming a self-taught geologist, and after his father's health failed in the sixties, backed by myriad investors, Marvin bravely went where the major oil companies wouldn't go—into the forbidding, unexplored landscape of the Rocky Mountains of Colorado, Montana, and Wyoming, where small pools of oil and gas, when they existed at all, were expensive to find and difficult to exploit. He and his team of geologists, who shared in his gross revenues, brought in enough so-called wildcat wells to feed his growing family and the insatiable appetites that saw him expand into a three-hundred-pound mountain of a man, as well as satisfy his investors even as oil prices stubbornly stayed low.

Things changed for the better in the mid-1970s, when the oil business boomed after the Arab-led OPEC (Organization of the Petroleum Exporting Countries) jacked up prices 400 percent in two years. Davis Oil ranked second in the nation in drilling exploratory wells and Marvin, the most successful independent oil man in America, became known as Mr. Wildcatter. He also controlled a local bank and started developing office buildings. So naturally, he and Barbara found themselves one of the most fascinating couples in the mile-high city.

Their private life grew elaborate. They expanded their already luxurious home in a posh Denver suburb to thirty-three thousand square feet, decorated it in a style described as Hollywood posh, bought vacation homes in Vail and Palm Springs, where their neighbors were political figures and entertainment celebrities, and drove around in a Mercedes in convoy with cars full of bodyguards. According to the author Alex Ben Block in *Outfoxed,* his account of two successive takeovers of Twentieth Century Fox, they not only bowled in a private alley and showed films in their private screening room, but also owned a nearby theater for those rare occasions when they couldn't get the first-run films they wanted to see; the Davis kids would sometimes work behind its concession stand.

Their public life accelerated, too, though instead of joining Denver society, they effectively created one of their own. In 1977, the Davises founded the Barbara Davis Center for Childhood Diabetes in Denver after their seven-year-old daughter, Dana, was diagnosed with the disease, and the next year, they hosted the first of their annual fund-raisers, initially called the Carousel Ball, to raise money for a diabetes-research foundation.

Davis lost his two mentors in the late seventies. First, Ray Ryan was killed when a massive bomb blew up his Lincoln Continental in the parking lot of a spa near his Illinois home; the blast was so strong it not only broke nearby windows, but also knocked out a nearby electricity substation. The perpetrators of the bombing were never found, but a mob hit was suspected.[29] Then, two years later, in 1979, Davis lost his father.

It was at that time that Davis seemed to grow restless, eager to find something more to do, something that would add a new dimension to his life. "He yearned to reach beyond the confines of the comfortable environment he had created in Denver," wrote Block. "He began to look beyond the next horizon . . . for fun." The same year Ray Ryan died, Davis made a deal with the owner of the Oakland A's baseball team to buy it for $12.5 million and move it to Denver. Though the deal collapsed, it gave Davis his first taste of national exposure. In that burst of attention, the Texas journalist Molly Ivins revealed that he regularly ripped ties off of friends' necks and replaced them with more expensive ones; that New York's 21 Club had catered the Denver bar mitzvah of one of his sons; that he counted former officeholders like Gerald Ford, Henry Kissinger, and Edmund Muskie among his friends and investors; and that he and a syndicate of investors had bought a 22,000-acre ranch, one of the largest in Colorado, from the Phipps family. He paid $13.7 million, and demonstrating that wealth hadn't dulled his edge, sold it two years later for $28.1 million.

Two and a half years after failing to land the A's, Davis had another trophy in his sights: He offered $75 million to $80 million to buy the *Denver Post.* Davis had an inside track; the paper's publisher sat on his bank's board of directors. And he said he was willing to spend millions more for new presses and to launch a morning edition of the afternoon paper. But again, the deal collapsed, for reasons never made clear. There were certainly arguments over the value of the newspaper's assets, and Davis worried about the drag of costly union contracts on the paper's bottom line. But around this time, he also underwent surgery for what was variously described as a benign growth and skin cancer on his lip; some said he was convinced he was dying. Adding to his woes, an oil wholesale firm he owned was under investigation by the FBI for overcharging drilling expenses and falsely calling old oil wells new in order to avoid price controls and thus jack up profits. Davis would ultimately resign as that company's chairman, sign a consent decree, and pay a $20,000 penalty; the company would be forced to cough up more than $17 million in refunds and pay a $3 million fine to settle the matter. He likely laughed it off, responding with belligerence backed up by expensive lawyers.[30]

Finally, early in 1981, Davis hooked a fish so big it changed his life forever. That February, he offered about $700 million to buy and take private Twentieth Century Fox Film Corp., winning control not only of the studio but also its valuable subsidiaries: Colorado's Aspen Skiing Corp., owner of Aspen, Snowmass, Buttermilk, and Breckenridge mountains; Pebble Beach, the legendary California golf course; three thousand acres of forest in Monterey, California; and the Midwest bottler of Coca-Cola. The deal—which he put together with bank loans as well as significant capital from New York–based commodities trader and, later, notorious friend of the Clintons Marc Rich, who agreed to leave voting control in Davis's hands—made him the first private individual to own a major movie studio since Howard Hughes sold RKO in 1955. It was assumed that Davis planned to pay for it with the proceeds of the sale, a month earlier, of 830 wells and 767,000 acres of Davis Oil's exploratory gas and oil properties for $630 million to Hiram Walker, the Canadian distilling company that also owned an oil-production concern. It's unclear whether he knew that oil prices had peaked, but at that time, few doubted his perspicacity. He'd renewed his rep as a man with an unfathomably acute sense of market timing.

After he was feted by Cary Grant and roasted at a Friar's Club banquet ("I can't tell you how much I've enjoyed watching him eat a Buick," said Milton Berle in a nod to his ever-expanding girth), Davis started commuting to L.A. from Denver every Thursday in his private Boeing 727 jet, renting a $1,000-a-night bungalow at the Beverly Hills Hotel on an annual basis. He spent his Fridays playing with his very expensive new toy, which he ran from the largest, best-situated office on the lot, and lunching in the studio commissary, and his weekends indulging in the myriad pleasures available to the new movie mogul in a town that valued only novelty as much as it did immense wealth. Mr. Wildcatter had hit a gusher of fun and he loved throwing his considerable new weight around: torturing his executives as they jockeyed for position, stacking the Fox board with his powerful cronies, having his ring kissed by agents and producers, dining in a chair specially designed and reserved for him at Wolfgang Puck's Spago (and later, on chic Monday nights at Morton's, in an extra-wide throne his bodyguards would bring over before he arrived), and hobnobbing with stars who, now and then, would even invest in his oil wells—and shrug it off when they came up dry. His investors included CBS boss Bill Paley, the *Star Wars* creator George Lucas, Lucille Ball, and Sinatra's lawyer, Mickey Rudin. Only one of them, Henry Kissinger, was discourteous enough to let it be known he was distressed by his losses and, the *Los Angeles Times* reported, "severed his once close relationship with Davis." The paper said that Davis bought back the interests of Lucas and the Greek ship owner Stavros Niarchos. "I love this stuff, the people and the glamour," Davis exulted. "This isn't just business, it's a helluva lot of fun."

A year after he bought Fox, Davis flew a batch of friends into Denver for the Carousel Ball and a separate gala five-course supper for a thousand "intimates," among them Bob Hope, Lucille Ball, the Sinatras, the Pecks, Diana Ross, Dolly Parton, Jack Lemmon, Dinah Shore, Mary Tyler Moore, James Caan, Joan Collins and Linda Evans (from the TV show *Dynasty*, allegedly based on the Davis clan), Maria Shriver, and Arnold Schwarzenegger. The ball décor included a ceiling carousel with two dozen horses and fourteen thousand balloons. Guests left with gift bags holding wine, silver, crystal, and watches.

Davis often wrote a personal check matching the total of what was contributed by everyone else at a benefit. He could afford it—*Newsweek* estimated he had a billion dollars and grossed about another million a week. And that was before he struck oil and gas in a huge new field in Wyoming. This didn't stop him from dismantling Fox, selling off its Coca-Cola bottler, its record and music publishing companies, and some of its real estate holdings. Some of the proceeds were "used to repay bank debts, but most went into [Davis and Rich's] pockets," wrote Alex Ben Block. The remaining debt was refinanced, and its burden shifted from the two owners to the studio.

In 1983, Davis bought out Rich for a song when his partner fled the United States after being charged with fifty-one counts of illegally trading oil with Iran during the 1979 hostage crisis, tax evasion, wire fraud, and racketeering. The government froze all of Rich's remaining assets and in October 1984, let Davis buy Rich's half of Fox for a paltry $116 million, considerably less than half what it had cost a mere two years before. Davis had already recouped the money he'd spent for Fox, cleared his debts, and "pocketed millions," according to Block.

Davis also bought a Davis-sized house in 1984, abandoning the Beverly Hills Hotel as well as Denver, after his sometime golf partner Kenny Rogers, who'd recently starred in a film at Fox, invited him and Barbara to a party at The Knoll and told him he couldn't afford to keep it anymore. "Marvin was a buddy, a great guy," Rogers says. "He heard I wanted to move and offered me $19 million. I said, 'That doesn't work.' He said, 'What are you looking for?' I said $22 million. He said, 'I can't. Forget it. Let's have dinner.' I said, 'I'll give you a break. You can have it for $21 million.' He offered me $19 million cash and $2 million more in a two-year note. He liked the game of negotiation. It was a way to hold his head up."

Rogers joked that Davis was trying to screw him. "That's how I make my living," Davis replied.

Rogers couldn't believe what happened next. "He threw everything out and totally redid it like it was when I bought it," he marvels. "Little fine furniture. I don't know how he sat in it!" Davis also added a mirrored gym, a security and surveillance room, a lower-level media complex with surround sound in addition to the separate thirty-seat 35-mm screening room (which boasted its own bar, kitchen, and entertaining terrace), a spa complete with massage, tanning, steam, and sauna rooms, a wine vault and tasting room, a separate "collection" vault, and a therapeutic indoor swimming pool with a skylit ceiling to complement the outdoor pool.

He'd moved to L.A., but his business there was faltering. Davis had doubled Fox's debt in 1984 when it lost $36 million, transmuting its losses into tax write-offs and justifying the bargain-basement price for Rich's half of the company, but the studio needed both fresh leadership and fresh cash, and Davis was loathe to part with his. That's when Barry Diller, then a wunderkind entertainment executive running Paramount Studios but in trouble with its owner, the Gulf + Western conglomerate, called asking if Davis would sell him half the studio. Instead, Davis hired him to run it; only later did Diller learn what desperate straits Twentieth Century Fox was really in. Wags who felt the pair would never get along dubbed the deal the Hitler-Stalin pact—and were almost immediately proved correct; Diller was shocked at being taken, infuriated by Davis's refusal to give him the funds he felt he needed to right the listing ship, and finally threatened that if Davis didn't sell the company to someone willing to run it right, he would sue for fraud.

Davis decided to sell half to the only buyer on the horizon, the same media mogul he'd preempted when he bought Fox four years earlier, Rupert Murdoch, who offered Davis enough money to pay down the studio's debt and inject millions for company operations. What Davis didn't expect was that Diller and Murdoch would immediately gang up on him; within months, Davis sold the rest of the studio to Murdoch, netting about $237 million, and also hanging on to Pebble Beach, half of the Aspen Company (he and Murdoch had recently sold the other half to Henry Crown, former owner of Greystone, and his son Lester), and half of the Fox Plaza office building in Century City, then still under construction, but later a set for the first *Die Hard* movie, and home to the executive offices of Fox, Davis, and former president Ronald Reagan. (Davis sold his stake in the building to Fox a few years later, then eventually bought the whole building from new owners in 1997.)

But Davis would never be happy as a mere real estate investor, even if he also co-owned property in Chicago, Boston, Virginia, and Denver. Bitter and angry at losing his finest toy, Davis forced Diller to personally carry the final sale documents to The Knoll for his signature. The attempted humiliation only served to further infuriate Diller.

A *Los Angeles Times* article that appeared just after the sale detailed "a string of problems and retrenchments" in the Davis empire, including notable declines in oil operations and profits. But Murdoch's money and another $180 million Davis made the same week the Fox deal was announced, when he sold the rest of his producing oil and gas wells and most of his remaining development acreage, kept him on the La-La Land A-List for years to come. In 1986, he gutted Davis Oil, turning it into what one of his children would later describe as "a checkbook" for him and his children's trusts. Though emptied of most of its assets, it continued to pay him $200,000 a year. In a reorganization, he created Davis Companies, which he wholly owned, and he paid it—meaning himself—for managing Davis Oil. He also managed the assets of his children's trusts, which would lead one of them to complain he was giving himself three paychecks for one job. He installed his sons, Gregg and John, in key executive positions. Gregg would henceforth run Davis Petroleum, a new oil and gas company, while John, who'd become a successful film producer (*Grumpy Old Men, Alien vs. Predator*), also served as Marvin's collaborator on new deals and on his own, headed Stone Canyon Venture Capital, financed in part by the family's trusts. "I never put a dime of my own into a movie," said John, who was clearly a chip off the old block.

The next few years saw a frenzy of deals announced but curiously, just like Marvin's first run at CBS in 1985 (which opened the door to the subsequent takeover of the network by the Tisch family), few were ever consummated, leading *Forbes* magazine to nickname the post-Fox Davis the Tire-kicker. But all the noise he made kept his name on lists of both the country's biggest deal makers and its most-wanted guests. He also claimed it made him profits. "All you have to do is look at a pretty girl and everyone thinks you're sleeping with her," he said. "You don't have to put up any money. It doesn't cost you."

Initially, Davis continued to divide his time between Beverly Hills and Denver, and continued to attract the prominent to Colorado for the annual Carousel Ball despite the sale of Fox. But inevitably, Barbara and Marvin's focus shifted to Los Angeles. The Davises' last fling in Denver was in 1985. The next year, it was announced that the ball would henceforth be held every other year, fueling speculation that the Davises were ready to leave Denver behind. They did and by 1987, Barbara was said to be looking for a Los Angeles cause to support. Instead, in 1990, she relaunched her diabetes benefit as the Carousel of Hope, and it has been held in Beverly Hills ever since.

Davis's shift in geographic focus was evident when he beat Donald Trump and Merv Griffin in a bidding war to buy the Beverly Hills Hotel from its latest owners, the New York arbitrageur Ivan Boesky, his wife Seema, her sister, Muriel Slatkin, and her estranged husband. Boesky concluded the sale as he was negotiating a plea bargain after he was indicted for insider trading; his in-laws had also sued him for misusing hotel funds in his illegal deals. A relatively small-stakes venture—Davis reportedly bid $135 million and promised to invest another $40 million in renovations—the hotel still held symbolic value for the Angelenos who flocked to The Knoll for the Davis Christmas party that year. The Pecks, the Sidney Poitiers, Elizabeth Taylor, Warren Beatty, Burt Bacharach, and Aaron Spelling were among those chowing down on twenty-eight pounds of caviar, oysters flown in from Florida, and a choice of three entrees prepared by the local in-crowd eatery Chasen's. "I like their style," declared the society columnist Suzy.

As it turned out, Davis held on to the hotel for only about eight months before selling it to the sultan of Brunei for about $200 million. He was less successful when he bought a Beverly Hills delicatessen in 1987 and, in partnership with New York's Carnegie Deli, tried to compete with Nate and Al's, a local institution where he was sometimes made to wait for a table. After Marvin and Barbara appeared at the opening and cut a salami in lieu of a ribbon, the new Carnegie failed, but by then, the Davises had themselves become local institutions. "Barbara, weighed down in diamonds, moving from group to group, introducing celebrities, kissing, and laughing, was a nice lady and a very good hostess," wrote *Vanity Fair*. "Marvin, a 350-pound hulk with a bad toupee who was thought to be worth billions, was always part of the show at their parties."

The selling and the posturing about buying continued through the end of the eighties. In 1988, Davis made a run at Lorimar Pictures that came to nothing but sold Breckenridge, an Aspen ski resort, to a Japanese company for an estimated $70 million. With some of the proceeds, he established The Little Nell, a small, celebrity-centric Aspen hotel, opening it with a Davis-sized party on Thanksgiving weekend 1989. The next year, he sold the Pebble Beach Company and its four golf courses for $841 million to another group of Japanese businessmen, and in 1993, he sold his remaining half-interest in Aspen to Chicago's (and Greystone's) Crown family.

Over the next decade, Davis would be reported as preparing to buy variously: Spectradyne, a pay-per-view company; the parent companies of Northwest, Continental, USAir, and United Airlines; NBC; MGM/UA; Vivendi; the *Los Angeles Herald-Examiner*; Carter-Wallace, the condom manufacturer; and various pieces of big-ticket real estate including the Plaza Hotel and several office buildings in New York and a Four Seasons hotel in Hawaii. None of the deals was consummated, but some made him greenmail profits (he supposedly netted $100 million on the United deal and $25 million to $30 million on Northwest) and all burnished his dealmaker image, as did regular appearances on the *Forbes* and *Fortune* rich lists, which pegged his wealth at $1.65 billion in 1990, $2.1 billion in 1991, $2 billion in 1994 (when he told *Forbes* he'd been sitting on the sidelines because "times were tough"), and $2.2 billion in 1996, when he'd made a big domestic oil strike.

Gossip columnists plumped his image even more. In the early nineties, the Davises gave a New Year's Eve party in Aspen that attracted half of Hollywood (including George and Alana Hamilton, Sylvester Stallone, and Ted Field) and a sprinkling of big names from Washington and New York's Seventh and Park avenues, and continued to entertain regularly at The Knoll in a style that even La-La Land considered something special.

"Everything changed with the Davises," says one social observer who was a regular at The Knoll. "There was always money here, but this was on a different scale. Old Society resisted them and they were more at home with movie stars. But they bought their way in and worked their way up, and they hung out the ham so much that eventually, they all came, from Betsy Bloomingdale to the Dohenys." And it wasn't only ham. "Every night, they fixed pork, lamb, veal, sirloin, burgers, baked, mashed, and French-fried potatoes, creamed and steamed everything, soufflés. I never saw so much food in my life, all delivered by liveried waiters. They changed social life here. They had a profound influence on this town."

Eventually, Davis started buying again, gaining a piece of Bally, the slot-machine maker, but he was soon back to his old tricks, briefly eyeing the Atlantic City casino business before deciding against it, and then, in 1997, agreeing to buy half-ownership of the Desert Inn in Las Vegas before backing out a few days later. By the midnineties, Davis's career as a deal maker was winding down—and not smoothly. A last late development, Water Garden, a seventeen-acre office complex in Santa Monica, begun in 1990 and not completed for ten years, "really hurt him," says a source close to the family.

Late in 1994, the Davises cancelled their annual New Year's Eve party in Aspen after Marvin was hospitalized—allegedly for knee replacement surgery, the first of many ailments caused by his weight, though some said he was really having another bout with skin cancer. Even as his constant health issues caused him to shed more than a hundred pounds in his last years, Davis still seemed larger than life. In 2004, *Golf Digest* was granted an interview with him on condition it be confined to the subject of golf, and writer Mark Seal described Davis "sitting behind a massive cockpit of a desk, in a peach-carpeted, crystal chandelier-strewn office" with "twin 'Personal Market Watch' screens" and "acres of frames of him posing with every dignitary on the planet." Davis, at seventy-four, was "every inch the dealmaker, a veritable mountain of a man, gargantuan both in weight and wallet," Seal rhapsodized.

Yet he'd developed diabetes, had a tumor on his spine, suffered from heart disease, had endured bouts of pneumonia and sepsis, was often confined to a wheelchair, and needed bodyguards and nurses to bathe him. This was all according to his daughter Patty Davis Raynes, who filed a lawsuit the next year because, she feared, he'd decimated his and his family's fortunes by living large while failing to make the kind of deals that might have revived the coffers. "Marvin made great deals," insists the source close to the family. "It's possible it would have turned around for him."

He wanted people to think it had. "My dad's quote is, 'We're back,'" Gregg Davis had told the *Rocky Mountain News* in 2000, announcing that with oil prices at a ten-year high, Davis Petroleum, which had been moribund for years, would be beefing up its Denver operations, and refocusing the company on natural gas exploration in Wyoming and Texas. But little more was heard about the company in the next few years, even though the Davis family continued making empty noise. Davis's last big bid, a $13 billion run at Vivendi in 2002, was rejected as too low and he lost it to NBC.

The family fortune was obviously shrinking; daughter Patty had moved to New York after marrying real estate developer and operator Martin J. Raynes in 1983. But in 1997, they sold their Fifth Avenue apartment and in 2001, they also offloaded their home on the ocean in posh Southampton, Long Island. The family was facing social challenges, too. Patty's sister Nancy's son Brandon had begun making the papers in 2002, when the *New York Post*'s Page Six reported that "the 21-year-old party boy . . . who has been in and out of rehab and does not have any substantial assets" was refusing to settle an $80,000 gambling debt after exceeding his $150,000 credit line at a Las Vegas hotel-casino.

Brandon would go on to gain a certain tawdry renown as a boyfriend of Mischa Barton, the television actress, a frenemy of Paris and Nicky Hilton, and the man who chased down red-haired Lindsay Lohan outside a nightclub, calling her firecrotch. "He's got a tremendous sense of entitlement," says Richard Johnson, then the editor of Page Six.

From 2006 to 2010, Brandon made more than a hundred appearances on that leading gossip page, a record run of epic bad behavior: frequent fights with friends and gambling casinos over money borrowed and unpaid; all-too-frequent trips to the bathroom and public displays of bagged white powder; offensive and belligerent behavior at parties, fashion shows, and nightclubs; and stints in drug rehab. The *Post* alleged that he'd been cut off financially by his family, popularized his nickname Greasy Bear for his sweaty, off-and-on flabby appearance, and described him at different times as "out of it," a "pudgy party boy," an "oily heir," "unctuous," "obnoxious," "lowbrow," "homophobic," "dangerous and out of control," "broke," and "a moocher."

His brother Jason was dubbed Gummy Bear and his stints in drug rehab and retaliatory threat to write a tell-all book about his family were chronicled, too. "I love my family," Jason told the column. "I wish they loved me the way I love them. If they want to play with fire, they are going to get burned." Their older brother, Alex, has wisely or luckily stayed below the media's radar, though Page Six did report that he'd become a real estate broker and had sold Lionsgate, Kenny Rogers's starter mansion. In 1985, it had passed to Mark Hughes, founder of the Herbalife nutritional supplement business, for $6.9 million. ("I finally got rid of it," Rogers says now. "Timing is everything.") Three years later, Hughes put it on the market for $12 million and Marvin Davis bought it for his daughter Nancy.[31]

The ailing Marvin Davis died of natural causes at The Knoll in September 2004. Davis's obituaries noted that since moving to L.A., he'd given Cedars-Sinai Medical Center a research building that carried his and Barbara's names and that he ranked third in wealth in Los Angeles; *Forbes* had recently estimated his fortune at $5.8 billion. But those claims would soon be questioned. "There was a time when there was real money and a lot of it," says the source close to the family. But that time had passed. And the family, who were all at Marvin's bedside when he died, were also at each other's throats.

Patty Davis had briefly worked at Twentieth Century Fox in New York as a production executive although her father allegedly wouldn't pay her, telling her that owners should not be employees. Then, after she married Marty Raynes, her father turned against her, she claimed in the 169-page complaint that was the opening and, eventually, only salvo in *Raynes v. Davis,* a lawsuit she brought a year after Marvin died.

"This is a case about greed, theft, and betrayal," her complaint began. "This is a case about how Marvin Davis, who was one of the wealthiest men in America, systematically stole hundreds of millions of dollars from the trust created for his oldest daughter, Patricia Davis Raynes, to finance his own business interests, the business interests of his two favored sons, and a lavish lifestyle for himself, his wife Barbara Davis, and his other children. Acting out of greed, spite, and malice, Marvin Davis and his close cohort of coconspirators abused, isolated, and stole from Patricia because she dared to question Marvin Davis, and dared to leave Los Angeles for New York to live her own life. Patricia's brothers and sisters knew about, took advantage of, and greedily accepted the benefits from the wrongful, illegal acts of Marvin Davis, Barbara Davis, and their coterie of advisers and sycophants."

According to the complaint, instead of giving Patty her trust fund on her twenty-first birthday in 1973, as Jack Davis had intended, Marvin rolled it into a new one, which he claimed to have managed into about $300 million by the midnineties. The problem was, her complaint continued, he had comingled its assets with those of her siblings, his own trust, and his companies, and used that pool of money however he wished, even shifting losses from his and Barbara's trust to the children's, so that by the time of his death, her fortune had vanished. "A few days after Marvin died, Barbara informed Patricia that, contrary to what Patricia had always believed, contrary to what the defendants had told Patricia all her life, contrary to what Marvin Davis and the other defendants had repeatedly represented to the world, 'You're poor, Patty. You're poor.' "

Since that surprise, Patty had decided that Marvin, his wife, all her siblings, and a few key executives of the various Davis entities had conspired to loot her trust fund for twenty-nine years and fritter her money away on their lavish lifestyle, illegitimate business expenses, and Marvin's series of failed and "imprudent" takeover bids, which she charged were shams calculated "to create the illusion that Marvin controlled a vast financial empire in order to benefit [her brothers' businesses], to inflate Marvin's and Barbara's egos, to generate millions of dollars in improper" advisory fees—basically to enrich the rest of her family at her expense. Marvin had even committed her trust to pay her mother $15 million on his death.

Just beneath the surface of those charges lay Patty's suspicion that there actually was some money left, and certainly valuable property, and the purpose of her suit was to ensure that she got her share. The flip side of Marvin's rep as a quintessential deal man with uncanny timing was the fast and loose player with other people's money, who wasn't above screwing his investors, and was always looking out for number one.

Most shocking of all were Patty's claims of what Marvin had done to her: Not only had he lied to her and arranged for her signature to be forged repeatedly on trust documents, but after she got an inkling of what was going on, began asking questions, and refused her father's demands that she sign complex legal documents that would have given him complete control of her money until 2010, he'd threatened to make her and her family's life "a living hell." And then, after an argument in his bedroom at The Knoll, Marvin "struck Patricia, and continued to beat her until Barbara eventually interceded," the complaint said. "Barbara did not, however, resist Marvin's efforts to force Patricia to sign the trust documents; in fact, Barbara pressured Patricia as well, telling Patricia that she should 'just sign, you can always change it later. I've changed mine.' "

Forbes reported that an anonymous friend of the family called Patty's claims preposterous, vicious lies and said she'd received almost $100 million from her trusts. The case was settled out of court and closed, with all the participants barred from discussing it under a confidentiality agreement. But one observer describes an early mediation in the case, with all the members of the Davis family present, some of them eating take-out food in the courtroom, while a huge oil painting of the whole family, brought to the federal courtroom by Barbara Davis, leaned against the bar between the audience and the participants. "It was huge, huge, huge," says the witness. "Just bizarre."

Patty's wasn't the only family lawsuit. Another was filed in Texas by sister Nancy Sue Davis, alleging that Gregg, who'd been in charge when Davis Oil was forced into bankruptcy and sold to private equity investors for $150 million, was self-dealing, underestimating the company's value—Nancy claimed it was worth $1 billion—in order to deprive her, her siblings', and their mother's trusts of their fair share. The suit, seeking at least $50 million, was dismissed, but was still on appeal early in 2011.

So was there any money left? When her suit was settled, Patty seemed much happier. Divorced, she now lives with her daughter in an exclusive condominium on Manhattan's Upper East Side. Long before that, Barbara took a final bow at The Knoll and then put it up for sale with a 15½-inch-wide photo brochure that renamed it Grand Manor. The price—first $70 million, then marked down to $59 million—was available only on request. It went for a reported $46 million. Barbara now lives in a condo on Wilshire Boulevard and is still the life of the party, even if she can no longer afford to give the best ones in Beverly Hills.

The buyer of The Knoll was Eric Smidt, president of Harbor Freight Tools, which sells budget-priced tools and equipment through catalogs, the Internet, and retail stores. Though hardly as glamorous as the Davises, the Smidts have also ended up in court in a vicious family feud. Harbor Freight was founded in 1968 by Eric's father, Allan, in the family's North Hollywood garage when Eric was eight years old. He became president at age twenty-five, working under his father, but as he grew older, he came to want control of the company, according to a lawsuit Allan would bring against his son fourteen years later.

Eric's love of luxury real estate seems to have inspired that suit. In 1998, he bought 60 Beverly Park Terrace, an 11,000-square-foot, multiwing seven-bedroom, ten-bathroom mansion, complete with an infinity pool and tennis court. A few years later he paid $14.95 million for a weekend house right next door to Steven Spielberg on Broad Beach in Malibu.

In the interim, Allan turned seventy-one and sold the company to Eric at a price far below fair market after his son promised him he would continue to have the last word on major decisions. But in 2007, the company borrowed $500 million and paid it all to Eric and his family as dividends; he then bought a $100 million painting, a $20 million New York City apartment, and The Knoll for $46 million, announcing that he was going to restore the last—by then so run down one top mansion renovator called it uninhabitable—"even if I have to tear it down and rebuild it." Allan Smidt, who'd always been conservative with money, objected, and to placate him, Eric agreed to pay him $2.5 million a year, but made only one payment, the complaint continues. Then he began renovating Harbor Freight, too.

After Eric started firing and replacing executives in spring 2009, his father expressed concern to the company's outside lawyer; Eric then removed him from the board and cut off his access to Harbor Freight's computers. Finally, Allan alleges, he was escorted from the company's headquarters and told, "Don't come back." Two months later, he sued his son. Eric Smidt calls the lawsuit "incredibly sad" and his father's accusations "completely unfounded." His stem-to-stern remake of The Knoll—which was gutted down to its concrete and steel frame before its transformation into a classically proportioned white-brick Regency house on steroids—continues and Smidt, his wife, and two children are expected to move there from Beverly Park early in 2012.

45

Beverly Hills

Greenacres (1740 Green Acres Place)

Frederick Woodruff "Ted" Field and Marvin Davis shared show business ambitions and a taste for great houses, but had little else in common besides fraught familial relationships. Unlike Mr. Wildcatter, who wanted desperately to fit in, Field saw himself as a rebel and a maverick—and wanted to stand out. He did everything he could to separate himself from his famous family and its legacy, even though it gave him the money to pursue his own interests, which ranged from car racing to rap music. "Now, that might sound ungrateful," he once said, adding, "frankly, I don't care about that."

Field was born a great-great-grandson and heir to nearly half the fortune created by the iconic Chicago retailer, Marshall Field. He has built that into $830 million according to the *Los Angeles Business Journal,* which ranks him the forty-first-richest person in L.A.

His wealth aside, Field's family legacy isn't enviable. While building Marshall Field & Company into Chicago's top department store, the original Marshall Field sired a family that has, through five generations, been plagued by mental illness and exhibited a marked tendency toward both broken marriages and suicide. Field's wife had mental problems. His son and namesake died of a gunshot wound; many believed he'd botched a suicide attempt in a local brothel and just made it home before dying from his wounds. Marshall Sr. died broken-hearted within weeks of his son's death. All but 10 percent of the store was then sold to its executives by his trustees.

Marshall Jr.'s son Marshall III, the next most accomplished Field, abandoned Chicago for New York, where he leased an apartment at the prestigious 740 Park and, urged on by his psychiatrist, started a progressive newspaper called *PM* that led to his being fiercely denounced as a Communist. Though *PM* failed, Marshall III also founded the *Chicago Sun* and bought the *Chicago Times* (eventually merging them), Simon & Schuster, and *The World Book Encyclopedia*. One of Marshall III's stepsons died of a heroin overdose and two of his daughters were also suicides. He also married three times. "I don't know what it *is* about this family," said wife number three, who outlived him by thirty-four years.

Everything was inherited by his son Marshall IV, a Harvard cum laude graduate who carried a piece of shrapnel in his head from World War II, and later was treated with electric shock therapy and repeatedly institutionalized, as was his older sister. Marshall IV also drank heavily and was addicted to prescription drugs; he died at forty-nine with both in his system in what a relative called a "kind of sort of suicide," though the official cause of death was heart attack. Their younger sister abandoned her first daughter; her second married and divorced three times before she was murdered.

His father Marshall IV's death is "nothing that haunts or bothers me," Ted Field has said.

Marshall IV had already sold most of his father's acquisitions when he died. Afterwards, the family sold its remaining interest in its store to concentrate on real estate and newspapers. The family firm Field Enterprises was left to Marshall V and Ted under a trust set to expire twelve years later, when Ted turned twenty-five. The two half-brothers could not have been more different. Marshall V was a child of his father's first wife, the daughter of a New Hampshire governor. Eleven years older than Ted, he was a prep-school-educated conservative with a keen sense of familial duty and a taste for fly-fishing. He spent five years training before taking over the company in 1969. Ted, a product of his father's second marriage, was ten when his parents divorced and only thirteen when his father died. He was in public school in Anchorage, Alaska, at the time.

Ted's mother, Kay, had married Marshall IV when she was fresh out of Smith College, but soon tired of his society lifestyle, divorced her husband, and joined the Christian Science church. "My life was on a downhill slide," she said. "I needed to grab onto something solid and permanent." So she threw her kids into a station wagon and drove them to Alaska, where some friends lived, and when one of Ted's sisters proclaimed she wanted to stay, Kay sprang her trap and agreed. "Of course, the people in Chicago thought I'd gone completely out of my mind," she said. Her son may have thought so, too, though he was diplomatic in expressing it. "My mother . . . decreed we'd live an un-showy lifestyle, and we certainly did," Field told *Vanity Fair* many years later, calling his upbringing an "enforced middle-class life."

Kay Field was hired by the *Anchorage Daily News* to organize its library and later became a reporter. In 1966, on a trip back to Chicago, she married Larry Fanning, a former editor of the Field family's *Sun-Times* whom she'd dated just after her divorce, and the next year, they bought the *Daily News* and turned it into an investigative force that offended the powerful and advertisers but appealed to readers. Unfortunately, Larry Fanning died at his desk of a heart attack in 1971, just after Ted graduated high school and returned to Chicago to attend Northwestern, the first of more than a half-dozen schools he would enroll in and leave; he never got a degree. Older brother Marshall, who'd reportedly once forced Ted to watch as he snapped the heads off turtles, told him no one would respect him unless he graduated, but Ted didn't care. "I'll take the chance," he said.

Ted, who'd worked at his mother's paper as a teenager, apparently admired her and his stepfather's style of progressive journalism. Over the next seven years, as he fitfully continued his education, he poured $5 million from his trust fund into the *Daily News* to keep it alive and even thriving; it won a Pulitzer Prize in 1976 for a series on the Teamsters in Alaska.[32] But he disdained his mother's religion—as a teenager he was forced to read the Bible daily and attend church twice a week—and early on, his trajectory seemed plotted to escape it, as well as the duty, or the burden, of being a Field. Still, he embraced the privileges, perks, and pork that came with his storied name.

As a young man, Ted's chosen venue was race cars; he'd caught the racing bug at ten when his mother took him to Indianapolis. Symbolizing both independence and expensive indulgence, racing was a perfect fit for his personality. As a child, Ted had been impatient and aggressive; he loved a challenge, and would obsess until he excelled at whatever caught his fancy. He showed off his hard-won skills, too; he gloried in winning at Ping-Pong and when playing tennis with his sisters would conspicuously read novels between their returns.

As an adult, he continues to compete in a variety of athletics. He played chess against his father when he was five and still plays—but later in life, he hired champions like Garry Kasparov and Boris Spassky to play against him. He kept a set of drums for years, another legacy of a childhood preoccupation. As a child in Chicago he was unforgiving of friends who failed him, but also oddly needy. After he was beaten up for laughing about a baseball teammate's error, he bought the same teammate a new mitt.

In 1973, Ted decided to live one of his dreams—to drive cross-country. He left his latest school, the University of Chicago, and stopped only when he reached the West Coast at Balboa Bay in Newport Beach, California. "He just knew that he had found his place, his home," his mother said. At first he lived off investments, but within a year, while ostensibly studying economics at the University of California at Irvine, he bought two Formula 5000 open-wheel single-seat race cars—a Talon and a Lola—and devoted himself to auto racing.

He knew he had a lot to learn before taking the wheel, so he formed a company he called Interscope (he'd say he chose the name for no particular reason other than it wasn't Field) and hired two professional drivers to race for him while he practiced. Perhaps he didn't practice enough; on November 5, 1975, Ted's car died in his second-ever race at Riverside International Raceway. A tow truck came to pull him off the track, and the driver hooked a towline to the car's roll bar and asked Field to hold it. When he popped his clutch, the car flipped over and was dragged more than fifty yards with Field's hand caught between it and the track—mangling most of his fingers, and leaving only his thumb intact on the stump of his left hand. Field has hidden the injured hand in an Ace bandage ever since. He has called the freak accident, the excruciating pain he experienced, and his long recovery a defining experience. "If anyone thinks that I've had the ultimate, cushy, easy life," he said, "I promise you that that year and a half to two years would give the lie to that notion." Even though he could only hold the wheel with his left thumb while shifting, Field continued to race until he quit abruptly in 1983. His departure from racing coincided with several other signal events in his life. Long estranged from his mother, he separated from his wife that year—he'd married the daughter of a dentist in the midseventies and the pair had one daughter—and the next, abruptly severed ties with the rest of his family and its legacy, if not its money.

The trust that ran Field Enterprises after Marshall IV's death expired in 1977 when Ted hit age twenty-five. From then on, the brothers each held half the voting stock and were bound by a document called "the bible," which set the rules for their business relationship. It required they be of like mind on major corporate issues. They almost never were. Ted wanted to dissolve the company, cash out, and free up his money. So Marshall announced the immediate sale of the *Chicago Sun-Times* "with deep regret," adding, "Had this decision been mine alone to make, I probably would not have taken this action." Seven months later, the newspaper was sold for about $100 million to Rupert Murdoch—and the Field brothers stopped speaking to each other. Each wound up with a bit more than a quarter-billion dollars. Marshall would invest his share conservatively. Ted was more of a maverick.

Though some considered him a villain and a pirate, Ted did not see himself that way. He wanted to make a contribution to society, he insisted; he just wanted to do it his way. So he moved to Beverly Hills, where he and a staff of twenty supervised his investments (he owned a newspaper recycling company and invested in stocks and real estate) from a full floor at Murdock Plaza. Not only did Murdock rent Field an office, he sold him a house. Appropriately, given his ambitions, it was the David Selznick house, but Field never moved in, instead listing it for $4.2 million and selling it in 1986 to Ed McMahon, the *Tonight Show* second banana.

When he won his freedom from his family, Ted Field had already had a hand in producing a children's television series, *Marlo and the Magic Movie Machine,* and a Donald Sutherland film, *A Man, a Woman and a Bank.* He lost money on both. He'd also bought the rights to *Passion Play,* a novel about a polo player, and hired its author, Jerzy Kosinski, to write a screenplay. It was never filmed, but Ted had been bitten by the show business bug.

Ted divorced his wife then; he not only wanted to make movies, he wanted a different life. Barbara Stephenson, his future second wife, had come into the picture at the tail end of Ted's racing career; they met at a Florida track. *Vanity Fair* would later describe her as "a blonde from the Donna Rice school of social advancement," a reference to the party girl who brought down Senator Gary Hart's 1988 bid for the presidency, as opposed to first wife, Judy, who was described as "sweet, pure, virginal . . . [and] completely dismayed . . . by the lifestyle Ted adopted after he moved to L.A." He and Barbara moved into a house on Charing Cross Road in Holmby Hills and a ranch in Santa Barbara.

Ted may have wanted nothing to do with his family but its money still came in handy. Interscope Communications, founded in 1981, was a product of Field's first movie investment. Ted and a partner had formed a development company that was, *Premiere* magazine wrote, "heavy on style and light on substance. . . . Learjets and opulent offices furnished in mahogany," and defined by an insistence on financial independence that proved counterproductive to the task at hand—making movies. He bought a bunch of scripts at $50,000 each but got nowhere with them. But a new friendship with Skip Brittenham, a well-connected Hollywood lawyer who gave good advice and introduced him to industry power brokers, "enhanced Ted's ability to work the system," Brittenham told *Premiere*. "He was footing the entire bill," the lawyer explained to the *Wall Street Journal*. "He needed someone else to validate the nature of what he was doing." He couldn't go it alone; he needed experienced allies.

In 1982, Field hired David Obst, a former literary agent, as his chief creative executive, and it wasn't long before Peter Bart, then a production executive at MGM, sold him the treatment for *Revenge of the Nerds,* inspired by a story written by Bart's eleven-year-old daughter. Ted's sputtering film career was finally in gear. Studios began paying attention.

Simultaneously, Field demonstrated canniness in business that must have impressed even his hated brother. He invested in two Bermuda-based companies, one headed by swashbuckling British corporate raider Sir James Goldsmith, and then another begun by Goldsmith's right-hand man. Through the mideighties, he quietly played a large role in financing their bids to take over several companies, including Crown Zellerbach, Goodyear, and BAT Industries (aka British American Tobacco), which owned not only big cigarette brands, but also a number of major American retailers, including Saks Fifth Avenue and, ironically, Marshall Field. Field also invested with T. Boone Pickens and Carl Icahn.

In 1984, Field made another key hire at Interscope, bringing in Robert Cort (who'd left Fox when Marvin Davis took over) as president of Interscope's entertainment division, replacing his original partner, whom he reportedly bought out for $1 million. Their split resulted in part from Field's wandering eye for women. That partner, a British producer, had a cousin, the British actress Emma Samms, and according to *Premiere,* Field fell for her, left Barbara Stephenson, whom he'd yet to marry, and moved into an apartment he bought for Samms. "Then one day he decided the affair was over," *Premiere* reported, "and [he] never spoke to [Samms] again. He didn't even tell her himself but had [his producer partner] do it for him. Field then reunited with Barbara, who demanded [the producer's] resignation—and got it." Ted would eventually come to be known as intensely loyal to friends but capable of closing an iron door on anyone he felt had crossed him.

Cort and Field have gone on to become one of the most profitable producing teams in Hollywood, beginning with a series of low-brow but incredibly popular films like *Outrageous Fortune, Three Men and a Baby,* and *Cocktail* for Walt Disney's Touchstone Pictures, as well as television miniseries and movies of the week. Field took Hollywood players on annual yacht trips and lavish vacations where he cultivated his new relationships. He also made another acquisition that proved as profitable as Cort was. In partnership with a venture capital firm, Field bought Panavision, the company that developed and rented to studios most of the cameras used to make movies in Hollywood. It cost $52.5 million; Field would later buy out his partners and sell the company in 1987 for $142 million.

Field would generally wake at 6 a.m., trade stocks and commodities all morning, and then, once the East Coast markets closed, eat lunch at Murdock's Regency Club. Then, he'd turn his attention to his other interests. One of those was real estate, and Field made his most impressive, if not his largest, purchase early in 1986 when he traded cash and a beach house for Greenacres shortly after succumbing and making Barbara Stephenson his second wife. The deal with the Solomons, literally made in court, according to Field's broker, Paris Moskopoulos, was valued at $6.5 million. "It sold for forty percent less [than it was worth]," says another broker involved with the transaction. "Bernie just wanted out and walked away from millions because he couldn't bear to suffer any more."

Field, now bearded and sporting a ponytail (as well as his mangled hand—an eerie echo of Harold Lloyd), immediately announced his emergence as a society host, planning a series of fund-raising events for Joseph Biden, who was beginning a run for president. He also began making regular contributions to socially liberal, economically pragmatic Democrats and progressive causes; he'd become a financial mainstay of Norman Lear's People for the American Way; an early supporter of AIDS research, the Holocaust Museum, and rain forests; and a crusader against a more conservative Supreme Court. Greenacres was the stage on which his new ambitions would play out. Ted and Barbara lived on in Holmby Hills while they began renovations.

Right after Barbara convinced Ted to adopt another child, a girl, he left her. He'd recently run into Susie Bollman in Beverly Hills; a beautiful blue-eyed blonde like Barbara, Susie was the daughter of the man who'd helped design and build Ted's fiberglass race cars. They'd first met when Ted moved to Newport Beach—he lived in a house on the bay two doors down from her best friend—but he was then married and she was a teenager, ten years younger than he. Now, she'd grown up and had been seeing Rod Stewart when she bumped into Ted again; they became a couple.

After Ted and Barbara divorced, Susie took over the Greenacres renovation. She began with public spaces in order to get the house ready for the planned April 1987 benefit for Joe Biden. She worked with John Picard, an architect and environmentalist who had just finished renovating The Knoll for Marvin Davis. They relandscaped and relit the whole property, reconfigured the driveway for limousines, planted rose gardens, and, inside, added air-conditioning, fifteenth- to seventeenth-century antiques and tapestries, and a twenty-seat dining table carved from one piece of wood. They also refinished the woodwork, floors, and beveled-glass windows, replaced tiles and fixtures in the bathrooms, and redid the kitchen entirely. Picard even came up with a plan to ensure that the 450 lightbulbs in the house could all be changed at once. The only parts of Dona Powell's renovation left untouched were the restored ceilings and wall paintings.

The renovations continued after the Biden party. Aware that Beverly Hills might run out of water, Harold Lloyd had built a huge underground water tank beneath the house; Susie turned it into a gym. The basement also held a new security room where nineteen closed-circuit cameras were monitored, along with an elaborate electronic defense system. Field's guards were armed.[33] Nearby were Ted's gym and a locked room with enough musical gear for a basement jam session. The Fields also installed a Wurlitzer merry-go-round, a pool, and, in an outbuilding, a seventy-seat screening room. *Vanity Fair* later psychologized that it all fit "the image of a rich boy . . . playing with his toys alone."

Ted Field and Susie Bollman were married at Greenacres in September 1987, six months after Barbara filed for divorce, and at least as many months after Susie took over the renovations. Susie then gave birth to two daughters—one that November, the second in March 1989. In 1988, Ted had added to his real estate collection, trading a 14,000-square-foot house complete with indoor swimming pool in Aspen, an unfinished $7 million New York townhouse, and some cash for a larger Aspen house just off the

Little Nell ski run, two nearby condos, and four Jeeps in a deal valued at $30 million. Ted would shortly add the house next door to his Aspen holdings. Field's broker Moskopoulos, who would do a dozen deals with him over the years, considered him the biggest real estate client in the world and compared him to the young Howard Hughes, another wealthy heir with a taste for movies, mansions, and young girls.

The next year, Field bought a Paul Williams six-bedroom mansion on an acre adjoining the Bel-Air Country Club from Joan Rivers for $5 million for his ex-wife Barbara and their adopted daughter, and a new ten-acre ranch in the Malibu hills from the actor Michael Landon for Susie and himself for about $6 million. His extended family was all within driving distance—first wife Judy and their daughter lived in Bel Air in a $3.5 million mansion he'd bought for them. Then, in spring 1990, Susie, pregnant with their third child, filed for divorce. "We sort of grew apart," she says, "but we were only apart for a week and a half. We stayed married the next four [years]."

Back together, for the moment, they "realized we had too many houses," Susie continues. "Can you imagine having five maids on at a time, three security guards, secretaries in the house? It's not a whole lot of fun to walk downstairs and have to say 'Hello, good morning, how are you?' and chit-chat with six people before you get to the breakfast room."

So Ted put Greenacres on the market for $55 million and offered his Aspen compound for sale, too, for $29 million. He bought a modern house on Mountain Drive—directly behind Neil McCarthy's former mansion and across the street from the one once owned by Dolly Green—for Susie and her brood for about $12 million, though the estranged couple continued to live together in Greenacres, and Moskopoulos reported they were "on very good terms" and "dating each other." In fact, by late summer, when a *Vanity Fair* writer came to visit for an extraordinarily out-of-character profile of Ted, the divorce was off, even though "only a month earlier, Susie's hard-to-shock Hollywood girlfriends could be found trading stories of flagrant infidelities on Ted's part," and "Green Acres [*sic*] had come to seem too big, too much—a symbol for all that had troubled their marriage."

Vanity Fair also said that it was well known among Ted's friends that he wanted a boy after four girls; the couple had just learned their third child would be his fifth daughter. "The game is, she who has the first son wins," a friend of Ted's told writer Michael Shnayerson. "It's Henry VIII time." Susie hoped to have "two more children in quick succession, the hope being that both [would] be boys." The pull of primogeniture was strong. "He really did want a son," says Susie now, "but he loved his daughters."

Shnayerson, who got curious about Field when he put Greenacres on the market, suspects he may have been invited in to help sell the house ("No," says Susie) or else because the "very stiff and uncomfortable" Field, while still producing hit movies at a steady clip (*Bill & Ted's Excellent Adventure* and *Bird on a Wire*) had just launched a new venture—Interscope Records, a partnership with Warner Music's Atlantic Group—with the brilliant rock producer Jimmy Iovine in the top creative role. ("Maybe," Susie says.) Interscope was seen as a bid to create a nineties version of David Geffen's Geffen Records, an independent, noncorporate label that had just been sold for $550 million. It would be five years before Internet connections became commonplace, and the music business was still vital and promising. Ted was bidding to be a full-fledged entertainment mogul—and outdo Howard Hughes. Marshall V suggested to Shnayerson that Ted was running as fast as he could to stay ahead of the manic-depression that felled their father at Ted's age. He certainly had inherited the manic part.

By 1993, Ted had sired a sixth daughter and shed third wife Susie. They'd moved into the Mountain Drive house together for about a year, she says, then got divorced. "Nothing bad went on," she repeats. "Ted is like my brother. We had a lot of good years. It was amicable." Postdivorce, Susie moved out of town and Ted returned to the still-unsold Greenacres.

He had meanwhile demolished, rebuilt, and offloaded his Malibu home for about $8 million and, with Iovine, turned Interscope Records into a pop powerhouse; its first recording went gold and in its first year it released a Marky Mark and the Funky Bunch album that went platinum and signed Tupac Shakur, Nine Inch Nails, 4 Non Blondes, and No Doubt. In its second year, Iovine and Field helped finance Suge Knight and his producer-partner Dr. Dre's Death Row Records, and agreed to distribute the label's releases. Dre's *The Chronic* would shortly go triple platinum; it introduced Snoop Dogg, who immediately became one of West Coast hip hop's biggest stars. By 1994, shock rocker Marilyn Manson had joined Interscope's stable too.

Iovine and Field's choices shocked American families as Ted had shocked his own. Ted justified the often obscene and angry acts he recorded with paeans to their art and resolute comments on free expression—consistent with the progressive agenda that guided his political contributions. His acts were also popular and profitable, and Field enjoyed outraging powerful elements of the emerging conservative movement in America.

Field apparently had problems by this stage, though their precise nature is unclear. Sue Lloyd was told Field "had a breakdown and stayed in Harold's private quarters," refusing to leave his bedroom. She also understood that he had some unspecified "money trouble." A severe real estate slump may have hurt him; the *Los Angeles Times* reported that he'd lost control of his leasehold on Murdock Plaza in May 1991 and then sold control of his film division, suggesting that "Field's empire is feeling the pinch from his spending so hugely over the last 2½ years to launch [his] record company."

"He was never in a crunch," insists Field's broker Moskopoulos. Susie Field agrees. "Wrong information," she says, laughing. "Ted doesn't lose anything. He went from $800 million to $1.2 billion within six months of our divorce. He scaled down on his properties because property values started to go down. He knows when to buy and he knows when to sell. Ted is the smartest man I've ever known."

But the purchaser of Greenacres, Ron Burkle, who'd made more than a billion dollars buying and selling supermarket chains, "bought it as much from the bank as from Ted," says someone close to that 1993 transaction, which followed a $16 million price drop. Burkle had ended up at Greenacres after failing to buy Enchanted Hill at 1363 Angelo Drive, the house the cowboy star Fred Thomson and his screenwriter wife Frances Marion built after he was refused in Bel Air. Later owned by a mining magnate and then an engineer, the 120-acre, 10,000-square-foot estate in Benedict Canyon overlooking Beverly Hills had been designed by architect Wallace Neff. The seller refused Burkle and instead sold Enchanted Hill to Microsoft cofounder Paul Allen, who soon tore the immaculately preserved estate down to the ground.[34]

Whatever Ted Field's financial issues, they had no obvious effect on his business or his lifestyle in the years after he left Greenacres. His political career had hit its apogee shortly before when, in 1992, Barbra Streisand sang and Warren Beatty and Whoopi Goldberg were among the guests at his second presidential candidate's fund-raiser at Greenacres, this one for Bill Clinton, and a newly svelte Field sat for another of his rare interviews. He even allowed a reporter into his home, where a photo of him with Clinton was the first thing visitors saw upon entering the foyer. Clinton stood to Field's left in the picture; to his right was Tracy Tweed, a buxom blonde Canadian actress and five-time *Playboy* magazine model (and little sister of Playboy Playmate Shannon Tweed). She'd replaced Susie in Ted's affections, though not in his home; she always maintained her own residence, and though she'd go on to have several children with Field, including those long-desired twin boys conceived through expensive sperm-selection treatments that allow the sex of a child to be chosen, she never married him. He continues to support her, regardless, as he does all of his former wives. He is, one of them admits privately, their "meal ticket." And, however improbably, they have all become friends, says Susie Field.

Ted's ex-wives went with Ted and Tracy and stayed in nearby hotels when they traveled "so we could take the kids," Susie continues. Ted's first wife was in the room when Susie's third daughter was born, and Susie organized a wedding for one of Barbara's daughters and was a guest at the baby shower for Tweed's twins. "I know it sounds not normal," says Susie. "Other people have a lot of kids and they have animosity. Ted just didn't. He's logical . . . he's really easy to get along with, he's really funny, really great with kids, very generous, very giving in all ways. It's not odd to us."

In his interview with the *Times,* Field was in full roar, comparing the religious right in America to Nazis, and defending his campaign against Robert Bork, a Ronald Reagan appointee to the Supreme Court, calling him "the most dangerous kind of monster." That kind of talk and the kind of music Interscope promoted had put Field in the sights of then vice president Dan Quayle, who met with the daughter of a Texas state trooper who'd been shot by a fleeing suspect who was driving a stolen car and listening to Tupac Shakur's Interscope album, *2pacalypse Now.* The suspect claimed he only shot because the music had riled him up, leading Quayle to condemn its release as "an irresponsible corporate act." Pointing to Field's fund-raiser for Clinton as proof, he said, "Hollywood simply does not reflect our values."

The protests continued, along with talk of Interscope's over-the-top spending to sign up acts, after Clinton won the election and Field vacated Greenacres. Three of the company's stars were arrested on charges ranging from assault to murder, and though Field gave another interview to the *Times* in which he dismissed the criticism of rap as "plain old racism" and challenged his opponents to "kiss my ass," he also allowed that, henceforth, Interscope would be more careful. "There are some things we won't do here," Field promised, "and releasing lyrics that could be misunderstood to promote cop killing is one of them."

That didn't quell the criticism—and soon, conservative newspaper columnists were naming names of candidates Field supported and pushing the Time Warner conglomerate, which held a 50 percent stake in the company, to end its relationship with Interscope, which it did late in 1995, selling its share back to Iovine and Field for a reported $115 million. The next year, they sold the record company to Polygram, which had already bought the rest of Field's film division. Iovine and Field were named cochairmen of the company. Field kept that title until 2001.

In the intervening years, Field, in his forties, was the rare denizen of the Platinum Triangle who sold his trophy mansion *before* indulging in a second (or in Field's case, perhaps, third) adolescence. In the midnineties, he embraced his late bachelorhood with pride. Field's most notorious behavior was chronicled in *Once More with Feeling*, that account of Hollywood party girls and prostitutes. One, who called herself Lisa, wrote that the still-married Field was her very first "date" as a high-end call girl. For $1,000, she and a more experienced practitioner (who got $1,500) met Field at an apartment he kept for these purposes and alternated providing him with oral sex for a half hour. "Ted was soft-spoken, a gentleman," she wrote. "Over the years I've heard that he uses call girls regularly, but he only wants women who are in their early twenties. I never saw him again, but for me, Ted Field was an easy way to start out in the business."

Field's alleged taste for paid sex would be in the spotlight again years later when author-blogger Mark Ebner published a story on the Internet about Field and Ron Burkle, the buyer of Greenacres, claiming they shared a Steve Powers–like figure who found young women for them. Ebner quoted a retired prostitute, Elizabeth Jawhary, who claimed the two liked "to watch girls get it on, or get hand jobs or blow jobs. They wouldn't have intercourse because they were afraid of AIDS." A spokesman for Burkle denied the story but didn't ask Ebner to retract or remove it from the Internet. Ebner says he never heard from Ted Field.

Though the sale of Greenacres was said to be the end of the public period of Ted Field's life, it was actually quite the opposite. In 1998, the *New York Times* was allowed to cover Field's private New Year's Eve party on a 190-foot yacht, *The Other Woman*, which he'd docked in the port of Gustavia on the French Caribbean island of St. Barthélemy. Field had arrived on the island with fifteen beautiful girls who lived with him on the boat and went with him everywhere.

In 1999 Field flew back to St. Barth on a rented Gulfstream II with the girl-finder and half a dozen models; he made Page Six when one of the girls allegedly jumped ship in favor of a neighboring boatload of Mexican moguls, and was sent back to Miami in punishment. The next year, the *New York Times* was back to cover Ted again, lauding his parties where "the ratio of women to men is usually about two to one." Field had rented Studio 54 for New Year's Eve and recreated it in its heyday for a night—though the "B list of boldfacers" the *Times* said Field attracted might not have passed Steve Rubell's muster. Field, then forty-seven, Monique P. Yazigi wrote, was "a huggy-bear figure" who spent the night on a black leather couch "where he was surrounded by five women who looked to be 18 to 23" and embodied "a cross between impeccable, preppy manners and studied contrariness." *Forbes* had lately estimated his wealth at $1.2 billion.

That figure would drop in the years to come after his next investment of time and money—to start a new record company in league with a dot-com. Within a year, it had lost $171 million and its stock price had plunged from $94 to $10. The good news, Field said, was that Marshall V had called and asked to buy some stock. "That probably meant more to me than any compliment I've gotten," Ted said. It's estimated he lost $100 million when the company effectively collapsed, but he could afford the loss.

Field continued buying, selling, and moving between houses (including the house on Mountain Drive, which he lost money on, according to a realtor, and a six-level ten-bedroom house above Sunset Strip in the Hollywood hills that he bought from boxer Mike Tyson for a reported $6 million; it was later sold to Carlos Boozer of the Utah Jazz, who rented it to Prince) and making more movies through Radar Pictures, a new company that made remakes of *The Amityville Horror, The Texas Chainsaw Massacre,* and *The Heartbreak Kid,* as well as *The Last Samurai* and *The Chronicles of Riddick.* He continues to dream of running a fully integrated entertainment company. He still goes to nightclubs occasionally. But he visits with his kids by Tweed every single day.

Once described as a weirdo and wild man—albeit behind his back—Ted Field has settled down, at least a little. One business partner describes him as "fiercely loyal, smart and decent." Still churning out movies at an astounding rate, he's become one of the most prolific producers in Hollywood, though he's returned to operating under the radar. He can still afford to live wherever he wants. To his credit, he now chooses to do so out of the spotlight.

46

Beverly Hills

Grayhall (1100 Carolyn Way)

By the 1990s, extraordinary success had become the key prerequisite for entry to the Platinum Triangle. Mark Hughes, who'd bought Lionsgate from Kenny Rogers in 1983, certainly had that. He also had a yen for, even perhaps an addiction to, trophy real estate. When he traded up and bought Grayhall from Philippe Boutboul in 1992, it was just a step up a ladder; he would eventually accumulate more, and even more impressive property. But he didn't keep any of it long. Despite a nine-figure fortune made peddling Herbalife, a weight-loss and nutrition program, many thought Hughes an epic phony, an odd but compelling amalgam of Anthony Norvell–style new age huckster and Cornfeld-esque pyramid scammer, cloaked in a George Hamilton tan.

At rallies and in the infomercials he used to fire up his sales force, Hughes would later spin a prepackaged legend of how he'd grown up in a poor Latino neighborhood, abandoned by his father and raised by grandparents while his overweight welfare mother ricocheted from one fad diet to the next, mixing amphetamines to lose weight with barbiturates to sleep, causing her death from an overdose when Mark was nineteen.

The truth was less clear-cut, certainly less inspirational for a weight-loss guru—but much more interesting. He was effectively born to a single mother; his parents separated before his birth and divorced before he was one, but she immediately remarried and he was raised by a successful businessman, Stuard

Hartman, who sold aircraft parts to the government. He moved his family to a ranch house in upper-middle-class Camarillo, northwest of the former Janss ranch that became wealthy Thousand Oaks, California. The family had a housekeeper, a Chris-Craft Constellation cruiser boat, and a gold Cadillac. His boyhood name, Mark Stuard Hartman, honored the provider of all that largesse. (After Hughes became a multimillionaire, Hartman would insist he was Mark's blood father, but when he was five and then again when he was seventeen, Mark's grandparents introduced him to a man they said was his real father, Jack Reynolds, a Hawaiian plumbing contractor. Hughes's second wife says Reynolds denied it at the time—but he would eventually embrace his son, or more precisely, his son's fortune.)

By the time Mark was a teenager, though, with two younger half-brothers, his family was in deep trouble. His mother didn't take speed to lose weight, but she was addicted to painkillers—Darvon and Percodan—and so lost in a drugged haze she couldn't care for her sons or their home. Late in 1969, after she had a seizure, she left Hartman and returned to her hometown with her younger children, leaving Mark with her parents. A few months later, she filed for divorce, but was so debilitated, spending her days in bed, she was unable to attend hearings in the case. Though Hartman won custody of Mark's brothers, Mark stayed with his mother, and for the rest of his life would blame his stepfather for the breakup of his family. Anguished and uncontrolled, Mark took to drinking wine and popping pills, and was "completely out of control," a childhood friend later told the *Los Angeles Times*.

Shortly before Hughes's mother died of acute drug intoxication, in the words of the coroner, sixteen-year-old Mark, "a little delinquent" by his own account, was confined in a reform school. Fortunately for him, it was a progressive one that turned his life around and planted the seeds for his later success in business. Founded by a veteran of Synanon, a cultlike drug rehabilitation program that inspired countless self-help, recovery, and therapy groups, CEDU was a boarding school that attempted to reprogram its young charges through behavior modification, help them see and believe in themselves, and instill a work ethic that would allow them to emerge from their substance-abuse problems and recreate their lives. Mark Hartman became a star pupil.

Mark's imagination was fired by the school's fund-raising efforts, in which students dressed up in suits and ventured into well-to-do Southland neighborhoods, going door to door, explaining CEDU's program and using themselves as inspirational examples, all with the singular aim of leaving with a check. They quite accurately called it hustling. According to the Hughes legend, he even managed to get $500 out of Ronald Reagan, newly arrived in Bel Air from his two terms as governor of California. As an incentive, the CEDU students were allowed to keep 5 percent of what they raised. Mark liked the school so much, he stayed on at CEDU as a paid staffer after graduating. Compared to his broken family, it may have been a better place.

CEDU replaced Mark's need to get high with a desire to get rich quick. And he certainly did. After a last year at CEDU, he went to work for a so-called multilevel direct sales operation called Seyforth Laboratories, selling a liquid protein called Slender Now that was touted as a miracle cure for the overweight. The organization was structured somewhat like Cornfeld's IOS: Salesmen received no salaries or commissions, but instead bought products at a discount and not only sold them for a profit but recruited family, friends, and strangers as subdistributors, earning larger discounts when they sold larger volumes as well as getting a cut from sales generated by their networks.

Mark had learned to pitch at CEDU. At Seyforth, he learned how to build a money-making pyramid, and when it failed in 1979, he joined Golden Youth, run by Larry Stephen Huff, a direct-sales pioneer, who'd gotten his start with another similar organization that went out of business after it was sued by the SEC and found guilty of deceptive sales practices. When Golden Youth collapsed a year later, Hughes, undeterred, struck out on his own. To mark the occasion, he changed his name, grafting his birth father's last and his mother's maiden names together to become Mark Reynolds Hughes.

Now twenty-four, he approached the manufacturer of Slender Now's protein, vitamin, and herbal products, a former drug salesman, and suggested they go into business together; his concept was to pitch the supplements as a blend of Eastern secrets and Western science. In an interview with Howard Libes for the book *Among the Mansions of Eden,* the manufacturer recalled that Hughes, with his toothy salesman's smile, mesmerizing brown eyes, Prince Valiant haircut, and neon blue suit, looked like a drug dealer dressed up to go to court. He declined Hughes's offer to become his partner, but signed on as his exclusive supplier, creating and manufacturing the products. Thus, early in 1980, Herbalife was born.

Four years later, when Mark and his first wife, a former Miss Santa Monica whom he'd met on the beach the year before the launch, divorced, she claimed they'd founded the company together with a financial assist from her parents, and that they'd created the "new" Herbalife formula by adding herbs to an already existing weight-loss product. "He wanted to make money," she said. "He really didn't care about helping people. If the business hadn't suc-ceeded, he would have gone into real estate." At the time of their divorce, Hughes edited her out of his company biography.

By then, he was rich. Though he began selling his potions out of the trunk of his Cadillac through his only salesman, a former hotel bellhop, sales rose 100,000 percent in Herbalife's first five years. Besides owning 54 per-cent of the company, Hughes's cut of gross sales totaled $1 million a month. But he wasn't satisfied. "Nothing was ever enough for him—money, clothes, cars," his ex told *People* magazine. He'd sit in bed with a calculator, obsessing over his finances. "It was as if somehow having all the money would make his childhood all right," she said.

In 1984, when Hughes married his second wife, a twenty-three-year-old Swedish beauty queen whom he'd met when she passed him a note in a Hollywood disco, he hired the comedian David Steinberg, Wayne Newton, and Doc Severinsen and the *Tonight Show* orchestra to entertain their three hundred guests, many of them flown in from Sweden at his expense. By then, he wore $1,500 Brioni suits from Bijan and custom-designed jewelry, and owned four cars, including two Rolls Royces, as well as Kenny Rogers' former mansion Lionsgate (to which he added a disco, a game room, and a gazebo with an elevator). All of this wealth on display came from Herbalife, which had now moved to its own high-rise near Los Angeles International Airport. The regimen put users on one 1,000-calorie meal a day, with other meals replaced by two glasses of skim milk, protein powder, and a dozen herbal pills; the program cost about $300 a month and had a million adher-ents and, Hughes claimed, seven hundred thousand distributors. He'd also added treatments for everything from cellulite, age spots, and varicose veins to arthritis, herpes, and irregular menstruation.

Hughes had attracted critics, too: Pharmacologists said he was basically hawking laxatives, diuretics, and caffeine; the FDA declared that two of Hughes's herbs were unsafe (they were removed); Canada's Department of Health claimed Herbalife had committed two dozen violations of its Food and Drugs Act; and the California government sued him for making false claims and operating a pyramid scam. A Senate subcommittee held hearings at which some of his former acolytes said they'd been suckered, and one widow blamed her husband's death on Herbalife's pills and powders. Hughes

defended his products by attacking the scientific experts who appeared before the panel. "If they're such experts, then why are they fat?" he asked. But
in those troubled months, almost eight hundred employees were laid off or
furloughed.

Hughes blamed the setbacks on the media and the food and medical
industries, claiming Herbalife had hurt them and they were just striking
back. He got still richer. *Inc.* magazine declared Herbalife the fastest-growing
private company in America and its founder a "honey-tongued spellbinder."
The *Los Angeles Times* would later describe his sales rallies as "part revival
meeting, part Richard Simmons–style pep talk, part the Apostle Paul finding his vocation as a missionary." Hughes flaunted his wealth along with
his well-manicured life story to inspire others to try and emulate him. "He
could cry on command" when he told his false story about his mother, his
manufacturer recalled. "I watched him do it in a thousand performances, in
the exact same part of the presentation, every time." Inside the company,
the word *herbalized* was coined to describe the effect of Mark's mesmerizing
performances on audiences.

Wife number two didn't buy into the program, though she did like to
spend Mark's money; the marriage ended after a year and she returned to
Sweden. Like Mark's mother, she had a substance-abuse problem, and her
drinking would eventually kill her. That loss hardly slowed Hughes down.
He was usually on the road three weeks a month, working crowds and glad-
handing distributors. In 1986, he settled the charges with California by paying an $850,000 fine and took the company public, retaining 74 percent
of the stock. And then he refocused Herbalife on international expansion,
moving into Europe, New Zealand, Israel, and Mexico.

By 1985, Hughes had found his third beauty queen in a Sunset Boulevard restaurant. Suzan Schroder was a former Miss Hawaiian Tropic runner-
up and Miss Petite USA who'd gone on to found her own court-reporting
company. Mark married his latest blonde in fall 1987 and she sold her company to be his full-time wife. Mark's father, Jack Reynolds, the plumbing
contractor, attended the ceremony after Suzan reunited them, sending them
to Maui on vacation together just before the wedding. She did that even
though she remains unsure if Reynolds really was his father.

Suzan says Herbalife was in the red at that moment, losing $12 million a
month. That may be true, since Mark put Lionsgate on the market for $12
million, quickly selling it to Marvin Davis. They moved into a rental on

Benedict Canyon Drive. Suzan claims credit for creating new weight loss and skin care products that "exploded," she says. In 1987, thinking of starting a family and wanting to get out of Beverly Hills, Mark bought five acres on the ocean south of L.A. airport, and started planning a house there. But in the next two years, "we grew up a little bit," she continues, and they decided to move back to the Triangle. They left their rental for a $6.5 million spec house on Doheny Drive, north of Sunset.

To ensure he could pay for it all, Mark also made a deal with his old boss Larry Huff to amp up his distribution network after domestic sales of Herbalife products plummeted from $400 million in 1985 to $42 million in 1991. Huff was but one figure from his past who'd joined Herbalife; several of his executives were friends from reform school. But Huff's hiring in 1990 raised eyebrows, since he had recently been released from federal prison, where he'd served two years for his part in yet another Ponzi scheme that bilked twenty-seven thousand victims.

Nonetheless, it did seem that Hughes might be settling down. In December 1991, he and Suzan had a son they named Alexander. But the following October, Hughes decided to move again and bought Grayhall from Boutboul, who'd just completed a $10 million high-tech renovation. Boutboul and Hughes were introduced by Marvin and Barbara Davis at The Knoll. "Mark likes to look at homes; it's his hobby," says Suzan. "They started talking about real estate and I'm going, 'Oh, no.'" Boutboul invited Mark and Suzan to see Grayhall—"the first and only visitors." Mark said, "I want it." Suzan says, "I thought it was way too grand. I didn't want to move, but you know, you go along."

Mark offered Boutboul his house on Doheny Road, "and also land and cash and stock and whatever," Boutboul says. "I had no choice. That's the way they wanted to do the deal," which the *Los Angeles Times* later valued at $20 million. Hughes's house on Doheny was sold to Sharon and "Ozzy" Osbourne, who filmed their MTV reality TV show there in 2002. It was later sold to Christina Aguilera.

Hughes soon expanded his new estate, buying three adjoining properties for a total of 2.5 acres. One was knocked down, one became a guesthouse, and a third was later turned into a dojo for their son. "I had to make twenty-two thousand square feet a warm home," says Suzan. "I made it the belle of the ball in Beverly Hills." She and Mark "spent hours and hours shopping all over the world." Inside the main house, they mixed traditional paintings and tapestries with carved wood antiques, gilt mirrors, brass cupids, and sphinxes. There was also a fifty-extension in-house intercom system. Writer David Weddle, who later toured the house, noted shelves full of books on the rich and their pursuits, and family photographs everywhere that, he wrote, "look too perfect, the colors too vibrant, the wardrobe too well pressed, the smiles and embraces too perfectly posed."

Suzan's relationship with Mark looked good on the surface, too, and in that, it mirrored Herbalife throughout the nineties. The company moved to expensive new quarters in Century City in 1995. Gross sales climbed throughout the decade, hitting $1.49 billion in 1997, and Mark continued to rake in millions, but net profits were not rising as fast and the same problems that undermined Herbalife in America began to affect it in other countries as well. Sales would spike when Herbalife entered a market, then decline rapidly as its products failed to live up to their promise.

Mark had also started to show the strain of always appearing to be perfect. He refused to discuss his family history, even with those closest to him, flaring angrily when Suzan tried to broach the subject. And when one of his brothers died from the effects of years of drinking in 1994, one year younger than their mother had been when she died, Mark revealed more scars after the funeral. Inviting Stuard Hartman back to Grayhall, he gave the man who'd raised him a tour of the property, then turned to his surviving brother. "I showed him," he said. "I showed that bastard what I could do."

Two years later, Mark got a taste of what his decades of denial had done to him. Just after Thanksgiving 1996, he was pulled over by police for driving on the wrong side of the road en route to a strip club and failed a sobriety test, with an alcohol level in his blood three times higher than the legal limit. He pled no contest, was sentenced to three years' probation and a $1,500 fine, briefly lost his license to drive, and was ordered to attend an alcohol-education program. Three months later, he was arrested again in Malibu, reportedly drunk, but he'd only be charged for vehicle infractions and the misdemeanor of driving without a license. It would later emerge that Hughes had been drinking for several years and had been put on a drug that inhibits alcohol cravings, though only when coupled with a recovery program. Hughes, of course, could not risk being seen at Alcoholics Anonymous meetings.

By then, Suzan Hughes had had enough. That showed in an article in *Cosmopolitan* early in 1997 called "The Really, Really Rich Wives Club."

Grayhall, she told the magazine, was "my husband's dream house, that's why we live here." She also said she hated "the feeling of having no reason to get out of bed in the morning" in the cavernous place with its huge full-time staff, who left her feeling "always under siege."

But Mark wasn't ready to stop. He bought a 157-acre mountaintop high above Beverly Hills at the top of Tower Grove Drive. One of the last huge parcels of undeveloped land in the city, it had been owned in turn by Princess Ashraf Pahlavi, the twin sister of the late shah of Iran, and then, in 1987, Merv Griffin, who'd bought it the same year he acquired the Beverly Hilton, planning to build a 58,000-square-foot home for himself and subdivide the rest of the property into five more estates. After grading fourteen acres, promising to donate 104 acres to the Santa Monica Mountains Conservancy, and winning approval for a subdivision on the rest of the land, Griffin had changed his mind and put it on the market in 1989 for $25 million. When a recession hit, he dropped the price, which eventually fell to $11 million. Hughes finally paid $8.5 million, still a record for an undeveloped home site in the Southland. He started planning his largest house yet, a $50 million, 45,000-square-foot Italianate castle with a sixty-five-foot tower, twenty-five principal rooms, a million-gallon lake, a pool house, tennis pavilion, and guesthouse. He'd wanted even bigger. Suzan says she talked him down. "We'd reached his goal—a billion dollars," she says. "I thought it would bring a change."

It did. Herbalife stock was at $37 when she filed for divorce in September. "It wasn't working," she said. "It was my call. He wanted a bigger and better home. I knew I'd be in charge. That was not how I wanted to spend my days. You can have too much. He wanted to keep building. I wanted more time together. We didn't need anything. When do you stop to enjoy yourself?" The divorce took seven months; Suzan continued to live at Grayhall, but moved out as soon as it was final.

She says it was amicable, and they shared joint custody of their son. In exchange for $10 million cash, $120,000 a year in child support, and $400,000 a year in spousal support, Suzan agreed to keep silent about her ex. "I didn't take a salt shaker. I got enough. I'm happy. I left him Maui, Grayhall, the yacht, our furniture. I had the memories in my mind. I move on." She bought a $3.95 million mansion out of foreclosure five blocks away on Beverly Drive. "The house was called Sunshine," she says.

During the divorce process, Hughes had revealed that he planned to reduce his holdings in Herbalife and its stock price collapsed, dropping as low as $6. Hughes also gave a 50 percent discount on stock options to his corporate cronies, infuriating regular shareholders, who sued. That's when his longtime supplier suggested to several of his closest friends he be forced into rehab in Switzerland, but the plan blew up when one of them told Hughes about it. Hughes's plan to sell his stock was reconfigured to be more palatable to shareholders—he eventually got $18 a share for five million shares.

Mark and Suzan had started a foundation to help children, and two weeks after she filed for divorce, a mutual friend introduced her to the so-called Muscles from Brussels, the Belgian action-film star Jean-Claude Van Damme, who was starting a foundation himself and wanted advice, she says. After a first meeting, he started coming by their home often, just ringing the doorbell, and talking about more than charity. "I didn't like him," she says. He told her ugly stories about his wife. "I disbelieved him," she continues. "Nobody could be that bad." Three months later, the same friend set Mark up on a blind date with Van Damme's wife. "I don't think it was a coincidence," says Suzan.

Darcy Lynn LaPier Van Damme had been married three times, but still had the glow of youth, despite the miles she'd traveled since leaving the farm in Portland, Oregon, where she was raised by a full-blooded Cree father and a half-Cherokee, half-French mother. Like Hughes, she quit school, either in ninth grade or after tenth (sources differ). Then, she had breast enlargement surgery and started entering beauty pageants, winning local titles like Miss Miller Lite and Miss Portland International Raceway before rising to become a Miss Hawaiian Tropic, just like Suzan Hughes.

According to a *Details* magazine profile, her new breasts had been paid for by the local Portland boy she'd married in 1986. LaPier denies that marriage. "People have always said that, but no," she insists. But writer Nina Burleigh found court records indicating that her first husband had charged she was addicted to cocaine and had even used it in the powerful smokable form known as free-base. LaPier denied that, too, claiming the profile writer was repeating tabloid gossip.

She does admit to two marriages before she met Hughes. The first, when she was nineteen, was to Ron Rice, the founder of the Hawaiian Tropic suntan oil company, who was more than twice her age. They had a million-dollar wedding with two thousand guests at the Daytona Marriott in Florida, redecorated as a medieval castle for the occasion. The wedding followed the

1990 birth of their son. But the marriage didn't last and by 1993, "I wanted to live," she told *Talk* magazine. So when she had the chance, she seduced Van Damme, breaking up both their marriages in the process. Burleigh wrote that it was only then that Ron Rice discovered she'd never finalized her divorce from her first husband—and had their union annulled. She apparently completed that unfinished divorce as she then married Van Damme and had a son with him. But their life together was marred by constant distance, allegations of drug use, drinking, violence, homosexuality on Van Damme's part and infidelity on LaPier's, and three separate divorce filings, all of which left Van Damme publicly yearning to reunite with his first wife, a fellow bodybuilder. LaPier finally left for good in 1997, returning briefly to Rice and thinking she was washed up at thirty-three.

She wasn't. After their first date, Hughes took her to see Grayhall, but they never made it, so furiously were they kissing in his Rolls. "It was kind of love at first sight," she says. They finally made it to the house on a later date. "He took me through it," she says. "It was unbelievable. The ballroom was so beautiful. He explained that the dining room was a registered museum piece. He took me to the tunnel [to Pickfair] and showed me where it was blocked off." A cruise on his yacht to the south of France followed.

Mark and Darcy were married in church on Valentine's Day 1999. Mark flew in seven hundred thousand South American roses for the ceremony. Afterwards, a reception for five hundred was held in a tent in Grayhall's courtyard. The pool was tented, too, and a mammoth igloo was created within, with a stage, bar, and barstools made of ice.

Darcy moved into Grayhall, though she says Mark mostly used the big house for meetings. "He entertained there because the basis of Herbalife was Mark himself, that you could live like Mark," she says. "He'd bring in the top distributors for parties as a reward." Darcy says Hughes was trying to stop being a workaholic. Was trying, in other words, to become the man Suzan had wanted him to be. "I was told he didn't know how to relax but when we met, the company was at a point where he could relax and enjoy life," Darcy says. So he preferred to live in the guesthouse because "it was not so vast," she says. "It was more homey."

Mark demolished his son's dojo and "brought in trees native to Oregon because I missed it," Darcy says. "He made it as close to Oregon as he could for me." He loved remodeling. "Every house Mark had was being remodeled," one of his real estate attorneys said, "and he cared about every detail."

Darcy had also decided Grayhall was haunted. She was often spooked by slamming doors and the sense that "someone was crossing the landing," she says. "One time, I was watching a movie and I heard a noise upstairs." The glass shower enclosure had mysteriously shattered.

Suzan Hughes wasn't haunting the house but she did haunt Darcy's life, and vice versa. She was convinced Darcy wanted to gain custody of her son. Nina Burleigh revealed that in court documents, Darcy charged Suzan with libeling and stalking her. In fact, she'd hired a notorious private detective, Anthony Pellicano, who'd taped some of Mark's phone calls. Suzan was also alleged to have called Mark's vacation home in Maui during the couple's engagement and accused Darcy of raping her son and using cocaine. Darcy's lawyers threatened Suzan with police and litigation in return.

Just after Mark and Darcy's wedding, the Hugheses' future neighbors beneath their mountaintop went to the Los Angeles zoning commission to protest his building plans. Though he'd already adjusted the plans, removed a ballroom, and reduced the size and height of the house, they pointed to vast entrance foyers with separate men's and women's bathrooms, and what appeared to be office space, arguing that he really wanted a business showplace even grander than Grayhall. They hoped to stop construction. He invited some of the neighbors to Grayhall for a party, but that didn't impress them. One guest told a reporter he looked waxen under makeup, and had obviously dyed hair.

Hughes's plans were being disrupted by more than a neighborhood protest. He had two bouts of pneumonia early in 2000 and was taking steroids that disrupted his sleep. And he couldn't stop working after all; the company was not at a point where he could step back. Sales were slowing in some countries, competition rising in others. Herbalife was sending uncertain signals to Wall Street, and the stock was dropping again. In August, Hughes launched an attempt to take the company private using $500 million in borrowed money. The buyback effort faltered in the market and was extended several times. Hughes had haggled hard to get the deal and word of his machinations and self-dealing had leaked out—Herbalife's share price fell to $4.

As the deal foundered, Mark kept spending pathologically, buying a huge mansion on seven acres with three hundred feet of private beach at Malibu from the widow of the founder of Harrah's casino. He paid about $25 million. He'd also finally gotten permission to build on Tower Grove after downsizing his castle a bit further and agreeing to donate a hundred acres to the Conservancy. Mark sold his existing Malibu house, which had only ninety feet of beach, for $8 million, put Grayhall on the market, and he and Darcy moved to the new Malibu place full time after it was decorated in lightning speed—trucks full of antiques pulling into the driveway, where Mark stood, buying the things he liked. There were no offers on Grayhall, though. "Houses like that, only a few people can buy," Darcy says.

"I can't believe what's happened with all this," Mark had sobbed on cue that February—the twentieth anniversary of Herbalife, which Hughes celebrated onstage at the L.A. Forum arena. There was an oxygen tank stashed backstage in case he needed it. Two months later, he'd drop his bid to go private because of "financing difficulties," said Reuters News. A junk bond sale designed to aid Hughes's effort was cancelled.

Life went on. Mark and Darcy decided to try and have a child, and Mark started spending longer hours at home. In May, there was a party to celebrate Mark's grandmother's eighty-seventh birthday at the new house in Malibu. Mark had some glasses of white wine, and then when the guests all left, kicked off his shoes and had a cigar. Darcy went to bed on her office couch where she sometimes slept because Mark snored. The next morning, she walked into their bedroom to wake him. He was on their four-poster bed in black bikini briefs and a black T-shirt, looking unusually white for a preternaturally tan man. Darcy called their security guards—Mark Hughes was dead.

An autopsy found he'd died accidentally from mixing an antidepressant with alcohol. His blood alcohol level was two and a half times the legal limit for driving. It was said he'd been on a four-day drinking binge. After his death, Darcy insisted he was not a drinker.

Mark had signed a will amendment a few months before giving Darcy $10 million within forty-five days of his death. "I wish they'd look into it more," says Suzan Hughes. "They decided they couldn't get a jury to convict." Convict who? "Who do you think?" she continues.

The mountaintop property went up for sale quickly for $35 million and would eventually be sold for $23.75 million to a businessman from Atlanta. A first attempt to develop it went into Chapter 11 bankruptcy, but with the help of $7 million in financing provided by the Hughes estate, the Atlanta still hopes to market six estates there. Darcy stayed in Malibu for a while, summered as a guest of Barron Hilton's son Rick and his wife Kathy, Paris Hilton's parents, in New York's Hamptons, where gossip columns chronicled her public displays of affection with various men, then moved to Grayhall, while she tried to get an additional $30 million from Mark's estate. But early in 2001, she gave up, announced she didn't want to raise her kids in a city, and moved back to Oregon where she married again and is now a professional barrel racer at rodeos. She also breeds and trains barrel-racing horses. "I'm a full-fledged cowgirl," she says. "I rope and ride." She eventually roped $35 million from Hughes's estate.

Although some of its executives broke ranks and revealed corporate intrigues after Hughes's death—including his supplier, who sued for breach of contract—Herbalife continued under his closest cronies and was eventually sold to two venture capital firms for $685 million. It continues and thrives.

Suzan Hughes spent years in litigation with her ex-husband's estate, trying to wrest money and property for her son from the $254 million Mark Hughes Family Trust, which is run—she says mismanaged—by two of those Herbalife cronies and Mark's putative father Jack Reynolds. Hughes designed the trust to ensure that Alex would inherit only when he turned thirty-five, though he is entitled to a third of its income and a $35 million payment at twenty-five and two-thirds of the income at age thirty. "They got the goldmine and [Alex] got the shaft," Suzan's lawyer said. "Her wealth apparently falls short of what she believes she is entitled to," the trust's attorneys responded drily.

Trustees sold the Malibu house for $30 million in 2001 and Grayhall went on the market for $29 million after Darcy left. By late 2003, the price had dropped to $18.9 million. That's when Bernie Cornfeld's ex-wife Lorraine toured it with a broker. "I couldn't breathe," she says. "The vibrations were so heavy. I couldn't finish the tour. I had to get out of there." It was finally sold in March 2004 for under $18 million. The buyers were a Middle Eastern couple, Moussa and Mahnaz Mehdizadeh.

Beverly Hills

Ghazi Aita wasn't the first wealthy Middle Easterner to buy a high-profile home in the Platinum Triangle. Nine months before he bought 141 South Carolwood, Mohammed al-Fassi had purchased the onetime Max Whittier estate on Sunset Boulevard; he and the house almost immediately became media sensations and set off a social and legal tragicomedy that has faded from public notice but may never reach a conclusion.

Al-Fassi bought the estate from a Swiss corporation that hid the identity of the man who'd owned it since 1974, Dino Fabbri, a Milanese publisher and art collector who owned homes around the world. Like Dino De Laurentiis, who came to Los Angeles around the same time, Fabbri had come west from Italy, but unlike his Roman countryman, the Milanese multimillionaire had only a vague intention of moving to Los Angeles and venturing into moviemaking. "He bought it not to live in it, but to restore it," thinks his third wife and widow Wendy Fabbri Pagan. "He loved to restore white elephants. He collected art and houses." Beverly Hills had long been on his list of possible acquisitions.

Fabbri and his two brothers shared a passion for books and had started a publishing house after World War II. By the time it was sold in 1971, they'd built a classics- and art-publishing empire from a base of textbooks and serialized encyclopedias sold on newsstands like magazines. On finding the Whittier estate, Dino turned his formidable energies toward renovating it, spending $1.3 million on the house and grounds and another $9 million on Louis XV furniture. He had a peculiar distaste for bathtubs, so one of his innovations was to hide them all behind walls or under floors that slid away at the push of a button. He covered the walls in velvet to highlight his collection of Old Masters and added a new pool tiled to resemble a lake. But when the house was robbed while he was in Europe, "he was very upset by it," says his widow, and never moved in.

"He was quite a playboy, though he would have hated my saying that," Wendy continues. "He enjoyed his life. He never lived in any of his houses. He loved to keep moving and pass by." His second wife, a Ford model he met on an airplane, had a stroke at age twenty-eight. "He sold the house due to her illness," her successor says. He put the house on the market in 1976. When it hadn't sold a year later, "Dino finally flew to L.A. for less than a week and said, 'I'll take anyone. I'm in a hurry,'" she continues. "The first or second caller was al-Fassi. He arrived with cash in a briefcase." Though a newspaper reported the sale price was just under $2.5 million, she recalls Fabbri, who met and married her a few years later, saying it was "a very poor sale" of $1.5 million that closed early in 1978. And the subsequent fate of the house did nothing to make up for that loss: It became a laughingstock.

Mohammed al-Fassi was the eldest son of a sort of holy man in Morocco who moved to Saudi Arabia to open "an unusual one-man church" that attracted "malcontents from smaller tribes dispossessed by the ruling Saud family," said *People* magazine. Dr. Sheikh, as he was known, was soon jailed by Saudi King Faisal and in a rather clever response, the doctor's wife maneuvered Mohammed's sister Hindi into the orbit of Turki bin Abdul Aziz al-Saud, a son of Saudi Arabia's founder Ibn Saud and a minister in Faisal's government, with the hope of making a match.

Though her plan worked and Turki fell in love with Hindi, he couldn't marry an enemy of the king, so instead he took her and her family under his wing, and for the next seven years, they lived a nomadic existence, moving among the great cities and resorts of the world on private planes, taking whole floors of hotels wherever they went, and freely spending Turki's seemingly limitless cash. Though still a teenager, Mohammed became the traveling caravan's purser. Then, in 1975, when Faisal was assassinated and replaced by Turki's half-brother, Dr. Sheikh was not only released from prison, he went into business with the Saud family, and Turki finally married

Hindi. The al-Fassis were now not just rich, but royal. Turki gave young Mo-hammed control of his finances and, *People* magazine's William McWhirter wrote, his "lifestyle began to rival the prince's."

The entourage was living in London when Mohammed met an Italian student working as a salesgirl in a clothing shop in 1975. Though Diana Bilinelli was only sixteen and the daughter of a coal miner, Mohammed fol-lowed her home to Milan and asked for her hand in marriage. She converted to Islam and they were married a year later, first in a Muslim ceremony in Saudi Arabia and then a civil one in their new home, Los Angeles. Sheikha Dena, as she was henceforth called, enrolled at a Catholic High School while Mohammed took business courses and opened a local branch of Al-Fassi Trading, his family's shipping, construction, and commodities company.

Mohammed and Dena lived in a $200-a-month apartment at first, but after having two children, they bought the onetime Whittier estate and moved into the Beverly Hilton while renovating. They built a mosque and installed kennels for their purebred dogs in the yard, created rooms for their collections of antique model ships and jukeboxes, brought in furnishings from Europe—lots of mirrors (including one above their round peach-colored bed) and velvet couches—and installed a gold scallop-shaped bath-tub, a $1.5 million copper roof, and urns filled with brightly colored plastic flowers along the property's fenced perimeter. An Egyptian artist was called in to paint the mansion's exterior a color neighbors would later call rotten lime, and the chimney bright blue accented with gold. They also had Mo-hammed's portrait painted on the bottom of the swimming pool. But all that paled next to the way al-Fassi decorated a series of Roman-style statues on his veranda: They, too, were painted—with natural skin tones and lifelike pubic hair on the women and phalluses on the men that were clearly vis-ible through the iron fence on Sunset Boulevard. By spring, they'd become a tourist attraction, slowing traffic to a crawl in front of the house. Despite complaints, the city could do nothing about it; no law banned bad taste.

When the general outrage hit the newspapers, the couple gave a press conference. Mohammed, then twenty-three, said they'd come to L.A. seek-ing "the freedom of the United States. . . . What you see is exactly how we are," he said. "You can't let what other people say bother you," added Dena, nineteen. "We just wanted to make [the statues] more beautiful." Living on display makes you a target, however. By July, the statues had been draped and hidden, but the damage was done. Al-Fassi was an international joke. "It made him sick," says Dino Fabbri's widow, "to think this beautiful place had become a circus." In fact, the circus had only just begun.

One night in a disco, Mohammed spotted a girl sitting with the actor Hervé Villechaize, the dwarf sidekick on the TV show *Fantasy Island*. Taking a fancy to her, Mohammed sent Dena to Europe and Saudi Arabia and while she was gone, had his majordomo marry them in a three-minute ceremony in a restaurant. But not even a second wife (he was allowed four in his own country) made him happy, and at the end of the year, he abandoned Sunset Boulevard, returning to Europe with both wives (Dena, though none too thrilled at this turn of events, went along), joining Turki and the rest of his family in Cannes, then moving to Geneva, where the entourage spent millions on jewels and cars, and $1.4 million on accommodations. Two suites on their several floors at a Geneva hotel were reserved just for Mohammed's shoes.

While they were in Geneva, the house on Sunset was seriously damaged by a fire that caused the copper roof to collapse. The Beverly Hills Fire Department investigated and determined the cause was deliberate arson. It turned out that a former chauffeur for the couple had stolen $500,000 worth of furniture from the house and burned it down to cover his tracks. Beforehand, he'd walked a well-known Beverly Hills plastic surgeon through the place on an apparent shopping expedition, and some of the stolen goods were subsequently recovered from the surgeon's house. The chauffeur eventually pleaded guilty to grand theft and the plastic surgeon no contest to a charge of receiving stolen property.

Apparently unconcerned about all that, al-Fassi left Geneva that April, passing through the Canary Islands, Marbella, and Turkey, where he adopted an ailing child, discarding his second wife along the way (she sued for divorce, claiming he'd held her prisoner, "bitten her about the entire body" and beaten her, but settled out of court) and replacing her with a Saudi girl. Once again, he sent Dena away while he got married, this time at a $5 million party that lasted three days. Finally, that Christmas, Prince Turki and the al-Fassis moved en masse to Miami. All the traveling inspired the *Washington Post* to describe al-Fassi as "a modern day Bedouin, carrying his family and followers with him."

Mohammed bought several homes on Star Island on the condition the owners move out within a day, demolished them, and began planning a new palace to replace them. Meanwhile, he and his family and servants took over three floors of a hotel in Hollywood, Florida, at a cost of $25,000 a day; Dena was exiled to a floor far away from her husband and children. She finally fled and returned to Beverly Hills, where she moved back into the Beverly Hilton—and began plotting her next move.

Sheikha Dena showed her hand in January 1982, when she and her lawyer, the famous divorce bomber Marvin Mitchelson, announced she was suing Mohammed, seeking a separation on the grounds of his bigamy, and planned to file for divorce, seeking half of a fortune she estimated at $6 billion and custody of their two natural and two adopted children (al-Fassi had also adopted a Uruguayan orphan). She also asked for a restraining order preventing him from contacting her or disposing of any of their community property, which she figured was everything he owned.

She was quickly awarded $75,000 in immediate support, an equal amount to pay Mitchelson's bills, and the right to move into a six-room guesthouse on the grounds of the Sunset estate. This infuriated her husband, who complained that she knew what she was getting into when she converted to Islam to marry him. About a week later, Mohammed claimed to have sold the house and other property to a Dutch corporation, but it was quickly revealed to be a sham company that he controlled. Remaining on the offensive, Mohammed chartered two Learjets to augment his 110-foot yacht and get everyone to Nassau, where a judge granted him custody of the children. Mitchelson and Dena followed and after a shoving match between the lawyer and al-Fassi's bodyguards, she was granted visitation rights.

But Dena wasn't Mohammed's only problem: The Saudi entourage in Florida was being accused of trying to buy their way out of a number of jams. Moreover, he was being sued in Los Angeles for unpaid bills; a contractor working on his Miami house sued him, too, for overdue payments; residents of Star Island objected to his building plans; and then, after his patron and brother-in-law Prince Turki was accused of treating one of his servants as a slave, police arrived at his door, Mohammed's sister bit a policewoman, and family bodyguards finally fought off the cops, five of whom were injured. Damage suits were filed against Turki and Hindi, who countersued for $210 million, charging the police and a state attorney with "abusive, disgusting and violent" conduct. Though the prince held no diplomatic or official post, he was closely enough connected to vital U.S. interests that the State Department hurriedly arranged to give him diplomatic immunity. A flurry of gifts to local institutions followed. But King Fahd, who had succeeded

Turki's half-brother on the throne, was not amused. From Riyadh came word that he wanted the whole unruly batch of relatives home for Ramadan, the Islamic holiday of repentance. Only Mohammed refused; he took his retinue to Washington, ignoring an injunction Mitchelson had won to keep his and Dena's children in Florida.

In June 1982, Mitchelson won another round, an injunction barring al-Fassi's sham Dutch corporation from disposing of any of his property. A month later, the sheikh was arrested for skipping out on the $1.5 million bill at his Hollywood, Florida, hotel (he posted bond, paid up with a cashier's check, and then sued the hotel unsuccessfully for $1 billion for embarrassing him). Then in August, fourteen Miami Beach policemen besieged his latest home there, attempting to serve him with a court order to remain in Florida, and demanding he post a $1 million surety bond to ensure he did. He won a round a few days later, when the bond was dissolved, but then defied the court, leaving for Saudia Arabia in October and taking not only the four children but also Sheikha Dena's Saudi passport with him; its government, Mitchelson charged, refused to replace it without her husband's permission. Three months after that, Dena won a Pyrrhic victory in Los Angeles when al-Fassi was ordered to give her half his fortune. Mohammed, pointing to a federal arrest warrant issued against him for taking the children, refused to return to the United States and in June 1984, the court's judgment was finalized: Dena was awarded the Sunset Boulevard wreck, valued at $5 million, and another $76.5 million—if she could get her hands on it.

Dena immediately put the house on the market for $10 million, offering it as a development site for four to six houses. The same realtor who'd sold it to them predicted the neighbors wouldn't mind because they hated the Saudis that much; he was wrong and the sale process stalled. Finally, in summer 1985, the former Max Whittier estate was sold for $7 million and the house demolished as five hundred invited guests and TV crews watched and toasted with wine laid on by the buyer, a developer who planned to build a more acceptable two mansions there. (It would be another twenty-five years before new homes were finally completed on the property.)

Mohammed al-Fassi never returned to America, and his ex-wife was still without her money when he died of an infected hernia in Cairo in 2002 at age fifty. In the interim, he'd distinguished himself by broadcasting from Baghdad during the first Gulf War, supporting the Iraqi invasion of Kuwait, and condemning Saudi Arabia for siding with the infidel Americans he'd once admired. A year before his death, Egypt ordered his arrest and detained his latest wife on charges of trying to smuggle Islamic treasures looted from mosques out of the country. A year after his death, a superior court judge in Los Angeles ordered that Prince Turki or King Fahd or the Saudi government pay Dena $270 million to settle al-Fassi's divorce bill, which has continued incurring interest.

Dena has gone back to Italy and to using her maiden name. She has also tried to sell her judgment to investors at a steep discount, and offered a reward to anyone who can help her find Turki's assets. "We're still chasing it," her latest lawyer, Eli Blumenfeld, said in 2010.

The smaller of two huge new mansions on the former Whittier property, a 36,000-square-foot nine-bedroom home, was finally offered for sale in June 2010 at a staggering $68.5 million. The second house, next door, was nearing completion. Though others indulge in nostalgia for what's been lost, the Whittiers do not. "Our family feels, out of sight, out of mind," says Max's granddaughter Laura-Lee Whittier Woods, who now lives in Pasadena. "When it's gone, it's gone. Walk off and leave it."

Despite the bad press and ill will garnered by al-Fassi, the Platinum Triangle has continued to welcome Arab potentates in the ensuing years. In the 1980s, Eugene Klein, who had owned National General Corporation, a film and theater conglomerate, and the San Diego Chargers (which he bought from Barron Hilton), and transformed Burton Green's Tudor house on Lexington Drive into a Georgian manor and enlarged the estate by buying adjacent property, sold it to another sheikh, Mouaffak Bin Jamil al-Midani. Klein had been asking $12.5 million.

Al-Midani, a Syrian and the youngest of about six children of an impoverished imam, was an engineering graduate of the University of Lebanon who moved to Saudi Arabia in the 1950s, grew close to the royal family, and won a contract to create an alliance of local and European companies to wire Saudi Arabia for telecommunications.

Having made his fortune, al-Midani joined the wave of Arabs that moved to Europe, flush with oil money, in the mid-1970s. Living in Paris, he found his true passion in real estate and property development, buying and selling a stake in one of Britain's most prominent construction companies, Fairclough, and more publicly, snapping up exclusive hotels and resorts like London's landmark Dorchester (later sold to the sultan of Brunei, as were the

Beverly Hills and Bel-Air Hotels) and Spain's Marbella Club, and converting the Puente Romano apartments next door into a luxury resort. Though some in Spain complained of a tasteless Arab takeover, others pointed out that the Middle Eastern presence generated jobs and investments.

Al-Midani also bought many houses for himself, spending happy hours planning their décor. He owned more than a dozen Rolls Royces and Ferraris. "Pick a car," he once told his chauffeur on the man's birthday, evidence of a streak of generosity that saw him give half of his fortune away over the years, according to a relative. By the time he bought the Green mansion, he'd sired a second family with his second wife. She was about twenty years his junior, the daughter of a wealthy Syrian doctor prominent enough that a village there was named for her family. She also had family in Los Angeles and the relative says al-Midani bought Klein's house for her, though he didn't spend much time there until the last year of his life. His absence may be explained by the fact that around the time he bought it, his first wife of twenty-two years hired Marvin Mitchelson to sue him for divorce.

Not living there didn't stop al-Midani from making a splash in L.A. Shortly after buying 1601 Lexington and redecorating it to the tune of $40 million, adding a third floor created by a Spanish disco designer, which included a boudoir, disco, oversize sauna, and mirror-ceilinged bedroom, he was revealed, early in 1989, to be the mysterious host of a party described as "the social plum of the season," an "official" dinner for two hundred friends to welcome Ronald and Nancy Reagan home after their eight years in Washington. A guest described the event as "the most lavish I've ever been to and I have been to some pretty fancy White House parties." It later emerged that in 1985, al-Midani had donated $1 million to Nancy Reagan's antidrug campaign. Saudi King Fahd gave a similar amount at the same time the Reagan administration was considering (and subsequently approved) his request to buy AWACS surveillance planes. The two contributions, the *Washington Post* revealed, "amounted to more than half the assets of the [antidrug] fund."

Al-Midani died of pancreatic cancer two years later, and his widow put the Lexington Road house on the market seven years after that for $27 million, finally selling it for $21 million in 2001; the buyer was a local apartment house developer, Geoff Palmer, who still owns it. In the intervening years, al-Midani had not rested in peace. In 1996, five years after his death, the *Washington Post* revealed that while al-Midani was dying at Minnesota's Mayo Clinic, Alawi Darwish Kayyal, then the Saudi telecommunications minister, had rushed there accompanied by an English doctor ostensibly touting a molasses cure for cancer. But his real purpose was to collect commissions and kickbacks he was owed in return for arranging al-Midani's past government contracts, and, "with Midani under sedation and half-conscious," the paper reported, the duo had him redraft his will a dozen times "until he agreed to include a $150 million note payable to the minister and name him executor" of al-Midani's $700 million estate. A few days later, the *Post* continued, Kayyal sold al-Midani's private jet and luxury apartment in Paris and withdrew money from the by-then dead man's Swiss and Spanish bank accounts.

In August 1995, Kayyal was fired from his job (along with a dozen other ministers) in what was touted as a far-reaching anticorruption campaign. "But many Saudis are convinced," the *Post* wrote, "that Kayyal has been set up as a scapegoat to deflect public criticism from senior members of the Saudi royal family who are widely believed to have multiplied their wealth through the same practices" of taking kickbacks from nonroyal contractors.

The news hook for the *Post* story was a lawsuit filed in Riyadh by al-Midani's second family, seeking the return of the $150 million. But the scandal, which became very public when letters about Kayyal's actions were faxed throughout the kingdom—some said with the tacit approval of King Fahd—went further than that. A special board of grievances decided that the negative publicity and loss of his position were sufficient punishment and instructed Kayyal to donate a third of the money he'd received to charity; when he didn't, one of his government associates had a change of heart and also brought a legal action against him. Late in 2010, that partner won and, according to one of the lawyers representing al-Midani's second family, Kayyal fled the country after a warrant was issued for his arrest. The family "certainly didn't" get the money back, the lawyer adds.

That wasn't the only legal case involving al-Midani's two families. The children of his second wife also sued those of his first in England. The complex case also involved Kayyal who, before he lost his job, had arbitrated disputes among the various heirs, some of whom sided with him, and in 1994 produced what was purported to be a final agreement on the distribution of al-Midani's estate. The resolution of that case, too, went unreported.

One of the children of al-Midani's first marriage, Amer al-Midani, apparently emerged from the dispute financially intact, but did not remain so. After ten years as a member of the board of directors of Manchester United, the British football team, the secretive millionaire property developer was forced into bankruptcy in 2002 over $1.8 million he borrowed and then lost at the Rio casino in Las Vegas, though curiously, he was said to be worth almost $25 million at the time.

Al-Midani was neither the last nor the wealthiest man with Saudi connections to move to the Triangle. "The Saudis come in summer and rent two places," a noted realtor says, "one for their families, and one for parties. They don't assimilate and nobody wants to be next to them, so they're nothing here." King Fahd bought the Bel Air house of Barbie designer Jack Ryan, the broker believes, and "tore it up because he needed thirty-nine bedrooms for one month a year." Rebuilt in 1985, the "gaudy, gilded" palace—sources say it's two mirror-image homes in one, so men and women can live separately—originally went on the market for $53 million three years after Fahd died in 2005. It is currently listed at $40 million.

Beverly Hills

Grayhall (1100 Carolyn Way)

Despite their high profile, Arabs were not the most significant Middle Easterners to arrive in Los Angeles in the last four decades. When they bought
Grayhall from the Mark Hughes estate, Moussa and Mahnaz Mehdizadeh
were at the tail end of a profound shift in the local population. Though
they came from the same general region around the same time and have,
particularly since the Iranian hostage crisis of 1979, been ignorantly lumped
together with Muslim Arabs, newcomers like the Mehdizadehs were Iranian
Jews (though they often describe themselves as Persian). Beginning as early
as the late 1940s, they came to Beverly Hills in a trickle that turned into a
torrent after their country was taken over in the radical Islamist revolution
led by the Ayatollah Khomeini. They were the most significant wave of Jewish immigration to west Los Angeles since the arrival of the movie moguls of
the early twentieth century.

Persian Jews now "own a significant percentage of the property in Beverly Hills," says realtor John Bruce Nelson, who adds that Farsi is used as a
second language in local public schools and one Presbyterian church in the
city has a regular Farsi service. Trousdale Estates in particular is crowded
with Persians who have remodeled the predominantly midcentury modern
homes there in what many consider bad taste, characterized by columns and
copious use of marble and statuary. "You couldn't pay me to move there," a
prominent local decorator sneers.

On the plus side, the Persian Jewish community has brought fresh wealth and entrepreneurial zeal to Beverly Hills and kept real estate values high. It has also contributed Jimmy Delshad, who has twice been elected mayor of the city. But the Persians of L.A. are still considered an insular group. "There are exceptions to be sure, but my impression is that for the most part, they have remained unto themselves in terms of marriage, language, neighborhoods, schools, institutional loyalties, business," says a local European Jewish leader. "There are numerous very positive things I can say about the Persian community—they are very loyal to their synagogue, their rabbi, the state of Israel, their faith. But it will take another one or two generations for real assimilation to take place."

Nonetheless, the Persians of Beverly Hills have become an integral part of the community. "They've brought tremendous good," says David Wolpe, rabbi of Sinai Temple, where the congregation is half Persian. "As far as I know, they're the most successful immigrant group in the country. They have extended families that are by and large intact, which is rare in our day and age. And their children show extraordinary educational achievement. The hospitals here are filling up with Persian doctors." Wolpe acknowledges that their social attitudes can seem backward compared to the standards of the region. "But remember where they came from," he continues. "Some of them are two steps out of the Middle Ages, from a country whose leaders can stand up and say there are no homosexuals in Iran. Before the hostage crisis they were unknown and exotic. Afterward, they were reviled. So the mix is a little volatile. They're insular in the sense that they're afraid of the corrosive effects of American life on their traditions and their families—and they're correct to be."

Some of the leading members of the Persian community have now been in the Platinum Triangle for more than four decades. Saeed Nourmand has been a luxury realtor there since 1976. But he came to the area eleven years earlier at age seventeen as a student, against the express wishes of his family, drawn to California by movies and TV shows. Though his well-connected and well-off father offered him an apartment, a car, a butler, a vacation anywhere in the world—anything really, to keep him in Tehran—Saeed asked only for a one-way ticket, and by 1970 had settled in San Diego with a master's degree in structural engineering.

When oil prices suddenly spiked in 1973, "Iran's economy changed overnight," he says. "Persians became big by First World standards; we had millionaires and quite a number of them sent their kids to school in Los Angeles because of the desirability of the weather. The Persians believed that education was much better here, so it had higher status, and the Jewish community started growing."

By 1973, Nourmand had moved to Los Angeles after his father finally gave in and visited, and like so many of his countrymen, discovered that the Triangle reminded him of the suburbs of North Tehran "where there are hills and beautiful views and prestigious and desirable properties," Nourmand says. At the time, real estate prices in Los Angeles were "drastically lower" than back in Iran. "People started buying houses." Nourmand got a real estate license.

Among those investing in Los Angeles from Tehran was the Mahboubi family, which owned a chewing gum factory at home. The family patriarch, aware that "the paradise we experienced because of the shah might be short-lived," as one family member put it, sent one of his sons, Daryoush, to the University of California at Berkeley to study business in 1966. In 1969, while still a student, he began building condos in Orange County, backed by his father. Moving to Los Angeles for graduate school, he caught the scent of oil money and quickly focused on developing retail in downtown Beverly Hills, which had not yet evolved into the designer-boutique-filled international shopping mecca it has become, but was already attracting oil-rich Middle Easterners, European expatriates, and the local new-money crowd, eager to show off their success.

Mahboubi's first deal was a partnership with Bijan Pakzad (then the husband of David Murdock's future third wife) to open what was billed as the most expensive men's clothing store in the world; its gimmick was a locked front door. In 1976, Mahboubi and his three brothers, who'd joined him in L.A., bought five lots fronting on Rodeo Drive and six more on Cañon Drive once owned by Will Rogers's family; a year later, they bought a Rodeo restaurant and three adjacent parking lots, and a few years after that, opened the Rodeo Collection, a $35 million retail complex selling brands like Louis Vuitton, Yves Saint Laurent, and Gianni Versace.

By then, Trousdale Estates was being called the new Persian Gulf. Between 1976 and 1978, Persians were estimated to have spent close to $200 million on local real estate. "They bought and bought," says Nourmand, "and when the Persians started buying, prices went up, and Americans were resentful, even though they were the beneficiaries. . . . The problems really started when Khomeini came to power and the hostage crisis [and seizure of the American Embassy in Tehran] caused a backlash. Irrespective of who we were, why we were here, what we believed in, we were all the people in the embassy. Before 1979, I was welcome, desirable. Then, I became the worst thing walking the face of the earth." It was then that the Iranians of Beverly Hills began calling themselves Persians.

Still, the community continued to grow. "Where were we going to go?" Nourmand asks. "Could I work in the south of France? I don't like hostility but still, this is the American dream. Who am I married to? An American. My only child who's married is married to an American. To them this is home. The Arabs don't call this home. They come, they have fun, they go back."

Mahnaz Medizadeh, née Elghanayan, was a relative latecomer to the Platinum Triangle. She was born in Iran, where her father and his brothers were prominent in business and the Tehran Jewish community, with economic interests that stretched from refrigerator and plastics factories to aluminum refining and other commodities. Her parents brought their family to Forest Hills, Queens, in the late 1940s, after her father visited New York and came away impressed by the order and opportunity of American society. Though he commuted between Queens and Tehran for many years, Mahnaz and her four brothers, Houchang, Kamran, Fred, and Jeffrey came to feel quite American. Houchang became Henry, Kamran Tommy, and Mahnaz Lilli. The return trips to Tehran ended after May 9, 1978, when their uncle Habib, a prominent industrialist who'd been the president of the Jewish community in Tehran, returned there over the objections of his family and was executed—martyred, some submit—along with about a dozen other Jewish leaders by the new Islamic Republic, charged with being a Zionist supporter of Israel.

In 1970, the four Elghanayan brothers, a lawyer, an MBA, an engineer, and an architect, had gone into business together, backed by their father, first renovating buildings, then converting office buildings into rental apartments. They'd lived on Rockrose Place in Forest Hills and named their company Rockrose Development. By the time the brothers split it up and went their separate ways in 2009 (curiously, on the day after their mother died and the day before their father died), they'd amassed a $3 billion empire with eight thousand apartments, nine development sites, and nine office buildings in New York and Washington. Lilli Elghanayan was the only one of her siblings with no interest in real estate. "Like all Persian girls, she got married young," says a relative.

Moussa Mehdizadeh's father was "an entrepreneur in Iran," a successful businessman who sold art and antiquities. A photograph of Lilli "ended up in Iran with her mother," who showed it to Moussa, "and he came to the United States and courted her," says their son Robert Mehdizadeh. "It's a small community." Arranged marriages were not uncommon. Luckily for Lilli, she fell "madly in love," says another relative.

Moussa relocated and went into business importing and exporting gift-ware and doing real estate deals, becoming prominent in Great Neck on Long Island which, like Beverly Hills, began to attract a large Persian Jewish community in the late seventies. Moussa founded a local synagogue and he and Lilli bought a large Tudor house on about four acres in King's Point, New York, allegedly once occupied by Charles Chaplin.

"Los Angeles was a natural progression," says son Robert. Five of Moussa Mehdizadeh's siblings had moved there after the Islamic revolution; the Mehdizadehs saw themselves as bicoastal. There were Elghanayans in Los Angeles, too, among them a developer of apartment buildings on the Wilshire Corridor. Growing older and attracted by the warm weather, family, and the vibrant Persian Jewish community in what some now call Tehrangeles, Moussa and Lilli joined them.

Why did they buy Grayhall, a castle in which the dreams of so many have been invested, and so often dashed? "You have to understand where they come from," says Robert Mehdizadeh. "The families have lived this lifestyle for over a hundred years. They're big entertainers. Some people, like the last owner, do it for business. [My parents] enjoy it with family and friends. Tonight, there will be forty-five people. It's just a regular night." Moussa and Lilli still live in the house, by all accounts much, much happier there than most of those who have lived in it since Carrie Canfield Spalding broke up the estate.

49

Holmby Hills

In the 1990s, the American economy changed for the better. With the fall of the Soviet Union and its client states in Eastern Europe, trade boomed as technological advances brought revolutions in computing and telecommunications, and a growing economy paired with low inflation and low unemployment created huge corporate profits, turned financial markets into money machines, and spawned a new class of the megawealthy who brought home sums that would have been incomprehensible to earlier generations. One result was that most entertainment figures were pushed out of the market for the great estates of Beverly Hills, Bel Air, and Holmby Hills for good. Their places in the area's highest-priced homes were taken by the natural inheritors of the oil- and land-rich pioneers who had built the communities for their own ilk. Though the old-timers might be surprised at fortunes seemingly conjured out of the ether of financial manipulation or made on the backs of borrowed and other people's money, they would surely recognize their kinship with the latest sort of folk who surreptitiously compare the size of their mansions as if they were genitalia.

"Hollywood did itself in by becoming a subsidiary of multinational corporations," says another local rabbi. "Movie executives have become well-paid working stiffs." There are exceptions that prove the rule, but generally speaking, the Hollywood types who still dabble in these real estate waters are or were proprietors of entertainment companies, not working stiffs. The Bell brothers of Bel Air own lucrative soap-opera franchises. Misty Mountain, Fred Niblo's old eagle-eye-view estate high atop Angelo Drive, is owned by Rupert Murdoch of News Corp., and below it on the same street, the cofounder of Dreamworks, former music executive and beau of Cher, David Geffen, another collector of high-end real estate, bought the 9.38-acre Jack Warner property with its white-columned colonial mansion in 1990 for a reported $47.5 million; he is only its second owner.

The most famous remaining show business house in the Triangle was the monstrosity built in 1990 in Holmby Hills on the site of the Gordon Kaufmann house on South Mapleton Drive, which was previously owned by Edna Letts and Malcolm McNaghten, Bing Crosby, and Patrick Frawley. The wildly successful television producer Aaron Spelling and his wife Candy bought the property in the early eighties for a reported $10.25 million, along with an adjacent lot, at the suggestion of Marvin and Barbara Davis (both couples were eyeing The Knoll at the time). Its demolition, called a tear-down in Los Angeles, and replacement by a $55 million W-shaped, 56,500-square-foot behemoth that the Spellings called The Manor, complete with bowling alley and beauty salon, was memorialized in *The New Yorker* by Joan Didion, the most edgy and erudite observer of life in the Southland.

She wrote that The Manor became "not just a form of popular entertainment but, among inhabitants of a city without much common experience, a unifying, even a political, idea." While "people who make movies still have most of the status, and believe themselves keepers of the community's unspoken code—of the rules, say, about what constitutes excess on the housing front," Didion continued, things had, in fact, changed, a change she compared to "an anomaly in the wheeling of the planets." This sea change was enough to inspire bewilderment, denial, grief, envy, and other deadly sins among those who made movies: Despite their awesome self-regard, they were not the center of the universe in Los Angeles anymore (if they ever had been). Television moguls had overtaken them.

After Spelling's death, his widow put the house on the market for $150 million.[35] It was sold in June 2011 for $85 million to a trust benefiting Petra Ecclestone, a former model and British reality TV star and the daughter of Bernie Ecclestone, the billionaire owner of Formula One racing. The Ecclestones are throwbacks to an earlier generation of Triangle estate owners. More typical now are the men who bought Greenacres in 1993, 141 South Carolwood in 2002, and Hilda Weber's Casa Encantada in 2003. All three are mere businessmen, barely known outside the corporate worlds they sprang from, but like Ecclestone's father, they possess fortunes of a size only the rarest and most successful television producer could even imagine.

50

Beverly Hills

Greenacres (1740 Green Acres Place)

The next owner of Greenacres, Ron Burkle, first saw the estate at Ted Field's benefit for then candidate Bill Clinton in summer 1992. The owner of a private investment firm that bought and sold supermarkets, Burkle had a long involvement in California politics, and was then the campaign finance chairman for the newly elected senator Dianne Feinstein. He also had a long involvement in Southland real estate; Greenacres isn't the first house with ties to the early history of Beverly Hills that Burkle has owned.

Burkle was born in 1952 in Pomona, California, the son of a Stater Bros. supermarket manager with a ninth-grade education who worked long hours seven days a week. At five, Ron started visiting the store to see his father; after closing hours, they would sift through the day's take of change together, looking for rare coins, the first sign of his lifelong focus on money. He also worked in the store, unpaid at first, before joining the union at age thirteen and earning his first paychecks as a mop boy, stock clerk, and bagger at the checkout counter. By then, his father was a district manager, earning $36,000 a year. But Burkle père also owned a piece of his stores. "They let you buy in if you did well," his son says. When Stater Bros. went public some years later, his father came away with $200,000.

The Burkles lived in an 1,800-square-foot home in suburban Claremont and bought a new Chevrolet every third year. "We certainly were never poor," Ron says, "but we were never rich." Still, Burkle's father had an entrepreneurial streak and invested his annual $4,000 bonus in houses near his stores, fixing them up and renting them out for extra income.

Burkle left school at age fifteen after breaking both legs in a swimming pool during a game of Marco Polo with some larger boys. The school system discovered that he'd already earned sufficient credits from attending summer classes, and graduated him early. For the next few years he dropped in and out of several colleges, but realized he preferred to work. On the side, he'd begun his career in finance after his father made him a deal: If he saved enough money to buy a car but invested it instead, his dad would buy the car for him. He put the money—$3,000—into a silver company and quickly turned it into $30,000. "It grew out of coins," he says. "My dad and I talked a lot about how to invest. He liked companies that had no debts and paid dividends. He said to invest in things I liked or things I understood." The quick profit "was an accident," he adds. "It was just blind luck but it was the beginning of something."

Briefly, Burkle considered dentistry school. "My father worked six or seven days a week. I thought, that's not how everyone else does it. How can I do it? Everyone needs a dentist and no one calls them at night." But within six months, he'd changed his mind and decided to stay at Stater Bros. Over the next eight years, he'd rise to vice president of administration at its parent company, where he helped introduce computers and integrate systems at its various businesses, which included drug, clothing, and tire stores, alcohol rehabilitation centers, industrial laundries, and a construction company. "I was doing all the things I would later do to acquire companies and fold them in together," he says.

In 1974, he married Janet Steeper, a nineteen-year-old working in one of the Stater markets who happened to be a great-grandniece of aviation's Wright Brothers. "I married the first girl I kissed," he later said. They lived near Claremont in Upland, California, and bought a vacation house in Palm Springs. In his best year, Stater paid him $87,000 plus a $45,000 bonus.

But on the side, Burkle's investing had earned him almost $5 million. So when its parent put Stater Bros. up for sale and it failed to find a buyer, and one of his bosses suggested he buy the chain and offered to shepherd him through the process, he decided to take the leap. Unfortunately, the boss had failed to inform the company's board of his brainstorm, so even though Burkle attracted Charles Munger of Warren Buffett's Berkshire Hathaway to partner with him and his father in a bid for the store, when their offer came in 22 percent below the expectations raised by the company's investment bankers, not only was his bid rejected, he was also abruptly fired. Given that he'd made more money outside of his day job up to that point, he realized: "I shouldn't be working."

So, "I set up an office and invested for a couple years," he says. Burkle had good teachers. "Charlie and Warren thought I was a good kid; they liked me and they called companies for me." They also taught him the difference between buying them and running them. He bought a candy company, a car dealership, and some real estate. His first year on his own he made ten times his previous year's salary. "It wasn't horrible," he deadpans.

Years earlier, while still a teenager, Burkle had met Paul Whittier, one of Max Whittier's sons, who lived on a ranch outside Yucaipa, California, on the edge of the San Bernadino National Forest near a small apple orchard the Burkle family owned. While sweeping out Whittier's barn for an apple growers' picnic, Burkle discovered that he owned a Camaro—and Burkle's father bought it, keeping his promise to get his son a car. Burkle was a millionaire when he called Whittier again. After reminding him of that earlier transaction, Burkle got straight to the point: "I've always liked your house."

"Come on down," Whittier replied. "I'll sell it to you." Burkle bought it on the spot for $2 million, putting down $750,000. It was worth much more and Whittier even financed the balance, Burkle claims, because "he liked me." He and his wife moved to the ranch, had two kids, and in 1986, Burkle teamed up with some of his old colleagues from Stater Bros. and started buying up supermarket chains. He named their private equity holding company Yucaipa. "I'd never thought you worked because you liked to," Burkle says. "I realized I liked it and I started buying things." Investment banks invested in his deals and he networked his way into other useful alliances. Stanley Druckenmiller became his personal investment advisor, and other financial highfliers, Ken Moelis, Leon Black, and George Soros, his partners in various deals. By the early nineties, he wasn't just playing with the big boys; he was one himself. Yucaipa owned the second-largest chain of groceries in California, grossing $3 billion a year. *Forbes* estimated Burkle himself was worth $100 million.

When Burkle walked into Ted Field's house and met Bill Clinton that night in 1992, it was a life-changing event. The Burkle legend has it that Clinton took to him because, after the famous race riots that year in South Central Los Angeles, not only had many of Yucaipa's grocery stores (which were often located in poor black and Hispanic neighborhoods) survived the burning and looting, Burkle made it clear they would continue to serve poor neighborhoods; he formed a foundation, Food 4 Less, to work within them, built new stores, and won a reputation as a community activist. Though it's a fine story, often repeated, and the supermarket part of it is true, Burkle sideswipes it. "Clinton called not because I had good ideas but because I'd raised money for Dianne Feinstein," whom Burkle had first met when he was fighting unions trying to keep scanners out of supermarkets in San Francisco, where she was mayor.

Regardless, it was bromance at first sight. "I was blown away when I met him," says Burkle, who was soon invited to sleep in the Lincoln bedroom at the White House. "I thought he was a good man and I still do," says Burkle, a longtime Republican who admits he voted for Clinton's predecessor, George H. W. Bush, and remained a registered Republican, despite his work for Feinstein, for another four years until Clinton asked him to be a delegate to the 1996 Democratic Convention. What became, arguably, Clinton's most famous first friendship blossomed when Burkle moved to Greenacres the next year.

Burkle moved to L.A. because "I didn't want to be married anymore," he says. "I wasn't happy at home." He and Janet broke up for the second time just after they had their third child, a boy. He'd looked at forty or fifty houses in L.A. before walking into Greenacres for that fund-raiser. "The market was down, prices were a disaster," he says. But though he bought and held on to the Lloyd estate, he became a nomad, moving from house to house; he has had six or seven in California (among them, an oceanfront site that was once the home of TV's *Ozzie and Harriet,* and the futuristic ridge-riding home in Palm Springs featured in the James Bond film *Diamonds Are Forever*), two in New York, one in London, and one in Mexico he shares with his friend the actor Leonardo DiCaprio. He estimates he has about fifteen altogether. "I don't know, maybe more," he says vaguely. "They're just scattered around. I'm either by myself or with a thousand people. I travel all the time so I don't really live anywhere."

Those travels, as much as his star-studded fund-raisers at Greenacres (the first was held in May 1994) made Burkle famous and to some minds, a marked man. After Clinton's escapades with White House intern Monica Lewinsky were revealed (and Clinton found "solace" and privacy at Greenacres, according to the author Carol Felsenthal), the friendship, once a boon for both, became a burden for Burkle. Even as Clinton's reputation recovered, Burkle remained a punching bag for the right and the press. Making matters more delicate for the best friend of the first philanderer, Burkle was simultaneously under attack by his wife.

Janet Burkle eventually moved from Yucaipa to their hometown of Claremont after Burkle moved to Greenacres. "We got along fine and were great friends," says Ron. Then, he continues, Janet heard he was involved with a woman she didn't approve of—"it wasn't true at all," he says—and filed for divorce in 1997, "in a rather spectacular way—with private detectives" hired to pry into his finances.

The day before he was served with divorce papers, Burkle continues, he'd been thinking how much he missed his children. During the ensuing negotiations, they left their lawyers behind and went for a cup of coffee, "and we talked about it and we thought we should try, and for the next few months we kind of dated and thought about it." Over the course of six months, as they attempted their reconciliation, seventeen different attorneys negotiated a postnuptial agreement at Janet's insistence, and "at the end of all that she moved into Greenacres." She'd waived support and agreed to a $30 million buyout if they divorced. He also agreed to pay her $1 million a year and apparently did for the next three years.

He could afford it. Yucaipa's holdings were then estimated to be worth $14 billion, and it was the fourth-largest grocer in the United States. Burkle was on a roll, teaming up with the former agent Michael Ovitz on Internet ventures and trying to bring a professional football franchise to Los Angeles. Vowing to be more private and claiming he was getting out of the market business, he sold two of his grocery chains that year, making $880 million on one deal and $260 million on the other. "My guess is unless we do something public . . . no one will pay attention to us again, which is good," he said hopefully.

But whether he wanted it or not, owning Greenacres brought him attention, even though he's rarely stayed there in the eighteen years since he bought it from Ted Field. Like Field, he used Greenacres for events, political and charitable fund-raisers. "Politicians and causes almost came with the house," he says. So, curiously, did Bob Burkett, Ted Field's political advisor, who segued into a similar job at Yucaipa.

Of all the owners of Greenacres since Harold Lloyd himself, Ron Burkle is the only one Lloyd's granddaughter Sue seems to really like. "I'm lucky to have Ron Burkle taking care of that house," she says. He reached out to her. "He really put it back. My grandparents would be so pleased. He wasn't using it for his personal advancement." Unlike Dona Solomon, Burkle would truly behave as a custodian of Greenacres, restoring it for its own glory as much as or more than his; he was one of a small but significant new minority of Triangle estate buyers who valued the area's architectural history and refused to indulge in glitzy Trousdale makeovers or, worse, Paul Allen–style teardowns.

At an early meeting, Burkle told Sue Lloyd how he'd driven around Beverly Hills as a teenager, "wishing he could have one" of the grand mansions there. She liked him so much, she gave back some bronze baby gates she'd taken with her when the house was sold. Burkle restored the pipe organ, the doll house, and Lloyd's underground rogues' gallery. "I didn't want the place to feel haunted, but I wanted to be respectful and I liked the history of it," Burkle says. He also added some history of his own. When Bill Clinton stayed overnight, Sue Lloyd adds, he slept in her old bedroom.

Lloyd calls Clinton Burkle's "partner in crime." She's joking, but the line reflects the conventional wisdom about the men's friendship. Mostly kept quiet during Clinton's two terms in office, when he slept at Greenacres on about eighty separate occasions (Burkle even installed a quarter-mile jogging path for him—which he never used), the relationship burst into public view in spring 2002, when Yucaipa hired the out-of-office Clinton as a senior advisor, in large part to promote two progressive investment funds it ran, one working in impoverished regions and a second that focused on companies with good corporate practices. The fact that the pension funds of California's public employees had invested $760 million in one of those funds focused fresh critical attention on Burkle.

Suddenly, the press filled with tales about Clinton's stays at Greenacres and his flights on Burkle's private planes, which became notorious. In 1997, he'd bought a Boeing 757, complete with sleeping quarters; Clinton became a frequent flyer and as their friendship blossomed in the ensuing years, that jet won several nicknames, among them Ron Air, Air Force Two, and, most provocatively, Air Fuck One.

Burkle says he was stunned by all the attention. He'd flown around the world with former president Jimmy Carter, skied with him, and housed him at Greenacres as well, and "I never read about it, never heard about it, and frankly never got any grief or aggravation about it," he says. His friendship with Clinton proceeded the same way—at first. "We were friends the whole time he was in the White House. He spent a lot of nights in L.A. and, frankly, I never read about it. I went to Camp David and I went to the White House. Nobody was really paying attention. So I frankly didn't give a lot of thought to what the downside was. Maybe I should have."

After Clinton left the White House, his and Burkle's roles reversed. "I was kind of horrified that somebody who was so smart about the world was so naïve about how he was gonna make money. I came up with two things he could do that would be honorable," he says, and hired his friend. Burkle talked about his new hire to *Vanity Fair* in 2004. "He's invaluable," Burkle said. "President Clinton is probably a better phone call than I am. Without a doubt." *Forbes* would later report that Clinton stood to make "tens of millions of dollars" from the gig.

If Burkle wanted to stay below the radar, bragging about Clinton probably wasn't the way to do it; neither was befriending Michael Jackson, Bono, Sean "P. Diddy" Combs (whose clothing line Sean John he invested in), Jesse Jackson's son Yusuf (not to mention hiring the civil rights leader's mistress), Leonardo DiCaprio, and Gisele Bundchen, or hosting star-studded fund-raisers for presidential candidate John Kerry. Given his high profile, it probably wasn't surprising that two years after hiring Clinton, Burkle made headlines again when he went to court seeking to seal some of the paperwork in the second divorce suit Janet Burkle filed against him in June 2003.

Their 1997 reconciliation had finally failed. "We tried it and frankly it wasn't a great idea," Burkle says. The problems began when Janet Burkle tried to have their hard-fought postnuptial agreement thrown out, claiming Burkle had understated his rising fortunes at the time. During the eighteen-month-long battle that followed, Burkle alleged that a personal trainer with a criminal record whom Janet had been dating was a threat to his son's safety—he'd been charged with attempted murder, mayhem, and assault with a firearm during a drug deal, and was convicted of the latter charge. Burkle sued the trainer for harassment and he was ordered to stay at least three hundred yards away from Burkle, his home, his office, his car, and his children.

Janet responded that the trainer wasn't an exclusive boyfriend and had never met their son. The trainer's lawyer then entered the ring and alleged that Burkle had hired a private eye to install hidden cameras in his and Janet's homes. Janet believed she'd been under surveillance for more than a year. In an affidavit Janet and Ron's daughter Carrie Ann filed in the case, she said

Burkle had taped Janet and her trainer boyfriend having "really rough" sex. (Though Burkle's side admitted conducting surveillance out of concern for his son, one of his lawyers later denied the videotape existed.) Separately, Carrie Ann sued her father for almost $1 million in investments she claimed were owed to her.

At the end of 2004, a private judge hearing the case ruled against Janet and she appealed. Early in 2006, after the first California law to seal divorce records was struck down, the *Los Angeles Times* editorialized against another bill that was being considered, in part because, the paper said, it "would personally benefit billionaire Ron Burkle" and had been written just for him. Burkle's lawyer protested that characterization as "outrageous in the extreme." A judge later threw out the law. Janet still lives near Greenacres and they once again get along, Burkle says.

As it turned out, the divorce revelations were merely a squall before what the *San Francisco Chronicle* would call "the Desert Storm of publicity wars," Burkle's decision to pick a fight with the *New York Post*'s combative gossip column, Page Six, and its most important freelance contributor, writer Jared Paul Stern, the fedora-wearing frequent guest editor of the page. Burkle believes he came into the column's sights because it served the political agenda of its conservative owner, Burkle's neighbor Rupert Murdoch.

Truth be told, Burkle would have provided a juicy target even if the gossips cared nothing about his political friends, but his relationship with the "Big Dog" Clinton was often the focus. In an early mention claiming Burkle was buying Elite Models for his pal, the page noted, "Burkle is notorious for flying gaggles of willing models around on his private jet."

Although most of the gossip items simply made him out to be what he'd become, a bachelor billionaire having fun, Burkle says that many items were simply inaccurate. "As flattering as it might have been . . . " he sputters, "they accused me of being engaged to Gisele Bundchen. . . . It made me out to be something I wasn't! I was in a long-term monogamous relationship then so it wasn't fun to hear I was having sex with friends. It wasn't great for my relationship. It also wasn't true." (Bundchen was then seeing Burkle's pal DiCaprio.)

Burkle claimed he'd complained to the *Post* about being singled out and about issues of accuracy. Then he arranged a meeting with Stern where the FBI taped the writer allegedly attempting to extort him for a $100,000 investment in a clothing line he'd started and further monthly payments of $10,000 in exchange for guaranteeing him positive coverage on the gossip page. The story was leaked to the *Post*'s rival tabloid, the *Daily News,* which gleefully reported the reporter's faux pas. Burkle also wrote an op-ed piece for the *Wall Street Journal,* lecturing the media about declining standards. Ironically, Yucaipa had recently teamed up with newspaper unions in a failed bid to buy a dozen newspapers. So the story, as the press says, had legs, and all concerned seemed determined to keep it running, even Stern, who was fired but never charged in the alleged plot; he won a book deal, though the book was never published, and filed a defamation lawsuit, later dismissed, against Burkle, the *News,* and, among others, Bill and Hillary Clinton, who'd recently held another fund-raiser at Greenacres.

In the aftermath of the affair, Burkle found himself described as a "greasy grocer," a "paunchy merchant prince," and an "evil rich guy." Few noted that the prounion Burkle had recently been named the AFL-CIO's Humanitarian of the Year or that one union leader had called him "the best employer we ever dealt with." Instead, he became a poster child for the sort of hypocrites who publicly disdain publicity while seeming to court it when it suits them.

Though it cancelled its own brief-lived stab at a gossip column in the wake of the Stern affair, the *New York Times* shortly proved it wasn't above gossiping itself when it floated the notion, early in 2007, that Clinton's friendship with Burkle partly explained a rift between Burkle's Beverly Hills neighbor David Geffen and the ex-president that burst into public view when Geffen loudly sided with Barack Obama in his race for the Democratic presidential nomination against Hillary Rodham Clinton. The Burkle-Geffen feud may have actually predated that partisan moment. "Burkle thought to sell Greenacres ten years ago," says realtor John Bruce Nelson. "Paul Allen looked at it and almost offered $36 million, but Geffen bad-mouthed the house and killed the deal."

Geffen, a longtime grandmaster of Machiavellian tactics in business, politics, media relations, and friendship, unburdened himself about the Clintons to *Times* op-ed columnist Maureen Dowd. The paper followed with a story that dwelled on Bill Clinton's sleeping arrangements in Beverly Hills, pointing out that after the 1996 election, Clinton seemed to favor Burkle's crib over Geffen's, though it added that once, even though Geffen wasn't home, Clinton left the former's house to sleep at the latter's, "all to avoid offending Mr. Geffen." Despite this airing of their political laundry, Burkle hosted another fund-raiser for Hillary at Greenacres a few weeks later, a dinner for seven hundred that was his third event on her behalf. Burkle seemed to relish making enemies as much as he did famous and powerful friends.

But it wasn't long before the first cracks appeared in the first friendship, with reports filtering out of the Clinton camp at the end of that year that Bill either had "severed" or would "reduce or curtail" his ties to Burkle if Hillary won their party's nod to run for president. The potential for embarrassment had gone beyond sexual innuendo when it emerged that Bill's closest aide had facilitated a joint real estate venture between Burkle and Raffaello Follieri, a swindler who would shortly go to jail, and that Burkle ran the sort of Cayman Islands–based investment vehicles that Hillary Clinton had recently said should be shut down.

The Bill and Ron show was also central to a controversial profile of the ex-president that ran in *Vanity Fair* the next summer. Author Todd Purdum (husband of Clinton's White House press secretary Dee Dee Meyers) opened his story at the wedding of that same Clinton aide, pointedly noting that Burkle appeared with a girl "not much older than 19, if she was that," made several equally provocative observations about Burkle's "European" lifestyle, detailed Clinton's take from Yucaipa over four years ($15.4 million, representing 20 percent of his income), noted Burkle's financial ties to an Arab ruler whose regime had been cited by the State Department for human rights violations, and managed to reheat the guilt-by-association leftovers from the Page Six mess.

Burkle points out that even before the age of instant archival access to inaccurate reporting, lies that are repeated, as Vladimir Lenin once said, take on the trappings of truth. "I didn't create Clinton's reputation for issues with women but I became part of it," he says. So he probably wasn't entirely surprised when the politically liberal *Vanity Fair* took the billionaire bachelor ball from the conservative *Post* and ran with it.

After the article appeared, Burkle called Meyers, whom he'd known since she was Dianne Feinstein's press secretary, to complain, and she told him her husband had two sources. "I know David [Geffen] was probably a source for a lot of it," Burkle says. Looked at from a certain angle, it was literally only back-fence gossip, one neighbor talking about another, albeit with higher-than-average stakes—the advancement of one presidential candidate over another.

Finally, the other shoe dropped in spring 2009, when Clinton quit Yucaipa. A year later, reporters were still chewing over the bones of their relationship, reporting the claims of people close to Clinton who said Burkle had stiffed the ex-president out of millions. Burkle's spokesman denied it, but the stories showed afresh the damage that had been done to his reputation, describing him as a playboy and gossip-column fixture. Only then did Burkle admit that hiring Clinton was in some ways "the dumbest thing I ever did."

In the months that followed, Burkle would back a losing bid by the brothers Harvey and Bob Weinstein to buy back their Miramax studio from Disney; battle unsuccessfully with Leonard Riggio, chairman of Barnes & Noble, for control of America's leading bookstore chain; and, more promisingly, buy up the debt of both Barneys New York and the A&P supermarket chain, putting him in a position to win control of one or the other company.

Despite all the punches he's taken, Burkle seems both unbowed and, if not quite pleased to be in the public eye, also unwilling to give up his place there. In 2010, he moved to London, but not before buying several properties adjacent to Greenacres and planning a three-year renovation of the front of the house, restoring some of Harold Lloyd's garden.

Oddly enough, the idea came from his sometime antagonist and equally house-mad neighbor, David Geffen; as it had been for Bernie Cornfeld and Steve Powers, theirs appears to be a love-hate relationsip. After both looked at some property that had come on the market between their estates and agreed it was overpriced, Geffen suggested Burkle buy and raze other adjacent properties. "You don't have the front you want," Geffen told him. Says Burkle, "I thought about it and he was right."

So despite the insults it has suffered over the years, Harold Lloyd's Greenacres will have another act. It seems safe to assume that bag boy turned billionaire Ron Burkle will as well.

51

Holmby Hills

Owlwood (141 South Carolwood Drive)

Compared to Burkle, Gary Winnick and the late Roland Arnall mostly flew under the radar of the media, so their paths to the riches that paid for their Los Angeles palaces are not as well lit. What is abundantly clear is that both walked away with fortunes from the financial wreckage of corporations they formed during economic bubbles.

Arnall, the secretive buyer of Owlwood and the two homes flanking it on Sunset Boulevard in 2002, has been called the Johnny Appleseed of the subprime mortgage industry that almost brought down the international economy in 2008. So it seems oddly apt that his last home was built by the widow of the man who paid all cash for John Wolfskill's Rancho San Juan de Buenos Ayres.

Details of Arnall's life are sketchy at best; he rarely spoke to the press, gave interviews, or proffered personal information, but according to Michael Howard's book on predatory lending, *The Monster,* he was born in Paris to a Romanian tailor and a Czech nurse. During World War II, the Jewish Arnalls pretended to be Roman Catholics in a small village in the south of France; only when the war ended did the six-year-old learn who he really was.

After the war, his family relocated to Montreal until his father returned from a trip to say he'd found "a place where there were no poor people": Beverly Hills. Roland started out there selling eggs door-to-door, but it wasn't long before he graduated to buying and developing real estate, keeping the sharp elbows he'd needed to work the streets. In 1968, he was accused (and later cleared) of bribing a Los Angeles city councilman and in 1973, his development company REA Enterprises (his middle initial was Edmond) sued the Beverly Hills bank that was financing him over a failed development deal. Though he often teetered on the financial brink, he managed to make big loans to politicians and in 1979, opened a savings and loan bank that was used, said an ex-employee, "as a piggy bank." In the eighties, he was charged with intentional fraud in a lawsuit; the case was settled out of court, confidentially. That would become a pattern.

After the collapse of the S&L industry in the mid-1980s led to strict regulation, Arnall literally burned his bank's official charter to ashes he kept in an urn on his desk, telling regulators "to shove it," according to *Chain of Blame,* another history of the mortgage mess. Little did he know that his next act would light a fire that would scorch the whole developed world.

In 1994, Arnall created Long Beach Mortgage, a nearly unregulated business funded by Wall Street instead of federally insured savings deposits; it specialized in subprime loans to borrowers with bad credit or low income. Fascinated with technology, Arnall created systems to grade borrowers, who were charged increasing rates and fees based on the risk they presented. In 1995, Arnall created a subsidiary, Ameriquest Mortgage, to issue higher-quality mortgages and turned Long Beach into a sales network focused on subprime loans.

Arnall's allergy to public notice was such that he created a maze of corporations to keep his name from public documents when he finally went public in 1997 via Long Beach Financial Corp., raising almost $150 million. A holding company he created at the same time still controlled 70 percent of the public company and he walked away with about $100 million. He also kept his retail outlets. He'd gone from rich to seriously so.

It was clearly not a coincidence that just before the IPO, Arnall and his wife separated; they would formally divorce two years later in 1998 after thirty-seven years. He was brutal to her in the negotiated end of their marriage. He lied and hid assets and even bullied her to settle on the same day his mother died. They made a deal: He kept his corporate holdings, she got two homes, but only $11 million. A stay-at-home mom, she'd paid no attention to her husband's business and believed him when he told her what he was worth.[36]

In 2000, Arnall reivented Ameriquest as a subprime lender, undertaking a national expansion of the retail business he'd kept, turning it into the largest source of subprime mortgages in America. Though he stayed in the shadows, Ameriquest began to resemble Herbalife, with salesmen fired up at sales meetings, compensated based on the volume of loans they wrote—top salesmen earned millions—and rewarded with prizes like Porsches and junkets to Vegas and the Caribbean. Through the next half-decade, as recession caused interest rates to drop, subprime mortgages soared, their growth driven in part by another Arnall innovation, stated-income loans, also known as liar loans, that saw loan officers accepting as truth whatever income a borrower claimed. By 2003, Ameriquest and its subsidiaries would be originating $40 billion in loans, about a third of which were the liar or limited-documentation mortgages that would shortly begin defaulting in horrifying numbers.

Regulators weren't entirely asleep. In 1996, Arnall had denied wrongdoing but paid $4 million to settle federal charges that his lending operation charged higher fees to women, senior citizens, and members of minority groups than it did to young white males. Now, in spring 2000, protesters stormed one of the new Ameriquest offices, chanting about "loan sharks" charging excessive fees. A protest leader denounced the firm as "slimy mortgage predators." The Federal Trade Commission opened an investigation. The next year, federal prosecutors in San Diego indicted several Ameriquest loan officers for fraudulently raising appraisal values on homes in order to generate larger loans and larger fees for themselves. Arnall and his top executives would claim such actions were aberrations committed by rogue employees. Watchdogs would pointedly note his $1.2 million in donations to local Democrats in the preceding decade—and suggest he'd bought himself a free pass.

Arnall had always worked with members of his family. In 1998, he hired Dawn Mansfield, a blonde MBA twenty years his junior. She'd started her career literally selling the family farm, then worked in commercial real estate in Chicago and L.A. for twenty years before joining Arnall at Ameriquest. Two years after hiring her, he married her in a ceremony performed by California governor Gray Davis, another recipient of his contributions and fund-raising skill. Davis appointed Dawn, an animal lover, to a post on California's veterinary board.

After his second marriage, Arnall made the series of trophy real estate purchases that announced his intention to emerge from the shadows and begin leading a more public life. He bought the ten-acre estate on Carolwood from Ghazi Aita and Enge Humperdinck and two years later, the 650-acre Mandalay Ranch between Snowmass and Buttermilk ski areas in Aspen from the movie producer Peter Guber. It was another relative bargain. Guber initially asked $63 million for his land, 15,000-square-foot home, 3,500-square-foot guest cabin, barns, and outbuildings. Arnall reportedly bought it all for $46 million, still managing to set a local record.

Greg Hagins, Aita's estate manager, said Arnall signed him to a one-year contract worth $125,000 to continue working on the Holmby Hills estate. "He was the weirdest person I've ever known," Hagins said. "He kept me because I knew where the gas and electric lines were. He tore everything up within two weeks. He wanted it done quick so he could have fund-raisers for Bush and Cheney." Bush's response to 9/11 was said to have motivated Arnall's switch in loyalty to the Republicans, though their opposition to financial regulation probably didn't hurt.

"He took down the Pink Palace first, bulldozing everything except the pool," Hagins continued. "He did it without permits and paid fines." Hagins got word to the local historical society and there were protests, but Arnall "didn't care," said Hagins. Shortly after the tear-downs, South Carolwood Drive, once a public street, was closed off with a gate. Hagins thought Arnall used his political connections to accomplish that. "They called it a security issue but he didn't want regular people sitting on lawn chairs out there."

Arnall wasn't only buying; he was making changes in the volume and direction of his giving and fund-raising. He'd already won a reputation for philanthropy and public service, serving sixteen years on the board of California State University (appointed by Jerry Brown after he became governor) and cofounding and serving as chairman of the board of a Jewish human rights organization, the Simon Wiesenthal Center and Museum of Tolerance in Los Angeles. In 2001, Arnall became the first president of the American Friends of the London School for Jewish Studies and gave a plot of Beverly Hills land to his local synagogue. But in 2004, his focus shifted to reelecting George W. Bush. By bundling contributions from his employees and family members, he made Ameriquest the twelfth-largest contributor to the Bush campaign. The *Washington Post* called the Arnalls "the single biggest source of financial support for Bush since 2002."

Ameriquest had also begun advertising and promoting itself, spending millions on ads, buying naming rights to the Texas Rangers stadium, sponsoring NASCAR drivers Dario Franchitti and Danica Patrick and a tour by the Rolling Stones, and hiring Paul McCartney to play a branded half-time show at the Super Bowl. It was all so out of character for Arnall, it suggested that he might be gearing up to sell the company, and get out while the getting was still very good. In 2003, *Chain of Blame* authors Paul Muolo and Mathew Padilla noted, Ameriquest and its affiliates were grossing $1 billion a year through its thousands of employees and hundreds of retail outlets. Investment bankers were dying to take the company public.

If Arnall seemed inclined to sell, though, by late 2004 it was too late. A series of exposés were about to appear that signaled the beginning of the end of Ameriquest. The *Los Angeles Times* revealed that between 2000 and 2004, its customers had filed more complaints with the Federal Trade Commission than its two biggest competitors combined.[37] Allegations of fraud, deception, forgery, unfair practices, bait-and-switch sales tactics, and falsified documents and appraisals were piling up in other states' offices and courthouses, too. The *Times* noted the Arnalls' $3.8 million in campaign contributions in the preceding year, and listed who'd attended their most recent holiday party at Owlwood, from Governor Schwarzenegger and his wife Maria Shriver to California's attorney general. The writer then quoted a former loan officer to devastating effect, explaining how *Boiler Room,* a movie glamorizing stock swindlers, was assigned to Ameriquest employees as homework as an example of "the energy, the impact, the driving, the hustling" needed to make it in the subprime world. A follow-up story told how the bipartisan Arnall had financed a weekend at the Pro Bowl in Hawaii for the leader of California's assembly and four other Democratic officials.

Just as Ameriquest's troubles were mounting—more investigations across the country, the abrupt end of its attempt to go public, and reports Arnall planned to sell $1 billion in bonds in order to cash out—the Bush administration revealed Arnall's reward and his exit strategy by nominating him to become U.S. ambassador to the Netherlands. Democrats in Congress opposed the appointment; all of Ameriquest's problems, both domestically and overseas, were raked over again, and citizen's groups accused Arnall of buying government favors and access, as well as the job in The Hague. He did little to court public opinion—he even refused to release a photograph of himself—again blaming employees for Ameriquest's bad actions. "I have made 'do the right thing' my motto," he said.

All through the fall of 2005, Arnall's appointment to The Hague dangled in the wind as Democrats and Dutch parliamentarians pushed back against it. The required revelation of his investments (in everything from real estate and film to baby wipes and clip-on sunglasses), his offer to resign as chairman of Ameriquest and five other companies (including an oil company that allegedly paid him over $100 million a year) and hand the reins of all to wife Dawn, and his agreement to sell his holdings in ten corporations, including the Dutch brewer Heineken, Royal Dutch Shell, and the British-Dutch Unilever, proved insufficient to still the opposition. Finally, under pressure from senators Paul Sarbanes and Barack Obama, Ameriquest agreed to settle with the forty-nine states where it did business, and set aside $325 million to pay penalties and restitution and reimburse the states' legal fees. Again, the company admitted no wrongdoing, but under an injunction requiring it, said it would mend its ways.

Arnall was finally confirmed as ambassador in February 2006. That May, faced with steeply lower demand for its products, Ameriquest closed all 229 of its retail offices, slashing 3,800 jobs and claiming it would replace them all with four telephone centers (a plan that soon failed amid rumors the company was losing a fortune). And late that year, his wife (operating, presumably, as he'd promised, without consulting him as owner) put Ameriquest up for sale. Early in 2007, after Dawn agreed to put a seven-figure sum back into the company, according to a former Ameriquest advisor, Citigroup made a deal to buy its mortgage operations for an undisclosed price.[38] Not long afterwards, attorneys for more than twenty borrowers seeking to combine their lawsuits against Ameriquest into a class action asked a judge to add the newly minted ambassador's name as a defendant, causing his family's spokeswoman to note that he'd left the board "far in advance of the meltdown of the non-prime industry," as if he'd had nothing to do with it. "If you're building a Mount Rushmore of people who should be on the face of the mortgage lending crisis, I think Roland Arnall has a distinct place in that litany," commented Ira Rheingold, executive director of the National Association of Consumer Advocates.

Arnall moved to The Hague in 2006 and Owlwood "became a ghost town," said Greg Hagins. Then, in February 2008, less than two years after winning his diplomatic post, Arnall abruptly resigned and returned to the United States because his son had Hodgkin's lymphoma. They didn't have long together. Arnall soon fell ill himself and checked into a hospital, where he was diagnosed with esophageal cancer and died five days later at sixty-eight. As had happened with so many of his neighbors, litigation lived on after his death.

Not only did Arnall's longtime lawyer sue his estate but the next January, Arnall's brother, Claude, sued too, claiming Arnall owed him $47.6 million for his share of a mortgage company they owned. Dawn Arnall responded that the lawsuit violated a no-contest provision in Arnall's trust and threatened that if he didn't stop, Claude would be disinherited. Her lawyer added that the "alleged stake" was "in a worthless and defunct company," was "based on a secret verbal agreement," and that Claude's claim was "completely without merit." A decision in the case was pending as of early 2011.

In 2010, the last big litigation over Ameriquest ended with a stipulation that disposed of those class action cases with small payments to claimants (who were expected to net about $100 each) and their lawyers. "The profits," Michael Howard wrote, had long since been "transferred into Roland Arnall's personal accounts." Which were presumably inherited by Dawn Arnall, who continues to live in the homes she and Roland shared in Holmby Hills and Aspen. "She deserves some credit for the way she wound down the company," says the former advisor. "She made the decision to negotiate settlements that cost her a lot of money. . . . I'm not saying she's now poor by any means," he adds.

Greg Hagins died early in 2011, but shortly before that, he said, "she's letting [Owlwood] deteriorate. The lawns are yellow." A visitor attempting to confirm that pulled into the cul-de-sac off Sunset that was once South Carolwood Drive one afternoon not long ago to be greeted by a private security guard. Asked if it was possible to peek at what had once been a public thoroughfare, he replied, "The owner wouldn't like that."

52

Bel Air

Bellagio House (10644 Bellagio Road)

Gary Winnick is surely the embodiment of St. Teresa of Avila's injunction that "answered prayers cause more tears than those that remain unanswered." "Yes, I made a lot of money," he told Congress in 2002. "I'm both proud [of] and saddened by it."

Shortly after he bought Hilda Boldt Weber's Bel Air estate from David Murdock in that $94 million record-setting deal, it became a symbol of the excesses of the dot-com and telecommunications bubble of the late 1990s. A former junk bond salesman at the high-flying 1980s investment bank Drexel Burnham Lambert, Winnick founded Global Crossing, a visionary telecommunications company, in 1996, and watched its stock soar only to see it swoon by the time he bought the estate, and then collapse in the fourth-largest bankruptcy in American history. Aferwards, he was condemned as the worst kind of business buccaneer, lumped together with Bernard Ebbers of World-Com and Kenneth Lay of Enron, two other epic business failures of the era. But while they were both convicted of financial crimes (Ebbers went to jail while Lay died before he was sentenced), lucky Gary Winnick walked away from the wreckage he'd created, settled all the lawsuits he left in his wake, and retreated behind the walls of his Bel Air fortress to live another day.

Since then, Winnick has become a pirate of penance, giving away bags full of the money he took with him before his company's collapse and loudly touting his philanthropy, the postbankruptcy success of Global Crossing (which was sold for $1.9 billion in April 2011), and his latest venture, an environmentally friendly concrete company. In regularly issued press releases, his Winnick Family Foundation calls him a "financier and philanthropist" and "a patron of humanitarian and literacy projects worldwide," but makes no mention whatsoever of the scandal that made him infamous.

The grandson of a pushcart peddler and son of a small businessman from the Long Island suburb of Roslyn, Winnick was a lousy student, taking nothing seriously until his father died of a heart attack in 1965 at age fifty-one when Gary was a freshman at nearby C.W. Post College. "It had a very, very profound impact on my life and my outlook," he's said. "I got serious about my life because I had no fallback." He kept a card in his pocket on which he'd written $50,000, the annual salary he hoped to earn one day, while he worked his way to a degree in economics as a soda jerk, bus driver, salesman in a local ski shop, and caddy at a nearby golf club. He married on Christmas Eve 1969 and later boasted that he'd saved the cost of decorations because the catering hall was already decked out for the holidays. It would take thirty years for him to get more comfortable splurging on interiors, but when he bought his Bel Air estate, Winnick would not only hire the renowned decorator Peter Marino and home renovator Peter McCoy (husband of Kayce Doheny) to refresh the place for him, but would spend a small fortune trying to buy back the Robsjohn-Gibbings furnishings that David Murdock sold off. Like Ron Burkle, Winnick seemed more interested in the house itself than in using it for self-aggrandizement. "Winnick restored it to the way it was supposed to be," says McCoy. "He recovered a lot and remade the rest."

Winnick's mother called him the *mitten drinnen* kid, Yiddish for "in the middle of everything," and after a brief stint selling furniture, Winnick found himself in the middle of something big in May 1973, when he was promoted from trainee to account executive at Drexel Burnham & Co., a company that was the combination of a declining old-school Wall Street brokerage and a feisty, mostly Jewish one staffed by eager come-from-nowheres like Winnick hoping to make a mark and some money.

The firm was known as Drexel Burnham Lambert by the time Winnick was promoted to bond salesman and met Michael Milken, who ran a then backwater department selling high-yield securities considered so risky they were called junk bonds. Their first encounter in 1976 wasn't a good one, wrote James B. Stewart in his book *Den of Thieves*. Though Winnick was supposed to earn a preestablished cut of a deal he made through Milken, the more experienced trader cheated him out of most of it, leading Winnick to complain to Milken's boss.

Milken wasn't sanctioned; he was too important to Drexel's bottom line. And clearly, there were no hard feelings of any significance; two years later, he asked Winnick, by then Drexel's top high-grade bond salesman, to come to Los Angeles and join him in what became one of the most exciting ventures in modern capitalism—the junk bond revolution that financed the explosive cable television, cellular telephone, and media innovations of the early Reagan years. Winnick, who was making that $50,000 a year at the time, jumped at the opportunity. He and his wife Karen moved to L.A. Sitting at Milken's famous X-shaped trading desk as one of his key lieutenants, Winnick was soon bringing home a breathtaking $2 million a month.

Winnick and Milken parted ways in 1985, Stewart reported, after Winnick got hold of evidence that Milken was taking far more than his fair share of lucrative partnerships he'd created to ensure that his salesmen didn't worry about their own earnings. Confronting Milken directly this time, Winnick, by then thirty-eight and his chief assistant, came away unsatisfied and quit Drexel. Cleverly, the manipulative Milken offered to help finance a private equity fund that Winnick would ostensibly run; the newly formed Pacific Asset Holdings, based across the street from Drexel, was essentially a Drexel "adjunct," as the author Connie Bruck put it, with Winnick's decisions controlled by his general partner, Milken's lawyer.

Nine months after forming Pacific, Winnick's first try at a big deal failed but likely planted the seed that would later grow into an immense fortune. In 1986, Drexel was advising Western Union in an attempt to restructure its crushing debts when Pacific and a partner offered to take over the company. As a telegraph, telex, microwave radio, mailgram, money transfer, and seminal e-mail company, Western Union was, in effect, a rudimentary data transmission service. The deal failed, but Winnick made money and, more important, tasted the future.

Meanwhile, the same officials investigating Beverly Hills Hotel owner Ivan Boesky for insider trading had begun looking into possible securities law violations by Drexel and Milken. By early 1989, Milken had pleaded not guilty to ninety-eight criminal counts, including racketeering, securities fraud, and tax law violations. At the end of that year, it emerged that Winnick had been granted immunity from prosecution in exchange for his testimony against Milken. Though he didn't end up testifying—Milken made a deal to plead guilty to six securities felonies—Milken loyalists turned on Winnick. But he emerged otherwise untainted as Drexel was forced into bankruptcy.

By 1996, visionaries had been talking about an information superhighway for several years, the Internet was catching on thanks to new software that provided access to the World Wide Web, and deregulation was causing financiers to look afresh at telephone and cable television when Gary Winnick first heard of the idea of laying fiber-optic cables under oceans to facilitate communications. Winnick had the sense to grab the opportunity, raising funds for a company called Global Telesystems and announcing Atlantic Crossing, a venture to lay an underwater fiber-optic cable connecting the United States, the United Kingdom, and Germany. Late the next year, it changed its name to Global Crossing, better reflecting Winnick's evolving vision, which had grown to include Pacific, Mid-Atlantic, and Pan-American units. By then, Winnick's stake had earned him the number eighteen spot on *Los Angeles Business Journal*'s list of the richest Angelenos. Rupert Murdoch, Marvin Davis, David Geffen, Jerrold Perenchio, Beverly Park's Steven Udvar-Hazy, Ron Burkle, Barron Hilton, and Ted Field were all above him on the list—but not for long. He was hailed as quick-witted, audacious, and generous: It was said he gave stock to his housekeeper, rabbi, and architect and Aston Martins and Rolls Royces to business associates who pleased him.

Though it had yet to make any profit, Global Crossing was a sensation, raising $800 million by selling junk bonds and signing contracts worth half that to lease space on its cables; it then went public and saw its stock price soar immediately. Winnick continued raising—and making—money at a fabulous rate, both for Global Crossing (which spent some of it buying telephone and fiber-optic networks) and for himself. In less than a year, Winnick's personal stake rose from $1 billion to $2.4 billion.

Winnick next announced plans to buy US West, the smallest of the so-called Baby Bell phone companies created from the breakup of the original AT&T monopoly. In the wake of that news, Global Crossing stock passed the $60 mark. His original $15 million investment was worth $6 billion in mid-1999, a fortune bigger than those of any of his L.A. mogul neighbors. His record-setting accumulation of wealth brought comparisons to John D. Rockefeller. He was said to be so driven he held business meetings while running off his excess weight on a treadmill in his office, which was said to have been renovated as a copy of the Oval Office. Though the top-heavy Global Crossing had another chairman, two vice-chairmen, a CEO (its second), a president, and would soon hire its second chief operating officer, no one doubted who was in charge. It was said—though denied—that he'd once fired an employee when he realized she didn't know who he was during a shared elevator ride.

Then, as suddenly as it had grown, Global Crossing's momentum lurched to a stop. Qwest snatched US West from Winnick in summer 1999, causing Global Crossing stock to fall by a third. And though it recovered and hit its all-time high of $64.25 in September, nine months later it was trading below $30 again, and that fall its price sank close to $20. Further intimations of volatility and disarray came when a third CEO quit the company seven months after taking the job. That was just seventeen days after Winnick bought 10644 Bellagio Road.

Even as its hundred thousand miles of cable connected two hundred cities and twenty-seven countries, an influx of competitors plus falling demand due to that year's dot-com bust caused a glut in network capacity and, inevitably, a steep drop in the price of Global Crossing's services. Revenues fell by about a third between 2000 and 2001. By that October, in the wake of the 9/11 terrorist attack that caused all stocks to plummet, Global Crossing had drawn down all its credit and its stock price had dropped to thirty-eight cents. In December, attempting to save cash to service its $12 billion-plus in debts, the company halted its dividend payments.

From then on, there would be nothing but bad news for Global Crossing and its largest shareholder. Late in 2001, it announced it would cut spending and 3,200 jobs, just under a quarter of its work force. Then, in January 2002, the company filed for bankruptcy under a proposed reorganization plan in which two Asian partners offered to put up $750 million for a 60 percent share of Global; debt holders would get the rest. In the aftermath of the filing, it emerged that while the share price was falling, insiders had sold about $1.5 billion in stock. Winnick himself had made $350 million. In April 2000, he'd sold another 8.1 million shares for $261 million. A month later, he cashed out 10 million more shares for $123 million, even as employees were barred from selling stock in their retirement plans.

Outside shareholders, facing the prospect that their stock was now worth little or nothing—after it was dropped by the New York Stock Exchange, Global's shares were trading for 13.5 cents on the over-the-counter market—expressed outrage when the press reported that renovations on Winnick's new mansion, involving more than a hundred workers, were still ongoing, and would cost between $15 million and $30 million. He could well afford it. Aside from his stock profits, he'd been drawing an annual salary of over $785,000 and gave himself a $1.03 million bonus that year. Friends described the house as a philanthropic project, as if restoring a fenced-in estate somehow benefited the citizens of L.A. "Where do I sign up as a contractor?" one ex-employee griped on a protest website. "I need a job."

Once the darling of investors and the press, Global Crossing became a goat overnight, criticized for overspending (the company leased five planes, including a Boeing 737), inside dealing, and poor management; sued by dozens of investors and former employees for severance pay; and under investigation by both the SEC and the FBI, which had learned that in August 2001, a Global Crossing executive had warned its accounting firm that it should stop puffing up its revenues with balance sheet trickery. That firm, Arthur Andersen (which was also Enron's auditor), had "written the bible" on how to perform those tricks—booking revenues for complex deals in a single year while spreading expenses out over many—without breaking securities laws, says someone involved in the mess of litigation that followed.

Inevitably, accusations of political influence followed; it turned out that Terry McAuliffe, Bill Clinton's chief fund-raiser, who'd assumed the helm of the Democratic National Committee, had also sold shares before the stock collapsed, making $18 million on a $100,000 investment after a golf round with Winnick that inspired the executive to pledge $1 million to Clinton's presidential library. McAuliffe was unapologetic. "If you don't like capitalism, move to Cuba or China," he said. Reporters wondered if that deal hadn't influenced the Clinton administration's decision to give Global Crossing a $400 million contract to develop a special computer network for defense scientists, and relax security rules to allow that to happen.

More revelations followed, many in the *New York Times,* which seemed as obsessed with Winnick as Inspector Javert was with Jean Valjean in *Les Misérables.* In story after story, the *Times* revealed that Global Crossing had forgiven two-thirds of a $15 million personal loan to a top executive just before the bankruptcy filing; had not only given CEO number two a million stock options with a discounted strike price and $10 million as a signing bonus, but also a 1999 Mercedes 500SL and first-class tickets to Los Angeles for his entire family, including his mother—even though he never moved there; and had then given CEO number four a $3.5 million signing bonus, a $1.1 million salary, and a promise of an annual bonus of $1.4 million. Global Crossing had also made $2.8 million in political contributions during the 2000 elections, including a sum in excess of $200,000 to New York Republicans, given while Global was seeking to sell most of the assets of its telephone company there—a deal that brought in $3.6 billion in much-needed cash after it was approved. As a bonus, Global Crossing kept $700 million in pension funds from the company while offloading both its employees and its obligations to them.

Day after day, the stories got worse, with tales of arrogance, insider deals, and increasingly desperate attempts to prop up if not abandon the sinking ship. Playing defense, Winnick's spokesman told the *Times*, "He was the chairman and did not run the company." Few others thought him blameless. "As an example of callous, cold-blooded greed, Gary Winnick is hard to match," thundered an editorial in the *New York Observer*, which called the story of Global Crossing "a sickening display of gluttony and venal avarice." The editorial ended, "Now the only responsible thing to do is put Gary Winnick behind bars."

That's not where he ended up. Global Crossing was finally sold to those two Asian partners, but by the time the deal was done, it was so devalued the buyers paid only $250 million for a 61.5 percent stake. When it restated its results for 2000 and 2001, Global Crossing showed almost $26 billion in losses.

Winnick was hauled before Congress but it was powerless to do more than embarrass him, and after admitting only that he'd let his employees down, "not because we engaged in fraud or insider trading but because we ran into a difficult economic period," he went home to Bel Air to lick his wounds. In December 2002, he created a $25 million fund for employees who'd lost money in their retirement plans. He also agreed to kick in $30 million to a $325 million settlement of the class action suit brought by investors and ex-employees and put $25 million in escrow on behalf of the New

York telephone workers who lost $300 million in pensions. He settled again a few months later, just before jurors were set to award $116 million to a former Pacific Capital associate who claimed Winnick had stiffed him on a share of profits (just as Milken had allegedly once stiffed Winnick). Arthur Andersen (which went belly-up after it was found guilty of obstruction of justice in the Enron collapse), the law firm of Simpson Thacher & Bartlett, Citigroup, Goldman Sachs, JPMorgan Chase, Credit Suisse, Morgan Stanley, Bear Stearns, Deutsche Bank, Lehman Brothers, and Canadian Imperial Bank of Commerce all also settled class action suits over their role selling Global Crossing to investors.

But some of those same banks also sued Winnick and other top executives, seeking $1.7 billion in damages, accusing them of a "massive scam," lying about the company's performance late in 2001 to win loans and keep it going. The judge in the case described it as "a bunch of crooks getting sued by a bunch of bankers who are too dumb to stop throwing money down the toilet." But that wasn't entirely accurate. The Justice Department had dropped its fraud investigation of Winnick on Christmas Eve 2002, his thirty-third wedding anniversary. "There just wasn't a crime there," his lawyer said.

After several years of legal wrangling, the judge dismissed half of the JPMorgan suit but a conventional securities fraud claim survived and, finally, on the brink of trial, Winnick's side settled again. Ever since, he's kept his head down, going public only to invest in the Broadway shows *The Color Purple* and *The Wedding Singer* and, early in 2011, putting money into the investment group that bought Miramax Studios from Walt Disney. Mostly, he battled to improve his reputation, hiring crisis management PR teams on both coasts and drawing praise from Los Angeles police chief Bill Bratton, an appearance by New York mayor Mike Bloomberg at a political fund-raiser he hosted, an invitation to speak at Harvard University's Center for Public Leadership, and even a warm greeting at a fund-raiser from former federal prosecutor Rudy Giuliani, who'd pressed him to testify against Milken.

To make amends, he's put his name on buildings, rooms, and institutes at Cedars-Sinai hospital, the local zoo, and the central library in Los Angeles, New York's Museum of Modern Art, and at Stanford, Syracuse, and Long Island universities. And he now runs iCrete, his environmentally friendly concrete company, as well as the renamed Pacific Capital Group. Since 2002, according to its tax returns, his foundation, run by his wife, a children's book author, has given away more than $27 million to dozens of Jewish, children's, animal, art, music, educational, and medical organizations. Presumably, despite this symphony of giving, Winnick can still afford the $894,618 annual property tax bill on his lavishly restored and beautifully maintained house on Bellagio Road.

53

Beverly Hills

Sunset House (9481 Sunset Boulevard)

In his *Eighteenth Brumaire of Louis Bonaparte,* Karl Marx cited Hegel's re-mark that historical events and actors repeat themselves, noting that his philosophical father forgot to add, "Once as tragedy, and again as farce." Though many in today's Los Angeles might disagree, and the superficial dif-ferences are many, the fourth and current owners of 9481 Sunset Boulevard, the chateau in the palms that Francis Xavier Lourdou built with a Spanish land-grant fortune, personify that notion. They would seem quite familiar to the self-made, self-taught, and often tragic likes of Charles Canfield, Edward Doheny, Max Whittier, and Burton Green. Not only that, all their fortunes derive from the very same Kern County land that once oozed the *brea* that built Beverly Hills and Bel Air. When Neil McCarthy's widow Mary sold 9481 Sunset for $750,000 in March 1977, her glorious wreck came full circle.

Disdained by what passed for L.A. society when they arrived, and gently mocked behind their backs for decades afterward, the buyers, Lynda and Stewart Resnick, embody not just what their community stands for, but also its highest aspirations. The Resnicks own an empire of popular products: FIJI Water, POM Wonderful pomegranate juice, almonds, pistachios, and California citrus fruits. They came to Sunset Boulevard with an eye for a bar-gain, a long-term outlook, and fierce aspirations, both financial and social. They fulfilled the first goal easily, the latter not so much—therein lying the farce. For while they continue to inch closer to social success, they demonstrate that even in L.A., signifiers like a big house, fancy cars, and wads of cash aren't everything. Still, sifting through the wreckage of so many of the lives lived in the great estates of the Platinum Triangle, it's clear that, for a host of reasons, few manage to stay the course. In this sense, the Resnicks have succeeded where countless others have failed. They've not reached the mountaintop yet, but it's clear they will keep climbing.

"It's not home, but it's much," Lynda Resnick says when she greets new visitors to the estate she named Sunset House. That quip captures more than just an ad woman's glibness. The Resnicks themselves are considered too much, too crass, pushy social climbers too self-absorbed and self-satisfied to realize they're being laughed at by the very same people who've crowded their lavish parties ever since they bought the house, when they immediately opened their doors to what Lynda has described, without irony, as their four hundred "nearest and dearest" for a "before party"—that is, before the house was renovated.

The fete, complete with medieval food, strolling minstrels, and a semi-nude, fire-eating belly dancer, was stage-managed by none other than former owner Dolly Green, who showed up just after they bought to welcome them to the neighborhood. Lynda Resnick thinks, incorrectly, that Dolly grew up in Bel Air, and that her father came from Texas. Lynda also claims she recovered the codicil to Howard Hughes's will in the walk-in safe in the basement, though it was actually found the year before they bought the house. Never mind—history was never the strong suit of most Angelenos. That said, Lynda knew her house—effectively untouched since 1927—was something special and not only saved it from near death, but brought it back to the life it was designed for.

"We have had so many wonderful parties, entertained presidents, future presidents, all manner of politicos, movie stars and movie star-makers, pillars of society . . . and an array of fascinating houseguests," Lynda said in a description of the house she wrote for friends in 2004. Her pride is well deserved. Like Ron Burkle and Gary Winnick (and perhaps Eric Smidt), the Resnicks have saved and restored one of the greatest Triangle mansions, in the process ensuring the survival of a small but vital bit of the history of Los Angeles.

Stewart Resnick was born sometime between 1936 and 1938 (depending on the source) and grew up in Highland Park, New Jersey, where his father

David, a Yiddish-speaking immigrant from Odessa in the Ukraine, ran a bar, drank too much, gambled away his earnings, argued with his wife, Yetta, and often beat his son, says author and journalist Mark Arax, who interviewed Resnick for a never-written biography. Arax attracted Resnick's attention when he coauthored a book called *The King of California*, on the life of a cotton-farming magnate. "[Stewart] probably felt, 'Damn, *I'm* the king of California,'" Arax says.

Resnick "grew up with tremendous shame," Arax thinks. He repeated several times in their interviews that he grew up around the rim of the Jewish Mafia. "My father was a great negative role model," Resnick said. "The lessons I got from him were all what not to do. About the only positive [thing] he taught me was never let anyone push me around." He credits his drive to his financial insecurity. Though poor, he was an instinctual entrepreneur; at thirteen, he sold photos to local Christian families of their homes decorated for Christmas. He left home at eighteen, enrolled at UCLA, and paid his way through school by working as a janitor, waxing floors, cleaning carpets, and slowly building a janitorial business that operated variously as White Glove Building Maintenance, Clean Time Building Maintenance, and Service Group, Inc. They made him his first million before he graduated from law school in 1962. By 1969, Service Group was a public company with $7.4 million in annual sales. Early in 1970, Resnick moved into the security business, which had boomed in L.A. after the 1965 Watts riots, buying two central-station burglar alarm firms and taking over a fire-alarm company. The next year, he changed its corporate name to American Protection Industries to reflect his new focus on guards, vehicle patrols, and protection services. Stewart Resnick was a janitor no more.

Resnick had gotten married very young, to a school nurse who, he told Arax, was "a nice lady without a lot of appreciations." They soon had three children, but he decided the marriage wouldn't last when she spotted two older couples playing bridge and told Stewart that was what she saw them becoming. "That's not how I saw it," said Resnick. At that point, he was rich but didn't live that way, buying used—if fancy—cars and living in a Culver City condominium.

Lynda Rae Harris married her first husband, Hershel David Sinay, in Beverly Hills the same year Resnick got his law degree. Born in Baltimore in 1943, she'd grown up in Philadelphia, the daughter of a child vaudevillian and movie distributor. Lynda performed on the *Horn & Hardart Children's Hour,* a radio (and, later, television) show with a cast of children sponsored by an automat restaurant chain. "By the time I was nine, I was washed up," she told the author Amy Wilentz. Her father segued from distributing movies to making them. His first were religious films, but in 1958, he produced a low-budget hit, *The Blob,* a science-fiction film with Steve McQueen in his first leading role. When it grossed millions, he moved his family to Trousdale Estates in Beverly Hills; he would go on to produce several more pictures, including *The Eyes of Laura Mars* and two *Blob* sequels.

"We quickly had two Rolls-Royces in the driveway," Lynda wrote in her business memoir, *Rubies in the Orchard.* Despite that, her father refused to pay for her to attend art school, so she spent a year at a community college, "bored and frustrated." But she also worked in a dress shop, where she found she had a knack for creating advertisements. She moved to Sunset House—her later home's namesake—a mail-order catalog selling Sea Monkeys and other novelty gifts, and by age nineteen, had gathered enough freelance clients to found her own ad agency, Lynda Limited. Her husband—she'd met him during her year in college through a family friend—was also in advertising, selling ad space for the *Wall Street Journal.* But Lynda was the family dynamo, even appearing on a local television show about success.

The Sinays lived south of Beverly Hills in a small house in which they raised two sons. "But the marriage came under a lot of pressure," Hershel Sinay later recalled. "I think we married too young and she was very focused on her career. . . . I wasn't the ambitious businessman she needed. Lynda wanted . . . success. She likes the good things in life." By 1968, she was divorced. "I was twenty-four and I looked forty-two," she's said.

In 1973, Lynda Sinay earned her first round of national fame—some might say infamy—when military analyst Daniel Ellsberg, the Julian Assange of his day, went on trial for photocopying internal Pentagon documents about the Vietnam War and leaking them to the press. It emerged that four years earlier, he'd copied the seven thousand pages of the Pentagon Papers on a Xerox machine at Lynda's ad agency office on Melrose Avenue. Lynda was dating Aaron Russo, who'd worked with Ellsberg at the think tank where they got hold of the papers.

Though she'd demonstrated against the war, Lynda wasn't political. "She was always thinking about how to make money," Russo told Ellsberg's biographer, Tom Wells. But still, "she was all impressed" when they asked if they could borrow her copier and explained why. She even helped with the two weeks of all-night copying sessions, shooing away the police the first night when they accidentally set off her burglar alarm, scissoring the Top Secret stamps off the tops of the documents to "declassify" them—and getting paid by the page for the use of her equipment.

"I was so naïve," Lynda told Wells. At the time, it seemed more "like the Keystone Cops or something," she said. "It was just like a comedy of errors." So was her subsequent appearance at Ellsberg's trial, when she testified that she'd discussed the contents of the documents with him, but couldn't recall specifics.

In the years between the copying and the courtroom, "my personal life was crumbling," Lynda wrote in her memoir. Her elder son had developed neurological problems, her ex was withholding child support, and a recession began that slowed her until-then flourishing business. Though the case against Ellsberg would be dismissed, she went into debt, lost all her employees, and lost her enthusiasm for advertising. Stewart Resnick, who'd just left his wife, would refocus her.

According to her memoir, a business associate wanted her to meet a man in the janitorial business. In another version of the story, Resnick lured her to his office on an advertising job and then relentlessly demanded more meetings. She didn't get the account, she often quips, "but I sure got the business." Stewart told Mark Arax that he contacted her about a relative's chain of clothing stores. Regardless, they were well matched in size (both were tiny) and ambition (less tiny) and soon got married and moved into a rental in the Malibu Colony where, by 1974, they'd begun earnestly socializing, earning the first of many mentions in *Los Angeles Times* social columns.[39]

After their honeymoon in Malibu, Lynda and Stewart Resnick moved east to a rented Mediterranean house on three acres in Bel Air. Their landlady was a 105-year-old widow and the rent was cheap; they hoped to buy it when she died. Three years later, when she showed no signs of shoving off, Lynda started looking at houses, dozens of them, showing only a select few to Stewart, who hated them all; he liked a grandiose but run-down chateau he'd seen on Sunset. The very thought made Lynda want to scream, or so she'd say later. "I didn't want that house. I knew I'd have to do . . . all the work." Despite her objections, they bought 9481 Sunset at the asking price under the aegis of American Protection and Lynda adapted, turned the purchase into a well-honed schtick (it was "like the cake in *Great Expectations,*" she often said, "almost totally destroyed"), and quickly learned to love it.

Stewart tells a different story, having said to Mark Arax that he prefers to live below his means. "None of this is my idea," he said of Sunset House. "If I had my way, I'd probably be living in Culver City in a little ranch house. . . . This is Lynda."

After their marriage, faced with raising their Brady Bunch–like gaggle of children, Lynda gave up her ad agency and went into what she thought would be an easier business, decorating. Though she's said she and her partner had eight jobs when 9481 became their ninth, it was an irresistible canvas, particularly since the new clients had millions and were unlikely to say no to their decorators' ideas. Though she stands about five foot two, with an hourglass figure (Stewart is said to call her breasts "the girls") topped by a hive of curly dark auburn hair, Lynda imagined herself as Marie Antoinette, declaiming "Let them eat cake" from behind the balustrades around her mansard roof. It was also a perfect environment for the diminutive yet powerful Stewart's Napoleonic fantasies.

Over time, the room they chose for Stewart's vast gilt office would become a fit setting for a contemporary emperor—complete with a Bonaparte-as-Caesar bust—albeit one who typically wears jeans, corduroys, or khakis and workshirts (along with the red string bracelet that kabbalah adherents wear to ward off the envy of others and their own jealousy and resentment). Their private living quarters filled up with Art Deco furniture and modern art, the public ones they used for entertaining with an eclectic mix of eighteenth-century Bourbon and nineteenth-century Empire and English-Aesthetic furniture, art, and adornments. So a life-sized 1871 white marble statue of a brooding Bonaparte at Elba by Vincenzo Vela would dominate the furnishings in their Corinthian-columned drawing room along with a valuable Savonnerie carpet from the Botiller era, Fortuny cotton draperies, an English Regency parcel-gilt chair, and a Chinese lacquer coffee table. "They've tried to blend and upgrade over time, and have it all in keeping with the Beaux Arts background," says decorator Craig Wright. "There's everything from Louis XIII to Georgian. It's all over the place but it all pulls together." But there was lots more to do to pull the house together than just buying furniture and garniture. And the heavy lifting wasn't limited to reinforcing the floor with steel rebar to hold up that Napoleon statue.

At the end, Neil and Mary McCarthy had lived like their fictional neighbor Norma Desmond. The place was in ruins, filled with five decades of grime; it had never been repainted; there were still bees in the rafters (as well as hundreds of pairs of polo boots in the basement); the roof leaked; the floors had rotted and one day shortly after the Resnicks bought it, a bathroom ceiling collapsed into the kitchen; fixtures were broken throughout the house; the pipes and electricity were as antique as the furnishings; the boiserie was decayed; the curtains rotted at the bottoms; the furniture was moth-eaten and the floors sun-bleached. "It was in a really bad state," says Wright, one of a number of interior designers they would hire as they continued decorating and redecorating for years (in the late seventies they even moved one decorator into a guest room).

That first phase of renovation lasted a frantic six months. "People became old as the house got young," says Lynda. "I sobbed. I was thirty and looked like a grandmother." They rewired, repainted, regilded, and restored; installed soundproof double-glazed windows on the Sunset façade; turned the foyer into a sculpture gallery; and added a scrolled marble mosaic R to the stair landing outside their front door as well as a window atop the grand staircase in the two-story entry foyer. The basement got a workout room and cubicles for Linda's several assistants. Upstairs, they created new family quarters, adding two master bathrooms, a butler's kitchen, and a sitting room where they still dine and watch television when they're home alone. "It's intimate compared to the rest of the house," says Wright.

Then they moved in and had another party, a black-and-white masked ball for a mere two hundred guests, after Lynda's mother reminded her, "You have been groomed your entire life to live in a great house and be a legendary hostess." This time, she dressed as another of her heroines, Scarlett O'Hara—though Lynda had never been hungry. At some point during the daylight-to-dawn affair, she removed a pair of tap pants she'd been wearing beneath her antebellum gown and flashed the remaining guests. "What young Beverly Hills socialite exposed herself at her own masked ball?" the Hollywood Reporter asked a few days later.

Lynda would later refer to that moment as her debut in Beverly Hills society. "Shortly after we moved in," she wrote in her memoir, "we realized we were quickly becoming everyone's new best friend. . . . We were invited to parties given by people we didn't know. We soon tired of the sort of friends that love you for the wealth they think you have." Apparently, moving out of one of the fanciest mansions in Beverly Hills wasn't a solution she was willing to consider.

Money was never the Resnicks' problem—they had it in spades. Stewart had the Midas touch when it came to making it—and after moving to Sunset House, he made lots more, unlike so many who moved to the Triangle only to flame out financially and leave again. Stewart bought their first farmland—2,500 acres of citrus trees and a packing plant in Delano, California—in 1978. Lynda would later claim it was a calculated plan to develop businesses that were "good for people." Stewart, on the other hand, considered it a passive investment. They were more active in Teleflora (a small, profit-making competitor of the huge nonprofit, florist-owned cooperative FTD), which they bought the next year. It was the first example of the teamwork that would build their empire. "Stewart and I together make one perfect person," Lynda later said. "We're like little salt and pepper shakers." Stewart handles strategy, administration, and finance; Lynda, marketing and image. She came up with the concept of flowers in a collectible gift, a variation of the gift-with-purchase gambit perfected by the cosmetics industry. After she and Stewart tried but failed to buy FTD in 1994, Lynda would boast that they made Teleflora twice its size.

Stewart's investment in land became significant in 1981, when American Protection bought control of Paramount Citrus Association, a leading grower, packer, and marketer of oranges, lemons, and grapefruits. Three years later, they bought Franklin Mint, then mostly a manufacturer of collectible coins and medals, for $100 million in cash and $67.5 million in notes. Harking back to her days at her first Sunset House, Lynda turned it into a somewhat more upscale version, churning out, instead of Sea Monkeys, nine hundred new products a year, including Scarlett O'Hara tchotchkes, Elvis portraits in blue suede frames, porcelain figurines, Frank Sinatra musical plates, pewter gargoyles, and die-cast models of vintage cars.

In years to come, Franklin Mint would give the couple their first taste of national fame. Lynda would buy famous jewelry like Jacqueline Onassis's triple strand of fake pearls (for $211,500) and the Duchess of Windsor's panther bracelet (for $90,000) at auction, copy them, and sell them at affordable prices. They compared themselves to the Medicis, subsidizing artists, and the Mint to Louis Comfort Tiffany's nineteenth-century decorative arts studio.[40]

The Franklin Mint was nothing, though, compared to the Resnicks' next big investment. In 1986, their holding company, Roll International, bought twelve thousand acres of pistachio and almond orchards from Mobil Oil, named them Paramount Farming, and the next year, added seventy-seven thousand acres of farm and grazing land plus wine production and storage, almond hulling, and cotton ginning facilities from Texaco, getting it all for a bargain price due to a drought that hit California's agribusiness hard. Some of it had once been Belridge Oil property, owned by Max Whittier and Burton Green. That was the year Dolly Green's steep decline began, but she likely would have been amused by the news that the new owners of one of her old houses had also acquired some of the land that paid for them all. The Triangle was still, in a very real sense, a very small world.

That same year, the Resnicks also bought eighteen thousand acres from Prudential Life Insurance for $30 million. It included 108 acres of pomegranate bushes. For the next ten years, though they sold pomegranates in small markets, they basically ignored them in favor of their nuts and citrus fruits; by 1996, Paramount Farms, with net sales of about $1.5 billion, was the largest producer, processor, and marketer of almonds and pistachios in the world. In 2000, it attained the same status in fresh citrus products after the company paid $55 million to buy almost four thousand acres more from David Murdock's Dole Food.

Though others mostly run his farms, Stewart Resnick has a deep personal connection to what is likely his and Lynda's "greatest hit," POM Wonderful, the pomegranate juice. Lynda has come to personify the brand, even calling herself the POM Queen. But it is Stewart's passion that drove the business. He'd had prostate problems and high PSA levels, says Mark Arax, to whom Resnick confided that his daily intake of the stuff dropped those levels to zero. His doctor had told him of the pomegranate's place in folk medicine. Whether that motivated him to finance studies of the fruit is unclear, but he did, to the reported tune of $23 million. The couple expanded their orchards to six thousand acres and in 2002, introduced their high-priced fresh juice sold in a bottle shaped like two stacked pomegranates (but also like "Mother, it's the female form, it looks like me," Lynda said). It was backed by a loud and pervasive advertising campaign with giveaways, recipes for pomegranate cocktails, billboards, and more, touting the drink, Herbalife-style, as an antioxidant-packed elixir that would help everything from impotence to cancer.

In private, Stewart seems a little rankled by the attention paid to his wife over POM. "He let her have her glory and then some," Arax says. "But the fact is he was the mover and shaker when it came to pomegranates. The man's got tremendous vision."

By the late 1990s, the Resnicks could not be denied even though they were still disdained; as one experienced social arbiter put it, "They are vulgarians and vulgarians almost always rub refined people the wrong way." Nonetheless, their business success (*Working Woman* magazine named Lynda its third most important female business owner in 1995) and their inroads into philanthropy (they'd started getting the awards that signal big gifts) made them friends in Los Angeles. Generous political donations had made them friends in high places, too. Over the last quarter of the twentieth century, they and executives of their companies gave almost $4 million to candidates and various political committees, mostly in California. Between 1993 and 2009, they gave $1.6 million to California governors alone. Most, though not all of it, went to Democrats, so it was hardly surprising when, at the party's 2000 convention in Los Angeles, Sunset House was the scene of a fund-raiser for Senator Dianne Feinstein honoring generous donors. Howard Blume of *LAWeekly* briefly crashed the event and wrote what he experienced: "Inside . . . a living room that looks like a fine-art museum—only better kept. The tasteful opulence exudes a tincture of Versailles—only better kept. And, may I say, I have never been thrown out of a party with such courtesy and deference. One of the doormen even shakes my hand before bidding me goodbye."

Those political connections had likely played a part in what many consider the Resnicks' greatest business coup—gaining control of an almost incomprehensible amount of water, the vital element that sustains the Southland, its businesses, and residential communities. Water has always been a life-or-death issue in Southern California. In 1937, the California Water Project formed to redistribute water from the north into the perennially parched south. As William Mulholland had learned, such redistributions stirred controversy; promoted as helping small farmers and local economies, they inevitably enriched only the wealthiest landowners. Shades of Huntington, Harriman, Sherman, Chandler, and Otis in the Owens Valley.

In 1968, when federal and state agencies started to build a 444-mile-long, $750 million aqueduct to the San Joaquin Valley, many asked whether the chief beneficiaries wouldn't be big corporate farmers like those in Kern County at the valley's southern end. Nobody is more interested in Kern

County farmland than the Resnicks, who by 2009 would own more than 115,000 acres there, an area equal in size to four San Franciscos.

In the mid-1980s, the state's Department of Water Resources came up with a plan to store about a million acre-feet of water (an acre-foot is the amount of water it takes to cover an acre with a foot of water) in Kern County's alluvial fan: ancient underground river formations and aquifers of disintegrated rock. To create this water bank, which would fill up in wet years so it could be pumped during droughts, the department bought twenty thousand acres, and paid for planning and the initial plumbing needed to make the plan reality. But in 1994, after spending $74 million, the department decided it couldn't finish the job and, following a drought that caused Kern County farmers to scream that they'd received far less water than they needed (a problem exacerbated by slowdowns at the pumps to protect endangered fish), a compromise was struck, and the Kern Water Bank was handed over to the Kern Water Bank Authority—48 percent owned by the Resnicks' Paramount Farming. Another 9 percent was owned by a water district run by the president of Paramount.

The new authority finished the seventy ponds, six-mile canal, thirty-three miles of pipe, and eighty-five wells to pump the water out. As part of the complex deal, the water bank was able to sell some of that same water back to the state at a profit, even though the state was pumping so much water at the time, Resnick and the other landowners only needed to make paper transfers in their records, rather than physically delivering any water.

In a report called, portentously, "Water Heist," issued late in 2003, Public Citizen, the nonprofit consumer advocacy group, concluded that control of the bank rested in the hands of the Resnicks, the recipients of a $180 million giveaway of precious public assets—the market value of all that water—as well as an insurance policy against natural fluctuations in rainfall. The public till was subsidizing a billion-dollar farming empire; Roll International was able to double its acreage and production and was selling some of its water for a profit to developers who, in search of fast, sure profits, were turning what had been farmland into housing tracts. Fears rose that the Resnicks would do the same themselves.

Asked by author Mark Arax if that was his plan, Resnick insisted, "Our first loyalty is to our trees," but then admitted, "If there's some big opportunity for us to take a couple thousand acres and build a nice industrial park out there, we're going to do it. That's just life. But on balance, unless there's a really big opportunity, there's a continuity to farming that I like."

In other words, farming is nice, but if he sees a chance, he might take it.

The last big piece of the Resnick corporate puzzle fell into place in 2004 when the couple bought FIJI Water, the second-largest brand of imported bottled water in the United States, and started touting it as a symbol of Roll's corporate philosophy of selling only products that are good for people and the planet. That didn't mean they weren't interested in profit. "We sell food," Lynda told Charlie Rose a few years later. "People have to eat."

But the master marketer was positioning them as thoroughly responsible modern capitalists. Her latest famous friend was the author and conservative political wife turned progressive new media magnate Arianna Huffington, who had a party at Sunset House for her latest book that year. "We are so tired of being disenfranchised," Lynda declaimed from atop her grand staircase, rallying her liberal troops: Heather Thomas, Irwin Winkler, Judith Krantz, Willow Bay, Rob Reiner. "Community and transparency," Lynda told Rose, "that's the twenty-first century. Unless you give back to the planet, there's no place for you in the new culture." Once again, her attempt to fuse her and her husband's fortunes to the Zeitgeist would leave Lynda open to charges of abject hypocrisy.

Rainwater, pistachios, pomegranates, even pure bottled water "untouched by man," as Lynda's new slogan for FIJI had it—on the surface, none of it sounded the least bit controversial. Even if some of their customers disagreed with their liberal politics, the Resnick empire seemed unshakable, transparent as FIJI Water, and as community-friendly as a business could be. So when their ground shook, as it soon did, and storm clouds arrived and buffeted Sunset House, Lynda would blame their troubles on jealousy. They were rich and important, so of course people hated them.

What many of their detractors share is the feeling that just beneath their buffed surface are rapacious capitalists who will happily hurt little people who get in their way. That's true in each of the serial controversies that have dogged them through the first decade of the twenty-first century, beginning with the pistachios that were the origin of the Resnicks' accidental agricultural empire.

In fall 2005, Stewart Resnick sued to freeze the finances of the California Pistachio Commission, a twenty-six-year-old marketing, promotion, government affairs, and research group sanctioned by the state's Department of Food and Agriculture. Resnick was furious that as a majority producer, Paramount paid most of the commission's bills but had no seat on its board and no input into advertising it opposed and programs that, he claimed, favored small growers and "were actually doing harm to Paramount. That's not a situation we could tolerate for very long." Paramount offered aid to any small growers who took its side, but most of the supporters solicited by Resnick were rejected by the judge in the case, while hundreds of growers chose to stick with the commission. Nonetheless, the following year, the commission was killed. Though a clear majority of the state's producers wanted to keep it alive, Paramount's percentage of pistachio production volume (it either grows or processes and markets 260 million of California's annual production of 400 million pounds) won the day.

Paramount soon began running Lynda's typically over-the-top advertising campaigns for its nuts, flew international journalists and nutritionists in to tout their virtues, and planned a major marketing push into Europe—but the aggressive move left a bad taste in the mouths of rival growers. They considered Resnick a monopolist who would use any tactic to get control and protect his empire.

Seven years after Public Citizen's exposé of the "water heist," a series by Mike Taugher in the *Contra Costa Times* brought that issue to the fore again, alleging that, among other things, the Kern water agencies had collected $138 million in water sales and had then used that money for a variety of not very public-minded purposes, including suing the Department of Water Resources, the same agency that paid those millions to them, to lower its water bills. The Resnicks' water and farm companies sold more than $30 million worth of water to the state, and made $3.8 million from sales through other public water agencies. And meanwhile, endangered fish that the water bank program was supposedly designed to protect were being hurt by it instead: Because of water pumping, delta smelt dropped to near-extinction, and fishing for wild California salmon was banned for two years.

Two lawsuits, brought by environmental groups and water agencies, sought to reverse the transfer of the water bank and gain restitution of all private profits it had generated. "We paid for it," Stewart Resnick told *BusinessWeek* in a rare public response. "We own it."

"The transfer of the water bank was not a simple purchase of property, like Resnick claims," responds Adam Keats, senior counsel for the Center for Biological Diversity, one of the plaintiffs, "but rather a sweetheart deal made between political allies to divest the public of its property so that a small group of private entities could outrageously profit. This is exactly what the law prohibits and we intend to prove that with our suit." Another water district, south of the Kern bank, sued too, claiming Kern's pumping dropped the local water table and dried up its water supplies. The head of the Kern authority shot back that the rival district was mismanaged.

Then, there was Ali Amin, head of Primex Farms, a rival pistachio processor. He sued, claiming that Paramount was using the Kern bank water as a weapon to drive him out of business, selling water on the cheap to growers who'd been his customers in order to steal them, causing him to lose $5.5 million. A judge ruled against Amin in his first suit, but not before he'd accepted a $10,000 settlement from Paramount. His lawyer says that during discovery, alleged "wrongful conduct" on the part of Paramount came to light, inspiring Amin to file a retooled suit challenging Paramount's interference and violations of the public utilities code. Amin compared himself to David fighting Goliath.

To *BusinessWeek*, Resnick backhanded his accuser. Amin "wanted to be a major player and he continues to have a lot of animosity and he'll never change," Resnick said. And after Amin's first suit was filed, the Resnicks' companies filed a federal suit against him, alleging he'd advertised falsely to growers and cost Paramount $15 million in damages.

Then, the Resnicks were attacked on another front. Despite their claims and a program announced in 2008 to go carbon negative, environmentalists were taking aim at FIJI's squat, square bottles. *Mother Jones*, the anticorporate investigative magazine, blasted FIJI and the Resnicks for "typhoid outbreaks that plague Fijians because of the island's faulty water supplies," the company's tax-free status on Fiji, its alleged sheltering of assets in tax havens like the Cayman Islands where its trademarks are registered, its Luxembourg corporate headquarters, and "the fact that its signature bottle is made from Chinese plastic in a diesel-fueled plant and hauled thousands of miles to its eco-conscious consumers. And, of course, you won't find mention of the military junta for which FIJI Water is a major source of global recognition and legitimacy."

The Resnicks' response noted that Fiji was democratic when they bought the company and that they used 1.5 percent of FIJI Water's gross revenues to improve life on Fiji and had set up a foundation to do more. But that didn't still the outrage. One clever Internet commentator called their efforts "greenwashing." "Bottled water," said Michael Brune of the Rainforest Action Network, "is a businesss that is fundamentally, inherently and inalterably unconscionable." Long known as pugnacious and litigious in pursuit of their financial interests, the Resnicks now found themselves tarred as enemies of the environment. The attacks left them feeling betrayed and defensive. Their business is their life, so they take it all personally.

"Most people like me," Lynda says. "Some don't, and it hurts my feelings."

Live by image and you can die by image, too. Their complex blend of business and social ambition and their relentless, sometime ruthless pursuit of success in both public and private spheres have left the Resnicks occupying a weird space in the social strata of Los Angeles, even as their home remains a social magnet for the rich, the famous, and the on the make. Despite Lynda's claim of the couple's instant social acceptance in Los Angeles after they bought their trophy mansion, their social situation has never been simple; some say the Resnicks' social emergence was more of a slog—even before the bad press of recent years.

"She goes back a long way, performing and being noticed," says one Los Angeles philanthropist. "She gets what she wants when she wants it. She'd like to be powerful, to get the things she wants. She seems like someone who wants to be a part of everything. She gets upset if she's not invited. She never comes. She says, 'I'd still like to be asked.' "

In the early days, "they had no one to ask for dinner," says a journalist who has covered L.A. society for decades. "Stewart's best friend was their butler." Which of the many butlers they employed was that best friend is unclear. But one of the parade that passed through the staff apartment facing out on the garden beneath the Italianate loggia was Ian Ross, hired in the early eighties. Ross had married a British aristocrat whose father helped finance Radio Caroline, the most famous of England's offshore pirate radio stations in the 1960s. Ross ran it and for a time managed the band the Animals, but in the late 1970s, he moved his family to Los Angeles, where he became the front man for California's first roller-disco, Flipper's, which was his nickname (he'd lost his leg in a car crash and wore a metal one). When the club closed, Flipper, broke, went to work for the Resnicks, who are said to have hired him because they were impressed with his plummy accent.

Ross later lampooned the Resnicks in a novel, *Beverly Hills Butler,* that portrayed them as a matched set of foul-mouthed, arrogant, superficial, and frighteningly insecure heathens whose money couldn't buy taste. He described Lynda as a spoiled and lethal "Tyrannosaurus Regina" with a red rictus smile and a "death-lizard voice," alternately screaming at him and utterly dependent on the veneer of class she thought he gave them despite his towering ineptitude as a butler. He saw Stewart as a powerful man helpless before his shrewish wife and awed by the "liberating tyrant" Napoleon, whose seated statue had its own dedicated lighting system, and whose "grimness he strove to emulate, with some success, to keep at bay those who would part him from his money, or seek to prevent him from amassing more."

But the Resnicks didn't just amass money; they also continued to give it away, and not just to politicians and pomegranate researchers. Through their Resnick and Resnick Family foundations, they have sprinkled their fortune far and wide. And though they claim to be "low-key philanthropists," they've gotten their name out there quite well. You can't claim Arianna Huffington and the Clintons as close friends and expect to be invisible.

At UCLA, their name is on the Stewart and Lynda Resnick Neuropsychiatric Hospital, partly financed with a $15 million gift from the duo, and they've also given $3 million toward a new medical sciences building. They donated $20 million for a Resnick Sustainability Institute to study energy technology at Caltech, and have given generously to the Aspen Institute.[41] Less noisily, big money's gone to Conservation International and Bard College, which runs a charter school, the Paramount Bard Academy, one of a number of schools and scholarship funds for Paramount employee children that the Resnicks have funded in the Central Valley. Smaller amounts go to a range of causes, from the King Hussein Foundation and the Vaclav Havel Library to the United Jewish Foundation and the U.S. Department of Agriculture's research service, which has studied navel orangeworms in pistachios.

They also give their time. Lynda sits on the board of the Aspen Institute, where she chairs the Communications Committee; UCLA Medical Sciences; the Prostate Cancer Foundation; and the Milken Family Foundation. She is also a trustee of the Philadelphia Museum of Art, which got $1 million from the couple in 1987, when they owned the local Franklin Mint, to endow the gallery where van Gogh's *Sunflowers* hangs. Stewart is on the boards at UCLA Medical Sciences and Bard, too, as well as the J. Paul Getty Trust, Conservation International, and the California Institute of Technology.

"One can buy one's way in where there's no society," says a friend and admirer. "It wouldn't have happened without the money and the vacuum at the heart of L.A. It's a town where everything is boom and bust and Stewart has never had a bust. So for all her Jewish nervousness, they represent stability. They appear deep because they actually do good. They're among the most consistently generous people in L.A. They're not unimportant strivers; they're important strivers."

That matters in Los Angeles, where the old guard from Pasadena long ago abdicated public leadership to the entertainment business crowd of the Triangle. There, you're only as good as your last movie, TV show, or charitable contribution. So the Resnicks' potent combination of fierce ambition, huge new wealth, networking genius, new and old media friends (Lynda has blogged deep thoughts for *The Huffington Post*), and willingness to try and try again, has helped them build a local brand as the town's premiere postmodern Renaissance couple. They're not unassailable—far from it—but somehow, that makes them even more compelling.

That was clear in fall 2010 when the Resnicks had what can only be termed their coronation as members of the philanthropic and cultural royalty of Los Angeles. The venue for their enoblement was the Los Angeles County Museum of Art, better known as LACMA, a rambling campus next to the La Brea Tar Pits in the Mid-Wilshire district between Beverly Hills and downtown L.A. Lynda has been a trustee since 1992 and serves as chair of the Acquisitions Committee.

In 2006, LACMA announced that a $25 million pledge made anonymously the year before would pay for a new grand entrance to the multibuilding museum named for the Resnicks. Two years later, when the oil company BP gave LACMA a separate $25 million gift, the Resnicks agreed to give it the naming rights to the entrance pavilion, and instead up their gift to $45 million to pay for a new 45,000-square-foot exhibition space designed by the architect Renzo Piano that would bear their names. It was just behind Piano's Broad Contemporary Art Museum, which had opened a few months before. Behind the scenes, some said, the Resnicks' additional generosity was inspired by the chance to distinguish themselves from—and one-up—the Broad's benefactors, Eli and Edyth Broad.

Retired from a career in real estate, insurance, and finance, Broad dedicated himself and his $5 billion fortune to philanthropy. But he is a hands-on benefactor, known for micromanaging his huge gifts to institutions like LACMA, and he isn't always beloved. He doesn't care. After a fight with the museum's director, Michael Govan, he decided to foil LACMA's expectation that it would eventually receive the bulk of his prodigious art collection, and open his own museum instead. Museum folk lauded the Resnicks for being LACMA's anti-Broads and making no demands over how their money was spent.

The Resnicks' reward was a gala opening party at their new Renzo Piano–designed building in their honor, and "Eye for the Sensual," an exhibition of some of their collection as one of its three opening shows. Govan raved that their collection was "distinguished and diverse" and of "unusual quality," and noted pointedly that they planned to give many of their 3,500 works to museums, LACMA among them.

Despite Lynda's claim that their money isn't everything, they would be nowhere without it—not in La-La Land. Stewart generates the wealth that fuels Lynda's social mountaineering and her spending on both conspicuous display and conspicuous philanthropy. In the country of the blind the one-eyed man is king; so this two-trick couple have become social royalty in the Platinum Triangle, even if they aren't exactly loved.

Money must be driven like a train if you want to get places, and Lynda is driven to do that. To Stewart's amusement, she turned Sunset House into a clubhouse for the "pretty highfalutin'," she has said. "If I want to meet somebody, I find a way." Their cast of regulars features Huffington, Hollywood types like David Geffen, Mike Medavoy, Lawrence Bender, Norman Lear, Albert Brooks, Rob Reiner, Michael York, Warren Beatty and Annette Bening, Aaron Sorkin, Yvette Mimieux, Bill Maher, and Larry David and his activist ex-wife Laurie, as well as the writer Gore Vidal and the former financier Michael Milken. "It's a fuller life when you know, in the same life, Martha Stewart and Jared Diamond, Edgar Doctorow and Joan Didion and Sylvester Stallone," Lynda said when she was profiled in *The New Yorker*. Yes, *The New Yorker*.

What attracts them all? "To have dinner at the long table under the huge chandelier in the dining room," observed the author Amy Wilentz, "is to feel *as if* one were a part of some kind of modern aristocracy, of an entitled few.

It's like dining at the table of the Sun King. But it becomes clear as you look around that nobody here is really *a part of* all this. . . . The money is the most important guest."

But the money by itself really isn't *everything*. In fact, it would be nothing without Lynda's fierce ambition to be somebody, to make a difference, to be remembered (that most un-L.A. of desires)—and her skill in making that happen is just as important as the wealth that enables it. She is above all else a marketing woman. So everything the Resnicks do has an aspect of calculated self-promotion, from their home to their entertaining to their lavish collectible holiday gift boxes, bursting with all the various products they grow or manufacture and accompanied by cards that double as advertisements.

The Resnicks both knew that their chances of making it (making money for Stewart, making a name for herself for Lynda) were much better in Los Angeles than in their homes in the East. "California wasn't set in its ways," Stewart told Wilentz. "There was nothing established in place. It was so easy to open new things. I was able to build a new business without much trouble. And we could eventually do things socially that would never have been open to us on the East Coast. We were accepted easily." Lynda has said much the same. "I couldn't have done it in any other town, in any other state. I had no credentials with the Eastern Establishment."

The Southern California establishment, by comparison, was and remains a work in progress, requiring no credentials to get started, no bloodline, no essential syllabus of prestigious schools attended, important books read, sights seen, and subjects studied as prerequisites for advancement, and boasting only a list of its richest citizens to sanctify arrival, not an impossible-to-define-but-you-know-it-when-you-see-it social A-list like in New York, Boston, Philadelphia, and even Denver. You can be anyone—or perhaps more accurately, invent yourself as anyone—and make it in L.A. And it doesn't matter whether people like you or not.

Money and power are more than enough to balance out ferocious displays of ambition and greed. Los Angeles is America's last great place, where you can go when all else fails and make your mark because the canvas is blank and your pedigree (genealogical, geographic, educational, or religious) makes no difference whatsoever. It's the place where no one knows you and no one cares who you are—just what you can do for them. Even the sunshine symbolizes possibility: nine hours of daylight after Europe goes to sleep, three hours more than they have "back east," suggesting that someday, it might even be the late bird that catches the worm.

There is only one caveat to California's cult of opportunity: Don't fail, or you might fall off the edge of the continent and into the Pacific which, at twice the size of the Atlantic or Indian Ocean, is a big place to drown—as demonstrated by those many tragic lives lived, and forgotten, in the Platinum Triangle.

For a hundred years, lives of accomplishment left barely a trace on the palimpsest that is L.A., a slate wiped clean with each new home sale. Who remembers Doheny, Bell, Canfield, Whittier, and the Jansses, many of whom were people of great generosity of spirit and intellect?[42] If they are recalled at all, it's because they built railroads, drilled for oil, and turned scrubby foothills into citadels of wealth. The Resnicks are their modern inheritors—panning for pomegranates and water instead of gold and oil. Let their guests whisper behind the Corinthian columns, accusing the Resnicks of being phonies; the fact is they come when called, and just like Lynda, long to be invited when they're not. Simultaneously courted and scorned, the Resnicks embody the publicity principle that it doesn't matter what people say as long as they are talking about you.

But no matter what people do say about them, unlike so many who came before them in the great estates of La-La Land, the Resnicks have survived. And not only that, they've bettered their city, too. That takes more than money—it takes a little heart.

At their LACMA building's opening, Lynda, in a flesh-colored Dior gown in front of her portrait of Marie Antoinette by Elisabeth-Louise Vigée–Le Brun, greeted guests like Tom Hanks, David Geffen, James Franco, Nicole Richie, and Kim Kardashian. "A great deal of her bad press was manufactured by her enemies," Lynda said of the ill-fated queen of France.

There were no enemies in sight to blame for the reviews that followed the opening. In keeping with the Resnicks' problematic place in L.A.'s constellation, the evening wasn't entirely a success. L.A. society may have turned out to bow before them, but the pesky press wasn't rolling over. "This exhibition shows more skin than you'd see at the Playboy mansion on a Saturday night," wrote the *Los Angeles Times* art critic Christopher Knight. "But to what end? The collector is always the primary subject of a vanity show and LACMA is of course trolling for a major art gift." The *Wall Street Journal* deemed Piano's building unimpressive and the Resnicks' art "second-rate stuff, more at home in a manor house on Sunset Boulevard than a major art museum."

But the biggest insult came from a higher authority two days after the LACMA event when the Federal Trade Commission issued two official complaints charging that the couple had made "false and unsubstantiated claims" about the health benefits of their pomegranate products. Despite the millions they claimed to have spent on research, "the available scientific information does not prove" that POM Wonderful, or associated POMx tea, iced coffee drinks, pills, and other products, "effectively treats or prevents" heart disease, prostate cancer, or erectile dysfunction. The vote to approve the complaints against POM, Roll, and the Resnicks personally was unanimous.

A source close to the FTC says that the ubiquitous advertisements for POM brought the hammer down on them. "Cheat death," a famous one read. The fact that the Resnicks had again used lawsuits as a business tool probably didn't help. A onetime POM Wonderful executive was sued after he launched a rival juice that POM claimed had added sweeteners. POM also sued Welch's, PepsiCo's Tropicana, and Coca-Cola's Minute Maid brand for falsely advertising the benefits of their juices. And then POM preemptively sued the FTC, charging that new regulations on deceptive advertising were in conflict with the pomegranate's First Amendment rights. Credit the Resnicks with this: If nothing else, they are litigiously creative.

Exaggerated, extravagant, crude, ridiculous, a bit indecent, and vastly entertaining, Lynda and Stewart Resnick embody all the characteristics of farce—and even seem to be on course for an improbably happy ending, ending their days as Neil McCarthy did at their Sunset House. In recent years, they have amassed not just more money, but more land, buying the homes on either side of theirs in 2000 and 2001 for a total of $8 million, demolishing one and after the second burned down, adding a pool, an orange grove, a sculpture garden, a cabana and outdoor dining area, a greenhouse, a huge lawn, hedges and paths, and a parking lot big enough for dozens of cars—giving what had once been a large house on a small lot the land it needed to truly qualify as a great estate. Then, in summer 2010, they bought a fourth adjacent four-bedroom house on another acre for almost $8 million (the actor James Caan had bought it in 1974 for a mere $225,000). At a planning commission hearing on their earlier work, Linda had categorically denied that they had a standing offer to buy it. "We have no intention of buying that house," she declared. "We're not taking over Czechoslovakia or Santa Monica. This is enough."

Apparently, there is no such thing as enough.

Which is a belief the Resnicks share with the founders of the Platinum Triangle. And that's what makes them exemplars of their community today, even more than their Beverly Hills mansion or their Kern County land, which once gushed oil and now holds a wealth of precious water; that's what inextricably links these two Eastern transplants to the Southland's storied past and the promise it held, and still does, for those who dare to look to the west and dream.

Like the founders, the Resnicks came to California with little more than that dream, hoping to make their fortune; and like their predecessors, they did—through stubborn persistence, occasional belligerence, and an unquenchable, almost noir-ish lust for land and lucre. And like the founders, they link the two Californias that have, in vastly different ways, captured the world's imagination with the bounties they produce; the Resnicks' holdings straddle several mountain ranges, with one corporate foot in the Central Valley, the fabled California of dirt and water, and one on Sunset Boulevard, the ribbon running through the California of glittering image. Both of these Californias cultivate money and power, but the Platinum Triangle is where it lives.

More streetwise and resilient than they are smooth social operators, the Resnicks are unlikely to go the way of Hilda Boldt Weber, whose brief foray onto the social battlefield of the Triangle left her fatally wounded. The Federal Trade Commission notwithstanding, neither are they likely to be crushed like Edward Doheny; though their political connections couldn't keep them out of trouble, they are dexterous enough that even if they lose the pomegranate war, they will surely find new ways to win.

Edward Huntington, Charles Canfield, Max Whittier, Burton Green, Edward Doheny, Alphonzo Bell, the Jansses, and Arthur Letts were all men of their time, reflecting its virtues and vices. The cast of characters that passed through the communities they created in the years since were also creatures of their eras, albeit exceptional examples. Thirty-four years after they came on the scene, buying and restoring their French Renaissance wreck, the Resnicks remain exemplars of their time and place. Simultaneously crass and cultured, innocent yet corrupt, alluring and off-putting, superficial and sage, materialistic and high-minded, real-phony and phony-phony, they are environmentalists selling water in plastic bottles made in fossil-fuel-run Chinese factories, political progressives with fully paid all-access passes to the powerful. Sitting in their grand old mansion, surrounded by their seventeenth- and eighteenth-century French art and the celebrated, the connected, and the accomplished, they are everything we love to hate about twenty-first-century Los Angeles—and everything we love about it, too.

ACKNOWLEDGMENTS

The genesis of this book was a review I wrote for the *New York Post* of *The Legendary Estates of Beverly Hills* by Jeff Hyland, a native of Beverly Hills, architectural historian, and the cofounder of the Hilton-Hyland real estate brokerage. The mammoth coffee-table book covers some of the same estates this book does, and if you want to see them in luscious, oversized photos, I highly recommend it. But I saw an opportunity in what Hyland didn't do: use the houses as the foundation of a social history of the estate district of Los Angeles from its earliest days to the present. Hyland's generosity in encouraging me to build on his research, and his willingness to share his knowledge and some of his resources, were a harbinger of what I found throughout the two-plus years I worked on this book. After writing two similar ones—*740 Park,* the New York City equivalent of *Unreal Estate,* and *Rogues' Gallery,* the story of the wealthy patrons of the Metropolitan Museum of Art—on the sometimes cooperative, sometimes indifferent, but often outright hostile society of my hometown, the warm reception I received in Los Angeles was a very welcome change. I was always a New Yorker who loved L.A. I love it there all the more now.

A book like this inevitably starts with people who know and care about great real estate. Many of the top real estate brokers in the Platinum Triangle were also generous with their time and knowledge. Thanks to Rose Borne, Ron de Salvo, Russ Filice, Valerie Fitzgerald, Betty Graham, Jerry Jolton, Brooke Knapp, Drew Mandile, Linda May, Jade Mills, John Bruce Nelson, Saeed and Myra Nourmand, Marjie Oswald, Joyce Rey, Jonathan Sands, Stephen Shapiro, Mike Silverman, Heidi Tabib, and Shirley Wells, each of whom played a part, some large, some small, in helping me choose which houses to focus on. A New York broker and friend, Martha Kramer, made several vital introductions.

You don't need to be a broker to know great real estate. Many others guided me and my research. I owe particular thanks to my sister Jane Gross, who lived in and covered Los Angeles while working for the *Los Angeles Times,* Julie Payne, Robbie Anderson, Greg Fisher, Hutton Wilkinson, David Jones, David Netto, and Denise Hale, who lived in Beverly Hills as Denise Minnelli. Thanks, also, to Mark Arax, Peter Bart, Annabelle Begelman Weston, Ted Bensinger, Simon and Tina Beriro, Ann Brenoff, Jack Brown, George Christy, Maggie Clair, Ron Collier, Jill Collins, David Patrick Columbia, Peter Duchin, the late Dominick Dunne, Sandy Gallin, Bob Goldsborough, Bob Grossweiner, Caroline Graham, Gigi Levangie Grazer, Gene Gutowksi, Gay Harwin, Fred Hayman, Beverly Jackson, Diane Kanner, Victoria King, Jesse Kornbluth, Charles Lockwood, Ann Magnin, Peter McCoy, Dennis McDougal, Jerry Oppenheimer, Holly Palance, Bret Parsons, Degen Pener, Ann Rapp, Nat Read, Gus Russo, Ruth Ryon, Melvin Sokolsky, Gene St. John, Leonard Stanley, Reggie Sully, Michael M. Thomas, Mark Voss, Marc Wanamaker, Sam Watters, Bernie Weinraub, Bebe Winkler, Ann Zellars, and Paula Zinneman. I should also single out Steven Macallum Powers, who generously shared his knowledge of several of the great estates, and several chapters of the manuscript of his unpublished memoir.

Most helpful of all were the family members and friends of the pioneers of the Platinum Triangle and of the owners of the homes this book is about, who were trusting and generous enough to share their recollections. I was as delighted as I was surprised by how many of them were willing to take part. I was even happier that no one preemptively threatened to sue me, as several residents of 740 Park did, though one current homeowner pointedly copied a lawyer on an e-mail withdrawing her promise of cooperation a few days after giving it. So I am particularly grateful to Ron Burkle, the current owner of Greenacres (and his aide Frank Quintero), and to Robert Mehdizadeh, a son of the owners of Grayhall, for helping me tell their stories.

For information and insight into the founding families of Beverly Hills, thanks to Laura-Lee Whittier Woods and to Linda Blinkenberg of the Whittier Foundation for their aid in learning about Max Whittier. On the Green family and their various homes, thanks to Russell G. Allen, Rick Arthur, Bill Bell, Grant Bettingen, Dean Bok, Patricia Brown, Hernando Courtright, Jim Greene, Daphne Ireland, Joan Mackey Bronson, Frank Merrick, John

Perenchio, Jorge Schondube, Anna Lorena Ochoa Schondube, Enrique Schondube, Ricardo Schondube Baumbach, Otto Schondube Kebe, Arlo Sorenson, Diane Stockmar, Matilda Gray Stream, William Walker Jr., and Daphne Whelahan.

I learned about Alphonzo Bell's family and home from Marshall Hopper, John Pohlmann, Emory Rogers, Rex Ross III, Ralph Tingle Jr., Ralph Tingle Sr., and Douglas Waldron. Doors were opened to the Canfield, Danziger, and Spalding families by Franci Vodicka Ferguson, Jane Kenealy, Michael Mishler, Clair Vodicka-Taylor, Mary Warthin, Lucinda Zeising, and Deborah Caroline Spalding Pelissero. And Karen Candace Booth, Larry Janss, Dagny Janss Corcoran, Mike Lai, Patricia Gregson Millington, Lett Mullen, and Anya Patterson helped me learn about the Letts and Janss families.

The Botillers and 9481 Sunset came to life thanks to Janet Clifford, Rondi Frankel, Ernest Garcia, Bobbie Hofler, Bonnie Kane, John Lindley, Robert Patrick Melsted, Jeri Nixon, John Edward Powell, and Chuck Swift. Rosemary Bullis, Bridget Gless Keller, Michael Gless, Sharon Gless, and Horace Laffaye shared memories of Neil McCarthy. And I learned about Stewart and Lynda Resnick from David Gadd, John Gibler, Adam Keats, Nancy Reddin Kienholz, Douglas Reed, Mike Taugher, Walt Whelan, Lance Williams, and Craig Wright. I also consulted and quote from interviews I conducted in 1994 for my book *Model* with Jerry and Eileen Ford and Bernie Cornfeld. Thanks also to Philippe Boutboul, and for the Mark Hughes era, to Suzann Hughes and Darcy LaPier.

At Grayhall, thanks to George Hamilton, Alana Hamilton Stewart, and Susan Kohner Weitz for the Hamilton era. I learned Bernie Cornfeld's story from Jerry Brandt, William H. Brownstein, Henry Buhl, Jessica Cornfeld, Lorraine Cornfeld-Vidal, J. Stephen Hicks, Howard Mann, Brian Oxman, and David Rudich. I also consulted and quote from interviews I conducted in 1994 for my book *Model* with Jerry and Eileen Ford and Bernie Cornfeld. Thanks also to Philippe Boutboul, and for the Mark Hughes era, to Suzann Hughes and Darcy LaPier.

The estate known as Owlwood at 141 South Carolwood in Holmby Hills holds a lot of history. Thanks to Victoria King, Philip Magaram, David Price, Mark Young, Francesca Drown Keck, and William Frank Hopkins for helping me learn about Joe Drown; Jill Curtis and the late Tony Curtis, Christine Kaufmann, and Leslie Curtis for their memories of their time there; Renvy Graves Pittman, Tay Uhler, and Ron Wilson for their help with the Cher story; Eleanor Vallée for her insight into her late husband Rudy; Nicholas Brown and Douglas Warde, who told me about the Wardes; Byron Alumbaugh, Ben Schwartz, and Gene Walsh, who tried to find members of the Kanter family for me (if you're out there, sorry I couldn't find any of you), and Mickey Hargitay Jr. for discussing his father and mother, Jayne Mansfield.

Piecing together Harold Greenlin's story was made easier thanks to Habib and Nick Carouba, Frank and Gary Culver, Rose Joyce Huismans, Adele DeCampli-Cirkelis, Roger Forbes, Sharon Greenlin, Carmen Novack, and James Verdon. Michelle Phillips and Elizabeth Freund helped fact-check and eliminate Mama Cass Elliott and Ringo Starr from the estate's cast of characters. Esther Williams did the same for herself.

For Bill Osco's story, thanks to Kristine Debelle Trites, Jennie Rebecca Haiman, Sharon Kemp, Sally Kirkland, Jackie Kong Driver, Tony Perez, Stefani Kong Uhler, Howard Ziehm, and Osco himself. Chase Mishkin told me about her years on the estate, and the story of Ghazi Aita was told to me by Robert Balsimelli Jr., Roberto Balsimelli Sr., Federica Bigi, Thomas Childers, Vince Conti, Shurl Curci, the late Greg Hagins, Eva Klimas, Carol Ann La Vella, Gil Schwartzberg, Robert Shaheen, and Daniel G. Zerfas. Roland Arnall's family didn't respond to interview requests but Kelly Mullens, Barry Fink, and Vicki J. Greene helped with details.

Suzanne Lloyd was indispensible in recounting the story of Harold Lloyd at Greenacres. Tom Sheppard, Shahram Afshani, and Afshin Moghavem also deserve thanks. For the story of Dona Powell and Bernard Solomon, thanks first to Powell herself, and also to Martin Basart, Mark Chayet, Holly George-Warren, Herman Krawitz, Ed Litwak, Franklin Mieuli, Fred Nicholas, Stanley B. Schneider, Matty Simmons, Barbara Laykin Solomon, Teri Solomon, Cristina Solomon-Adams and Cori Solomon-Bornstein. Mark Ebner, Coerte Felske, Susie Bollman Field, Paris Moskopoulos, and Michael Shnayerson helped me capture the elusive Ted Field.

I learned about Casa Encantada and the so-called Beverly Hillbillies house in Bel Air from Patrick Barry, Pat Hilton, Trish Hilton, Mark Young, Arnold C. "Buzz" Kirkeby, Carla Kirkeby, Cynthia Duncan, Nancy Kirkeby, and John Ziffren. The Murdock era was opened up to me by Erika Brunson, Tracy Murdock, Lillie Murdock, and Nancy Stoddart.

I owe particular thanks to William H. Doheny for helping me learn about Greystone and The Knoll. Thanks also to Peter McCoy, Veronique Peck, and Kenny Rogers, who took time from a tour to talk to me. Sheikh Salah al-Heijalan and David Ottaway helped me learn about the al-Midani family; John F. Whitsett told me about Guy Atkinson; Wendy Fabbri Pagan generously shared memories of Dino Fabbri; Eli Blumenfeld told me about Dena al-Fassi, and Lee Miller and A. J. Rolls completed my understanding of Anthony Norvell.

Finally, thanks to the many individuals who helped me puzzle out the rich but twisty story of Beverly Park: Brian Adler, Jerry Breslauer, Lynne Davidson, Betty Dector, Robert Dewhirst, Allen R. Glick, Elliott Gottfurcht, Robert Trent Jones Jr., Mona Lands, Tom Naccarato, Nick Pileggi, George Santo Pietro, Dorothy Schoelen, Tim Tobin, Joel Wachs, Stuart Whitman, Ron Whitten, Dave Robb, Dick Brenneman, Dennis McDougal, Dan Moldea, and especially the altogether generous Gus Russo.

I owe another particular debt to Gail Stein, Archivist of the Historical Collection at the Beverly Hills Public Library, where I was able to gain access to the treasure trove of primary source and other material gathered by a writer named Patricia Eckhardt for a never-written book on Beverly Hills as well as "The Greystone Report," prepared while the city of Beverly Hills was deciding what to do with that estate. At other libraries and archives, thanks to Glen Creason, Map Curator at the Los Angeles Public Library; Betty Uyeda, Collections Manager at the Seaver Center for Western History Research at the Los Angeles County Natural History Museum; Dace Taub, Regional History Collection Librarian in the Special Collections department of the Doheny Memorial Library of the University of Southern California; Genie Guerrard, Manuscripts Librarian at UCLA; Jennifer Goldman, Suzanne Oatey, Deborah Johnston, and Steve Koblik of the Huntington Library; Brenda Gunn at the University of Texas at Austin; Tony Black, Appraisal Archivist at the Archives and Information Services Division of the Texas State Library and Archives Commission; Michael Redman of the Santa Barbara Historical Museum; Amanda Neal and Joe Cantrell at the Santa Barbara Public Library; Santa Barbara historian Teri Gabrielsen; Marion Gregston of the Montecito Association; Jeanette Berard of the Thousand Oaks Library; Laura Harris at the *New York Post* archives; Jeff Suess at the *Cincinnati Enquirer* library; Tina Reyes, Coordinator at Lane Community College at Downtown Center; Jenny Lynch, Senior Research Analyst for Postal History at the Corporate Information and Archival Programs of the U.S. Postal Service; Mark E. Young, Ph.D., Director of the Hospitality Industry Archives at the Conrad N. Hilton College of Hotel & Restaurant Management at the

University of Houston; John Reinhard of the Illinois State Archives, Yvonne Ng, Reference Librarian of the Arcadia Public Library; Adam Keats at the Center for Biological Diversity; and Bonnie Kane, of Ridge Route Communities Museum and Historical Society.

I have been blessed with great fortune in finding interns and researchers to help me with each of my books. This time, thanks to Kerry Lee Barker, Marusca Niccolini, Maria Eugenia Miranda, and Joshua Lormer in New York; Jill Boberg, Max Zimbert, and Massiel Bobadilla in Los Angeles; and Ralph Elder in Texas. I also thank Margo Evashevski, who led me to Albert Ghazarian, whose legal research was incomparable.

Just as important to the process was Janis Kaye, whose home was my home-away-from-home during several long research trips. Russell Kagan was both tolerant and kind about my intrusions. I am also indebted to Stephen Brandman and the staff of the Thompson Hotel and Jonathan Morr and his team at Bondst, who let me give Janis a break now and then, and to the rest of the best L.A. friends a fellow could have, David Netto, Liz Dalling, Wesley and Marla Strick, Richard Buckley, Ellen and Ian Graham, Sharon Day, Pam Stanley, and the late Marianne Page. I'd also like to thank the staff of the best bookstore on Sunset Boulevard, Book Soup, particularly the delightful Fawn Hall.

Most journalism involves anonymous sources as well as identified ones, and a number of people helped me out in exchange for a promise I would withhold their names. They know who they are and I thank them, too. One I should single out is the blogger known as Your Mama at Real Estalker. If I have left out anyone else, it was inadvertent and I'm sorry.

Finally, thanks to my wife, Barbara, who not only lets me work at home, but designed the desk where I write, and to my editors at Broadway Books, Peter Gethers and the meticulous and inspiring Claudia Herr and their assistant Christina Malach, and my agent Dan Strone at Trident Media Group. The four of them have given me the great gift of safe harbor in the choppy seas of contemporary book publishing. I'm also grateful to Stacy Creamer, who convinced me to write this book, and to Diane Salvatore, who helped to shape it.

A bibliography follows after the endnotes, but does not include the thousands of newspaper and magazine articles that I consulted and quote from in the text. Significant information is usually presented in a way that makes it clear where it came from, but in general, I have not interrupted the narrative by sourcing periodicals, nor included voluminous endnotes that would have made a hefty book even fatter. Suffice it to say that most quotations presented in the present tense (i.e., those followed by "she says," or something similar) were spoken or written directly to me during my reporting, while those from previously published texts are attributed in the past tense (i.e., "he said"). The only exceptions are quotes from people who died between our interviews and the book's publication.

NOTES

1. Real estate sources who recall the incident with more precision than Schoelen say Stallone topped Knight's offer by $1 million and snatched the house away, buying it himself (albeit in the names of his lawyer, Jake Bloom, and a trust). Knight, Stallone, Bloom, and Valerie Fitzgerald did not respond to requests for comment.

2. In the interim, the Los Angeles and Santa Monica Land and Water Company had given 150 acres to the federal government, today the home of the Veteran's Administration Cemetery, a federal building, and a UCLA parking lot.

3. When it opened in 1904, the Pacific Electric headquarters was the biggest building west of Chicago. Today, it contains more than 300 residential lofts.

4. A year later, Harriman seemed to back away from competing in the street rail business; he died in 1909, effectively ending the feud.

5. Famously, Ince died under mysterious circumstances in 1924, two days after embarking on a weekend sailing party celebrating his birthday on the publisher William Randolph Hearst's yacht. Hollywood gossip had it that—in the most common of several versions—Hearst shot Ince after mistaking him for Charlie Chaplin, whom the married Hearst suspected of sleeping with his mistress, the actress Marion Davies. Ince's body had been immediately cremated and members of the sailing party gave contradictory, squirrelly accounts of the event. So the public was inclined to think that Hearst had covered up a crime, and several subsequent fictional accounts of the incident—including one coauthored by Hearst's own granddaughter, Patricia—have kept the apocryphal story alive. Ince's doctor's declaration that he died of heart failure was deemed unsatisfying.

6. That year, Warner Bros. co-owner Jack Warner added a pitch-and-putt golf course to his adjacent property and over the years to come, he and Lloyd would sometimes open the gate between their courses to let friends "play through." A later owner of the Warner estate, David Geffen, eliminated his course.

7. Greenacres was about 32,000 square feet and San Simeon's main house, 60,645 square feet.

8. Battson had previously sold the remaining Doheny oil properties for his mother-in-law for about $35 million. After a lifetime of philanthropy, including endowing a memorial library named for Ned at the University of Southern California, Estelle Doheny left about $30 million, mostly to charity, on her death in 1958.

9. Canfield's wastrel son Charles (who would eventually marry three times) received $1,200 a year, though his spendthrift trust fund earned $50,000 annually, and an adopted daughter thought by some to be his own out-of-wedlock child got a $250,000 trust fund. An additional $1 million was left in trust to endow a school for girls named for Chloe Canfield.

10. Bell also helped create the famous Riviera Country Club west of Bel Air, investing in the syndicate to which he sold the land.

11. Davies ended up owning a substantial amount of Beverly Hills real estate, as well as a thirty-four-room Georgian beach house in Santa Monica, the remains of which are now a public beach club. There was a mansion near Burton Green's on Lexington Road that had belonged to the studio head Harry Cohn, another Lexington Road estate that belonged to Walter McCarty, builder of the Beverly Wilshire Hotel, and finally, the home of banker Milton Getz at 1011 Beverly Drive, which Davies later loaned to John and Jacqueline Kennedy, who spent part of their honeymoon there. The property, subsequently downsized, was sold for $1.6 million in 1976 to Leonard Ross, a banker who briefly put it on the market in 2007 for $165,000,000, a world record for a private residence. When the world economy collapsed the next year, it was taken off the market.

12. In 1926, the year Peter Janss died and left the Janss Investment Company to his sons, they also sold a large tract to the Fox Film Corporation, which built a new studio where Century City stands today.

13. The exteriors of Desmond's mansion were shot at a house at 641 South Irving Boulevard on the corner of Wilshire in downtown Los Angeles. It was owned by the divorced wife of J. Paul Getty.

14. Singleton commissioned first a modernist Richard Neutra house on Mulholland Drive in Bel-Air later owned by Vidal Sassoon, then a house by Wallace Neff on Delfern Drive in Holmby Hills, which was listed after his death in 1990 for sale for $85 million or for rent at $50,000 monthly.

15. The third and current owner of the seven-acre, twenty-two-room Wallace Neff estate high above the city on Angelo Drive is the media mogul Rupert Murdoch.

16. Robbin Green Perenchio would end up in court in 1957, sued for support by her mother, from whom she'd been estranged. She admitted that she and her husband shared a $1,400-a-month income (about $10,700 today). Her mother, who'd been hit by a car not long before, came to court on a walker and testified that she lived in a motel room and sometimes couldn't afford to eat. The judge called it "one of the most tragic cases it has been my misfortune to hear." Robbin Perenchio was ordered to pay her $200 a month. At the time, a rumor went

through Blue Book society that Robbin was actually Burton Green's illegitimate daughter, brokered to relatives by a lawyer.

17. Katleman had recently been divorced from Lee Cohn, niece of Columbia Pictures' chief Harry Cohn. She would go on to marry Lewis Rosenstiel, the distiller and founder of Schenley Industries, after her uncle bought Rosenstiel's Beverly Hills mansion at 1000 North Crescent Drive in Beverly Hills. That house would later be owned or occupied by Laurence Harvey and Mike Douglas and, most recently, by Georges Marciano of Guess, the jeans designer. After a second divorce, Leonore Cohn Rosenstiel married Walter Annenberg, the publisher.

18. Many owners later (among them, H. R. "Bob" Haldeman, Richard Nixon's chief of staff), the house now belongs to mainland China and there are guardian Fu dogs on the front walkway, but the shamrocks are still there.

19. After the last of the Green sisters died, the family staff, which mostly managed oil leases and other business affairs of the Greens, "all retired," says Gene St. John, the Hammel heir who now runs the Beverly Hills Land Company, collecting royalties on oil wells that are still pumping and managing its share of the right-of-way property. "Over the years, pieces have been sold off, primarily to the city," he says. "We've invested in other real estate." Beverly Hills Land rents an office in the same building where the living Dohenys run their family interests.

20. De La Vega was the inspiration for the character Hector Paradiso, who split his time between high-society ladies and low-life rent boys in Dominick Dunne's roman à clef about Los Angeles society, *An Inconvenient Woman.*

21. In fact, Liliore had been friends with Dr. Roy Menninger, the president of the Menninger Foundation, which ran the clinic, a psychiatric facility. Her late husband had gone to law school at Loyola, which saw its endowment triple thanks to Liliore's gift. Pomona's Chancellor guessed that a nephew's attendance there inspired its bequest and that Good Samaritan had been chosen because Liliore had once been treated for a minor injury there.

22. Like Dolly, Bell has a sibling neighbor, his brother and coproducer Bradley, who would buy 391 North Carolwood in Holmby Hills, a 17,000-square-foot Italianate villa built in 1927. Bradley Bell bought it in 1992 from the singer Rod Stewart, who moved to Beverly Park. Bradley also bought the house next door, the longtime home of Harold Janss and, later, the movie star Gregory Peck, and demolished it to add four acres of gardens to his estate.

23. Years later, a John Dahlinger would write a book claiming to be the illegitimate son of Henry Ford.

24. Among the so-called phone phreaks who built and sold the gadgets were Apple Computer founders Steve Jobs and Steve Wozniak.

25. In 2010, a small house in West Hollywood, occupied by Elijah Blue and reportedly owned by a trust associated with his mother, was sold at a $300,000 loss—one of the few black marks on Cher's otherwise stellar record as a real estate investor.

26. In 2008, that apartment was put on the market for $6.5 million by its third owner, Rosemary Stack, widow of the well-born actor Robert, who sixty-four years before had bought Colleen Moore's Bel Air mansion. Two years later it remained unsold and the price had dropped to $2.95 million.

27. Osco would later recut the film and insert hard-core sequences.

28. Alagem built a Robert A. M. Stern house there, and almost simultaneously bought the 582-room Beverly Hilton Hotel in Beverly Hills from TV talk show host Merv Griffin, paying about $130 million for it.

29. In 1964, Ryan had testified against two men accused of threatening to kidnap him to force him to pay a five-figure gambling debt; both men were convicted of racketeering and extortion.

30. A few years later, Davis would make another, far more significant, settlement on the courthouse steps, after an investment subsidiary of Aetna Life & Casualty put $182 million into Davis Oil, lost two-thirds of it, and sued him for $100 million for fraud, misrepresentations, and irregularities. Aetna's chief financial officer told *Vanity Fair* he believed that Davis gave them "essentially what we were charging" in order to avoid bad publicity.

31. Years later she listed it for about $30 million. After dropping the asking price to $23.95 million, her eldest son finally sold it for $12.2 million in 2010, said Page Six, adding "before it was foreclosed on." According to a well-placed real estate source, the buyer was a Malaysian businessman.

32. Later, Field told his mother to sell it or close it. She managed to sell it, and moved to Boston, where she became editor of *The Christian Science Monitor* from 1983 until 1988.

33. A few years earlier, Field had begun installing a chute from his fourteenth-floor office at Murdock Plaza to the ground equipped with blasting caps to speed his descent. After moorings were installed, the project was called off.

34. Allen bought a lot next door as well, then cleared the site. But it has sat empty ever since. "There's nothing there now but a $10 million driveway that runs through a tunnel from Benedict Canyon," says a real estate broker who knows the property. When he is in Los Angeles, Allen, who owns property all over the world, is said to live in a Mediterranean-style mansion on Beverly Crest Drive that he bought from the director John Landis. It was built on the same property where Rock Hudson lived and died of AIDS in 1985.

35. Spelling announced plans to downsize into the top two floors of The Century, a condominium tower designed by Robert A. M. Stern in Century City, which she'd agreed to buy for a mere $47 million. After a year of rumors that she was backing out of the deal, Spelling ultimately closed on the apartment for $35 million. Representatives of The Century say the price drop reflected her desire to buy it as a "white box," somewhat smaller than originally expected.

36. Long Beach Financial was later sold to Washington Mutual for $360 million,

double its IPO price. When Arnall's ex-wife subsequently saw him listed in the *Forbes* 400 as a new entrant, worth $2 billion, she asked a judge to reconsider their property settlement, claiming she'd been misled. After two years of legal maneuvering, on the third day of trial, she and Arnall reached an undisclosed settlement.

37. The FTC investigation had been called off after Ameriquest committed to making $360 million in low-interest, low-fee loans in minority neighborhoods.

38. In May 2008, Citigroup announced it was shutting down and incorporating the Ameriquest units, eliminating 1,860 of its 1,930 employees.

39. Though his new wife clearly loved attention, in years to come, Stewart would actively disdain the press. One source of his animus was likely what happened when he hired former Los Angeles chief of police Tom Reddin as the boss of American Protection's 1,100 security guards, who watched over facilities stretching from downtown L.A. to the airport, where they screened passengers and guarded incoming flights. A year later, Reddin resigned after an argument with Resnick. Six months after that, in a sting operation likely initiated by the embittered former top cop, three of Resnick's former employees at LAX were arrested on charges they'd sold two pounds of pure heroin to undercover officers, and a federal organized crime task force and state and local authorities were reportedly looking into American Protection's role in what appeared to be a case of massive fraud against an airline, possibly involving New York Mafia figures. Resnick denied any involvement and said that rogue employees had been dismissed months before. Two weeks later, American Protection sued Reddin for stealing customers and trade secrets. Reddin called the suit baseless, explaining that he never solicited customers, though he had taken on some "who could no longer condone [their] business practices." Years later, Resnick volunteered to Mark Arax that "Reddin was fucking with me" and had hired a private eye to investigate him and started rumors he was laundering money for the mob. "He turned out to be a putz and I fired him," Resnick said. "He went to his cop buddies." Reddin's eighty-nine-year-old widow says that "putz" comment sounds like something Reddin would have said about Resnick.

40. In 1997, Lynda paid $151,000 at a charity auction for a strapless white silk crepe dress and matching jacket once worn by Diana, Princess of Wales, and the Resnicks filed a trademark application for the name "Diana, Forever a Princess." Unfortunately, two years later, after Diana's death, Stewart and the Mint were sued by the trustees of the princess's charitable Memorial Fund for exploiting Diana's name and likeness illegally when they reproduced that dress among a batch of Diana-related items. The fund compared them to "vultures feeding on the dead." The case wasn't clear-cut. The fund's trustees had already licensed margarine tubs carrying her signature, and other questionable items. Though their suit was tossed out, it infuriated the Resnicks and in 2002, they struck back with a suit of their

own, charging the trustees with malicious prosecution. Some British newspapers took the Spencer family's side, calling the American schlock merchants "not only the kind of people with whom [the trustees] did not wish to do business but the sort of people they would usually avoid." But the *Times* of London called the trustees "crass" and "sniffy." In 2003, in a Machiavellian maneuver, the fund announced it was freezing its assets and suspending its giving, setting off more Resnick bashing and a lengthy recounting of their adventures in litigation, including several unsuccessful suits against them by aggrieved ex-employees. A year later, on the day the case was to go to court, a settlement was announced. The Diana fund dropped its suit and the Resnicks agreed to donate the proceeds of the Diana products they'd never stopped selling to a "mutually agreed international program of humanitarian work." The Resnicks had effectively made themselves Diana's philanthropic partners. Battered by several years of declining sales and competition from eBay, the Resnicks laid off two-thirds of the Franklin Mint's employees in 2003 and sold it three years later.

41. In 1997, the Resnicks moved into a new vacation home they'd built on seventy acres outside Aspen, but as in many high-end resort communities, they were disdained by locals as part-time residents—and showy ones at that. Even after the couple made large donations to the Aspen Institute (along with the Aspen Skiing Corporation, one of the two tent-pole institutions in the former mining town) and Lynda was named to the board of the liberal think tank in 1999, the local newspaper continued to call them part-timers. Some of the animosity stemmed from lawsuits filed by the Resnicks in 2000 and 2001 to stop Aspen from building seventeen units of much-needed low-cost housing for local service employees a half mile from Little Lake Lodge, as they call their vacation home, claiming it would devalue the property. The lawsuits led to local protests, including a letter to the *Aspen Times* accusing them of "dubious moral standards." After their suit was rejected, the Resnicks continued to maneuver to delay construction and the imbroglio came up again three years later when the Aspen Institute announced plans to renovate an auditorium on its campus and name it for the Resnicks. Previously, it and the building around it had been named for Chicago businessman Walter Paepcke and his wife Elizabeth, who created modern Aspen when they founded the institute and the Skiing Corporation in the 1950s. The name change decision outraged many Aspenites. One of the institute's supporters called it "unspeakably rude and vulgar." Institute officials said the whole thing was their idea, approved to thank the Resnicks for their $4.2 million gift to pay for the renovation. Then Lynda threw gasoline on the fire. "Everybody else gets a naming opportunity, and this was the biggest gift the institute has ever received," she said. "It isn't like I want my name in neon everywhere. I mean, it's going to be a small plaque, for God's sake." Soon, a local wit covered the word *Aspen* on a city limits highway sign with a sticker reading *Resnick,* and below it, the phrase *Elev. $4.2 Mil.* Finally,

the institute's president withdrew the proposal, and Lynda announced that she and Stewart were withdrawing their contribution and rethinking their gifts to the institute. "We have never had such vitriolic things said about us," she complained. As with the Diana Memorial Fund kerfuffle, time seemed to salve the Resnicks' wounds. Less than a year later, the institute announced that the Resnicks would give $3 million after all, and two other couples matched their gift. The restored auditorium opened in summer 2010.

42. Here, Edward Huntington is the exception who proves the rule, as his Huntington Library is a monument to both his acquisitiveness and his generosity—but it is, of course, in San Marino, not L.A.

SELECTED BIBLIOGRAPHY

Albert, James A. *Pay Dirt: Divorces of the Rich and Famous*. Boston: Branden Publishing, 1989.

Antonian, Armen, and Lisa H. Iyer. *The L.A. Sensation*. Haverford, PA: Infinity Publishing, 2004.

Arax, Mark. *West of the West: Dreamers, Believers, Builders, and Killers in the Golden State*. New York: Public Affairs, 2009.

Artunian, Judy, and Mike Oldham. *Movie Star Homes*. Santa Monica, CA: Santa Monica Press, 2004.

Bai, Matt. *The Argument: Inside the Battle to Remake Democratic Politics*. New York: Penguin, 2008.

Bartlett, Donald L., and James B. Steele. *Howard Hughes: His Life and Madness*. New York: W. W. Norton & Company, 1979.

Basichis, Gordon. *Beautiful Bad Girl: The Vicki Morgan Story*. Santa Barbara, CA: Santa Barbara Press, 1985.

Bates, Joseph Clement, ed. *History of the Bench and Bar of California*. San Francisco: Bench and Bar Publishing Company, 1912.

Beardwood, Jack. *From Browns to Greens: A History of the Los Angeles Country Club 1898–1973*. Los Angeles: Los Angeles Country Club, 1973.

Beauchamp, Cari. *Without Lying Down: Frances Marion and the Powerful Women of Early Hollywood*. Berkeley and Los Angeles: University of California Press, 1997.

Bego, Mark. *Cher: If You Believe*. New York: Cooper Square Press, 2001.

Bel-Air Country Club. Charlotte, NC: Delmar Printing, 1993.

Bell, Alphonzo, with Marc L. Weber. *The Bel-Air Kid: An Autobiography*. Victoria, Canada: Trafford Publishing, 2002.

Benedict, Pierce E., and Don Kennedy, eds. *History of Beverly Hills*. Beverly Hills, CA: A. H. Cawston–H. M. Meier, 1934.

Block, Alan A. *Masters of Paradise: Organized Crime and the Internal Revenue Service in the Bahamas*. New Brunswick, NJ: Transaction Publishers, 1998.

Block, Alex Ben. *Outfoxed: Marvin Davis, Barry Diller, Rupert Murdoch, Joan Rivers, and the Inside Story of America's Fourth Television Network.* New York: St. Martin's Press, 1990.

Bolton, Whitney. *The Silver Spade: The Conrad Hilton Story.* New York: Farrar, Straus & Young, 1954.

Brooks, John. *The Go-Go Years.* New York: John Wiley & Sons, 1973.

Broven, John. *Record Makers and Breakers: Voices of the Independent Rock 'n' Roll Pioneers.* Urbana: University of Illinois Press, 2009.

Brown, John Jr., and James Boyd. *History of San Bernardino and Riverside Counties.* Vol. III. Chicago: Western Historical Association–Lewis Publishing Company, 1922.

Brown, Peter Harry, and Pat H. Broeske. *Howard Hughes: The Untold Story.* New York: Penguin Group, 1996.

Brown, Peter Harry, and Patte B. Barham. *Marilyn: The Last Take.* New York: Dutton, 1992.

Bruck, Connie. *When Hollywood Had a King.* New York: Random House, 2003.

———. *The Predators' Ball: Junk-Bond Traders and the Man Who Staked Them.* New York: Simon & Schuster, 1988.

Cantor, Bert. *The Bernie Cornfeld Story.* New York: Lyle Stuart Inc., 1970.

Carr, Harry. *Los Angeles.* New York: D. Appleton–Century Company, 1935.

Cassini, Oleg. *In My Own Fashion: An Autobiography.* New York: Pocket Books, 1987.

Cher, and Jeff Coplon. *The First Time.* New York: Simon & Schuster, 1998.

Churchwell, Sarah. *The Many Lives of Marilyn Monroe.* New York: Picador, 2005.

Colacello, Bob. *Ronnie & Nancy.* New York: Warner Books, 2004.

Curtis, Tony, and Peter Golenbock. *American Prince: A Memoir.* New York: Crown Publishers, 2009.

Cusic, Don. *Gene Autry: His Life and Career.* Jefferson, NC: McFarland & Co., 2010.

Dabney, Thomas Ewing. *The Man Who Bought the Waldorf: The Life of Conrad N. Hilton.* New York: Duell, Sloan and Pearce, 1950.

Davis, Genevieve. *Beverly Hills: An Illustrated History.* Northridge, CA: Windsor Publications, 1988.

Davis, Margaret Leslie. *Rivers in the Desert: William Mulholland and the Inventing of Los Angeles.* New York: HarperCollins, 1993.

———. *Dark Side of Fortune: Triumph and Scandal in the Life of Oil Tycoon Edward L. Doheny.* Berkeley and Los Angeles: University of California Press, 1998.

Davis, Moshe. *Zionism in Transition.* New York: Arno Press, 1980.

Dunne, Dominick. *Fatal Charms and Other Tales of Today.* New York: Crown Publishers, 1987.

———. *An Inconvenient Woman.* New York: Crown Publishers, 1990.

Durham, David L. *California's Geographic Names.* Fresno, CA: Quill Driver Books, 1998.

Edwards, Allan E. *Franklin Canyon: A Microhistory*. Beverly Hills, CA: The William O. Douglas Outdoor Classroom, 1991.

Edwards, Anne. *The DeMilles: An American Family*. New York: H. N. Abrams, 1988.

———. *The Reagans: Portrait of a Marriage*. New York: St. Martin's Press, 2003.

Elder, Jane Lenz. *Alice Faye: A Life Beyond the Silver Screen*. Jackson, MS: University Press of Mississippi, 2002.

Elisofon, Eliot. *Hollywood Life: The Glamorous Homes of Vintage Hollywood*. Los Angeles: Greybull Press, 2004.

Evans, Robert. *The Kid Stays in the Picture*. New York: Hyperion, 1994.

Eyman, Scott. *Lion of Hollywood: The Life and Legend of Louis B. Mayer*. New York: Simon & Schuster, 2005.

Faris, Jocelyn. *Jayne Mansfield: A Bio-bibliography*. Westport, CT: Greenwood Press, 1994.

Felsenthal, Carol. *Clinton in Exile: A President Out of the White House*. New York: HarperCollins, 2008.

Fitzmaurice, Victor. *Bel-Heirs*. New York: Vantage Press, 1981.

Fleming, E. J. *The Fixers: Eddie Mannix, Howard Strickling, and the MGM Publicity Machine*. Jefferson, NC: McFarland & Co., 2005.

Frankel, Jennie Louise, and Terrie Maxine Frankel. *You'll Never Make Love in This Town Again*. Beverly Hills, CA: Dove Books, 1995.

Friedrich, Otto. *City of Nets: A Portrait of Hollywood in the 1940's*. New York: Harper & Row Publishers, 1986.

Gabler, Neal. *An Empire of Their Own: How the Jews Invented Hollywood*. New York: Crown Publishers, 1988.

Gebhard, David, and Robert Winter. *Architecture in Los Angeles*. Salt Lake City: Peregrine Smith Books, 1985.

George-Warren, Holly. *Public Cowboy No. 1: The Life and Times of Gene Autry*. New York: Oxford University Press, 2007.

Gill, Brendan, and Derry Moore. *The Dream Come True: Great Houses of Los Angeles*. New York: Lippincott & Cromwell, 1980.

Golden, Eve. *Golden Images: 41 Essays on Silent Film Stars*. Jefferson, NC: McFarland & Co., 2001.

Gordon, William A. *The Ultimate Hollywood Tour Book*. Lake Forest, CA: North Ridge Books, 2002.

Guiles, Fred Lawrence. *Legend: The Life and Death of Marilyn Monroe*. New York: Stein & Day, 1984.

Guinn, James Miller. *A History of California*. Volume II. Los Angeles: Historic Record Company, 1915.

Hack, Richard. *Hughes: The Private Diaries, Memos, and Letters*. Beverly Hills, CA: Phoenix, 2007.

Haden-Guest, Anthony. *The Last Party: Studio 54, Disco, and the Culture of the Night.* New York: William Morrow, 1997.

Halberstam, David. *The Powers That Be, Within the Kingdom of the Media.* New York: Alfred A. Knopf, 1979.

Havill, Adrian. *The Last Mogul: The Unauthorized Biography of Jack Kent Cooke.* New York: St. Martin's Press, 1992.

Herzog, Arthur. *Vesco: From Wall Street to Castro's Cuba: The Rise, Fall, and Exile of the King of White Collar Crime.* New York: Doubleday, 1987.

Higham, Charles. *Howard Hughes: The Secret Life.* New York: G. P. Putnam's Sons, 1993.

Hilton, Conrad. *Be My Guest.* Englewood Cliffs, NJ: Prentice-Hall Press, 1957.

Hoover, Mildred Brooke, Douglas E. Kyle, Hero Eugene Rensch, and Ethel G. Rensch. *Historic Spots in California.* Stanford, CA: Stanford University Press, 2002.

Hopper, Charles Blauvelt. *Memoirs of a Full Life.* Los Angeles: Privately printed, 1963.

Horton, Joseph K. *A Brief History of Bel-Air.* Los Angeles: The Bel-Air Association, 1982.

Hubner, John. *Bottom Feeders: From Free Love to Hard Core—the Rise and Fall of Counterculture Heroes Jim and Artie Mitchell.* New York: Doubleday, 1992.

Hudson, Michael W. *The Monster: How a Gang of Predatory Lenders and Wall Street Bankers Fleeced America—and Spawned a Global Crisis.* New York: Times Books, 2010.

Humperdinck, Engelbert, and Katie Wright. *Engelbert: What's in a Name? The Autobiography.* London: Virgin Books, 2004.

Hyland, Jeffrey. *The Legendary Estates of Beverly Hills.* New York: Rizzoli, 2008.

Kanner, Diane. *Wallace Neff and the Grand Houses of the Golden State.* New York: Monacelli Press, 2005.

Kashner, Sam, and Nancy Schoenberger. *Furious Love: Elizabeth Taylor, Richard Burton and the Marriage of the Century.* New York: Harper, 2010.

Kelley, Kitty. *Nancy Reagan: The Unauthorized Biography.* New York: Pocket Books, 1992.

Kezich, Tullio, and Alessandra Levantesi. *Dino: The Life and Films of Dino De Laurentiis.* New York: Miramax, 2004.

Kilner, William H. B. *Arthur Letts, 1862–1923: Man and Merchant, Steadfast Friend, Loyal Employer.* Los Angeles: Young & McCallister, 1927.

King, Tom. *The Operator: David Geffen Builds, Buys, and Sells the New Hollywood.* New York: Random House, 2000.

Knight, Arthur, and Eliot Elisofon. *The Hollywood Style.* Toronto: Collier-Macmillan, 1969.

Krantz, Judith. *Dazzle.* New York: Crown, 1990.

Lawson, Kristan, and Anneli Rufus. *California Babylon: A Guide to Sites of Scandal, Mayhem, and Celluloid in the Golden State.* New York: St. Martin's Griffin, 2000.

Leaming, Barbara. *Marilyn Monroe*. New York: Three Rivers Press, 1998.

Lee, William F. *American Big Bands*. Milwaukee, WI: Hal Leonard, 2005.

Levins, Hoag. *Arab Reach*. New York: Doubleday, 1983.

Lewis, Judy. *Uncommon Knowledge*. New York: Pocket Books, 1995.

Lockwood, Charles. *Dream Palaces*. New York: Viking Press, 1981.

———, and Jeffrey Hyland. *The Estates of Beverly Hills: Holmby Hills, Bel-Air, Beverly Park*. Beverly Hills, CA: Beverly Park Gatehouse, 1989.

Longstreth, Richard W. *City Center to Regional Mall: Architecture, the Automobile, and Retailing in Los Angeles, 1920–1950*. Boston: MIT Press, 1997.

Louvish, Simon. *Cecil B. DeMille: A Life in Art*. New York: Thomas Dunne, 2007.

Mailer, Norman. *Marilyn, A Biography*. New York: Grosset & Dunlap, 1973.

Mann, May. *Jayne Mansfield: A Biography*. New York: Pocket Books, 1974.

Marion, Frances. *Off with Their Heads! A Serio-Comic Tale of Hollywood*. New York: Macmillan, 1972.

McDougal, Dennis. *The Last Mogul: Lew Wasserman, MCA, and the Hidden History of Hollywood*. New York: Random House, 1998.

———. *Privileged Son: Otis Chandler and the Rise and Fall of the L.A. Times Dynasty*. Cambridge, MA: Perseus Publishing, 2001.

McFarlane, Malcolm. *Bing Crosby: Day by Day*. Lanham, MD: Scarecrow Press, 2001.

McGroarty, John Steven. *Los Angeles from the Mountains to the Sea*. Vol. 3. Chicago and New York: American Historical Society, 1921.

McWilliams, Carey. *Southern California: An Island on the Land*. Salt Lake City: Peregrine Smith Books, 1946.

Miller, Judith. *God Has Ninety-Nine Names*. New York: Touchstone, 1997.

Monroe, Marilyn. *My Story*. New York: Cooper Square Press, 1974.

Mulholland, Catherine. *William Mulholland and the Rise of Los Angeles*. Berkeley and Los Angeles: University of California Press, 2000.

Muolo, Paul, and Mathew Padilla. *Chain of Blame: How Wall Street Caused the Mortgage and Credit Crisis*. New York: John Wiley & Sons, 2010.

Murray, William. *Previews of Coming Attractions*. New York: World Publishing Company, 1970.

Niklas, Kurt. *The Corner Table*. Los Angeles: Tuxedo Press, 2000.

Ogden, Tom. *Haunted Hollywood*. Guilford, CT: Globe Pequot, 2009.

Oppenheimer, Jerry. *House of Hilton*. New York: Crown Publishers, 2006.

Parla, Paul, and Charles P. Mitchell. *Screen Sirens Scream! Interviews with 20 Actresses from Science Fiction, Horror, Film Noir and Mystery Movies, 1930s to 1960s*. Jefferson, NC: McFarland, 2009.

Parrent, Joanne, and Bruce W. Cook. *Once More with Feeling*. Los Angeles: Dove Books, 1996.

Paz, Maria Emilia. *Strategy, Security, and Spies: Mexico and the U.S. as Allies in World War II*. University Park, PA: Pennsylvania State University Press, 1997.

Pohlmann, John O. "Alphonzo E. Bell: A Biography." *Southern California Quarterly* 46 (1964): 197–222, 315–350.

Porter, Darwin. *Hollywood's Silent Closet*. Staten Island, NY: Porter and Prince Corporation, 2001.

Powdermaker, Hortense. *Hollywood, the Dream Factory*. Boston: Little, Brown & Company, 1950.

Powers, Steven Macallum. *Once Upon a Time*. Unpublished manuscript.

Raw, Charles, Bruce Page, and Godfrey Hodgson. *Do You Sincerely Want to Be Rich?* New York: Viking Press, 1971.

Regan, Michael. *Mansions of Los Angeles*. Los Angeles: Regan Publishing, 1965.

———. *Stars, Moguls, Magnates: The Mansions of Beverly Hills*. Los Angeles: Regan Publishing, 1966.

Resnick, Lynda, and Francis Wilkinson. *Rubies in the Orchard*. New York: Doubleday, 2009.

Rivera-Viruet, Rafael J., and Max Resto. *Hollywood . . . Se Habla Espanol: Hispanics in Hollywood Films*. New York: Terramax Entertainment, 2008.

Rodriguez, Clara E. *Heroes, Lovers, and Others: The Story of Latinos in Hollywood*. New York: Oxford University Press, 2008.

Ross, Ian. *Beverly Hills Butler*. London: Heinemann, 1991.

Russo, Gus. *The Outfit: The Role of Chicago's Underworld in the Shaping of Modern America*. New York: Bloomsbury, 2001.

———. *Supermob: How Sidney Korshak and His Criminal Associates Became America's Hidden Power Brokers*. New York: Bloomsbury, 2006.

Shapiro, Harry, and Caesar Glebbeek. *Jimi Hendrix: Electric Gypsy*. New York: St. Martin's Press, 1995.

Shumway, Burgess McK. *California Ranchos*. San Bernardino, CA: Borgo Press, 1988.

Sims, Edwin C. *Capitalism: In Spite of It All*. New York: Gordon & Breach, 1989.

Sloper, Don. *Los Angeles's Chester Place (Images of America)*. Charleston, SC: Arcadia Publishing, 2006.

Spalding, William A. *History of Los Angeles*. Vol. II. Los Angeles: J. R. Finnell & Sons, 1931.

Sparling, Earl. *Mystery Men of Wall Street*. New York: Blue Ribbon Books, 1930.

Spelling, Aaron, and Jefferson Graham. *Aaron Spelling: A Prime-Time Life*. New York: St. Martin's Press, 2002.

Spelling, Tori. *sTORI Telling*. New York: Simon Spotlight Entertainment, 2008.

Stewart, James B. *Den of Thieves*. New York: Simon & Schuster, 1991.

Strait, Raymond. *The Tragic Secret Life of Jayne Mansfield*. Chicago: Regnery, 1974.

Summers, Anthony. *Goddess: The Secret Lives of Marilyn Monroe*. New York: Macmillan, 1985.

Taraborrelli, J. Randy. *Cher*. New York: St. Martin's Press, 1986.

Thompson, Dave. *Black and White and Blue: Adult Cinema from the Victorian Age to the VCR.* Toronto: ECW Press, 2007.

Thorpe, James. *Henry Edwards Huntington: A Biography.* Berkeley and Los Angeles: University of California Press, 1994.

Tosches, Nick. *Dino: Living High in the Dirty Business of Dreams.* New York: Dell Publishing, 1992.

Towner, Wesley. *The Elegant Auctioneers.* New York: Hill & Wang, 1970.

Wagner, Walter. *Beverly Hills: Inside the Golden Ghetto.* New York: Grosset & Dunlap, 1976.

Wallace, David. *Hollywoodland.* New York: St. Martin's Press, 2002.

Wallach, Ruth, et al. *Historic Hotels of Los Angeles and Hollywood (Images of America).* Charleston, SC: Arcadia Publishing, 2008.

Wanamaker, Marc. *Beverly Hills, 1930–2005 (Images of America).* Charleston, SC: Arcadia Publishing, 2006.

———. *Early Beverly Hills (Images of America).* Charleston, SC: Arcadia Publishing, 2005.

———, and Robert W. Nudelman. *Early Hollywood (Images of America).* Charleston, SC: Arcadia Publishing, 2007.

Wasserstein, Bruce. *Big Deal: 2000 and Beyond.* New York: Warner Books, 2001.

Watters, Sam. *Houses of Los Angeles, 1885–1919.* Vol. 1. *Urban Domestic Architecture Series.* New York: Acanthus Press, 2007.

Watts, Steven. *Mr. Playboy: Hugh Hefner and the American Dream.* New York: Wiley, 2009.

Wayne, Jane Ellen. *Marilyn's Men: The Private Life of Marilyn Monroe.* New York: St. Martin's Press, 1993.

Weddle, David. *Among the Mansions of Eden.* New York: HarperCollins, 2003.

Wells, Tom. *Wild Man: The Life and Times of Daniel Ellsberg.* New York: Palgrave, 2001.

Westbrook, Alonzo. *Hip Hoptionary.* New York: Broadway Books, 2002.

Wilentz, Amy. *I Feel Earthquakes More Often Than They Happen.* New York: Simon & Schuster, 2006.

Wolfe, Donald. *The Last Days of Marilyn Monroe.* New York: William Morrow, 1998.

Zerfas, Daniel G. *The Middleman.* Bloomington, IN: 1st Books Library, 2002.

PHOTO CREDITS

page 54: Botiller mansion under construction (*courtesy of Bobbie Hofler*)

page 136: Hilda Boldt Weber residence, Bel Air (*photograph from the Maynard Parker Collection, reproduced by permission of the Huntington Library, San Marino, California*)

page 226: Mickey Hargitay and Jayne Mansfield in The Pink Palace (*By permission of UCLA Charles E. Young Research Library Department of Special Collections, Los Angeles Times photographic Archives. Copyright © Regents of the University of California, UCLA Library.*)

page 352: The Lynda and Stewart Resnick residence, Beverly Hills (*photograph by Michael Gross*)

INDEX

Page numbers in italics refer to photographs.

ABOUT THE AUTHOR

MICHAEL GROSS is the bestselling author of *740 Park: The Story of the World's Richest Apartment Building; Rogues' Gallery: The Secret History of the Moguls and Money That Made the Metropolitan Museum; Model: The Ugly Business of Beautiful Women;* and other books. A contributing editor of *Travel + Leisure* and a columnist for *Crain's New York Business,* he has also written for major publications around the world, including the *New York Times, Vanity Fair, New York, Esquire,* and *GQ.* He lives in New York City.

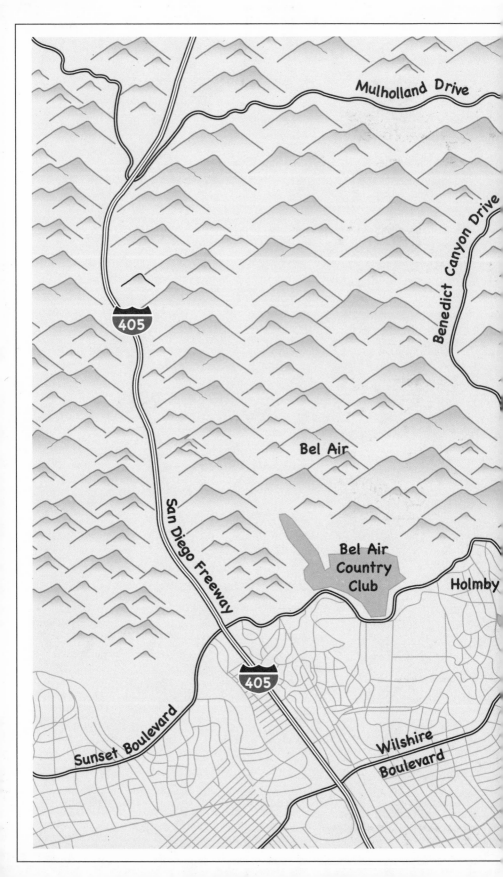